Awful Splendour

The Nature | History | Society series is devoted to the publication of high-quality scholarship in environmental history and allied fields. Its broad compass is signalled by its title: nature because it takes the natural world seriously; history because it aims to foster work that has temporal depth; and society because its essential concern is with the interface between nature and society, broadly conceived. The series is avowedly interdisciplinary and is open to the work of anthropologists, ecologists, historians, geographers, literary scholars, political scientists, sociologists, and others whose interests resonate with its mandate. It offers a timely outlet for lively, innovative, and well-written work on the interaction of people and nature through time in North America.

General Editor: Graeme Wynn, University of British Columbia

NATURE | HISTORY | SOCIETY

To Sonja, who understood both the fire and the ice, and Karlie, Ashley, Lindsey, Colten, and Julie, the new growth in the ash.

It is like a volcano in full activity, you cannot imitate it, because it is impossible to obtain those gigantic elements from which it derives its awful splendour.

Henry Y. Hind,
Narrative of the Canadian Red River Exploring Expedition of 1857

Contents

Contents

Figures

FOREWORD

Mon pays, c'est le feu

by Graeme Wynn

I n August 2003, Canadians watched nightly television news coverage of the "firestorm" ravaging British Columbia. Hundreds of fires burned simultaneously. Most dramatically, three large, aggressive "interface fires" threatened (and destroyed) homes, businesses, and communities near Alexis Creek, Kamloops, and Kelowna. When the fire tally for 2003 was complete, it revealed that almost 2,500 blazes had burned some 260,000 hectares across the province. Most of the damage was in the east and especially the southeast of the province, where the fire atlas charted a dense concentration of burns. In truth, there had been years with more fires, even in the preceding decade. Over 4,000 were recorded in 1994 and well over 2,500 in 1998. But only once in that period, when 75,000 hectares burned in 1998, did the affected area significantly exceed 50,000 hectares. By most accounts, the blazes of 2003 constituted the biggest, most intense, most expensive, and most devastating wildfires in the history of British Columbia.[1]

In October, Rob Dinwoodie, an agrologist in the Okanagan Shuswap Forest District who also played the cowboy music circuit with his band Dogwood Road, released a CD dedicated to those who had fought the blaze centred in Okanagan Mountain Provincial Park, a blaze that destroyed 239 Kelowna homes and caused losses that exceeded $100 million. Accompanied by Fire Information Officer Kirk Hughes on blues harp, Dinwoodie sang, "Put on your boots, boys, / We're going to fight a fire tonight" and continued, in his effort to raise money for the Fire Relief Fund,

When a fire threatens our community,
We will work in perfect unity.
Our only focus, our only aim,
Is to put that fire out.[2]

The sentiment was entirely understandable. Tens of thousands of people had been evacuated from their homes. Firefighters, municipal officials, and provincial politicians lived on tenterhooks for days. Provincial premier Gordon Campbell found it "truly staggering" to look down on the seemingly endless smoke from the air. On 23 August, Lieutenant Peter Cole of the Kelowna Fire Department admitted that he and his colleagues were "pretty apprehensive" and that "The dragon's just woke up." Others had already identified it as a "double-headed monster." Planning for the worst, workers on the front lines and officials in back rooms saw it happen.[3] Soldiers were brought in to assist the thousands of firefighters already deployed across the province. Many expressed disbelief at the power and speed of the flames that roared hundreds of feet into the air.

As people wrestled with nature's fury, they also pondered what had brought it on. It had been particularly dry throughout British Columbia in 2003. In Vancouver, smoking was banned in parched recreational areas, and many feared that extensive, heavily treed Stanley or Pacific Spirit parks might ignite. Hikers were warned to stay out of the back country of southern British Columbia. This was an El Niño summer, and fluctuating water surface temperatures and shifting atmospheric circulation patterns over the Pacific Ocean were held at least partly responsible for the flames threatening interior towns. Some pointed to an even longer pedigree of unusual environmental circumstances that helped to establish the preconditions for fire. According to Environment Canada, parts of the Pacific coast and southern interior were experiencing their worst drought in a century. The years from 2000 to 2003 were the driest three-year period ever recorded in southern British Columbia. Stream flows were at near-record lows and ground water stocks were seriously depleted in many areas.[4] On this evidence at least, the fires could be interpreted as a consequence of long-term climate change, or global warming.

Of course, each fire had a specific, more proximate cause. Lightning strikes – for some acts of God, for others natural occurrences – were identified as igniting some of the fires. Others were started by the careless, or foolish, behaviour of humans. Yet it was widely understood that however fires began, their development was shaped by chance. If the wind blew to fan initial flames, if the fire got a hold in a relatively remote area, or if the fire grew large enough to generate its own winds, then a significant blaze could emerge quickly in the hot, dry conditions prevailing. In some sense big fires were the products of fate. "People," concluded the firestorm review team established by the provincial government, "can do very little about these forces of nature" – except try their utmost to "put the fire out."

The fires, most people agreed, were a natural disaster. Or were they? To describe events or circumstances as "natural" places them beyond the realm of human responsibility by invoking a long-standing distinction between the "natural" and the "artificial," or human-created, elements of the world. Thus fish, oil, clean water, and gold are widely regarded as "natural resources," the products of biophysical processes over which humans had and have no direct influence; they are parts of the earth's "natural" environment that happen to be useful for humans. But students of economic geography long ago recognized that so-called natural resources were more accurately thought of as "cultural appraisals." Different cultures, different societies, have different attitudes toward their environments; different technological complexes differentiate societies' capacities to identify and make use of different parts of the biophysical system.

Consider two illustrations of this principle. The spruce forests of northern Canada were regarded and utilized in very different ways by indigenous peoples, early-nineteenth-century settlers, and pulp-mill interests. Oxides of uranium were used to colour glass and ceramics almost 2,000 years ago, but the element, named late in the eighteenth century, was not isolated until 1841; its radioactive properties were not understood until fifty years after that; and the process of nuclear fission that made uranium an invaluable resource for the development of atomic bombs was not discovered until 1939. Spruce trees and uranium atoms are created without human interference, by processes that are entirely "natural," but the uses to which they are put depends on the value humans place upon them. Their identification as "resources" is, in other words, a cultural construction subject to various influences and thus change.

We need to be cautious in describing catastrophic events as "natural disasters." Think of a massive flood, a volcanic eruption, a powerful hurricane, or a large earthquake. The event may be natural enough in the sense described above, but the "disaster" associated with it probably owes as much to human actions as to natural processes. People build their dwellings on the fertile, flat banks along the lower reaches of major rivers, in areas that they may even understand and describe as "flood plains," only to be surprised when rising waters inundate their properties. Volcanic eruptions, earthquakes, and the tsunamis sometimes associated with them are all capable of changing the face of the earth, but the perceived disastrousness of the reshaping they produce is largely determined by the amount and type of human activity in the affected vicinity. The Indian Ocean tsunami triggered by the Banda Aceh earthquake was indubitably tragic; but would it have been a disaster had it rolled into and across uninhabited shores? Clearly most of the human and financial costs associated with Hurricane Katrina were products of human decisions to inhabit the Mississippi delta, to build a city, to drain and dyke, and to establish in New Orleans a settlement and society particularly vulnerable to a certain combination of physical circumstances.[5]

By the same token, the disastrous qualities of the Okanagan Mountain fire owed much to an economic boom in the Okanagan valley, a rapid increase in the population of Kelowna, societal attitudes that valued large homes on the outskirts of cities (and especially, in the hot, dry Okanagan, in well-wooded settings), and a series of decisions by local officials and land developers that extended tentacles of suburban construction into the pine-clad hills beyond the city and above the lake. By encouraging the location of expensive homes in forested country, these developments blurred the distinction between urban and rural, suburb and forest, and produced an extensive, complex interface between cultural and natural realms. That blurring proved both costly and dangerous when fires erupted.

But there was more to it than this. The Okanagan Mountain fire began in a provincial park set aside in 1973 as a wilderness preserve. Over 110 square kilometres in extent and accessible only on foot or horseback or by bicycle or boat, the area is classified as a Class A park, in which neither resource exploitation nor forest management is permitted. When trees in the park were killed by a mountain pine beetle infestation, foresters and others warned that accumulating deadwood was creating a significant fire hazard, but park officials, mandated to preserve the area in its natural state, were reluctant to remove the dead trees. Ironically, there had been conspicuously less unwillingness to interfere with another natural process in the park since its inception. For thirty years, provincial employees had done their utmost to suppress fires in Okanagan Mountain Provincial Park and other forested areas of British Columbia. "Put the fire out" had been the mantra of the BC Forest Service for decades, and in the park, as elsewhere, firefighters sought to detect fires early and hit them hard to avoid the loss of valuable timber and/or recreational values. In this they differed little from those charged with responsibility for forests across the country. Early in the new millennium, the Canadian Forest Service claimed that 97 percent of all forest fires in Canada were extinguished before they burned 200 hectares.

In the ponderosa pine forests of the Okanagan valley, this policy of early intervention and fire suppression had significant ecological consequences. Long before European settlers and expert foresters entered the region, low-intensity ground fires burned through open stands of mature pines underlain by native grasses at intervals of between two and fifteen years. When these burns were extinguished early, seedling trees – which would otherwise have been killed by fire – survived. The forest became denser as thickets of young trees grew and litter accumulated on the forest floor. Under these conditions, fires that gained hold raged much more fiercely than before and occasionally blew up into catastrophic, stand-destroying crown fires. Far from being a simple "force of nature," the firestorm that burst out of Okanagan Mountain Provincial Park in August 2003, almost precisely thirty years after its establishment, was just such an occurrence. It was fuelled by easily forgotten and oh-so-human decisions and policies: to create a park, to eliminate fire, to reject the removal of dead trees. The dragon that caused such apprehension among Kelowna firefighters was indeed a double-headed monster, an extraordinary hybrid of "natural" and "cultural" elements.

This fusion makes fire a fascinating subject for environmental historians and others interested in the relations between humans and nature. Few people understand this better than Stephen Pyne. A distinguished and prolific scholar who is known around the world for his ground-breaking books on fire, he spent fifteen seasons fighting wildfires on the North Rim of Grand Canyon National Park between 1967 and 1981. He has been writing about them more or less ever since. Pyne has held fire in his historian's eye from the rim of the Grand Canyon to Australia; he has written of the great fires that ravaged the United States in 1910, produced a cultural history of wildland and rural fire in America, and authored such sweeping and ambitious works as *World Fire: The Culture of Fire on Earth* and *Vestal Fire: An Environmental History, Told through Fire, of Europe and Europe's Encounter with the World*.[6] Elsewhere, Pyne has reflected that his pursuit of fire has been an unusual and even rather solitary endeavour: whereas "the other Aristotelian 'elements' – air, water, earth – have academic departments to study them" he notes self-effacingly, "the only fire department at universities is the one that dispatches emergency vehicles when an alarm sounds."[7] *Awful Splendour*, in which Pyne brings his characteristically vigorous prose style, powerful capacity for strong narrative, and evident ability to bestride large and complex topics to bear on Canada is his eighteenth book. A dozen of these explore the story of fire through the ages and around the world, and six of them form a suite – known as the Cycle of Fire – that surveys the history of fire. It is fortunate that Pyne has now brought Canada into this mix, because (as the pages that follow reveal) fire has played an integral part in shaping the diverse ecologies and human histories of this extensive territory. Moreover, efforts to limit and control fire, especially in the twentieth century, have shaped the practice of forestry in Canada as they presented both federal and provincial forest services with challenges and opportunities for adaptation and innovation.

Writing the history of fire in Canada is no easy task. This, as Pyne was immediately forced to recognize when he turned his gaze northward, "is a big country with abundant fires and a literature to describe them" (p. xxv). Fires have affected the vegetation of northern North America for millennia. Started by lightning strikes in the absence of any human presence, natural fires ran through the terrain periodically. Grasslands probably burned every decade or so, on average; in the boreal forest the interval was about a century; and in the moist old-growth forests of the Pacific coast it was closer to 500 years. Grasses and trees adapted to these fire regimes and many species became fire dependent, requiring regular cycles of fire for regeneration and renewal. In some northern parts of the continent Native peoples set fires to clear land for settlement and cultivation. In the Great Lakes basin, such burning, undertaken every few years, began fewer than 2,000 years ago. Elsewhere, indigenous use of fire to assist in the hunt – either to drive animals in particular directions or to improve the browse for the herds upon which Native peoples depended for subsistence – had a longer history. There are no literary records of these early fires, but their histories are written in the scarred trunks of long-lived trees, in accumulations of carbon in the soil, and in other physical traces.

When newcomers from Europe began to settle in the territory that became Canada, they quickly came to understand both the great value and the malevolent power of combustion in this broad and heavily forested land, and developed an ambivalent relation to fire. Contained and managed, fire was essential to survival, providing heat for warmth and the preparation of food. It was also an enormously powerful tool. Clearing the forested land for agriculture was arduous and would have been overwhelming without fire's capacity to kill trees and consume slash. Later, as railroads were extended across the continent, fire helped to clear rights of way. Elsewhere, mining prospectors exploring the northern fastness often put forests to the torch to make their work easier. With trees stretching beyond imaginable horizons, little thought was given to the waste entailed by their incineration. When J.H. White, one of the first graduates of the University of Toronto School of Forestry, travelled through the Ontario north country before the First World War, he reported on the devastation that had ravaged the area. "From Sudbury to Port Arthur [on Lake Superior], generally speaking, the country along the [Algoma Central] railway has been burned at one time or another for the entire distance of 550 miles. Not much has escaped except the spruce swamps. The burned areas have been partially recovered by temporary stands of poplar, white birch and jack pine ... But to a vast extent the country has been burned so repeatedly that there is nothing left but bare rock."[8]

So long as it ran where intended or through what contemporaries described as waste lands, fire was an invaluable ally, whose foibles (so to speak) could be overlooked. Gone wild and running amok where settlers had invested labour and capital in "improvements" though, fire was a threatening, frightening, unmanageable menace, and it was both loathed and feared. From the beginnings of European settlement, anxious residents had watched smoke billow from clearings and written in diaries and newspapers of the "dark days" and "evil nights" produced by escaped fire. When an enormous blaze blew up in the tinder-dry woods of New Brunswick and destroyed settlements and lives along the Miramichi River in 1825, contemporaries were quick to describe it in apocalyptic terms. By one account, the fire resembled "the eve of the General Assize of Mankind," lacking only "the blast of a TRUMPET, the voice of the ARCHANGEL, and the resurrection of the DEAD."[9] Neither the first nor the last massive conflagration to rage across Canadian space, the Miramichi fire became the notorious archetype among dozens of calamitous and costly fires that ravaged the landscape as Canada industrialized.

In the final decades of the nineteenth century, rising concerns about the loss of timber to fire and the depletion of North American forest reserves spawned a conservation movement encouraging the "wise use" of resources. As trained "experts" assumed positions of authority in various walks of life, professional foresters staffed newly created branches of government dedicated to managing Canada's forests and changing prevailing spendthrift attitudes toward them. Fire quickly became the main focus of their attention. The "red menace" was destroying nature's wealth and blighting the prospects of Canadians. Together, the Dominion Forestry Branch and its provincial counterparts began the first tentative steps toward what would become a full-fledged war on fire in the woods.[10] Early in the twentieth century, Ontario required railroad companies to employ fire rangers along their lines and mounted fire patrols in provincial forest reserves. Other jurisdictions followed suit. The results were mixed. The forests were vast and travel through them was difficult. There were few rangers and their capacity to fight fires was limited. By one account, fire rangers "covered" barely a third of the 1.1 million square kilometres of federal forest, and in northern areas around Lac La Ronge, the Peace River and Great Slave Lake, individuals were supposedly responsible for thousands of square miles.[11]

Arthur Lower, who went on to an illustrious career at Queen's University, and was the first serious student of Canada's forest history, spent several undergraduate summers as a fire ranger in Ontario, thanks, he said, to his father "being a good Conservative and to nothing else," and his account of his time in the north woods effectively suggests the limits of early fire protection efforts. To become a ranger, Lower reflected, "One used what pull one could to get the job, received an impressive-looking letter of appointment, went up north to the place indicated and found the chief ranger. The latter just said, 'So-and-so will be your beat,' and that was that." In 1910, Lower and another student were assigned as partners to patrol Barrington Lake in the Nipigon territory by canoe. Their work entailed "making contact with the other rangers, putting out small fires, nailing up warning signs, displaying our badge conspicuously, and in general acting as conservation officers." But they were given no more specific instruction, and as most of these university students serving as rangers in rugged northern expanses realized, as "youngsters," their "personal authority did not go very far."[12]

During Lower's second summer in the bush an enormous fire burned almost 500,000 acres (200,000 hectares) of forest and killed at least 70 people in and around the town of Porcupine, near Timmins, a hundred miles north of Lower's camp.[13] Five years later, a similar area was burned, half a dozen settlements were destroyed, and over 200 people were killed by the Matheson fire near Cochrane, Ontario. The provincial government responded by passing the Forest Fires and Prevention Act, and the following summer almost 1,000 rangers were patrolling provincial forests. Similar intensification of effort was seen elsewhere. New approaches, borrowed from the Americans, included the construction of lookout towers, recognized as "the most economical method of securing early discovery and prompt action upon fires which occur at random throughout a broad territory." According to the *Canada Lumberman* of 1924, forest lands between the Gulf of St. Lawrence and the upper Ottawa had been "dotted with steel lookout towers." The usefulness of these and other lookouts across the country was increased by the introduction of new technologies such as the Osborne Fire Finder, which allowed observers to pinpoint fire locations with greater accuracy, and heliographs and telephones that quickened the dispatch of firefighting crews. The recruitment of idle air-craft and experienced pilots into fire detection after the First World War further revolutionized the fight against fire, and it soon evolved into an all-out war in both rhetorical and practical terms. As many have noted, even the language used to describe efforts at detection and suppression assumed increasingly "combative overtones: fire fighting, water bombing, first strike, initial attack, mopping up" and so on.[14] Those charged with managing the forest allowed little room for doubt about the importance of preventing and controlling fire.

After 1945, great effort was devoted to improving "the tools and tech-niques of ground-based fire suppression," and these methods were increas-ingly supplemented by airborne assaults on Canadian wildfire. Aircraft patrols superseded lookout towers; "smokejumpers" (parachute crews) led the attack on remote blazes; helicopters delivered firefighting crews to hot spots far more quickly than did canoes; and air tankers (water bomb-ers) capable of dousing developing fires with water or chemical retardants became indispensable in the fight against fire. Seeking every advantage that technology could provide, Canadian fire scientists quickly deployed satel-lite imagery and enlisted both advances in telecommunications and the power of computers to their cause. They also combined reports from offi-cers on the ground with data from automated weather stations to calibrate the risks of fire (expressed in the Canadian Fire Weather Index System), to reduce the threat of conflagration by closing forests to the public, and to deploy fire detection and suppression crews in hazardous areas.

Risk reduction, early detection, rapid responses, and quick and con-certed attacks on fires became the operating standard as agencies sought to extinguish every wildfire they could reach as quickly as possible. Fire eradication became the guiding principle of fire management, and the capacity of modern-day forest services to find and fight fires would have astonished Arthur Lower and his fellow rangers.[15]

Yet costs continued to rise. In the 1970s wildfires cost the Canad-ian economy an average of $50 million each year in detection, control, and damage, but this was merely a fraction of the account in the 1980s. Drought conditions meant that four to five million hectares of forest burned each summer between 1979 and 1981, and the cost of suppressing the 9,000 or more fires that burned in 1980 alone topped $100 million. New equipment was purchased and efforts to share firefighting resources efficiently were redoubled. One recent estimate suggests that Canadian agencies are spending between $400 and $800 million a year planning, preventing, and fighting fires. Eventually, even the most fervent enemies of fire in the forest have come to realize that they face the law of diminishing returns. As one fire scientist put it, "to suppress the last 3 percent of fires that cause 97 percent of the damage, we would need a firefighter behind every tree and a helicopter on every mountain slope."[16] Equally important, public opinion and official policy have begun to heed the opinion of fire experts that aggressive fire suppression, which effectively increased the time between burns, has only made fires more catastrophic when they occur. New strategies of forest management, more sensitive to ecological considerations than were earlier managerial regimes designed to maximize economic returns, have opened space for more holistic views that regard forest fires as "integral to the health, structure and diversity of forest ecosystems."[17] In this view, Canada, as one of the world's most heavily forested nations is manifestly a country of fire.

This story is much easier to outline in half a dozen paragraphs than it is to treat as thoroughly and systematically as Stephen Pyne does. Coming to the study of this northern territory as an outsider – an expert on fire but a newcomer to the details of Canadian history – Pyne had the experience to recognize the importance of finding an organizing principle for his narrative and the inestimable advantage of being able to transcend the clutter of generations of accumulated historical scholarship on the country. But he also had to learn the hard lesson confronting all who seek to understand more than federal or particular provincial political histories of this large country. Canadian fire history – rather like the country itself – is "an uneasy confederation of stories and sources without an obvious national narrative" (p. xxvi). Variously overlapping, competing, and co-operating federal and provincial interests in the forests of Canada make any full historical account of the management, exploitation, and significance of this resource (and others) a challenging task. Canada is, moreover, an artificial country, as the nineteenth-century historian and political commentator Goldwin Smith had it: its productive areas are set apart by "great barriers of nature, wide and irreclaimable wildernesses or manifold chains of mountains."[18] This configuration poses great difficulties for those writing environmental or resource histories at the national scale, forcing them to grapple with the disjunction between the administrative power containers defined by provincial and national boundaries and the contrasting bioregional characteristics of the land itself. In the end, Pyne found his organizing device in that significant influence on bioregional patterns and favourite topic of casual Canadian conversation – the climate. This helps, but it cannot answer all organizational questions. To address this, Pyne has crafted a complex of what he calls nested narratives.

The result is a bold and unusual book, one that begins with the ice of the last continental glaciation and ends with global warming threatening the lives of polar bears as the world of fire extends its dominion over the last remnants of the Pleistocene world of ice to which they are adapted. Between these symbolic beginning and end points, Pyne carries his story forward vigorously, sketching the biogeoclimatic characteristics of the country's geography as a series of "fire rings," tracing the environmental impacts of pioneer settlers whose axes transformed woods and grasslands and "remoulded their capacity to receive flame" (p. 68), and describing – in the longest and most complex section of the book – the ways in which "industrial fire remade woods, waters, soils, and even air ... [and] caused fire regimes ... to realign" (p. 137). The story of changing attitudes toward fire and the forest parallels, and is woven into, these narratives, charting the shift from the days of indigenous firesticks, when fire regimes were shaped by "what nature presented and what people desired," through care-less disregard of loss and waste in pursuit of development and profits, to the development of machines and institutions to manage and control fire in the years after Confederation. Finally, a brief essay considers the chang-ing relations between people and fire, institutions and attitudes, econom-ics and culture as fire prevention was reorganized and reconceptualized in an ever-greening and yet ever more fire-susceptible Canada.

So here we have it, the nearest thing yet to a comprehensive study of fire in Canada. Of course there are gaps in what Pyne has achieved, and read-ers may quibble about the emphasis he affords particular topics. But these are hair-splitting concerns against the magnitude of his accomplishment. *Awful Splendour* is a sweeping interpretive synthesis that does much to address a significant void in Canada's historical literature. It also places an important aspect of the Canadian story on the international map by fill-ing a gap in Pyne's global Cycle of Fire series. Third, it offers a compelling argument that an understanding of nature – of biology, botany, chemistry, climate, geology, and geomorphology – and of the interactions of people with nature can enrich (indeed is essential to) an understanding of Canada and its past. This book takes its place in the UBC Press Nature/History/Society series alongside other exemplars of this basic claim. It provides a remarkably detailed, richly documented foundation for all future discus-sions of Canada's fire history; its audacious scope and courageous ambi-tion should act as stimuli to more grand and daring work in Canadian environmental history and historical geography. Above all, *Awful Splen-dour* should rekindle and clarify much-needed national debates about fires, forests, and people in Canada, le pays du feu.

A Boreal Burning Bush

This is a book about fire and Canada. It describes why (and how) fire exists in Canada, or what might be termed fire's Canadian condition. Equally it narrates the story of Canada as viewed by fire, recasting Canadian history with fire as an organizing conceit. The fires of interest are those of field and forest, not those of the city. The span of interest lies between an era in which ice banished fire and a time, today, in which other forms of combustion are challenging open flame and driving off ice. If the historical geography of Canada says much about the character of such fires, the fires speak with equal force about the character of the culture that has responded to, kindled, and otherwise shaped the terms of their sustaining settings. They illuminate the hand and mind of those who tend them. *Awful Splendour* hovers between these purposes, at once symmetrical yet often competing.

The book exists for the same reason that Canada does: because Canadians willed it. Ever since I published *Fire in America* (1982), Canadian colleagues have pressed for a Canadian version. But it was clear the project could not be a casual one. Canadian fire history could not be done on the cheap – not intellectually, not archivally. It is a big country with abundant fires and a literature to describe them. Its history stood on its own. It demanded time, funding, and willing collaborators, and the right combination never aligned. Still, Dennis Dubé of the Canadian Forest Service would press in a friendly way, becoming the project's godfather. Then the

circumstances jelled: I had a sabbatical year, and Brian Stocks and Marty
Alexander of the CFS renewed the query, and Brian offered travel funds.
The National Humanities Center proposed one of its MacArthur Ecological Humanities Fellowships, suddenly making the project doable. Parks
Canada contributed a pack trip tutorial through Banff. And the Canadian
Studies Program of the Canadian embassy kicked in a small grant sufficient to complete the travels not covered by the CFS. Thereafter, the project relied on the unfailing hospitality and efficiency of Canadian hosts,
librarians, and archivists. I had almost all I needed.

What I lacked was an organizing principle. I found instead an uneasy
confederation of stories and sources without an obvious national narrative.
The closest environmental analogue was Australia, and I began to conceive
of a Canadian fire history as a boreal version of *Burning Bush*, my fire
history of Australia. The example had serious liabilities, however. Whatever
the political weaknesses of its federal centre, Australia the nation filled
Australia the continent and acquired a wholeness that Canada could
never equal, while exhibiting both a clarity of settlement and a shock of
encounter that Canada could not match. But the experience of starting
with outside events such as climate suggested a way to frame the master
narrative. As it happens, outside forces, of which climate is the archetype,
are a Canadian obsession. I could shape the text by appeal to them. The
result is a complex of nested narratives: a narrative of climate, a narrative of
fire, a narrative of imperial and confederated Canada, and narratives of the
institutions and ideas that direct what Canadians do and think about fire.
Henry Hind's description of a free-burning fire in its full-throated howl
seemed to capture the necessary sentiments and thus furnished a title.

The outcome is structurally complex – as uneasy as the political
equilibrium that allows Canada to go about its daily tasks. The fundamental
choice was whether to relate separate histories of the provincial and federal
fire services or to merge them. My reading of the scene was that I needed
to tell the stories separately. The outcome became a confederation of
narratives. That made for a longish manuscript, a cumbersome master
narrative, and a constant struggle to avoid the commonplace and the
repetitious. From the onset, however, it has been my ambition to write
something that would serve as a basic repository of Canadian fire history,
that would identify in a single volume the major themes, institutions,
individuals, and events. I could devise no other way to achieve these goals.
Still, there are lapses. The decision to end this approach in the mid-1980s
and telescope the past two decades into a common narrative has meant
that many provincial reforms have been glossed over. But a change did

occur in that decade that warranted a more national perspective, and I could not introduce it and then renew the separate agency histories without the text becoming unpublishable in its length and unintelligible in its conclusions. The story needed closure, and as with all art, endings introduce distortions.

The provincial chapters remain awkward. As readers, principally in the Canadian fire community (organized by Brian Stocks), submitted comments, fissures widened, not only between federal and provincial perspectives but also among the provinces and between those who wanted an integral history and those who wanted a full rendering of the particular parts. Provincial critics thought too much ink went to federal institutions, whose presence was marginal; federal critics, and historians of national Canada, thought the provinces claimed too much thematic territory and ruptured any pretence of a master narrative; others wondered why Albertans should care about New Brunswick, or Quebec about the Yukon; and all were dismayed about the length. Arguments that the manuscript approximated the dimensions of *Fire in America* and that Canadians deserved no less fell on deaf ears. The text had to be shortened, and the provinces bore that burden. One pass reduced them to encyclopaedic mini-histories, still repositories of data, names, fires, and reorganizations; another pass reduced them to essayist micro-histories that would try to identify only the defining traits and contributions of each. Literature, like politics, is the art of the possible, and I could not devise a means to hold all the details I wanted with the coherence and flow that readers deserved. The text is a compromise that will satisfy no group wholly and represents an ascendancy of geography over history, or of parts over an organic whole, but which works. In that, perhaps, it may also speak to Canada.

Thanks to all those who have helped on the ground and on whose scholarship I have relied. Anyone familiar with the subject will appreciate that my particular contribution lies in the synthesis I provide to published sources, supplemented by fresh archival evidence where relevant. In particular, I am indebted to Peter Murphy for his study of fire institutions in Alberta, Patrick Blanchet for Quebec, John Parminter for British Columbia, Stephen Janzen for the Northwest Territories, and W.C. Wilton and C.H. Evans for Newfoundland. For the remainder, I have relied on the unfailing assistance of librarians, fire officers, and the just plain generous to mill the details I required from the archival and grey-literature sources; to half a dozen colleagues, I have incurred an insurmountable debt for working through a very long and very rough draft. That substantial numbers of Canada's fire establishment (and countless ranks of Canadian librarians and archivists) would assist an American to write a fire history of their country speaks volumes for vigour and adaptability of that community and, through them, of Canada itself. Simply listing all those who have contributed hardly conveys the particulars for which I owe each one thanks in a different way. I trust that the book itself will compensate a bit and that I will have a chance in the future to thank them in person. I'm grateful for their help and humbled by their hopes.

Special thanks to the instigators – Dennis Dubé, Brian Stocks, and Marty Alexander – and to the staff at the National Archives of Canada: Sophie Tellier, Isabelle Fernandes, Michael McDonald, Alfred Deschênes, and Karla Benoit. Others include Kelvin Hirsch, Ian Campbell, Doug McCreary, Mike Weber, Brad Hawkes, Steve Taylor, C.E. Van Wagner, Cliff White, Mark Heathcott, Stephen Woodley, Raymond Quenneville, Blair Pardy, Steve Malcolm, Ian Pengally, Celine Racette, Mike Etches, Ian Stirling, C. Allan Jeffrey, Keith Barr, Al Beaver, Jeanette van Esbroeck, Aimee Ellis, David Milne, John Parminter, Jim Price, John Flanagan, Sylvia Gautier, Julie Fortin, Patrick Blanchet, Michel Chabot, Dan McAskill, Shirley Mah, Allison Welch, Peter Harding, R.J. Buck, M. Christopher Kotecki, Angela Batistte, Glenda Goetzner, Paul Maczek, Bruce Boland, Cal Best, Dan MacKinnon, Kris Johnson, Jeff Patch, Cordy Tymstra, Brian Amiro, and Rob McAlpine. Kelvin Hirsch and Peter Murphy gave especially helpful readings of an early draft, and Peter rescued the illustrations when I sank into an Albertan muskeg. Others who assisted with figures must include Yuri Shimpo, Allen and Barbara Place, Betty Biesenthal, Marc-André Parisien, Dave Lemke, Bob Stevenson, and Brenda Laishley. And I need to extend heartfelt gratitude to Camilla Blakeley and Dallas Harrison for their care and patience in working through a fractious manuscript with an unorthodox organization. They have made the text both sharper and stronger.

And as always there is Sonja. Always there, always tolerant, always the ideal reader. This is for her and the grandkids she so warmly deserves.

For what readers may find admirable in the text that follows, they should congratulate those sponsors who made the work possible. For what they find objectionable or erroneous, they should blame me.

Measurements
The text is binumerate in that I have retained both SI (metric) and imperial measurements. Whichever system the original source cited, I repeat it. In a scientific paper, it would be worth converting all measurements to an SI standard, but the numbers are secondary to the narrative, and the text would become unreadable with parenthetical potholes if I included both.

Institutional Names

Name changes within agencies are so widespread and frequent that it could only confuse the reader to include each change, particularly when used perhaps once before another change arrives. I have tried to compromise for sense. Often I simply refer to the responsible institution as the "agency" or "department," avoiding the label du jour. In some instances, I have projected the current title back a few decades (e.g., Parks Canada instead of Canadian Park Service). In a few prominent cases, I have allowed the name changes to appear, primarily with regard to the Canadian Forest Service, except for the most recent years and where it seemed calculated only to confuse. The full chronicle of name changes for that agency looks like this:

1906-23	Dominion Forestry Branch
1923-48	Dominion Forest Service
1948-60	Dominion Forestry Branch
1960-69	Department of Forestry
1969-88	Canadian Forestry Service
1988-mid-1990s	Forestry Canada
mid-1990s-	Canadian Forest Service

PROLOGUE

WHITE CANADA

White Canada

T heir rivalry is ancient. It dates at least as far back as the Devonian when a planet that had known only ice first began to know fire. From then onward the Earth, at least in portions, began to swing between times of frost and times of flame. The two could not co-exist. Ice is inorganic, tolerating at best micro-niches for bacteria around its fringe, while fire is a creation of the living world, for which life furnishes its fuels, its oxygen, and eventually its most abundant ignitions. At any place, at any time, one or the other must prevail.

During the Pleistocene, the epoch before today's, the climatic cadence quickened, and for almost two million years, the land that would become Canada whipsawed between a world smothered by ice and a world fluffed with combustible hydrocarbons, with uncertain, oft-violent, and sudden transitions between them. Some 20,000 years ago, the ice seemed supreme.

The ice was everywhere, and everywhere it was immense, inclusive, and implacable. The Laurentide ice dome rose over two miles above the western shore of Hudson Bay. The ice lay 3,800 metres over present-day Churchill, 3,000 metres over Winnipeg, 2,500 metres over Quebec City and Edmonton. The two great ice mounds were somewhat in sync. The Laurentide sheet swelled most fully around 18,000 years before the present (BP), the Cordilleran, spilling down the Rockies, roughly 15,000 years ago. Only a wedge along the Yukon Valley was spared. The place that became Canada was that most marvellous of narrative openings, a blank page.

When the ice collapsed, its geographical matrix was reloaded, although the great sheets left a legacy, a geophysical palimpsest of their presence.

The lands, long scoured and depressed, now filled and rose. The waters, long held frozen, now melted and fed an ephemera of streams, ponds, and inland seas, helping to raise the level of the world ocean nearly sixty metres, flooding most of the continental shelves, and sundering the land bridge to Asia. The air, long blocked by the ice dome, returned to a circumpolar circulation, with a mobile sweep of wind, storm, and turbulence. Yet here too the towering ice left an atmospheric echo in the form of the Hudson Bay High, an atmospheric dome that redirects the larger sweep and can block the flow of moisture into the interior for eight to fifteen days or more.[1]

This reconstituted matrix, and how it happened, shaped the character of the fires that followed by its capacity to arrange combustibles and coolants. Glaciated land and liberated waters left the Canadian Shield textured with a dense array of ponds, lakes, rivers, sloughs, muskegs, all of which could check the untrammelled spread of fire. The waxing and waning of the Hudson Bay High created ideal conditions for combustion: warming, drying, and readying fuels for burning, while along its margins shedding dry, downrushing winds, not unlike those that formerly spilled off the ice, and when the High broke down drawing in fronts from the west to hurl storms, turbulent winds, and lightning over the desiccated land. These were the moments of critical fire weather, and nearly all of Canada's great natural fires and outbreaks of large-fire swarms have occurred under precisely these conditions. Eerily the dynamics of the advancing fire world often mimicked those of the retreating ice. Just as the ice withdrew in fits, in lurches and spasms that mocked averages, a convulsion of rupturing ice dams and melts, interrupted by stalled ice fronts and insulated domes, so boreal fires exhibited a cadence of cataclysms and calms, a pattern not meaningfully expressed in averages.[2]

For all this, however, there was one imponderable and unblinking difference between the two elements. The ice could come and go without the slightest regard for anything living; it ebbed and flowed according to an inorganic logic: the wavering of solar radiation, the orbital mechanics of a wobbling Earth, the arrangement of continents and oceans, mountains, and plateaus. But fire was more subtle, complex, and variable, a phenomenon of life. What it eats, what it breathes, even (though not exclusively) the spark that births it, all rely on the living world. The character of the life that colonized the ice-liberated lands was fire's character as well.

The biotic reclamation of Canada, from microbes to megafauna, moved, with the exception of a few niche refugia, from the outside in. There were two primary sources. One was Beringia, the land bridge that spanned the Bering Sea and plunged inland in a twisted, narrowing wedge roughly along the Yukon River. As the ice receded, the corridor widened, unzipping along the eastern front of the Rocky Mountains. It funnelled and filtered, and through it came the biota of Eurasia, especially its tundra and grassland creatures. But the dominant source – so vast as to render the others nearly trivial – was continental North America to the south. It served, through the long night of the glacial epoch, as a biotic reservoir from which raw species probed and pushed northward.

As the means varied, so did the outcomes and the chronology of colonization. Some species could move quickly and over long distances. Some could barely advance beyond their own canopy. Some could thrive in barren ground, even creating their own nitrogen; others demanded a textured soil, a complementary ecology, a suite of conditions only possible after the tough pioneering species had broken the land for life. Certainly for plants, the process was less a migration than a progressive propagation that depended on how, exactly, grasses, forbs, shrubs, and trees reproduced themselves. Spruce could generate from wind-borne seeds carried over long distances. Oak relied on squirrels to carry and bury acorns away from the source. Chestnut could advance, on average, about 100 metres per year; lodgepole pine, 200 metres per year; spruce, 300 metres per year. Each species had its own rate of spread, its unique requirements for propagation, its peculiar ecological demands. The populating of the formerly iced lands was less a paced migration than a slow land rush, a sprawling, jostling, biotic bumping along of species amid a still-flexing crust, an unsettled hydrology, and a turbulent climate. The upshot was less a grand ecosystem in equilibrium than an evolving confederation of biotic conveniences.[3]

With the coming of life – the massing of hydrocarbons subject to oxidation – also came fire. The patterns of burning were as unstable as their setting. One reason, of course, was that the setting was in upheaval for thousands of years and never truly fixed, and fires could not assume regularities until their sustaining circumstances did as well. But another reason is that fires fed on organic combustibles, organized according to ecological and evolutionary principles, and had to assume the complexity of those fuels: they took on the character of their context. Tundra, boreal forest, muskeg and bog, mixed woodland, prairie, mountain forest, and coastal forest – each burns according to its unique, unstable mingling of organic matter, weather, and terrain. And while it is possible to discern patterns, or fire regimes, those regimes are a statistical composite; individual fires occur within a regime much as individual storms do within a given climate. In this way fires appeared, as tepid as scattered alder and bunchgrass, as robust as congested stands of black spruce and jack pine, as sullen as drought-drained muskeg. They were as prominent or hidden as their sustaining conditions, particularly ignition, could make them. They were the biochemical sum of many rhythms not easily compressed into mechanical formulas.

Nor were those new-kindled fires wholly passive, a self-combusting afterthought of post-glacial recolonization. They could open up lands to newcomers and renew lost sites for pioneers. They could shatter ecological inertia, those logjams in which early arrivals, establishing claims under one climate and soil, could hold on and resist later immigrants; they could scour out bogs and strip insulating mosses away from permafrost and thus create, if only temporarily, new habitats; they could put creatures into motion, abandoning patches of burned-out lichens or seared spruce, searching for the renewed nutrition of forbs, grasses, and berries on fresh-burned sites. The fires forced change; they reflected change. They stirred and kept simmering the whole biotic cauldron that was colonized Canada after the ice.

The Pleistocene ended, from a geological perspective, with remarkable abruptness as several grand trends converged suddenly around 11,000-10,000 years ago. Atmospheric carbon dioxide, whose concentration had been rising since the glacial maximum, began to decline. The water temperatures of the oceans rose. The world warmed and kept warming for several thousand years more, and probably the seasons sharpened. The composition of biotas became scrambled: a sudden, southern decline of spruce restructured landscapes as substitutes seized abandoned sites from Minnesota to Nova Scotia; jack pine spread vigorously in the east, while Douglas fir appeared in the west; prairie thrived in the wake of vanishing plains woodlands. And perhaps most spectacularly between 12,000 and 9,000 years BP, a menagerie of megafauna went extinct. Some thirty-five to forty species of large mammals disappeared, among them mammoths, giant beavers the size of ponies, Shasta ground sloths, and galloping, short-faced bears.[4]

This evolutionary quenching was an old story. North America had acquired and lost throngs of large creatures as it had piled up and melted away ice sheets, and filled and drained lakes, and raised and levelled mountains. The Pleistocene had witnessed several waves of extinctions, roughly synchronized with the climatic whip-sawing between glacials and interglacials. Yet this one was different. Almost no small creatures expired, for example. More tellingly the great die-off occurred, with uncanny fidelity, in pace with the emergence of a megafaunal arrival, *Homo sapiens,* with the proven capacity to wipe out whole species with unthinking aplomb. Were the North American losses the last of a long legacy of nature's evolutionary extinctions, or were they among the first of humanity's ecological wreckages?

Probably the latter. Not only did humans hunt those species, but they also tampered with the larger habitat and overall were a powerful catalyst amid an epoch of radical biotic restructuring in which every act sparked synergistic reactions. The extinctions are global, if variable, and everywhere they are out of sync with climate (only mildly so in North America, wildly so in Australia). Yet uncertainties abound. There is clear evidence of human hunters, of Clovis vintage, well south of the ice around 11,500 years BP. A long-held assumption is that they migrated from Beringia through the ice-free corridor that wedged open between the Cordilleran and Laurentian ice sheets. But around the world humans have travelled quickest along coastlines; it may well be that Clovis hunters did likewise or that pre-Clovis peoples clung to well-stocked shores, hopping between coastal refugia, or even ventured inland. Whatever triggered the extinctions, regardless of whether people were the prime agents or just enabling associates, Clovis and its successors accompanied the upheaval that swept over the continent.[5]

For upper North America, however, the dispute over ultimate origins matters little. What matters is that, from whatever source, humans were present as the ice faltered and ebbed and that they were part of the vast, brawling recolonization of post-glacial Canada. What matters, too, is that they carried in their toolkits and genetic heritage a power no other creature possessed. They could kindle fire. They could affect the land far beyond the elimination of a species or two, for fire had two vital properties unlike nature's other physical disturbances or humanity's toolkit. Unlike a thrown spear or a club, it could propagate, and unlike a flood or a glacier it spread not against a biota but through it. Fire was different. For a landscape like the boreal forest, where fire was also fundamental, this difference rendered fire unlike anything else, bonded not only to life but also to humanity. In a fire-prone landscape, the torch is what made humanity potentially implacable.

The tipping point between Pleistocene and Holocene, between tenacious ice and intrepid life, marked the end of a beginning. The great forces that warmed and cooled the Earth, that buckled and flooded and drained continents, that spawned and suppressed species and scattered them into migrations, that placed a restless, fire-wielding creature amid a land rapidly becoming combustion prone, all abided and impressed themselves on the land. But with the ice swiftly imploding, there was room for interactions. Ice no longer met ice but now encountered fast-tumbling figurations of waters, stones, storms, droughts, plants, and animals. The pace and variety of contacts multiplied. The ecological epic quickened. What would become Canada adjusted.

There was, first, a deepened warming. The greatest intensity of sunlight, as defined by the convergence of Milankovitch cycles on the northern latitudes, occurred almost precisely at the boundary between Pleistocene and Holocene, roughly 10,000 years ago. But plenty of ice remained, and the ecological maximum came later, probably 6,500 years BP. While the Great Warmth was a presence far less ruthless than the Big Chill, it prompted a crisis nonetheless, for it forced massive relocations; because the era was dry as well as hot, life had to seek sanctuaries, finding them on such biotic nunataks as the Cypress Hills and Turtle Mountain, where higher elevations meant cooler and wetter conditions.

Then the climatic wheel turned again, gradually cooling and wetting over the past 4,000 to 5,000 years. Within that broad trend, however, there were ample bumps and veerings, episodes of cold and warm, wetting and drying on the order of decades or even centuries, all mediated by local terrain and floral refugia. In particular, the gears of this atmospheric clockwork meshed to yield a Little Climatic Optimum that peaked some 1,800 years ago and a glacial echo, the Little Ice Age, dating from AD 1350 to 1870. The optimum was, not surprisingly, an era of extraordinary burning, especially during a span of 500 years, as a warming and drying climate acted on a rank vegetation that had blossomed during the preceding millennia. The resurgence of cooling, wetting, and glacial ice reversed that process until recent decades. In the Rockies, after 1760, the frequency of fires plummeted from about 60 years to 175 years (although this sharp transition comes uncomfortably close to a period of collapse in indigenous demographics, which might point to ignition rather than climate).[6]

While fires responded to these climatic arrhythmias, it was not a simple correspondence by which a physical prompt kindles a physical reaction. Something was mediating. That something was humanity and its capacity to control combustion. Here was a means by which to modulate climate. With their fires, they could resist the cold, dry the wet, enhance warmth, arbitrate between an indifferent geophysics and a nurturing ecology. With fire – applying it, withholding it – they could make the land more to their liking; they could convert prairie to woods, and forest to brush, and brush to raw rock. Fire alone could rarely force such revolutions, but fire as catalyst, fire as spark to tindered land and a spreading technosphere, could.

The linkages are such that fires in autos can now affect fires in woods. It is impossible to imagine humanity's vast reach without a torch in hand.

Yet, paradoxically, the last of the ice's lingering legacies may be a curious disbelief in such power. The continental glaciers left a vision of nature responsive to immense forces before which humanity is puny. Those grand cadences and implacable pressures, and they alone, all well beyond humanity's grasp, account for the fundamental character of the country and all within it. Even regarding fire, humanity tinkers, but climate drives. The historical record suggests otherwise. It suggests that people have, in truth, affected such vast extents of the planet that thoughtful observers have proposed that the Holocene might more suitably be renamed the Anthropocene, the age of humans. Through the torch, the future passed to people, who used their fire power generally to enhance burning, which is to say a world in which the torch could exert even greater leverage. Still, the rivalry over ideas endures, metamorphosing into other realms of human endeavour, although perhaps not for much longer. The old border between the hand and the vast machinery of climate is dissolving. As people have found new means to increase their fire power, they have discovered that they can compete with climate itself. The Earth's apparent wheeling into a greenhouse atmosphere is largely an outcome of combustion set loose from the fidgety fingers of humanity.

In this way, White Canada has evolved by sweep and spasm into Green Canada. The grand narrative of this transformation is not simple, not direct, not even contained within the confines of Canada. It is, rather, a chronicle of forces from outside interacting with the particularities of places and peoples, a plexus of causes and consequences, a complex of nested narratives.

For this transubstantiation of ice into life, fire furnishes a distinctive index. It was an inevitable after-effect of life's reclamation from the ice, a tracer of ecological cycling and biotic vigour, a measure of cultural power and human choice, a presence so fundamental that Canada's future must itself become a contest over combustion – the combustion people confront in nature, the combustion they control in machines and megalopoli, and the combustion they fecklessly unleash wherever they appear. As the mounding ice once created more ice, so the mounting fire is creating more fire. Before those flames, the ice continues to melt, and humanity finds itself challenged to devise means to cope with a rivalry between fire and fire, between nature's fires and its own.

Book 1

Torch

Kindling

The rudimentary requirements for fire are simple enough. Combustion demands something to burn, adequate oxygen to combine with the raw fuel, and sufficient heat to kindle the process into being. Post-glacial Canada had all these ingredients in abundance.

Oxygen was plentiful enough, saturating the atmosphere to the amount of 21 percent, marinating the exposed surfaces of vegetation. So, too, there was ample fuel. While large chunks of Canada's crust hold lakes, stony hummocks on the Shield, and swatches of ice and rock, even its most formidable landscapes typically have some vegetation: mosses, lichen, tussock grass, organic mats. What of this biomass is actually available to burn varies considerably according to the fraction of small particles and the internal moisture of those particles. Or put differently, natural fuels are dynamic. They change over time, especially as moisture flows into and out of the scene. In particular, the quantity of combustibles varies largely according to rhythms of wetting and drying; these rhythms may be seasonal or secular, bobbing on the waves of spring greenup and autumnal dormancy, or the longer swells of drought and deluge; the dialectic is what matters. In both circumstances, oxygen abundance and fuel availability, people could do little to alter what nature made available.

Still, even masses of small-particle fuels, well cured and fluffed, do not spontaneously combust. They require a burst of concentrated heat, and after its reclamation from the ice Canada has had two primary sources of ignition. The return of post-ice circulation restored lightning-laden storms, while the colonization by life brought fire-wielding humans. Each created a distinctive geography of ignition, though there have been numerous places of overlap. To them might be added a third, which is really a means to extend those sources: the ability of fires, once kindled, to bury themselves in organic soils, propagating by simple pyrolysis (the combustion equivalent of anaerobic respiration), holding the heat of ignition until it can be liberated to the surface. In Canada, a spark can persist for months.

The geography of lightning mirrors that of climate generally: the regions most prone to burning are also those subject to relatively dry lightning. The gross cartography of average thunderstorm days in July shows none at Baffin Island, two to three at Churchill, and seven to eight at Thunder Bay, while along the western slope the gradient moves from zero at Queen Charlotte Islands inland to seven to eight in the Palliser Triangle. The effective storms, however, are those that flail the land with dry lightning or that blast a landscape well cured by drought or dry spells. These storms track the seasonal recession of Arctic air and typically accompany the first flush of unstable moisture that wedges eastward or northward after the breakdown of an upper-level ridge, that moves along the margins or into the vacated site of a Hudson Bay High. One- to two-week bouts of critical fire weather can easily end with lightning. Around the Rockies, the geography of lightning, like climate, fractures into more complex patterns and a trickier history. The broad arrangement concentrates lightning fire west of the divide, but nearly everywhere that fire is possible lightning is there to kindle it.[1]

The origins of anthropogenic fire are murkier, and its presence required a longer, stickier period of adjustment. Human colonizers had fire in their toolkits, knew how to use it along with rock scrapers and fluted spearpoints, and learned and relearned how to cast it upon the land. Since the landscapes were continually morphing, sometimes violently, the process of adjustment was equally continuous and arduous. The extinction of the megafauna, for example, shook up the arrangement of woods, shrubs, and grasses, which meant the configuration of fuels. Moreover, fire on the land was not as tractable as fire in the hearth or furnace. Not all sparks caught; not all fires behaved as their kindlers wished; not all ignitions were willed.

Yet no people doubted the power that fire granted them. In their myths, they reside, among the creatures, as a poor and suffering lot, unable to cook food or warm themselves. Some cultural hero grants them fire, sometimes as a gift, more often as an act of theft. The North American Prometheans tend to be animals such as raven, deer, mink, muskrat, assorted birds, fox, eagle, or beaver. By various means, they trick and filch their way to fire, often at great cost as the hoarding creature pursues and kills them. Typically they bequeath fire not to humans directly but by scattering it during their fiery flight into the woods and grasses. The power thus suffuses nature. The trick becomes the knowledge of how to conjure it up again, a capacity only humans possess. But the outcome is clear. Fire is everywhere in the forests and prairies, and with it people can survive in the hostile north, provided they learn how to coax it from the woods and command it to their own ends.[2]

What both ignitions share is that neither can, by itself, cause self-sustaining fires. They can only act on what nature makes available by way of combustibles. Most lightning expires amid rain showers or is wasted on lakes, rocks, and green boles. Most human ignition thrives only where people nurture it with fine, dry kindling and shelter. For either to free-burn over the countryside, the land has to be ready to receive it. In particular, humans can kindle where nature, by itself, reliant on lightning, cannot, yet they cannot force combustion in circumstances that nature otherwise hardens against burning. The firestick is a lever; it can move only so much as the fulcrum nature provides. This is the defining condition of "aboriginal" burning, a fire technology that made it possible to start but not to sustain flame. (For fire history, aboriginal thus refers to a kind of burning, not a tribe of people.) To force fire beyond ignition required the techniques inherent in agricultural or industrial burning, a capacity to tinker with fuels or air. That required the additional leverage of axe and engine. In aboriginal times, the fire regimes of Canada were a negotiation between what nature presented and what people desired.

Fire Rings of Indigenous Canada

Gradually there emerged a series of concentric arcs, a biotic banding that merged two geophysical gradients. One, a spectrum of sunlight, ran north and south; the other, of moisture, spread from the coasts inland. Together they meant that warmth increased to the south and wetness with proximity to a sea. Like a kind of biotic concretion, these tendencies combined to form broad rings around Hudson Bay, the grey, dead heart of Canada. Each ring had its characteristic fire regimes. Collectively those rings closest to the bay and those fringing the ocean held the least fire, and those with sufficient light and moisture to grow combustibles while subject to bouts of drying held the most.

Fire and Frost: Tundra
Nearest the residual ice, outside the range of invading air masses from west and south, beyond the border of trees, the tundra arcs across the northern tier of the continent and over the Arctic archipelago. It is a complex biota and a historical one. Lichens, grasses, sedges, dwarf shrubs, here and there a patch of black spruce, alder, or birch, a dash of forbs – in places it resembles a boreal shortgrass prairie, a starved tussock grassland, a cold heath, an upland peat bog. Over Canada the tundra today fronts cold seas or ice, gently rippling over lowlands underlain by permafrost. Fire is present – continues to simmer and occasionally flash. Its character, however, fits its context; it appears as low-ground fires that smoulder rather than roar, letting smoke drift along like meltwaters rather than erupt into the sky.

But the mix is also contingent on history. The tundra's composition has varied and remains a work in progress. Elements appeared shortly after the ice loosened its grip and have joined and parted and roamed ever

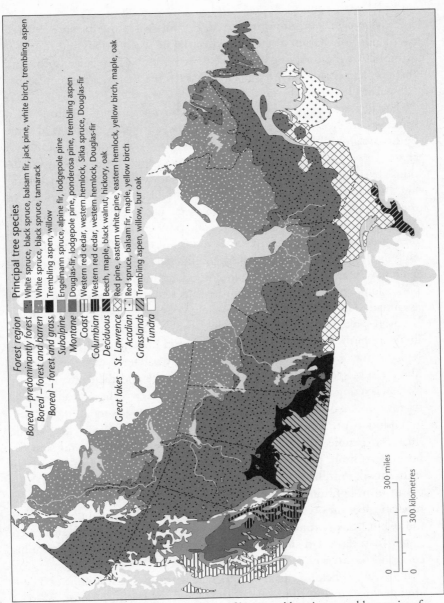

Forest region · **Principal tree species**

- Boreal – predominantly forest — White spruce, black spruce, balsam fir, jack pine, white birch, trembling aspen
- Boreal – forest and barren — White spruce, black spruce, tamarack
- Boreal – forest and grass — Trembling aspen, willow
- Subalpine — Engelmann spruce, alpine fir, lodgepole pine
- Montane — Douglas-fir, lodgepole pine, ponderosa pine, trembling aspen
- Coast — Western red cedar, western hemlock, Sitka spruce, Douglas-fir
- Columbian — Western red cedar, western hemlock, Douglas-fir
- Deciduous — Beech, maple, black walnut, hickory, oak
- Great lakes – St. Lawrence — Red pine, eastern white pine, eastern hemlock, yellow birch, maple, oak
- Acadian — Red spruce, balsam fir, maple, yellow birch
- Grasslands — Trembling aspen, willow, bur oak
- Tundra

300 miles

300 kilometres

Fire rings of Canada. The broad arrangement of biotas and burning resembles a series of rings, somewhat skewed, around Hudson Bay.

since, wherever conditions permitted. In times past, too, forests expanded over lands now barren of taiga: the frontier between woods and tundra is as mobile as the bobbling air masses that hover over the Far North. And there is plain ecological inertia, which has left fragments of past landscapes still embedded amid the new.

The historical geography of fire has shuffled accordingly. A study from southwestern Keewatin, west of Hudson Bay, chronicles a northward surge by forests around 3,500 years ago, followed by a recession, then a revival about 900 years ago, with another collapse leading to present-day conditions. These movements align roughly with known waves of climatic warming. But the record of buried podzol soils and black carbon testifies also to the stickiness of the process. Bigger fires were possible because denser fuels fed them, which allowed a richer residue of charcoal. Those more robust fires, moreover, may have jarred the woods out of comfortable niches that no longer agreed with the prevailing conditions. Once burned, with the climate now altered, the woods could not reclaim their sites, and tundra took possession. The actual tree-line border thus reflects a history of fire as well as climate. Those marcher-land fires can give as well as take. One researcher has even spoken of a "pyrogenic tundra," the outcome of fires in forests that lie temporarily beyond the true tree limit and that can lead to a full-bore replacement of woods by tundra. Occasionally patches escape the burning, like the odd spot of black spruce that evades fire and then propagates by asexual layering under conditions that would otherwise have prohibited its regeneration, a historical monument to a bygone biotic time.[1]

Thunderstorms occasionally penetrate beyond the border and kindle fires. But people are present, at least along routes of travel and sites for hunting, fishing, or foraging, and they too leave fires. A five-year study from Inuvik near the Mackenzie Delta recorded eleven fires, of which three began from lightning. Other observers have witnessed lightning busts of nine and five fires respectively. The fires were small; probably there were more, but because tundra fires are tiny, and even when large in area creep rather than dash and smoulder rather than pile up into thermocumulus columns, they passed without comment.[2]

The reasons behind the anthropogenic ignitions are not known. There are references to Inuit burning of individual shrubs (to promote berries) – this over still-frozen ground, a kind of pyric horticulture. Broadcast burning, however, is not practised and is probably undesired in caribou-dominated landscapes since the lichens that form the principal winter diet recover slowly from burns, and a large fire could deflect migration patterns. The power of anthropogenic burning has waxed and waned with the ebb and flow of settlement, which coincide with larger climatic tides; at least three times cultures have colonized the northern tier and twice have been driven back. Still, fires will escape, and campfires will settle deeply into drying organic soils, then spread if and when conditions permit. Burning will lightly dapple the landscape.[3]

The variety of tundra makes for a varied ecology of tundra fires. Burns are patchy, even the permafrost cleavages of patterned ground may sufficiently bar spread, and the severity of burning depends keenly on the depth of fuel and its dryness. (In 1968 outside Inuvik, some eighty-six days passed without precipitation.) Rich with ether extractives, heath plants burn brightly, while woodier patches, perhaps in a wetter swale, may escape fire altogether. Afterward, most low shrubs, heath, and tussocks (like cottongrass) simply resprout from roots safely below the burn. Lichens take the biggest hit. Lacking roots, water storage tissues, and vascular systems, they dry quickly, and being fine branched and ventilated they burn crisply and completely. They regenerate slowly, propagating on organics, which require time to restock and do so at diverse rates. They quickly surrender the post-fire terrain to the grasses and shrubs, which thrive in mineral soil and can tap deeply with preserved roots. On average, restoration takes about a century.[4]

The biotic competition overlays an abiotic one. Burning alters the albedo, the surface temperature, the thickness of the organic mat insulating permafrost, soil moisture, the presence of alleopaths, and the fertility of the ground. Heating the surface and stripping away its insulating shield cause the permafrost to thaw more deeply, sometimes leading to a thermokarst landscape of frozen mounds and melted cavities and sinks. This fire-induced shock liberates water and nutrients from the soil, adding to the boost of phosphorus and calcium (in particular) unlocked by combustion from woody matter on the surface. The brew is congenial to the microbial production of nitrogen. The upshot is a biochemical boost to those plants that can quickly seize upon the boon. The vascular plants can; the lichens cannot and must wait until an organic layer evolves on which they can thrive. Old lichens may succeed to mosses or become decadent. Since the lichens drive the most vigorous fires, those that can span the minor ridges and ravines of the landscape, the cycle of lichenous fuel helps to shape the larger cycle of burning.[5]

There exists, then, a hierarchy of fire rhythms or ecological pulses. The short-term outcome, on the order of years and decades, is to promote grasses and shrubs; the longer-wave effect, a century or two, is to enhance lichens and, along frontiers, trees; and the still broader-swell consequence can perhaps shape the bolder geography of the tundra and its dual borders with ice and forest. The question exists whether, because fire happens, the biota has passively adapted to it or whether the tundra, which seems so hostile to fire (and fire to it), might require pulses of burning to renew itself. The query may be academic. Between climatic change, species migrations, and fires, the tundra has never been stable long enough to find out. Certainly it is not immune to fire; clearly it has accommodated itself to episodic burning. Whether it could thrive without combustion may never be answered. It is enough that even here, close to an inner frozen core, fire finds its way.

Fire and Water: Boreal Forest

Between the Arctic and the Cordilleras, between the cold-dry climes of the tundra and the warm-dry and warm-wet climes of the grasslands and mountain woodlands, stretches the boreal forest, Canada's vastest woods. The belt narrows between James Bay and the Great Lakes, and nearly doubles toward the Rockies, but its sweep encompasses the bulk of continental Canada. Within its immense arc resides Canada's largest fires, its greatest fire problems, and its most distinctive fire regimes, the ones that best define Canada as a fire nation. Its boreal forest is to Canada what the arid Outback is to Australia. Over 90 percent of the country's big fires, which account for over 97 percent of its burned area, lie within the boreal belt. Without its burning boreal bush, Canada would be a middling fire power. With that flaming landscape, however, Canada becomes a global presence for earthly fire ecology, fire science, and fire institutions. A red maple leaf may decorate its national flag, but a crimson crown fire swelling through its boreal conifers would be a more apt symbol of what makes Canada biotically majestic.[6]

Yet all this staggering burning occurs mostly within a matrix of water. The bulk of the boreal forest overlies the Shield, pocked with endless lakes, ponds, wetlands, and streams; the rest intercalates with muskeg, bog, floodplains, paludifying landscapes, and thawing permafrost, all in all, the greatest expanse of freshwater on Earth and perhaps its most intricately fashioned system of firebreaks. The climate sharpens the scene, being cold and wet, with long winters and short, explosive summers. This is, on average, not a place to burn. But averages mean little in the boreal belt. It is a place of extremes, of sudden ecological eruptions, and of fires that burst wildly and widely across a vast quilt of landscapes.

This paradox of fire and water has precisely such a rhythm: long, ambient periods of cool and wet, ruptured by sharp spikes of dryness and spark. Its wetness allows for fuels to grow; its cold stalls their biological decomposition, such that more and more of a site's ecological wealth gets stuffed into the biotic equivalent of mattresses and tins buried in backyard gardens, locked up in woody debris and standing trees, deposited in peat, moss mats, and shrubs. That is what makes fire necessary. What makes it possible, however, are the drying rays of the summer's endless sunlight, the bouts of seasonal dryness within live vegetation before greenup and after dormancy, and especially the migration of the Hudson Bay High or its minor echoes around the arc. The sudden drying wrought by the wandering ridge quickly transforms sodden biomass into combustibles. Combined with a spark, fire becomes possible, and granted a stiff wind flames may ramble far and wide, broken only by the waning weather and the intricate etching of the Shield's crustal waterways. And outside the Shield, on the western plains clothed with a boreal biota, fires can roam almost unchecked by any geographic impediment, roaring like a prairie fire on woody steroids.

From afar, the boreal forest appears uniform. That illusion crumbles upon close inspection, as the North American taiga fragments into a landscape mosaic – an overused expression but one entirely apt for boreal Canada. What matters is the clustering of biomass on the surface and in the canopies and the ways in which combustion might link them. That patchiness helps to sculpt fire behaviour. When combined with patterns of ignition, a characteristic rhythm of burning emerges, a cadence that underlies a chronicle of fire history. But the action is reciprocal. Since the driving fuels are organic, the product of a living biota, the fires help to select and mould them as much as they do fire.

A small suite of trees dominates the overstorey: birch, aspen, jack pine, and black spruce. Alder, white spruce, balsam fir, and others occupy minor niches or thicken upon the borders of the boreal belt, but the big four define the fire scene. Birch and aspen are deciduous, flushing with growth in the spring and shedding their leaves in the autumn. Canopy fires are impossible, and surface burning depends on grasses, forbs, lichens, shrubs, or conifer reproduction that may underlie groves; such fires can burn briskly in the spring, prior to greenup. Mostly the trees flourish on sites stripped by large fires – the birch reproducing by wind-borne seed, the aspen by some seeding but primarily by suckering from buried rhizomes. Overall, they dapple the larger landscape with fire-resisting blocks.

It is the conifers that power the heavy burning. Crown fires soar through the canopies of jack pine and black spruce. The closely packed jack pine, growing gregariously in dense swaths, can carry fire, even crown fire, throughout much of its life. It grows on good sites and bad, in moist but especially arid soils, matures quickly, resists frost, burns fiercely. In the west its cousin lodgepole pine, with which it hybridizes, assumes this role. The masses of fine fuel that carry fire lie within the canopies, which is where the flames rush. Yet those who study Canadian fire often reserve pride of place for the black spruce. It saturates the boreal belt and flourishes across a gamut of conditions, both wet and dry, rising above mossy understoreys and landscapes lathered in lichens. Those surface fuels provide for the necessary continuity of combustion, while the separate spruce torch like a mass field of immolating candles.

Yet this very intensity ensures perpetuation, for both species boast serotinous cones that open when heated, a formula ideal for flashy crown fires. A seared jack pine stand may shower a burned site with up to five million seeds per hectare; and the more burning it endures, the more it drives off competitors, and the more fire hardened the landscape becomes. Typically jack pine grows on previously burned sites, over large areas where wind and terrain hammer vast crown fires, over scattered pine barrens where more moderate surface burns carve up or gut larger forests. Among Canadian trees it is reckoned the most fire adapted overall.

Black spruce is more subtle, hosting semi-serotinous cones, bunched like grapes at its crown, that spray seeds over ash and char for several years. While those seeds can establish themselves on organic as well as mineral soils, they prosper best where the ground is exposed, where the fire has swept the soils clear of moss, lichens, needles, woody debris, and duff. Black spruce flourishes best, that is, where the fires are most vigorous and all consuming, where, paradoxically, the fires are most broadly lethal. Nowhere has a black spruce stand been found that does not originate from a burn.[7]

These biotic blocks furnish the fuels. Lightning supplies most of the ignitions and sparks most of the large fires, accounting for roughly 60 percent of all ignitions and 80 percent of the entire area burned. The contours of thunderstorm days overlay nicely Canada's broad fire rings: lightning increases steadily to the south, thickening along with the boreal forest that it pummels. Lightning-caused fires, however, are patchier. Lightning varies considerably in its electrical properties, only some of which are favourable to kindling (those with negative charges and long-continuing currents). Moreover, the bolt must strike something combustible, which exists because of local site conditions and past history. Lightning fires will thus cluster around drier shards of landscape, which may be more prone to burning because of soils, terrain, microclimates, and the broader lumpiness of storm tracks. Dry slivers such as the rain-sheltered base of a tree may burn, while a lightning-drenched regional storm may spark nothing. In this way, some regions burn frequently, some rarely; some are places of fire origin, others more likely to receive far-ranging fires from elsewhere. It is remarkable, in the end, how much burns and how little of the boreal belt escapes fire. It is believed that contemporary statistics on lightning-kindled burning could well be doubled (or more) to capture the magnitude of historical burning.[8]

Probably lightning by itself could eventually burn off most of the boreal forest that is susceptible to burning. But lightning did not have to carry that duty alone, and across much of the boreal belt, over many millennia, humans added their own ignitions to help twist the kaleidoscope of this evolving biota. How their fires worked while ice and lakes and earth lurched into something like their current status and to what effect remain unclear, save that they almost certainly did happen. Within historical times, however, a record of aboriginal use has become, if haltingly, recorded and recovered. The best summary comes from northern Alberta, from the research of Henry Lewis among the Athabascan Beaver and Slavey peoples, the Algonkian Cree (who arrived in the region in the early eighteenth century), and various Métis.[9]

Of course, domestic fire was mandatory. No one could long survive the subarctic winter without the heat and light it infused or the summer without the smudge fires that abated somewhat the plague of mosquitoes and blackflies. Then, too, wildfire was an erstwhile and far-flung presence to which humans had to adapt. Probably they scavenged through its recent burns and later hunted, travelled, and foraged among them. But it is that intermediary fire, set by people yet free burning over the land, that intrigues observers – the domestic fire carried to the surrounding landscape and the tame flame that, once let loose, becomes feral.

The evidence is clear: the indigenes used fires deliberately to make their environment more habitable. They burned to shield themselves from nature's threats and randomness, to derive the benefits of fire, on their own terms; they competed with natural fire, burning in the spring (or less often in the fall), outside the prime lightning season, and burning in places and for purposes that mattered specifically to them, rather than accept lightning's lottery. They sought to replace fires of chance with fires of choice.[10]

The grand cycle began with burning around habitations, which were typically in open, grassy patches. Removing the old, dry grass protected their residences from wildfire while sanitizing and cleaning up their near

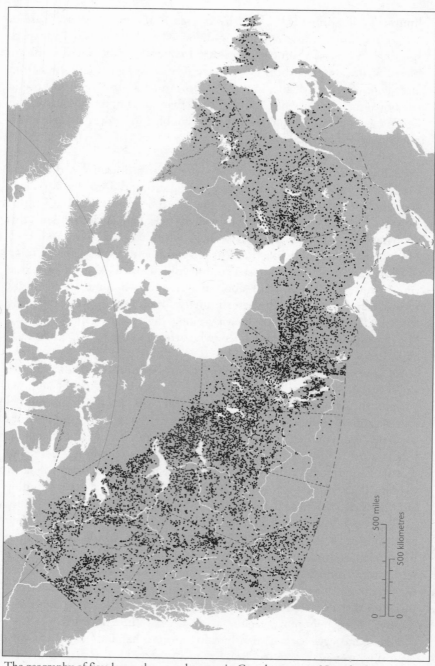

The geography of fires larger than 200 hectares in Canada, 1959-99. Note the concentration in the boreal belt.

surroundings. The thick fringe between meadow and forest became a frontier rich in berries and a place of both covert and clearing, welcome to wildlife. A newly burnt forest, moreover, provided a cache of ready firewood, far better than cutting, stacking, and drying, which in any event was as far beyond their technological capabilities as it was their needs. Writing from the North-West Territory in the 1860s, Émile Petitot explained that, "if drywood becomes scarce, the Indian does not hesitate a moment, he sacrifices beauty to necessity, by setting fire to the forest. The fire will spread over the land, will ravage the country for many leagues. Little cares he. 'What a beautiful country,' he will cry some years after, 'it can be traversed without the branches putting out your eyes, and we have plenty of firewood.'"[11]

The burning proceeded in the spring, as soon as the snow had left the grasses but still resided in the outlying woods or left them soggy. The fires flashed crisply through the stalks and then expired against the damp edge. But the technique could be applied to any and all nearby grasslands and was, in all likelihood, the reason those prairie patches still flourished. The surveying geologist George Dawson reported in 1879 that, whatever theory one might adopt for the origin of the western grasslands to the south, "the origin of the prairies of the Peace River is sufficiently obvious. There can be no doubt that they have been produced and are maintained by fires. The country is naturally a wooded one, and where fires have not run for a few years, young trees begin rapidly to spring up. The fires are, of course, ultimately attributable to human agency."[12]

Wherever they travelled, people burned, fighting back scrub with their flaming axe, opening paths to early drying. A Fort McMurray fire ranger following a Cree crew watched with dismay and outrage as spot fires littered a trail like breadcrumbs until, after "a few years, I realized that those [trail-side] fires weren't going to go anywhere. They only did it in the spring and the fire burned to the wetter stuff and went out ... and that's the way they kept trails open through the muskeg areas." Those corridors existed because they ran along routes for hunting, trapping, or harvesting, and what people sought from these places they could enhance by appropriate fires. They burned along sloughs, marshes, and lakeshores to improve prime habitat for ducks, geese, and muskrats. The intention was to fire the rank sedges and overgrown willows in the early spring, before nesting, but there are accounts of burning to expose nests for ease in harvesting eggs. They burned to increase berries, particularly strawberry and raspberry (and in the east blueberry), though not for saskatoon.[13]

They burned especially to promote favoured wildlife, which feasted on the fresh sedge, grass, sprigs, saplings, and berries that ripened rich with protein and nutrients. They fired grasslands for bison; reeds and marsh grasses for muskrats and waterfowl; riverine willows and aspen for beaver; berry patches for bears; deadfall and brush for deer and moose; strips of grass and shrubs along traplines for snowshoe hares, mice, and voles, in turn prey for fur-bearing marten, fisher, fox, wolf, and lynx. Moose sampled widely from the smorgasbord; there are even reports of them browsing on fresh char (possibly for the mineral "salts"). The creatures that fed on recent fire sites were, Natives agreed, healthier. An elderly Beaver woman observed that "sloughs, where there's rats, muskrats, that's where they used to burn. And where there's heavy brush, you know, like a windfall and things like that. All the young trees would grow (and) attract animals like moose and things. Where there is timber and moss they don't burn (because) the fire lasts and lasts. And, furthermore, the fur-bearing animals like marten and mink and lynx, that's where they mostly stay in wintertime so they don't want to destroy that."[14]

They burned deadfall and windfall forests, the tangled aftermath of storms or recent wildfires, sites prone to dangerous wildfire. The new burns, rightly timed, brought the land back to productive life, opened paths, and attracted wildlife. "Windfalls – where there's all dead trees – those aren't good places," a Slavey observed. "Nothing lives there, nothing is any good. We set fire to those places in the spring. That way the fire makes the forest live again."[15]

So also their fires roused human society to life, a rite of spring that proclaimed the end of winter, the return of warmth and plenty. If animals followed the syncopated cycle of patch burns, so did people, or they shaped that round of gathering and hunting through their burns. They moved with seasonal opportunities, seizing the selective meats and fruits of different sites in turn. They erected their movable teepees one place in the spring, another in the fall. Over time, such regular settlements would exhaust their firewood, make game animals wary and scarce, and become burdened with the aggregate effluent of human presence. They would move to a new site, open it with fire, while the old one returned to bush, perhaps fired for a while as part of an ensemble of useful environs. The boreal kaleidoscope turned anew.

The premise behind aboriginal fire practices was that their calculated burns did more good than harm. They allowed people to extract more and do so under safer and more predictable conditions. They had to be controlled; they had to yield the proper biotic outcomes. The techniques for burning thus melded fire's behaviour with fire's ecology. That merger argued for spring burns when the desired fuels were dry enough to combust but the surrounding landscape was not. Summer fires were dangerous for the same reason that lightning fires could, from time to time, break free and swallow huge woods. Autumn fires lacked the checks and balances that the spring moisture regime furnished. Burners preferred certain conditions, such as a light wind; wetlands, streams, snow, or sodden surface mats with which to contain flames; flashy fuels that would not hold a smouldering fire until a later time when it might erupt on its own; isolated stands of tough scrub after the surrounding grasses had burned off. The settlement meadows the men burned collectively; the smaller strips individual men and, where foraging rather than hunting was the object, women could treat. Winter campfires, on snow, were kindled over sites known to end in rock or mineral soils. "Fires had to be controlled," an old Cree recalled. "You couldn't just start a fire anywhere, anytime. Fire can do a lot of harm or a lot of good. You have to know how to control it." A Beaver informant added, "They must be very wise, eh? Those people? That time?"[16]

Yet the indisputable fact is that fires did escape. Perfect control was impossible. Campfires burned through snow into mossy duff or peat and then erupted during droughty springs. Logs smouldered for days, even weeks, then rekindled. Grasses burned around lakes and sloughs to expose muskrat runs might break free. Routine fires blew up when they struck treelines that, because of exceptional dryness, lacked adequate moisture barriers. A light wind could become strong; a cold front could blast past with winds that blustered and veered. Fires could be used viciously, wantonly, foolishly. In 1796, from what would become northern Saskatchewan, David Thompson observed that "the Natives" were "frequently very careless" in putting out their fires, and a high wind would stir the embers widely, and the flames would gallop "until stopped by some large swamp or lake; which makes many miles of the country appear very unsightly, and destroys many animals and birds especially the grouse, who do not appear to know how to save themselves, but all this devastation is nothing to the Indian, his country is large."[17]

Such fires were only as powerful as their surroundings – even arson is no better than its capacity to propagate – but they added to the overall fire load. Most landscape-scale burning occurs during episodes of short-term dryness over a handful of years, a few days amid a few years, the probability demanding not only proper fuels and weather but also ignition. Anthropogenic burning, the sheer volume of fire littering, meant that ignition was almost always there. Just as their calculated spring burns shifted the fire regime, so too did the conflagrations that sprang from their mistakes.

As a general conception, this one has limits, both geographical and

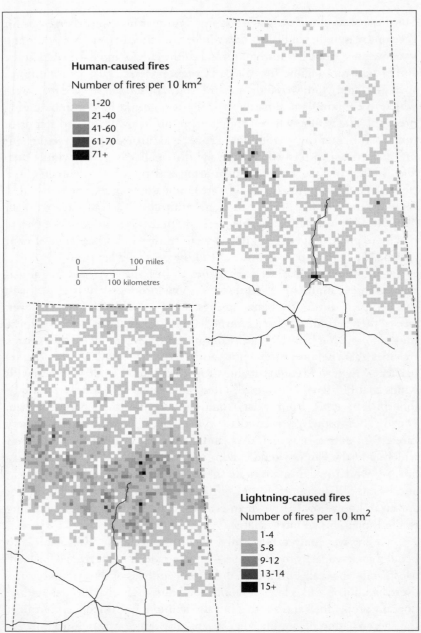

Human-caused fires

Number of fires per 10 km^2

- 1-20
- 21-40
- 41-60
- 61-70
- 71+

0   100 miles

0   100 kilometres

Lightning-caused fires

Number of fires per 10 km^2

- 1-4
- 5-8
- 9-12
- 13-14
- 15+

Torch and bolt, the geographies of people and lightning as ignition sources in Saskatchewan. Note the distinctive patterns, as anthropogenic fire concentrates on routes of travel and places of activity, while lightning is both more random and more clustered.

historical. The Shield, underlying so much of boreal Canada, proposed a more formidable landscape for burning. It featured many lakes and few prairies, forced travel by canoe rather than on foot, offered more wet edges and fewer drier ones. Still, where people went, so did fires, and where they sought to extract something from the land they found in fire a nearly universal catalyst. Fires probably crowded around well-travelled shores and hunting haunts, occasionally erupting into the deeper bush.

The schema says nothing about caribou, the hoofed larder that migrated seasonally, often between woods and tundra, and that feasted on lichens during the arduous subarctic winters. Unlike the fire-fluffed browse that sustained the creatures of interest to Albertan indigenes, or the prairies that fed bison and elk, lichens are devastated, not renewed, by fire; they may require decades to recover (sixty to eighty years in the west, forty to sixty years in the east), which depresses the sizes and deflects the movements of herds and hence of hunters. The scientific and political denunciation of lichen burning dates back to eighteenth-century Scandinavia and continues today. The literature suggests that fires might not have burned as widely in the past and that aboriginal fire practices may have been more closely checked for fear of wiping out a critical creature. The issue remains muddled. Yet another reading suggests that the condemnation of lichen burning is political and ritual, that, while caribou much prefer lichens, they are cosmopolitan in taste, capable of surviving on boreal hardtack instead of gourmet meals, and that, over the span of centuries and biotas, fire is a necessary rejuvenant, without which even the fire-abhorrent lichens would eventually starve. Clearly, indigenes would not burn lichen prairies as they would meadows, but clearly, too, those lands could absorb a good dose of fire, which in any event would happen from lightning.

The Hypsithermal and the Neoglacial, too, altered the patterns of anthropogenic fire. At the height of the Great Warming, the grasslands and seasonally dry woodlands pushed farther north, rendering those lands more susceptible to burning. Probably some of the large prairies embedded within the boreal forest are residual from that era – not originally created by indigenous burning so much as maintained by it. The fire practices of near-contemporary peoples may likewise be relicts, seeking out those niches that preserve patches of past habitats, holding onto techniques previously well suited to broader and more favourable landscapes. First Nations demographics had changed: diseases had decimated whole tribes, peoples had migrated and morphed into new clan confederations, market trapping upset arrangements of beaver ponds and browse, and outright European colonization had pushed a wandering folk into fixed

reservations and restricted the old ways. Over the past century in particular, governments deliberately sought to rein in indigenous fire practices; in northern Alberta, authorities officially banned burning in 1910.
It continued, whether surreptitiously or in open defiance, but gradually
anthropogenic fire for habitat became snuffed out. By the 1970s, when
anthropologists such as Lewis could interview them, even tribal elders had
grown up under a regimen in which ancient fire practices were suspect and
never truly practised.

Yet it beggars belief that Canada's aboriginal peoples, alone among the
forest dwellers of the Earth, would not have burned where they could and
did not alter the larger geography of fire by the burns that fled their restless
hands. What is problematic is to sift out the wholly natural from the
anthropogenic, but that is a problem of our construction. Humans have
been in the biota since it congealed; both castes of fires have interacted. If
contemporary aboriginal practices do not portray past ones, then neither
do the statistics of contemporary burning. The hegemony of lightning
fire is in part an outcome of removing people as active fire agents, which
statistically boosts the proportion allotted to lightning. Contemporary
residents and travellers start fewer fires, and those fires tally fewer hectares,
because people are either discouraged or divorced from the fire-foraging
that probably characterized their previous economies and are admonished,
under pain of law, not to set and leave fires. There are, in brief, few patch
burns and fewer escapes. When newcomers have suddenly appeared,
however, as prospectors, road construction crews, or professional trappers,
an outbreak of far-ranging fires has typically resulted.

The issue is not whether fire would scorch the boreal forest – it would.
The ecological concern lies with the fire regimes that have evolved, the
historical geography behind more recent conditions. Some hundreds of
years ago the boreal belt overall probably had more fires, more spring
fires, a finer texture of burns along major routes of travel and patches of
habitation, with splotches erupting when those fires broke free. These fires,
too, would originate from corridors and seasons of human occupation.
What these fires burned, lightning could not. Probably the grand sweep
showed a mosaic of larger and smaller tiles; the bigger pieces were far
removed from human settlement, with a fine-grained landscape of intricate
shards near habitations. While the pattern was not that of underburning
typical of temperate climes, it would be foolish to dismiss the power of
anthropogenic fire. Where aboriginal burning has ceased, the scrub has
thickened and overrun grasses and non-woody patches. The prairies that
the Great Warming spread northward, and that anthropogenic burning

held in partial preservation, the suppression of fire has allowed the woods to roll over. "The country has changed from what it used to be," said an old Cree, eleven years old when the fire ban was formally announced, "brush and trees where there used to be lots of meadows and not so many animals as before." The people who reside in (or visit) that forest today do so equipped with firesticks of internal combustion.[18]

What has emerged in recent centuries is a fat-patched quilt of fire regimes stitched into the boreal belt. They obey trends, north and south, west and east, according to the two geographic gradients that broadly plait Canada. Fires occur most vigorously where biomass builds most rapidly, and they bolt most frequently when dryness and spark most often meet. In this way, the cycle of burning is shorter in the south than in the north, and quicker in the west than in the east, the fires revisiting more often in jack pine than in black spruce, at a faster tempo in dry sites than in moist ones. On average, large fires – and the powerful burns, those that work the most ecological effects – traditionally arrive roughly every 100 to 120 years in the boreal biomes of the east and every 60 to 80 (or even 40 to 60) years in the west. Compared with those of African savannahs or Mediterranean brushlands, this is a long wave of burning; compared with rainforests and sodden peatlands and near-empty deserts, it is a brisk one; but mostly it is a pace well matched against the deep swells of the far northern climate. It is one to which the boreal biota has adapted, one that it expects, one for which ecologically it hungers.

Fire and Grass, Fire and Leaf:
Great Plains Prairies and Great Lakes Forests

That exquisite mix of the wet and the dry that shapes the boreal forest breaks down farther south. One tendency or the other prevails. To the southwest, the Great Plains show annual dry spells, a predictable rhythm of seasonal aridity, over which longer waves of drought appear; trees find it harder to thrive, while grasses find it easier to burn; fire becomes not merely possible but also routine. To the southeast, however, around the Great Lakes and the St. Lawrence, wetness prevails. Each month shows roughly the same quantity of precipitation as every other, and even the atonal beat of drought becomes rare. Biological decomposition, not open combustion, drives the recycling of nutrients. Fires burn, if at all, with the benign, brief colouring of autumn leaves or simply shrivel in the perpetual shade.

The prairies were many. They were tallgrass, fescue, aspen, and mixed; they graded into assorted shrub and woods; they spread over wetland

and sandhill; they fronted montane forest, woodland, and boreal forest. They jostled within a skewed bubble between the drying lands west of the Great Lakes and a stark rain shadow east of the Rocky Mountains. What they shared was a relatively level, little-broken terrain; a climate given to regular, typically annual dry spells; powerful winds; and a biota dominated by grasses and forbs, with sprinklings of woody scrub and gallery forest. It was a landscape prone to burning, and the question that has gripped so many observers, from European explorers to modern ecologists, is whether those fires are a necessary process and even, from a historical perspective, a causative agent. In brief, do these grasslands need fires, or do they simply sustain them, as they might occasional outbreaks of grasshoppers? And are they primarily climatic, or do they result from cultural activities, which is to say from anthropogenic burning?[19]

There is no single ecology of prairie fire because there is no single kind of prairie and no exactly replicating fire. Each grassy and forb-choked patch has its own regimen of responses, varying according to season, frequency, intensity, and scale of burning, the amount of soil moisture and the subsequent onset of rain or drought, the character of pre- and post-burn grazing, the salting of woody species within the biome. They will differ according to whether the fire that passed through was slow or fast, backing or heading. A fire in the spring yields different results from one in the fall; a fire in late April from one in mid-May; a fire crackling through shortgrass stalks after a long drought from one through tallgrass and aspen after several wet seasons. A patch heavily grazed and trampled will burn differently from one untouched for several years. A parcel of greenup will respond according to which species rush in to crop it, and how many, and how soon.

Put simply, fires clean out dead debris, liberate nutrients, expose the soil to warming and drying, select among species, and check or clear away woody scrub. Fires promote richer forage when they occur on moist soils or are followed by gentle rains; they best sustain grasslands, and beat back brush and trees, when they burn through dense grass swards after droughts; they promote the greatest variety of plants when they burn in the early spring, perhaps with snow still spotty, and do not burn too often. Burning after seasonal flowering, particularly in plants stressed by drought, reduces their productivity and variety; not burning where woody plants abound allows scrub to overtake the prairies. Paradoxically, the beneficial outcomes – as judged by people – are more likely to happen from routine firing outside the summer lightning season.

What is generally true of fire adaptations is especially true for prairies:

species display a suite of traits that adapts them to a suite of conditions. The classic stresses on the grasslands are browsing and grazing, bouts of dryness, and fire. By storing most of their biomass underground, by becoming dormant during times of stress, by resprouting from rhizomes – these properties serve to protect against the collective assault on the above-surface stalks, tillers, and leaves. The stresses themselves are interdependent. Drought promotes fire, spring fire stimulates new growth more succulent to grazers, grazing varies according to the moisture and alters the quantity and arrangement of combustibles. The choreography is complex, even chaotic, yet rhythms and regimes emerge. This is true whether events come from people or nature but exponentially so when the two interact.

That lightning can and does start fires is unquestionable. The situation is not unlike that on the tundra: when people look for lightning-kindled burns, they find them. It is difficult to imagine why such fires should be lacking, and in fact they aren't. Even early explorers such as John Macoun witnessed lightning-kindled fires. They occur with the summer storms, roughly from May through August (although Peter Fidler cites spring and fall origins, which he may have confused with human sources). The timing is curious because it coincides with the period of full-flushed growth – that is, burning can be difficult except through the dry debris interweaving with the green, or if the storm arrives after a severe drought the resulting fires often savage the grasses, diminishing their growth and diversity. Yet they happen and have helped to shape the biome.[20]

Far more abundant are human fire starts. They were many, varied, and expected, such that flaming prairies were a common feature of the plains. Quickly explorers came to expect them, as they did bison and antelope and an incessant wind; if the prairies didn't freely oblige, then the travellers could coerce them. In his *Tour of the Prairies*, Washington Irving blithely recorded the wish of one member of his party to witness the fabled spectacle, to which their French Canadian guide exclaimed, "by Gar, I'll set one on fire myself!" The scene was little different north of the forty-ninth parallel. At Pigeon Lake, Alberta, John Palliser noted, "we set fire to the grass, just to say we had done so."[21]

These burns merged, like salt in the sea, with all the others, for which pragmatic reasons abounded; the prairie tribes needed fire and adapted fire practices to their purposes. The likelihood of escapes was ever possible. Even winter could be fire season if the snow was sparse and ignition abundant. Feral fires from seasonal encampments were rare since special care was taken not only with the fires but also with the surrounding fuels, even to first burning over a campsite or grazing it. But transient fires from travellers were more likely to break free. Signal fires were common, either to warn of strangers or to announce the arrival of visitors, or according to pre-established codes such as those suggested by Bacqueville de La Potherie: "It is the custom of the peoples who inhabit this continent that, when they go hunting in spring and autumn, they light fires on those prairies, so that they can ascertain each other's location." Travellers kindled fires to clear out thick growth and thus ease access. Indigenes also set fires to harass intruders – burning out ahead and around of parties to deprive them of forage and perhaps pick off a clumsy straggler. Army parties in the United States in particular took precautions, sometimes even burning out around their evening campsites to prevent an ambush by fire during the night. Such burns could ramble widely. And of course there was the usual fire littering. Those who merely travelled through a place were never as careful as those who lived there, and careless fires mingled with those resulting from malice.[22]

In short, there could be fires at nearly all times and at nearly all places and for nearly all purposes. But fire was too powerful to leave to happenstance; fire was a good servant only if people were good masters; and the Natives had ample reasons for burning. The most fundamental – and ecologically pervasive – was fire for hunting. Louis Hennepin, perhaps the first European chronicler of the vast prairies, wrote from the headwaters of the Illinois River in 1679 that, "having passed through great Marshes, we found a vast Plain, on which nothing grows but only some Herbs, which were dry at the time, and burnt, because the Miamis set them on fire every Year, in their hunting wild Bulls." For the next two centuries, until agricultural colonization finally ended that world with the near extinction of bison, prairie, and indigenes all, that iconic observation was repeated. As fur traders and naturalists probed into the Canadian prairies, they discovered a commonality of fire practices to match that of grasses and grazers. Bacqueville de La Potherie, Nicholas Perrot, Alexander Hendry, Peter Fidler, Henry Sibley, David Thompson, Alexander Henry, Henry Boller, John Macoun, John Palliser, Henry Hind, Paul Kane, Colonel S.B. Steele – all noted the fiery prairies and tallied the reasons for them, of which the hunt loomed largest.[23]

There was a smattering of outright fire-driving: some fire-forcing of the herds to move where hunters wanted them, some advancing upon their prey with torches and smoke or outright flaming fronts. Such tactics could help to drive them over cliffs or into bogs or relatively unburned patches. Lewis and Clark describe how early firing pushed some bison onto river ice, whose floes toppled them or brought them near banks, where they could be slaughtered. Colonel Richard Dodge, in the central plains, relates how, with the game scarce, a band of hunters, "taking advantage of winds or streams," fired off the prairies some distance from camp such that the herds ambled to the unburned grasses nearer the camp, where they could be harvested. Near Pembina, Henry Sibley observed similar techniques, such as pushing bison to a hilltop bare of grass. Both La Potherie and Perrot describe fire rings "from which the animals cannot escape." Elk, deer, bison – some could slip through the fiery noose, some would be killed as they fled a gauntlet of hunters, some (in deep fuels) would perish. But the scale could increase. When conditions allowed, tribes could deflect herds away from rivals and toward themselves and did so. But what happened deliberately could also occur accidentally. Palliser, for example, described the "serious misfortune" that could result when such fires, or accidental ones, went wrong: "They cut off the buffalo sometimes from a whole district of country, and thus often are the cause of great privation and distress."[24]

These strategies hint at the richer reason for burning: to control the geography of foraging and hence influence the migrations of herds. A Hidatsa from North Dakota, Waheenee, stated the matter simply by recalling the words of his father: "Every spring, when I was young, we fired the prairie grass around the Five Vallages. Green grass then sprang up; buffalos came to graze on it, and we killed many." The underlying logic is simple. The fresh growth sprouting from burns is more palatable, nutritious, richer in protein, and vastly more attractive than old stalks. Equally land fired in autumn and left blackened over the winter lacked forage. The upshot is that herds move with the pattern of burns. They seek out greening-up patches in the spring and unburned patches over the winter, and they avoid sites just fired but not yet regrown and sites extensive with over-wintering burns. The most desirable of all forage was one burned and now freshly sprouting on moist soils. From Palliser again: "Places where fire had consumed the grass in the previous autumn, after that season's growth had ceased, now became green in the course of a few days, as the snow always disappears from these spots first."[25]

If a creature could control that geography of burning, it could control the herds, not only the bison, but also the antelope, elk, deer, and their carnivorous camp followers, grizzly, wolf, coyote. But that is precisely the power the North American indigenes possessed. They could kindle fire, and they had every reason to do so and to ensure that their fires, not those of lightning, moulded those migrations that so determined whether they thrived or starved. As best constructed, the rhythm seems to reconcile the seasonal movements of hunters and prey, forcing the herds to cluster on unburned landscapes near winter encampments and then to attract them to fresh-burned sites elsewhere in the spring. Astute observers echoed Colonel Richard Dodge (from the central plains) that "the Indians burn portions of the prairie every fall, setting the fires so as to burn as vast an extent of country as possible, and yet preserve unburned a good section in the vicinity where they purpose to make their fall hunt." This was basic fire ecology, known by all who inhabited the grasslands. The speculation even exists that it was the pressure of human hunting that helped to drive the bison into gregarious throngs.[26]

It is not easy to control free-burning flame over lush, dry grasses with a stiff wind behind it, which is why aboriginal hunters avoided such times and places. They burned when the dead grass came out from the snow, often still damp or flanked with snow banks; or they burned grazed and trampled parcels, where the flames could not flare wildly; and, everywhere possible, they burned against streams and lakes or old burns or verdant swards. They burned against the wind as well as with it; they banked one burned patch against another. The sheer history of firing and grazing created a collage that helped to quell any tendency toward conflagrations. Most prairie fires were not roaring tidal waves; they flashed and fizzled with gusts and greenery, most winding in long serpentine threads through modest carpets of combustibles. At night, they lit up skies with savage sublimity, more spectacular than threatening.

Aboriginal peoples had no reason to kindle fires and let them ramble senselessly wherever the flames could reach. The ferocious conflagrations of record, blazing "as fast as a horse could gallop," ran through bottom lands or valleys, rank with rough growth. Typical grass fires burned with lower flames and less pace, buffeted about by the winds, wending in long twisted strips over hills and wallows. The immense burns often reported were a cumulative quilt of multiple firings, or the outcome of accidental or arson fires, often set for military advantage, or the outbreak of lightning. They were also dangerous. Escaped fires threatened camps; malicious or drought-powered broadcast burns could endanger forage for winter herds; fast-sweeping flames could kill slowly moving parties caught suddenly in dense, dry swards. If the fire broke out in a temporary camp, the response was to swat it out with blankets, hides, or even chunks of dry meat. If amid the grasses, the standard technique was to kindle a counter fire or more simply, as Alexander Ross recounted, "to burn the grass around him, and occupy the centre of the little clearing thus formed; in which case he will have only the smoke and ashes to contend with." In this way, reported Paul Kane, they "escape all but the smoke, which, however, nearly suffocates them."[27]

Even when the burning was deliberate, control was never complete. Seasons varied, and years were more notable for their extremes than for their averages. Some years burning was difficult because there was too little grass due to drought or too much that was too wet due to relentless rains. And because the burns attracted grazers, the herds helped determine what forage might survive as fuel. Ecological equants and epicycles overlay any putative cycle of fire and combustibles. Areas heavily cropped would have less fuel and hence experience less vigorous burning and so reduce their attractiveness the next year, while areas not grazed might burn keenly and thus draw grazers to their green pick and be chewed to nubbin. The interplay of animals, plants, and fire is a biotic three-body problem, without a strict solution. Aboriginal hunters and foragers were probably little better equipped to forecast, precisely, what their burns would yield than modern researchers, whose models seem so much conceptual clutter.

Nor was the torch applied with the mechanical rigour of a piston sparking at top-dead centre. Tribal demographics varied, particularly as peoples felt the first tremors of European disease; they quarrelled with other peoples, affecting the movements of each group; they made mistakes, they let fires escape, they miscalculated. Certainly Canada's grasslands could be burned more readily and for more explicit reasons than its boreal forest, but the climatic lumpiness underwriting both never departed. The dry spells that made burning possible segued into wet ones that made it difficult. In 1914, rangers with the Dominion Forestry Branch reported, in dismay and outrage, how the local indigenes were furiously firing the eastern slopes, the reason given that, the past three years having been too wet to burn as they wished, they intended to seize the geographic moment and cram as much fire as they could into the slots made available.[28]

So fire there was and anthropogenic fire in abundance. Often annual, nearly everywhere, the flames were among the prairies' defining features. No other Canadian biota had so many fires so often and so widely cast. The history of Canadian grasslands is a history of fire, of places burned and sites spared. But were those fires merely a property of the prairies, an ecological decoration, as it were, that painted the night sky with orange and yellow? Or, more boldly, were they a generative agent without which the grasslands could not exist, a flaming axe that hewed back the original forest?

Probably both. Certainly the origin of the grand prairies was a popular debate in North America. Many early observers noted the power of repeated fire to check woody growth, and Macoun summarized these opinions when he reckoned that "the only cause of this absence of trees" in southern Saskatchewan was "the ever recurring fires which burn off the grass and shrubby plants almost every season." From the northern Saskatchewan, Palliser went further, also echoing a cadre of naturalists, and declared that "the great pine forest" that had previously clothed the country had been "removed by successive fires." Accepting the obvious facts as he saw them – the frequency of burning on even small scales, the seasonality of burning (May and October), the presence of buried char on what are now grassy plains – Ernest Thompson Seton even sought to calculate the rate at which the prairie must have advanced. His conclusion, that "this was once a wooded country; it was cleared by fire; the fires were the work of man; it would take between five and ten centuries of such fires to effect the present clearance, and their starting point must have been in the direction of the Coteau du Missouri."[29]

Such claims harbour both fact and hyperbole. A grinding drought could allow fires to enter normally immune woods and replace it with prairie, but a round of wet seasons could permit the trees to reclaim that lost ground. The frontier between tree and grass was ecologically elastic. The power of anthropogenic fire was only as great as its power to propagate, which depended on circumstances beyond human control, save the capacity to decide when to kindle. One could ignite a fire to sweep through an understorey like a gentle broom by burning in low winds, damp fuels, snow-patchy woods. Or one could scythe a stand by kindling during times of acute aridity, overstocked fuels, and high winds. Fire could perform both tasks, but to argue over its might as a generative agent is to miss its greater power as a preserver; it could hold grasses against woods, so long as weather allowed for dry spells and people wished to burn. Curiously, just as the boreal forest held pockets of prairie, so the grasslands surrounded bundles of forest. The one existed because the sites were burned, the other because they were spared.

The reason is historical. The grand fringe between the boreal forest and the prairie grasslands had, more than once after deglaciation, shuffled north and south. There is an argument that some of the largest prairie swaths such as the Peace River region exist in and of themselves as a product of present conditions. Perhaps they do, but many of the smaller chunks survive only because they are burned. They are relics of a past prairie that had once surged farther north at least during the Great Warmth. Similarly, along streams and atop rocky mounds, copses of woods thrive. On larger rises such as the Cypress Hills or Turtle Mountain, the elevation captures enough rainfall to sustain a woods-preferred climate. The rest survive only because they escape the flames. They grow in marshes or wet bottoms, preferably on the east sides of streams that serve as fuel breaks against the wind-driven flames; or amid rocky outcrops and cliffs, again stony on their west and so immune to east-racing fires; or on barren sandhills or sodden wallows; or in areas that shelter herds and thus find their understoreys so grazed that intense fires cannot blast through. Their wooded range ebbs and flows with the tug of climate, but without regular burning much of what swelled with grasses at the time of European contact would have sprouted trees.

Fire and prairie were joined like surf and sea. Over and again, observers, both Native and newcomer, declared the indisputable fact that, when the fires retreated, the woods advanced. Those carefully tended flames were biotic dikes that kept the ponded woods from overflowing the land. This much was self-evident. Even the most obtuse traveller could witness, with his or her own eyes, the consequences of fire's presence and removal. The only debates were whether aboriginal burning had originally carved the prairies out of the woods and whether the plains shared the same scenario as the prairies. And these are perhaps less revealing for what they say regarding the physical geography of the grasslands than for the impact the prairies' fires had on the imagination of those, typically from sodden, fire-intolerant lands, who were witnessing such burning on a subcontinental scale for the first time.

Writing in 1874, A.R.C. Selwyn of the Geological Survey distilled the observations of several generations of trained naturalists when he observed "the gradual destruction of the forests over large areas, by fire," that "there is no doubt that at different times almost every square mile of the country between Red River and the Rocky Mountains has been subjected to them [fires]; and that hundreds of miles of forest have thus been converted into wide and almost treeless expanses of prairie." What the conjecture missed is the prospect that those prairies might be a climatic relict, an older scene preserved by fire, and thus a cultural landscape. What it foresaw, however, was that, when the fire dike was breached, the land would flood with trees.[30]

Addressing the Royal Geographical Society eighteen years later, as settlement squeezed the last of the old ways, and as trees were slowly surging south, Miller Christy summed up the case for fire in this way: "That the fires, by gradually killing and consuming the forests, have caused the treelessness of the prairies; or, in other words, that the prairies themselves are, largely at least, due to fire." The evidence, he concluded, was the "clearest" possible. "If the fires have not caused the prairies, they

are at least now extending them in numberless places; that trees still grow
on the prairies on spots that are to some extent protected from the fires;
and that, over large portions of the prairies, young trees spring up annually,
only to be at once burned; but, if protected from the fire, they would grow
and in due time reproduce the banished forest-growth.[31]

In arguing his case, Christy carefully distinguished between tallgrass
prairies and the shortgrass of the high plains. The Canadian prairies he
traced from Manitoba and "all the North-West Territories" south of the
Saskatchewan River as far west as Regina. On these lands, the grasses
flourished only with fire's constant tending. In the remaining geographic
wedge, what became known as the Palliser Triangle, he believed that other
causes prevailed, both "soil and climate" uniting to establish "a sterile
region." The plains were treeless for reasons other than solely flame.[32]

Yet flames were not absent and not without ecological power. They were
common if no longer necessary to hold back the crowding woods, passing
over the plains with the insouciance of the winds. While these grasslands
could thrive as grasslands with or without burning, the abundant fires
shuffled the black and green tiles of a landscape mosaic, around which
the deer and the antelope played. Moreover, if these grasses would persist,
so would their fires. In the prairies, the relationship was reciprocal.
Extinguishing fires extinguished the grasslands, but quenching the grasses
also quenched fires. On the more arid plains, both could continue. It
was from precisely this fire citadel that Seton believed the aboriginal fires
must have emerged that had flailed against and driven back the ancient
forest. And even here, along the foothills of the Rockies and amid moist
patches, when fire ended, scrub sprouted. What intervened, however, was
settlement. What here replaced the grasslands was ultimately not forest
but farm.

The mixed forest arrayed north of the Great Lakes is the prairies'
complement. Cartographically it inverts the prairie wedge, and climatically
it grades not into a rhythmic aridity but into a smeared moistness.
Precipitation of some kind – rain, sleet, snow, drizzle – falls month after
month. The cracks of dryness through which fire can enter are here sparse,
and fire must seek out those moments when seasonal rhythms are slightly
out of sync, particularly in early spring and late fall, especially around the
western lakes, where rain falls preferentially during the warm months.
The bioregional uniformity becomes greater as one moves east and south
toward the triangle's apex, as the biota brokers between the eruptive fires
of the boreal forest and nearly incombustible fringes, patchily grading

between a coniferous forest and a deciduous woodland. Less frequent than on the prairies, less explosive than in the boreal forest, fires are as mixed as their fuels.

Red and white pine dominate the conifers. The red pine overlaps with jack pine, while the white pine overlaps with other biomes tracking along the Appalachians far to the east and south. Both are fire species, but this means they accommodate nicely fire regimes of a particular sort. Both species generate well after fires; severe burns, scrubbing the surface to mineral soil, promote pine over hazel, balsam fir, aspen, dense herbs, and birch. After fifty years, both red and white pine become inured against surface fire as thick bark plates their trunks; they can then slough off brisk-running fires through the duff and shrubs, including hot burns every twenty to thirty years, that help to trim back competitors. Even relatively light burns can cause growth rings to widen in response to lessened stress. If crown fires come more often than fifty years, then jack pine, birch, and aspen – the boreal medley – tend to predominate. If the fires withdraw for more than 150 years, then northern sites will edge into a boreal mix of spruce and fir and southern sites into hardwoods such as maple and hemlock. The fire-carrying understorey is a rich stew of shrubs, moss, and grass, with hazel, raspberry, honeysuckle, and blueberry particularly prominent. Mosses and lichens often appear after burns and become nurseries for pine seedlings. Fire keeps the cauldron bubbling. The patch geography of the Great Lakes forest is largely a geography of its fire history.[33]

So, too, the hardwoods run a gamut of species from the fire-thirsty to the fire-shunning. Of the former there are, of course, the weedy birch and aspen that dapple the landscape. But more specifically, there is the red oak that thrives with fire, regenerating from basal sprouts, seizing released nutrients to lay on thicker growth rings. It can tolerate frequent light fires and revive after severe ones; in the absence of disturbance, however, of something to crack open the shade canopy of neighbouring sugar maple, white ash, and basswood, the oak withers away. Once converted to mature hardwoods, especially maple or beech, only a profound jarring from the outside will rattle that woods sufficiently to allow oak to revive. Once such a shade forest firmly roots, dense as a tumulus, even fire must struggle to enter or simply becomes an autumnal broom to whisk away dry leaves.

The fuels, like the landscapes that hold them, are a jumble, sprouting on the deranged hydrology of the Shield and the glaciated lowlands. A jostling throng of trees typically replaces vast stands dominated by one or two species. There are pockets and peninsulas of boreal forest from the north, and the same of hardwoods from the south, the berm and

flotsam of past climatic tides. The region is rife with legacy forests, broken
into shards, shaken, and tossed over the land. The understorey is a shag
carpet of moss, needles, branchwood, shrubs, grass, and, where the soils
allow, lush reproduction of shade-tolerant hardwoods. There are splashes
of grassy meadows and sedgelands, fields of sun-craving berries, canopy
cavities, and jack-strawed timber ripped from the woods by wind, ice,
insect, and disease. But there is little of the vast, fire-imposed uniformities
of the boreal forest or the prairie. Fire is spottier, more inclined to pass
over the surface than through the crowns, less habitual than amid wind-
swept, sun-drenched plains, more varied and subtle as it probes rather
than punches through a patchy terrain.

What often assists the burning is a prior slashing. It helps if something
can open up the canopy and expose the surface fuels to dry. The means are
several: windstorms, icestorms, weevils, blister rust, scleroderris canker,
root rot. Such events reverse the thickening of the woods with young
growth, particularly of hardwoods, that, if not halted, will eventually
overtop the original grove. The dominant conifers respond to such stresses
differently. Red pine better resists disease, white pine wind. But once
standing trees are trashed, they move from living biomass to available fuel,
a further jumble on the land. When arid spells come, they find something
to dry, and fire can find something to burn. Such patches are useful points
of ignition and accelerants, but if they make fire possible they also tend to
limit its range.

Overall, the size of burns depends on the fuels available and hence on the
dryness that readies them. Most of the large burns occur after light winters
and early springs, during which fires can sprint across large landscapes. The
deeper, more severe burns happen in the fall, after drought combines with
dormancy to drain even organic soils of moisture, such that fires burn deep
as well as wide. The western expanse, around Lake Superior and toward the
Manitoban prairies, packs more of its seasonal moisture into the summer,
thus cracking open a bit wider the scope for early spring and late fall fires
and encouraging larger and more fierce burns. To the east, and especially
in southern Ontario, the cracks are tinier and fewer, the forest less prone to
broad shattering, the shards of broken woods smaller. This complexity of
fuels makes for a blotchy fire regime of light fires, intense fires, petite fires,
mass fires, surface fires, crown fires, smouldering roots, flaring shrublands,
torching thickets – the most intricate of Canada's indigenous fire provinces.
The charcoal chronicle left in lake sediments is both common and stirred,
lacking "distinct layers with well defined boundaries."[34]

Even the driest, fluffiest fuels still need a spark to kindle. The Great

Lakes forest holds two known foci of lightning fires, both in the west. The largest centres on Kenora, splashing out to Red Lake and Quetico Park. The other, less intense, hovers over Sault Ste. Marie. Like concretions around these cores, the fires drop off in number toward Hudson Bay and the Ontario peninsula. In brief, the more the province resembles the southern boreal forest, the more naturally disposed it is to burn, while the more it trails into maple and beech, the less it is. A prominent reason is the gyration of the Hudson Bay High, which often settles in northwest Ontario, drying, blowing, sparking. Here lightning and woods converge, but when the High moves south, it beats harmlessly against tumulus hardwoods.[35]

More difficult to determine is the regimen of anthropogenic fire. A reconstruction is confusing because the first-contact explorers, fresh from Reformation Europe, were little interested in fire; because, quickly, Native societies morphed under the impress of trade, war, and disease; and because, by the moment of the first encounters, some of the indigenous peoples had the axe as well as the torch. Aboriginal fire regimes must remain conjectural, a plausible supposition from first principles, an extrapolated ecology, an argument from analogy.

Burning probably clustered then, as today, around settlements, at sites of intensive hunting, fishing, or foraging, and along routes of travel. Compared with the boreal forest, there were more people, more places of harvesting and routes to get there, more purposes for firing. The matrix of fire was probably more intricate, the escapes less prone to roar hugely. Anthropogenic burning etched along shorelines and riverine campsites. Grassy patches, attractive to deer, would be burned routinely, along with oak savannahs. Probably berry shrublands were extensive and fired every two or three years, a pyric horticulture. Spring burns along overland paths would keep the corridors open. Fields around seasonal or semi-permanent camps would be fired annually; frequented shorelines became in effect immense open hearths. Carpets of autumnal leaves may well have been fired to assist a fall hunt. Escapes were abundant – there is no reason to assume otherwise. But the jumbled character of the landscape meant that fires would quickly jam against biotic baffles and buffers, except where blowdowns and insects had opened swaths. East of Lake Superior, the region is not prone to large burns.[36]

Historical documentation from indigenous Canada is sparse; almost nothing predates contact. South of the St. Lawrence, however, Thaddeus Harris in 1803 described how, for "more than fifty miles," the Allegheny Mountains were aflame, kindled "by the hunters, who set fire to dry leaves and decayed fallen timber in the vallies, in order to thin the undergrowth, that they may traverse the woods with more ease in pursuit of game." Peter Kalm, around Lake Champlain, reported how at one site the "natives themselves were very careful" with fire, while elsewhere the woods were mindlessly thinned by means of "the numerous fires which happen every year in the woods, through the carelessness of the *Indians,* who frequently make great fires when they are hunting, which spread over the fir woods when every thing is dry." And Timothy Dwight explained how "the aborigines of New England customarily fired the forests that they might pursue their hunting with advantage."[37]

All these citations are of course doubly dubious. Harris describes white hunters three centuries after contact, Kalm was travelling along a deeply entrenched corridor (often used for war), and Dwight generalizes over New England as a whole from scenes probably hacked to serve agriculture. Yet all ring true: this is how hunting and foraging societies practise fire around the world. There is little justification to believe that those in the Great Lakes forest would not have set fires where burning would help or that their fires would not have routinely escaped. Everything they did would have added to the overall fire load. Yet their fire power was limited by the transient and scattered nature of their travels, the coarse patchwork of landscape fuels, the fleeting seasonal portals for burning. They added and amplified; their fires could prune, trim, cleave; but by ignition alone, they could not wrench the province into a wholly new state.

Fire on the Hills, Fire on the Mountains:
Acadian Woods and Cordilleran Forests
Outside the Shield, beyond the boreal belt, the next fire ring rises like the rims of a bowl. The ring fractures once more into two paired arcs, east and west. These are again oddly symmetrical, two ranges of mountains, one old and wet and one new and seasonally dry. Between them, they neatly frame the subcontinent with complementary fire regimes, one as sluggish as its hills, with big fires bursting out like monadnocks, the other as robust and volatile as its peaks, as spiked with fires as its jagged summits.

To the east, the Acadian forest clothes the Appalachians. The ancient mountains, worn and rounded, here meet a rising sea, and the two so intermingle that the land becomes a cluster of islands and peninsulas and the sea a suite of bays, gulfs, and channels. Geologically old, climatically wet and cold, linked by a shared history of the Laurentide ice sheet and by boreal sinews to the great interior of Canada, the forest is an ecological collage. There are patches of outright boreal forest, dominated by black spruce and birch. There are swaths of the Great Lakes forest, ripe with red and white pine, oaks, hemlock, maples, shrubs. Some reflect local conditions – the boreal woodlands nesting preferentially on New Brunswick uplands, for example. Some are the outcome of staggered, stalled migrations or the relics of past colonizations. Bogs, barrens, and berry shrublands further dapple the scene. Toward the sea, and especially northward, other species like balsam fir become prominent, the fog-bound fringe of the Canadian forest. Overall, the two general woods, Acadian and boreal, make for a biotically bilingual landscape. Its indigenous peoples clung particularly to coastal habitations. As the proportion of sea to land increases, so the power of fire declines.

Yet throughout the forest's evolution, fire has loomed as a consistent presence and at times a decisive power. The sedimentary record displays sharp peaks of charcoal at 9,700, 9,200, 8,300, 6,700, and 4,400 years BP, immediately followed by floral inundations and a "resorting" of the forest. Each fire spike is thus the biotic equivalent of a ruptured ice dam that floods the landscape with a new wave of woodlands. The chronicle of the Acadian forest resembles a stream broken by waterfalls and pools, of fire spasms succeeded by sometimes long eras of smouldering. Some quiet periods were extensive, notably those between 6,000 and 4,400 years BP and 3,400 BP and the present. Even then smaller fires undoubtedly splashed through the region, a sorting out of combustion akin to that which was occurring among species. But by 4,000 years BP (although in many locales not until 2,000 years BP), most of the components of the modern forest were present, along with its characteristic fire regimes and a steady drizzle of charcoal, while the cataclysmic, landscape-upheaving conflagrations that had invited wholesale colonizations had faded.[38]

Still, there were suitable fire rhythms of wetting and drying, including longer-wave periods of paludification and drought. New Brunswick bogs retain charcoal that testifies to province-wide burns in 2,200, 1,750, 1,550, and 400 years BP. Black spruce in the northeast burned on a probable cycle of 60 years, jack pine in northern Nova Scotia burned roughly every 65-70 years, and the mixed red pine woodlands in southwest Nova Scotia with a syncopated regime saw the understorey burn every 20-40 years and the crown every 150-200 years. Researchers at Kejimkujik National Park estimate an average fire cycle of 78 years. These figures agree with others generally in Canada; fires in the Acadian probably differ from those elsewhere by being smaller in scale and somewhat less frequent. The complexity thickens because fire interweaves with other events, such as storms and insects. A further complication to the chronicle, however, is the fact that virtually all the old forest disappeared during the course of European settlement, and most hard records – from fire-scarred trunks to age-stand distributions to shallow bogs – disappeared along with it. Modern reconstructions are guesses, derived from the much-disturbed landscape that survived.[39]

Ignition, too, is a mix. Historical records from the twentieth century estimate lightning fires at roughly 7 percent of all starts in New Brunswick and 1 percent in Nova Scotia. The fires favour the continental over the maritime, clustering in the mountains and interior uplands while avoiding the coast. Still, lightning, remote from habitations, can ignite large fires, and probably in times past, during those periods of intensified drought laden with charcoal, lightning fires kindled more often and ranged more vigorously. In 1672, Nicholas Denys reported huge fires, ten to fifteen leagues wide. "Unless rains fall sufficiently to extinguish it," he affirmed, there was nothing to stop the wholesale conflagration. "At evening and at night, one sees the smoke ten and a dozen leagues away. On the side to which the wind is carrying it, it is seen very far off. From such places, the animals flee widely, and if near the sea, the runoff will so poison the coast that fish and fowl will flee." As to origins, Denys cited "the thunder [that] falls sometimes in fire" as well as careless people. In 1677, Christien LeClercq described a conflagration that began when the "heavens, being one day all on fire, full of tempest and thunder," and when "the dryness was extraordinary," sent a thunderbolt that joined the two, and not merely set in flames all the woods and forest between Miramichis and Nipisiquit but also "burnt and consumed more than two hundred and fifty leagues of country in such a manner that nothing was to be seen except very tall and quite blackened trunks of trees, which showed in their frightful barrenness the evidence of a conflagration widespread and altogether astonishing."[40] (Trekking on snowshoes through these forlorn solitudes, LeClercq managed to lose his way.)

Yet the main fire season, pre-greenup April and May, lies outside the thunderstorm season. By volume, people kindle the most fires; they ignite them at the prime periods for burning, outside the summer rains. The difficulty is that aboriginal Acadians resided preferentially along the coasts, and the geography of their burning may have been out of sync with the preferred timing. But the fire practices of the Mi'kmaq are unknown in detail. That they valued fire is certain; they never travelled without the means of calling it forth. A Mi'kmaq informed Abbé Maillard how they kindled their requisite cooking fires: "At night when we met together, we would feast on meat roasted on a fire, a fire we lighted by briskly rubbing sun-dried pine-wood in our hands for a long time. Sometimes, if the fire did not start as soon as we wished, we would go to the seashore to gather those white pebbles that are so abundant there. We would each take two of these and strike one against the other over powdered rotten dried pine wood. We had fire then, without fail." But keeping a fire is easier than reigniting it endlessly. This led to the nurturing of a perpetual hearth fire, as explained, again, to the abbé: "To preserve the fire, especially in winter, we would entrust it to the care of our war-chief's women, who took turns to preserve the spark, using half-rotten pine wood covered with ash." The fire could last for months; if it survived "the span of three moons," it became sacred and magical to us, and we showered with a thousand praises the chief's woman who had been the fire's guardian during the last days of the third moon." Such occasions called for a general convocation; young men would be sent to fetch those who were missing. "Then, when our numbers were complete, we would gather round and, without regard to rank or age, light our pipes at the fire."[41]

Those fires, however, moved with the Mi'kmaq, who moved with the seasons, harvesting shellfish and fish during the summer, then establishing camps inland over the winter, although it is suggested that European contact brought them to the coast earlier and for longer periods than previously. Probably they resembled those peoples in the boreal forest, who burned berry patches and fired along traplines and forage sites attractive to game. (Such early season grass fires are still common today.) Probably they shared the fire habits of their western-mountain counterparts, enflaming sites of special harvest. Undoubtedly fires littered corridors of seasonal travel; camp and smudge fires smouldered through snow and peat; flames caught dune grass and blitzed into the woods; fires escaped. Their seasons for travel, early spring and late fall, coincided precisely with the prime seasons for burning. Surely small fires crowded around them, and larger fires ranged when conditions permitted.[42]

From the geological record, it is impossible to discriminate, during periods of upheaval, among those fires set loose by people and those released by nature. At such times, any fire, from any source, could ramble and roar. Undoubtedly fires from all sources did.

The western mountains are higher, wider, fresher. So imposing is their mass that they become an informing principle for the fire regimes that carpet their valleys and drape their slopes. Their bulk interrupts the flow of moisture from the Pacific, trapping most on the western flank and parching the eastern slope, while warping the tracks of storms. Within its bulk, the Cordillera repeats over and over internally that grand texture, with bands of north-south-running ranges, each displaying its own patch quilt of dampness and aridity. The blockiness of the land underwrites the blockiness of the biota, as terrain shuffles, sorts, and stratifies and as borders slide up and down slopes, ever messy and mobile.

As always, fire follows fuel. The potential combustibles are patchy, however, their internal moisture set by intricate sculptings of shade, snow, and sun; propelling winds are distorted by peak and gorge; and fire regimes are fractal. Still, a few general features stand out. The geological tectonics find a biological equivalent, as the mountains inscribe a lumpy zone of collision between rainforest to the west and either semi-arid grassland or boreal forest to the east. Where Pacific moisture funnels into interior corridors, a damp forest, notably of western hemlock and western red cedar, chokes out routine fire in shade and fern. Along the eastern slope, however, grasses splash up the flanks and spill through long valleys. Lower elevations are more arid and exposed for longer periods than higher ones, such that montane woodlands resemble steppes; their fire regimes behave more like those of the prairie, gently washed by regular flame, than the explosive conflagrations of forests heavily stocked with combustibles. Farther north, the prairie surrenders to the boreal forest, which fronts the Rockies, and farther north still the boreal woods sweep over the subdued hills altogether, such that fires burn with boreal rhythms, checked and quickened by slopes and summits instead of muskeg and streams.[43]

Two coniferous forests most characterize the region: lodgepole pine and interior Douglas fir. Both grade into ponderosa pine to the south, which in turn segues into savannah. Lodgepole is the western expression of jack pine, with which it can interbreed. The Douglas fir of the interior mountains – distinct from its habit along the sodden coasts – behaves much like the Acadian pines. Both accept surface fires; both can immolate from crown fires. Since each extends over a range of landscapes, the choreography of combustion is complex: fires are one tumult among many. Avalanches, windstorms, dwarf mistletoe, and bark beetle infestations – all churn up the landscape and ready fuels. The resulting regime is a composite, as rugged as the ranges they clothe.

In many respects, lodgepole is a woody fireweed. It grows widely, from Colorado to the Yukon, claiming sites "too dry, too wet, too cold, too infertile, or in some other way beyond" the reach of other conifers, avidly reseeding after self-immolating burns, inextinguishable in its tenacity. It can tolerate surface fires, often sprouting amid dense swards of grass. Such fires thin groves, scar survivors, purge the seedlings of competitors, and clean out understoreys. Surface burns may come as often as ten years or as rarely as sixty. On the Chilcotin plateau of central British Columbia, they occur between twenty and forty years or in some sites every ten years. But lodgepole, like its jack pine cousin, is also prone to crown fires. The rhythm of such fires obeys the curious ridge-and-swale cycle of canopy fuels. In their early years, a thick carpet of evenly aged, closely packed seedlings furnishes an ideal medium for fire, which blasts through as if through brush. As the forest ages, the canopy, while rising, remains squarely within the range of surface fires, and crown fires can flourish. With maturation, however, trees self-prune, the canopy thins, and the understorey carries heavy poles rather than light kindling; fire burns, if at all, over the ground, perhaps from fallen trunk to fallen trunk. Then, roughly at the century mark, the aging forest spans its canopy gaps, an understorey thickens with ripe fuels, and crown fire again becomes the norm. Where crown fires are particularly frequent and widespread, serotinous cones dominate, shedding seeds after the gust of flame melts their seals. The rhythm of burning thus rises and falls with the rhythm of the fuels, which reflect the chronicle of past burning. The landscape is lumpy with lodgepole of different ages, the progeny of different fires.[44]

What lodgepole does not dominate, Douglas fir does. Over much of the interior Rockies, it is both pervasive and stable. Its understorey is more open and semi-arid, flushed with grasses and a sparse suite of tough shrubs, locally thickened with the reproduction of tree competitors. At lower elevations, it grades into grasses and scrub, at higher ones into subalpine forests, typically of fir. South of Kamloops, ponderosa and larch replace it. North of the Chilcotin plateau, the boreal forest chokes it out in favour of aspen, lodgepole, various spruces and firs. These are, broadly considered, climatic provenances, but in the Rockies climate is never far removed from fire.

Its local borders bulge and shrink with the character of burning. Too little fire where it meets steppe-grasslands, and Douglas fir invades. Too much fire where it meshes with ponderosa, larch, or aspen, and Douglas fir retreats. Too frequent fire, even where it flourishes better than the rest, and the seed source for regeneration may burn away, leaving an ecological rubble of brush fields. The regime consists mostly of surface fires, with pockets torched or spared as local conditions warrant. Unlike the great swells of flame that ripple over the boreal belt, fire here breaks like waves on a rocky shoreline, sometimes gentle, sometimes savage, yet always fracturing the large into the particular. It is a zone of high biotic tectonism,

and even when the burning is extensive the flames are full of peaks and
ravines, shelves and gorges. What the Rockies are to geology fire is to the
Rockies.

The Cordillera poses a great divide of ignition. From the west, Pacific
storms slam inland, and summer moisture boils up into thunderstorms.
Fuels are dense, lightning frequent, and from time to time there is enough
drying to encourage the two to spark into episodic eruptions of fire. The
interior belts more evenly balance wet and dry, so that lightning fire is
abundant amid the drier flanks of ranges. But the heavy electricity seems
to evaporate along the last summits: the east slope rainshadow becomes
also a lightning shadow. Fuels are lighter and lightning less abundant; yet
prehistoric fires were routine. The most plausible explanation is that those
fires were kindled by people.[45]

Here, as elsewhere, humans created lines of fire and fields of fire. They
wanted open corridors where they and the creatures they desired could
travel, and they sought open, fire-tended landscapes where they could
hunt, harvest, and seasonally reside. Probably the great grassy valleys that
laced the Rockies and bound it, like biotic sinews, to the Great Plains were
maintained, if not created, by fire-wielding humans. Probably aboriginal
burning helped to perpetuate conditions established during the Great
Warmth, fostering firestick refugia for people and their preferred prey.
Elsewhere, even in the wetter west, smaller burns applied to specific sites
dappled the scene, a weirdly gardened landscape of pyric horticulture.

The torch complemented the spear. The prairies abounded with game;
the trick was to lure them into the mountains, away from rivals but close to
winter encampments. The means was to extend tentacles of prairie into the
Rockies proper, beyond the parklands of the foothills, along river valleys,
and until they could coil into great meadows and trench valleys. Mary T.S.
Schaeffer's classic observation of Cataract Creek, "a favourite highway for
centuries, as the well-worn trails show," linked hunters, fires, and bison.
The "red hunters' camp-sites, many tepee-poles, and bones galore lined
the route; fires for years have swept hither and yon." Migrating bison in
particular would drift into or be enticed by the fresh grassy bait into the
grassy corridors, and then, after winter snows sealed off the passes, they
would be trapped, close to encampments and easy prey for hunters. The
grassy streams and steep stony flanks thus acted much like a fishtrap. The
seasonal firing of the corridors kept the routes open, the grasses and forbs
succulent, and the hunters in control.[46]

Some fires were set in the spring, lapping at the snow along the woody
fringe. Others, associated with fire-drive hunting, occurred in the fall.

Father Pierre de Smet reported one such drive from Lake Coeur d'Alene in northern Idaho. "On both ends of their line they light fires, some distance apart, which they feed with old garments and worn out moccasins." The deer, disoriented and frantic, "rush to right and left to escape. As soon as they smell the smoke of fires, they turn and run back." But with fire on both sides and the hunters to their rear, they have no recourse save to "dash toward the lake" and jump in "as the only refuge left for them." This simplifies the hunters' task. "They let the animals get away from the shore, then pursue them in their light bark canoes and kill them without trouble or danger."[47]

Other accounts, also of the Salish and Kootenay, describe classic fire surrounds. The hunters divide into two groups, organized in a huge circle. One group carries torches, occasionally igniting "brush and trees" along the way as they compress the circle, while the other group, armed with bows, fire at any deer attempting to escape. One area of the ring remained open from flame, and as deer (and sometimes bear) dashed there a gauntlet of hunters awaited them. Another observer described how the tribes fired high slopes in the autumn to remove "a certain kind of long moss" on which deer browsed (and which was believed to be "parasitic" on the local pines). Doing so forced the deer into the lower valleys, closer to patient hunters. Even more spectacular was the "Valley of the Jasper," as R.M. Rylatt described it in 1873. It was "good feeding ground," thick with the whitened skulls of bison, he observed, and his party's "line of travel" was free from underbrush; but the evidence of fire was everywhere, fires that had flushed out the floor of the trench, fires that had raced out of the valley up the slopes to "the line of everlasting Snows." Why, Rylatt asked, this "devastation by scathing fire?" Look to "the redman; he can answer it," for "he it is who has lighted the fires that ha[ve] devastated spots in the Valley; that have robbed the mountains on either hand of a portion of their forest garment, and the cause is clear, the cunning savage year after year crept past the herds as they fed, and attained the upper end, then fired the long grass during the heated term, driving a thundering living mass in terror to the only Outlet at the end of the Valley, where the main body of their enemy waited to destroy as many as the opportunity offered."[48]

But the flames that swept across the broad meadows, birch bogs, shrub fields, and lower flanks of the mountains helped to feed a veritable menagerie of megafauna and the creatures that hunted them. None ate old-growth forest; all feasted on forage and browse that grew in sunlight, not shade; all favoured the fractal edges where woods, brush, and grass met. Elk thrived on small aspen and bunchgrass, grizzlies on berries and roots, goats and sheep on high-elevation swards. Left alone, those edges blur into a hegemonic forest whose closing canopy throttles light from the surface, as through a glass, darkly. Fire cracks that coniferous belljar, stirs the ecological brew, refreshes the stale, and sparks the exceptional. What matters is not fire per se but its regimen: enough fire at the right time and place, fires that brighten the mosaic without wiping it out.

Aboriginal fire also catalyzed plants directly consumed by people. Prairie patches and hillside meadows speckled even wet landscapes. Seasonal migration for the Salish involved moving up and down mountains and plateaus, with different crops harvested at different months. There were spot burns around hazelnut sites, pruning burns amid berries, broadcast burns over meadows, fallow-field burns over root crops, opportunistic burns as needed or possible. The particulars under fire cultivation differed by local climate, soil, and the like, but an overall pattern persists. Among the crops were berries: serviceberry, wild strawberry, raspberry, huckleberry, and others. Among the nuts, hazel; among the green vegetables, bracken and balsamroot; among fire-stimulated fungi, edible mushrooms. Among the roots, they sought, according to particular value, the bulbs, corms, rhizomes, tubers, and taproots of nodding onion, balsamroot, avalanche lily, tiger lily, Indian potato, and others. (But not the camas, the manioc of the northwest, which grew farther south.) They gathered medicinal plants. More than 300 species in all the regional tribes apparently exploited and did what they could to promote. Most of that they cultivated with fire somewhere as a catalyst, much of it burned in the fall, prior to the rains.[49]

The Lil'wat elder Baptiste Ritchie aptly summarized the empirical character of this indigenous fire philosophy, why the forefathers "always did well wherever they went for the purpose of picking all the berries and roots like potatoes that they ate." They would "burn one hill and use the other." They would prevent "bushes" from reclaiming land otherwise cultivated by fire for berries and tubers. After a fire it took "around three years" before "those things grew there again. Then there were lots of berries. Everything was all really fertile." Big trees were rarely burned, for there was no reason; the point was to prod and prune the proper roots and shrubs. His forefathers' managed hills, he concluded proudly, were "just like a garden."[50]

Even this firestick farming hardly exhausted the cornucopia of fire practices. Smoky fires drove off mosquitoes and sent messages. Controlled field fires protected encampments from wildfires. Hot fires created future fuel wood. In wet weather, fires dried the harvest. Campfires dotted trails like caravanserai. All this is to say there were ample opportunities for mistakes, for violence, for fire littering, for escapes. Fire-scarred trees in the northern Rockies suggest a fire frequency twice as great along corridors as in more remote settings.[51]

Those fire threads and fire blocks laid out a grand quilt for burning, but it was only that. Not everything burned within its assigned matrix with deliberation and constraint, not everything fired with calculated purpose behaved as predicted, not every year intended for burning could sustain a burn. A rough-hewn land made for rough-hewn burning. The shards of this landscape mosaic less resembled ceramic tiles, fixed immutably in their places, than immiscible liquids, flowing out and back. Throughout, what people didn't claim lightning could. Large chunks could evade flame for decades, but little eluded it altogether.

Fire and Fog: The Incombustible Fringe

Northward along the coasts, the cold and the wet increase and become more uniform. Cold currents press along the shores. Winter rains cycle into summer fogs. Few breaks occur in the weather to brighten and dry; few occasions allow the rhythm of fuels to align with the rhythm of flames. Fire-intolerant flora thicken and become dominant – species damaged by even light surface burns, species capable of regenerating without fire. Sitka spruce replaces Douglas fir; red spruce, red pine. The necessary conditions for fire wash away. Here Canadian fire finds its outer limits.

In the Pacific Northwest, the extinction of fire proceeds in stages as the sheltering mountains thin relative to storms. On Vancouver Island, the eastern tip, lying within a mild rain shadow, features fire regimes similar to those of the interior Rockies. In particular, it boasts patches of Garry oak savannah, acorn-rich prairies believed to be anthropogenic, an outcome of aboriginal burning. Farther west and north, increasingly wet and progressively unbroken in their moisture, coastal forests grow to immense sizes over the course of centuries, the rhythm of fire lengthening steadily.[52]

Coastal Douglas fir dominates, but it intermingles with western hemlock and western red cedar, pinching off quickly to the misty north and up steep valley slopes. Douglas fir can live for a thousand years, but fire drives down that life span and helps to ensure its competitive survival because it can reproduce profusely after big burns, while hemlock regenerates on a surface of decaying biomass. The exuberant vegetation – the slopes heavily laden with wood, shrubs, mosses, ferns, the very thickness that makes it celebrated as a temperate rainforest – can stoke holocausts when a fire breaks out.

The geography of coastal Douglas fir remains a geography of fire, though one of a slowing tempo. In southern locales, particularly where subject to outbreaks of dry weather and stiff, off-shore winds, conflagrations can return as often as once a century. In the Nimpkish Valley of Vancouver Island, over a period of 950 years, eight major fires ripped through the landscape, one on average every 135 years. But fires become more rare with each leap farther north. Big fires return about every 500 years, then 700-800, then hardly if ever at all. The Douglas fir must compete with species capable, as it is not, of reproducing in shade and dank litter and thriving under a shadowed canopy. It grades into hemlock and especially Sitka spruce.[53]

So, too, aboriginal fire practices shrivelled. Tribes such as the Gitxsan, a near-coastal Tsimshian people, and the Wet'suwet'en, Athabascan speakers in the Bulkley Valley, reside in a transitional landscape – one dominated by hemlocks – between the coast and the boreal interior. They burn for berries, deer meadows, clearing around habitations, kitchen gardens; they burn on foothills, on slopes, where possible, on floodplains. But the opportunities for fire become fewer, and the capacity of flame to spread compresses; even escapes become rare. The closer to the coast proper, the more the dominion of individual sites shrinks, and the less robust the archipelago of such sites becomes. The coastal economy was as maritime as the climate: peoples lived off the sea and the streams, not off the dark, cloud-scudded mountains behind them. The Haida may have perpetuated the salal and huckleberry patches of Guten Island, in the Queen Charlotte group, with regular fires. But little flame otherwise pushed beyond their villages.[54]

This is a province of winter rain and summer fog. Disturbances derive from flooding, sodden soils, blowdowns; fog drip, not routine fire, sustains its understorey. The distinctive trees are the western hemlock and the majestic Sitka spruce. In Oregon, where it is a minor constituent, the Sitka spruce lives for 200-400 years before being swept away; in western Washington, and parts farther north, where it lords over others, it can survive for up to 1,146 years. Here variety, even a variety of potential disturbances, has been rinsed away in the relentless wet. For the indigenous peoples, the problem was not to control fires on the environment but to shield fires from that environment. Here even fire needs its shelter.[55]

The Cape Breton Highlands are an anomaly. Within a subcontinent that nearly everywhere, at some time, burns, it does very rarely. Combustibles don't accumulate; climate doesn't allow for open combustion. Fires don't start within it, and fires that originate outside it expire when they enter. In place of fire, there is the spruce budworm.[56]

Balsam fir makes up 90 percent of the highlands forest, with the rest mostly white spruce and white birch. The fir appears elsewhere in eastern Canada, a minor component of the boreal belt, a somewhat larger constituent of the Great Lakes forest. In such circumstances, it burns as its surroundings do. But on the highlands, it dictates those circumstances, and the moist, cool clime allows the balsam fir to undergo an entirely biological cycle of regeneration, growth, and decay. It has, weirdly, no fire history and no apparent fire future. Insects kill, fungi decomposes, mosses provide a seedbed. A new balsam fir forest arises out of the rotting ruins of the old.

Its fire immunity underwent a major test in the 1970s when a spruce budworm epidemic of catastrophic proportions defoliated all but a few minor patches. The defoliation repeated year after year; after four to six years, trees began to die. Between 1978 and 1988, a live forest disintegrated into a dead one, shedding branches, bark, and tops and finally falling to the floor. The highlands became a vast necropolis. Anywhere else such a swath of slash would be a tinderbox, prone to an explosion from a stray spark. But not here. The small fuels simply didn't accumulate. They fell apart, decomposed, sank under a pall of ferns and fungi into a dense layer of wet and putrid cellulose, a reminder that biomass does not equate with fuel. Regeneration and light-eager shrubs proliferated, adding to the overall moisture captured on the surface. Only during a fleeting two- to three-week window prior to spring greenup did the fire proneness flicker. While surface biomass increased, the proportion available for burning dropped. Combustibility plummeted.

Climate made that decomposition possible; it also meant there were few occasions for overcoming that condition. In early spring, prior to leafing out, the weather is almost always unsuitable for burning. Then, during late summer's flush, when moments of dryness might strike, the canopy shelters the surface, lightly laden as it is with damp, scant fuels. Between them, those processes cover the few windows for burning with shade. Even an exotic drought could probably not shatter the sodden scene enough to feed a fire. This assumption was challenged in the summer of 1981 when a fire broke out in nearby logging slash and again in 1982 when a fire raced over a nearby heath land near Christie Ponds and struck the wooded border. Both fires were snuffed out. They burned outside, they expired within.

It is possible to burn this landscape – the two wildfires show that. In 2001, lightning succeeded in kindling a blaze on the plateau, and had the pinprick of drought deepened fire might have shoved through the dense woods. But such events are rare and appear outside the core dynamics of the biota. Historic large fires such as those of 1921, 1947, and 1968 flared along the highland margins, at lower elevations, amid disturbances more powerful than budworms or even icestorms and the occasional hurricane. Something more ruthless has to intervene to shatter the woods and ensure that the timing of fuel and flame match. That had to await the axe and a hand willing to use it.[57]

Tongues of Fire:
Black Spruce and High Plains

The story of fire in Canada has always been one of nature and people. The core conditions, nature laid down, but they are no more than the genetic coding embedded in the environment. Their expression, and the meaning granted them, have depended on people. The grand narrative of Canadian fire unfolds not only amid evolving climates and colonizing biotas but aburst with witnesses that grant them expression. That cavalcade of observers plays alongside and against the physical chronicle of fire. Every reconfiguration of Canadian pyrogeography has its exemplary fires, those that typify in heightened form the fires that most characterize an era. And each has its epiphanous fires, those for which people gave exceptional expression, and for which the observer cannot be separated from the scene observed. This fugue of culture and geography began early, as advancing humans crowded against abating ice. Both, the exemplary and the epiphanous, the record of defining fires and the record of fire defined, deserve to be heard. But the most extraordinary moments have come when those tongues of flame have descended on witnesses prepared to speak in the foreign tongues of literature, art, and science.

Nowhere has a black spruce stand been found that does not originate from a burn. This extraordinary observation belies a complicated cadence of biology and climate. The short needles that power high-intensity burns through the crowns congeal into mats when shed, so the standing spruce require surface combustibles, mostly moss and lichens, to drive the primary flame. Each has its own rhythm of growth and fire readiness; each must then converge with exquisite timing with drought, wind, and ignition. The odds are long, akin to pollinators in the Amazon finding a single species amid thousands. Yet it happens. And when it does, perhaps no other fire scene has so mesmerized observers.[1]

In 1861 Henry Hind plunged into the Labrador plateau and began a relentless register of old burns and active fires. They culminate in a breathless gush, a long passage perhaps unprecedented by an on-site observer:

> A spruce tree flashes into flame from the bottom to the top almost instantaneously, with a crackling hissing roar, which when viewed close at hand rivets a breathless attention, not unmixed with anxiety and fear. The light which it casts is vivid and red, the noise sharp, quick, and loud, like an infinite number of snaps repeated with just perceptible intervals. The awful but splendid light thrown through the forest casts the blackest shadows wherever its rays cannot reach. The birch trees flame steadily, pouring forth huge volumes of dense smoke, which whirling high in the air form an opaque screen above the burning forest, from which a lurid light is reflected; at intervals gusts of wind sweep through the trees, followed by a train of smoke and sparks which, winding through the charred trunks or meeting with violent eddies, rise up in a spiral form to rejoin the black clouds above. When the wind is favourable, a burning spruce forest viewed from an eminence is awfully impressive; from ten, twenty, to fifty trees at a time columns of flame shoot up, wildly twisting and darting high above the trees, and then subside; a few minutes later another outburst illuminates rocks and mountains, which appear indescribably vast, silent, and immovable. Wild-fowl, disturbed and bewildered by the dazzling light, fly in great circles high above the burning forest, and sometimes, descending rapidly in spiral flight, plunge into the fires; others drop from an immense height like a stone into the flames, probably suffocated by the hot air and smoke in which they have been wheeling round and round for hours, fascinated like moths by the fitful glare below them.[2]

Among boreal nations Canada is unique for not having a visual art of forest fires. There are paintings of prairies aflame, and some of the Group of Seven were attracted to the axe- and fire-wrecked landscapes of Ontario, but fire soaring, flames twisting up through woods and sky, fire racing with the wind like billowing sails – images of such moments are lacking. What exists instead are occasional word paintings, of which Hind's is a premium. While its fires could inspire, what spares his purple prose from self-parody is the felt reality behind them. Its eruptive fires escaped expression as they did control.

But fire was also mundane. It was for most landscapes simply an inextricable part of quotidian ecology. For such scenes, a more vernacular prose might better suit fire's presence, and for illustration, consider Peter Fidler's November 1792 to March 1793 trek from Buckingham House along the High Plains, a chronicle of blizzards, buffalo, and burning. Although Fidler believed that lightning "in the Spring and Fall" frequently kindled grass fires, there was no question that winter burns arose solely from the "Indians."[3]

Week by week the spectacle of burned and burning land unscrolled. On 12 November, Fidler reported "grass all burnt this day." On 4 December, the grass was burned "in several places in the Plain." On the 18th, the grass was "all lately burnt the way we have passed this Day towards the Mountain." To the south, the land was "now burning very great fury, supposed to be set on fire by the Cotten na hew Indians." With a gale howling and tent fires of buffalo dung mixed with what tiny quantities of firewood the party had hauled along, Fidler pondered the scene: "Every fall and spring, and even in the winter when there is no snow, these large plains either in one place or other is constantly on fire, and when the Grass happens to be long and the wind high, the sight is grand and awful, and it drives along with amazing swiftness." The flames rushed along "like the waves in the ocean in a storm." So rapidly could they move that "several Indians" had reportedly been burned to death in their sleep. The only escape was for the threatened party to "immediately" set fire to the grass around them and then move themselves, horses, and gear into that black patch.[4]

On 28 December, grass was burning "very briskly" some miles away. The next day grass to the west was afire, reportedly set by some Blood Indians returning from a horse raid on the Snakes. On 13 January, "2 Tents" joined the party to the eastward, and when they left "they did not put out their fire," which promptly spread "& ran with great velocity and burnt with very great fury, which enlightened the night like day, and appeared awfully grand." A fresh wind drove it "a great distance in a little while." Such escapes were most dangerous, especially in evenings. This fire had broken loose around midnight, but fortunately the wind billowed the flames away from Fidler's camp and spared the men from anything worse than mild panic. The next day, with still-brisk gales, the fire continued its long sprint. Fidler observes that the Indians "very much disapprove" of burns near them, not only because of the immediate threat posed but also because the smoke is an "excellent guide" by which to direct enemies to their location.

Yet the fires had their value too. On 15 January, observing long lines of flame threading both to the southwest and to the northeast, Fidler noted that the burning of the "old grass" made for "excellent sweet feed" for the horses and buffalo and other creatures of the plains. If there were reasons to fear the accidental fire, there were reasons to celebrate the calculated burn.[5]

On 19 January, fresh gales arose, and grass fires raged "still very furiously." On the 22nd, the fires were "all around us and in some places pretty near" and forced the party to keep a watch over the horses to prevent their flight or harm. On the 31st, the land they traversed was "all burnt"; on 1 February, the same; on the 3rd, fires had swept the "most part" of the scene; on the 4th, "all burnt ... as yesterday." Fidler then unwittingly violated tribal norms – a "heinous offence" – by adding some coal to the tent fire, contaminating the flame and compelling a "much affronted" chief to avoid his tent for two nights.

By the end of February, new storms drove more burns. On the 26th, the land was "mostly all burnt" from the Red Deer River southward. On 8 March, Fidler found the surrounding plains "lately burnt." On the 11th, they endured heavy rain and high wind amid a landscape "all burnt," and on the 12th "grass all burnt as before." The same held for the 13th, the 14th, the 15th, and the 16th, so extensive that it caused some hardship to find enough feed for the horses. On the 19th, amid uneven, hummocky ground, the grass was burnt "in several places." The next day the party returned to Buckingham House.[6]

Of such stuff is a culture of fire created.

Conflagration and Complex

Each of the great reorganizations of Canadian fire's historical geography has characteristic conflagrations that can stand as exemplars of that epoch. In the context of torch and bolt, two varieties figure most prominently: the single mass fire and the complex of simultaneous fires. Each reveals those "gigantic elements" that, when slammed together, create the awful splendour of fire's Canadian condition.

Chinchaga, 1950

It may not be the largest Canadian fire of history, but the Chinchaga River fire is the most monstrous of record, accorded archetypal stature. From 1 June to 31 October 1950, in a series of rushes and pauses, it burned a swath of 1.4 million hectares across northern British Columbia and Alberta. Its immensity exceeds such better-known North American holocausts as the Miramichi fire, the 1871 Great Lakes burns, and the Big Blowup of 1910, all of which were composites of lesser burns. Combined with other regional fires, the Chinchaga flung its smoke over the northeastern United States and on to Britain and the Netherlands. Yet its novelty was one of size, not of kind. It behaved on a larger scale exactly as boreal Canada's lesser large fires, and as they have probably done since life replaced ice.[1]

The simple factors were these: for fuel, the boreal forest; for terrain, the northern plains between the Rockies and the Shield; for climate, drought; for weather, a series of upper-level ridge buildups and breakdowns. Once launched, there was nothing to stop the flames, which managed to roar between Fort St. John and Keg River. The fire had the entire summer season to ramble and would burn as nature willed.

That will expressed itself in a sequence of rushes and rests. In all, there

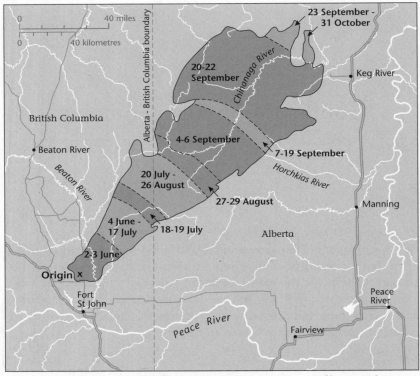

History of the Chinchaga fire. Observe the characteristic signature of surges and pauses as weather systems sweep through.

were five major runs, each larger than the preceding one, with four minor runs separating them. The rests occurred during periods of high pressure – stable, drying, allowing for vigorous residual burning. When those domes collapsed and east-rushing cold fronts pushed through the region, the forward edge of the burn burst into a front that surged northeast until stalled by the arrival of another blocking high. There was one such prolonged rush at the time of origin, 1-3 June; another from 4 June through 17 July; another from 20 July to 26 August; yet again 4-6 September; and a last, the largest, from 20 to 22 September, which probably accounted for a third of the total burn. An anomaly of atmospheric structure left a layer of air sandwiched between upper and lower strata, and it was this channel through which the smoke streamed.[2]

People could do little save stay out of the way. In truth, no one tried to do anything more, and the history of the Chinchaga River conflagration is the product of painstaking scholarship, based on scattered observations, aerial photos of the burned area and the age-class forest that regrew over it, and the recorded trace of its smoke, spreading like a foreboding pall across the northern hemisphere. The fire testifies to the immensity of Canadian fire; its vast forests, its undeflectable climate, its scope for untrammelled combustion, against which people seem tiny and their presumptions puny.

Yet the fire may be more typically Canadian than even its celebrants admit because it was the outcome of a curious interplay between nature and culture. The extraordinary reach of the Chinchaga River fire was the result of a prolonged season for burning, which became possible because of its early-season origin, which happened because people caused it. Ignition began not in a clump of decadent black spruce or overripe lodgepole but in logging slash, and it started at the hands of humans. The reason for the kindling is unknown – perhaps to clear away the debris, perhaps to prepare for agricultural planting, perhaps simply as an accident, a hunting fire set to warm or cook that sprang into the accelerant slash. With the fire but one of many in the region, no attempt was made to suppress it, and it burned freely And for all this, not solely as an exemplar of a fire untouchable to humanity, it can stand for many burns during the *longue durée* in which a kindling torch has prowled over a tindered land.

Ontario, 1980

The 1980 fires in northwestern Ontario are, as a fire complex, what the Chinchaga River fire is as a solitary burn. The setting is again boreal, a quilt of mostly jack pine and black spruce; this time in the Shield; at a favourite haunt of the Hudson Bay High, often squeezed into drought, synoptic dry spells, wicked winds; a scene of exceptional ignition. Probably dry lightning blasts the woods here more than anywhere else in Canada. But permanent settlements at Kenora and Thunder Bay, and seasonal settlements such as those around Red Lake, texture the land with roads and encampments and human ignitions.[3]

The boreal is notorious for the lumpiness of its fire history, but in the decade leading to 1980, big fire seasons had broken out in eerie echoes. Large fires and fire complexes had branded the 1970s as Ontario's worst decade for serial conflagrations. The 1974 season had shocked, but then came 1976 and then 1979. It was some comfort that most of the bad fires and the bulk of the area burnt occurred outside the zone of active fire suppression; those within the pale of protection fires had spread only modestly. Still, these were the most severe fire plagues in memory, and it appeared to fire officials that they must represent an upper limit to burning. The 1980 season blasted that belief for the ignorance and hubris it was.

Part of the shock was simple scale. Impressive as the 1970s had been, their averages shrivelled when compared with 1980. Over the decade, the region had experienced an annual average of 670 fires, with a burned area of 56,667 hectares and an average fire size of 85 hectares. In 1980, the number of starts increased by 50 percent to 994; the burned area exploded by almost an order of magnitude to 515,232 hectares; and the average size increased sixfold to 518 hectares. In the preceding decade, some 2.3 percent of all fires had exceeded 200 hectares. In 1980, that percentage doubled to 4.3 percent. For the epochal 1980 season, there were more fires, proportionately more big fires, and a vastly bigger area burned.[4]

But what most stunned officials was the power of anthropogenic fire. During the 1970s, only 4.5 percent of all fires had occurred outside the zone of protection, and these fires – virtually all lightning caused – accounted for 60 percent of the burned area. In 1980, lightning kindled more than its average number of fires, but the greater proportion of area burned resided within the pale of protection, and what overloaded the system was an epidemic of human ignitions. Canada is an industrial and largely urban country and Ontario its most industrialized and urbanized province; these were not the classic sparks from flint and firestick struck from "aboriginal" fire practices. Yet the resulting patterns were remarkably similar. The fires clustered around the towns, they popped up along roads and at waystations, and they bubbled up at the scattered habitations around lakes and campgrounds, the temporary sites of seasonal transients to the bush. In that respect, the colossal outbreak probably did resemble those of the prehistoric past.

Clearly, boreal Canada could burn without the hand of humanity. But people multiplied nature's sparks, they amplified its capacity to burn widely, and they juggled the fire regimes that resulted – and they have done so since fire began its colonization after the ice. Canada has always had a mixed-combustion economy. The 1980 season was large. It became stupendous when people, through malice or accident, added to the load. Even so, the combustion-related drama that most held Canada's attention at the time focused not on remote forests openly aflame and the cost of containing them but on an eruption in the cost of oil and its impact on the internal combustion that drove the national economy. What paralyzed the national government was not the spectre of liberated boreal fuels but a throttled flow of fossil fuels. Such considerations, of course, were specific to industrial, not indigenous, Canada. But in the complex choreography between torch and bolt, and in the judgment on which combustion was good and which bad and why, that mixed ensemble spoke across millennia.

BOOK 2

AXE

Creating Fuel

Bolt and torch were powerful – they chiselled many of Canada's landscapes, and for its vastest woods, the boreal belt, they sculpted the forest root and branch. Yet while over much of Canada the kindled fire was an indelible environmental presence, it was one immensely limited. Spark was only as explosive as its tinder; flame could only propagate as its surroundings allowed; burning could ecologically catalyze only what it could actually combust. Fire was no more powerful than its fuel. The chisel needed a hammer, the torch craved an axe.

The limitations on aboriginal burning, which is to say the power of fire-kindling, were overcome by the capacity to make fuel as well as spark. The process of creating combustibles by slashing woods into kindling, growing fallow, and rearranging landscapes of hydrocarbons began before the arrival of Europeans. A maize-based agriculture pushed north of the Great Lakes and skipped, here and there, across the plains. This was a variant of swidden, based on slashing and then burning, and it redesigned the landscapes it touched with fire. Compare the regimes of northwestern Minnesota, without agriculture, with those in southern Ontario, where axe and torch joined. Over the past 750 years, the Minnesota chronicle waxes and wanes with that of the Little Ice Age, showing frequent fires (every 8.6 years) during the warm and dry phase of the fifteenth and sixteenth centuries, and a lengthening pause (13.2 years) for the duration of the neo-glaciation. In the fire-prone years, fire broke out regularly when a spark struck; during the slumberous era, fires demanded drought or wrenching dry spells. While people could add to ignition, the larger environment, particularly climate, determined which fuels were available to carry a blaze. During the same era, in southern Ontario, however, fires swelled and sank with the advent and destruction of the Iroquoian tribes. The chronicle of charcoal traces a history of anthropogenic fire regimes in which people could set fires over wider areas and longer seasons because they could control not only the timing of ignition but also the combustibles that had to sustain a flame.[1]

Europeans arrived centuries after the slashing had commenced. Their impact was both direct and, more significantly, indirect. Their fire-kits were, by themselves, no more trenchant than those of the indigenes and their founding agriculture no more expansive. They carried strike-a-lights, held fires in the holds of their ships, and introduced new fire technologies, most spectacularly gunpowder. (A defining moment in Canadian history occurred at the battle near Ticonderoga when Champlain fired his arquebuses decisively into the fray, an omen of how the newcomers' firepower might amplify the assault on the North American forest, like an atlatl adding thrust to a spear.) But ignition was already plentiful and not limiting in the fire dynamics of the Canadian landscape. The deeper driver was not the firestick, however magnified with chemical additives such as gunpowder; it was the axe and the muscles and markets that swung it.

The reformation came not from the strike of steel on flint but from that of steel on tree, which set in motion a train of environmental effects for which the expression "disturbance" is an ecological euphemism. Their impact cascaded, beginning slowly, then with a quickening force that shattered woods and grasslands and profoundly remoulded their capacity to receive flame. Claims on wood for heating and construction for even seasonal settlements altered local forests. Traffic in furs affected the distribution of creatures, particularly beaver, and thus the geography of browse and ponds, the landscape mosaic of combustibles. Later the creation of farms and pastures, and especially a trade in balk timber, would begin the wholesale recasting of wooded Canada. Yet the most violent shock of encounter remained the conversion of forest into kindling, because the proliferation of available fuels stoked a proliferation of controlled burns and uncontrolled conflagrations. Increasingly, the frontiers of European contact – where the axe met the woods – redefined the fire regimes of Canada.

Fire Frontiers of Imperial Canada

They came by water, they carried fire. Contact with Canada began, for Europeans, with islands, and more often than not it involved an exchange of fire. Europe's far voyagers, from Vasco da Gama to James Cook, tracked their progress along discovered shores with smokes by day and fires by night. Approaching the Bahamas, Christopher Columbus had seen through the night's gloom a flicker of light, as though from a candle, before sighting land the next dawn. (Probably he spotted the fires carried on fishing canoes or perhaps torches along the shore, associated with crab hunting.) Before he spotted land along northeastern America, Giovanni da Verrazano smelled the smoke from its fires. His successors, probing around Canada's Atlantic headlands and into the Gulf of St. Lawrence, tracked habitation by the glitter of its coastal flames.

Their intent was trade, not settlement, certainly not colonization by broadcast immigration. Europeans came as transient fishermen and traffickers in furs; they clung to the rocky littoral; they sited outposts preferentially on islands or bays that offered shelter or bold rocks like Quebec that promised protection by and for ships. They moved inland by boat – Native canoe, bateau, York boat, and where saltwater allowed brigantine. They sailed up the St. Lawrence and into Hudson Bay, crossed the Great Lakes, paddled over the Shield's skein of waterways, tracked the great rivers to the Rockies and the Arctic, threaded along the Pacific's tangle of islands and fiords. Yet the means were never adequate to their ends. The St. Lawrence was no Mississippi or Rhine; Hudson Bay, no Baltic; the Great Lakes, no Mediterranean. Routes were seasonal, subject to freezing. Rivers broke with rapids and portages and outright falls. European power was limited by what muscle, wind, and current could penetrate. Europe's Canadian commerce thus relied on what would be caught or cut and exported by ship, the celebrated northern economy of fish, fur, and later forests and farms.

The Gulf of St. Lawrence defined the European entry to Canada. So, too, its chronicle of settlement tracks the entry to Canada's European-catalyzed fire history.

New Found Land

Canada's fish, not its forests, first drew Europeans. The Grand Banks with their immense swarms of cod early became the scene of annual voyages between Europe and America. John Cabot and the Real brothers explored the area in the 1490s, and it is possible that fishing fleets were visiting the region before Columbus sailed, the heirs of Norse colonists who had hopped from the Faeroes to Greenland and of the Portuguese who had settled Madeira and the Azores. At L'Anse aux Meadows on its far northwest tip, a seasonal Viking settlement had once thrived. The shores soon swarmed with English, French, Portuguese, and Spanish ships, taking provisions, drying and salting cod. In this sense, Newfoundland was less an outlier of continental Canada than the farthest of those islands that arced between Europe and America across the north Atlantic.

Like those other isles, this one had its founding fires, for fire would make it possible to smelt and forge habitable landscapes out of raw lumps of wood and rock. The most famous, however, was a fire forestalled. It happened on the voyage of Humphrey Gilbert in 1583. A letter to Richard Hakluyt from Stephen Parmenius, a Hungarian poet travelling with the party, describes the event. "We put in to this place [St. John's] on August 3, and on the 5th the admiral [Gilbert] took these regions into the possession of authority of himself and of the realm of England, having passed certain laws about religion and obedience to the Queen of England." So far, so good.[1]

Parmenius admitted that he ought to describe "the customs, territories and inhabitants" yet found he could not because he could see "nothing but desolation." The terrain was hilly, the woods impenetrable, the grass tall, the view obstructed. Accordingly, "we made representations to the admiral to burn the forests down, so as to clear an open space for surveying the area; nor was he averse to the idea, if it had not seemed likely to bring a considerable disadvantage. For some reliable people asserted that, when this had occurred by accident at some other settlement post, no fish had been seen for seven whole years, because the sea-water had been turned bitter by the turpentine that flowed down from the trees burning along the rivers." (The "reliable" source is unclear; possibly it comes from Madeira, where legend held that first colonists had set a fire that burned for seven years and nearly consumed them in its fury. Regardless, the incident reappears consistently, always from some reliable but elusive source, in the subsequent natural histories of Atlantic Canada.)[2]

So the fire was not kindled, and this time the new found land did not blaze with imperial fancy. It did burn, by design or negligence, elsewhere and undoubtedly at Gilbert's landing some later time. The fishing fleets lay to during summer and fall, when fires are most prone to ramble. With the chartering of the Newfoundland Company in 1610, the English began establishing permanent (if small) settlements on shore to support the fisheries. Fire, too, became a permanent feature. In 1619, for example, the cod fisheries reported that "fishers" had "maliciously" burned 5,000 acres of woods in the Bay of Conception, "with many more thousands of acres burned and destroyed by them within these twenty years." Probably the "rinding" of trees around settlements was immense – 50,000 around Ferryland in 1622, it was estimated. The deading timber amassed belts of combustibles. The same year Daniel Powell reported that "the woods along the coasts are so spoyled by the fishermen that it is a great pity to behold them, and without redresse undoubtedly will be the ruine of this good land."[3]

But this time self-interest stayed the hand. Gilbert's crew replenished their water and wood and, anticipating greater discoveries in a more favoured land to the south, sailed on. Whatever they found vanished when the *Squirrel,* carrying Gilbert and Parmenius, sank on its return voyage.

For several centuries, this remained the pattern of Newfoundland fire. A large flake of the continent chipped off into the Atlantic, the island was in truth a virtual monolith of stone, cracked and scraped by glaciers, lightly dusted with soil, crusty with a boreal biota, its rims branded by the fires of its fleeting fishermen. A closer inspection would reveal three subregions, each with a fire regime that reflected its peculiar natural history.

None was naturally prone to fire: overall, the climate was cool and humid, and the prevailing winds carried more, not less, moisture. Yet fire in different ways could enter each. To the southeast, the "English shore," the climate was chilly and frequently foggy but with enough dry breaks to accept a spark if any was cast at the right time. The flora hovered on a knife edge between forest and heath. So precarious was the balance, however, so thin the soil, and so abundant the sparks that, as the decades passed, the landscape became more and more heath-like. The southwestern and western ("French shore") third of the island was likewise damp, with a bit less rainfall overall than the eastern shores but that rainfall more evenly distributed. This made for thicker soils and a crop of balsam fir, not readily burned without more effort than tossing a torch. The central region is classic boreal forest, somewhat more continental in climate, subject to outbreaks of fire when ignition and drought combined. But there was little reason to penetrate deeply into the interior beyond the seasonal culling of caribou. The Mi'kmaq remained along the coast. Whatever the indigenous Beothuks did with fire died with them.

Accounts are few: no naturalists probed far into the woods; settlers looked to the seas. But in the 1760s, warrants were issued by Governor Hugh Palliser to apprehend whalers and fishers who wantonly fired the woods. In 1772, Governor Shuldham wrote that "irregular crews from the colony and other places resorting to this coast" were guilty of heinous crimes, among them "firing the woods." In 1810, Governor Erasmus Gower, alarmed "by the repeated fires" surrounding St. John's, proclaimed that "any person who shall be convicted of having a fire which shall communicate to the woods will be punished with the utmost rigor of the law." Even so, fires continued, and where settlements expanded by way of woods farms and pastures the greater piles of fuel invited greater fires. Fires erupted at Plate Cove, Kings Cove, Broad Cove, Brigus, Colliers, Cupids. In 1862, with a "very high wind," fire burst forth between St. John's and Kelligrews, while other fires roared around Steady Water, Petty Harbour and Bay Bulls roads, and Freshwater. "Southside Hills on fire all day." The surer record lay in the land itself: the blotchy heaths that ate away at the forest.[4]

Of the interior, less is known. In 1822, W.E. Cormack traversed the island on behalf of the Boeothick Institution. The fires that concerned him were two. One was the campfire, without which travel was impossible. "A large fire at night is the life and soul of such a party as ours," he observed. He noted in some detail the proper ritual for deciding a site and laying tinder ("made by pulverising a small piece of dry rotten wood and a little gunpowder together between the hands"). The availability of firewood was in fact a consideration in selecting a locale. Prudence demanded also that the covering moss not overlie a hollow between boulders, lest the fire, in burning down, fall into the cavity and "swallow up any slumberer who might chance to slide into it." Critically, the smoke afforded "instant relief from the constant devouring enemy, the flies." Each morning, having camped near summits, they rose before dawn to discover the smoke of others' campfires, and, "to prevent the discovery of ourselves, we extinguished our own fire always some length of time before day-light."[5]

The other fires were those that splashed across the interior forests. "The ravages of fire, which we saw in the woods for the last two days," Cormack concluded anxiously, "indicated that man had been near." More deeply, the breadth of burning had transformed large portions into "savannas," as Cormack termed them – steppes of peat, the province of which was "destined to become a very important integral part of Newfoundland." Cormack found abundant evidence that these lands had once been wooded but "are now partially, or wholly, covered with savannah fires, originating with the Indians, and from lightning, which have in many parts destroyed the forest." For the forest to return, he estimated, would require a century. In the meantime, they found wild currants, gooseberries, and raspberries, "the latter, as in all other parts of North America, only where the woods have been recently burnt."[6]

So it remained. The spread of settlement along the littoral intensified the perimeter fires, while the passing of the Beothuks probably lessened fire pressures in the interior. In 1825, Newfoundland became a British crown colony, with representative government in 1832. Little changed. The Geological Survey of Newfoundland summarized the fire scene by remarking that "enormous destruction has been affected at nearly every part of the Island from time to time by fire." It had found evidence of "great conflagrations of a very early date," originating from the "wild aborigines" or lightning or what it passed off as spontaneous combustion. The abundant wildfires of recent years it attributed to the "culpable neglect" of trappers, lumber explorers, and rinders, who failed to extinguish their camp and smudge fires. The very structure of the Newfoundland forest – young woods sprouting amid the charred wreckage of old forests – testified to the antiquity and pervasiveness of burning. Often the same sites reburned, driving the landscapes into a blasted heath, sprinkled with dwarfed trees and scanty woods. The survey reported one immense fire that occurred around 1859, originating in the Gander River "about 40 miles above the lake and then swept nearly the entire space between the two rivers until checked by the intervention of the Great Lake which saved the lower valley." There the fire split, each branch laying waste to a vast strip of countryside. Since then several fires "of less magnitude" revisited the region, "still further enlarging the burned area which taken altogether cannot be said to be less than 2,000 square miles in extent."[7]

Then came 1867. While on the mainland bonfires celebrated the merging of British North America into the Confederation of Canada, Newfoundland, politically aloof, was scourged by conflagrations. There were large fires and "incalculable damage" long "raging in all directions, in the country." In some instances, "noble forests of timber, where the sound of the woodsman's hatchet has never or seldom been heard, have been utterly swept away" along with houses and perimeter farms. Some fires burst out of the interior, driven by shifting winds; around Trinity Bay, telegraph lines were burnt, and over 150 men struggled to keep the remaining lines open. The Geological Survey noted that, along the valley of the Terra Nova River, a succession of devastating fires, of which the 1867 outbreaks were only "the most recent," had made "sad havoc" and spared, as forlorn relics, only isolated patches of the timber, a "representative of the past." Except around settlements and routes of transit, fire was not frequent in Newfoundland, and save for extreme years not widespread, but the island was a chip from the boreal block, and when it burned it did so brilliantly.[8]

Acadia

Throughout Acadia the coast dominated as well. The lands were islands or peninsulas; the seas were the great arbiter of climate; along the Bay of Fundy, mammoth tides were the ruling presence of daily life. Shores and streams furnished fish and fowl at least seasonally and, for Europeans, a maritime lifeline to the Old World. Revealingly, the earliest French settlers along Fundy farmed by diking the tidal flats.

Among the first accounts of indigenous fire practices were some peculiar to life along the littoral. Nicholas Denys described both in his 1672 *Description and Natural History of the Coasts of North America*. The Mi'kmaq fished at night, paddling up the streams where the salmon and trout gathered during their ascents, collecting at night in pools behind falls. "To these places of rest the Indians went at night with their canoes and their torches." The fish, "seeing the fire which shines upon the water, come wheeling around the canoe." There they were speared, 150-200 in a night. (This is a common method throughout the world, including Europe, and one sufficiently successful to be later outlawed by fishing regulations.)[9]

The other technique involved a "rather interesting" hunt for ducks and geese in the closed coves where the flocks slept at night, safe from foxes. "To those places the Indians went, two or three in a canoe, with torches which they made of Birch bark; these burn more brightly than torches of wax." As they approached the sleeping fowl, they lay down in the canoes and drifted unsuspectingly into the flocks. "When the Indians were in their midst they lighted their torches all at once." Surprised, the birds rose, but darkness and the brilliant light of the torches confused them, and they fluttered about the flames like moths. "They all proceeded to wheel in confusion around the torches which an Indian held, always approaching the fire, and so close that the Indians, with sticks they held, knocked them down as they passed." Others became dizzy and fell, and the hunters then seized them and wrung their necks. "As a result in a single night they filled their canoe."[10]

Denys noted, however, that all he said "about the customs of the Indians, and of their diverse ways of doing things, ought to be understood only as the way in which they did them in old times." Already, European contact was provoking irreversible changes. European diseases were shredding Native populations; European fire appliances – from metal cookware to muskets – were altering the dynamics of hearth and habitat; and European fire practices, leveraged by the axe, began actively reshaping the land. Agriculture required that forests be hacked and burned into fields. Whether by accident or design, those fires could bolt beyond their slashings. A great fire raged about Miscou when "a cannonier, who drying his powder ..., set it afire in using tobacco, and the fire reduced to cinders a good part of the woods of the island." Even Denys felt their impress. In 1669, his house and dwellings burned, leaving him to retire to Nipisiquit, where he put down gun and axe and picked up a quill to write his *Natural History*.[11]

The process was slow. Acadia was the contested middle ground between New France and New England, between the winter-frozen St. Lawrence and the ice-free seaports to the south, a tangle of seas and lands alternately threatened and shielded by Louisbourg and Halifax. Settlements were forts, trading posts, entrepôts, with a smattering of hinterland to help sustain them. Movement into the interior was tentative. Yet as the region sorted itself out into three separate colonies under British rule, each acquired a distinctive character relative to land and fire. Nova Scotia remained tied to the sea, an administrative centre, a sentinel, and a largely ship-borne culture; it became a seaport. Prince Edward Island evolved into a farm. New Brunswick became a timber colony. Fishing village, garden, logging camp – each fashioned its own fire regime. What made them differ from the preceding state was their relative abilities to cut into the mixed Acadian forest and the incentive to burn those slashings.

Time and Tide: Nova Scotia

Nova Scotia was a country of coasts, almost an island itself, combined with the Isle of Cape Breton. Settlement grew to support traffic for fish and fur and, along the Bay of Fundy, the farming of tidal marshes, but trade, not colonization, was its intent. The land was also a guardian to the gulf, the scene of endless squabbling between England and France, symbolized by the great forts erected at Louisbourg (1713) and Halifax (1749). Incentives to break into the back country were few, since the soil was poor, transport feeble, and resources lacking. Villages were strung along the coast like beads. British or French, national traditions made little difference on the land except as war and forced emigration settled and unsettled human habitations. Nova Scotia was known for its harbours, not its hinterland.

Where harbour and tide lands combined, as they did at Annapolis, Minas Basin, and Chignecto Bay, a distinctive pattern of agriculture emerged, made by diking the marshlands. This was a reclamation more easily wrought than that from the upland forest and a far more productive one. The settlements fashioned to support fishers, traders, and garrisons thrived on such landscapes, and when they sought expansion they did so by colonizing further tide lands rather than cracking open the dense woods behind. The spade was more valuable than the axe; water did here what fire did elsewhere. Livestock of all sorts – cattle, oxen, sheep, horses, swine – were let loose into the countryside. It was a system calculated to infuriate those who identified colonization with clearing.

Besides, most settlers farmed only part time. The seasons forced farmers and fishers into competition; both lay claim to summers. Trapping (and later logging), however, were jobs best done in the winter. Woods farms would be limited, neither necessary nor possible without external pressures, mass immigration, artificial fertilizers, robust markets for farm produce, and a transport network beyond birch-bark canoes and coastal schooners. The Sieur de Dièreville summed up the case against farming the interior succinctly when he observed that "it costs a great deal to prepare the lands which they wish to cultivate; those called Uplands, which must be cleared in the Forest, are not good, and the seed does not come up well in them; it makes no difference how much trouble is taken to bring them into condition with Manure, which is very scarce; there is almost no harvest, and sometimes they have to be abandoned."[12]

Thus, there were few inroads when, in 1755, the Acadians were forcibly evicted, and the process of colonization had to begin anew with fresh drafts of immigrants. The Acadian legacy on the land had been scanty. Much of the countryside had become, in the words of Andrew Hill Clark, "a *tabula rasa*." Formal British suzereignty came with the 1763 Treaty of Paris; Cape Breton was annexed two years later. The process of large-scale reclamation did not come until almost another century passed.[13]

What brought the axe to the woods was logging, and the earliest prohibitions against reckless burning were to protect reserved timber as much as farms. A sawmill (the first in North America) appeared at Lequille in 1612. A policy of restrictions against felling trees suitable for ship masts, first promulgated in 1688 for New England, was extended to Nova Scotia in 1728. The practice of marking such pines with the King's Broad Arrow became, in fact, one of the irritations that festered into the American Revolution, but it would also, over the coming decades, ripen into the wholesale reservation of crown land. About the time of the Acadian expulsion, the English felling axe was introduced. In 1762, the Legislative Assembly passed Nova Scotia's first fire ordinance, an attempt to restrict settler burning to particular seasons, an adaptation of English common law. In 1774, setting fire to lands reserved for the Royal Navy became a felony. Exempt, however, were coastal woodlands within half a mile of the shore, a concession to the fisheries.[14]

The new geography of fire followed that of settlement. In 1783, as Loyalists and freedmen piled into Nova Scotia, ramshackle towns appeared along with some desultory clearing and desultory (if damaging) fires. At Port Mouton, 2,500 people, including soldiers, huddled through a wretched winter in log and sod huts and canvas tents, until in mid-May a fire broke out that swept the cantonment and, driven by southwesterly winds, ran through the forest and scattered the settlers to the sea. The Loyalist diaspora, following the American Revolution, sparked the first serious roads into the country, another form of clearing and an invitation for yet more. In hallowed fashion, the new fuels soon found new ignitions.[15]

The task of highland clearance was arduous. Trees were felled, helter-skelter, then lopped and chopped into twelve-foot segments, the debris piled and fired. From New England came the simpler practice of girdling, by which bark was stripped or chipped away around the trunk, thus killing the tree. This practice opened the canopy to sunlight and allowed planting (and later grazing) amid the standing boles. (Girdling worked with conifers; some of the hardwoods, however, could sucker below the girdle while the roots yet lived.) After five to six years, the trees had rotted enough that they could be neatly felled, which the skilled axeman did in parallel rows. Subsequently, the bole was bucked not by steel but by fire; hacking a notch into the trunk, the farmer laid a single burning stick within it, renewing the fire as necessary, while the slow burn cleaved its way through the bole. With an ox, he piled the logs, gathered the new debris to it, and fired the mound.[16]

A careful settler would surround the slashings with a firebreak, or call neighbours to help with the burning, or trust to his knowledge of the season to keep the fire within its bounds. But the work was tedious, colleagues scant, and experience hard won, so it happened that wildfires could enter the drying slash and that controlled fires burst out. Throughout the 1790s, the quickening pace of settlement inspired a hastening outbreak of fires. They were particularly serious to the southwest. In June and July 1792, Simeon Perkins reported fires "in all quarters" around Liverpool. In 1800, nearly every settlement in southern Nova Scotia reported fires, while over Liverpool smoke hung heavily throughout the summer. There were wide swaths burned south of Lakes Rossignol and Jordan, fires within Annapolis County, predatory flame wherever tinder, which lay along the isle's margins like carrion in the woods, found a scavenging spark.[17]

The first flush of growth could last, with proper crop sequencing and weeding, for several years. A second burn a handful of years later could prolong the flush. Those settlers blessed with good soils could then pluck out stumps and haul off stones and nurture their crops with manure, lime, or fishbone meal. But many had land less fertile; unless they could convert arable land to pasture, they abandoned the plot and moved to another. Had steam not intervened, colonization might well have followed the boreal farming practices of Eurasia, with a long-fallow swidden cycle in which the young, regrowing woods became the scene for a second round of clearing and firing. Instead, the land went feral, much reclaimed by white spruce, which today accounts for nearly 10 percent of the Nova Scotia forest. If farmers abandoned the land, however, fire did not. The resprouted patchwork of woods redefined rather than dismissed the geography of fire.[18]

In 1801-2, Titus Smith, Jr., on commission from Governor John Wentworth, surveyed the lesser-known interior. His specific charge was to identify sites suitable for growing hemp, part of what was evolving in the colony (along with masts) into a naval stores industry, but in truth it was a natural history reconnaissance, in the vogue of Linnaeus and Humboldt. Smith traversed the mainland along several compass bearings and then summarized his conclusions. He estimated more than a million acres of "burn," most of it having occurred within the past decade. Additionally, he identified 1.3 million acres of "barren" – that is, older burns now covered with huckleberries, blueberries, and sheep laurel, only lightly sprinkled with scrubby hardwoods. Clearly, this boreal heath had resulted from repeated burnings, well before the recent push for roads and clearings. Most of it, in fact, had probably been deliberately kept as berry fields through regular firings. He noted, too, the curious choreography of lichens and caribou. Around the LaHavre River, he concluded that "the caribou are more numerous than the moose but are very few compared to what they have been heretofore, owing to the fires which have burnt over the open barrens and destroyed the reindeer moss which is their principal food." (By 1830, caribou were returning to the lands so ferociously burned in 1800.) West of the Mersey River, he found across swamps burned in the 1800 conflagrations the tracks of moose and bear, the latter probably grateful for the abundant whortle and blueberry. And he documented the colossal wreckage wrought by the Great Storm of September 1798. Here was nature's slashing, soon followed by burning, kindled either by nature or by people. A settler, William Burke, reported that the Mi'kmaq had told him about a great blowdown some eighty years before (1720) that had inspired a burn over a region thirty miles long and twenty miles wide.[19]

In the end, hemp mattered less than timber. Nova Scotia was a potential woodlot. In particular, Smith discovered great pines around Medway and Pictou that could serve as masts, although most of the trees he found too stunted or warped and hence better suited for spars. Overall, however, as he observed around Shelburne, the pines were defective, retarded by the too-frequent fires. The alliance between logging and fire proved critical for the future of the woods. The imperial jostlings between England and France heightened into the deadly rivalry between Britain and Napoleon, and this contest would be fought partly over wood, for Canada's stock of timber became an imperial resource, the sustenance of the Royal Navy. Sword and fire gave way, in Canada, to axe and fire, the heartless burning of villages and forts to a relentless firing of slashed forest.[20]

Garden in the Gulf: Prince Edward Island

It was small, an island, and frozen in the Gulf of St. Lawrence half the year, and those facts argued against trapping, fishing, and logging but meant that even a skein of settlement could cover the interior with farms. The permanent settlement of Île Saint-Jean (later renamed Prince Edward Island) began with a proprietary grant in 1719. By 1739, a census reported 440 people, 166 oxen, 337 cows, 402 sheep, 14 horses, and arable land (including wet meadows) of 1,000 acres. The figures should include an abundance of fires. Colonists used fire to prepare land for crops, to burn off the fallow, to promote rough pasture, and simply to clear and clean, all practices typical of European agronomy.[21]

The procedures were crude. In 1732-34, Jean-Pierre Roma described the "method" of clearing as follows: "Cut down the trees, remove their branches, burn the branches in a fire, choose the trees that could be of some use, carry them to a convenient spot along extremely cluttered tracks, chop up and move the rest, retaining what is good for burning in the house or burning on the spot that which makes too much clutter with the aim also of making room." Where the purpose was to plant, there was little incentive to clear-cut, only to mince up the smaller brush and girdle (or "rind") the larger timber before burning, and then sow in the ash amid the stumps. Plough cultivation came later, after the arduous extirpation of stumps (often following years of rotting and slow burning). Where timber itself had a value, it was felled, trimmed, and hauled away, and the debris was burned where it lay. Elsewhere the natural grasslands along the shore, dappled meadows, and grassy understoreys were probably fired for pasture and berry patches for fruit.[22]

It did not take long for the burns to break loose. Extensive fires were recalled by residents for 1724. Sébastien-François-Ange Le Normant de Mézy recounted a disastrous fire in 1736 that savaged lands, crops, and seed, so much so that the garrison had to tide the colonists over the winter with provisions from the king's stores along with twenty hogs' heads from Canada and then supply wheat seed for spring sowing. Still worse came in 1741 when a fire swept through the vicinity of St. Peters-Savage Harbour. Both Louis Duchambon Du Pont and François Bigot reported the outcome. A sudden wind had carried flame "from all parts of the woods which surrounded the houses of its residents" and trapped several families, killing thirteen or fourteen people. (A later account from Captain Holland claimed that it burned "all the fishing vessels" as well.) The wider landscape bore the scars for decades, although some of the scorched lands ripened into blueberry barrens that became a robust foodstock in its own right (and a source of recurrent burning thereafter). In 1751, Louis Franquet reported the aftermath of extensive firing around Port La-Joie. For some, this burning caused hardship, the inhabitants having to travel a "long distance" to secure fuel wood. But for others, it was a blessing. "There are areas of a large size that fire has laid bare and that one can put under cultivation at little expense and without much work." Elsewhere settlers reported that, the woods having "previously been burned in part, they had less trouble in clearing them." The burned woods, moreover, burst with blueberries. A year later Joseph de La Roque noted that the region around East Point was a "desert owing to the occurrence of the fire." He reported, too, a fire remembered by residents from 1738. And Thomas Pichon in 1760, also inspecting East Point, reported lands "deserted, because a fire had obliged the inhabitants to abandon" the site. The nearby coast, he reported, was "a country laid waste by fire."[23]

By the time the British assumed sovereignty in 1763, the island remained largely wooded and, where burned, not likely to have been fired beyond its range of ecological tolerance. The Acadians had been reluctant clearers: the rough pasture mattered as much as the arable land, and tidal meadows were a good source of fodder. Settlement had proceeded little farther than a farm-length from tidewater, like barnacles clinging to the littoral. Without fire, settlement was impossible, and unquestionably fires had sprung free and rambled, like some livestock. But the conversion of the island into a garden had only begun; after the Acadians were expelled, it would have to begin anew. Île Saint-Jean, like the rest of Acadia, had more strategic than agricultural value. William Cobbett famously dismissed the region as "wretchedly poor": mounds of rocks covered chiefly with fir trees. Prince Edward Island itself was a "rascally heap of sand, rock and swamp," bearing "nothing but potatoes."[24]

Over the next century, this perception changed utterly. Recolonization rekindled in earnestness after the American Revolution, filling with the various dispossessed peoples of British North America. The 1798 census tallied 4,372 persons. A year later the island acquired its new name. By 1805, it had a population of 7,000; by 1827, 23,000; by 1841, 47,000. Land clearing and burning commenced apace, as the island evolved its famous mixed-farm economy. By 1833, it boasted 30,000 cattle, 50,000 sheep, 20,000 pigs, and 6,000 horses. Pasture was easier to create than arable land, and – as especially the Scots immigrants knew – fire was an ideal means to do it. By the 1820s, girdling and burning replaced clear-felling. Long-fallow could be grazed and kept moderately fresh by repeated burning. Outright logging supported a small timber industry, which in turn sustained shipbuilding. By the time the island reluctantly joined the Canadian Confederation in 1873, it held a population of a little fewer than 100,000, and indigenous births had replaced immigration. The wild woods were largely gone, the forests absorbed as woodlots into a regimen of agriculture. The island would soon have the character for which it became famous: the Garden in the Gulf.[25]

Its evolution of fires tracks nicely the evolution of settlement. In 1755, Thomas Curtis visited the isle. The vessel foundered, and although the party struggled to shore in a leaky boat they survived thanks to a "Mr. Fry," who had the "presence of mind to put in his pocket some instruments for making a fire which we soon kindled and got of trees that lay down a good fire." But while drying themselves, the wind blew hard, sparks scattered on their clothes and skin, and a "very disagreeable" smoke billowed up. They spent the night "standing round the fire." Subsequently they erected a shelter of fir boughs, which "caught fire about 12 o'clock at night and in a few minutes was redused to Ashes having only time to run out and save their Blanketts." Later in their travels, the misfortune repeated itself. The party sometime thought "of going in the Wood and make a fire." They met Indians as bad off as themselves, "under great aprehensions for some time of being freezd to death for want of Wood ... Their Whole employ to fetch fireing." Still, they had a wigwam, and the Curtis party thought to erect one of their own in the woods. They did not, however, make a sufficiently large hole for the escaping smoke, so the heat built up, and the boughs caught fire, and "in a few minutes was all redused to Ashes."[26]

That was the crude fire story of survival, of fire as shelter. The story of settlement required that fire be applied to the land, that the woods themselves be converted into a habitable abode. This process, more calculated, Walter Johnstone described in a series of letters written in 1820. He makes clear that colonization means clearing: new settlers begin at the place where they intend to erect their houses, using the felled timber for construction. "This step is absolutely necessary to ensure the safety of the dwelling, and place it beyond the reach of the flames that may arise from the burning of the woods." The felled timber is limbed and cut into twelve- to fourteen-foot lengths, a process called "junking." Thus, "when the space intended to be cleared is cut down, junked, and all lying in a promiscuous manner over the whole surface, fire is applied to it in as dry and windy a day as can be selected, and if the fire runs well, the greater part of the small branches will be consumed, but the trunks will only be scorched." So much is basic fire behaviour: the fine particles drive the fire. The heavy pieces are next rolled together into piles, to which are added any small branches remaining to quicken a second burning. "The stronger part of the family then go on to make up more piles, while the weaker part set fire to those which are thus prepared. In this way they proceed till the whole of what was cut down is gone over; then when the piles go out they are kindled again, and those that continue to burn are thrust closer together, till all is consumed." Johnstone concluded that he had "to say this is a piece of work of the most dirty and disagreeable nature ... After the wood is all burnt, the stumps are left standing about two feet high, scorched black with the first burning, like so many blocks, of a blacksmith's anvil."[27]

Into this ash settlers commence to sow, potatoes being the preferred first crop. The burnt ground is hoed into small mounds with four cuttings each. The work is hard. The ground is laced with roots, and the wood, "which will not burn early in the season, ... as well as the land, is rendered extremely damp by the melting of the snow." Yet the burning quickens the growth. It is possible to plant later on burnt land and still yield a crop, and a first burning "enriches the land greatly, and their first crop, as well as the succeeding ones, are, in this case, very luxuriant." Subsequently they plant wheat and then timothy, and if the land is good and "has been well burnt" they mow it for several years among the stumps for rough hay without need for manure. The greater part of the land, Johnstone observed, had in fact been converted to pasture. Most livestock were turned out into the woods to forage for themselves. (Even when penned, herders assisted cattle and sheep by fire, in this instance by smoke against "flies in the night.") "This," he concluded, "is the whole history of clearing the land upon this Island."[28]

It was not an ideal system, certainly not for an educated Improver, keen to rotate crops, fertilize, and upgrade breeding. Johnstone admitted, however, that the islanders of the New World enjoyed a privilege denied many in the Old World. They got a quick return on their labour. That flush could not last, he insisted: "But they have all need to be taught this lesson, that their success in agriculture must spring from the dunghill." That was the collective wisdom of European agronomy speaking, that only the slow cycling of organic matter built up the soil's capital, that fire robbed nature's principal rather than spending its interest, that a fire-flushed agriculture made for rich parents and poor children. It was a judgment reinforced by J.L. Lewellin, who in 1826 dismissed "the general mode of conducting a Farm [as] slovenly, often wretched," even as he marvelled at "what returns are obtained." He disliked, in particular, the turning out to the woods of the stock, whose gathered dung should go to the field. Instead, the islanders burned, and even the "fern" that grew profusely "where the fire has run" they failed to convert into organic mulch.[29]

There were practical considerations, too. Escaped fires were dangerous and their aftermath unsightly. "When the fire gets hold of woods much mixed with soft wood, it runs sometimes several miles, and forms in its progress, I am told (and I partly saw it)," Johnstone assured his readers, "one of the most awful scenes in nature; flying when the wind is high with amazing rapidity, making a noise like thunder, and involving the neighborhood in a dense cloud of smoke." It sometimes killed cattle and wildlife, rightly alarmed newcomers who had to defend their hasty wooden cabins or flee outright yet "not knowing where to find safety." Such "burnt woods are to be seen in the neighborhood of almost every settlement, some of them of considerable magnitude."[30]

Yet awful as the wild flames were, their consequences were worse. The burnt woods "form, in reality, a scene the most ruinous, confused, and disgusting, the eye can possibly look upon." The passage of time improves the wreckage little or slowly: "If a few years more have elapsed since the fatal flame passed through it, a scene more revolting remains yet to be described." The trees, their roots destroyed, topple over, churn the earth into hideous mounds, and form an impassable tangle of trunks. The evil continues, for a land overrun by fire "is damaged in more than one respect." If not immediately cultivated, the land springs back with fireweed, fern, and "rasp bushes." It dries under the sun and becomes "unfit for any crop, without summer fallowing," redeemable only by dung. The lost hardwoods deprive the settler of firewood, and instead of an attractive limning of green and ornamental woods the "borders of almost every settlement have been more or less destroyed by fire." Only someone who has seen it, Johnstone concluded, can appreciate how "unpleasant and revolting" is the outcome.[31]

As clearing continued, there were ample opportunities for people to judge for themselves. An 1821 fire around St. Margarets destroyed the church and parochial house. In his 1905 *History of Prince Edward Island,* Alexander Warburton recorded how, "occasionally, in a generation, so great is the summer drought" that if a fire kindles "it sweeps everything before it." For illustration, he cited the "conflagration" that occurred "around the year 1840" and threatened settlers' houses near Conway and Ellerslie, searing "hundreds of acres of woodland almost bare." In 1870, the land was yet recovering from the shock. Blackened tree trunks, still standing, had worn to grey, and the district was chocked with fields of post-burn blueberries, while scattered spruce and fir had gradually reclaimed niches.[32]

That was the crisis of colonization. Yet eventually, like all other aspects of the island, fire became disciplined into an agrarian order. Its fires became those of spring burning for pasture, the firing of the fallow, the scorching of blueberry fields, the occasional clearing burn, and the ever rarer wildfire. The rhythms of burning were those of cultivation and seasonal herding; the scales of fire belonged with field and woodlot. There was less hinterland for escapes to break free from this regimen. Here its character as an island mattered. Even settlement that pushed weakly away from the coast – a few farms inland from tidewater – could overwhelm the landscape because there was so little interior land relative to the deeply embayed coast. Elsewhere in Old Acadia, there remained a backcountry, little broken until the advent of steam. Prince Edward Island, however, converted with axe and open flame instead of iron and internal combustion.

The Torch in the Timber: New Brunswick

In 1807, Napoleon and Britain had declared mutual blockades, and by 1808 the continental system had severed Britain from its ancient Baltic sources for naval timber and tar. Desperate, Britain turned, instead, to what remained of British North America. Heavy duties on European sources further encouraged the promotion of Canadian timber. In 1800, Nova Scotia exported 565 loads of fir to Great Britain; by 1812, that trickle had become a torrent of 25,203. The new province captured, too, some of the West Indian trade that pre-revolutionary New England had dominated. The real action, however, lay across the Bay of Fundy, where intense lobbying by elite Loyalists had flaked off from the Acadian legacy a separate colony, New Brunswick. It quickly established itself, at Saint John, as an ice-free rival to the traffic in St. Lawrence timber. By 1815, it had become, in Graeme Wynn's phrase, Britain's pre-eminent "timber colony."[33]

After the revolution, the growth of European population was rapid. From 4,000 in 1780, numbers rose to 25,000 in 1800 and to 200,000 in 1851. This increase still left it holding the second-smallest population in British North America, and with 640,000 acres cleared for agriculture by mid-century even Prince Edward Island boasted a broader farmland. What New Brunswick had was trees: the red (and especially) white pine and spruce of the Acadian forest. In early Canada, only the Ottawa River region rivalled it for richness and access. A great timber frontier, gathering along the gulf, moved inland like a tidal bore up the St. Lawrence and into the Great Lakes. But its colonial epicentre lay in New Brunswick. What cod and beaver had done previously, timber would now do for Canada's export economy. Between 1802 and 1805, British North America had annually exported to Britain some 9,000 loads of balk timber; by 1809, that volume had swelled to 90,000. What A.R.M. Lower famously called "the North American assault on the Canadian forest" had begun.[34]

New Brunswick had less coast proportionally than the other Maritimes, half its shores along the Bay of Fundy, half fronting the Gulf of St. Lawrence. But a system of broad rivers, particularly the Miramichi and St. John, opened the pre-industrial interior to logging. The streams were ideal for floating timber. All winter loggers would cut and pile along the icy banks, the frozen land making hauling relatively easy. Come spring, with the waters high, they would dump the logs into the streams and drive them to market, like transhumant sheep in the Mediterranean or longhorn cattle on the Great Plains. It was possible for settlers to both log and farm, and many did so, although a jack-tar of logging emerged, the lumberjack, who increasingly did the heavy labour. The early traffic was in balk timber; later sawmills arose to add value to the less-raw wood. Farms took hold on the better-soiled lands after logging.[35]

These were the features, environmental and economic, that would flow up the St. Lawrence and stamp the Canadian timber industry. A seasonal rhythm of labour, of winter cutting and spring driving; a backcountry of raw natural wealth, of vast pineries laced by streams suitable for floating logs; a commodity economy of booms and busts, like a climate of extremes rather than of averages, that promoted the large firm and a corporatist polity – these traits had also characterized the fisheries and fur trade and would long continue to shape a Canada committed to raw materials, from wheat to minerals to petroleum. Business cycles adumbrated climatic cycles and the wild fitfulness of biotic populations. Survival favoured the big, the rich, the well connected, and over time the relentless uncertainties would force small colonies, like small companies, to merge.[36]

The explosive growth of logging badly stressed the politics of land tenure. In principle, the Broad Arrow system, seeking to reserve prime timber for the navy, granted royal authority over the woods. The policy made agricultural settlement technically illegal. After Loyalists spilled into the region, eager to claim land, the issue could no longer be ignored. In 1783, the authorities thus sought to protect the Royal Navy's prerogatives by reserving to the crown any timber suitable for naval use, even on land otherwise sold to private persons, and by establishing, on premier forests, reserves from which settlement was excluded. The result was confusing and unpopular – just such actions had contributed to revolutionary unrest in New England (where it seemed to be an environmental analogue to impressment). Once the timber boom had begun, settlement became a means of logging, and logging a prelude to settlement, and the authorities, in any event, were largely powerless to prevent folks on the ground from culling out good timber from reserves and buying farmland in order to strip it of pines. Having to refer to London for decisions was hopeless.

In 1816, with the crisis of the Napoleonic Wars ended, Britain devolved administration of the forests to New Brunswick, and within a year local authorities, divided uneasily between those who sold lands and those who sold only timber, issued guidelines. By 1824, these guidelines had congealed into a system of timber-licensing that restrained access to crown forests. But enforcement was weak, speculation (with the boom cresting) rampant, the reserves unpopular, and the government interested primarily in revenue. Grievances mounted, the reserves were disbanded in 1833, and a strategy of longer-term leases came into force. All this favoured loggers over settlers and, among the timber barons, the large, well-capitalized owners, able to bid generously at auction, influence colonial officials, and weather economic and ecological instabilities. By 1846, critics denounced the outcome as a "monstrous monopoly." A commodity economy of exports had triumphed over agricultural colonization. The cutover lands grew back into woods, not farms.[37]

Even so, the axe radically restructured the land. The usual colonizing fires popped up, with burning for charcoal and potash and later the burning of sawdust. But the big story was wildfire. Especially where the boreal forest dappled the countryside, lightning fire had existed, and to this one should add the fire-littering of the Mi'kmaq. Surveying the Saint John River, Charles Morris alluded to an immense fire that ravaged Washademoak and Grand Lake in 1761. "All the timber," he concluded, "has been burnt by the Indians." Loyalists along the Saint John settled on the "Intervale lands by the river" because, Bates reported, "the highlands had generally been burned by the Indians." Surveyors in 1797 reported evidence of recent burns around Charlotte County and the Magaguadavic River. These were only the most obvious manifestations amid a pattern of woods – patches of even-aged pine, "snarls" of charred and fallen trunks, swaths of birch, fields of blueberry – that spoke to fire's enduring presence. As cutting quickened, however, so did burning. Nature's economy adjusted to an exchange of fuel for flame; even as New Brunswick exported timber, it effectively imported fire. A felling binge was followed by a flaming bust.[38]

The logging rush reached a peak in 1825, then promptly crashed and burned. In October 1825, the first great conflagration of North American colonization, and the largest of historical record, savaged New Brunswick from Fredericton to Miramichi. Vast tracts of slashings burned; uncut but drought-blasted woods burned; towns burned; vessels at harbour burned. The Miramichi fire founded a lethal pantheon of Great Fires. A witness, later a regional historian, Robert Cooney, declared that "a greater calamity ... never befell any forest country." As Graeme Wynn has observed, "the devastation seemed to lay bare the frail foundations of provincial prosperity."[39]

So it had. Thereafter, cutting dropped to a still-high but more sustainable level. Fires, too, fell into a rhythm, as climate and slash combined in smaller outbreaks. There were plenty of promiscuous sparks in the woods, for every hunter, trapper, traveller, and pipe-smoking logger scattered campfires, warming fires, and matches with abandon. James Johnston described how, "winding round the trunk," a flame could ascend "in one continuous rushing pyramid of fire." It was a "very beautiful sight in the day-time" and even more "singularly so in the dark woods at night." While confessing that "of course" such a spectacle destroyed the trees, he added that, "in these forests, trees are of no value; and it is the making of such experiments that, in very warm and arid weather, the firing of whole tracts of forest are often to be ascribed."[40]

Never again, however, did conditions collude so hugely as in 1825, and the frustrations of farming meant that, unlike around the Great Lakes, the land would not experience routine clearing fires ever ready to leap into fresh slash and explode across the countryside. Its fires, like its heaps of sawdust, were the residue of a logging economy; they "lumbered" up the woods as square balks did wharves. Fire obeyed the same logic as logging, and its control followed from similar principles of political economy. That the land did not convert into fields but regrew to forest meant, too, that fires would return, even if, like those woods, they had changed their character.

The Canadas

The axe arrived from the south, clearing the way for maize, beans, and squash (and later sunflowers and tobacco) and the colonizing peoples who planted them. A new breed of short-season corn encouraged a surge northward during the seventh century AD; by 1000 AD, much of the lowlands around the Great Lakes and St. Lawrence were under some form of swidden cultivation. The human geography divided between Algonquin speakers on the Shield and Appalachians, devoted to an aboriginal economy of seasonal hunting, fishing, and foraging, and Iroquoian speakers in the lowlands, who practised a mixed economy of horticulture and hunting and a political economy of trade, settled villages, and confederation. A new mosaic of fire regimes jostled into order.[41]

The strategy behind swidden is universal: create fuel, burn it, and plant in the ashes. But the techniques vary according to local circumstances; the best known for Canada are those of the Hurons. Samuel de Champlain related how a group would "strip the trees of all their branches which they burn at the foot of the said tree to kill it." Between the boles they would plant the seed, "a pace apart." Gabriel Sagard elaborated. The men would fell the trees at a height of two to three feet, then gather the branches along with brush, weeds, and other debris to burn at the stump, in this way not only burning the ground but preventing resprouting from the trunk. This occurred during March and April, and what was not needed for agricultural burning was hauled off by women for firewood. Granted stone axes, the technique worked best with small trees; the big ones they would strip of bark in order to kill and then burn down. The planting itself occurred in small mounds, a technique that, while common throughout the Americas, had the additive benefit of sparing the young plants from ground-hugging frosts. Overall, the scene was kept "quite clean," not only the specific fields but also the landscape – astonishingly so, as it appeared to early explorers.[42]

A village could thrive for ten to fifteen years before a move became necessary. The reasons for relocating included exhausted soils, depleted firewood, the vigour of weeds and pests, and a general buildup of waste. The primary effect of the burning was probably less to fertilize than to fumigate, but after a handful of years the indigenous vegetation simply overwhelmed the efforts to contain it. The creeping dispersion of fields also made the women vulnerable to summer raids. One could probably add, too, the need for regeneration through a new fire, which could only come by reaccumulating fuel – that is, by allowing the site to go fallow for two or three decades. Upon returning, it would be possible to reoccupy the old clearings, having to cope only with the younger, more easily felled trees. In this way, the initial shock of clearing could become part of a system of long-rhythm cultivation, and the decadal cycling of agriculture could rest lightly atop an annual cycle of aboriginal hunting and harvesting (which abounded in berries and even had dogs and captive bears for meat).[43]

But, in the end, how much land could such practices touch with fire? Not all the land could be swiddened; estimates place perhaps a third of Huronia into the network, adjusted by soil, microclimate, and site characteristics. This is a significant fraction of the tract between the lakes, but what is equally significant is that swidden made possible a penumbra of other fire practices. It had, in fire's economy, a multiplier effect, not only through the inevitable escapes into wild wood beyond the stumps but by sustaining a higher human population that also had to hunt, gather berries, and otherwise fuss over the land. It meant that most of the forest on dry soils was actually fallow. It meant that the land bore the oft-grassy scars of the abandoned swiddens.[44]

The old clearings, frequently fired, left a landscape that, in Champlain's words, was "for the most part cleared." Sagard agreed, as usual refining the description: "a well cleared country, pretty and pleasant ... The country is full of fine hills, open fields, very beautiful broad meadows bearing much excellent hay." These became prime hunting grounds, probably sustained by regular burning. Even in the 1830s the origin of these fields remained in collective memory. Catharine Parr Traill recorded the opinion that "these plains were formerly famous hunting-grounds of the Indians, who, to prevent the growth of the timbers, burned them year after year" to stop the forest from reclaiming them. "Sufficient only was left to form coverts," which the deer required; the deer thus swarmed in "great herds" to feast on the plains-clothed "deer-grass, on which they become exceedingly fat at certain seasons of the year." It was not the deer alone, however, that benefited. "Almost all wild animals are more abundant in the cleared districts than in the bush," she reported. So they had no doubt been in the heyday of the Hurons, whose judicious clearings had bolstered their prey.[45]

European settlers rarely doubted, as later sceptics would, the power of Indian burning. If anything, they credited it with too much rather than too little. Traill, for example, had to dismiss as "absurd" the "notion entertained by some travellers, that the Indian summer is caused by the annual conflagration of forests by those Indians inhabiting the unexplored regions beyond the larger lakes." Those languid days of cool sun and filtered sky settlers had long associated with burning, for it is when many Europeans did some of their own firing amid leaves and logs desiccated by long summers, and undoubtedly some of those grey fumes did rise from Indian burning. Autumn skies were smoky skies. The particular tradition that identified Indian summer with Indian burning had migrated from the coast to the interior and from early explorers to settlers later disturbed by the persistence and grim terror of dark days, when palls blotted out even the sun. It was a legend to which Europeans were especially prone, since it conflated all fires with those set by people.[46]

Yet what they saw, as distinct from what they supposed, was already a shadow of its former glory. The thrust of Meso-American agriculture northward had come early enough to ride the climatic warming of times a millennium ago. Probably it had advanced wherever the soils permitted; then it receded. Even as the European first bobbed offshore to fish or to trade iron for furs, the great tide of Iroquoian agriculture had ebbed. By the 1540s, when Jacques Cartier probed into what the Natives called "Canada," the Iroquoian peoples of the St. Lawrence Valley had vanished, driven off by combinations of threats, diseases, quarrels, famines, and internal unrest, to which a deteriorating climate was probably a contributor, if only to toughen the rivalry between the swiddeners and their surroundings. Their disintegration isolated the Hurons, and, if powerful because they controlled important trade routes and could barter in corn, they were also vulnerable. The collapse created an agricultural vacuum precisely at the time the French explored, sought posts to traffic in furs, and announced majestic claims for king and church.[47]

The arrival of the Europeans changed this world, irreversibly. Trade segued from fish to fur; outposts moved into the gulf and down the St. Lawrence; small settlements arose to support the coastal factories, garrisons, and missions. Champlain established Quebec in 1608; the Dutch erected a competing post at Albany in 1614. The numbers of Europeans were trivial but their impacts immense because they carried diseases that swept through Native populations like a scythe and because their rivalries fed into those already present and sparked a series of lethal wars and relocations, the most famous of which, in 1648-49, led to the near extinction of the Huron.

The indigenous population collapsed, particularly along the St. Lawrence; by 1650, there were more French than Natives. Their cultivated lands went feral; a wilderness of fallow grew up. No longer was it possible to rely on Native trappers and traders to supply furs, whose annual exports became as erratic as burned areas. The French would have to immigrate, interbreed, and expand territorially, themselves become the middlemen, and support their own population by agriculture. In 1663, New France became a royal colony for which immigration was a goal. Gradually the felling axe replaced the tomahawk.

"Almost as soon as the French and Indians came in contact," R.L. Jones has observed, "they borrowed from each other's agriculture." The French adopted maple syrup, maize, squash, and tobacco, while the indigenes planted peas, swung iron axes, and eventually acquired some livestock. Authorities laboured to relocate friendly tribes and fragments of broken ones to missions and reserves within the colony, encouraging hybrid practices. The pioneering stages of agricultural colonization closely resembled swidden: slashing, piling, burning, planting, then beginning anew. Even in France, after all, agriculture was a fire-fallow system in which the farm no longer cycled through the land but had the landscape, as it were, cycle through the farm in the form of crop rotations and fallowing. The later agricultural revolution reduced the amount of fallow and fire but never eradicated it. Condemned as slovenly – leaving half the fields in fallow, turning out swine and cattle to free-graze on wet prairie and woods pasture – French Canadian farmers were simply adapting old ways to new crops and a setting in which there was room for slack.[48]

Yet the amount of arable land was small, crowded within the valley of the St. Lawrence and its near hinterlands. There was scant incentive to break into the backcountry. That did not change with the British ascendancy in 1763 and only commenced seriously after the American Revolution twenty years later sent some 7,500 Loyalists trekking across to the Niagara Peninsula to settle on lands ceded by the Mississauga. Allies among the Six Nations Iroquois were also resettled near the Bay of Quinte. More free grants of land became available, immigration was encouraged, and by 1790 the population had swollen to 14,000 to 20,000, boldly outdistancing the resident demographics of Quebec. A dynamic of Indian land cessions, immigration, and agricultural colonization, not unlike that characteristic of the United States, became established. The Quebec Act (1774) assured old Canada of some basic institutions, but the surge around Lake Ontario quickly created a distinct society, and in 1791 the Constitutional Act recognized these implacable realities and created two Canadas, Upper and Lower. After the Napoleonic wars, British immigration poured in. By 1842, Upper Canada boasted a population of 450,000. That influx was housed and fed by a commensurate colonization of fire.

Over the centuries, a mixed geography of fire had evolved. One domain nature laid down, one was tied to an aboriginal economy, and another bonded to agriculture. Settlement thus shifted the gradient between lightning and torch. Around Algonquin Park, lightning starts an estimated five fires a year per 400,000 hectares; in southern Ontario, it kindles fewer than one. Yet studies from fire-scarred trees in central Ontario register between 58 and 200 fires a year per 400,000 hectares – a difference most reasonably attributed to people. (Similarly, across the Great Lakes, researchers have found an average of 100 fires a year in coastal pine forests.) This era of quickened burning, an ecological shadow of human passage, may have caused fundamental shifts in the forest itself, in south-central Ontario nudging the land into red oak forest.[49]

But settlement itself had its seasons, and its great climatic swings, and fire regimes swayed with those slow rhythms. Even within a given site, mean fire intervals varied between six and twenty-nine years, and five and seventy-six years. As one might expect, the routes that connected the various economies were themselves often the most consistently burned domains because every economy had its trade; and traders – whether Hurons and Algonquins trafficking in maize, or coureurs de bois and voyageurs hauling furs, or farmers and loggers moving wheat and lumber – left fires. Not the density of settlement but the density of travel determined the fire regimes of such corridors.[50]

Consider, first, the chronicle of burning near the Jocko River, not far from one of the dominant routes of travel in pre-industrial Canada, the Ottawa and Mattawa Rivers corridor. Until logged, the site held mostly white pine with some oak. The scarred pine reveal between 1721 and 1937 a relatively constant fire frequency that exhibited low-intensity burns on a roughly fourteen-year average. The site weathered the worst of the demographic turmoil because its fires resulted from travel, and there was always movement for some reason or another, and because its terrain could allow for far-ranging fires, not squeezed into small patches by a dense matrix of lakes and watercourses.[51]

By contrast, a chronicle from the Muskoka River, another travel corridor in central Ontario, shows wide swings in burning. Tree-scar dating begins at 1664, after the worst of the Iroquois wars, and it documents a seventy-six-year fire-free interval otherwise unprecedented amid this white pine woods. The cause of fire's disappearance seems to be the population implosion of indigenes: there were few people left to swidden, burn berry patches, and fire-litter. Ojibwa replaced Hurons; a commitment to fur trading and warfare supplanted that of farming and harvesting. The forest regrew. By the mid-eighteenth century, a process of reclamation had commenced, announced by an apparent conflagration in 1761. Thereafter, settlement accelerated, and fire frequencies plummeted, with a rhythm of burning as short as five years. The once white pine forest returned as oak. At Algonquin Park, near Lake Opeongo, a similar study recorded only one fire from 1636 to 1779, then a rapid quickening, along with recolonization, to yield a mean fire-free interval of seventeen years.[52]

Elsewhere in Algonquin Park, near Basin Lake, a fire-history chronology from 1665 to 1856 recorded low-intensity fires, on average, "every 26 years, moderate intensity fires every 47 years, and stand-replacing fires every 200 years." The major phase of burning occurred between 1733 and 1780, both years that experienced stand-replacing fires in red pine, between which rippled quieter fires at roughly twelve-year intervals. Unsurprisingly the big outbreaks corresponded with drought. The more routine burning, however, revealed "no relationship" between flame and climate. These were probably anthropogenic fires, perhaps reflecting an acceleration in fur trading during the mid-eighteenth century. Before 1714, fewer than 40 traders held permits; by the early 1740s, more than 400 had permits, and the actual number is believed to have been five to six times greater. More transients almost universally translates into more fires.[53]

For New France's human residents, however, the most memorable fires of that conflagrating era were those associated with the havoc of the Seven Years War. In particular, the invasion of Quebec in 1758 followed a scorched earth strategy in which General James Wolfe instructed General Robert Monckton to "burn every house and hut," while at Kamouraska Major George Scott reported that he had marched fifty-two miles "and in that distance, burnt nine hundred and ninety eight good buildings, two sloops, two schooners, Ten Shallops and several Batteaus and small craft." Surely some such fires bolted free, and the firing of villages and fields, an old tactic of Indian warfare, no doubt followed, with victims escaping into the woods. The French retaliated with two massive waves of fireships, loaded with "pitch, tar, and every manner of combustible, mixed with fireworks, bombs, grenades," and old firearms. While the visual effect was "terrific" – Captain John Knox termed it "the grandest fireworks that can possibly be conceived" – the practical outcome was nil. But the mix of natural and contrived combustibles, and the violence of the display, foreshadowed the fiery assault to come on the Canadian forest.[54]

So, also, two patterns of agricultural burning thrived. There was the initial clearing, an event full of wild flame, often recorded – this is the fire front of settlement. But there was also a more subtle regimen of subsequent burning in fallow and rough pasture. This phase is poorly documented, for the routine is never as glamorous as first contact, and maintenance is less exciting than the shock of the new. In fact, a class of backwoodsman emerged, as in America, who broke the land, then quickly sold it to others better suited to farming, while they decamped to new locales. For those first fires, there are, in fact, two classic accounts, the outcomes of two sisters who emigrated to Canada in 1832.

Thomas and Catharine Traill pioneered their land near Peterborough responsibly. The slovenly approach was to fell the woods helter-skelter, or into tangled windrows, and then fire the debris as soon in the spring as they could burn – a sure formula for wildfire. Traill described a more prudent strategy that began when her husband "let out ten acres to some Irish choppers" who lived in a shanty over the winter and received fourteen dollars an acre for their labour. "The ground is to be perfectly cleared of every thing but the stumps: these will take from seven to nine or ten years to decay." In general, there were two approaches to the slashing. The New England method, which the Traills adopted, was the most common in Upper Canada and required total clearing. The southern method, however, mostly confined in Canada to oak plains, simply required girdling the trees. This technique was considered hazardous in thickly forested sites because the trees, to say nothing of their decaying limbs, were liable to fall in subsequent years; better, it was thought, to fell them at the start. The timber went to erecting a log cabin and split rail fences, with the rest committed to the flames of hearth, potash pile, and field. The Traills expected to have "about three acres ready for spring-crops, provided we get a good burning."[55]

There were two slashings and two burnings. "Those that understand the proper management of uncleared land," Traill continued, slashed the small brush and scrub during the summer, allowing it a full season to dry. "Windfallen trees" they bucked into suitable lengths, some to be hauled to burn, some for stockpiling with the winter's felled timber. These caches of lighter combustibles were fired in April and May, with a brisk wind. The larger woods, now scorched, were then reduced by a process of systematic stacking and burning. The Traills organized a "logging-bee": neighbours brought oxen, and together they yanked and yarded the larger trunks into a vast heap. Typically a team consisted of yoked ox and four men; they would pile the wood against a large log until a mound seven to eight feet tall and ten to twelve feet wide arose and toss loose debris on it. One such team could "log" an acre a day. Then the heaps were fired.[56]

When it came, the burning was "glorious," a "magnificent sight to see." Traill was uneasy to have open flame so close to their log shack, but the crews had taken care that the winds blew away from the house, and accidents, she observed, were of "rarer occurrence than might be expected, when we consider the subtlety and destructiveness of the element employed on the occasion." If the fuel was dry, the fire would "run all over the fallow." At night, the spectacle increased in splendour. Sometimes hollow pines and tall stumps would catch embers, soon aswirl with "exceedingly fine and fanciful" scenes, while firewhirls shot sparks like rockets and some stumps flared like "gas lamp-posts newly lit." On a dark night, with many settlers firing their slash, a great glow spread over the sky. The fire could burn for days.[57]

Then they did it again. They reyarded, or relogged, the scene, scraping the unburned debris together with the charred trunks and rekindling the heaps. "Strange as it may appear to you," Traill insisted, "there is no work that is more interesting and exciting than that of tending the log-heaps, rousing up the dying flames and closing them in, and supplying the fires with fresh fuel." And so it continued, collecting and consuming every remnant until the ground "be perfectly free from all encumbrances," save the standing stumps. It remained only to scatter the ashes "abroad" for the "great work of clearing" to conclude.[58]

It happened, from time to time, that the flames sprang beyond their hearth heaps and roared through "many hundreds of acres." This, too, was a "magnificent sight" – the "blazing" trees, the "awful" rush of a "conflagration," hurrying on, consuming all before it, "or leaving such scorching mementoes as have blasted the forest growth for years." Yet with her characteristic common-sensibility, Traill noted that such occurrences were "not considered favourable for clearing," since they destroyed the underbrush and light scrub that "are almost indispensable for ensuring a good burning."[59]

Susanna Moodie had a darker experience of Canada, and a more novelistic flair, and her founding fires leaped "madly up, like serpents in the dark, Shaking their arrowy tongues at Nature's heart." In brief, the burn was botched, and bolted, and nearly swallowed their small cabin amid the "hollow roaring" and "hideous hissing" of its "ten thousand flames."[60]

Dunbar Moodie had already fired the acres immediately adjacent to their cabin. With hired "choppers," he then cleared another twenty acres. The summer of 1834 came with drought and withering sun, but those with experience recommended he hold his torch until a good wind could help push the flames through the bush and ensure a fuller burn. A stiff wind meant, also, better control because the fire would go where the wind directed it. When he had to leave for business in Toronto, he left strict instructions with "old Thomas and his sons," their choppers, not to fire until he returned. Susanna had no special concerns. "I had never seen a fallow burnt," she confessed, "but I had heard of it as a thing of such common occurrence that I had never connected with it any idea of danger."[61]

Old Thomas took sick, however, and one of his sons, John Thomas, "surly [and] obstinant," assumed charge, and during a sultry day, with a strong wind blasting around noon, smoke sprang up around them. "The swamp immediately below us was on fire, and the heavy wind was driving a dense black cloud of smoke directly towards us." Susanna and her servant-girl, Mary, confronted John Thomas, who confessed that he had thought the time right to burn but that the fires had burst out of control, and he regretted the act. There was no one to fight the flames, nor was escape possible, for the "blubbering" boy had kindled the fields "in fifty different places" all around them. "Behind, before, on every side, we were surrounded by a wall of fire, burning furiously within a hundred yards of us, and cutting off all possibility of retreat." There was no open passage, and if one had existed the smoke was so dense they could not have seen their way through it, and if they had somehow forced a passage, "buried as we were in the heart of the forest," they could not have escaped the fire's ravenous fury, a "spectacle truly appalling."[62]

Sparks showered down upon them like snowflakes; the wind "rose to a hurricane"; a "tempest of burning billows" surrounded them. "I thought our time had come," Susanna despaired. Perhaps she thought her husband would return to find his wife, children, and house reduced to ash. Then a "terrific crash of thunder burst over our heads," and the long-delayed rains came in a torrent, "like the breaking of a waterspout." Providence doused them with the only storm of any consequence that summer. The flames sank. But for "a long time" afterward, the great burn, Susanna wailed, "haunted me in my dreams," as she imagined herself and her children fleeing from the flames, their clothes catching fire just as safety was within sight.[63]

Yet her trial by fire had not ended. The fires of winter could match those of summer. In the winter of 1837, the thermometer plunged to -30° Fahrenheit ("and it would have been much colder if the thermometer had been longer," as one wit put it), the Moodies had but green wood to burn, and they "complained bitterly" about the chill. A new servant girl, young, hired the day before, never having seen a Franklin stove, determined to help by gathering up cedar chips from the yard and stuffing them into the appliance. The stove soon turned red, a "suffocating smell of burning soot" spread, and the stovepipe carried the extreme heat right to the roof. Susanna thrust a wet blanket into the stove and cooled it down, then turned to the roof, covered the day before with a blanket of snow. But too late: "the roof was in flames." The heat of the fire had melted the snow; a spark had settled on the wood shingles. There was no one to help them, with the nearest neighbour a mile and a quarter away.[64]

She sent the servant girl after Dunbar, then turned to rescue what she could – the children first, then bedding and clothing, and whatever else she could salvage. She stuffed the smaller children in drawers from a chest, lined with blankets. By now, "the roof was burning like a brush-heap." Suddenly, once again at the limit of hope, she spied two men running at full speed, Dunbar and her brother-in-law. They quickly raised a ladder, plastered the roof with snow, emptied a barrel of beef brine on the flames, and slowly, improbably, as more hands gathered, quenched a fire that, only minutes previously, had seemed unstoppable. "This fact shows," Susanna affirmed, "how much can be done by persons working in union, without bustle and confusion, or running in each other's way." Modestly, Susanna concluded that "these circumstances appeared far more alarming, as all real danger does, after they were past."[65]

In fact, wildfire had not yet finished with Susanna Moodie. The experience had given her a "shock for which I did not recover for several months, and made me so fearful of fire, that from that hour it haunts me like a nightmare." A subsequent fire, savaging their residence after they had moved to town, defying the efforts of 400 persons and a fire engine, "consumed almost all we were worth in the world." The burning of Canada's new towns, in truth, followed almost as often as the firing of its forests. Thereafter, Susanna could never retire to bed without ensuring that every stove was shut up and every ember covered with ash, while the "sight of a burning edifice" was guaranteed to make her "really ill."[66]

Here were two sides of Canadian fire in the backwoods: the essential flame of hearth and field, the ruinous blaze that could, in minutes, threaten life and wipe out every possession. In the two sisters' accounts, the several themes of careless fire shine through. There is the danger of inexperience, the potentially lethal education of fire in the woods, and the hazards of new settlement. The villains were newcomers, more ignorant than malicious, the scenes of eruption places of fresh slashings or wood-crusted cabins or raw towns erected out of reconstituted forests and prone to burn like their origins. In the two sisters' reactions the two prospects of the colonizing future. Catharine, pragmatic, could lay out the prescriptions for chopping and burning, relish the hard labour of reburning, and savour the (literal) fireworks the occasion displayed; Canada's fires were a means of rendering the country habitable, its burning heaps a kind of landscape hearth. Emigration was an opportunity, the beckoning of a kind of independence, a domestic chore on a grand scale. She delighted in the birds and flowers that abounded in the fields and woods. Susanna, more breathless, given to poetry and novelistic scenes, could only react and, thrice scarred, hold fire as nightmare, an apt symbol of all that was alien and hostile about Canada. For her, emigration had been "a matter of necessity." Appropriately, when the fires threatened, Susanna sought to salvage memories, while Catharine imagined a less arduous future beyond ugly split-rail fences and charred stumps.

Pioneering was a deed not repeated. Once cleared, the woods did not return, apart from a certain amount of bush-fallowing. The logging axe, however, could replay its saga over and over, felling whatever new forest grew on the old. For both, fire followed the axe, but unlike farmers, who piled the debris in order to burn it, loggers feared the fires that might seize their untamped slash, and unlike settlement, where the land burned once, logging fires could reappear with every cutting; and, while soils decreed that only so much of the Canadas could be farmed, nearly all of it, even the formidable Shield, could be logged.

A certain amount of lumbering had accompanied settlement. Instead of burning all their timber, settlers turned the choicest slabs to cabins, barns, and fences, and then to milled lumber, or sold prime timber to jobbers for hard cash. Alternatively, in the agro-forestier system, lumber companies owned farms and hired tenants to work them as well as to log, thus supplying both labour and food. Farming and logging could reconcile their seasons, the one a summer occupation, the other a winter one. The sawmill took its place alongside the gristmill. But wholesale cutting – logging for an export market – gathered momentum only with the preferential opening of the British market in the wake of Napoleonic blockades. Eventually a mercantilist network emerged, a trans-Atlantic traffic in which ships carried immigrants and goods to Canada and returned with timber. It was a new triangular trade, based on "ships, colonies, commerce." Timber supplemented, then replaced, furs as an export staple.[67]

The main centre of operations for the Canadas was the Ottawa Valley, already a corridor for the fur trade. The river system that carried voyageurs soon jostled with timber rafts. Quebec quickly became a major entrepôt for the export trade in square timber. Without railroads, bulk transport required rivers or lakes, which Canada had in abundance, as it did woods. Providentially the timber most in demand, white pine, was precisely the dominant tree of the region. A wave of cutting, a timber frontier similar to but separate from the settlement frontier, spread outward. By 1835, it passed through most of the Ottawa Valley; by 1850, it had reached Lakes Huron and Erie; by 1880, Lake Superior.

The economics of the timber trade was similar to that for fur, and like their peers timber merchants sought stability amid the wild swings of the market. There would be no continent-spanning royal charter, no grant of a Rupert's Land, but there evolved a kind of partial monopoly in the form of leases. The crown retained ownership of the land and sold its timber. The state became, in effect, a rentier. While settlers and loggers often competed for land, a political feud that persisted until the twentieth century, the general population agreed with the arrangement because it meant that tax fell on remote timber, not on persons. The state's operating revenues came from its silent rents, not from more overt levies of the sort that inflamed citizens. Thus evolved the famous corporatist character of the Canadian timber industry. The state guaranteed access to timber (and, where possible, to markets), while industry guaranteed a hefty return of revenue in the form of rents. As with the fur trade, a small number of firms, though not an outright monopoly, tended to dominate.[68]

Over the coming decades, the market boomed and busted. A depression in Britain caused a crash in Canada. The end of imperial preferences in 1841, culminating in the free-trade philosophy of 1846, which finally dissolved the Corn Laws and Navigation Acts, destroyed a principal advantage of Canadian timber, and Baltic timber reclaimed the British market. Instead, Canada turned to free trade with the United States, climaxing in the Reciprocity Treaty of 1854. Its huge reserves of forest and its proximity to an insatiable American demand caused new booms, to be followed by further busts with the panics of 1837 and 1857. Stability required access not only to markets but also to supplies in the form of cheaper, longer-term leases, which could serve as collateral to raise additional capital.

The system evolved piecemeal. Not until 1824 did the crown assert its ownership of timber. Outright land purchase had, in truth, little appeal to the lumber merchants since, on the Shield, they could extract nothing further from the land by selling it to settlers; no one could farm it; there was no additional revenue possible, only the costs of nominal ownership and taxation. The two Canadas thus both appointed surveyors general of woods and forests, Lower Canada in 1826, Upper Canada a year later. The resulting rules proved unworkable. The basics of a usable licensing system appeared with regulations in 1832, along with a commission of inquiry. The Canadas were joined following the Union Act of 1840, but a mechanism to manage timber did not congeal until the Crown Timber Act of 1849. This survived the remainder of the century, and after Confederation it became the exemplar for other provinces.[69]

Stability also required some protection against threats to that supply caused by fire, for nature's economy had its cycles, as vacillating as those of the commodity market. When threats were few and untapped timber berths vast, industry could shrug off the occasional burn, as a farmer might an accidental fire in the fallow. But as the land crowded with settlers, as profit margins shrank, and as cycles of drought and depression overlapped, wildfires compromised timber stocks, a matter as vital to the state as to its corporate clients. Such fires heightened, in particular, the competition between those who wanted to buy the land and farm it and those who wanted only to lease and log it. Mixed, they made a metastable compound, not only as a matter of principle and legal title but also because settler fires could not be contained within fee-simple slashings and could broadcast like a rebellion. An era of great fires commenced in 1833 and 1851, when conflagrations boiled over the Ottawa Valley, becoming both more numerous and more ferocious. The more cutting, the more fires.[70]

Wildfires thus joined other threats to the security of tenure. Already the argument thrived that a tree uncut was a tree wasted, that it would simply burn and be worthless to merchants and governments. Better to harvest than to leave to the untaxed flames; better still to quicken the tempo of harvesting to stay ahead of the fires that swarmed like mosquitoes. "The ravenous sawmills in this pine wilderness are not unlike the huge dragons that used in popular legend to lay waste the country," W.H. Withrow explained, "and like dragons, they die when their prey, the lordly pines, are all devoured." Like dragons, too, they belched fire and cried out for some champion to fight them. Lumbermen became advocates of government protection for forests – protection against squatters, against trespassers, against the vicissitudes of forest destruction, against fire. Forest conservation required that settlers be prohibited, that wasteful logging end, that land regenerate, and that fires be prevented. But controlling people was politically tricky, and regulating settlement was ideologically risky. Instead, attention focused on what became the one common point of agreement: conservation, however construed, demanded fire protection.[71]

Naturally such tasks, it was argued, were the duty of government. Loggers had not the power to regulate settlement or control wildfire. If the united provinces wanted the economic profits of lumbering, they had to shoulder its perils as well. There were strong economic reasons for doing so. By 1867, the timber trade was the Canadas' largest source of revenue, and it involved, "in one way or another," half the adult male population. In 1892, E.H. Bronson, logger and a member of Parliament, succinctly summarized the reason behind the evolution of lease auctions: "WE WANTED THE MONEY."[72]

Over the next century, these forces continued to play out. The clearings got bigger, the slashings got vaster, the hastily erected wooden towns got more shambolic, the fires grew more violent. The multitude of littered flames was astounding, needing only the right collusion of weather and woods to burst across the landscape.

"It is remarkable," observed George Head in 1829, "considering every Indian and traveller usually lights his fire against the trunk of some prostrate tree, and leaves it burning, that conflagration should not be more general and frequent." After all, the Canadas were a whole country of travellers, rapidly filling with immigrants, flush with repeated internal migrations, and plunging, axe in hand, into the bush. Even nominally settled areas thus experienced seasonal fires with little more concern than they did the falling of autumn's leaves. "As it is, however," Head continued, "few summers pass away without instances of such accidental combustion (one, indeed of late years, most serious and fatal in its consequences,) when volumes of smoke, proceeding from a spot distant and unknown, envelope in thick fog the inhabitants of the settled parts of the country, who pursue their daily avocations without enquiring from whence the winds have wafted the gloomy curtain, although the air is obscured and darkened as if by a natural mist." The flames would not quiet until the people did, until the campfire had become a hearth.[73]

Still, not everyone saw those flames as bleeding wounds of nature. Elizabeth Simcoe, wife of Upper Canada's lieutenant governor, John

Graves Simcoe, wrote how she had been "this Evening in a wood lately set on fire, by some unextinguished fires being left by some persons who had encamped there; which in dry weather often communicates to the Trees." She was enchanted. The "pleasure of walking in a burning wood" she found so astonishing that she contemplated having "some woods set on fire for my Evening walks." The smoke screened away mosquitoes; hollow trunks lofted flames and sparks like royal fireworks; small flames and dark woods made a "picturesque appearance a little like Tasso's enchanted wood." In Canada's fired woods, there was beauty as well as beastliness.[74]

Colonizing fires, often lethal, persisted into the 1920s, generally immune to state-sponsored measures for control. (The first conviction of a settler for illegal fire-setting occurred in 1921.) But the fire front slowed, heaps of felled trees shrank into scrubby litter of fallowed fields, the uncut forest became a woodlot for the stove. Upper Canada, in particular, became wheat country, the grain becoming yet another of the country's long succession of export staples. Over and over farmers planted and replanted wheat, and because "land was cheap and abundant," when fields shrivelled with "symptoms of exhaustion," "a new clearing was commenced, and the old pretty much abandoned to nature." Those who rotated crops did so with abundant fallow, in early times perhaps half the fields, around Toronto about a third. The more progressive improvers sought to restore the untilled land through multiple ploughings and harrowings, but at some point they normally had to burn it in an act that recapitulated the original clearings though on a diminutive scale. The fired fallow was not mere symbolism: the ecology of grain, a domesticated grass, often demanded a return of flame. Probably the rough pasture through which swine and cattle were left to forage also burned. The remaining farm woods were saved, as long as possible, for firewood. Dunbar Moodie estimated, for example, that a house with two or three stoves would consume an acre of fuel wood a year. By the 1840s, Upper Canada was burning a million acres a year simply for home use; the free-burning fires of colonization were literally becoming domesticated.[75]

Yet away from the farms, there was plenty of forest. The united provinces fronted a vast backcountry. After Confederation and the purchase of Rupert's Land, and its parsing among the provinces, the hinterlands of the now-fissioned Canadas swelled even more. Their backcountries, especially northwest Ontario, became internal colonies to the provinces. They held wood, water, and minerals in abundance; the trick was to extract them with the motive power of wind, water, and muscle, and this proved impossible away from the major streams. The exploitation of the deep bush needed steam to move wood to market. The Shield, in particular, would not yield to the plough, although it could fall before the axe, and labourers freed from seasonal bondage to the farm could provide those needed hands.

The emerging towns, too, had their fire regimes. Largely wood, they were in effect reconstituted forests, and they burned accordingly. Most settler towns could expect to incinerate at least once and did. From fire's perspective, they were little different from log pilings, and suburbs often resembled better organized slashings. The outlying communities of even large cities were de facto frontier villages, bloated with wood houses, barns, shanties, and fences, dappled with garden plots, saturated with open flames from hearths and candles. Montreal's Saint-Laurent and Sainte-Marie suburbs burned savagely in 1852. Quebec's Saint-Roche suburb incinerated in 1845, wiping out 1,630 homes and 3,000 workshops – and then reburned in 1866.[76]

The scene was not unique to Canada or solely to North America. What ended the sorry spectacle were municipal requirements (and insurance stipulations) that changed the composition and design of cities. Stone buildings replaced wood ones, streets were widened, fire-protection measures from water mains to fire companies appeared. By the end of the century, a "fire gap" became apparent, and fires no longer swept cities proportionally to a city's size. Cities grew, while their burning shrank. Such reforms were ultimately an aftermath of industrialization. They were also, as with the quelling of settlement fires, an outcome of a maturing social order.[77]

The future of Canadian fire belonged with the evolution of that order or its disorder. On 25 April 1849, a blaze, set at the hands of a Tory mob, broke out in the Canadas' Parliament building at Montreal. By morning, the building lay in ruins and the pretence of a unified Canada along with it. Politics had its pioneering phase, no less than agriculture, and in a new country restlessness in either yielded fire. The mixture of French and British institutions (and peoples) proved as volatile as the mix of bush and field. They were together yet apart. Previously, imperial contests had dictated, and somewhat resolved, those internal rivalries; increasingly the United States applied those stresses, less through threats of outright annexation than through commerce, and left it to British North America how to cope. The Canadas experienced a succession of wars, rebellions, riots, and reunifications, all typically ending with the firepower of guns and torches.

Economic and political pressures pointed toward a confederation, separating the two Canadas into distinct provinces and then combining them within a grander alliance. Two fires illuminated that creaky if necessary drive for unification. One was the haunting spectre of the Canadas' burning Parliament building, the threat of political arson, the incineration of civil society. The other was the black smoke belching out of locomotives and steamboats, the appeal of coal as a motive power for a continent-spanning Canada, a proposition that British North America might sublimate its political fires through internal combustion. The future argued for a confederation of combustion – the slash fires of industry and settlement to claim the land, the fossil fuels powering steam and industrial capitalism to link them together.

Far Countries

There was yet more to British North America. Especially there was Rupert's Land, the somewhat vague catchment to which the Hudson's Bay Company charter of 1670 gave that company of adventurers proprietary rights. There was the North-West, stretching from Selkirk's hardscrabble settlement on the Red River to the Rockies and perhaps along the Mackenzie River to the Arctic itself. There were trading posts dotting the Columbia River, Vancouver Island, Queen Charlotte Island, and across the Rockies. There was, in brief, a vast subcontinent north and west of Lake Superior over which the United States and Britain and, with lesser urgency, Russia squabbled.

To the extent that this archipelago of presences had coherence, it resided with the fur trade. The Hudson's Bay Company, asleep, as James Robson, one of its factors put it, "by the edge of a frozen sea," nonetheless claimed the watery hub of Canadian watercourses, while a series of Montreal-based competitors, notably the consolidated North West Company, ranged far around the southern rim of lakes and rivers. The rivalry sparked an outburst of exploration in the North-West, but it also threatened both companies with ruin. In 1821, they merged into a consolidated Hudson's Bay Company. As the only British institution west of the Canadas, which still clung along the St. Lawrence corridor, the company functioned in western North America much like the British East India Company in India. At its height, the company oversaw roughly a fourth of the continent, more than three million square miles. A chartered monopoly, with almost no contenders for its hegemony, and with Rupert's Land as its own, the company became a de facto political institution and, more, an "imperial factor" in negotiations with the Americans and Russians.[78]

Environmental diplomacy was less easily negotiated. The consequences for fire, in particular, were both local and diffuse. There were impacts directly around posts and settlements, and for gold-rush camps like those along the Fraser the upheaval could be dramatic. But until steam transport arrived in the guise of boats and railways, agricultural settlement would be slight. Prospectors were notorious for burning, but they would pass through a countryside like pine beetles. They came, they wrecked, they left. The enduring impacts had to wait for the axe and the axe, for steam.

Until then, major changes rippled through northwestern North America indirectly through the medium of demographic eruptions and crashes. First Nations, beaver, bison – all collapsed, at least locally. Wars of trade shattered tribes and sent their fragments westward, which sparked new explosions. But vacuums created by such losses were filled by others; horses, in particular, burst into the northern plains around 1700 and began restructuring the pattern of traditional burning. All these population swings affected fire regimes, although the details are unclear and perhaps unknowable. A shrinking company of indigenes meant fewer torches and perhaps less control of those that remained. The diminished beaver left a landscape with fewer ponds and meadows, a countryside, that is, less broken with watery firebreaks. The near-extinguished bison freed more grasses for burning, deferring to a competition of horses and flames. And so it went: each push encouraged a reactive shove, a plexus of unanticipated and largely unwitnessed changes.

Explorers ranged from Hudson Bay to the limits of North America. Some moved northward, tracking the great-laked rim of the Shield, to the Arctic Ocean. Others paddled up the majestic rivers that drained the Rockies, then plunged over the mountains and probed for routes to the Pacific. Their journals provide transects of regional fire regimes, a sampler of practices.

Samuel Hearne's improbable quest in 1771-72 sent him to search for a northern Quivira, a rumoured land of copper mines and furs. His trek ranged from Prince of Wales' Fort Churchill to the Great Slave Lake and then along a chain of lakes and streams that ended with a descent down the Coppermine River to its Arctic delta. The first part of the journey sent him and his Chippewyan guides through the Shield, the latter part through the Barrens. These were formidable lands, the river unnavigable, the glittering copper mines a handful of lumps, much of the landscape a starving tundra. Worse, Hearne mislocated the mouth of the Coppermine by four degrees latitude.

What Hearne reported of fires was common enough. He described the methods that various tribes had to make it; he noted its absolute necessity.

Even hunters running down a moose would take with them, along with a "knife or bayonet," a "little bag containing a set of fire-tackle." He describes the care with which a party travelling through their own lands might make camp, even amid snow. "When a convenient spot is found, the snow is then cleared away in a circular form to the very moss; and when it is proposed to remain more than a night or two in one place, the moss is also cut up and removed, as it is very liable when dry to take fire, and occasion much harm to the inhabitants." And so it did. In July 1771, with his band of men trying to catch up with their wives, they sighted "a large smoke to the Southward." They crossed the river and found the abandoned camp of their women, who "at their departure had set the moss on fire, which was then burning, and occasioned the smoke we had seen." They continued, "saw another smoke at a great distance," and again came to the next camp, where again, upon leaving, they had "set fire to the moss which was then burning." Unsurprisingly, they passed through plenty of burned forests. Upon reaching the Coppermine River, Hearne observed that "some wood" grew near the water's edge, but there was nothing "on or near the top of the hills between which the river runs." Formerly there was a forest; now, after a "fire some years ago," ten burned "sticks" lay on the ground for every green one still standing.[79]

Yet the upshot could be beneficent. In sketching the biotic wealth of Rupert's Land, Hearne waxed long on the strawberry. It was "most remarkable," he pondered, how "they are frequently known to be more plentiful in such places as have formerly been set on fire." Other products of nature also wanted "some assistance," he concluded. "It is well known that in the interior parts of the country, as well as at Albany and Moose Forts, that after the ground, or more properly the underwood and moss, have been set on fire, that Raspberry bushes and Hips have shot up in great numbers on spots where nothing of the kind had been seen before." The older residents had understood this for centuries, and it takes a considerable leap of faith to believe that they would not have kindled some helpful fires to encourage such a rich food source.[80]

Alexander Mackenzie added little but detail to this fire reconnaissance. On his trek to the Arctic, he noted that the indigenes "universally" carried a bag with pyrites, flint, a "piece of touchwood," so that "they are in a continual state of preparation to produce fire." Like so many others, he identified smoke with the presence of Natives – less a misreading of the Canadian fire scene than a recognition that, along routes of travel, most fires would in truth signify camps. "We saw many places where fires had been lately made along the beach," he observed, "as well as fire running in the woods," one of which "had spread all over the country." He noted typical examples of spreading fire, often contrasting the appearance of burned and green woods and marvelling – because "it is not easy to be reconciled" – that "any thing should grow where there is so little appearance of soil." Yet berries flourished, and they drew bears, as they did people. Along the Fraser River, worried over sparse provisions, he cached ninety pounds of pemmican by burying it "in an hole, sufficiently deep to admit of a fire over it." The Canadian fire scene, it seemed, was one of both accident and necessity.[81]

Revealingly the burns best recorded are those that greeted the major portals of the great journeys. As they plunged through the mouth of the Mackenzie River, debouching out of Great Slave Lake, Mackenzie noted that the land was "covered with large quantities of burned wood, lying on the ground, and young poplar [aspen] trees, that have sprung up since the fire that destroyed the larger wood." He thought it curious that the old woods, when "laid waste by fire," should subsequently produce "nothing but poplars, where none of that species of tree were previously to be found." So, too, when he departed from his winter camp in May 1793 to cross the Rockies along the Peace River, his party struggled through "country ... entirely overrun by fire." Trekking across the land was "toilsome," for while parts were forested with large trees and little underwood, they struck an old burn, a tangle of fallen trunks, and dense copses of "close growth" and "briars." On 11 July, as they breached the Coast Mountains on their way to the Pacific, they struggled through country "laid waste by fire, and the fallen trees added to the pain and perplexity of our way." Yet fire was their heartiest voyageur, their most indispensable tool, without which they would both freeze and starve. In May 1793, paddling the Peace River, they found themselves so cold that they had to land in mid-morning "in order to kindle a fire." This was "a very uncommon circumstance at this season," however, and the party was able to tap, as "an adequate substitute," an ample quantity of rum.[82]

There was no ready surrogate on the plains. The fires were everywhere; they were integral to the lives of the bison and their hunters and thus to those who sought to trade with them. The greatest of the era's explorers, David Thompson, filled his journals, year after year, from Pembina on the prairies along the Red River to Kootenay House in the grassy valleys of the Rocky Mountains with a chronicle of prairie fires. "The plains on fire in every direction," he wrote from the Pembina River, "and smoke darkens the air." In April 1801, he reported smoke on all horizons – "this is caused by the Indians returning from their beaver hunts." But fires were as likely in the fall as well. "The plains are burned almost everywhere; only a few small spots have escaped the fury of the flames." Thompson noted those attached to people: hunters, travellers, warriors, the careless, the malicious. In 1805, he attributed the fires to a "war party." At Fort Vermilion, he elaborated on a buffalo hunt in which the herd would be driven to a "pound." It was a "tedious task which requires great patience, for the herd must be started by slow degrees. This is done by setting fire to dung or grass." But wherever one turned, at almost any time of year, the fires appeared, as threat, spectacle, and ecological force, as routine as autumn frost or spring blossoms, as thick as grasshoppers. "Fire is raging at every point of the compass; thick clouds of smoke nearly deprive us of the sight of the sun, and at night the view from the top of my house is awful indeed."[83]

Because of the burning, the grasslands were "constantly increasing in length and breadth, and the deer give place to the Bison." Such fires affected the "whole of the great Plains." Thompson pondered their meaning amid a "Providence" that had granted the grasses a "productive power" allowing them, unlike the trees, to shrug off the endless fires such that green land became black, the rains fell, and the land shone with a yet brighter green. Without such capacity, "these Great Plains would, many centuries ago, have been without Man, Bird, or Beast." Assisted by fire, the grasslands even twisted into the mountains along the primary corridors of travel. Constructing Kootenay House on the upper Columbia, Thompson recorded that "the Ground was set on fire by the Kootanaes 8 days ago below, and the Fire now fast approaches us."[84]

The indigenes had adapted to the flaming prairies by moving with the seasons. But the fur trade demanded a permanent presence, which meant fixed posts, typically with garden farms, which meant that forts and flames would collide. That frontier met most often along the North Saskatchewan River, where a string of posts resided in the awkward fringe between the prairies and the woodlands. To the north lay pelts, to the south pemmican; the Hudson's Bay Company trafficked in both. It soon found itself an imperial factor in the political economy of fire.

One problem was simply the physical threat of free-burning fire. The forts were wooden and thus susceptible to flames that might rush out of a near-annual "ocean of flames." Paul Kane observed one such storm surge that swept nearly to Edmonton House in 1846. When the fire appeared ready to cross the river, he knew it would threaten the fort, which "must in that case" succumb. "The scene was terrific in the extreme," he wrote in awe and then recorded it in watercolour and oil. The fiery ordeal began early and continued until bison, Indians, and their fires were gone, which meant as well the senescence of the fur trade. The company issued no universal directives but left a solution to its posts' chief factors. A suite of informal fire prevention measures evolved. Residents cleared debris from around the palisades and houses, kept water on hand, and conducted some prophylactic burning, particularly around fields and haystacks. If a fire did appear, they fought it. Against a blaze surrounding Carlton House, J.P. Pruden directed all hands to the Saskatchewan River, where they beat down flames with "bunches of old leather fixed on poles of about six feet long."[85]

More devastating were fires that sapped the posts' economic foundations. The rhythm of fires helped to set the rhythm of buffalo. Tribes reasoned that by controlling pemmican they could control the overall trade and that they could manipulate the herds by burning. As early as 1779, while William Tomison and Robert Longmoor erected Hudson House, they wrote that the local tribes of Cree and Assiniboine were firing the prairies in order to push the bison elsewhere, believing that the company would then have to trade goods for food, as starvation gnawed at them. Unfortunately by 1781 the strategy had propelled the bison so far that the local tribes themselves could no longer hunt them, and they, not the company, faced famine and had to beg for aid. Longmoor wrote that "the Ground is all burnt, and no buffallo, the Natives burnt it as they were nigh hand in the fall and far from the Beaver Country, in purpose that they might get a great price for provisions, but great part of them has payed for it since, by Hunger and oblidged to go far off."[86]

A new logic of economics smashed against an older logic of ecology. The problems were complicated during drought years, which sparked massive burns, such as those in 1812, 1828, and 1836, and by the fact that the indigenes themselves were, by their desire for trade goods, being drawn into a new geography of settlement, and by unsettling combinations of trade wars and extensive burnings pushed into new territory. As one factor noted in 1814, "the Plains for sixty miles round this place were entirely ravaged by fires last fall and the consequence has been that we have neither seen an Indian from that quarter nor heard of a buffalo since that time." And when indirect fire measures failed, the disgruntled were not above direct action, like those of the Stoneys, who responded to a reprimand by firing the plains around Edmonton, or the Assiniboines, disgraced for stealing, who departed behind a screen of flames. Before the two companies merged, factors from one even charged counterparts at rival posts with arson.[87]

Paradoxically, the real threat to the fur trade was less the ravenous flames than the becalmed ones. The real disturbance in the force lay with Selkirk's 1811 agricultural colony at Red River, which not only interrupted the seasonal flow of hunting and commerce, and eventually its political justification, but also undermined its ecological existence. A land that grew crops was not a land that would accept the seasonal fire flooding that, like the Nile's annual inundation, renewed the biota. Settled farming distrusted free-burning fire, and with reason, for wildfires could consume wheat before harvest, destroy the winter range of livestock, and burn down barns and houses. So, while fire had its place, it was in the hearth or fallow, not in the countryside. Slowly but inexorably the spread of agriculture and fee-simple land ownership dampened the ancient flames, draining the prairies of fire as their British ancestors had drained the fens of water.

That was what was needed, or so enthusiasts of settlement argued, and that is what happened. The Red River region had, prior to the Little Ice Age, grown maize. At the height of the medieval warming, the corn belt had swelled northward; then it had collapsed, sagging southward, as the cold shortened the growing season. So, too, the new settlers had struggled when they had to match their grains against the cadences of a hostile climate. But as the century aged, they acquired a new combustion source, a power sufficient to challenge even that climate, a fuel not dependent on the biomass that could be grown annually under the unsteady sun. Steam made settlement possible.[88]

Writing in 1882, after the railway promised to boost prairie farming, John Macoun observed that "prairie fires are dangerous both to settlers and travellers, but especially to the former." Fires were easily started and were known "to run over 100 miles without stopping." One such conflagration threatened Macoun's party, then raced northeast to burn the hay harvested by Red Pheasant's band 130 miles away before continuing "between the two Saskatchewans" and burning up the tent of sleeping mounted policemen. But agricultural colonization could no longer tolerate such events. Macoun concluded simply that "settlement will cause the fires to cease, and the groves of young wood scattered everywhere over the country will soon become of great value for fuel and fencing." In this view, he echoed John Palliser and virtually every other naturalist who travelled through the region. And exactly as they predicted, the general suppression of fire allowed the boreal forest and its woodland fringe to creep steadily southward, advancing roughly a kilometre a year over the course of the twentieth century.[89]

Across the mountains, a pattern of contact emerged along Pacific Canada that mirrored the earlier evolution of Atlantic Canada. Traffic in fish, furs, and later timber led to a strategic sprinkling of outposts along the coast. In the summer of 1793, overland and maritime explorers narrowly missed each other at Echo Harbor – Vancouver departing by ship on 5 June and Mackenzie struggling to a tidal river on 21 July. That failed linkage suggests the difficulties of connecting the scattered patches of British North America, a task that would ultimately demand a railway.

After 1821, the Hudson's Bay Company sought a proper monopoly in the far west. Its imagined centre was Fort Vancouver, sited where the Willamette joined the Columbia, a place with which to tap the whole of the region, and a challenge to both Russians and Americans. But James Douglas spoke for all the factors when he observed that agricultural settlement and fur trading would "never harmonize." The American overlanders to Oregon proved his point, formalized in the Oregon Treaty (1846) that drew the international border along the forty-ninth parallel and forced the company to relocate to Fort Victoria in Puget Sound, with outliers at Fort Langley, Fort McLoughlin, and Fort Simpson.[90]

In 1849, imperial competitions in the region elevated Fort Victoria into the status of a formal colony, Vancouver Island. To ensure economy, Britain chartered the company as the fledgling colony's "true and absolute lords and proprietors." Its charter required the company to establish "a settlement or settlements of resident colonists," the kind of occupation expected under international law to enforce a claim but also one the company required to feed a permanent post with more than seasonal fish. But the soil was poor, enticements weak, and immigration feeble. Still, the colonial reach expanded to the Queen Charlotte Islands in 1852. What finally pitchforked people into the region was a gold rush to the Fraser River in 1858, which then cascaded throughout the Rockies. With the mainland, overseen by Fort Langley, portending another California, the authorities quickly proclaimed it as the colony of British Columbia. Apart from a handful of treaties on Vancouver Island, local officials ignored making treaties with the indigenes. The two colonies fused in 1866; their collective boundaries soon swelled northward and eastward. Five years later, with a promised link by rail, British Columbia agreed to join Confederation.[91]

What these developments meant for fire was mixed. Native populations crashed and somewhat rebuilt, but the coastal regime argued for either massive fires on a cycle of centuries or none at all. Most scenes of regular indigenous burning, like the Garry oak savannahs of Victoria, were rapidly absorbed into the outposts of European settlement, and there was little agricultural colonization of the sort typical in the old Canadas, for farming and herding had little promise, and even the markets created by gold rushes passed as rapidly as they had come. Legislation, moreover, left almost all the landed estate with the crown. The economy was based on export staples, notably furs, gold, some fish, some coal, and slowly, although eventually, in huge gulps, timber. The colony resembled a Pacific Maritimes. Until the market boomed for its green gold, its coastal woods, penetration by the axe was partial and slash-stoked conflagrations few. Industrial-strength forestry had to wait for steam, at which point British North America on the Pacific acquired industrial-strength fires.

With Fire in Their Eyes:
Gabriel Sagard and Henry Hind

xplorers saw what they had eyes to see. The early journals document fire spottily, not because it wasn't there but because it mattered little. Samuel de Champlain's *Voyages* mentions fire often, though it is the fire of camp and of battle or of tortured prisoners. He refers in passing to the field firing of the Huron but elaborates on attempts to burn down the palisades of the Onondaga. What mattered was survival. By the time John Palliser conducted a well-outfitted survey of the western plains (1857-60), fire could be seen as an interesting natural phenomenon, even a spectacle worth recording at length, like "the magnificent fire" they had contemplated on 5 October 1857. Palliser documented the burning prairie from Manitoba to the Rockies, speculated about the influence of the "frequent fires" on the geography of the northern forests, lamented that he had "never, in all my experience of life in the prairies, witnessed the awful wonders of a prairie on fire" up close and personal, was content to quote windy passages from a "brother-sportsman" who found himself in the middle of the conflagrating grasses, and finally, near Pigeon Lake, Alberta, "set fire to the grass, just to say we had done so." The change is not merely one of geography, from the fire-mixed Great Lakes forest to the routinely burning prairies. That change represents a new syndrome of thought, a tectonic shift from the world of the Counter-Reformation to that of the Enlightenment, from soldier and missionary to natural historian.[1]

Consider two examples, both representative of their times: one, Brother Gabriel Sagard Théodat, a lay missionary to the Hurons in 1623-24; the other, Professor Henry Hind, a natural historian who toured the plains from 1856 to 1858 and then the interior of Labrador in 1861. Between them, they traverse the geographical extremes of Canadian fire and, equally, two and a half centuries of how Canadians saw those landscapes. In simple terms, Sagard, motivated by religious enthusiasm, placed fire within a moral geography, while Hind, a secular scientist, fixed it within a physical one. Each ignored much of what the other had brooded and exulted over.

Sagard was a member of the Recollets, a branch of reformist Franciscans, and a devout disciple, even adopting as a surname "Théodat" (God-given). Of his early life, little is known. He was French, he knew the classics as well as Scripture, he had a passion for an apostolic ministry in Canada. At last that request, long withheld, was granted, though his tour in New France lasted only from June 1623 to the autumn of 1624. In that time, he journeyed to Huronia. The record of his experience, *The Long Journey to the Country of the Hurons,* published in 1632, claimed to "fully" treat "everything relating to the country," its peoples, their social order, their beliefs, the natural history of the country, even a "dictionary of the Huron tongue" to instruct those who might follow. The *Long Journey* was a guidebook for future missionaries.[2]

Ultimately, it is a book about character: it is about how a people live (and one might add, a missionary). Their fire practices matter as a means toward that description. Thus, Brother Sagard explains how they kindle fire by rubbing sticks, how they pick campsites with an eye toward firewood, how they cook their maize-broth (*sagamité*), how they bake earthenware pots, how they heat their longhouses, how they dry meat and fish over smoke, how they prepare sweat baths with red-hot stones, how they purge furs of lice and fleas over a fire. He describes how their "councils" sit around a "great fire." He elaborates how, in preparing for war, they clean around the fortification and lodges, even as to "soot and spiders," for "fear of fire" that their enemies might launch against them with various incendiaries. He recites the wretched ways they torture by fire, "so cruel that nothing could well be more inhuman" – and the surprising means by which prisoners occasionally escape, by kicking about the lodge the coals they are sometimes made to walk through, causing both darkness and smoke, and fleeing in the ensuing panic. He recounts their fire superstitions; that, for example, "if any of the fat [from game] drops into the fire, or any bones are thrown into it, they will be unable to get any more"; how, in response to disease or injury, a "medicine-man" handles heated stones, even chewing them, before rubbing his scorched hands on the afflicted part; how, during their "feast of souls," the celebrants cast offerings to the flames; why they fear burned bones, and, "if fire should break out in their village and in their cemetery, they would first run to extinguish the fire in the cemetery and then the fire in the village."[3]

His most justly famous fire references are those that pertain to the Hurons' swidden agriculture. Sagard amplifies far more than others do, particularly the clipped, telegraphic references of Champlain. Agriculture mattered: it fed the Hurons, it shaped the geography of villages, it sustained their trade and relations with neighbouring tribes, and it was, for a Frenchman, a practice to which he could relate better than the raw travails of the hunt and the trading voyage. Because they farmed, the Huron lived in semi-stable communities, precisely what proclaimers of the gospel needed or its missionaries would become little better than coureurs de bois who carried Bibles instead of pelts.

Each family had what land it needed. The uncleared woods were common property, but once brought into cultivation a patch remained the possession of the cultivator until abandoned. Clearing was "very troublesome" because the Huron lacked metal tools. Instead, they cut trees high, stripped bark and branches and burned them, the fires intended to kill the trees to their roots. The women cleaned the ground and sowed the maize. They returned "every year" to the same spots and replanted them. The remainder of the land was "only cleansed of noxious weeds," so that it seemed "as if it were all paths," and the openness caused Sagard, when he travelled between villages, to lose his way, "usually in these corn-fields more than in the meadows and forests." At virtually every stage, fire entered into the cycle of agriculture, from readying the field to cleaning it after harvest to boiling, baking, drying, or otherwise preparing the meal.[4]

All in all, an odd survey of fire practices. But as Brother Sagard-Théodat's purpose was to preach, so his book's purpose was to instruct those who might follow his footsteps. As the Hurons' diverse fires made their life possible, so Sagard's register of their uses illustrated the kind of folk they were. Those recorded flames illuminated an inner life, as their hearth fires did lodges. The reported fires are those that shape a terrain of manners and mores. They inhabited a moral ecology, a web ultimately spun by God, "praiseworthy in all things, without whose permission not a single leaf falls from a tree."[5]

Two hundred and twenty-five years later, Henry Youle Hind journeyed from England, by way of Toronto, to the Great Plains. He was a man of his time, as Sagard had been of his. An emissary from a century still rent by religion and war, Sagard had travelled as a missionary, but Hind's was a century dazzled by steam and science, and Hind ventured as an explorer of natural history and technological improvement. He stands

Henry Hind, an aspiring explorer-naturalist and perhaps the first Canadian to sense the full geography and significance of Canada's fires.

as a curious latter-day version of Sagard: a lay professor and scientist, a traveller to the Canadian west, a promoter of the faith, which by the mid-nineteenth century meant the gospel of commerce and progress. Like other seventeenth-century emissaries to New France, Sagard returned to Europe. True to the immigration that spilled into Canada in the nineteenth century, Hind stayed. Like the observant Recollet, Professor

Hind recorded fire, but they were fires that informed nature and those that might restructure a new society busily extracting nature's wealth.

The contours of Henry Hind's education are these: grammar school in the classics, commercial and technical training at the Handelschochschule in Leipzig, followed by private tutoring and a year at Cambridge, without a formal degree. In 1846, Hind sailed to North America, wandering through the prairies of Louisiana and Texas before settling in Toronto. There he began a career as a professor of natural science at the Normal School and later at University of Trinity College. Gradually he slid into tracks that would lead him into a career as a geographical explorer through self-training in geology and chemistry, an interest in climate, railways, and the economic development of the western lands by means of mining and agriculture. He joined the Royal Canadian Institute, where he rubbed shoulders with William Logan and Sandford Fleming, the one encouraging him in geology, the other inviting him on a summer of western surveying for a railway line along the Saugeen River. The summer was a slow epiphany. Hind determined that his future lay in the geographical reconnaissance of new lands.[6]

Throughout the 1850s, Americans had fielded expeditions to survey possible routes for a trans-continental railway. In 1857, British North America sponsored two of their own. The British government dispatched an elaborate party under Captain John Palliser, intending to span from Lake Superior to the Pacific. The Canadian government sent a leaner expedition with a narrower purpose, to survey the valleys of the Red and Saskatchewan Rivers; this tour was repeated in 1858. Hind joined both as "Geologist and Naturalist to the party." His published account, *Narrative of the Canadian Red River Exploring Expedition of 1857 and of the Assiniboine and Saskatchewan Exploring Expedition of 1858,* was typical of the genre: a revised journal of an era that specialized in geographical reconnaissances, dense with names, places, observations of flora and fauna, and particularly information pertinent to settlement, sources of fuel, patterns of frost and soil fertility, the abundance of game and mineral deposits.

But Hind was particularly sensitive to fire. He recorded it everywhere. In October 1857, he described how, at night, "the sky in the northwest began to assume a ruddy tinge, and finally a lurid red, produced by the fires in the rich prairies beyond the Assiniboine," which lay over ninety air miles distant. The next year he witnessed "the whole country of the Saskatchewan ... in flames." His party traced that particular blaze "from the 49th parallel to the 53rd, and from the 98th to the 108th degree of longitude. It extended, no doubt, to the Rocky Mountains." The "grandeur of the prairie on fire," he exulted, "belongs to itself. It is like a volcano in full activity, you cannot imitate it, because it is impossible to obtain those gigantic elements from which it derives its awful splendour." His fascination went beyond the fact that such fires were vast and impressive and thus amenable to literary flourish. Hind described how and why they were set and how, on scales vast and tiny, they shaped the countryside. Their primary source was the Indian, "putting out fire" under various pretexts. One such purpose was "to turn the buffalo." Another was as "a telegraphic mode of communication," such as those the Cree set "to inform their friends that they had found buffalo." Other fires resulted from simple carelessness, or outright hostility, "so numerous" as to defy calculation. The capacity of people and fire to move expansively meant that the region was regularly aflame.[7]

The consequences Hind saw clearly, for there could be no doubt that the "sterility" of the plains overall was as much an outcome of abundant fire as of scanty rainfall. The destructive fires had "converted into sterile areas an immense tract of country which does not appear necessarily sterile from aridity, or poverty of soil." The evidence was everywhere and "remarkable." The relentless fires cut down woods as ruthlessly as the settler's axe, but instead of growing farms they yielded a vagrant hunt. Where fires stalled, however, saplings strengthened their grip, for example oaks near Crooked Lake, oak and aspen around Riding Mountain, willows at Touchwood Hills. Trees grew on one side of a river but not on the other, the result of different regimens of burning, because the "Indians often travel along the valley on the north of the river, which accounts for the fires being on that side." This "lamentable destruction of forests is a great drawback to the country," Hind insisted, "and a serious obstacle to its future progress." So long as the indigenes ruled, their fires would remain a presence "beyond human power" to contain. Still, he concluded that "reclamation" was possible. Remove the causes of burning and their effects would recede; Indians and buffalo would go, and the forests that had previously flourished would return. This process, he assured his readers, was already happening "with great rapidity."[8]

Such observations were not unique to Hind; Palliser's parallel trek recorded many of the same phenomena. What made Hind unusual was that he turned next to Labrador. The role of explorer, geographer, promoter, and littérateur appealed to him. But while he wished to seek out new lands, he lacked the formal contacts and, as the century moved ahead, the credentials to lead a government-sponsored survey. A year before his *Narrative*, Darwin had published *On the Origin of Species,* and the simple geographical reconnaissance seemed increasingly insufficient, the apparent amateur progressively inadequate. Instead, Hind organized a private foray up the Moisie River during the summer of 1861. It proved a hard slog. The science was less vigorous, and the written account more sensitive to the party's personalities, since the publication of *Explorations in the Interior of the Labrador Peninsula* would have to pay for the expedition.

There is, throughout the *Explorations,* a long roster of fire technologies – the mandatory campfire; matches, flint-and-steel strikers, fire drills; smudge fires; fires to heat gum to repair canoes; firearms; fire "superstitions" of the Montagnais and Nasquapee Indians. Twice fire announced the party's entry into the interior. The first incident occurred while they were portaging. A campfire, "notwithstanding every precaution," escaped into the moss, where it spread "with amazing rapidity." The fire came to a fast boil, and the party, scattered over the portage, barely rescued their canoes – and then themselves – from the conflagration that rose into a pall of smoke and ash and danced through the scene with whirlwinds. The fire then continued unabated for several days; they still saw its smoke "when nearly thirty miles away." Not until the flames slammed into the wet moss surrounding Lake Iash-ner-nus-kow did it quell.[9]

But the gripping texts are those that recount wildfire in the woods and the sense, quite startling, in which conflagrations in boreal Labrador mimicked those in the prairie west. Both shaped their landscapes; both moulded the habitats of their region's principal game, caribou and bison, respectively, and hence the livelihood of the indigenes; both were unmistakable and indelible features, as fundamental as frost and wind. The appearance of fire in two such disparate geographies recommended it as one of the grand motifs of Canadian life.

That insight led Hind to consider the history of such burns and to ponder whether fire worked in the boreal plateau as it had on the Great Plains. Captain George Cartwright had written about large fires in eighteenth-century Labrador. Those had happened early in the season, "when the ground is wet," and skimmed across the surface. Those that came in droughty late summers could burn broadly and deeply. Large fires with some documentary record behind them had apparently roared through Labrador in 1785, 1814, 1840, 1857, and 1859. W.H. Davies had recounted a signal fire his party had kindled on the summit of a hill "to ascertain if any Indians were in the neighbourhood," a practice as common in Labrador as in Manitoba. The fire blew up, with a "noise like thunder," and before it calmed, it had burned for three weeks and "completely destroyed an area covering some hundreds of square miles." Even so, Hind had seen enough fires to remain sceptical. "The extent of fire is generally very much exaggerated in a thickly wooded country," he observed. Most burns, moreover, confine themselves to the "main line of communication," primarily along the region's great rivers. Still, he had witnessed for himself how a spark could explode and a single fire "run for an immense distance, probably for some hundreds of miles." Unlike on the prairies, fires did not have to occur often to sculpt the boreal forest.[10]

These researches inspired Hind to ask if fires had become more frequent. The generally fire-hostile biota and sheer age of many forests suggested that fires happened rarely, if hugely. The reliance of the indigenes on caribou hinted as well that fires could not have a short cadence or there would be few lichens for the herds to feed upon, for which reason "the Indians generally exercise great caution in putting out their fires." Yet the magnitude of the burned woods through which he passed argued for a quickening tempo of fire. "It must have been in recent times," he concluded, "for the charred stumps are standing over immense areas, many thousand square miles being now a burnt country." He thought the introduction of new ignition devices was one reason; left unsaid are wandering Europeans such as himself and the breakdown of Native society under the hammer blows of epidemics, smallpox not least; and, as he and every other traveller to Labrador illustrated, campfires and signal fires escaped. Even a few such errors could yield ecological earthquakes sufficient to topple whole forests. Native traditions were full of accounts of "extensive conflagrations."[11]

As they plunged into the height of land, which lay at the heart of Labrador, they passed through a portal, the aptly named Burnt Portage, for the geographical core of Labrador was indeed a "burnt country." They surveyed the horizons. To the east, they spied a "vast forest" that had evaded the "numerous fires." Elsewhere, they overlooked only "an awful scene of desolation, far surpassing anything we had seen before." The "wild and inhospitable appearance" of the land "dismayed and scared" Hind's voyageurs, whom he sought to hurry along. Trudging through this "black wilderness," the portagers became "nearly as black as the ground they walked on, and looked like a procession of weary chimney-sweeps." The burnt country resembled a "land of the dead; and everything, in fact, is dead." There was scant relief. The heart of Labrador was a charred stump. "What desolation! What dreadful ruin all around! Not ruin from fire only, but ruin exposed by fire."[12]

The two regimes shared only fire's implacable presence. Otherwise, prairie Manitoba and interior Labrador presented inverted images. For the prairies, regular fire was essential to spark fresh grass, while the boreal forest obeyed a far longer rhythm of immolation and regeneration.

Without those renewed grasses, the bison could not have thrived in their unfathomable herds; without some restraint over the burning of their lichen pastures, the caribou would collapse. The indigenes of the prairies scattered fire freely, confident that the land could absorb it like a summer rain. Those of the Labradorean highlands exercised more care. What both frontiers displayed, and what Hind recognized, was that fire belonged with any tally of Canadian natural history, as much as geese, bison, white pine, and sugar maple.

Virtually alone, Hind appreciated that its fires also belonged among Canada's inextinguishable sights. "The grandeur of the prairie on fire belongs to itself," he had rhapsodized in 1857. This, by itself, was not unique: most observers with any literary or aesthetic sensibility had lavished similar praises on the flaming prairie. What Hind did was analyze how it achieved its effects. But his real triumph came in Labrador, where he realized that the western fires were not unique. "A burning forest of spruce and birth is a spectacle of extraordinary sublimity during the night," he marvelled. "It is like a magnificent display of fireworks on a stupendous scale, and far surpasses the conflagrations of the heavier forests in more temperate climates."[13]

Such prosy outbursts are not found in the *Jesuit Relations* or among the sailing instructions in Champlain's *Voyages* or amid either the ledgers or the astronomical recordings of Hudson's Bay Company clerks and surveyors. They are the product of a Romantic sentiment, an age inclined toward operatic landscapes, yet an era informed not less by an exploring natural science, keen to answer Humboldt's exhortation that it capture the sense of a landscape as well as its measurements. A great era of geographical reconnaissance had tabulated Canada's rocks and minerals, fish and furs, timber trees and farmlands, birds and scenic monuments, but it had not, until Hind did so, included in that survey its free-burning fires.

So when Hind came to write a geographical summary of his adopted country, *The Dominion of Canada,* on the occasion of Confederation, fire figured. It did so within the context of national development. Agriculture could not flourish on the plains until it swept fire from the horizon; forestry could not thrive so long as fires consumed "millions of magnificent trees which would now command a fabulous price" and drove loggers farther into more remote wilderness at greater cost in search of poorer-quality timber. "Thousands of square miles of the forest timber have been ruined by this ruthless destroyer," Hind noted. In *Explorations,* he had elaborated on the Dark Days of early Canada, which he attributed to far-ranging conflagrations. Now he included lengthy passages from an eyewitness account of the Miramichi holocaust of 1825. And to complete the ensemble, he tabulated among Canada's mineral resources its wealth of lignite, coal, and oil. Canada's future would depend on its ability to reduce its free-burning flames while enhancing its internal combustion of fossil fuel.[14]

For Henry Hind, however, *Dominion* was a coda to a curious career. His expedition to the Red River and beyond had inflamed his imagination: this was what his training and temperament told him he did best. But he had been unable to obtain real support for his Labrador venture and, when it concluded, could find neither sponsorship for another expedition nor a permanent post as a field scientist. The age of the amateur explorer was fading; the professional scientist, ensconced in a university or a government bureau, would succeed him. To his bewilderment and frustration, Hind failed to make that transition, not in the political arena of post-Confederation institutions, certainly not in its burgeoning scientific organizations. His travels had involved a mix of steamboat and canoe, horse and railway, natural history survey and economic promotion – the expeditions are an apt symbol of the ardent nation-building that swept past him. Yet Hind had almost but not quite made that passage. He became bitter, isolated, crotchety, eccentric, fending off charges of plagiarism, embroiled in pointless disputes with the Fisheries Commission. As W.L. Morton concluded, "the scientist became the polemicist, the promoter the anti-promoter, the publicist the fantasticist." The English emigrant who became a Canadian explorer ended his life in Nova Scotia as an officer of the Edgehill School for Girls.[15]

But before that sad denouement, he had done something no one before him had. He had begun surveying, if patchily but with thematic consistency, the human and natural history of fire in British North America. As a confederated Canada searched for suitable institutions, it had need of advice about what kind of place it was, and especially what kind of remote lands it was eagerly absorbing, and what it might make of such terrains. Henry Hind had told those who would listen. And if in the end the dominion had no professional niche for him to fill, it could not so easily pension off or dismiss as a crank of nature his observations about fire. Instead, those problems proliferated as the axe bit deeper into the Canadian countryside. By the time Hind died in 1908, untrammelled burning commanded national attention, Ontario was on the verge of a decade of hideous and lethal conflagrations, and the dominion was scrambling for scientific advice and an institutional order by which to contain them. Even in a merged political economy of steam and confederation, fire would again find its way.

"Burning Most Furiously"

Captain Thomas James Kindles a Signal Fire

In 1631, Captain Thomas James, forlornly seeking the South Seas, found himself in the frozen south coves of Hudson Bay, locked in ice for the winter. Come the following spring, the *Henrietta Maria* and her crew remained jammed against Charlton Island by the remorseless ice. As June ended, bright with sun, the ice gripped them still. On the 24th, midsummer's day, Captain James celebrated by cutting down a "very high tree," making a cross of it, then fastening a shilling and sixpence of his majesty's coin, along with an inscription of the king's arms and the City of Bristol; then he raised the tree on the summit of a bare hill where they had buried those crewmen who had died during the winter ordeal and took formal "possesion of these Territories, to his Maiesties use." Providentially the wind shifted to the west and blew away enough pack ice that they contemplated a departure.[1]

The next morning, as the boat was being rerigged and reprovisioned from their winter camp on shore, Captain James took a lance and a companion outfitted with a musket and "some fire" and went to the island's "watch-tree," from where he could spy across the scene. His intention was to make a fire "on the eminentest place of the Iland: to see if it would be answered." He had done this on other travels as a means of locating indigenes and did so now to see if any of the "Saluages" might have "some intelligence of some *Christians*, or some Ocean Sea thereabouts." Perhaps they could point him to Tahiti.[2]

They laid down their lance and musket. Captain James proceeded to climb up the tree while instructing his companion "to put fire into some low tree therabouts." He did so "(unadvisedly)" to the windward; the fire kindled the lichens like "hempe," soon blew up, and raced toward the watch-tree. As the flames cascaded up, James frantically hustled down, and before they met he leaped, tumbled down a steep hill, and fled. "The mosse on the ground was as dry as flaxe: and it would runne most strangely, and like a traine along the earth." The musket and lance both burned, but the two men escaped, "leauing the fire increasing, and still burning most furiously. We could see no answer of it."[3]

That night the captain slept little, and the next morning he ordered his crew to move powder and beef quickly to the ship and to ready the sails to be dumped into the bay if need be. Then he climbed the hills to observe the fire, "where I saw how it did still burne most furiously." Leaving an observer, he hurried to the ship to exhort greater haste. About noon, the wind shifted to the north, and "our Sentinell came running haome, bring vs word that the fire did follow him at hard heeles, like a traine of powder." The fire roared down upon them with "a most terrible rattling noyse: bearing a full mile in breadth." The crew fled to their ship; the flames swept over their winter's camp and "burnt it downe to the ground." The winds shifted, and the fire ranged on, "seeking what it might deuoure." All the while, amid "this combustion," the ship's dogs sat down on their tails and howled.[4]

Captain and crew gave thanks for their deliverance. Canada boasted one more incinerated island, and Europe's explorers chronicled one more fiery encounter with a landscape they naively thought too barren and cold to burn. They had much to learn.

Dark Days

"Accounts of extensive conflagrations" were, Henry Hind noted, "traditional among the Indians." They would soon become no less a feature of European settlement lore. But like fires, the legends had a reach beyond the flames themselves; they spread with the winds, blotting the sky with immense palls, black portents far removed from their origins. They gave rise to the fabled Dark Days.[5]

The earliest reports from British North America date to New England. There were dark days, so named, from 1716 onward, in which the sky grew dim, and the omens (to a credulous folk) foreboding, and under extreme cases caused candles to be lit at midday. Occasionally observers reported soot or ash and sometimes even the smell of burning. Clearly these were the fallouts of fires. Some were probably close, those that brought tangible sensations of burning. But the deeper burns were distant, their soot lofted and trapped high in the atmosphere like smoked glass. These were less obviously attributed to the fires that rose up as often as autumn leaves fell; they were the spawn of conflagrations perhaps hundreds of miles away. As the smoke pall thinned, dark days gave way to dry fog, coloured rain, the haze of Indian summer, and copper skies. Given the clockwise circulation of winds around a Hudson Bay High, the source for these New England smoke apocalypses probably resided along the Gulf of St. Lawrence and beyond.[6]

No doubt some of the forcing fires belonged with indigenous Canada, with conflagrations sparked by lightning, escaped campfires, malicious and careless littering. That their chronicle appears with European settlement may simply be an artefact of recording as they moved from legend to literature, but there are good reasons to associate them with wildfires, especially from slashings. One of the most celebrated of New England's dark days – Black Friday, 19 May 1780 – occurred after forest slashings, stalled for several years by revolution, renewed themselves; the relocation of the Loyalists soon coincided with more. One of the most famous, however, pressed down from north of Quebec. The 1785 outburst excited "much apprehension among the ignorant and speculation among the learned." Quebec witnessed obscurity on 9 October, "the heavens" exhibiting "a luminous appearance upon the line of the horizon of a yellow tinge." The spectre was repeated on the 15th. The next day began with fog, which a northeasterly wind blew away, followed by "black clouds" that made reading impossible. There followed a "second period of obscurity," then "a third, and a fourth, and fifth, at intervals: at half-past four it was dark as midnight." The obscurity, Hind concluded, extended from Fredericton, New Brunswick, to Montreal.[7]

The most extensively studied episode occurred in 1814. It inspired four accounts, one from the Bay of Seven Islands above Anticosti, one from a transport ship resting at anchor in the St. Lawrence at Cape Chat, a third from another ship similarly located, and one from Chief Justice Jonathan Sewell at Newfoundland. Together they trace the movement of a vast pall. At the Bay of Seven Islands, the black clouds approached from the north. "About 9 P.M. a sort of dust or ashes commenced falling, and continued during the night; towards the morning the whole atmosphere appeared red and fiery to a wonderful degree, and the moon, then at the full, not visible; the appearance through the cabin windows as crystal lights singular in the extreme, as if surrounded by a mass of fire; the sea sparkling much, and in a manner not usual in these latitudes." With the dawn, the wind died, and ashes covered the sea. The darkness at noon crept eastward.[8]

Chief Justice Sewell pondered the consequences and reasoned about their causes. The third of July was "a most extraordinary day." The morning had brought "dark thick weather, and fog of a deep yellow colour, which increased in density and colour until 4 o'clock P.M., at which hour the cabin was entirely dark, and we dined by candle-light." Riding at anchor, well into the Atlantic, the chief justice from a Britain that considered burning piles of leaves dangerous and an occasional moor burn a catastrophe could scarcely conceive of a cause other than volcanic and concluded that there must reside an Etna or Vesuvius deep in the obscure interior of Labrador. "It seems impossible to suppose," he reasoned, "that the conflagration of a forest could have produced a mass of smoke so dense and so extensive as to overspread … the surface of a territory exceeding certainly 300 miles in length, and probably 200 miles in breadth, and producing at its utmost longitudinal extremity, and at mid-day, the obscurity of the darkest night." Better to consider it a volcano, like those someone on the Grand Tour might witness in Italy.[9]

Such august opinion Hind took seriously. He tabulated lists of earthquakes that might be an index of volcanic eruptions and quoted the ruminations of Captain F.H. Baddely, who in 1828 explored the Saguenay country and wrote that "it is not perhaps generally known that there exists highly respectable evidence of a volcanic eruption" in the region. The captain then quoted the reconstructed journal of an M. Gagnon from St. Paul's Bay, who recorded how, sighting up a valley between two mountains, he "saw a continual eruption, mixed with smoke and flame, which appeared very plain on the horizon." Such outbreaks were followed by shocks, and "a dark and *yellowish* day." As for the eruption itself, a "most beautiful spectacle," the "whole atmosphere was in flames and agitated, one's face suffered from the heat, the weather was very calm, the eruption continued the whole night with flames." Hind even tested the idea that the "fire mountain" of Nasquapees' lore might be, in truth, a volcano.[10]

Yet he decided for fire. There was too little proof of a volcano, and he had seen for himself that one did not need close-packed forests to produce countrywide conflagrations. The ground was thickly lathered with lichens and mosses, and they were disposed to burn more rapidly and with more vigorous outpourings of smoke than mere forests. He had seen such fires with his own eyes – had in fact fled before them. The Labrador interior was a lichen savannah, burning much like the prairies. There was ample country, more than abundant combustibles, and no lack of evidence for past burns on a huge scale. "No valid reason" existed "why a fire should not stretch from Hudson's Bay to the Gulf of St. Lawrence in a few days." Only the profusion of lakes broke up such a prospect, and only shifting winds kept the fires aboiling, or the fractured geography would leave those burns strictly "local" in their effects. Instead, they could swell to elephantine sizes, big enough, he might have told the chief justice, to blacken all of England itself.[11]

Day of Judgment: Miramichi

There are big fires and great fires; benign fires and malignant fires; founding fires, defining fires, memorable fires; fires that announce eras, fires that symbolize eras, fires that end eras. The Miramichi fire of 1825 – the Great Fire of New Brunswick – was all of the above. Canada had long abounded in giant fires, but not until the Miramichi had it spawned a monster, one capable of savaging whole settlements and worthy of written records by eyewitnesses. So, too, Europeans had, from their earliest encounters, experienced threatening fires, most from their own slovenly habits and ignorance, and they had chronicled a long litany of fiery portents, of dark days and the rumble of distant flames. But not until the autumn of 1825 did that seasonal roll call of slash fires and smoke palls suddenly reach a critical mass and explode with almost apocalyptic violence. The Miramichi fires did more than torch wild forests, rude farms, logging camps, and rough-hewn towns: they announced a new regimen of fire in Canada, and they inscribed, literally, a new set-piece of Canadiana. If the clearing fire was the celebratory bonfire of colonization, the conflagration was its evil twin, and the Miramichi fire, like a Dark Annunciation, first showed the face of that horror.[12]

The fire was multiple and, in its origins, pedestrian. Nothing was more common than flames feasting on the scraps of slashings as settlement scythed its way into New Brunswick. "Fires in Canada," observed Major Samuel Strickland, a settler, "are of frequent occurrence." A chronicler of the Miramichi conflagration concurred: "Fires in the woods are usual every summer in the British provinces." They inspired no great apprehension. Even extensive fires late in the fall aroused little "alarm" among the folk, a fact that can "hardly be accounted for except for the circumstances of their never having experienced the sad effects of fires any former instance." Most were kindled by settlers, many spread into the surrounding woods through unpiled debris cast against the uncut scrub, few damaged more than the occasional barn or cabin. The torch followed the axe, and the axe cleared along the major thoroughfares of commerce, which here meant its wending rivers. In the mixed Acadian forest, the vigorous fires spread through the conifers, not the hardwoods. But Nova Scotia and New Brunswick could be exceptions. There "extensive conflagrations often devastate the country for miles round." In fact, fires had "raged" through Nova Scotia in August and September, though sparing the well-cleared farm country. On 19 September, Government House in Fredericton ominously burned to the ground. The land was primed. It needed only a spark, a suitable gust, to jar that meta-stable mix into an explosion. The worst struck on 7 October 1825.[13]

Everything converged. Drought had gripped the region; "scarcely any" rain had fallen since July; everything organic, living or dead, rooted or felled, was drained of moisture. Debris littered whole landscapes. Logging still boomed, with exports overreaching to their wobbly pinnacle that very year. Mostly lumber meant square-hewn balks, so trimmed that roughly a third of the trunk and its branches remained, parsed and broken, on the ground. Logging, that is, removed the large boles that were heat sinks and left the smaller branches, chips, needles, and rail-flakes that acted as heat sources. Around and within those vast, reckless slashings, settlers added their own choppings. The landscape was chocked with combustibles: this was a supply-side conflagration. Equally to the point, those who wielded the axe also waved the torch. Farmers burned their piles, their fallows, their rough pastures; loggers kindled cooking and warming fires and dropped matches where they smoked; travellers and hunters abandoned fires as they did a butchered carcass or hemlock-bough bed. For the settler, the drier the woods, the better the burn. For loggers, the fire litter was a matter of studied indifference. Few fires blew up. Once flame finished its rush through the slashings, it typically quieted when it struck mature woods, often well adapted to surface burns. Besides, there were always more woods; logging was a kind of industrial swidden, slashing and burning and moving on. For the transient, escaped fires were a lost memory. Whether lightning might also have contributed is unknown. Clearly it wasn't necessary.

Across New Brunswick, from Fredericton to the Bay of Chaleur, from the delta of the Richibucto River throughout the watershed of the Miramichi River, the land crackled here and there with eager flames, waiting only for some triggering jolt to become critical. A resident of Newcastle, Robert Cooney reported how, on 6 October, "the fire was evidently approximating to us." Throughout the day, "fitful blazes and flashes" were observed variously about the countryside. The weather stirred. Probably the Hudson Bay High that had clamped down on the region for so long and dried everything under it like a bell-jar broke down. A smoky mist gave way to a gloomy pall, the heat became crushingly oppressive, a "deep and awful silence" descended. Then a front moved through, the winds first rising in the southwest before shifting to the north. The gusts, rising to a "hurricane," fanned flame into conflagration. An immense pillar of smoke towered like a malevolent burnt offering. "Suddenly," Cooney recalled, "a lengthened and sullen roar came booming through the forest, ... driving a thousand massive and devouring flames before it." A frontier society collapsed under its assault.[14]

The full scope of the Great Fire is unknown. Fires fused, and fires fissioned. Flames coalesced into veritable firestorms, while embers hurtled high into convective columns that were spotted miles away. Observers confused local fires, whipped by winds, with the crown fires miles distant. What got reported were points where flame and people collided, samples in what was almost certainly an immense patch quilt of the burned and the unburned, the immolated and the partly incinerated. The fire blasted settlements along the Bartibog, Nappan, Black, Richibucto, St. John, and Miramichi Rivers; swept cottages and hamlets along the Bay of Chaleur; gnawed through the suburbs of Fredericton; destroyed Douglastown, Newcastle, and Nappan; even enflamed ships at anchor at Miramichi. Probably the most reliable estimate of the total land involved is that of Cooney. He thought the fires burned a sloppy ellipse 140 miles long by 60-70 miles wide, encompassing some 6,000 square miles, or more than 3.8 million acres. For years afterward, estimates with better or worse data ranged from 5,000 to 8,000 square miles. Still, the regional complex was yet more colossal. Other fires burned in Upper and Lower Canada, and still more consumed chunks of the Gaspé Peninsula – known to have been fired in the "early part of the season" – and contributed to the smoky murk that clotted the skies over Prince Edward Island and Nova Scotia. An estimated 832,000 acres burned in northern Maine, and the Penobscot River was described as resembling "a sea of fire for thirty miles." Its first chronicler judged it a "universal conflagration," an "ocean of fire that we may conclude to be unparalleled in the history of forest countries, and perhaps not surpassed in horrific sublimity by any natural calamity from this element, that has ever been recorded." By any standard, this was an immense fire complex.[15]

These were intense fires, not simply burns widely cast, and their damages were commensurate with their fury. Its core area, roughly 400 square miles "of once settled country" along the Miramichi, Cooney dismissed as "one vast and cheerless panorama of desolation and despair." Forests were charred, like a spectral graveyard; houses and towns were blackened husks; fields and pastures were devoured as though by a horde of fiery locusts. Some 160 people died, a figure that, if the backwoods habitations were reckoned fully, might swell to 500. Whole families had perished or been rent by their flight. "Lumbering parties" had perished in the woods. Some had died where they stood; some fell as they fled; some drowned as they sought salvation in the tempest-swept waters. Graphic accounts described bodies "so horribly mangled that nature recoiled at the spectacle." Those who survived were cold, hungry, homeless, dazed, frightened, frequently burned, and often destitute. Their misery was genuine, and winter would soon replace flame with an equally savage frost. The destruction of whole communities, and these on a hastily erected frontier, left them with reason for despair.[16]

Within days, a pamphlet appeared, *A Narrative of the Late Fires at Miramichi, New Brunswick,* that sketched the horrors of the event and the grievous plight of the survivors. Governor Sir Howard Douglas called a public meeting "to devise measures and raise funds for the relief" of the sufferers, then quickly organized a tour of the burned areas around Fredericton to see for himself this "scene of woe" and to carry to its inhabitants "consolation and advice." Letters went out to Halifax, Fredericton, and St. John recounting the horrors and pleading for aid. Legislatures assembled to debate what measures they might extend to help. Newspapers in the United States ran lurid, heart-wrenching accounts. A Central Committee for the Relief of the Sufferers was organized at Fredericton, which also issued an appeal to the "British Nation." On 31 October, Governor Douglas arrived in Chatham, the one community spared the flames, and exhorted the region's residents at a public assembly. The contrast with their former prosperity was "awful." No more terror and desolation could have occurred had "the whole globe ... been in combustion." Yet he counselled against "groundless despondency," against an urge to emigrate, and against a repetition of those practices that had contributed to the destruction, notably an overdependence on logging, a shiftless agriculture, and the lack of commercial consolidation afforded by towns. The subscriptions succeeded impressively. From British North America, the committee received some £19,290 in cash and goods; from Great Britain, £12,246, plus £1,400 from the crown; and from the United States, $11,704 and £93.[17]

The colony rebuilt. Loggers moved into the many unburned islands and felled the surviving timber. The lumbering economy crashed less from ecological reasons, the fires, than economic ones, a depression in Britain. The seared forests regenerated to hardwoods. Great swaths of blueberries clothed many charred hillsides. Travellers reported reburns or burns among those sites originally unscathed. A year after the Great Fire, the Chatham *Mercury* described fires "of great magnitude" and dense smoke "all last week," though they seemed remote. Trekking through Greater Acadia, James Alexander bemoaned "a most difficult country," as far as could be seen flooded with "naked and grey" snags or "raft-like" heaps of blowdown, the flotsam of an 1827 reburn. But these were aftershocks; the Big One had shaken its full measure. Still, settlement revived; a year after the horror, townsfolk observed a day of fasting and thanksgiving and held special church services. By 1833, however, the memorial observances ceased, and when 8 October was declared a general day of thanksgiving by the governor the fires' living memory had passed. Families buried their dead, societies built over the ruins, the forest regrew.[18]

Its memory survived in literature: the printed memorials, a poem, some ballads, the ledgers of the Relief Committee, the formal histories of New Brunswick and later of North American forestry. There it morphed from an event into a symbol and then into an archetype. It even entered, as an object lesson in reckless forestry, into George Perkins Marsh's *Man and Nature*. It survived, paradoxically, not because it was singular but because it became the paradigm for a century of horrific settlement fires that plagued the Great Lakes; very little that occurred at Peshtigo, Hinckley, Cloquet, Porcupine, Cochrane, or Haileybury did not replay the Miramichi scenario. The advent of steam accelerated the process because it pushed the axe beyond the banks of navigable streams. The Great Fire became, for this era, for these colonies, for the Acadian and Great Lakes forests, the fire of reference.

It became the standard and type by which, for a century, all other colonizing fires were measured, the progenitor of a sickening litany of settlement-catalyzed "great fires." At the time these fires erupted, almost no institutions existed to regulate fire practices, to fight wildfires, to provide relief, to rehabilitate towns and woods, and no genres thrived by which to narrate the horrors or memorialize the losses. There was no agency charged with measuring, studying, and describing either campfire or conflagration. Every response was unique and spontaneous. By the mid-twentieth century, however, Canada had a suite of governmental institutions to administer fire-prone lands, a fledgling science of forestry to analyze and even forecast fire's behaviour, and a cadre of professionals committed to fire's containment. Fire became explicable by means other than allusion to an "awful visitation" that an Almighty God had permitted, and the response could exceed general appeals to "Christian charity."[19]

On 7 October 1825, none of this existed. The forest heaved, and the heavens seemed to open floodgates of flame. A ship's master – watching the twisting streams of fire, deafened by the roar – opened his Bible and compared the "sights and sounds" to the predictions of the last day and "believed firmly at the moment that it was indeed the end of all things." He was not alone. Robert Cooney concluded his own historical account thus: "All it required, to complete a picture of the GENERAL JUDGMENT, was the blast of a TRUMPET, the voice of the ARCHANGEL, and the resurrection of the DEAD."[20]

BOOK 3

ENGINE

Containing Combustion

As the nineteenth century unfolded, a new species of combustion matured, one of such immense power that it forced a tectonic shift in the dynamics of fire throughout the planet. Paradoxically it was the least visible of burning, for it occurred in specially contrived chambers; to control over spark and fuel, it added the control over oxygen. So voracious did it prove that it soon exhausted biomass fuels and commanded a more unbounded source, which it found in the lithic crust. With fossil biomass, exhumed as coal, and later as oil, lignite, and gas, industrial combustion began to burn whole landscapes from the geological past. A new ecology of combustion crept, then sprawled, across Canada and restructured wholesale its regimens of fire.

Steam and steel joined a suite of other forces impinging on British North America. Imperial pressures remained; from the onset of European colonization, the politics of Canada had followed from the wars and treaties of Europe. Perhaps the central event of Canadian nationalism, the loss of the lands south of the Great Lakes, happened without much say from Canadians. To these forces was added the brazen expansionism of a United States that had deliberately severed linkages that would allow Europe to contain it. There were economic pressures, too: a search for markets, a scavenging for capital for internal improvements, the tremors of a revolution in transportation and industry powered by the new combustion. Immigration boomed. Scientific ideas, arts, and literary conventions poured into the country. And of course climate, the archetype of Canada's external stresses, hovered over the land like a dark angel. These strains forced an internal adjustment.

The politics congealed during mid-century. The need to keep the United

States out, Quebec in, and railways financed argued for a "continental Canada" that would, like its rival to the south, stretch from Atlantic to Pacific. The Oregon Treaty of 1846 set the US border along the forty-ninth parallel. The American 1867 purchase of Alaska began defining Canada's Pacific domain. That year the united provinces, New Brunswick, and Nova Scotia, under considerable pressure, joined in a national alliance, another of a long series of confederations of convenience to protect against forces they otherwise could not resist. In 1868, Britain and Canada negotiated the cession by purchase (though not completed until 1870) of Rupert's Land, placing the North-West under Canadian sovereignty and opening the prairies, in particular, to agricultural settlement. That process precipitated a political crisis that ended with the admission of Manitoba in 1870. In 1871, British Columbia, in reality a gaggle of trading posts and gold-rush camps, signed on. Two years later Prince Edward Island reluctantly joined.

British North America now had its own interior empire and created a national policy, a program of internal mercantilism, to replace the imperial preferences it had previously enjoyed and to which it had owed the founding prosperity of its staple economy. The scrapping of the Reciprocity Treaty with the United States in 1866 gave further urgency to the settlement of the new lands. What made Canada's "national program" practically possible, however, was the promise of a dominion-sponsored railway to link east with west. Rails could bond Ontario with an ice-free port and a quasi-colonial hinterland eager to trade grain and wood for manufactured goods; could connect British Columbia to Nova Scotia, giving credence to a continental nation; could help to reorient Canada away from unstable commodity markets in Europe and from politically risky markets in the United States. The desperation for railways profoundly shaped politics by warping the capital market and provincial finances; steel and steam were the costs and promises of Confederation. Individual provinces could not underwrite the Intercolonial Railway between Halifax and Quebec or the Canadian Pacific Railway that joined Vancouver and Toronto. The collapse of its own railway scheme is what forced Prince Edward Island to seek a merger. The debts of its island-spanning rails nearly compelled Newfoundland to do the same. No colony could survive the perils of industrialism alone. The political power of the rails became patently evident in 1885 when, even though not quite complete, the Canadian Pacific Railway allowed the rapid movement of troops to put down the second Riel rebellion in the North-West. Combustion and Confederation became the two prime movers of Canadian life.

Industrial combustion touched nearly everything with its peculiar fire. Landscape by landscape, industrial fire remade woods, waters, soils, and even air. Like an additional wobble to the Earth's axis, shifting the intensity of sunlight, this new combustion caused fire regimes everywhere to realign. Steam sawmills slashed through forests; steamboats and steam locomotives hefted lumber from once-remote outbacks and hauled in people for settlements. Steam made wholesale colonization of the prairies possible, and steam powered factories whose manufactures lifted the Canadian economy, for the first time, out of a cycle of export commodities. Steadily Canada underwent the pyric transition typical of industrializing societies. As new ignitions piled on to old ones, the population of its fires erupted, dangerously.

Yet Confederation sought to counter this extravagance, as it sought to discipline capital and to bring, in the time-honoured phrasing of the British Colonial Office, "peace, order, and good government" to an outpost of empire. Canadian fire and Canadian politics, it seemed, shared a similar logic, a parallel macroeconomics, and a common need to seek mergers for mutual protection against larger threats. Sometimes sturdily, sometimes feebly, industrial fire would be channelled through institutions, a hierarchy of organizations and bureaucracies that ultimately pointed to Confederation. New social instruments appeared and decided what kinds of fire practices would be acceptable, how fire would manifest itself on the land, and which precepts would guide the hand that worked the levers on the throbbing engines that, overtly or more often covertly, shaped the character of fire in the dominion. Between them, Confederation and internal combustion seemed to promise the means to contain the free-burning flame so characteristic of Canadian nature.

Those means were institutions. Some were federal in that they spanned the dominion in intention if not in fact and were able to muster collective imagination and national funds to fire's control. But most were provincial. The original provinces administered their lands and the natural resources on them, directly if those lands were crown. After 1930, the western provinces did so as well. What began as a commanding national narrative spluttered and then splintered. The story of Canadian fire has always been one of parts – of concentric fire rings, loosely organized by climate and geological history; of scattered fire frontiers, shambolically clustered by imperial impulses. Now it became one of fire provinces, loosely federated around a national ideal and the weak-valence cohesion that such politics brought to fire's management.

In its origins, however, the dominion experiment was crucial. Few prov-

inces could muster the funds, or even the ambition, to cope with a population explosion of settlement fires that was almost Malthusian in scale. The
dominion government could – had to, in fact, because it held large chunks
of the national estate in the west for which it claimed active administrative responsibilities. It could also inspire and educate through institutional
devices such as the Commission of Conservation, which sought to rally
applied science to national problems. And not least the dominion government sponsored research in the guise of natural history reconnaissances
more probing than simple prospecting, land surveys more rationalizing
than squatter stakes, and laboratory investigations more thorough than a
folk knowledge scrambled in crossing the Atlantic.

These institutions could, as it were, command some Canadians'
attention all of the time, and all Canada's attention some of the time,
but little more. They existed in a political force field that trapped them
between external hammers, from climate to global economics, over
which they had little control, and provincial anvils, from local politics
to practices, over which they had no more influence. Small surprise that
they found themselves constantly battered and reshaped. The narrative of
their passage is an awkward one, for while the dominion might survey the
course, only more local bodies could do the work, and the outcome often
resembles a log corduroy bridge wobbling across muskeg.

There are many ways in which societies may connect to fire; the fires they
use, the fires they wish to remove, the fires from which they seek to protect
themselves. Some, in ancient times, made fire a god, some worshipped it,
some made it a philosophical principle. The Akkadians had a fire deity
in marsh reeds, the Zoroastrians had temples of pure fire, the Greeks and
Romans had pyrtaneums where Hestia and Vesta nurtured the hearth fire
into a symbol of the state. Some let fire's symbolism saturate the culture
as its use did daily life. Some, in more secular times, put fire at the core
of alchemy and later natural philosophy and especially chemistry. Some
expressed their firepower through military might; some through factories;
some, even in modern times, through arts and literature. There are societies
rich in fire paintings, fire poetry, fire as a theme and symbol in literature.
There are peoples who have debated the place of fire in landscapes close
to their national identities. Canada is not among them. Canadians have
instead expressed their connection with fire through machines and
institutions; their fire culture has been instrumental and commercial. Fire
lore is applied knowledge, directed largely through organs of government
and the devices of internal combustion.

This has become the fundamental dialectic of Canadian fire: the rhythms of the boreal environment against the dynamics of political Confederation. The first assured that averages meant little, that the big fire and the big fire year would do most of the ecological work, account for most of the damages and costs, and define the character of fire's administration by people. The second assured that institutions would struggle to become large enough to cope with those outbreaks. Even the dominion government could, for decades, make little more than token gestures, and then in 1930 it removed itself from the arena. The provinces, even the largest, lacked the power to counter the exceptional – which were really the defining – years. The institutions that sought to mediate between Canadians and Canadian fire would thus prove unstable, the grip of society over geography tentative if tenacious. The story of Canadian fire is the story of that dialectic, which is another variant of Canada's *ur*-story, the quarrel between its history and its geography. While the history is there, it does not emerge organically so much as it is held together by the presence, or perceived threat, of outside pressures. The master narrative is in reality a confederation of narratives, each centred on a geographical matrix. One group clusters around the Gulf of St. Lawrence, and another around the plains and mountains of the west, with Ontario becoming an accidental transition between them, the territories a skewed variant, and Newfoundland a skewed synopsis of the whole.

Reconnaissance by Fire:
Robert Bell and Bernhard Fernow

The new dominion found itself both pushed and pulled into fire protection. Wildfires posed a clear threat to settlers, to the vital lumber economy, and to crown lands for which the state owed basic obligations of ownership. Towering smoke plumes did not convert wood into wealth; incinerated villages did not encourage immigration. All these concerns pushed the government into some calculated response or at least some public reaction. But there were pulls as well, especially the emergence of a political philosophy of conservation, which quickly became an axiom of "good government" throughout the British Empire and, before long, within the United States, however flawed and fumbling its application.

Conservation was one among many such rationalizing practices, but it acquired a special cachet as a model of how an industrializing nation coped with the wrenching transitions from pioneering pastoralism, subsistence agriculture, and an extravagant plundering of natural resources. Paradoxically, environmental wreckage and conservation programs marched to the same modernizing drummer, and they pointed to the need to transcend local politics, which seemed incompetent to resist the coercion and rapacity of a global economy. Some larger institution of state had to intervene, if not national then imperial.

Much attention focused on the woods, for the felling of forests wholesale was the most visible emblem of havoc. In reply, forest conservation promised not only a steady stream of timber but also a more stable climate, a dampening of floods and droughts, and a boon to public health. Whether or not rain followed the plough, drought seemingly followed the axe. Felled and fired woods meant soil erosion, climatic desiccation, and a deficit of fuels. The protection of existing woods, the planting of new ones – this was the essence of wise use and rational exploitation. It was a public service for a commonwealth, precisely the sort of thing progressive government could do that individuals, acting alone, could not. In his 1864 classic *Man and Nature*, George Perkins Marsh ranged widely for examples, pointing not only to the collapse of ancient civilizations by their environmental abuses but also to contemporary terrors such as the fresh torrents of alpine-logged France and the reclaimed sands of Jutland. Nor, on the eve of Confederation, did this crusty New Englander ignore Canada. The 1825 Miramichi fire loomed, for him, as a lurid example of a broken and burned world.[1]

While on most conservation issues political rivals found little agreement, there was one decisive exception: the all-pervasive hazard and too-frequent horror of wildfire. The emissaries of conservation saw flame everywhere. It flourished in the European heartland, in the settler colonies of New Worlds from North America to Australia, in imperiums from India to Algeria. Fire followed axe and plough and rail. It ransacked woods more ruinously and indifferently than logging; it savaged settlements as though they were so much hammered slash; it mocked nationalistic rhetoric of present visions and future glories; it threatened wealth and challenged pretensions of administrative order. Fires sprang from faulty brakes and wayward torches, fire simply dropped from the sky. Forest protection, conservation philosophies, practical colonization all meant nothing unless fire could be shackled. It was a kind of stubborn, simmering, sullen ecological insurgency that threatened rule and order, an environmental equivalent of Thuggee bandits or Berber Bedouins. It was not so much that government institutions, committed to conservation, demanded fire control as that the perceived need for fire protection made compelling the case for state-sponsored conservation.

Thoughtful observers understood the need instinctively. In 1871, Prime Minister John A. Macdonald, Canada's first, pondered the "sight of the immense masses of timber passing my windows every morning constantly," a spectre that questioned the unbounded future of "this great trade." Logging was one source of forest depletion, but "fires in the woods" – regularly "destroying millions of money" – were the other. Axe and torch were the shears of an environmental scissors that cut the Canadian woods into shreds. At the time of Macdonald's musings, the dominion government had no direct interest in the issue, lacking lands it could administer directly to that end, but Macdonald thought it would be "a very good thing" for a commission to explore what he regarded as an impending crisis. He thought a solution would require regulation over cutting, a program of replanting, and a means of "protecting the woods from fires." His formulation of the problem would remain for more than a century as the core of a Canadian creed for fire control. That no commission appeared – that the dominion government proved unable to muster the political clout to enforce such a project – also established a standard.[2]

Slowly, however, the political planets came into alignment. The dominion did acquire territory for which it had continual oversight in the immense sweep of the North-West Territory, acquired by the purchase of Rupert's Land from the Hudson's Bay Company, and a forty-mile-wide tract in British Columbia, that province's contribution to the transcontinental railway project, along with a block in the Peace River region. In response, the federal government passed a series of ordinances to establish a governing structure. The Dominion Lands Act of 1872 authorized the permanent reservation of timber lands from sale and settlement and enjoined timber companies to prevent fires and fight those that did occur; neither provision was enforced. A year later the North West Mounted Police were authorized, soon adding fire control (where possible) to their duties to maintain public order. The North West Territories Act of 1875 established a governing council for the territory, which quickly enacted legislation to prevent wildfires in woods and prairies. In 1876, Parliament created a Department of the Interior to oversee the dominion's estate in the territories. Outside settlements, there was little means (or will) to suppress fire. Crown timber agents existed to collect royalties.[3]

Something else had to shake up governmental lethargy. That happened when forestry and the forest industry found common cause in conservation, the one a guild with academic credentials in Europe and an emerging bureaucratic power within Britain's empire, the other concerned about the stability of its business. Together they promised to bridge a concern for future generations with the contemporary necessities of logging. Interestingly, among the earliest Canadian advocates were timbermen, such as James Little, a lumberman with experience along Ontario's Grand River and the St. Maurice district of Quebec. In 1872 and 1876, he published two pamphlets, *The Lumber Trade in the Ottawa Valley* and *The Timber Supply Question of the Dominion of Canada and the United States of America*, together a jeremiad about how overcutting and fire were stripping North America of its woody wealth. His solution was better regulation of logging, restrictions on settlement, and fire control.

On all counts, Little's pamphleteering was prophetic. There was, first, the corporatist alliance between business and government that has so defined Canadian exploitation of natural resources. Specifically an implicit bargain was struck, that the government would guarantee preferential access to timber, while the timber industry would guarantee a steady flow of revenue to provincial coffers. A relatively small number of large operators would deal with a relatively small number of officials. There were fewer quarrels between government and industry than, say, in the United States. Canadian forest conservation proceeded by political negotiations – an understood commonality of interest in revenue and order – between lumbermen and officials, while American conservation involved a more factious amalgam of scientists, intellectuals, professors, and professional foresters, all of whom had different designs on the national estate and were prepared to protest and if necessary rebel. Second, conservation was coupled to settlement. In the east, this meant that farmers and loggers had to be segregated in order for the felled woods to regrow to forest or to be replanted outright after agriculture failed. In the prairie west, the need was to create forests where none existed; settlers required tree plantations as a source of timber, fuel, and climate abatement and relied on protected catchments to supply waters for irrigation. What threatened all parties was fire. There were too many sparks in the settled lands and too much slash in the logged areas, and they too often merged into the environmental equivalent of nuclear fusion. Farmers, loggers, foresters, officials, all agreed on the need for fire protection if on little else.[4]

By 1875, there was enough North American interest to sponsor an American Forestry Congress in Cincinnati, which led to the founding of the American Forestry Association; both included Canadian delegates, the Little brothers among them. A bit recklessly, the Canadians promised to host the next congress, in 1882, in Montreal. What made that sequel a rousing success was that Quebec lumbermen found common cause with the Little brothers and particularly that it claimed the attention of Henri Gustave Joly de Lotbinière, a member of Parliament, amateur forester, and Liberal broker between industry and government. As chair, Joly ensured that the fire question became the first item of business placed before the congress.[5]

This required no special attention; already the fire crisis had become a commonplace. Writing in 1878 for the Montreal Horticultural Society, A.T. Drummond noted the threat by fire to settlement at its fringes, the western prairies and the eastern pineries. That recurring fires had "much to do with the scarcity of trees" in Manitoba and westward was "beyond question." The effect cascaded, contributing to aridity, lack of fuel, a hostile environment generally. But the cutover lands were worse yet, for fire wreaked even more havoc than axe. "No person who has visited the Saguenay District, the Upper Ottawa, the shores of Lake Superior, and the Albany River Country, can be blind to the fact that forest fires have been a source of vast ruin." Forest preservation demanded not simply staying the axe but preventing the conflagrations that outstripped it. "So important is this question" to all – governments, lumbermen, bankers, settlers – that every crown land agent should be deputized as a "fire inspector." Laws, certainly fire laws, did not enforce themselves. Fire protection was simply the policing demanded of a civilized state.[6]

Of course, fire was a vital matter, almost universal among delegates, perhaps uniquely so. Yet that so many had so much to say caused the organizers to fret that this one issue might monopolize the congress altogether. In fact, it fell to a Committee on Forest Fires jointly staffed by Canadians and Americans, including Joly and Little, for the former, and Franklin Hough, C.S. Sargent, and Bernhard Fernow, among others, for the latter. During the final session, the committee presented its recommendations for endorsement by the congress. Specifically, it urged the creation of dedicated forest reserves, the prohibition of debris burning during risky months, and the creation of an agency that could both enforce legislation and fight those fires that did occur, paid for by a fire tax on the industry. This was, almost wholly, the corporatist agenda, although the provisions, so far as they went, aligned with a vision of forest conservation accepted by the imperial powers. The committee said nothing about regulating cutting, reforming timber leasing and land tenure, or establishing inviolate nature preserves.

Instead, it reduced the varied forest crises to a crisis of fire. In the east, the problem was overcutting and too much fire, which prevented regeneration; in the west, it was too few forests, further thinned by reckless burning; and everywhere it was incinerated future timber berths and threatened prairie settlements. If, then, fire was the universal cause of distress, fire protection might by itself provide a universal antidote. "Fire conservancy" might not be simply an axiom of conservation but its primary task, one for which the dominion government had both a duty and an opportunity, a duty because it administered a large chunk of the national estate and an opportunity because state-sponsored fire protection could become a means for possible regulation on other matters at present too politically contentious. The dominion's official response was to appoint, in February 1884, J.H. Morgan as a commission of one to "examine into and make a Preliminary report on the subject of the protection of the forests of the Dominion." An amendment to the Dominion Lands Act, meanwhile, allowed the governor-in-council to create forest reserves along the Rocky Mountains as a means to stabilize catchment areas and otherwise assist settlement.[7]

But east and west, national or provincial, the question of fires drove the agenda of forest conservation. Joly characterized the issue well: Canada had fires on the scale of Canada. "The difficulty of guarding against fire in such immense and distant forests as ours is enormous; and as for extinguishing it when once fairly started, the power of man cannot succeed. It will sweep onward as long as it can find food, leaping at one bound over such rivers as the great Ottawa and Miramichi, and will only stop when brought to bay by large lakes, or when it reaches rocky or barren ground, with nothing to burn; it will run riot for weeks, until starved for want of food or drowned under torrents of rain." The only solution was to prevent those fires from starting or, once having started, deliberately or otherwise, from escalating to the proportions that the elemental matrix of Canada allowed.[8]

Principles met practice when in 1885 Ontario and Quebec moved to create a system of "fire ranging." After the Northwest Rebellion, the NWT Council legislated a system of fire districts for prairie settlements, and the Department of the Interior argued for a program of fuel breaks, fire guardians, and volunteer fire brigades. (Interestingly the United States at this time adopted some measures for fire control, one based in the states, another in the federal domain; New York's Adirondacks Preserve, now subject to fire protection, and Yellowstone National Park, for which the US Army assumed administrative responsibility.) In 1887, Morgan officially became "forest commissioner," charged with devising ways of "preserving and protecting the forests of the Dominion." Two years later he published his conclusions in the annual report for the Department of the Interior, reasoning that stewardship had to begin with a serious investment in fire protection.[9]

Morgan's supervisor, D.M. Burgess, disagreed, however, arguing that an aggressive – and undoubtedly expensive – program of fire control was unnecessary. Burned forest regenerated without any assistance from the government, and the very process of settlement would, by converting wildlands to domesticated landscapes, eliminate wildfires as it matured. To this reasoning, also common in America, there were several replies. One was biological. The forest did not always come back to what had grown before or within a timeframe that the timber industry needed. Another was that the crisis was upon the country and demanded immediate attention. Still another argument, advanced by Morgan, was bureaucratic. This was not how matters were done in Europe or within Europe's more progressive imperium. Laissez-faire was not conservation. But the question of how much protection was necessary, who should do it, and, especially, who should pay for it would no more go away by itself than would fires.[10]

Of course, commissions, reports, ordinances, and orders-in-council did not mean much on the ground. In its annual report for 1897, the Department of the Interior cited settlers burning to clear land and firing off hay meadows for the "disastrous fires which occur annually." Provincial and territorial laws were "excellent … were they enforced," which of course they were not. A.O. Wheeler, dominion land surveyor in charge, elaborated for the foothills of the Rockies: "By far the largest area," he noted, was *brûlé;* the "bush fires" were in truth denuding land faster than new growth could cover it. For causes, Wheeler identified the usual suspects, pointing to lightning, "parties requiring dry timber for market purposes, prospectors wishing to examine rock outcrops, ranchers who have none too much pasture land and, chief of all, carelessness in lighting and extinguishing campfires when high winds are in season." Sending in the Mounties was "very much like locking the door when the horse has gone." Needed was a pre-emptive "system of guardianship." To his political minders, this system seemed expensive. But since the federal government sought to quicken the pace of settlement, and since settlement brought more fire, which threatened settlement, at some point those flames would touch political powder.[11]

By the 1880s, the fuse had been lit. The political stakes were real, for whichever institution controlled fires would become powerful. Yet as the conservation era unfolded, the country barely comprehended the extent of its national estate, much less the full magnitude of its fire hazards and the range of responses that might be appropriate to them. It needed to know, exactly, what kinds of fires it confronted and what sort of government agency might be best equipped to oversee a response to them. The competition to acquire and apply that information was keen.

Robert Bell was, as a memorialist put it, "especially fond of investigating and exploring regions hitherto untraversed." In truth, he excelled at such expeditions, perhaps the last man to have the opportunity to tramp over vast stretches of the Canadian outback while possessing the training to report in scientific language what he saw and commanding the institutional setting to make himself heard. As an observer of Canadian fire – the flames that raged beyond the pale of settlement – he was prophetic, not the first to report that the remote north burned, but the first to apply some system toward understanding those fires.[12]

Bell was at heart a pioneer – an explorer, a nationalist, a forger of ideas and institutions, a master of the natural history reconnaissance and of those agencies, notably the Geological Survey of Canada, that both sponsored and assimilated such undertakings. He accomplished for the Canadian north what Humboldt did for the South American tropics. In these tasks, he had rivals, both scientific and political, though no field scientist could match his range of traverses, and few could hope to equal his fifty-two years with the survey. As an observer of boreal fire, however, he nearly stands alone. For decades, he had trekked meticulously through the violent heartlands of Canadian combustion, and he recognized that fire was not merely a seasonal presence, like mosquitoes, but a shaper of the vast northern forests, a force as powerful as the droughts and winds with which it was associated. His observations stand to those of Henry Hind as Hind's do to those of Gabriel Sagard.

If Bell saw more than Hind, he also saw with more sophistication. He had education, connections, a heritage as the son (and grandson) of Church of Scotland ministers that translated into a secular mission. In 1856, his father, a keen naturalist and friend of William Dawson, chief of the Geological Survey of Canada, helped to secure for the young Robert a post with the survey. He was sixteen years old. That apprenticeship set the direction of his career. He became an artful practitioner of the scientific reconnaissance so characteristic of the Second Great Age of Discovery, eventually receiving a King's Gold Medal, the highest award of the Royal Geographic Society. The rhythm of his life he thus set early, with a season in the field followed by another at a desk. That tempo continued for another fifty-two years.[13]

Bell bent his studies accordingly. He acquired a degree in 1861 in civil engineering from McGill University, skills useful for surveying and mapping. He returned for an MD in 1878, knowledge valuable to someone tramping in remote and hazardous locales. He picked up a baccalaureate in natural science and embellished it with graduate studies at Edinburgh, training essential for executing the survey's charge. In 1863, at the age of twenty-one, he accepted an interim professorship at Queen's University in chemistry and natural history. But the call of the wild sounded louder than the groves of academe. After five years, he resigned to work fully for the survey. In 1877, he was appointed assistant director; in 1890, chief geologist as well; and from 1901 to 1906, acting director, all the while writing copiously about Canada's natural wealth and the promise of its development, an ardent, early advocate for railways. He went north and grew up with the country. His singular achievement, however, was to trek over more of "the north" than anyone before or since.[14]

Year by year, his reconnaissances sprawled over the Canadian outback. Bell explored Hudson Bay along its eastern shores and then around its interior with three ship-borne expeditions (*Neptune*, 1884; *Alert*, 1885; *Diana*, 1897) and, of special interest, the straits that guarded its entrance; this led to surveys along northern Quebec and southern Baffin Island. He traversed, along its major rivers, the hinterlands of Quebec and, especially, Ontario. He toured the prairies of western Manitoba and inspected potential rail routes from Lake Winnipeg to Hudson Bay. He organized expeditions into the Northwest Territories, inspecting most of the vast lakes that hang like a thick-chained necklace around the Shield, most spectacularly Great Slave and Great Bear Lakes. Bell swung briefly into the Yukon and British Columbia. Partly these arduous treks sketched the rough geology (and cartography) of the Shield; partly they identified useful deposits of minerals and coal; and partly they assessed routes of travel potentially important to national development: Hudson Bay as a shipping outlet for western wheat; railway paths to the bay and around the Great Lakes; rivers potentially navigable by steam. With Confederation, he argued early for a transcontinental railway. The Grand Trunk Pacific Railway (the portion between Quebec and Winnipeg) largely followed from his reconnaissances.

Bell understood, as perhaps no one else in Canada did, certainly no one from such a cache of personal knowledge, the natural wealth of the country, the ways in which it might be made accessible and exploited for the good of the dominion, and the power of institutions such as the Geological Survey to oversee that process. He found lignite, tar sands, petroleum, gold, diamonds, silver, iron, every conceivable geological resource. But while minerals and transportation were his prime subjects, his curiosity seized on all of Canada's natural history; he wrote on the birds of Hudson Bay, molluscs in the Gulf of St. Lawrence, soil fertility in the northwest, butterflies in Keewatin, mammoth fossils, glacial moraines, even the Canadian porcupine. For his labours collecting Indian legends and folklore, he was made an honorary chief of the Algonquin peoples of Grand Lake, Quebec.

Unsurprisingly, he included Canada's forests within that majestic sweep. The Shield was largely water, rock, and trees; the water meant routes of travel; the rocks, mineral deposits; the trees, timber. Its woods were the soft ore of the Shield. Bell mapped the boreal forest, particularly its limits, as he did the strata of the Huronian group. He prepared his first national forest map in 1873, then updated it for 1879, and continued to modify it on the basis of his (and others') reports. (For this "large map," the International Forestry Exhibition in Edinburgh awarded Bell a special diploma.) Of particular interest were those borders where the woods met prairie and tundra, those two treelines, south and north, that traced the shores of Canada's climate. But the woods had a second factor almost as powerful: they burned. In their internal dynamics, they responded to fire as their gross geography did to water and temperature. His curiosity about fire may have stemmed originally, as so much of his career did, from the example of William Dawson, who had denounced Canada's extravagance of burning.

In his first sketch, "The Geographical Distribution of the Forest Trees of Canada," Bell noted that the white pine, which had once stretched from Ottawa to Lake Superior, locally had been "entirely destroyed by extensive forest fires" and, except for "small groves," replaced by other species. He amplified that aside for a major address to the British Association for the Advancement of Science when it met in Montreal in 1884. "The Forests of Canada" was largely a survey of Canadian fire. "The amount of timber which has been lost through forest fires in Canada," Bell asserted, "is almost incredible, and can only be appreciated by those who have traveled much in our northern districts." Fire far outstripped logging as a despoiler; the quantities lost were "almost incalculable" and of "serious national consequence." Bell cited his own traverses as testimony. "Nearly every district was more or less burnt, the portions which had been overrun by fire usually exceeding those which remained green." Worse, the fired woods became susceptible to beetle attacks that further ravaged them, and various shocks meant that the burned commercial forests came back to aspen and birch.[15]

While the fires' causes were many, Bell lashed out especially at "white settlers and demoralized Indians." In colonizing lands, settlers often lost fires while burning brush and logheaps; lumbermen confronted grudge fires, often submitting "to a species of blackmail from discharged employees and pretending settlers in order to keep them off their limits"; Indians, too, sometimes burned other tribes' hunting grounds "from motives of revenge," although most of their fires sprang from sheer "carelessness or indifference." Such outrages, he insisted, should be preventable by segregating agricultural from timber lands and through a proper system of forest conservancy patrolled by "forest guardians." Even the Indians, Bell believed, were amenable to friendly cautionary warnings or, if necessary, to economic incentives. Their annuities could be withheld as a punishment for woods burning, or a "bounty might be paid each year that no fires occur," goads that would soon rally the Natives in favour of fire protection. While such measures would be meaningless against that other cause of northern fires, lightning, presumably a suitable system of patrol would handle these as they would the others.[16]

The need was immense; already the classic white pineries of the united provinces were exhausted. Still, the country could thrive on its immense stock of timber on the Shield, provided it would still be standing when needed. "If the vast northern forests can be preserved from fire in the future," Bell concluded, "our supply of small timber is practicably inexhaustible." That supply, however, required fire control, and it demanded appropriate institutions of the state. True, laws against careless fire existed, but they were unenforced and perhaps unenforceable. "The time has arrived for more vigorous action by the general Government and the Local Legislatures looking to the improvement and preservation of the forests which still remain in Canada, and for the partial restoration of those which have been destroyed." What the dominion required were "educated and intelligent conservators of forest," appointed "by the Government," to oversee both the protection and the propagation of its timber estate.[17]

This was the commercial argument – that fire wasted natural resources, that timber was, in the end, no more unbounded than coal, that it was the duty of good government to prevent both dangers and losses. But embedded in the essay was a discussion of how, exactly, fire behaved in the boreal landscape and some hints of how nature had accommodated fire's relentless outbursts. Bell thus identified the linkage between "mossy ground" and "dry tops," the thick mingling of small trees with large, the close coupling of dense branches among adjacent trees, the blow-torch blast of high winds. He noted, too, the patterns of response to a sweeping burn. Recovery began with the onset of "shrubs and bushes," then with aspen and birch, and finally with slow-upthrusting conifers, until "at the end of a hundred and fifty years or more they regain possession of the burnt tract." Such a process "appears to have been going for centuries." Here was an analysis based on biology, if one still cast within the narrative of wreckage, although a waste absorbed within nature's economy rather than the dominion's. If the northern forest rebuilt itself after such conflagrations much as cities did, fire was no more necessary for the one than for the other.[18]

In 1888, Bell addressed the American Forestry Congress specifically on fire. "Forest Fires in Northern Canada" is his fullest statement, elaborating his earlier essays and serving as the core text for his later work. He opens by making the case for fire's extent, antiquity, inevitability, and evolutionary independence from people. The model of large fires that had become commonplace in conservationist jeremiads – fires devouring towns and logging slash – did not here apply. "Notwithstanding its immense extent," Bell says of the boreal, "it may be said that fire has run through every part of it at one period or another." The "normal condition" of those woods is "patchy," precisely because they are burned. Bell assures his readers that he "has crossed the entire breadth of our northern forests in many parts and has found the above condition to prevail everywhere." It could hardly be otherwise since the conditions within which the forests flourish make them "peculiarly liable to destruction by fire," and, more, the repeated fires have fostered conditions that make further fires possible. "These fires have had an effect on the formation of the soil, on the rotation of crops of trees, so necessary to their healthy condition, and on the dispersion of seeds."[19]

Remarkably, Bell lays out the ecological scenario, selecting his favourite fire species, the "Banksian" (jack) pine, for illustration. He describes its serotinous cones, needing the "scorch" of flame to open; the "fire-fall" of killed trunks that encumbers a site; the comparative outcomes of different scenarios of reburns; the effects of burning and fire-charred windfall on soil fertility; the patterns of biotic succession; the relationship of burned land to beetles, so loud on a *brûlé* that "in a still evening, the creaking noise of the millions of their larvae may be heard for considerable distances in all directions." Repeatedly, smoke had shut down surveying operations. Ecology thus conspired with climate to account both for fire's behaviour and for its inevitability. All this, Bell notes, occurred quite apart from human meddling since lightning was more than sufficient to kindle the woods on a vast scale. He estimates that a third of the boreal forest consisted of recent burns, a third of young growth (much under ten years) recovering from burns, and a third of relatively mature growth (perhaps a century old). The northern forest had to accommodate such realities, just as it did frozen soils and dry spells. The miraculous adaptations he described were measures by which the woods assured their perpetuation in the face of fire's implacable and recurrent threat. Fire was something the forest responded to, sought to shield itself against, as it would an early frost or a plague of defoliating moths.[20]

Bell did not invert that relationship. He did not explore the necessity, as distinct from the inevitability, of fire. He knew that fire was integral to the forest, that apart from its grand borders, set by climate, the structure and composition of boreal forest reflected the rhythms of fire; he dismissed objections that only people started such conflagrations; but he could not imagine that fire was so built into the constitution of the boreal forest that its removal could be disruptive, that it might not be simply unavoidable but also necessary. To demand such insight was to expect too much, for Bell was a creature of his time. The vast fires were catastrophic, they cast immense smoke palls, they destroyed animals (even overtaking birds), they consumed with mindless vandalism a vast stock of useful timber and fuel, they killed people. (They also tested his resourcefulness when a bush fire burned over a food cache, forcing him to exist on very light rations for nine days, one of his few misadventures in the field.) When witnessed raw in the wild, their mix of "distant solitude" and "wide-spread destruction" conveyed a deep impression of "weird grandeur"; they were "one of the wildest and grandest scenes of destruction which can take place on the face of the earth." Yet the forests existed to serve Confederation, not the other way around. Bell as pioneer and nationalist ended with thoughts appropriate to his age: "Can anything be done to prevent or lessen this terrible waste?"[21]

His answer was yes. Agents could instruct the Natives, who, Bell now decided, had "always" been careful with fire prior to degenerative contact with whites; governments could pass laws and then install "the necessary machinery to carry them out"; pioneer farming could be segregated from logging; forest guards could call out local populations to help fight fires. Bell himself illustrated how to live in the backcountry without incinerating it. He always built campfires on stone or sand, not where embers could touch any kind of buried organic debris, which could hold fire tenaciously. He camped on islands. He lectured – hectored – his Native guides and contacts about the need for care. And "many a time" he stopped his party "for hours or even for a whole day to put out fires" he found burning "during the dry season." His sensitivity was such that he even claimed that, on a hot day, "you can smell the turpentine given off in the form of hydro-carbon gas everywhere, so much so that an experienced man will not light a match among these trees." For Bell, the lesson of boreal ecology was that fire would not go away by itself. Its chronicle resided in soil charcoal, in the structure of the forest and the evolutionary adaptations encoded in the genes of its trees, in the spark of lightning. People would have to intervene. What prevented them was "want of executive force."[22]

His subsequent addresses repeated and developed these arguments. Bell included a generous review of fire for an audience in Edinburgh (1897), the meetings of the Canadian Forestry Association, and especially the Canadian Forestry Convention of 1906. His address, on "The Alarming Destruction of Our Forests by Fire," was notable for two points. First, he claimed that, since the onset of his travels, he had made "careful notes of burned areas." Upon assuming the directorship of the survey, field parties had followed his example, such that he had prepared a map of burned areas, with dates of the burns coded into thirty-year intervals by different colours. Bell assured his audience that the fires were universal, beyond what anyone who had not traversed the country as he had could imagine. The northern forests, he concluded, have been "so often overrun by fires of greater or less extent that we cannot say with certainty that there is any fully grown forest in that country." Rather, the land was in various stages of recovery from the last burn and thus preparing for the next. This lost map was the pyric double of his geological surveys, and it shared a like purpose, to provide intellectual underpinning for government action.[23]

That was his second point, the urgency of a response. At the time director of the Geological Survey of Canada, Bell insisted, "I do not know of any other subject of greater importance to the government than this matter of the alarming destruction of our forests by fire and the means to be taken to prevent a continuance of that destruction." Of course, he recognized that fires could not be wholly prevented; lightning would work its inanimate will regardless. But the indigenes could be bribed and cajoled and at a minimum disabused of their notion that their wildfires did a "service by scorching the trees and making plenty of dry wood for your camps"; negligent fire kindling by whites should be treated as the criminal act it was. Still, if people had only limited control over fire's start, they could attack its spread. The proper strategy was to increase "our force of foresters," as the Dominion Forestry Branch was then attempting to do. "Surely, it is most important for the government to take any reasonable means to prevent this destruction and loss."[24]

Most of what the world knew of Canada's boreal fires it learned from Robert Bell. He offered not only his personal testimony but also that which he gleaned from his agents on the survey. Along railway lines and within the raw pale of settlement, commentators were as thick as the fires; abusive burning was visible to all. Almost uniquely, however, Bell scrutinized the fire scene beyond the lines of axe and steel – that is, across the immense mass of Canada. His observations offered a unique descriptive geography of early Confederation fire yet were so astute that most can still stand today, more or less unrevised.

The brute drive that made Bell such an indomitable force in the field could prove hard to bottle within an office. The bureaucracy of the survey under Alfred R.C. Selwyn bridled Bell, who thought the British import too genteel, too sluggish, too English to suit Canada's energetic nationalism, and too restrictive of Bell's own ambitions. Clearly Bell thought he, not Selwyn, should have been appointed director, and their sparring over the years festered into a bureaucratic blood feud that led, to no one's credit, to damaging parliamentary inquiries in 1884. Eventually Bell did advance to the directorship, but only in an "acting" capacity, in which role he nonetheless nearly doubled the survey's productivity as measured by survey parties sent into the field and maps printed. This internecine dispute only crippled the survey at a time when it nearly alone oversaw an inventory of Canada's vast natural estate.[25]

The other limitation was that the Geological Survey of Canada was an agency to study, not to govern. It did not sell the lands it surveyed, did not dredge or dam the rivers it mapped, did not mine the ore and coal it identified. It served a staff function to the dominion government: it researched, it advised. Similarly, it could not act on Bell's astonishing assessment of Canada's northern fires, for that required an agency with political power, which could only come routinely by exercising direct control over the land or resource in question. The task, as Bell recognized, had passed to Elihu Stewart's Forestry Branch in the Department of the Interior. Foresters claimed specialized knowledge beyond the ken of natural history reconnaissances and surveys conducted to trace rocks, plat townships, and assay minerals. It was thus no accident that Robert Bell, shortly before retiring from acting directorship, addressed his pleas to the Canadian Forestry Convention in the same year that the Dominion Forest Reserves Act granted administrative responsibility over large extents of land to the Forestry Branch. While the Geological Survey could cope nicely with rocks and waters, it passed the torch to foresters.

Foresters were only too keen to seize that torch and believed themselves uniquely endowed to control it. By the latter nineteenth century, forestry had joined that Earth-spanning sprawl of engineering cadres that busily surveyed railways, dug mines, erected bridges and dams, and fortified military cantonments; that promoted a rational reconstruction of landscapes and societies; that sought to ground its practices in an iron web of applied science, government agencies, academic learning, and professional societies. Foresters conformed to this formula exactly, doing with woods what mining engineers did with rocks. Fast-colonizing countries such as Canada, Australia, and America, recognizing that European political and social conditions (to say nothing of environmental conditions) offered few practical examples, took cues from overseas experiments in places such as India and Algeria and sought to import their own authorities, typically from central Europe. For Canada, no one symbolized that transfer better than Bernhard Fernow.

Early rivals, institutional and intellectual. *Top*, Robert Bell in the field, Témiscamingue and Abitibi districts, 1887. *Bottom*, Bernhard Fernow, standing at right, by the Rocky Mountains, 1915. Others from left to right are R.H. Campbell, Walter Potts, and Mrs. B.E. Fernow.

Born in 1851 into the Prussian aristocracy, educated broadly (even to competency in classical piano), destined to manage an uncle's estate, Bernhard entered the Prussian forest service and then studied at the forest academy at Muenden until the Franco-Prussian war sent him to France for a year as a lieutenant. After mustering out, he read law at the University of Königsberg before returning to the Muenden academy and eventually earning a licence as a forester and acquiring a conviction that the Prussian system of forestry was supreme. Meanwhile, he had met Olivia Reynolds, an American whose brother attended Königsberg, and when she returned to the United States in 1876 Bernhard, to his family's intense displeasure, joined her. He became an American citizen in 1877; two years later he and Olivia married. America had acquired its first professional forester. Fernow set up shop as a consulting "forest engineer."[26]

Thereafter, virtually every development of importance in North American forestry felt his touch. Forestry conventions, professional societies, journals, the drafting of model legislation, the creation of forest reserves, the promulgation of silviculture on private lands, artificial plantations, professional education, experimental stations and forest-product labs, forest surveys, consulting at state, provincial, national, and even international levels – Fernow did it all. His connections were endless, his sense of mission indefatigable. He helped to nestle forestry within government by directing the US Division of Forestry (1886-97); he installed forestry education by serving as the first dean of the New York State College of Forestry at Cornell; he founded and edited the *Forestry Quarterly;* he became a force behind the American Forestry Congresses and a founder of the Society of American Foresters; he wrote a monumental, globe-sweeping history of forestry. He even travelled to Alaska with the 1899 Harriman Expedition. The one omission in his curriculum vitae as a cameo of global forestry was his lack of direct contact with British India, where so many policies and protocols had been bred; in effect, Fernow reinvented the process for himself, doing for North America what Dietrich Brandis had accomplished for imperial Britain. In brief, his vision was comprehensive, from ideas to institutions, from formal education to journal editing to paradigmatic field surveys. He did for American forestry what Franz Boas did for American anthropology, fusing state, academy, and profession into one collective enterprise.

Then, having assisted the emigration of professional forestry to the United States from central Europe, he carried it to Canada. In a series of lectures at the School of Mining at Kingston, later published, he laid out a systematic agenda for Canadian forestry. When a Faculty of Forestry was endowed at the University of Toronto in 1907, as the natural candidate for dean, Fernow was selected. The school was the first for Canada and remained its forestry flagship. Soon afterward Fernow helped to found the Canadian Society of Forest Engineers, a professional organization to complement the more popularly based Canadian Forestry Association. For the association, he chaired a committee to promote a uniform body of fire legislation throughout the dominion. He became active in the Canadian Commission of Conservation, again promoting fire protection, particularly along railways. Under the commission's aegis, he organized a forest survey of Nova Scotia, which served as a model for others conducted in British Columbia, Saskatchewan, and Ontario. The *Forestry Quarterly,* while remaining in New York, overflowed with Canadian subjects. Fernow incorporated Canada within his broader scholarship on the history of forestry. He consulted with British Columbia, so rife with fires, and plumbed the prospects for cross-border arrangements and co-operative fire control. At the request of Robert Campell of the Dominion Forestry Branch, he conducted a long tour of its western forest reserves in 1915 and then organized an advisory council for forest research. He spoke tirelessly, recommending policy, suggesting models (he thought Sweden particularly apt), fulminating against the absurd and unbounded burning that so stamped the Canadian woods. Almost immediately, he became a point of integration, linking the concerns of east and west, of America and Canada, of North America and Europe, of forestry as plantation silviculture and forestry as the administration of wooded wildlands. He seemingly knew everyone; many officials were colleagues, many of them former students, all of them associates.

Throughout, close links existed between American and Canadian conservationists, with forestry a primary conduit. Oddly, Canada's normally binocular vision, part British, part American, was, for conservation, biased toward the United States. There were the joint American Forestry Congresses; the sheer volume of the cross-border timber trade, so critical to the Canadian economy; the transfer of people; the free traffic of ideas. Early Canadian forestry relied on consultants such as Carl Schenck at the Biltmore School and later Fernow or G.C. Piché and T.W. White, who trained at Yale. Each country's forest reserves co-evolved out of common precedents in the British Empire (and, to a lesser extent, with the French Empire), but, once their systems were created, American and Canadian administrators looked across the border and brought them into closer alignment. The alliance strengthened when the US Forest Service was established in 1905. (Oddly, Britain's imperial influence was refracted

through US foresters such as Gifford Pinchot and Henry Graves, the two
founding chiefs of the US Forest Service and both students of Brandis.)
The major distinction was that Canada attempted to protect public
lands outside reserves, while the United States did not; these fire-ranging
districts amounted to almost 80 percent of the land under protection and
helped to account for the chasm in staffing between the two countries.
Still, the challenges to American and Canadian state forestry were almost
identical. Each sought to disentangle agriculture from logging, to ensure
new forest crops either by natural regeneration or by artificial planting
and, the sine qua non, to protect them from fire. If the model for Canada
was essentially the same as that for the United States, then Fernow was a
prominent reason why. "Every principle" that has been "found to work
elsewhere [can] be put in practice in Canada," he insisted.[27]

What Fernow and forestry thought of fire thus matters. It particularly matters that his ultimate vision of forests was agronomic, that forestry
was agriculture for trees, that silviculture meant, literally, the cultivation
of woods by planting, pruning, weeding, harvesting. It was a business that
had its peculiar engineers, its entrepreneurs, and its economics. Conservation overall was itself "a business proposition pure and simple." It differed
from most businesses, however, in that its investments demanded a long
time to mature and because many of its goods were public, and for both
reasons it became the interest of the state to ensure policies that would allow
forestry to flourish. Ideally, the state would itself administer considerable
lands reserved for forests and their "influences," an expectation often easier
to promulgate in colonies than in the nation-states of Europe, although it
meant that forestry would have to oversee often vast expanses of wild, not
cultivated, land. Certainly, this was the case in North America. Forestry also
existed because previous practices had collapsed into crisis. In the inaugural
edition of *Forestry Quarterly,* editor Fernow quoted Heinrich Cotta, who
had observed in 1816 that "formerly we had no forestry science and enough
wood; now we have that science, but no wood." His explanation was simple:
forestry is "only a child of necessity or need ... We have now a forestry science because we have a dearth of wood." For North America, that crisis was
a forecasted famine in timber and an ongoing orgy of burning.[28]

In a wooded garden, fire had no place. It is one of the core ironies of
conservation that the public administration of fire came into the hands
of foresters, a guild that collectively hated and feared it, that sought with
every means possible to extinguish and exclude every vestige of flame.
They saw fire as mining engineers might see gangue, and, unlike civil
engineers who could distinguish between a flood and an irrigated field,

they refused to discriminate between a wildfire and a controlled one. For such attitudes, Fernow was synecdoche. Fire was a veritable definition of waste. It symbolized the irrational and the barbarous, and its ravenous flames epitomized all that conservation intended to suppress. In America, Fernow had condemned the burning as simply the outcome of "bad habits and loose morals"; in Canada, he denounced fires as both the country's "worst enemy" and its "national disgrace." Not only was fire intrinsically reprehensible, but it also magnified every other misdeed, just as repeated burnings led to rock deserts; tolerating folk firings only encouraged slovenly husbandry and a disdain for government and social order all around. In 1908, Fernow outlined the requirements of a national forest policy. Such a program should insist that farms and forests be separated, that the state administer its public timbers for "the interest of the future," which meant state oversight if not state ownership, and, as a rock-ribbed precondition to any such policies, that administrators ensure a "reduction of the causes of forest fires" and an "increase of the forces" available to prevent burns and fight those that occurred. Forestry and fire protection fused like the two heads of a double-bit axe.[29]

Yet paradoxically, Fernow did not consider fire control fundamental to the art and science of forestry. "The protection of forests from fire," he explained, wearily, "is no more forestry than the preventing of the burning of your house is architecture." Fire control was a necessary precondition for forest management, like owning the land; it was not itself true management; and his dismay over the fire plague was its effect in continually stalling genuine silviculture. Henry Graves, chief of the Forest Service, declared in 1910 that fire protection was 90 percent of American forestry. But he understood that the reign of fire would, with a proper system and political will, eventually diminish, for fire was something a raw country passed through, like a childhood disease. Forestry's pioneers would have to grapple with it, as settlers did wild animals, until a truly rational system could prevail. While fire protection might obsess forestry's founders, it would be of historical interest only to their grandchildren. Good management would contain it as good silviculture would an outbreak of beetles or blight.[30]

That vision reflects forestry's origins in temperate Europe, a place alien to natural fire, a practice grafted onto the great rootstock of European agronomy. Yet fires abounded in Canada on a scale inconceivable to Europe. No native forester believed that fire would pass quickly, although many accepted, if implicitly, that it might fade over many decades. Instead, flame remained. Much as Robert Bell recognized fire as a pervasive presence but failed to imagine it as an ecological essential, so too Bernhard Fernow appreciated fire's omnipresence yet failed to understand how integral fire was for forestry in fire-prone biotas like Canada's, as a matter not merely of biology but also of administration. It was less forestry that brought fire protection than the perceived need for fire protection that prompted state sponsorship of forestry. Fire made forestry powerful, and ultimately forestry could not banish flame because it needed it.

No forester of Fernow's age appreciated that paradox. Each knew in every fibre of his professional being that his first charge was fire control; without it, nothing else he might do mattered. Even as fire proved trickier than they anticipated, even as costs mounted and techniques became more complicated, even as the utopian prospects for a fire-free era faded, foresters continued to accept as a legitimate and necessary goal the abolition of fire. The end was certain, a conviction that freed them to pursue, with ever greater efficiency and ingenuity, the means to make it happen.

The diaspora of forestry around the globe had its echo in Canada. Foresters transferred among the provinces as they had throughout the empire. What created a common language and institutional medium in the dominion was not shared policy or a national vision but, as often as not, a shared fraternity of foresters. That civil society bonded more tightly than politics. They were, by and large, a homogeneous crowd, all trained in the same texts, all sharing similar values, all viewing their work through a collective professional prism. What Canada could not achieve through direct political institutions it did acquire through the indirect rule of its foresters. That was Fernow's deepest legacy, and he would have wished for none better.

Fire Provinces of Industrial Canada

F ire regimes in industrial Canada reconciled, or tried to reconcile, boreal fire with modern institutions. This was a political project, not simply a matter of policy but of that raw politics that determined means as well as ends. With fire's scale vast and its power seemingly primordial, only the state could apparently stand against it. But government had its own dynamics, and while the contest would begin at the highest levels, the fight would occur within smaller polities and the selective collectivities they could tolerate.

Dominion of Fire: Canada's Quest for Fire Conservancy

Forestry Takes Command: Dominion Forestry Branch

In 1899, the dominion established a Forestry Branch within the Department of the Interior and appointed Elihu Stewart, a former departmental land surveyor and Liberal politician, as chief inspector of timber and forestry. Stewart knew the west, knew politics, understood the agenda that reform had to pursue. "The whole forestry problem of our Northwest," he summarized, "may be included in two words: conservation and propagation." As it did for Fernow, conservation for Stewart meant use. "It would be as unwise to refuse to cut a forest as it would be to allow the ripened grain to go to waste by neglecting to harvest it." Public use, however, was possible only if existing stocks were protected and new ones added, and preserving what already existed had to begin with fire protection. A panorama of the dominion's reserves identified fire as a hazard everywhere, even in an "exceptionally wet" season. Especially needed were "fire guards" (fuel breaks) along roads and railways. Protecting woods in

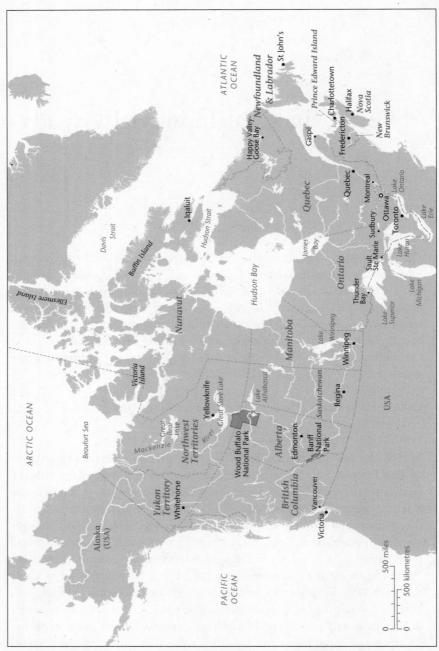

Fire provinces of Canada. The geography of primary political entities, and their relative proportions of forest. Only the two units of Parks Canada most relevant to fire history are included.

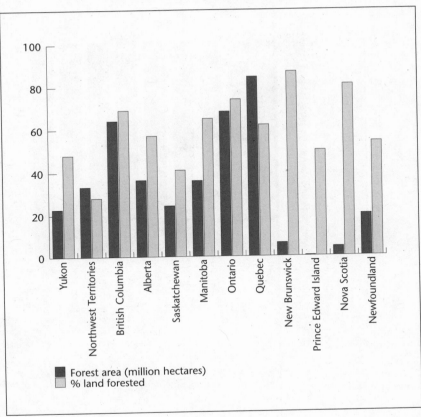

Forest area by province

the mountains, planting trees on the plains, what linked both was that they required fire protection. Whatever exalted credos the conservationist elites might proclaim, or grungy politics that parliamentarians in Ottawa might concoct, the practical reality was this: conservation required fire control.[1]

It had been the "burden of every report," Stewart said with exasperation, to document the forests' "rapid destruction by fire." This wreckage had gone on for so long that he regarded it as "not only useless but unprofitable" to estimate the losses. What was demanded was action. Stewart urged a dominion program of fire ranging like that developed in Ontario and Quebec. He cited the recommendations of the 1899 Royal Commission on Forestry in Ontario, which praised its effectiveness and had urged that it be extended and made compulsory. He quoted, too, from W.C. Edwards, MP and lumberman, who observed that prior to this system wildfires had

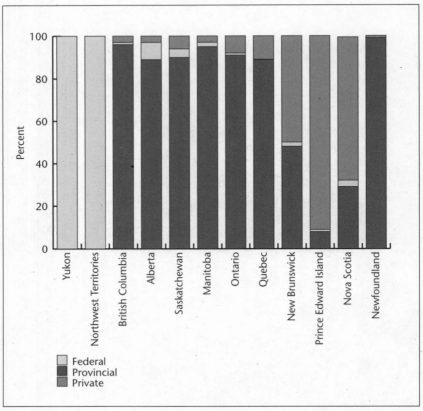

Land ownership

raged unchecked, and since adoption no serious fires had occurred. "Such testimony," Stewart argued, "seems conclusive and is sufficient to warrant the Dominion in adopting a somewhat similar system." So much had been said for so long; too much for too long. It remained only to act "before the next season arrives."[2]

Until he retired in 1907, Stewart, assisted by Robert H. Campbell, tirelessly campaigned for forest conservation similar to the American model. The administration of Wilfrid Laurier was sympathetic. Almost immediately, Stewart had written to Gifford Pinchot for advice and then visited his American counterpart in Washington, DC. Recognizing quickly the alliance between professional forestry and political forestry, he revived the consortium of interests that had sustained the earlier forestry congresses, which led in 1900 to the establishment of the Canadian Forestry Association. Their two agendas, reflecting their shared memberships and political ambitions, converged nicely. At its inaugural meeting, the association heard Robert Bell speak at length about fire in the "northern forest"; Thomas Southworth elaborate on fire and regeneration in Ontario and how, without its fire rangers, "our system of forest reserves would be impossible"; John Macoun describe lightning as an ignition source on the prairies and the pattern of burning at Moose Mountain and elsewhere in the northwest as it related to water; and William Pearce remind his colleagues that, although "bush fires have done incalculable damage to Canada, prairie fires have and continue to do also an appalling amount of injury." He then laid out what the alliance already understood completely: "Forestry and fire protection must go hand in hand. The latter might be carried into effect without paying any attention to the former, though the former would be greatly assisted by giving effect to the latter; but the former cannot be given effect to without the latter." In brief, forestry needed fire control more than fire protection needed forestry.[3]

Stewart of course had no intention of dissociating them. As promised, he acted. Before his first season ended, he travelled through Manitoba, the territories, and the railway belt with an eye to appointing fire rangers and discussed extensively with the North West Mounted Police a suitable division of labour for fire protection, which the Mounties had "always regarded" as one of their duties. Still, the NWMP were small in numbers and restricted largely to the prairies; they were most useful in educating the public. Other forces had to attend to the settlements, the forests, and those regions in British Columbia and Manitoba outside the North-West Territory proper. Quickly, rangers were hired; fire guards were constructed around vulnerable portions of the Moose Mountain and Turtle Mountain reserves; plans devised to shield the Rocky Mountains Park from wanton burning; steps taken to dampen the havoc caused by locomotives. The next year Stewart elaborated on the corps of fire rangers. They were selected from men residing in or around the district of employment; they worked as needed, when notified by the crown timber agent, forest ranger, or homestead inspector; they were provided, when called up, with "copies of the Fire Act, a copy of general instructions defining their duties, and [fire] notices … warning the general public against the careless use of fire." They furnished their own horses. They earned three dollars a day. When the fire risk abated, they were discharged. Not much, all in all: the fire force for the North-West Territory could probably not have staffed a hockey team. By the next year, however, Stewart documented how even this minuscule force had saved "millions of feet" of timber in British Columbia and spared Riding Mountain from incineration, and the deputy minister insisted that "there can be no ground for questioning the wisdom of the policy inaugurated." The Dominion Forestry Branch had become, in fact, a fire service.[4]

Steadily, Stewart consolidated his gains. The reserves grew, and the staff of fire rangers notched up to forty by 1905. To bolster prevention, the Forestry Branch enlisted the services of the Mounties, the Hudson's Bay Company, and the Canadian Pacific and Canadian Northern Railways, all of which distributed fire prevention posters in suitable locales. Stewart reported how travellers on the Peace and Mackenzie Rivers had met such notices "everywhere in conspicuous places throughout their travels." Rangers scrutinized the sources of recurring fires. Locomotives were a category by themselves; so was lightning, particularly in southern British Columbia. But although the railways kindled many fires, they were easily reached, while lightning set fewer fires but made them far more difficult to find and attack, and made them unpreventable, even in principle. Still, "carelessness" accounted for most burns. Prospectors were prominent incendiarists, along with ranchers burning for pasture, legitimate settlers firing brush, and squatters infesting nominal reserves and timber berths. At Turtle Mountain, the international border, which cut across the forest, complicated matters because undisciplined Americans constantly fired the land, and the prevailing winds blew them into the reserve. In fact, hardly a year passed without some fraction burning; a chronicle of large fires would include those of 1879, 1881, 1885, 1897, 1903, 1905, and 1906. The 1903 fires reburned much of the landscape of 1897, and it was evident that multiple ignitions had intended to make "a clean job of removing the forest so that the land would be thrown open for settlement." The merged blaze burned all summer, defying every attempt to quench it. A similar story unfolded at Moose Mountain. Here, too, "the devolution from forest to prairie through fire can be seen in all the stages along the edge of these mountains and the Indians tell us that the forest once extended over a large area which now through fire and grazing is a rolling prairie." The Indians, too, added to the load. Around the Shuswap Lake district of British Columbia, agents reported that the Natives were "known to start fires in the woods with the intention of encouraging the growth of wild berries." In southern Alberta, ranger Joseph Stauffer reported widespread burning. "I always understood that Indians would never set out fires in the forests," he wrote, "but this year I was convinced that they do; for hunting purposes, in season or out, in the Banff Park and out of it. They set out fires in the spring on their fishing and hunting trips in order to draw deer later for grazing." The fires' numbers varied; some years they were as common as poppies or mushrooms and in others sparse. Mostly, particularly away from places with easy access, the rangers could hold them or not, as wind and drought allowed.[5]

Its fires, though, made Canadian forestry distinctive. "The spectacle witnessed by the traveller passing through our unsettled forest country is sad indeed," mourned the chief inspector. "On every hand he beholds the charred remains of the old time forest. He sees this as he journeys through Nova Scotia, New Brunswick, Quebec, Ontario, the Northwest Territories, and, sad to say, this destruction is not least if not greatest in the giant woods of the Pacific slope. Everywhere this destruction of public property is before his eyes, and it is humiliating to confess, as we must do, that the fires which caused this great loss were not only permitted but in most cases caused by our own people." Hence, while he toured Europe in 1905, with particular attention to the forestry schools at Cooper's Hill in England, Nancy in France, and Munich in Bavaria, he concluded that "the conditions in these older countries were so different from those existing in Canada" that "I am decidedly of the opinion that we will have to work out a system essentially our own." The closest analogue was the United States, which that year transferred responsibility for its forest reserves to the US Forest Service. Like the Americans, Canadians needed their own schools of forestry and their own apparatus for fire control. They routinely had fires the size of shires and European duchies.[6]

The political tasks were as formidable as those confronted by the rangers. Weirdly, the Department of the Interior had long separated "forestry" from actual "leasing." It thus had a Forestry Branch (under Stewart) responsible for protection and a Timber and Grazing Branch (answerable to the chief clerk), which auctioned leases and collected royalties. In 1905, Stewart managed to merge these functions under his bailiwick. That year the North-West Territory spun off into two new provinces, Saskatchewan and Alberta, restricting the department's forestry to the federal lands. These bureaucratic movements culminated the next year with two stellar events: the first Canadian Forestry Convention, which Prime Minister Laurier himself called to order, and passage of the Dominion Forest Reserves Act, which set aside some 13,965 square kilometres as permanent forests of the federal government. Stewart celebrated his triumphs by embarking on a vast reconnaissance of the northwest along the Mackenzie, Porcupine, and Yukon Rivers. The year following, his ambitions realized, Stewart resigned, and his protégé, Robert Campbell, succeeded him. Stewart's timing was precocious. Stewart left not only while the Laurier Liberals still rode high but also after a largely wet cycle in the west. Fires there had been, some ferocious, a few mushrooming into conflagrations, but the horror years were to follow.

In addressing the 1906 Canadian Forestry Convention, Prime Minister Laurier had exhorted that "our labours are just commencing." So they were. These were heady times for Liberal politics, conservation, and the foresters who claimed for themselves special status as the agents of reform. Under the capable Campbell, the Forestry Branch rapidly assumed the status of an all-purpose conservation agency for the dominion. In 1907, it acquired responsibility for western irrigation and for dominion parks, and a year later it formed a Forest Economics Section, which promptly compiled the first statistical survey of Canada's forest estate and its international traffic in timber. It dispatched surveys beyond the reserves into the formidable, and well-burned, north. Meanwhile, Stewart's call for homegrown forestry helped to inspire forestry schools in Ontario, New Brunswick, and Quebec. By 1915, these had graduated forty-one BSc foresters, of which the DFB hired thirty-one.[7]

Institution building boomed. The American example loomed even larger in 1909 when Laurier participated by invitation in the North American Conservation Conference in Washington, DC, the successor to President Roosevelt's spectacularly successful Governor's Conference on Conservation. Out of that experience came the formation of a dominion-wide Commission for the Conservation of Natural Resources, an advisory body that paralleled what the Forestry Branch was attempting on the ground. In 1911, a Dominion Forest Reserves and Park Act expanded the scope of the Forestry Branch and nearly doubled the size of the reserved forests; a 1913 revision further enlarged the land reserved. Before the Campbell era concluded, most of the prominent figures of Canadian forestry – and of Canadian fire protection – did a tour of duty with the Forestry Branch. Even the ravages of the Great War, when enlistments stripped away many experienced field officers, did not long stall its momentum. Its graduates reincarnated in industry, universities, and provincial forestry services.

Campbell's was a broad vision, extending beyond the mechanics of ploughing fire guards and erecting political alliances. Most powerfully, while untrained in science himself, he trumpeted the need for research. Applied science was essential to the mission, and the Forestry Branch would have to do it. Forest product laboratories were one outcome; a forestry advisory committee to the Dominion Council for Science and Industrial Research, established during the war, was another; and not least, based on CSIR recommendations and with the United States as a model, was the creation of a network of field stations, the foremost of which became possible in 1918 when the Department of Militia and Defence asked the branch to assist with managing its forests on the Petawawa military reserve in Ontario. A survey was quickly succeeded by a plan for fire control, what became a prototype and later the training ground for dominion fire scientists.[8]

Certainly the fire threat loomed over every newly gazetted forest reserve and dominion park, and it practically defined the rhythm of life for rangers. In 1908, virtually every reserve bore the brands of repeated burns, against which stood forty-seven fire rangers, twenty-one of whom laboured along the railway belt. The northern districts, beyond the realm of formal reserves, were in worse shape, suffering "heavily from fire and the danger is increasing with the advance of settlement, the increase of travel and the extension of the railway systems." Without aggressive fire control, those nominally protected woods would succumb to the fate of so much of the dominion and "present but a blackened and almost barren waste." The promotion of railways, such as that from Winnipeg to Hudson Bay, would expose an already fire-scourged land to further flagellation. The more settled countryside, particularly along rail lines near the American border, suffered extravagantly that summer, both in British Columbia and in Manitoba. As Abraham Knechtel, the branch's chief inspector, stated bluntly in 1910, following another bout of conflagrations, "all other work on the forest reserves has been held subservient to that of guarding the forest against fire." Yet while the US Forest Service had an appropriation of $4,640,000 and a permanent staff greater than 2,000, its dominion counterpart was funded at $100,000 and fielded a staff of 40. That the Forestry Branch under Campbell even conceived of fire protection on this scale was both heroic and quixotic; that it overcame so many challenges to that vision was perhaps its most outstanding and practical achievement.[9]

It did so first by targeting the reserves, whose unblinking asset was their exclusion of people. Where squatters encroached, they were evicted. This strategy left most of Canadian fire well beyond the branch's political script, for the branch could influence those realms of colonization, cutovers, and the boreal outback only through exhortation and example. The alternative was illustrated by R.H. MacMillan's observations at Crowsnest Pass, on the east slopes of the Rockies. "Of the 240 square miles included in the valley, 212 were originally covered with a fairly dense forest of spruce, pine, Douglas fir and balsam. At present only 33 square miles remain unburned, 179 square miles having been burned over. Of this latter area 60 square miles are covered with young growth, 34 square miles with dead standing timber, and 85 square miles have been so badly burned and so frequently, that only a few scattered trees remain. It must be a very long time before another forest can be produced."[10]

Having brought some legal level of protection, the branch needed to secure its physical borders, excluding fires that might originate outside the reserve and burn into it. Mostly this meant permanent "fire guards," principally by ploughing, grading, and burning. Ploughed guards might involve four or so furrows or two with the intervening land burned off, or they might mean a single furrow alongside rail lines, with the right-of-way burned out. Double guards were typically sixteen feet wide and the intervening swath two rods. Built fire guards were roads or trails tracing boundaries, particularly those subject to frequent incursions by fire from the outside. The cheapest, simplest, and often most effective, however, involved selective early burning, "which we know saved the reserves several fires." Inspector Knechtel explained that it was "a well known fact that, in the early spring, the fields become bare and the grass dry before the snow is all gone from the woods. While such conditions existed the forest rangers burned the meadows along the reserve boundaries. Fires, coming in from the prairie, met this wide fire line and died out for want of fuel." The trick was to manufacture such fire guards to shield reserves. "Around the Riding mountains the meadows were burned for ninety miles, around the Duck mountains for forty-two miles, and around the Porcupine mountains for thirty miles; all these in the most dangerous places." Knechtel drew the obvious conclusion: "It is advisable to extend this practice to all the reserves wherever it is practicable, and to carry it out upon an extensive scale," even through sloughs and along higher ground covered with "a rank growth of hay and peavine." Done at the right time – "just as soon as the snow is off the fields, but before it is out of the woods" – such guards were not difficult to create and could be recleared annually.[11]

Beyond that was simple firefighting. The fire ranger, it was agreed, "should live on the reserve and should be a man who can easily secure the co-operation of the settlers in preventing and extinguishing fires." The work itself was unglamorous. The most effective system, W.R. McLeod explained from Prince Albert, was "to work at night when the air is heavy and moist, and dig a trench in suitable places where the fire has too far to jump so as to make it a ground fire. The ordinary garden hoe and wet sacks where water can be had we find to be the most effective." Along the eastern Rockies, rangers added long-handled square- and round-pointed shovels, axes, grub hoes, galvanized pails, and brooms. By such simple means, the Forestry Branch sought vast changes.[12]

The railways constituted a special case; often they behaved like a mechanical firestick on rails. But clearing debris from the right-of-way, installing spark

Fire lookout, Brazeau Forest, Alberta, 1912.

Packing to the Cameron Lookout, Burke Mountain, Alberta, 1929.

arrestors, and patrolling the tracks could dampen their impact. Since the dominion controlled the railway belt through British Columbia, it applied its energies to the task, while other institutions (notably the Commission of Conservation) wrestled with the problem nationally, and everywhere legislation sought to coerce the railway companies into maintaining guards. Over the rails themselves rangers traversed with velocipedes and speeders; along the Grand Trunk Pacific from Prince Albert, the strategy called for the ranger to patrol about twenty miles along one side of the right-of-way one day and then patrol the other side the next day in return, in the process meeting "the rangers of the neighbouring patrols." Meanwhile, the construction of the Hudson Bay Railway promised a monumental rash of fires. In May 1910, J.T.G. Whyte inspected its route by river; "except on the islands," he concluded, "the whole country has been overrun by fire, in a few districts once, in the majority of cases many times during the past forty or fifty years, and any timber now standing dates from the last fire and is therefore small." The shores of Split Lake had been burned over "on an average of once every season."[13]

Of special concern were the eastern slopes of the Rockies, where many of the prize reserves and parks lay. During the 1910 season, the southern Canadian Rockies were ablaze over an estimated 494 square miles: "At one time there was a line of fire more or less continuous of over seventy-five miles." The worst burns were incendiary or the product of wilful carelessness. Fire protection would succeed, that is, only insofar as it shaped public opinion, and outside the reserves proper that meant the indigenous peoples. Fire prevention sowed its message with the abandon of jack pine seeds showering ash. It enlisted the Mounties, missionaries, and Hudson's Bay Company factors to cajole the Natives and printed warnings in the syllabic alphabets of Cree and Chipewyan. (To deal with European wanderers it posted notices in the tens of thousands, translated into the tongues of polyglot western Canada, including Icelandic, French, and Galician.) Even small bands could inflict serious damage in drought years. "The fires of the past years," the branch's chief fire inspector determined, had largely resulted from "the thoughtlessness and ignorance of the Indian." He cited the report of a fire ranger who observed that, while only "four or five families of Indians" lived in the country, they moved whenever the dry wood disappeared from around their camps and in fact were suspected of creating, by the torch, more dry wood. Officials believed them responsible for vast fires.[14]

The success of fire protection by the Forestry Branch, however, derived less from swatting out fast-moving blazes than by shutting off their sources. Ultimately rangers argued for control, by permit if necessary, of human traffic through the reserves. Even infrequently travelled routes such as the Nelson River between Split Lake and Hudson Bay showed the effects of careless campers. The north side, more heavily trafficked, with greater camping places and portages, displayed more burning than the south, which had a higher load from lightning. When one appreciated that such fire littering "has been going on for scores of years and the fires are left to burn themselves out," the scant timber visible came as little surprise, as the Forestry Branch summarized. With meagre resources for actual firefighting, rangers pushed for prevention; the need was urgent and desperate; after all, fire was, as one of them succinctly put it, "the worst enemy the forest has."[15]

It was tough work for tough men, and the hard-pressed, underpaid staff prided themselves on their achievements. They had to be young, fit, skilled in bushcraft, and literate, and if possible educated in rudimentary forestry. The Forestry Branch struggled to find enough men to fill its quotas. With no little pride, Abraham Knechtel reprinted in his report for 1911 passages from an article in the *Saturday Evening Post* that tracked a "fire guardian" along his rounds. He contrasted with Americans, for unlike them he possessed the mental discipline that embraced "the restraints of the law." He was a Steele of forestry, a fire Mountie, bringing an order unknown south of the border. "All alone, a sturdy and self-reliant figure – representing the law, representing civilization even in the wilderness, representing a decent regard of organized society for the organized society that is to follow us – he set out on foot for his wilderness journey across an untracked country. In all of one's experience with outdoor men, rarely has one met a better, simpler and nobler figure than this one."[16]

But fire protection in so vast a domain required more than skilled canoeists, however taciturn, burly, and civilized to Canadian norms. It needed system. The Forestry Branch needed to "settle" crown lands in the name of conservation, which drove it to push forward on all fronts. It fielded surveys. It pressed for control to issue permits and regulate settler burning and then for logging slash as well. It requested authorization to impress locals during fire emergencies. It erected "permanent improvements" such as roads, trails, cabins, telephone lines, and lookouts over a reserved domain greater than Nova Scotia and Prince Edward Island and one expanding steadily. It shielded vulnerable reserves with fire guards. It extended fire ranging beyond those reserves proper, such that by 1914 protection embraced a vast domain of 205,344 square miles, organized into twelve districts and patrolled by 186 rangers, largely by

Fire ranging, overland by a corduroy bridge on the Bow River Reserve, Alberta, 1925.

An idealized, latter-day voyageur travels by canoe, as recorded on the cover of the
Canadian Forestry Journal, 1916.

canoe. It beat down the locomotive-fire menace, with the help of the Commission of Conservation, by forcing engines to use diesel fuel rather than coal, compelling clearance along rights-of-way, and transferring actual duties for fire control to the Board of Railway Commissioners and the railways themselves. For the big-river and lake backcountry, it launched a small fleet of steamboats. It held annual meetings among its rangers. And in 1912 it hired E.H. Finlayson, a forestry graduate of the University of Toronto who had "considerable experience" with fire ranging in Ontario. The Ontario model would become the norm for the territories as well. Finlayson immediately oversaw a reorganization of fire ranging beyond the reserves proper.[17]

Then came 1914. The fire season was severe in the Rockies, the worst since 1910 and the first truly bad season with which the Forestry Branch tried to wrestle on any scale. The crisis exposed a number of weaknesses, most regrettably "the numerous incompetent men on the staff." Before the season ended, Canada was at war, and both fights proved to be gruelling wars of attrition. The early euphoria quickly chilled; the proud reductions in burned area attributed to good organization wilted before the renewed flames. Officials admitted that favourable weather, not a sound system, had accounted for the good statistics. Even Native burning revived, at least locally, suggesting that it, too, had dampened because of environmental conditions, not from a conversion of fire convictions. At Salmon Arm, British Columbia, rangers observed how "particularly troublesome" the Natives had proved. The reason was that the past few seasons had been too wet to burn the mountain sides "for the purpose of securing berry-picking grounds," and "a luxuriant growth of brush" had consequently encroached on the sites. With the return to dry weather, the indigenes drove back the brush with torches, and of course not all the flames stayed benignly in their berry patches. Resistance, however, increased resolve. The Forestry Branch dug in. "We must constantly keep before us," Finlayson warned, "the distinct vision of the ever-lurking enemy, fire."[18]

Fortunately for the agency, the truly villainous fires hammered eastern rather than western Canada. Ontario, in particular, suffered an extraordinary decade of conflagrations, from the 1911 Porcupine fire to the 1922 Haileybury burn. Western Canada skipped through several benign seasons, although British Columbia's railway belt always seemed, year by year, to have an "exceptional" season, whatever the measured outcome. There was an attrition of staff through enlistments, which created an "extreme shortage of trained men for the technical features" and starved supervisory staffs to "a skeleton basis." Some railways reverted to inferior coal, once again heaving sparks like a fiery spoor. Slash built up; fire-killed snagfields and jackstrawed windfall lined too many horizons. Every outbreak of fires diverted attention, staff, and funds away from programmed tasks into emergency operations, at the end of which few improvements had been made, save perhaps for fewer burned acres.[19]

And of course there was the wildly improbable spectacle of the fire ranger as coureur de bois, outfitted with canoes and steamboats and occasionally a York boat, patrolling millions of acres or more properly snuffing out smouldering campfires along major routes of travel and hammering fire notices onto trees. They understood only too well that, like their fur trade predecessors, they had to rely on the Natives for the real work of prevention. Chief Inspector Finlayson understood, too, that fire ranging was a temporizing measure, good only to establish an administrative presence, that, like itinerant missionaries, his bold rangers could do little more than baptize those born since their last visit and rekindle the passion of the faithful for prevention. Eventually such crown lands had to be transferred into formal jurisdictions, either to towns or to forest reserves, where they could be subject to more intensive administration. Fire rangers had responsibility for too much and power over too little, for they had no authority over the lands other than fire control, not including "the provision of adequate transportation facilities and other improvements, upon all of which any successful fire protective organization is absolutely dependent." By 1917, however, the Forestry Branch oversaw a vast empire, a kind of Hudson's Bay Company of fire protection, with 23 million acres in gazetted forest reserves, 132 million acres of fire-ranging districts outside reserves, and 6 million acres in the railway belt, all stitched together by the annual circuits of its fire voyageurs.[20]

. Still, the work went on. The Dominion Board of Railway Commissioners successfully regulated private companies, while the Forestry Branch assumed responsibility for publicly owned railways. Proper engine fuels, adequate spark arrestors, suitable clearance of debris, regular patrols – these soon dampened the problem of rail fires. Exceptions were newly hacked routes or rogue companies such as the Edmonton, Dunvegan, and British Columbia Railway, which managed for a time to defy official demands for responsible maintenance. The Hudson Bay Railway went from a million burned acres in 1916 to 1,640 burned acres in 1917. Favourable weather was a prime reason, of course, but so was passage from rude pioneering to regular administration, and in that way the railway fire problem was a model for organizing the untrammelled backcountry. Success meant bringing a system to bear, and that meant greater control over the movement of people and practices. Always the branch kept before it the credo that it was "directly concerned only in the *protection of the timber resources of the country.*" Its defining mission, however expansive, was economic.[21]

The bad news came in 1919: a monstrous fire year, the worst since 1910; labour unrest, including a general strike in Manitoba, that compounded difficulties of mustering crews; rampant incendiarism as settlers and ranchers seized on the dry conditions to catch up on years of poor burning; a residue of improvements not done and debris untreated because of the war; functional dissolution of the Commission of Conservation; Director R.H. Campbell head-injured on an inspection tour, thus absenting his charismatic leadership. Writing for Saskatchewan, District Inspector MacFayden spoke for much of the west when he characterized the past year as "the most unfavourable, from the fire-protection standpoint, [of any] experienced since any thought was given to this matter." The branch's postwar slump was stunning, pervasive, serious.[22]

Yet it ended quickly with powerful boosts, administrative and technological, from the war. Canada gained a new appreciation for the magnitude of its timbered wealth. The war had shown, in particular, Britain's vulnerability in a critical war material, wood, all of which it imported. The Imperial Reconstruction Committee noted that "Canada contains the only large reserves within the Empire," even as those stocks were "rapidly being depleted by fire," and urged their "effectual conservation." A year later London hosted the British Empire Forestry Conference, in which wooded Canada figured mightily. South of the border, too, demand for forest products soared. Like water over a rapids, research quickened over a few short years as the Petawawa experimental forest opened and the formal dissolution of the Commission of Conservation meant a transfer of staff to the Forestry Branch. The western provinces fortified their fire ordinances, encouraging co-operation to the point of allowing DFB rangers to oversee burning by permit.[23]

For those in the field, however, the most dramatic reforms were mechanical. Fire protection found in internal combustion machines the controlled power it needed to counter free-burning flames. Here was a classic Canadian solution to a classic Canadian problem: the application of technology to overcome vastness and doing it so successfully across the Confederation that those shared means replaced many incommensurable ends. In rapid stride, a great era of fire appliances took to the air, dipped into the Shield's plenitude of waters, hauled fire crews hundreds of miles, and broadcast messages over wire. In 1920, the branch consolidated its knowledge of telephony with a manual, *Methods of Communication Adapted to Forest Protection.* The single-wire, ground-return system, often strung through trees, that patrols could tap into with portable phones made modern communication possible. Gasoline-powered pumps ("portable" only in rude comparison with mounted fire engines) became available, the origins of effective firefighting on the Shield.

Most spectacularly, though, the branch inaugurated a co-operative program of aerial reconnaissance with the Dominion Air Board. One patrol flew out of Morley, Alberta, another out of Kamloops and Sicamous in British Columbia. Although complications delayed both enterprises until November, well beyond the fire season, the experiment convinced officials that aircraft promised a simple, economical solution to the problem of discovering fires in remote landscapes and even delivering firefighters to the scene. Even better, the Sicamous incident involved an HS-2L seaplane, which not only "functioned perfectly" but also took the "Right Hon. Arthur Meighen, Prime Minister of Canada," for a politically helpful joy ride. Roy Cameron, forest inspector for British Columbia, gleefully rattled off a roster of potential uses: "Exploration and sketch-mapping of timber areas in inaccessible location, aerial photographic reconnaissance, investigation and exploration of insect infestations, grazing reconnaissance and patrols, fire patrols supplementary to the lookout system, initial and progress reports on fires, especially lightning fires occurring in high, inaccessible places, emergency transportation of supervising officers, check-mapping of burned areas in accessible location, restocking lakes by the transportation of fish eggs or small fry." Soon afterward Cameron transferred to the Ottawa office as a fire protection specialist.[24]

The next year the program expanded into Manitoba as well, whose numberless lakes and rivers offered abundant landing sites. The "most successful results" came from aircraft capable of transporting eight to ten persons. For small fires, the pilot and a "helper" landed and suppressed the blaze; for larger fires, they flew to a nearby settlement and carried a troop of firefighters along with their tools to the burn. Alberta added a wireless telegraph that could communicate new fires to headquarters, which could then telephone the information to the closest ranger. BC pilots discovered they could fly nearly at treetops to gather information, which proved particularly useful on smoky days, opaque to lookouts. Nearly half of all agency flight hours went to fire operations. Not least, officials celebrated the "moral effect" of the patrols. Slash burners and travellers felt as if they were under surveillance, while planes dropped cards "printed with suitable messages" over "camps and picnic parties" and, in certain cases, "fairs and sports meetings." Aerial fire protection had come to Canada. It would never leave.[25]

The hard-slogging work in the field went on. It went on through good seasons and bad, through war and peace, through boom and bust, through benign or hostile administrations, all in all one of the most tenacious and astonishing acts of pioneering and institution building in Canadian history. Patrols by canoe, by mounted ranger, by velocipede patrolmen, by lookouts who acted on their own smoke sightings, this was the hard reality of fire rangering. Annually, "improvements" strengthened their hand, at least within reserves in the form of new trails, better roads, remote cabins, fire-tool caches, lookout towers, telephone lines, and lengthened fire guards. Saskatchewan developed a "rather ambitious programme" of infrastructure to serve local residents and travelling visitors as well as fire rangers by upgrading portages, marking frequented routes, identifying suitable campsites, building "inexpensive" log cabins, erecting timber lookout towers, even digging two canals that shortened the Montreal River by five miles ("work ... not likely to go unnoticed or unappreciated by a traveller"). From Manitoba, recently outfitted with aircraft and a headquarters on "Forestry Island" on Lake Winnipeg, came a reminder of how old practices could clash with new purposes. Winter trappers had traditionally camped in the bottom of dense spruce muskegs to shelter from the wind where their warming fires burned down into moss and peat, and during dry years, smouldering for months, the banked embers might break out in a rash of free-burning bushfires. Fire prevention meant educating this hard-bitten corps and following the traplines. From Kamloops, meanwhile, returned war veteran D.A. Macdonald brought further system to lands not so inhabited by devising new standards for the mountain cabin, by introducing a more elaborate scale of fire-control plans, and by staging training camps for seasonal rangers, filling a practical need for education overlooked by university schools of forestry.[26]

A seasonal journal from the Shuswap Forest Reserve along the BC railway belt showed how fire ordered the lives of DFB staffers. In April, Ranger Aiton spent five days locating the Scotch Creek trail and bridge, two days inspecting a new timber sale, six days examining settler slash and issuing fire permits, a day himself in brush burning, two days overhauling gear, and three days travelling, including a meeting at Salmon Arm, while his assistant went on fire patrol and posted notices. In May, he worked on the Scotch Creek trail and laid out another along Ross Creek, and the rest of the month he spent in fire patrols, timber sales, and overhauling his fire canoe (*Mabel*), while his assistant helped on the trails but trekked eighteen days on fire patrol. June found the two on the trails, mostly on fire patrol but with some trail work, packing supplies, burning brush, handling sheep-grazing applications, and a day fighting fire. July they spent on trails, relocating and resupplying camps, doing some fire patrol, touring with Inspector Barnes, and repairing tools. In August, Ranger Aiton spent sixteen days on fire patrol and twelve days fighting fires, with two days spent repairing his car, while Assistant Ranger Gray spent ten days on fire patrol, eleven days on fire lines, eight days packing supplies, and a day on car repairs. For September, they worked on trails, burned brush, collected seed, and hiked fifteen days on fire patrol. All in all, a very quiet year.[27]

By 1923, as it prepared for its twenty-fifth anniversary, and rechristening as the Dominion Forest Service, the DFB reigned over a domain of 273,000 square miles, an estate larger than western Europe. It had brought to this wild territory both social order and commercial purpose. Extraordinarily, for confederated Canada, it had established a national agenda that seemingly transcended the ceaseless sparring of provincial politics. It readied for a confederation-spanning conference on forest fire protection, a unique, and uniquely nationalizing, event. It helped to align Canadian interests in conservation with those of the United States, especially through the shared, mirror-image institutions of federal forestry. It prepared to bring Canada into international prominence by hosting the second British Empire Forestry Conference in Ottawa. The chief vehicle behind this astonishing dominion – its political imperative – had been fire protection. When Robert Campbell resigned that year, it was no surprise that his successor was the redoubtable E.H. Finlayson, a man whose entire career had been a study in practical, unremitting fire control.

Protecting the Parks

While small in area, their significance could be huge, and while negligible in revenue, their importance to politically thriving urban constituencies could be immeasurable. While by the onset of the twentieth century, Canada's parks were symbolic and decorative, by the onset of the twenty-first, they were a major force in fire management. Especially as the dominion forest system collapsed, Canada's national parks became the primary means to float discussions beyond the political calculus of axe and dollar. But that narrative began inauspiciously.

It commenced in the Bow Valley, where the Canadian Pacific Railway sought to bond a hot springs on Sulphur Mountain with a lavish hotel. An order-in-council established the Hot Springs Reserve in November 1885. The American inspiration was less with Yellowstone, with which

Banff, as it was renamed in 1930, would be compared, than with Arkansas Hot Springs. Canada's fabled national parks began as a resort. But as the gazetted lands expanded to embrace monumental scenery and charismatic fauna, the model shifted to that of the forest reserves that could treat wildlife as the reserves did old woods and could develop recreational resources by analogy to timber berths. The chief obsession of both was to shut out agriculture and its ungainly sprawl. The hot springs, enlarged, became Rocky Mountain National Park in 1887.

That Banff was awash with fire boosted the argument that it needed fire protection on the model of state-sponsored forestry. Natives, trappers, explorers, transients of all kinds left the great valleys of Banff and the surrounding hillsides in black stumps and ash. Construction of the railway left slash and sparked fires along its roughshod right-of-way and apparently stimulated burning wherever its shadows fell. In 1884, Dr. A.P. Coleman, a professor of geology at the University of Toronto, contrasted the views from Mount Whitehorn near Lake Louise. To the rising crest of summits, there was "clean air" and majesty; to the valley, "a trail of smoke," burning timber, and "sullied" view. Crossing to the peak, he had passed through "a swath of burnt woods – an abomination of desolation made up of black soil, black standing trunks, and black fallen logs." Superintendent G. A. Stewart agreed, declaiming in his first report how "in past years forest fires have ravished portions of the Park and left spots of desolation and extensive bands of dead timber, disfiguring the natural beauties of certain tracts." He proposed to sell off the charred residue as firewood and to construct roads as firebreaks, while others suggested that dams would help to staunch the flood of flame.[28]

The 1889 outbreak questioned whether even such measures could break a full-blown conflagration. Superintendent Stewart redirected "all the men on the works" and warned "the inhabitants" to fight the "demon" by hewing firebreaks and watching for spot fires. Through the heavy lodgepole pine around the park's western border, "no human efforts could avail to arrest the flames"; only the bare summits arrested their surge, leaving firefighters to swat out "the sparks and masses of burning wood carried by the wind over the mountain peaks." Miraculously, the park proper mostly escaped. Over the next decade, however, four more major burns branded deep scars, while an 1891 fire managed to burn over much the same terrain as the main flames of 1889. Banff village narrowly escaped a serious fire in 1897, although it could not evade serious flooding that followed as the burnt slopes became "chutes" that channelled runoff into a "wild torrent."[29]

Throughout the coming decade, threatening fires, mostly kindled along the railway, almost annually caused a callout of men and frightened villagers. By 1908, the scene demanded attention. Parliament approved funding for a Warden Service to provide protection for timber and game and placed dominion parks under the Forestry Branch since the crucial tasks of the two agencies seemed to be indistinguishable. A 1909 survey of what would become Kootenay National Park by H.R. MacMillan documented a landscape abraded by burning: "The mouths of all the larger valleys have reverted to prairie as have the foothills, though proof is not lacking that both were once heavily timbered." Flames swept along the valley channels, then overflooded into the hills. "Fires have also cleared the whole of the rest of the territory within the last thirty years." Administration can mean "but one thing, fire protection," which is precisely what the Warden Service was intended to provide.[30]

Banff Superintendent Howard Douglas quickly observed the encouraging consequences. A new "plan of fire and game guarding," "a competent staff" of experienced men under a chief, careful monitoring of the cutting, mining, roading, and tramping abundant throughout the park, all made fires less frequent and damaging. The deputy minister of the interior noted approvingly that "special attention was given in all the parks to the perfecting of the fire and game protective organization and to the development of the system of roads and trails." Superintendent Douglas concluded presciently that, if the system matured, and if "chance" fire were further dampened, it would be "only a question of [a] few years" until the threat would vanish, save along the railway proper.[31]

That is more or less what happened. By 1919, despite the war years, the Warden Service in the Rockies had expanded from a staff of four to forty-six; avidly adopted power pumps; experimented with fire retardants; and launched serious publicity campaigns to abolish careless fires. Soon the Rocky Mountain parks found themselves under the aerial fire patrols mustered by the Forestry Branch. The big fires in the Rockies – 1910, 1914, 1919 – passed over Banff like a summer breeze. An outbreak in 1920, probably from embers lofted over the Continental Divide from the west, forced the park to call upon the RCMP for assistance, while Banff itself began to mumble that complacency had allowed the perimeter fire guards to overgrow. Revealingly, a large fire along the Red Deer River in 1921, its record inscribed in the stand ages of lodgepole, went unreported, while smaller fires from locomotives were tallied religiously.[32]

When the Dominion Parks Branch joined the 1924 Forest Fire Conference, they did so intrepidly, unwilling to yield significance or competence to forest reserves, either federal or provincial. Commissioner of Dominion

Parks J.B. Harkin freely boasted that the lands under his administration, while not strictly commercial, were nonetheless in the business of "selling or exporting scenery." These days, he admitted, one had "to put the commercial side of things forward in order to get appropriations." That meant that Dominion Parks, although "only the small brother of the Forestry Branch so far as forest protection" was concerned, had an even greater imperative to protect their wooded estate, a prime feature for tourists, "for if we do not protect our forests we have nothing."[33]

So the parks insisted on intensive protection, relied on a common staff to watch game and timber, and applied fundamentally the same methods as their siblings in the Forestry Branch. By 1924, fire claimed 60 percent of the protection budget, while game tallied 40 percent. A Dominion Parks fire inspector oversaw the medley from Ottawa. Park fires originated from the usual sources, although prospectors and trappers were morphing into recreationists. The railways faded as a fire cause once the construction phase had withered and the Railway Commission had clamped down on stray sparks and imposed right-of-way cleanup. Lightning, mercifully, did not much afflict the crown jewel of the system, Banff. Mostly park staffs fretted over their visiting throngs, every member of which was a "potential cause of fire." Accordingly the staff relied on publicity, "education," and close patrols, particularly for motorists. And the parks invested heavily in infrastructure and equipment. All their experience, Harkin explained, went "to prove that it pays to go in for equipment." The parks spent almost as much on cabins, trails, telephones, hoses, and pumps as on the salaries of its wardens. As measured by burned area, the outcome amply justified that policy.[34]

Banff remained the flagship, and the exemplar, but the Rockies boasted other parks as well. In 1919, a dry year complicated by postwar adjustments, the parks collectively had 119 fires; by 1923, that number had plummeted to 38, half of which were associated with the Canadian Pacific and Canadian National Railways but spread negligibly and came under the tightening vice of railway suppression. Averages can mean little in the Canadian context, and comparing one year with another even less, but the plunge in the parks' burned area was real. It represented an absolute reduction in fire load; in the number of starts, in the areas blackened. The chief reason lay less with aggressive fire control than with a shift in human occupancy, a rapid replacement of aboriginal firebrands, wandering woodsmen, migratory loggers, and slashing settlers with a more compliant clientele of urban-based tourists, willing to restrict their flames to designated campgrounds and firepits.[35]

Among its most effective propaganda, Harkin pointed to a stretch of three to four miles along the Banff-Windemere road, the "most ghastly burn I think I ever saw," a mature forest reduced to gaunt snags and blackened stumps. It reminded him that *brûlé* was to the dominion parks what slash was to the national forests, "the most serious menace we have." Much of that mess the parks had inherited. Worse, Harkin believed that slash, broadly defined, could never be overcome until its disposal could pay for itself. Although Banff could not sell it off as salvage, or convert it to dendrochemicals, it could turn the scene to profit through propaganda. The park posted notices at each end of this melancholy spectacle, alerting motorists to the horror of wildfire, a "bit of advertising" about which "everybody" talked. The commissioner of dominion parks avidly confessed that nothing in his experience with fire control had affected him so much as that dismal scene. He reasoned that impact on visitors, particularly children, was probably incalculable.[36]

A few favourable years did not, however, constitute regime change. The parks' statistics were a moving target, reliant on politics and weather. In 1922, Wood Buffalo National Park was established, the largest wildlife preserve in North America, a colossal patch of highly flammable boreal forest. Over the coming decades, it would become the black hole of fire protection in the Canadian park system, both an anomaly and a dark paradigm. Meanwhile a cascade of droughty seasons rolled over the Rocky Mountain parks, especially those west of the divide. In 1925, roughly 20,000 hectares burned through them, mostly in a single conflagration in the Chaba-Athabasca River region of Jasper. Official reports cited extensive *brûlé* as an impediment, along with the peculiar geography that had "the fire coming in from four valleys" to a common focus. The next year dry lightning blasted Yoho and Kootenay. The six-week firefight that resulted drew in help from the provinces, the RCMP, the CPR, and other parks, and, while officials argued that the "opening up of the forest" along the Banff-Windemere road would be "an improvement from the scenic point of view," most observers considered the outbreak an embarrassment and a challenge. A conference of superintendents and chief wardens later that year, chaired by the supervisor of forest protection from Ottawa, led to the development of a new portable power pump but no structural reforms.[37]

For a while, Banff itself seemed blessed. The parks overall had not yet learned the truth that fires, like droughts, came episodically and that a few favourable years did not by themselves constitute a permanent revolution. The park suffered through big fires in 1928 and 1929. Meanwhile, Wood Buffalo began to expand. Once protected, the remnant herd of 500 wood bison quickly multiplied and outgrew the designated habitat. In 1925 and 1928, several thousand plains bison were shipped from southern Alberta to co-occupy the reservation. The park proved too small and in 1926 was enlarged to encompass the Delta region, to which the introduced herds migrated. If they fretted at all, officials worried more about bovine tuberculosis and possible culling than about fire, for over such a remote and immense terrain, fire ranging was a cosmetic gesture. Administratively, Wood Buffalo resembled a forest reserve to protect wildlife rather than woods. There was scant choice but to leave unculled its ancient rhythms of burning.

By 1930, there was little by way of fire administration to distinguish between the dominion's parks and its forests. Both applied similar means to similar ends, and if the parks measured success by tourist days instead of board feet they no less tallied fires and burned areas as a protection standard. Politically, however, the chasm widened. Parliament reverted the forests to the provinces, effectively gutting the Dominion Forestry Branch, but it enacted a National Parks Act that granted special status to those lands and explicitly chartered that they "be maintained and made use of so as to leave them unimpaired to the enjoyment of future generations." In that double stroke, the big had become tiny, and the tiny had become durable. The parks emerged as the sole fire agency of the dominion, the only one that actually managed fires on its own lands, which was the only meaningful expression of political power. Whatever authority the federal government might exercise by way of reforming fire policy would have to come through the parks. A practical outcome, however, had to wait until most of the century had passed.

Fire Conservancy by Commission

The Forestry Branch had ample rivals. Mostly, of course, it quarrelled with the provinces, which, outside the west, held forests, towns, and crown lands in their tenacious grip and remained deeply jealous of federal ambitions. But national competitors also appeared, of which the Commission of Conservation was for a while the most formidable. The forces behind it blew from the south, the implacable stirrings of a climate of reformist opinion. The American conservation movement had found national political expression in the 1908 Governor's Conference, which inspired further efforts to translate the progressive agenda into a more durable form. One outcome was to create an autonomous National Conservation Commission to prevent Congress from meddling too unhelpfully; another was to broaden the project beyond the United States. This led to a North

American Conservation Conference, held in 1909, which urged upon all three countries (and Newfoundland) similarly permanent commissions. The proposal was delivered by Gifford Pinchot as a personal emissary of the soon-retiring President Roosevelt. That alone guaranteed that forestry would figure hugely.

National politics soon shredded this exercise in premature continentalism. Mexico and Newfoundland did nothing. A revanchist Congress refused to fund the National Conservation Commission, which stumbled along with academic reports and little political clout. But the Laurier administration – seeing in the scheme "a good political measure for a government long in office and a little short of ideas" – bulled ahead. The proposal finessed around provincial objections by denying the commission any real powers. It existed to investigate and advise, rather like a quasi-permanent royal commission. It relied on a small budget, which it leveraged by research contracts with academics and co-operative agreements with provinces.[38]

Initially the commission found common cause with the Forestry Branch, supporting most of Campbell's initiatives and chastising its political challengers. What they most shared was a horrific fire scene, particularly railways that had often become corridors of cinders, their adjacent lands burned not once but over and again until even berries shrivelled. Writing in 1912, J.H. White, the first forester graduated from the University of Toronto, sketched the appalling wreckage possible: "From Sudbury to Port Arthur, generally speaking, the country along the [Algoma Central] railway has been burned at one time or another for the entire distance of 550 miles. Not much has escaped except the spruce swamps. The burned areas have been partially recovered by temporary stands of poplar, white birch and jack pine, either pure or in mixture. But to a vast extent the country has been burned so repeatedly that there is nothing left but bare rock." Such locales were the poster child for fire conservancy, particularly appalling to urban constituencies.[39]

Together the commission and the Forestry Branch argued for a common agency to control all aspects of public forestry and even oversee its extension, through suitable regulations, onto private lands. It was not simply the provinces and the dominion that were out of sync, for the institutional inconsistency extended to dominion crown lands as well since within the Department of the Interior the Forestry Branch oversaw "forestry" and protection, while the Timber and Grazing Branch allocated timber berths and collected revenue. One program spoke to ideals, which Canada could project to the world, the other to a grubby politics of rough logging and royalties. Here was Canadian forestry's Potemkin village. The Commission

Fire follows axe and rail. *Top*, typical slash left after logging. *Bottom*, land burned to barrens by repeated fires along rail rights-of-way.

of Conservation, full of thoughtful, earnest reports, yet without powers to enact them, belonged with the visionaries.

Yet in its authority to investigate issues of its choosing by hiring independent researchers, in its capacity to transcend entrenched bureaucratic interests, and in its ability to publicize and hence appeal to public opinion, the commission did hold implicit powers. Its Committee on Forestry quickly became one of its crown jewels, a perfect test case for the application of state-sponsored engineering to correct wasteful practices. The committee chair, Bernhard Fernow, lent it both credibility and professional authority. (Fernow himself recognized that, while the commission was "educative" and "without executive functions," it had "some good men ... and as usual some blowers.") Within forestry, moreover, no topic was more powerful and less contentious than fire protection, so Fernow easily ensured that a national fire survey would become among the first topics addressed, a task that folded smartly into the Committee on Forest Fires that he chaired for the Canadian Forestry Association. Quickly, shrewdly, the committee latched onto the railway fire problem for special attention. The issue promised technical fixes, it overleaped provincial politics, it was publicly visible. Snuffing out rail fires could become an exemplar for resolving all the disputes that vexed Canadian forestry.[40]

The task fell, with fitting symbolism, to Clyde Leavitt, an American forester, a former secretary to Fernow at Cornell, a supervisor with the US Forest Service, and in 1912 a man ready to become a professor at his alma mater, the University of Michigan. When he queried Fernow about accepting the post, his mentor advised him that forestry education in the United States was "being overdone" and urged Leavitt, instead, to enlist in the Canadian fire campaign. He did, becoming chief forester for the Commission of Conservation and, simultaneously, chief fire inspector for the Board of Railway Commissioners. This split appointment (with his salary from the commission) meant that Leavitt could fuse the rupture between the commission's ability to advise and the forests' need for action. On behalf of the commission, he published two treatises, *Forest Protection in Canada, 1912* and *Forest Protection in Canada, 1913-1914*, marvels of synthesis and practical wisdom about suitable legislation and field operations. Their core was the orgy of railway-related burning, of course, but they included reports from the committee on allied topics such as brush disposal, co-operative fire protection with provinces and industry, statistics, forest reserves, and forest surveys.[41]

What made this particular problem inspired was that virtually all the

Fire protection rides the rails. A fire patrolman rides a velocipede, a bicycle on rails, searching for the endless sparks left by early trains.

railways had national rather than provincial charters. The problems could be addressed through federal institutions, thus making it amenable to conservationist visions. In 1912, the Railway Act expanded provisions of its 1903 antecedent. The Board of Railway Commissioners then issued Order 16570, which laid out an ambitious program of detailed prescriptions to prevent fires along rights-of-way; the next year it extended these provisions to most of eastern Canada. As chief inspector, Leavitt had the authority to enforce those provisions, and he did, initially with the assistance of the Forestry Branch and select provincial entities. The outcome was remarkable. Within a handful of years, the railway fire issue had gone from a free-floating crisis, a hysteria of rhetoric, to a fixable problem, the very paradigm of how an efficient corps of technocrats could reform sloppy habits and wasteful apathy. The most stubborn difficulties remained with those railways that lay outside federal jurisdiction, and thus a vivid reminder of how thoroughly conservation relied on a national body to overcome deep local inertias and how feeble the commission could be in the absence of a conduit to genuine power. For provincially chartered railways, the commission depended on moral suasion, a compound of showing how reform could pay while shaming the slackers into passing separate legislation modelled on Order 16570. What made the program

Fire patrolmen on a speeder, a motorized velocipede.

work was Leavitt's dual bureaucratic citizenship and his membership in the professional caste of foresters. The future of Canadian fire protection, as had proved true for the United States, lay with formal co-operation among agencies.

Naturally, the committee sought to extend this paragon to other arenas. If railways could clean debris from their rights-of-way, then loggers could scrub their cutovers of slash, and settlers, under a proper permit system, could contain their clearing fires. As settlement wound down from its own exhaustion, the provinces sought to emulate what they understood as the dominion model, catalyzed by a series of violent firequakes and their smouldering aftershocks in the clay belt of Ontario. Singular conflagrations were less catastrophic, however, than the continued abrasion of serial burning. Under commission sponsorship, C.D. Howe scrutinized this phenomenon in Peterborough County. His conclusions were dismal. Bad as the lumbering had been, the burning that inevitably followed was worse, and even more distressing was the train of fires that passed over. Only a third of the logged pinery had been burned once; another third had suffered twice, a sixth had been burned three times, and another sixth had been burned "many times." Each fire stripped away the capacity of the land to recover; fewer saplings, fewer seed trees, less soil survived. Under such conditions, forestry was impossible. Howe concluded, "it is clear, the forest has been a very unsafe place for trees."[42]

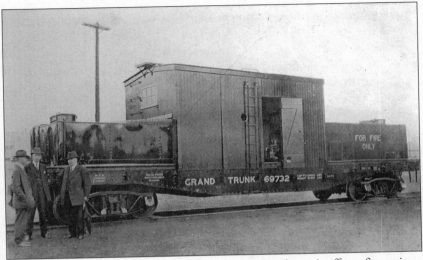

A special fire tank car designed to combat fires alongside railways, in effect a fire engine on rails.

Yet as with railways, the fire problem seemed solvable, granted the proper system and sufficient political will. In fact, it was mandatory if conservation was not to be a chimera. What the committee meant by conservation was clear: conservation sought to reduce waste, to spare critical resources for future generations, to apply "technical knowledge" to yield "revenue forever." Forestry was scientific agronomy for trees. It was "merely the business of handling timberlands in an improved way for perpetual revenue," a species of "regulated lumbering," whose "intensity of practice is in direct co-ordination with the status of that industry." On such a political economy, government, industry, academics, professional engineers, and conservation propagandists could agree, as they could on the unblinking necessity for fire protection.[43]

They did not, however, agree on much else. Foresters insisted that no sensible choice could be made without formal inventories. The venerable Dr. Fernow devised the model, a two-year survey summarized in *Forest Conditions of Nova Scotia,* published by the commission in 1912. The next year British Columbia and Saskatchewan launched studies, assisted by both industry and the DFB, although the latter faded away when illness wasted its investigator. An effort to replicate the effort in Ontario failed to leap beyond the Trent watershed. Yet with or without adequate statistics, there was much the committee could advocate based on existing field knowledge. Both the dominion and the provinces could expand formal reserves, industry and government could co-operate in establishing fire protective associations like those in Quebec, loggers and settlers could contain slash burning. In its first annual report, the commission identified as a "fact," indisputable and self-evident to all, that "the devastation of forests by fire is going on at a rate that is simply appalling when one considers the ultimate and not far distant result." Fire protection would not sit obediently and quietly to the side while learned philosophers and grasping politicians quibbled over abstract principles and dallied over constitutional quirks.[44]

Fire of course transcended the forest, and most Canadians experienced it not free-burning in the boreal forest but in their homes and towns, and it is no surprise that the rationalizing impulse of the commission should also extend to cities. The commission quickly learned that Canada's record of fire protection was no better in its towns than in its forests. Against the historical grain elsewhere, North America experienced an increasing fire loss that exceeded, "per unit of population, the waste of any other five civilized countries combined." Every year, as J. Grove Smith of the Canadian Fire Underwriters' Association informed the commission in 1916, "flames consume a value equal to 11,000 dwellings worth $2,000 each and housing 50,000 people, or, in effect, more than all the dwellings in London, Ontario." There were places where wildfire violently fused town and country such as those that had blasted new settlements in the clay belt earlier in the year. It was less obvious how the burning of the Parliament building and the burning of Banff might be coupled.[45]

The links were several, which Grove identified as the three "great factors" that resulted in fires: "physical hazard, moral hazard, and temperamental hazard." Physical hazard referred to the built environment, which in Canada consisted largely of wooden structures, which not coincidentally burned like the forests from which they came. Moral hazard included bad behaviour that led to deliberate fire setting. While the specific reasons for incendiarism differed in woods and towns, they shared a common criminal intent. By temperamental hazard, Grove meant "the habit of the people, the state of mind which condones carelessness, is indifferent to its effects, and frequently denies its very existence." This was "undoubtedly" the principal "cause for the immense number of fires in Canada," a dominion of burning of which the public was largely unaware or, if knowledgeable, unconcerned.[46]

Thus, the two realms of fire did in fact partake of common elements in the guise of sloppy practice, vicious acts, and appalling apathy. Solutions required some engineering standards, economic incentives, a quasi-governmental organ of oversight; these were the identical needs of Canada's forests. What was good for the woods was good for the towns and vice versa. Treating slash was equivalent to installing codes for city dwellings. In truth, it was less the case that bush fire protection became a model for urban fire services than the reverse. What the coupling suggests is that urban perceptions became the standard for judging "waste" in the woods. The idea that fire might have a legitimate role in urban ecology would have seemed preposterous or worse to the commission, even as cities renewed themselves on the awful ashes of their last conflagrations. The commission's charge was to identify and reduce the wastage of precious resources. In the end, governments and their scientific specialists argued for conservation as a means to prevent economic losses, of which flame and smoke were so egregious an example as to become an archetype for all the rest.

The task of practical reform fell to municipalities, insurance companies, and education. Government responsibility remained where the government had unique responsibilities, notably crown lands. It was one thing for political entities, like a threatened community in the clay belt, to rally against the flames. It was another for government organs at the local or provincial or even national level to agree to surrender sovereignty and patronage after the flames had passed. Speaking with the authority of European forestry, Fernow thundered that forestry was a "*distinctly State business,*" that those forests thrived best that existed under public ownership, and that, on an implicitly Prussian model, a single bureaucracy was the ideal medium for administering technical knowledge over the long term. Confederated Canada offered a very different realm, one of jealously guarded political frontiers that even the threat from fire could not break down.[47]

Whatever value agencies such as those proposed by Fernow had for shielding the woods from public passions, they seemed to have little for shielding them from rival agencies. The provinces were not about to yield control over woods and waters to institutions in Ottawa; the Timber and Grazing Branch refused to submit to the Forestry Branch; the Forestry Branch openly challenged the Commission of Conservation for control over the agenda of forest conservation. When the commission's chairman, Clifford Sifton, overstepped himself in a controversy involving hydropower, the postwar Tory government found ways to strangle the Liberal viper in its midst. The commission could study, advise, harangue, but its power depended on the willingness of Canada to listen. It had committed to a higher standard of research and had forced rivals such as the Forestry Branch to conduct their own; it had worked well as an institutional flywheel, helping to smooth the lumpy, separate pistons of forest conservation across the dispersed jurisdictions of confederated

Canada; it had sought indirect rule, a governance by example and standard. But all this could work only to the extent that the institutions with power were freely willing to be synchronized or could be made willing by their political minders or the voice of public opinion.

National institutions thrive amid pressure, particularly from the outside. After the Great War and its postwar slump, those institutions declined, and a sorting out occurred amid the institutional rivals for control over fire. Sifton resigned in 1918; the commission was dissolved in 1921. The immediate outcome was a "rush for the spoils." Increasingly, particularly after 1923, the Dominion Forest Service, under the energetic leadership of E.H. Finlayson, became the self-appointed and singular voice of forest conservation. It amassed more and more of the functions of a national forestry institution. The primary means by which it seized more authority was fire protection, which everyone could agree was a national problem but which no one else could do much about. The power behind the Forestry Branch was precisely its ability to field a firefighting force, and that it could do because it held a vast estate.[48]

Fire Conservancy by Machine

From the beginning, the Canadian scene was a paradox, matching the world's most savage fires against its most advanced machines, as free-burning flame met internal combustion. For Canada, however, combining the primitive with the technologically modern was far from unusual. Harold Innis had early pointed out the apparent incongruity of the Canadian Pacific Railway, the industrial tip of global capitalism's spear, thrusting through the Canadian wilderness, and later observed the necessity, for a country that was both modern and dispersed, to seize the latest developments in communication and transportation. Donald Worster, less kindly, pointed out the industrial basis for Canada's exploitation of its natural wealth, likening the country to a technological crack baby. Fire protection by machine had a long pedigree.[49]

Fire's hazards and fire's controls fed one into the other. Industrial logging, powered by steam, required, as it made possible, industrial fire protection. The locomotive as a source of ignition also morphed into the locomotive as a means of rapid access and pumps; the smokechaser on a velocipede was as common as rail section patrols. Automobiles brought access to visitors; converted to forest fire engines, they carried firefighters to the scene. Telephones and especially wireless shattered the distance that had left remote fires to burn for days. It was the quintessential Canadian conundrum: vast distances, costly labour, expensive capital, bulk commodities. But what forested Canada had in abundance, save along the eastern Rockies, was water. Eastern Canada, notably the Shield, was awash with ponds, bogs, streams, and later reservoirs; the northwest was laced with rivers and muskegs; the Rockies shed streams; and British Columbia, west of the Cordillera, was practically a rainforest. If Canada had fire, it also had fire's natural retardant. The apparent solution, and a magnificent expression of Canadian genius for directed knowledge, was to apply capital to acquire equipment to move water. Canada became the world authority on portable pumps and hoses.

Without such devices, fire protection was quixotic. But the technology only worked as a system in that each part demanded the others. Pumps were meaningless unless they could be moved to the fire; they could not be moved until they shrank and their mode of transport bulked up; they were, in any event, worthless unless the fires could be fought while small, which required the capacity to find them quickly and communicate their locations. Beyond the bold but largely symbolic era of fire ranging by dog sled and canoe, fire protection demanded a package of machinery. That fire suppression was so firmly welded to logging meant that the access and technology each required could advance together. Perhaps more fundamentally, industrial machinery provided a common medium for the Canadian fire community that politics never could. Canadian fire officers would come to share technology, the ends to which they would commit technology, and the belief that efficiency was the measure of success; they would not share institutions. That technology imposed its own politics of power was a consideration they ignored in their determination not to surrender the levers and throttles that governed the relationship between province and dominion.

A mechanical pump had to be tough, light, and powerful. The earliest engines were none of these, but in a mechanical age when cars, motorcycles, outboard motors, and airplanes boomed, technological advances came quickly. While fire control had only to adapt general developments to its peculiar needs, it went beyond modifications, for it saw that mechanical leverage made possible what was otherwise primitive. Axes, shovels, mattocks, and water buckets could not overcome slash burns or face down flames in the boreal woods. Pumps and the means to get them to the front could.[50]

Locomotives hauled early generation pumps, which ran off steam, and later more compact models, which burned gasoline. The Fairbanks-Morse Company advertised gas-powered machines in 1911-12. Where fires were common, special cars with pumps and tanks, like urban fire engines on rails, were positioned for rapid response. The Railway Commission created a robust market. In 1915, H.C. Johnson, a fire inspector with the commission, worked with Fairbanks-Morse to create a more truly portable pump for dominion parks. Weighing 130 pounds, the prototype could be hauled by a small locomotive or a suitably engineered automobile or even by hand or horse over trails with a special wheeled truck. It was promptly shipped to Banff, where it spent the fire season splashing twenty gallons a minute onto slash burns. It exceeded anything anywhere "in Canada or the United States," Johnson exulted.[51]

Orders poured in. The dominion parks wanted another six units; the Ontario Forest Protection Service purchased pumps; so did the St. Maurice, the Laurentide, and the Ottawa River Forest Protective Associations. Competing companies arose, including Evinrude, distributed by Watson and Jack Company of Montreal. The BC Forest Service worked with the Wonder Pump and Engine Company of Vancouver to produce a single-cylinder model and bought thirty-four in 1919. Modifications continued. In 1921, British Columbia's chief forester declared that "the use of this mechanical means" marked "the greatest step forward" for fire control in recent years. The agency realized that its crews could "not go out and fight a fire with their bare hands, a shovel and a wet sack," so it invested in hardware "as fast as funds became available." That year alone BC foresters pumped an estimated five million gallons of water; by 1923, they had sunk a quarter of a million dollars into pumps and "other permanent equipment," which required another "$50,000 a year to keep that up to standard." When float planes demonstrated they could haul such pumps, the range of accessibility seemed boundless. Even along the semi-arid Rockies, smokechasers were as likely to haul portable pumps as shovels. Canadians enthusiastically staged demonstrations to awed colleagues touring with the British Empire Forestry Conference.[52]

More orders, more companies, more improvements. Within a decade, engineers had shrunk the bulky, often temperamental machines into progressively more compact, lighter, and reliable units. Relay pumping allowed ever longer lines of hose to run; indeed, the hose became more a limitation than the engine. Linen hoses were costly, easily damaged, cumbersome to carry, awkward to recover in the woods, and tedious to prepare for reuse. Pumps could be interchangeable – fire services typically had units from several manufacturers – but hoses and their couplings often were not. Thus, when during the 1930s the National Research Council created a subcommittee on fire protection, it devoted an extraordinary amount of attention to hoses. An outsider might well have considered the focus obsessive, but Canadian fire control depended on Canadian water, and the pump and hose were the means to connect quenching agent with flame. Over time, Canadian foresters turned more and more to Canadian manufacturers. Watson and Jack Company (later Wajax) ultimately came to dominate the global market for portable fire pumps.

At least pumps were a product; companies were willing to invest in improvements. Other research had no commercial payoff. Its development devolved onto state forestry organizations or the dominion. On the example of the US Forest Service, the Forestry Branch had sought a research mission, and with a recommendation from the Dominion Council for Scientific and Industrial research Cameron got one in 1917.

The silvicultural argument was simple: Canada could not sustain a modern economy of forest products with a folk culture or mere commercial enthusiasm. The same applied to fire protection. A major boost came in 1919, when the Department of Militia and Defence solicited help in managing its forests around the training camp at Petawawa. It had first appealed to Clyde Leavitt, then forester with the Commission of Conservation, but the scheme for converting Petawawa into a full-service experimental station went to Cameron. The breakthrough came, however, after the collapse of the Commission of Conservation. The Dominion Forestry Branch quickly mopped up the commission's extensive research projects in Ontario, Quebec, and New Brunswick and, when it reorganized in 1923, created a research division under H.G. Wright, which continued traditional inquiries into silviculture. New projects were added, all intended to transfer research into applications. The outcome pleased Finlayson, who discerned "considerable significance" in the enlightened public's recognition of "the practical application of scientific methods" and by implication the role of the Forestry Branch "in the scheme of economic development throughout Canada." The Petawawa site evolved into a major forest experiment station.[53]

Fortuitously, however, that year two American foresters, J.V. Hoffman and W.B. Osborne, published the results of a multi-year investigation into the role of relative humidity as a measure of fire danger. While their concern was slash, the Berkeley fire of that year provided a vivid demonstration of how plunging relative humidity could magnify fire hazard. The hope soared that in relative humidity, which could be measured simply with sling psychrometers or more elaborately with fixed-station hygrothermographs, fire officers had a robust index by which to evaluate the threat from fire, especially in slash. On this count, they could look to the United States, eagerly applying relative humidity as an objective criterion to regulate logging during periods of high danger. When the relative humidity dropped below a certain point, officials could close the woods to further work, thereby avoiding the random spark or rubbing chain that could ignite parched debris.

Granting such authority to relative humidity put a premium on better weather forecasts so that agencies could anticipate, not simply react. This the federal Meteorological Service should have been able to provide, and a stream of petitions from fire and forestry organizations beseeched the dominion to strengthen its network of weather stations and, no less urgently, to broadcast that information in a timely manner. All parties seemed to agree that this was a good idea. The problem, as always, was getting the political parts to align and to nail down funds. Some provinces bulled ahead, some lagged behind, the feds talked. But the hard-data linkage between ambient humidity and how vigorously slash burned welded fire behaviour to weather predictions.

In 1925, John Patterson of the Meteorological Service and James G. Wright of the DFB reviewed the requirements for a more systematic program. Afterward, Wright proposed to Finlayson a formal research project on fire danger rating. Field trials with duff hygrometers did not commence until 1928, when Herbert W. Beall, a young forester, joined him as an assistant. A year later Wright and Beall began a full-bore inquiry that sought to identify the quantitative relationship between all the readily measurable meteorological factors and the actual moisture of fine fuels, which they understood to be the critical factor in a fire's behaviour. Finlayson happily reported that, "as a result of this work, it is now definitely known precisely what effect a given set of weather conditions has upon the inflammability of the forest fuels in the white pine and the red pine type." That exercise marked the embryonic origin of modern Canadian fire research.[54]

The real breakthrough – what became both the instrument and the emblem of industrial fire suppression – was aircraft. They did for the political economy of fire what the railways did for wood, wheat, and minerals. The effect on fire officers was galvanic; from the first dazzling demonstration, they insisted that only aircraft could solve the problem of fires remote from railways and villages. Interest swelled as, during the Great War, planes evolved beyond the status of a novelty or toy. In 1915, an American fire reconnaissance flew in Wisconsin. Quebec foresters were keen to experiment in 1916-17 but could not work out arrangements. P.Z. Caverhill, chief of the BC Forest Branch, recalled how he had "got a machine that had been making a few flights there, and after the second or

Early aircraft, trial and error, east and west. *Top*, Stuart Graham, left, with his wife and mechanic in *La Vigilance*, for the St. Maurice experiment, a public sensation in 1919. *Bottom*, British Columbia's aborted 1918 experiment, which deposited the pilot in an upstairs bathtub.

third flight it had made for us we crashed it – that was our first experience."
A more official version held that the BC Forest Branch had contracted with
a Vancouver company to make a plane based on the Curtiss H-2. After
the plane crashed (into a roof), the province calculated the full costs of
aerial protection and decided to postpone its rush into the air. Enthusiasts
would have to fight budgets before they fought any fires.[55]

The larger agencies moved in quick-step. The Great War had prodded
the research behind flying, boosted its public appeal (even with the war
grinding on, pilots lectured about the future of forest aviation), and
with the armistice liberated planes and pilots. The idea mesmerized the
Commission of Conservation; the Dominion Parks Branch investigated
the unlikely possibility of zeppelins; in Quebec, the St. Maurice Protective
Association agreed in November 1918 to purchase a "hydroaeroplane" for
patrol. For the next season, it hired a former RAF pilot, Stuart Graham, to
fly two Curtiss flying boats (HS-2L) from Halifax to Three Rivers before
commencing regular patrols.[56]

What made aircraft a working proposition, not simply an exercise in fire-
reconnaissance barnstorming, was the donation by Great Britain of over a
hundred war-surplus aircraft to Canada in June 1919. Hoping to jumpstart
a civilian air-transport industry, the dominion established an Air Board,
charged with both stimulating and regulating civil aeronautics. The board
convened an interdepartmental conference in January 1920 to recommend
projects, with the Dominion Forestry Branch an enthusiastic booster.
The outcome was a constellation of bases located in British Columbia,
Alberta, Manitoba, Ottawa, Quebec, and Halifax. By 1920, there were
reconnaissance flights for British Columbia and Alberta and a year later
similar patrols out of Roberval, Quebec, and Manitoba. New Brunswick
"experimented" with an airplane in 1920 but otherwise contented itself
with observing the results elsewhere in Canada and the United States.
The next year, with enthusiasm still high, the Air Board staged a second
interdepartmental conference and increased operations, especially for fire
patrols and transport. On 1 January 1923, the Air Board was dissolved and
incorporated into a Ministry of National Defence; thereafter the Royal
Canadian Air Force flew any missions required by the dominion. On
the eve of the 1924 Forest Fire Conference, forestry constituted about 60
percent of Canadian flying, and firefighting its largest proportion.[57]

The planes investigated were seaplanes, since Canada's lakes furnished an
endless array of landing areas. The preferred planes were Curtiss HS-2Ls and
later DeHavilland Moths and Vickers Vikings. Across the dry interior west,
boasting only graded landing sites, there was little opportunity for more

than aerial reconnaissance, which Alberta demonstrated enthusiastically but which, all parties agreed, could not pay for itself. (The Alberta flights continued until the DFB erected a network of towers.) Probably British Columbia determined that, much as it craved aircraft, it could not justify planes simply for reconnaissance, although the dominion still flew over some critical landscapes of the railway belt. When, in 1923, the dominion's contribution ended for Quebec, the province paid for the service itself. Ontario first flew in 1920, quickly appreciating the ability of aircraft to extend protection into its own immense northwest, briskly establishing a base near Sudbury and another at North Bay. Subsequently the province decided that it would create its own Provincial Air Service by purchasing the Laurentide Air Service (inheritor of the St. Maurice program), believing that it would ultimately reduce expenses and appreciating no doubt the fickleness of dominion support. Overnight, Ontario acquired the whole package, not only planes but also pilots and service crews.[58]

The costs of aerial fire protection were staggering. They meant that fire detection alone could not justify such a program, nor, in truth, could fire suppression, particularly when seasons were prone to wild swings of booms and busts. Contract planes had to do other jobs, of which mapping was the most suitable, and when fighting fires planes had to deliver men and pumps, not simply observe. Only the largest, most prosperous, most timber-dependent provinces could afford to dabble; the others either had only residual patches of crown land (Nova Scotia) or already established protection systems (New Brunswick) or no perceived fire threat (Prince Edward Island). The prospect had happened at all only because the dominion had inherited a fleet of surplus aircraft and wanted to boost a new mode of commercial transport.

For this ambition forestry, and particularly fire protection, was an obvious outlet. E.J. Zavitz, provincial forester for Ontario, put the matter directly: "In the outlying regions it works out to a question whether you are going to get fire protection or not get it." Either you relied on aircraft, or you had no basis for fire control. Alberta's aerial reconnaissance under the DFB was the only detection possible for the Bow River and Crowsnest reserves. "The solution is aircraft," Zavitz concluded, although the expense is "very great."[59]

Where aircraft triumphed was over the Shield. Colonel H.I. Stevenson, district inspector for the Forestry Branch, explained what aerial protection meant to Manitoba. Citing The Pas as an example, he observed that the district sent out, annually, twelve canoe patrols. His experience was "that a fire always occurs when the patrol is at the opposite end of the three hundred mile district" or that high winds forced the patrols to tie up along the larger lakes "sometimes for a week at a time" until they could cross. "They travel along these narrow waterways and it is impossible for them to know the nature of the country, impossible for them to observe fire at any distance from the rivers and small lakes unless it happens that the wind is blowing in their direction and carries the smoke to them." Sensing a fire was only the beginning, however. They still might "have to hunt a couple of weeks before actually locating the fire. They would travel up on a line of waterways and find the fire twenty miles to one side of them; they would spend a week going up another river, only to find it twenty miles off in some other direction, and, as happened in one case, by that time rain came along and they did not have to reach the fire." So as a practical matter of fire protection, he judged that "canoe patrols are absolutely useless and should be wiped out." (Others disagreed. Gustave Piché from Quebec, for instance, argued for early-season canoe patrols in the mining district to open up portages and contact residents, though he conceded the overall superiority of aircraft. Zavitz agreed.)[60]

This situation changed instantly when, once the Air Board experiment donated planes, fires could be quickly spotted, men and pumps flown to an adjacent lake, and the fires promptly attacked. (That a third of the province under protection was also under water gave float planes virtual carte-blanche entry.) Like others, Stevenson exulted in the "moral" effect of aerial reconnaissance on local populations otherwise indifferent to set-ting or leaving fires. There was nothing that planes could not do. His experience "thoroughly demonstrates the fact that the seaplane can pre-vent fires, can do police work, can detect fires, and that in our part of the country it is the quickest method of getting men and equipment to the fires." If the government wanted fire protection, then it needed planes. The only issues were the proper selection of aircraft and of course perma-nency, which is to say, paying their cost.[61]

On such matters, the conferees deferred to the Royal Canadian Air Force. Wing Commander J.L. Gordon elaborated his understanding that civilian and military requirements were different. The military needed fast, light planes, most of which would be ground-based, while civilians required float planes heavy enough to haul pumps, crews, and supplies. Even the two tasks of fire protection, detection and suppression, led him to believe that each would evolve a machine particularly fitted to its distinctive usage. There was no existing fleet of military aircraft that could be transferred precisely to the purposes of fire control. Clearly, too, each province had special needs that directed it to special suites of aircraft, not easily interchangeable.

Worse, most of the planes dated from 1917 and were barely serviceable for any kind of flying. Either they were replaced quickly, or the program had to be scrapped. In brief, military aircraft differed from what civilian agencies needed, civilians needed more than one kind of aircraft, and each province needed a different mix of aircraft, none of which, not incidentally, was manufactured in Canada. The daring experiment of the past few seasons had been an expedient rather than a precedent.[62]

Then Gordon came to the crux: "Each one who has spoken has expressed a desire for the use of aircraft, and each one has complained about the cost." He reviewed the brief experience of the Air Board. The dominion had wanted to develop a civilian, commercial program of air transport but recognized the exorbitant expense of starting one. The compromise had been the creation of an Air Board to which the RCAF would contribute planes and pilots for several years, a boost that lifted the experiment beyond provincial tinkering. The prospects were dazzling. Everyone thought that aircraft had a future in fire protection, that perhaps planes would *be* the future of fire suppression, and everyone believed that someone else ought to pay for it. Typically that someone was identified as Ottawa. "The problem," concluded Wing Commander Gordon, "appears to me to be absolutely one of costs."[63]

The provinces wanted the federal government to continue the subsidy, while the dominion expected the provinces to assume the burden. Mighty Ontario was willing to try commercial companies in the hope of driving down costs. Commercial Quebec might download some of the charges to private associations such as the St. Maurice. British Columbia, however, argued that its forests were "not merely a Provincial asset but were sources of great national wealth and great national benefit," and hence the dominion should bear "the entire cost of any forest patrol work." A subsidized air service would be a modern version of the subsidized CPR; the BC aerial protection force would provide a nucleus from which "wider expansion" around the dominion could evolve as circumstances warranted. The other provinces were willing enough to use airplanes but not to contribute financially to a national infrastructure.[64]

Even the Dominion Forestry Branch found it impossible to pay for an air fleet and had relied on the Air Board. Wing Commander Gordon himself mused over the possibility of moving military personnel into civilian service, "provided that we do not insist, as we do not intend to, on their trying to play the part of the proudest regiment with their drills and fatigues, snappy uniforms, and so on." He saw no reason why this shouldn't work, "just as the mounted police, being a strictly service unit, if you like, go out and do work of a civil nature." But for that he needed new planes, and they cost serious money. He admitted that he "knew of no way we can bring any greater pressure to bear on the Government in regard to the providing of increased appropriations." Still, Roy Cameron felt justified in arguing to press ahead regardless since in some cases you either "have air patrol or no protection at all" and since, with use, the outlays ought to drop.[65]

There the issue stood, in classic Canadian fashion, deadlocked over the relationship between national and provincial ambitions, expressed by who should pay for what. The various departments of the dominion, including the Air Force, as Gordon put it "on a very plain basis," could not "get the money to do their work." J.J. Lyons, minister of lands and forests for Ontario, then asked whether this state of affairs might not be "evidence that the provinces themselves should take hold of this problem and develop it." His counterpart from British Columbia, T.D. Pattullo, quickly disabused him. "No," he insisted. "The very reverse." While centred on aircraft, the discussion was the archetype of a debate – every Canadian debate – about who should set the purposes of fire protection and who should fund them. This particular discourse about aerial fire control would continue, on precisely these terms, for another sixty years.[66]

The stalemate involved more than posturing and pettiness. It went to the political-economic heart of fire protection. Throughout this era, and well into recent times, Canada's economy remained one that produced staples for export, an economy that demanded cheap transport, which meant canals or later railways, which the provinces separately could not afford; nor could they control the price of commodities, which boomed and collapsed according to global markets. The only solution, as Harold Innis emphatically analyzed, was to merge. Confederation was, in a sense, quite apart from cultural issues and felt senses of identity, a political response to the peculiarities of Canada's relationship to its extractive industries and export markets. Canada needed railways. It needed Confederation to underwrite those rails.[67]

The same logic of macroeconomics applied to fire protection. Fires behaved like staples; burned areas, and hence the costs of fighting them, fluctuated wildly while fixed costs remained high. Over those erratic expenses, driven mostly by weather, Canada had little control; what it could do was dampen the costs of the equipment needed to fight them. In this regard, aerial fire protection did resemble Confederation's early national network of rails, arguing for consolidation rather than separate provincial systems. Particularly with vast extents of western Canada under dominion control, there was a compelling case for a federal subsidy.

The differences, of course, were that fire control could not make the same political claim as wheat. The protection of vacant lands, eventually suitable for timber berths, could not compete with the need to populate the prairies. There were ample berths available; the future could wait. The thesis also demanded that the dominion hold dearly to its western forests as a national asset, a commitment that could provide the nucleus for a national fleet, available to the co-operating provinces. But the provinces were not willing to co-operate in that way. Overall, the political pain would have to exceed even that of the 1921-23 seasons before the provinces would consider cutting a deal with the dominion. When that deal eventually happened, it was, unsurprisingly, the cost and apparent necessity of aircraft that drove it.

Fire Conservancy by Conference: Empire and Dominion

Even a strengthened Dominion Forest Service could not hope to do it all alone. The commission showed abstractly the power of alliances and the danger of political isolation. The US Forest Service, so often a model, demonstrated the practical leverage possible by co-operative programs with state and private institutions and through the use of national conferences. But Canada had other assets as well, unavailable to its American double, by virtue of its status within the British Empire.

One was the institution of the royal commission, an investigative body that could be called upon to inquire into tricky political issues in, ideally, an impartial, quasi-judicial fashion. Commissions offered a medium for analyzing and discussing controversial issues without themselves becoming, as the Commission of Conservation had threatened, permanent bodies with sovereign powers. Although no royal commissions were convened for fire alone, they were arraigned for forestry and, by defining relationships between provinces and the dominion, contributed to the ways and ends of national fire protection. In fact, two such commissions frame the era. The first, in 1923, strengthened the Dominion Forestry Branch. The second, in 1928, eviscerated it.

In August 1923, the Liberal government under W.L.M. King created a royal commission to investigate a political crisis over pulpwood. The incident contained all the essentials of recurring Canadian dilemmas – restrictions in the export market to America, jurisdictional confusion between provinces and the dominion, a clash over current felling and future conservation, spiced by the presence of agricultural settlers. That Finlayson became secretary to the commission enhanced the voice of the Forest Service and allowed it to push for a federal role in all matters pertaining to forests. Shrewdly he channelled the commission's needs for staff and research through the DFS, rushing into the institutional void left by the disbanded Commission of Conservation; he wrote the final report; he argued, in print and by his presence, that the Forest Service was the de facto institution of state-sponsored forestry. In return, the King government rewarded "Finn" by making him the service's new director. The service had, in effect, embarked on a program of expansion by commission and conference.

The timing of the royal commission was almost preternatural, for that year the second British Imperial Forestry Conference convened, offering another web of alliances, with vigorous support for forestry as an instrument for state-sponsored conservation that could also offer a code of best practices. Dominion foresters could look to the empire for advice and sustenance, and as a counterweight to the gravitational distortion of the United States, and throughout the 1920s they did so, often from a position of considerable strength. Britain had early fostered an informal empire of forestry bureaus, beginning with the grand Indian Forest Department, before spreading virtually everywhere, even to such unlikely colonies as Sierra Leone, Trinidad, and Hong Kong. Both the United States and Canada took inspiration from the model. (Forestry even came to Britain itself as part of the backwash from its colonies; the first chair in forestry, at Edinburgh, had gone to William Schlich, previously governor general of the Indian Forest Department and author of the multi-volume *Manual of Forestry.*) Like Fernow, professional foresters had become almost a caste unto themselves, often having more in common with colleagues across oceans than with their proximate government. The oft-knighted foresters, men like Dietrich Brandis and David Hutchins, became grandees of empire; foresters served as the bureaucratic rationalists who reduced wild or primitive woods to productive industries as civil engineers did raw landscapes with railways and dams. They became, by default, the engineering corps of free-burning fire.[68]

Most of these developments occurred after the India Forest Act of 1875, well after Canada had confederated. What prompted Canada to add its link to the chain was the internal empire to the west it acquired at that time and the emerging belief among elites that state-sponsored conservation was an essential program of good government. It was no longer enough to have a pact with loggers that simply exchanged timber for revenue. In this ambition, however, it found itself more in accord with the United States than, say, Cyprus (although Gifford Pinchot, founder of the US

Forest Service, brazenly declared that he hoped to achieve in America what Dietrich Brandis, founder of the Indian Forest Department, had in Asia; the ties were present if diffuse). Nor did the empire much concern itself with Canada as it did with forestry laggards such as arid Australia and new timber colonies such as British Honduras and Burma.

What changed this arrangement was the Great War, which quickly stripped Britain of its own woods and sent it scrambling to secure supplies from its colonies. A royal commission had toured the empire during the war, surveying a cornucopia of natural resource issues, but wood as a strategic material repeatedly haunted its imagination, and while postwar Britain established a Forestry Commission for the home islands, and commenced afforestation projects, a program that would take decades, it had to look elsewhere for its immediate needs. On that score, Canada loomed. Its proximity, size, and history as an exporter meant that it soon dominated the imperial traffic in timber. It was the world's great hewer of wood. In 1920, Britain convened, in London, the first of a series of imperial forestry conferences, partly to rationalize this vital trade, and partly to disseminate, under the doctrine of conservation, shared best practices. The Canadian delegation included Clyde Leavitt and E.H. Finlayson but also the foresters for the Laurentide Paper Company and the provinces of British Columbia and Quebec, the dominant exporters. It was a perfect collusion of politics, money, and woods; its theme was the responsibility of the state for forestry.[69]

Finlayson used the imperial pulpit to browbeat his internal rivals, reserving special scorn for the Commission of Conservation and of course his blood feud with the Timber, Mines, and Grazing Branch. Canada's confusing confederation of responsibilities, he asserted, accounted for its dismal record in forest conservation. What Canada needed was what other forest colonies had (or seemed to have): a unified policy under a single administrator, preferably a forester. The only institution that could satisfy that goal was, of course, the Dominion Forestry Branch. Here, although the US Forest Service remained an exemplar, Finlayson recognized that the empire, with its circuit of state-sponsored forestry bureaus, offered moral support and political cover.

When the delegates met next, in 1923, they did so in Ottawa, with field tours across Canada. The 8 August session, with Lord Lovat, chief of Britain's Forestry Commission, in the chair, commenced a survey of fire protection around the empire, as foresters from Australia, India, Cape Colony, and Cyprus sketched their fire problems and solutions. But none held a candle to Canada. As its forests were the lushest, so its fires were the most extreme. Roy Cameron laid out, in brutal detail, the extent of the crisis. The bill for fire damages, on an average year between 1918 and 1922, he assessed at $14,500,000. Here, in bare economics, lay the justification for fire protection. The forest industry was second only to agriculture in generating the national wealth, and its future "stability" depended on fire protection. Every other administrative problem of forestry was, and "must be," Cameron asserted, subordinate to fire protection. It was "probably safe to say," he concluded, "that 90 percent of the activities of every forest service or organization in Canada" were directed "to organization for, and actual fighting of, forest fires."[70]

As always, their causes were many and familiar. Some were simply due to a natural geography that slammed together coniferous forests, droughts, wind, and lightning. But 90 percent were attributable to the "present state of civilization," namely the pioneering that defiantly and needlessly persisted. People started almost all the truly damaging fires, and the flames gorged on the slash left by land clearing and logging. Canada's outrageous fire scene was attributable not to "government lethargy," Cameron insisted, but to "public apathy." The Railway Commission demonstrated what could be done with sufficient will, for while right-of-way fires were many they were small and amenable to control. The imponderable hazard was slash. Canada's fire problem was, in truth, largely a slash problem, since an estimated 60 percent of a logged forest ended up as slash, which was "the banker's excuse for withholding loans, the insurance company's reason for prohibitive premiums on timber insurance, the fire-fighter's all-but-insurmountable obstacle, the forest community's deadly menace, the lumberman's own worst enemy." No forestry was "possible," Cameron concluded, "where slash exists."[71]

The slash had to go deliberately, or wildfire would take it. The complications were that settlers needed, legitimately, to burn it off and that logging companies could only do likewise if all were subject to the same, uniform mandate. The solution of the first was not merely to regulate burning with a permit system but also to assist, to ensure that what had to get done got done properly. The solution to the second was to legislate slash removal as a universal standard, a stipulation of tenure or logging contracts. All companies had to share the cost, or else those who treated their debris would absorb expenses that would bias their standing in the market, with the cost of their lumber higher than that of competitors who shrugged off the burden. Fire protection, Cameron insisted, must "eventually stand or fall as a business proposition." That meant the cost of slash disposal must be borne equally by everyone.[72]

For all Canada's continental difference and internal variability, he continued, there were universal principles that applied here as everywhere. At their core was the need for any forest service to exercise "complete control of all forest activities on the lands within its jurisdiction" and for a "single direct line of authority" from office to field. In this, Canada had achieved some successes. The Railway Commission was one; so were the better provinces with serious forest departments; but the supreme case was the Dominion Forest Service. It oversaw some 110 million acres of forest, of which 20 percent was gazetted into permanent "forest reserves" or, "as we now prefer calling them, national forests." Because it exercised such administrative control with a permanent infrastructure and staff, progress toward sound fire protection within the DFS was "much further advanced" on the reserves than elsewhere. On dominion lands outside the reserves proper, the branch relied on temporary "fire-ranging staffs" hired as needed or, where traversed by railways, on co-operative agreements with the Railway Commission. The worst situation involved settlers burning along the reserve borders, where not only did slash and reserved woods mingle but dominion and provincial jurisdictions also became murky. The DFS, however, regarded such arrangements as "merely ... a temporary expedient designed to hold fires in check, to a certain extent, until the day comes when all absolute forest lands can be placed in national forests and proper fire-protective organization developed on a permanent basis." In this, Cameron echoed the professional axioms of state-sponsored forestry everywhere.[73]

But his was only one voice in a chorus. The conference heard also from Clyde Leavitt, representing the Railway Commission; from E.J. Zavitz, G.C. Piché, P.Z. Caverhill, G.H. Prince, and J.A. Knight, provincial foresters from Ontario, Quebec, British Columbia, New Brunswick, and Nova Scotia, respectively; from private foresters; and from J.A. Wilson, representing the Royal Canadian Air Force. Dan McLachlin of McLachlin Brothers observed that Champlain himself had reported the country outside Ottawa burning. "So in 1614 the country was on fire; it has been on fire ever since." Fire protection was vital for the contemporary Canadian lumberman because "once a forest has been burned and the seedlings and the soil, to a certain extent, destroyed, you may write that area off your books for one hundred years." Otto Schierbeck of Price Brothers agreed. The "fire situation was the most important question" before the Canadian forest industry. "There is no sense in talking about forestry as long as this fire situation exists." Even foreign guests who thought they had seen a lot of fire were impressed. C.E.S. Cubitt from the Federated Malay States found himself "very much struck by the immensity of the task which the Canadian foresters were attempting," although he politely wondered if "perhaps they are really attempting too much." The consensus of the conference was that perhaps they were.[74]

But no Canadian forester believed that. Fire control, while daunting, was their fundamental charge, "the primary duty, not only of all foresters, but to all true patriots in Canada" and, by implication, to the vitality of the empire. Canada had dutifully contributed to the Great War; it now sought reciprocal help, if only moral, for its own campaign against fire. It looked to the conference "with its great influence and its great authority for exceedingly effective aid and assistance." What the ambivalent example of the United States could not convey, and what the confused politics of the dominion could not instil, perhaps the inspiration of the empire could. Lovat responded by recommending, in time-honoured bureaucratic fashion, that a committee be appointed to produce "constructive suggestions" and that Cameron submit names to constitute that committee.[75]

Such a project suited Ottawa. The imperial recommendation merged smoothly with the royal commission's. In January 1924, with Minister of the Interior Charles Stewart presiding, the Liberal government convened the first Canada-wide forest conference, and not surprisingly, it focused on the one item to which all parties, public and private, provincial and dominion, would willingly submit, fire protection. Following a bitter decade of lethal conflagrations – some practically outside the doorstep of Parliament, the smoke from the most recent fires throwing an embarrassing pall over the scheduled tours of the empire's forestry conference – politicians were ready to listen.

Fire Conservancy by Conference: Dominion and Province

The group that gathered outside Parliament on 7-11 January 1924 for Canada's first Forest Fire Conference assembled, in the words of the official minutes, the "Ministers, Deputy Ministers, Foresters and Officials of Provincial and Federal Forest Services," all gathering "at the call of the Minister of the Interior" to confer on matters "relating to forest fire prevention, protection and control." Nothing like it had happened before, and certainly nothing like it has happened since. Its ranks made it as prominent in its realm as the 1908 Champlain tercentenary was in its.[76]

The incentives for the gathering were many. The convocation brought to life the arid resolution of the 1923 British Empire Forestry Conference. The American example was, as always, ambivalent, if ardent, the "extent of the devastation of the forest wealth of our neighbours to the south" being a spur to preserve Canada's "splendid heritage" by "definite and immediate action." Surely more compelling was the horrific cascade of conflagrations that had ripped Canadian settlements from 1908 to 1923. It probably helped to focus the minds of politicians that the past two decades had witnessed a parallel epidemic of urban fires, blasting provincial capitals in Victoria, Toronto, Quebec, Halifax, offshore St. John's, and not least, on 3 February 1916, the Parliament building itself. Protection from fire of all sorts could claim a significant fraction of the public's attention, and of course it obsessed those charged with administering dominion or provincial crown lands. On this, if on anything, lay a basis for co-operation.[77]

Certainly the dominion hoped as much. Minister of the Interior Stewart noted that the dominion had "some well defined ideas" about how to protect its holdings, and his department, at least, was prepared "to recommend that [a] reasonable amount of assistance be given to the provinces if that should be necessary." Roy Cameron concurred. The importance of fire protection was self-evident: "For a good many of us, it is our life work." Without it, the "practice of forestry" was impossible, and without sound forestry conservation was a hollow shell, and without conservation Canada placed its export economy at risk. That, insisted T.D. Pattullo of British Columbia, was the "whole thing in forest conservation." They were "in competition with other countries and, as between province and province, with ourselves, and the result is that it is impossible for us to do many of the things we would like to do." The conference was, perhaps, a device by which to replace some of that competition with co-operation. Stewart proposed, and the conferees accepted, that they should bar the press from the meetings, issuing a news release at the end of each day while producing a full transcript at the conclusion. He wanted a "heart to heart talk" that they might get what "we are so desirous of obtaining – better protection."[78]

For the first day, each province and the various dominion agencies described their fire organization. The second day concentrated on problems related to settlement and forest reserves. What they sought was to disengage proper agricultural land from forests and with it the slash and fires that settlers, both genuine and bogus, kindled. The flip side of land classification was to firm up the gazetted forest reserves, which the conferees, on the American example, wanted to rename as national forests. The remaining sessions targeted fire prevention, slash disposal, and fire control techniques and concluded with aerial protection and its political valence, "assistance from [the] Federal government."[79]

Almost from the outset they had to confront an uncomfortable paradox, that despite years of experience and increased expenditures 1922-23 was for many agencies their worst season on record. More equipment, more effort, more prevention programs, more funds – and more fires. They all had explanations, not unreasonable. The hazard, as made manifest by forest debris, was expanding, and fires followed the slashed spoor of settler and logger; beetles and budworms turned forests to kindling; even the residue of past burns, the boreal *brûlé,* attracted fires because "people believe that they are valueless" and did not take the "same precautions" they would elsewhere. Much of Canada had been hammered by drought, with 1923 in Quebec, for example, being reckoned by "astronomers [as] ... one of the worst years." Part of the increase, it was argued, was only apparent, the outcome of superior statistics; there were not more big fires, only better reporting about them. And the investment in fire protection remained far below what the situation called for. The woefully understaffed US Forest Service was an order of magnitude better off than its Canadian colleague. Regardless, it was apparent that there would be no simple political equation that linked more funds with fewer burned acres.[80]

The exchanges, as hoped, were candid and for the conferees informative. When the committee on resolutions presented their text, there was unanimous agreement on all fourteen save one. The conference approved upgraded training, better methods to segregate settlement from reserved forests, improved land surveying and classification, an expansion in reserved forests, co-operation with schools on fire prevention, reliance on the DFS as a clearinghouse for fire publicity, the universal use of burning permits, better means of slash disposal, a unified administration of forest authority, an expanded exploitation of aircraft with "substantial assistance" from the federal government, investment by the dominion in researching and disseminating meteorological information relevant to fire, a common format for reporting fire data orchestrated by the Dominion Forest Service, and a concentration of prevention efforts on Save the Forest Week.

The sticking point was the call for direct dominion cost sharing toward the creation of a fire-protection infrastructure. Roy Cameron reminded the conferees that the gathering had been called "for the purpose of asking the Dominion Government to do things; whether they can do it or not they must decide." Resolution Thirteen, on forest improvements, urged the conference to record "its conviction that the forest authorities should immediately undertake a programme for completion of such forest improvements within the shortest time possible and that the Federal Government should assist in financing such programme to the extent of." The reading never got beyond this point. Secretary of the Interior Stewart intervened "to point out that so far as possible it would be well for the various provinces and the Federal Government to keep their services within their own control." Co-operation was welcome, and there might well be ways to keep the Air Board aloft for a while longer, but direct subsidies were unlikely and unwelcome. Even Pattullo agreed and proposed an amendment that would remove the feds from financing a provincial task, which would also remove them from influencing how the provinces went about their jobs. The conference then approved the amended resolution.[81]

There was much over which the conferees could boast. They had talked civilly; they had exchanged experiences and data and at the highest political levels; they had found points on which to co-operate; but consensus broke down when the time came to put cash on the table. Ottawa wanted the provinces to practise conservation, for it was of national interest in two vital industries, logging and settlement. But it would not (or could not) itself pay for such practices. The provinces wanted the dominion to pay but would not (or could not) yield to Ottawa any substantial or even symbolic control over what they might do. Even with regard to aircraft, which all parties desperately wanted, no compromise was possible. Good will did not fly planes or mount pumps on pickups.

Whatever glow the empire evoked, whatever use Canadians could glean from the resolutions of the British Empire Forestry Conference, Canada's fire community knew that its real international links were across its southern border. On some projects, there was more co-operation between British Columbia and the northwestern American states than with the Maritimes and more mutual concerns between New Brunswick and Maine than with the Northwest Territories. When the Dominion Forest Service measured Canada's investment in fire protection, it compared output with that of the United States, not with those of India or South Africa. Some leading figures such as Clyde Leavitt were emigré Americans, and Canadians studied in US schools. Canadian foresters could view with collegial horror (and a touch of cultural smugness) the waste, extravagance, and violence to the south. Yet there was also a tinge of regret that they could not match America's industrial might applied to fire control or the American capacity for crafting co-operative political institutions.

Several conferees alluded to the Weeks Act, which, since 1911, had established a program of federal-state co-operation in forestry, centred on fire protection and financed by grants-in-aid. It was their hope that the dominion might sponsor something equivalent. In fact, even as the conference met, America was rushing to expand that program and did so in June, with enactment of the Clarke-McNary Act, which eventually brought all the states voluntarily under its aegis and committed them to some common standards of protection. The real distinction across the border was not that Americans had more fire guards and fire trucks but that the capacity of American federalism to promote systematic co-operation proved impossible under Canadian federalism, even with a convocation such as the Forest Fire Conference.

There was a bond even more fundamental, however. From its founding, the Dominion Forest Service had looked to the United States for models, practical advice, rhetorical styles, inspiration, and not least personnel. The renamed DFS was, even in its title, a Canadian clone of the US Forest Service, and it sought to expand its influence, as its American colleagues had, through co-operative programs, with industry, the states, and other bureaus. The US Forest Service had evolved beyond a minor advisory bureau when, in 1905, it acquired responsibility for the administration of the growing domain of forest reserves. That was the source of its political might. Likewise, the DFB could command government support because it administered the immense crown domain carved out of Rupert's Land. It was not simply an advisory or disbursing bureau or a meddlesome oversight committee of Parliament; it was, like its American exemplar, an *imperium in imperio,* the overseer of a vast territory. Without that land base, the DFS would collapse like a tent with its centre pole yanked out. The agency could wait over questions of co-operative fire protection; there would be ample opportunities to work through the quirks of Canadian federalism. What it could not tolerate was an assault on its land base.

Fire Conservancy by Confederation: Fire's Canadian Condition

When the Dominion Forest Service departed from the Forest Fire Conference, it was as institutionally powerful as it would ever be. But even as it continued to push boldly out – extending fire ranging into the remote northwest, acquiring responsibilities for national research, claiming more authority as the government's voice on conservation – it was, like an old fir, rotting from within. Its territorial acquisitions came amid a political divestment. Two gatherings in 1928 demonstrated both its outward strength and its inner weakness.

The Third British Empire Forestry Conference convened in Australia and New Zealand from August to October 1928. Roy Cameron described the progress Canada had made over the past five years. The 1923 report had identified the "incalculable damage" wrought by fire and "recognized, as all forest officers in Canada recognized, that the forest fire problem is the

besetting difficulty in, and obstacle to, the practice of forestry in Canada."
Cameron proudly summarized what Canada had achieved since then.[82]

There was, for starters, the seminal 1924 conference that had germinated
as a direct consequence of the imperial recommendations and whose
"personal contacts" he reckoned as vital as the ensuing resolutions. The most
striking development was the rise of "fire-prevention work to a position
of primary importance," with national co-ordination booming, not only
among the provinces but also with industry, and even synchronization
with American colleagues. On technical matters, Canadians could point
to rapid mechanization, such that pumps, automobiles, fire trucks, and
"the use of every possible mechanical facility" were no longer novelties but
indispensable armaments in forestry's cache. The use of carbide headlamps
allowed for firefighting at night. Fire-weather forecasting, based primarily
on relative humidity, was developing rapidly; British Columbia shut down
logging operations, and Manitoba and Saskatchewan scheduled air patrols,
based on such forecasts, while co-operation between the Meteorological
Service and the Forest Service had led to an expansion in recording stations.
The DFS had created model forests, subject to maximum protection and
sustained-yield logging, in each of the provinces for which it controlled
the crown lands: Sandilands (Manitoba), Nisbet (Saskatchewan), and
Cypress Hills (Alberta). Other high-value lands were being "fire-proofed"
as fast as "funds will permit."[83]

No mountain was too remote, no portage too onerous, no conifer-fringed
lake too distant for the intrepid fire rangers of the DFS. They trekked
into the Canadian outback by horse, canoe, York boat, and steamer; they
tracked traplines looking for abandoned campfires, intercepted modern
voyageurs at portages, posted notices at Hudson's Bay Company stations,
and fought fires, remaining in the bush for weeks if not months; and
they generally established an administrative presence. If they turned to
the RCMP for assistance, it was equally true that the Mounties found in
fire rangers fellow travellers in the quest for order. All in all, the Forest
Service's fire mission was a commitment several times grander than that
any other bureau in the empire could claim.

Most spectacularly, aerial fire protection had advanced beyond timid trials,
now supported by the Directorate of Civil Government Air Operations.
For northern spruce forests ("the foundation of Canada's pulp and paper
industry," the loss of which to fire would be "little else than a calamity to
the Dominion"), the "advent of aircraft has provided an instrument for
effective protection at costs justified by values involved." For those presently
remote but progressively accessible timber reserves, anything other than

aerial protection was "quite defective." For Manitoba and Saskatchewan, aircraft were the "entire basis of fire protection." Ontario had created its own provincial air service. In 1927, Saskatchewan flew a plane equipped with skis with which it could land on still-iced lakes in order to connect with spring trapping operations, for "trappers have the custom of setting fire to meadow and marsh land to locate rat houses and runs, and, with the high price at present for rat pelts, many persons are engaged in rat-trapping, scattered over the north." These meadow and marsh fires become "the forerunners of more serious fires later in the season." Canada had pushed well beyond the tenuous experiments of the Air Board.[84]

It was all truly impressive, as Cameron had intended it to be, and it established Canada as the foremost practitioner of fire protection in the empire. In his peroration to the conference, Cameron proudly inserted a statement contributed to Canadian Forest Week by William Lyon Mackenzie King. "We are the trustees, not the owners of our forest heritage," intoned the prime minister, and "to keep faith with the future we must use it wisely, and guard it from waste through preventable forest fires." Unknown to Cameron, the "we" in his remarks did not, apparently, to the mind of the prime minister, include the Dominion Forest Service.[85]

What government commissions gave they could also take away. In 1928, the Mackenzie King government commenced a suite of royal commissions on the transfer of natural resources to Manitoba, Saskatchewan, Alberta, and British Columbia. The matter involved both practical and constitutional politics. The Liberals needed support from the west, and a reversion of lands was popular, but inevitably, this being Canada, the issue foundered on questions of confederation. The British North America Act clearly left natural resources within the purview of the original provinces, and as Canada carved new provinces out of its western territories they should be, it was argued, entitled to the same privileges as those who signed the founding documents.

The loss of their lands was of course anathema to dominion foresters and to those who regarded sound forestry, on a dominion scale, as the basis for Canadian conservation overall. This was America's Transfer Act in reverse; the Dominion Forest Service in all its capacities would shatter. (Cynics might wonder what practical difference the change would make. In its last hurrah, the DFS had to report that, despite its herculean efforts, "all directorates report[ed] a very hazardous season." In Manitoba, the 1929 season "was the longest ever experienced, and the worst since the inauguration of organized fire-fighting." Without aggressive action, every province would have been horribly hammered, inspectors insisted – that was why the Fire Protection Service of the DFS was indispensable.) Over Finlayson's ferocious protests, however, agreements were signed in 1929, even as the royal commission worked through hearings and details. By the time the recommendations required action, the Great Depression allowed the dominion to shed a heavy burden of expenses to the provinces.[86]

Thus, Canada followed the example of the empire, whose other dominions were undergoing similar devolutions, rather than the United States, whose federal government, under the crisis of Depression, was about to invest heavily in conservation, forestry, and fire protection. Whatever their common interests, the Canadian and American fire communities operated under fundamentally different political regimes. The United States had much earlier confirmed the ultimate power of the federal government, first through the failed experiment with the Articles of Confederation and then by a brutal civil war. While Canada had not suffered the rupture of war, neither had its national institutions reknit, like bones once broken, into a tougher tissue. Political power lay suspended, like an oil drop, between the alternately charged poles of national and provincial interests. In the larger scheme, the Dominion Forest Service was a minor endeavour, noble but costly. It would be abandoned to the wayside when the wheels bogged down in political sand.

Canada's reversion acts bonded fire protection to the provinces. Fire control became more narrow, focused on efficiency, lashed to revenue-generating enterprises such as logging. The opportunities for dominion-wide co-operation crumbled. When the dominion pulled out of its lands, it pulled out of fire protection, save for niche assignments in the Yukon and Northwest Territories and for a specialized nook in fire research. The American exemplar, too, lost its claim, as the US Forest Service embarked on a vastly expanded role, a prime vehicle for the mutual rehabilitation of American society and American land, soon to become the premier firefighting institution in the world.

In 1929, Charles Stewart and E.H. Finlayson attempted a final gesture to claim national leadership on forest issues, calling for a kind of successor to the Forest Fire Conference, this time a Conference on the National Inventory of Forest Resources. No firm resolution followed since no serious funds were contemplated. Platitudes about co-operation were cheap; on-the-ground surveys, like subsidized aerial patrols, required hard cash. Power shifted to the provinces, and as the Depression deepened this meant that effective fire protection, once the glory and vanguard of forest conservation and of dominion noblesse oblige toward the national estate, receded. To counter the slashed woods, state-sponsored forestry could only point to slashed budgets.[87]

Sea and Shield: Fire Provinces of Eastern Canada

The provinces bordering the Gulf of St. Lawrence easily self-identify as a suite. The gulf links them geographically, and the experience of colonization joins them historically. Collectively, they summarize the founding economy of Canada – farm, forest, fur, and fishing village. All were settled before the Confederation era of state-sponsored conservation; all lacked dominion-governed lands. None was a miniature Canada; none had extensive hinterlands awaiting exploitation, save Quebec, whose immense outback for long lay fallow apart from furs. Yet each had a distinctive character shaped by the province's proneness to fire, the extent of forestry and a forest industry within it, and the relative strength of the state. In this micro-confederation, Newfoundland stands to one side because it came so late to Canada, and Ontario stands to another because it held its own northwestern colony and, by acting as a conduit for fire institutions, joined the eastern provinces with the western ones. Newfoundland and Ontario can thus, in different ways, serve as synecdoches for Canada overall.

Nova Scotia

At the time of Confederation, Nova Scotia's identity remained with the sea, and most of it was already settled or as fully settled as the economy of the day allowed. The land lay almost wholly in private hands, and all of that was sculpted into farms, pastures, woodlots, or the penumbral gardens of fishing villages. There were backwoods for hunting, and there were forests well timbered but too remote for logging. There were sweeping landscapes of berries, bogs, and barrens, some natural but most the scabbed legacy of hard use, lost soil, and too-frequent burns. The maritime climate made explosive fire rare, helping to buffer anthropogenic burning. Without a forest economy or forested crown lands, there was no occasion for state-sponsored forestry, and without foresters the province lacked the more hard-bitten proscriptions against fire or the institutional power to battle it.

There was fire aplenty, but it was confined within fallowed fields and between roads, or over the scrubby hillsides of blueberry, and within the seasonal rhythms traditional for burning. Spring grass burning could bolt beyond the fence line, and fall hunting fires escaped into windfalls. Even fuel wood was rendered into charcoal, the process of contained distillation serving as a metaphor for treatment of the cultivated landscape. Where flame ran loose, it did so in wasteland. Wildfire joined a gallery of natural hazards, including windstorms, insects, ice, and drought, although, unlike the others, fire came mostly from the hands of humans. In 1865, for example, log-driver Daniel Moody set a smudge fire along the banks of the Mersey River. He succeeded in driving off the black flies, along with scorching 20,000 acres.[1]

All this began to change with the advent of steam. A new wave of settlement commenced. (Interestingly the earliest steam engine served as a pump at the Stellarton coal mine, neatly demonstrating the collusion of new fuel and new combustion. The old hardwoods that had made the best charcoal now had higher economic value as sawtimber.) Railways punched through the landscape with the Windsor to Annapolis Royal line in 1869, the Intercolonial in 1872, the Nova Scotia Central Railway in 1889; rails laced the landscape like baling wire around hay. Sawmills turned to steam first in 1845, but not seriously until the 1860s, while loggers adapted locomotives to wooden rails to replace oxen and built tug steamers to replace log drives. Overseas trade quickened, stirring demands for natural goods that forced a re-evaluation of once overlooked or discarded sites. Trees scorned because of remoteness or scant value for sawtimber became invaluable as pulp. Over the next few decades, steam powered a slow recolonization of the Nova Scotian scene. The provincial economy morphed from fire-fallow agriculture to fossil-fuel industry.[2]

That meant a renewed, more powerful wave of fires. Fresh forests were felled and stale or regrown ones reharvested. The spreading slash met the propagating sparks of engines, especially locomotives but also the steam donkeys used by loggers to yard and run portable mills. The debris of milling, including sawdust, became further points of combustion infection. Like some ancient plague, fires returned and then turned on their new handlers. During its first eight years, the Transcontinental Railway reportedly destroyed by its fires twenty times the timber that it hauled out. The rest of the new landscape plunged down this cascade of combustion as fire incinerated mills and their adjacent wooden towns. Hastily assembled factories and hamlets burned almost as often as the woods from which their boards came. In a macabre way, loggers birthed a vicious fire cycle in which they found themselves in competition with fire to see who could harvest the standing timber first. The more the loggers cut, the more their locomotives puffed through the cutover, the more fires broke out, which then rushed into the uncut woods.[3]

This eruption of flame was, by itself, unremarkable. What distinguished

Classification of land, Nova Scotia

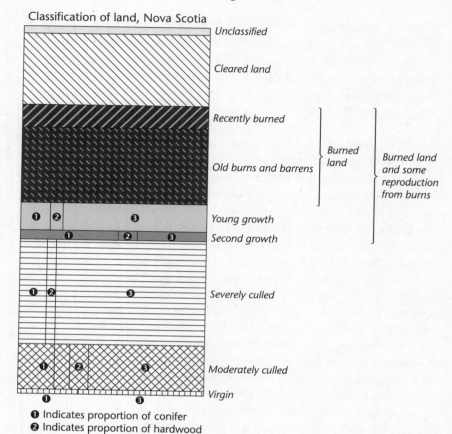

The fire factor in Nova Scotia as recorded in Fernow's 1912 study. The crucial issue was not area burned once and abandoned, but areas repeatedly fired. Accompanying maps showed a typical geography of anthropogenic burning, with lines and fields of fire, the largest proportions being blueberry "barrens."

Nova Scotia was the absence of a corporatist structure that made fire protection a common cause for industry and the state. The sparsity of crown lands, the lack of dominant timber companies, the stubbornly rural character of the countryside and its fires, all meant that fire protection had to evolve outside a commanding presence by forestry. As an official later lamented, every spring the province simmered with flame: "Rubbish heaps, leaves and lawns are being burned, fields and meadows, the embankments of the roads and railways," and worse, "and all this burning is, nearly everywhere, being conducted by children." Fires would quell to the extent that the land went to other purposes (reacquired by the crown if necessary) and was overseen by foresters in the service of the state.[4]

The quest for a new order of fire took decades after Confederation. It meant control over locomotives, control over rural burning, and control over slash. Fitful legislation and episodic conflagration continued in a flaming fugue until Canadian conservation intervened. In 1912, *The Forest Conditions of Nova Scotia,* written by Bernhard Fernow, assisted by C.D. Howe and J.H. White, conveyed the full magnitude of the problem. Howe reckoned that over half a million acres of recent burns (including those of 1902) would cripple forestry for years and that the lavish *brûlés* and too-promiscuous "fire barrens," at present "practically worthless," were the greatest challenge to future forestry. Fernow's survey classified 2,992,908 acres as recently burned, old burn, or barren. This number exceeded by half a million acres the estimated land base farmed or grazed. Probably 25 percent of the province thus showed the open ravages of fire. Unsurprisingly Fernow insisted that the "first, most needful step" toward reform was fire protection, pursued until Nova Scotia's woods were as well insulated as its cities. He recommended the standard measures, beginning with the erection of fire towers, permits for setting fires in the woods, lopping tops of felled trees, controlled burning of brush, the proper organization of a firefighting force, and liability of railways for fires they start.[5]

What the situation demanded was a system – vision and will, moral as much as practical ambition – and this was always the grand promise of government-sponsored forestry, which rose to the challenge in Nova Scotia as elsewhere. For the next seventy years, the province groped, stalled, lurched, and finagled toward stronger institutions primarily by allowing state forestry to oversee more and more of the rural scene. A long chronicle of bureaucratic adjustments, amended acts, reorganizations, name changes, infrastructure improvements, and modernized fire control commenced. As even successive Department of Lands and Forests commissioners admitted, the details were "tedious." The responsible agency appeared and vanished; the number of fire districts expanded, the number shrank; staff came, staff went. Irritating rural burning persisted; big fires, from time to time, broke free. Most years another lookout tower went up, a few pumps and shovels were added to caches. On a per capita basis, the province had more fires than any other. While at the 1923 and 1924 conferences, J.A. Knight considered Nova Scotia's strategy "fairly successful," he admitted that climate and the absence of forests "very remote from settlers" were the primary reasons.

Gradually even that responsibility was transferred to state agencies.[6]

What made the problem distinctive was the need to retrofit a new order onto one long established but fast delaminating. A critical breakthrough came in 1921 when an act established a commissioner of forests and game, who, among other duties, was to "conserve and protect the forest from fire." The enterprise was shaky since funds derived from royalties on fur, the towns collected the fire levy, and the staff (the entire Department of Forests and Game) could be, and was, dismissed with each change of government. This situation improved in March 1926 with enactment of the Lands and Forests Act, which consolidated all affairs involving crown lands, forests, and game into a common bureau, a Department of Lands and Forests, with stiffened responsibilities, a chief forester charged "to conserve the forests and protect them from fire," and a year later the power to collect the fire tax and to use surplus funds, not spent on wages, to purchase equipment. The agency administered crown lands, provided fire protection across all forested land (crown and freehold), and enforced game laws. The chief forester actually announced that the province would be practically free of forest fires "if the question of the burning of blueberry barrens could be solved, and if the citizens of Halifax would show reasonable care when picnicking."[7]

That was the official line. After long service, however, Owen Barr recalled his early memories of fires. The first occurred in 1919, when he was eleven years old. It was twenty miles away, burning the Walton barrens, and with a telescope "flames could be seen high in the air along with great clouds of smoke." He concluded it was put out by wet weather "as there was very little fire fighting equipment at that time." The next outbreak came in 1923. It was an acre, burning slowly, but close enough that he had been called out to help, which he did with shovels and pails of water. "The ranger from the area came with horse and wagon." In 1933, he was "told to go by a voluntary ranger (you went or else!)." He had to take his own equipment; a promised motor pump never showed up; he was paid and fed. (A day's labour earned $1.50. Meals "of a sort" consisted "mainly of bread, butter, tea, sugar, jam, bullybeef and bologna.") "In the end, wet weather killed the fire." The next year he assisted a large burn in Rawdon, in which a pump sank in a lake before being recovered. "As all these fires were in a very small area," he pondered, "think of all the other fires that were in Nova Scotia in those years. With very little equipment and also very little skilled help to fight them, what a problem it was."[8]

In 1933, following the dismissal of the entire staff after an election, Wilfrid Creighton, a forester trained at the University of New Brunswick and subsequently in Germany, assumed the post of provincial forester, thus granting to Nova Scotia one of those patriarchal foresters so critical to Canadian fire history. The department acquired authorization to purchase land (at twenty-five cents per acre), in this way creating a critical mass of crown lands that could support a forest industry and grant political power to the department that also furnished fire protection. From time to time, big fires – 1934 and 1947, for example – exposed the flimsiness of the apparatus but prompted reforms that allowed the program to leap to a new level. By 1959, it could even boast three airplanes for fire duty. This was, after all, a program not to assault fire in the remote bush but to oversee a resmelting of the land in an increasingly industrial furnace.[9]

In 1969, after thirty-five years with the department, Dr. G.W.I. Creighton, first hired as provincial forester, retired as deputy minister. Two great problems remained – had persisted – he thought, "public apathy and fire hazards." Fire protection "continued to demand too much time and expense," he grumbled, "but some slight progress was evident." That fire mission had been forced on Creighton, as it had on the province. With his European training, he had always longed for a world beyond burning, where silviculture and economic land use would guide decisions, not a casino climate and the happenstance of fires at the hands of arsonists, children, and berry pickers, where a knowledgeable public treasured its forest wealth. Toward the end of his tenure, he had joined a delegation to Sweden and noted enviously that the Swedes were "free of the enormous sums spent here on fire protection," money they could invest to more productive purposes. One reason was that their forests were free of debris, either natural or slash. Another was that, while their young plantations were vulnerable to fire, the "fires did not start"; the people didn't set them. These were conditions that Creighton, and the Department of Lands and Forests, had never known. He had instead learned patience and that "if you could look back over a 10-year period and see reasonable progress you had to be content." Whatever the vision of a rationalized landscape, the reality was otherwise. The reality was that even Nova Scotia had to invest seriously in fire protection before it could advance to something like the putative norms of western Europe. But by the time he retired, Creighton might have thought that he, and his department, were close to achieving them.[10]

The next year the department reorganized into three branches, following management concepts that affected Canadian provinces generally. The modernization proceeded, roughly proportional to that elsewhere; Nova Scotia could boast a fire organization more or less interchangeable with those throughout the country. On a decadal scale, average fire size continued to shrink. Fewer problem fires broke out, and fire officers could match them with ever-greater counterforce. Yet success could be ironic. Since its origins, state-sponsored forestry had regarded itself as the highest imaginable use of the land, certainly as measured against its rural forebears. Those assumptions were, by the 1970s, barely verbalized. They were simply there, like the Precambrian Shield.

But a letter to the editor two years before clearly expressed the contrast and the choices involved. Writing from Shelburne, Daniel W. Bower began with a discussion of deer, wildcats, and rabbits, all of which led to his core theme, "spring burning." Years ago, he observed, "the country people, each spring, before it became dry enough to be dangerous, burned their meadows, swamps, and barren lands to produce grass for their livestock and berries for the family larder." Those practices sculpted a habitat that also favoured the game animals that rural areas relied on for meat, not sport. It made the land habitable; it kept the scrub under control. Then the Department of Lands and Forests intervened, criminalized the fires as mere incendiarism, and "clamped down on spring burning for the sake of waiting for 50 to 60 years for some scrub spruce or pine to grow on some rocky barren where they never grew before." In return, the "country people" forfeited their crops of blueberries, raspberries, huckleberries, rabbits, wildcats, and deer and acquired an "invasion of ticks." Many old timers would reply that spring burning done right – not too soon, not too late – was "the answer." Bower concluded with tongue only slightly in cheek that "maybe the department should institute a controlled and supervised burning of some of our scrub lands, barrens, savannahs and swamps." But the old quarrel with spring-burning farmers and blueberry pickers meant less and less. The province had exchanged a rural fire problem for a wildland fire problem.[11]

The real competition lay with the tectonic shifts in the Canadian economy, nudging away from staples and into services, its lands more valued for amenity pursuits than raw goods, its forest industry competitive only by increasing the scale and intensity of its harvest, which probably meant government subsidies. Lands were becoming more valuable as national parks than pulp-producing forests; rural habitations, more attractive to exurban recreationists and second-home fanciers than berry pickers, cabbage growers, and coarse-forage cattle herders. The capital-intensive industrial forestry of Nova Scotia found itself in crisis not because of renewed competition from country folk or lack of pulp but from urban wanderlust, cheap-labour rivals overseas, and the demands of industrial combustion. The fires that commanded public attention were those that blasted the Sydney coalfields, reopened after the double oil embargoes of the 1970s. Six mine fires later, one every two years, the mines were finally shut, thanks to a global oil glut that even government subsidies could not overcome. The Springhill mine disaster, not Nova Scotia's conflagrations, captured popular memory.

Thoughtful observers might pause to ponder whether the challenges themselves had not fundamentally changed. The regional environment that had sustained the old northern economy was, like the Grand Banks, fished out. Much as government subsidies could not keep the coalfields open, so the new machinery, even if drawn from across Canada through institutions such as the Canadian Interagency Forest Fire Centre, might not match the requirements of a society that was being recolonized once again, this time by exurbanites and electronics. Fire protection had been adequate to assure the survival of an industrial economy based on forest products. It did not look sufficient for the new landscapes quietly unfolding.

Prince Edward Island

Its wildfires, like its wild woods, were fast vanishing from Prince Edward Island when the founders of Confederation debated the issue at Charlottetown. Some clearing remained; some field fires escaped into as-yet-uncut conifers. For several decades after Confederation, island newspapers described smoke palls. By 1900, however, the landscape was domesticated. The island had become a garden, in geographical fact as much as popular imagination. Its forests were woodlots; its fires were those of cultivation. Residents burned debris piles, dry grass around habitations, fallow fields, berry patches, and occasional land-clearing slash, all in all a pyric burst of spring cleaning that shook out the landscape like beating the winter dust out of a rug.[12]

A Forestry Commission, charged with assessing the state of the island's woods, reported in 1904 that "a timber famine is in sight" and urged the provincial authorities to initiate a campaign of tree promotion and outright reforestation. Nothing happened officially. But unofficially the island began a slow reversion to its woody past as emigration replaced immigration. One wave passed between 1900 and 1910, another after the Great War, and a third after the Second World War. Once the young had left and the elderly had died, one farm after another, now here, now there, succumbed to woody weediness. The 1901 provincial census had listed 756,285 acres of farmland; seventy-five years later those cultivated lands had declined to 486,000 acres, an annual rate of reversion of 1.9 percent. By mid-century, the logic of compounding interest had become irresistible. The land was lapsing into coniferous fallow. By 1980, forestry (or at least arboriculture) seemed plausible, with some 48 percent of Prince Edward Island once again wooded.[13]

A revanchist forest could lead to revanchist forest fires. Still, the problem remained small and hidden, like a creeping shabby gentility, and it took not merely forests but also foresters to define a fire problem. The island had not identified itself as a forest province so had not participated in the 1923 Second British Empire Forest Conference or the 1924 Forest Fire Conference. It had no forests, it had no foresters. In 1938, Deputy Minister of Agriculture Walter Shaw had sent a delegation of twenty-eight young men to the Acadia Experimental Station at Fredericton, New Brunswick, for an eight-week course in forestry, but that led nowhere save for the employment opportunities offered by the short-lived National Forestry Program the following year. In 1950, with trees sprouting like ragweed, the island passed a Forestry Act. Within a year, the province had a Forestry Division within its Ministry of Agriculture, headed by J. Frank Gaudet. Forestry agreements with Ottawa followed. Meanwhile, between 1951 and 1981, the number of farms had fallen from 10,137 to 3,145. The proportion of real-farmer islanders among the population plummeted from 50 percent to 10 percent.[14]

The division's ambition was to graft silviculture onto the island's fundamentally agricultural scene. The islanders could become tree farmers. Accordingly it sought a forest inventory and worried how to improve scattered pockets of crown land, the parcels no one had wanted – all this the normal tasks of forestry bureaus. Yet it also promoted trees as an adjunct to farms, as a means to stabilize soil against desiccation and wind, to which end it fostered a forest nursery, plantings, weedings and prunings, and improved tree breeding by replacing poor stock with better. Between 1952 and 1976, the Forestry Division planted 4.25 million seedlings from its Beach Grove nursery. It addressed, particularly, the conundrum of the white spruce that had willy-nilly reclaimed most of the abandoned fields, a poor tree (from the forester's perspective), of inferior stock, feral, prone to spruce budworm infestations, and alien to the primeval Acadian forest. In 1975, a budworm outbreak, carried by prevailing winds from a New Brunswick epidemic, led to severe defoliation, confirming foresters in their determination to do with the haphazard forest they inherited what original settlers had done with the Acadian, namely to wrestle it into cultivation.[15]

Its fires thus mirrored its land use. Even at the end of the twentieth century, Prince Edward Island had more fires per forest area than any other province. Those fires, though, tended to be small; they clustered in the spring, part of a customary freshening up of the landscape; grass burning typically expired in snow banks. But as its coniferous forests spread, thickened, and interleaved, so did its flames. Some sprang from their hedgerows and became dangerous. In August 1960, after a prolonged drought, packs of fire ran wild. One began around Enmore, supposedly from a woodcutter burning out a nest of wasps; others overwhelmed attempts at control and incinerated "quite a number of houses and other buildings." A second group kindled around Victoria West and rushed into Port Hill and Tyne Valley, blasting 20,000 acres of forest. A third broke out near Dundee and raced across 2,000 acres. The Department of Industry and Natural Resources downplayed the crisis, identifying only six fires and 17,000 acres burned. It concluded that, even with its "limited amount of equipment," none of those fires should have occurred "had they been reported in time."[16]

That was the erstwhile voice of the public forester speaking. More equipment, more public sensitivity, more attention to silviculture, more system – and the fires would be squelched. The Forestry Division duly acquired vehicles, pumps, and tractors and assigned personnel to local fire brigades; it ploughed firebreaks around provincial properties, particularly lands acquired by the crown and stocked with silvic plantations; it worked closely with the RCMP, which both reported fires and investigated suspicious origins; it sought to harrow flame into traditional social furrows. In 1970, another autumn fire escaped. It hid in 500 acres of peat bog around North Cape, and while the department noted gratefully that "very few commercial trees" were harmed, it also reasoned that suitable equipment for operating in such terrain was a "must." When 3,000 acres of grass and scrub burned "near and in the area of the National Park" in 1977, the episode only demonstrated the logic of cultivated fire, for this was a site that, as a matter of policy, stood outside that order. Two 500-acre fires at Savage Harbour and Hermanville in May 1978, driven before winds of up to 100 kilometres an hour, were contained with help from the Canadian Armed Forces base at Summerside. Such fires, however, were envisioned as extraordinary events, like hurricanes or a terrorist attack, something that called for a constabulary, not an integral feature of island life.[17]

By the mid-1980s, two trends seemingly defined the island's fire scene. One absorbed Prince Edward Island into national fire institutions; the other modernized its traditional practices. The first unfolded, like a sudden spring blossoming, in 1983 when a new Fire Prevention Act updated provisions of the Forestry Act of 1974. Even more powerfully, that year the province joined the Canadian Committee on Forest Fire Control and later the Canadian Interagency Forest Fire Centre; this was akin to construction of the Confederation Bridge, linking its fire institutions with national norms. A province that fifty years earlier had shunned imperial and dominion conferences addressing forest fire protection now integrated itself within a national infrastructure. In the spring of 1986, it hosted a special fire training course with an instructor from Nova Scotia. Two months later, as so often in Canadian history, a buildup in fire suppression forces was followed by major fires. Frozen ground, winter dryness and an arid spring, high winds, human ignition – the formula was primordial. Officials foresaw even more outbreaks as the extensive old-field white pine forests "collapsed" into more crown-fire-prone status.[18]

Against this likelihood was a modernizing of the rural landscape. For most provinces, the historical problem of fire had been to hold off the expansionist instincts of agriculture, with its fiery threats to forests. In Prince Edward Island, the issue was reversed. The problem had been for agriculture to absorb an expansionist forest (and the fires it brought). Now that countryside was again being remade; the reforestation of the island was being matched by an exurban reclamation, a makeover by metropolitan migrants, particularly around the larger towns. So, too, was its fire scene transformed, as fossil-fuel engines began to replace traditional spring burning, aptly symbolized by farmers who burned blueberry fields with a harrow-like apparatus arrayed with propane-fuelled torches and pulled by a tractor. Whether this was a genuinely agricultural economy, even if subsidized, or a rustic façade, a kind of historical theme park, the story-book world of Green Gables, time and fire would tell. But the intensity of the island's cultivation, however defined, would decide, as it had for three centuries, the intensity of its flame.[19]

New Brunswick

If Prince Edward Island was a big farm, New Brunswick was a big woodlot. By the end of the twentieth century, it remained 85 percent forested. What in most provinces were hinterlands was here the core. Agriculture was sparse and scattered; mining had come late and hydro power was comparatively timid; industry remained bound to the woods; and cities, like farmlands, were cast about, without the gravitational pull of a major metropolis. New Brunswick went from timber colony to timber province without missing a beat.

Along the way it perfected the fundamentals of corporatist forestry in which the crown would retain ownership and lease rights of harvest. Potentially this was a slick solution. Logging companies would clear the land, settlers would then occupy it, and the government would collect the revenue from both leases and sales. In practice, much of the land proved unsuitable for agriculture, and as forest industries became more capital intensive, long-tenure rights migrated to a small cabal of large companies. In most provinces, there were competing sources for economic development, revenue, and political influence that helped to contain these distortions. Not so in New Brunswick. What had been devised as an expedient of pioneering here became permanent. If Nova Scotia suffered from too little forested crown land and Prince Edward Island from too few forests, New Brunswick suffered from an excess of both. So, while a forest industry thrived, the state remained feeble and needed Confederation and conservation to stiffen its resolve and to force industry into a condominium for fire protection.

A wave of settlement conflagrations had risen sharply, then fallen as abruptly. The province could boast one monumental holocaust, the iconic but singular 1825 Miramichi fire. Thereafter pioneering fires clung to the fringes of towns, and railways never branded the scene as cruelly as they did where the slash from farms, mines, logging, and the general chaotic bustle of settlement allowed fires to fester and break free. The Miramichi disaster itself became a convenient memory with which one could argue for fire protection. No subsequent fire has come anywhere near it in size or damages, in part because it was less a provincial archetype than an anomaly. Instead of more settlement, there was less; vast forests, not small farms, would define the province; long tenure for logging, not the gnawing flames of land-clearing pioneers, would sculpt the land. The conditions that made Miramichi possible were not likely to be repeated. Where Nova Scotia had struggled to birth state forestry out of a rural countryside, New Brunswick sought to absorb rural fire within a condominium of state and industrial forestry. Whatever climatic pushes and ecological pulls might shape fire, those flames would increasingly occur within the shackles and halters of that corporatist arrangement and were bottled so effectively that New Brunswick became, for all of Canada, an institutional nursery for fire control by professional forestry and its sponsors.

New Brunswick had entered Confederation reluctantly, like the other Maritime provinces alternately badgered and bribed. Its forests seemed to confirm those doubts, for even as legislation was passed in 1870 for railway construction, conflagrations raged, gorging on the slash left by the Saxby Gale of the previous year. Overall its fire scene remained less serious than elsewhere, for although forests proportionately dominated its landmass, a large fraction fell under a maritime climate, much consisted of the less fire-prone Acadian woods, and their absolute scale was minor compared with the boreal belt sweeping across the continent. In northern Manitoba, fires would rip and roar with no more concern than icebergs around Antarctica. They couldn't in New Brunswick.

While it took a few years after Confederation for the province to reorganize its crown lands department, it took no time for that department to identify fire as a rival. In 1875, the surveyor general concluded that, "to a large extent, the immediate cause of the falling off of the timber product of the districts referred to, is chargeable to forest fires." Preventing such losses, though, seemed illusory in a country where settlers burned for land clearing, railways cast sparks to all sides, and travellers exercised little care to extinguish the fires "necessarily made by them." His gloomy conclusion was that "in the present state of public sentiment" little could be done. A succession of further reports fingered the usual suspects, and some token legislation followed. There was an 1885 Fire Act, an 1890 Forestry Commission, legislation in 1897 that provided for a corps of fire wardens. In 1903, even the Lumbermen and Limit Holders Association appointed a committee that proposed a permanent staff of wardens and a permit system for travel. And a fundamental cycle of analysis appeared, as endemic as white pine, that attributed good fire years to the work of institutions and bad ones to climate.[20]

Something had to jolt the separate self-interests of government, industry, and settlers. That something was the conservation movement, then gaining momentum in Ottawa before spreading to New Brunswick, where it found ready tinder. Scientific, state-sponsored forestry promised a way to rationalize the timber industry, to assert the authority of government, and to channel the virulent politics of the province. The key was to have fire protection, about which all parties could agree, substitute for regulations on logging, on which an implacable partisanship prevailed. What didn't burn could be cut. In 1906, the legislature passed a Public Domain Act that called for a provincial survey and, surprisingly, a public convocation to review critical issues, which, this being New Brunswick, meant forestry. The Forestry Convention duly met in February 1907 in Fredericton, attended not only by New Brunswick's elite but also by notables from Ottawa, elsewhere in Canada, and the United States. As a result, the province commenced mapping, collected statistics on fire and forest industry (other than a simple record of revenue), established a

School of Forestry at the University of New Brunswick, and pondered a plan for comprehensive fire protection throughout the province, including the appointment of a permanent corps of wardens to enforce both game and fire laws, assisted by county staffs.[21]

The solution was the usual one – system. There were Fire Act amendments; there was the creation of a bureau devoted to crown lands and forestry; there was a prescribed source of revenue for fire programs; there was the long reign of a patriarchal forester, in this case G.H. Prince, a rabid fire abolitionist. The provincial oddity was the creation of a Forestry Advisory Commission that included emissaries from industry, thus helping to bureaucratically bottle the dangerous rivalry between the state, which held the lands that industry demanded, and industry, whose leases funded the state. The burned woods were their common ground; and if reforms were to happen, they would sprout up from the ash. P.Z. Caverhill, director of the forest survey, unabashedly declared that "the Act as now constituted is a step in advance of any law of a similar nature in any Province in Canada." The Committee of Forests of the Commission of Conservation agreed. "No Province of Canada," it asserted, "has a more progressive forest policy than New Brunswick." Provincial Forester Prince resolved to use that program to crush fire. "There is no more destructive agent in New Brunswick," he thundered, "and I may say in the whole of the Dominion." If only fire could be removed, nature's forested bounty would bloom. By the time the British Empire Forestry Conference met, New Brunswick could boast of a robust forest industry, including major new pulp and paper mills and an infrastructure for fire control probably as sound as any in the dominion. In the slipstream of fire reforms, however, came massive fires. The 1923 conflagrations, savaging 650 square miles, were the worst for decades.[22]

Yet the 1923 Restigouche fires were more than an order of magnitude smaller than the Miramichi burn, and the response to them demonstrates what a century of "system" could mean. In the words of Prince,

> Volumes could be written to the credit of those men who gave their best to control the fires – the fire pump men who stuck to their pumps for days without relief, the wardens who never had their boots off for nearly a month, the men with blistered and sore feet, worked and endured the heat and smoke until exhausted; the lumbermen, who realizing more than any other what the loss of timber really meant, redoubled their efforts in the face of discouraging daily reports, providing every facility possible to combat the fires, even visiting the fire lines to encourage the men; the railway authorities who provided special accommodation in transporting supplies and equipment;

the Municipal Councillors who organized many crews on private lands; all joined together in trying to combat the heavy odds started by the careless acts of a few and carried on by the abundance of highly inflammable forest material rendered such by unusual weather conditions.

No wonder Provincial Forester Prince considered fire "without doubt" the "greatest problem in the administration of our public lands and perhaps the least realized by our people." Yet had he stepped back from the flames, he might have focused less on what remained to be done and appreciated what had been accomplished.[23]

As everywhere, the task was enormous, the means at hand meagre, and the political will fickle. Slowly, a suite of agencies evolved including the Forest Service, private landowners, municipalities, the National Railway Commission (over rights-of-way), and a special arrangement for select counties, notably Westmorland. For all its distinctive liabilities, New Brunswick held equally distinctive advantages. Its compact size and ready access to transport, relative to most Canadian provinces, meant that intensive management was possible. What remained was to unify forestry under an organ of the state. What made New Brunswick distinctive, however, was the alliance, through forest industry, between private owners and crown agencies. And while there were disparities among foresters, particularly granted that private landowners and limit holders were less inclined to invest in fire control, all accepted protection as a common cause in ways that the towns and rural landowners did not, and while they might quarrel among themselves, in a kind a sibling rivalry, they locked arms against foes to forestry.

The core agency was the Forest Service, which had jurisdiction over crown lands. Directing it was an Advisory Commission, consisting of the minister of lands and mines, the deputy minister, the provincial forester, a representative of crown land licensees, and a representative of private landowners. The service had a field staff of thirty-six, plus temporary wardens hired during the fire season, although much of the equipment and many of the men used on fires came from lumbermen, with whom the Forest Service enjoyed "excellent co-operation." In effect, through their shared norms embedded in forestry, the state and industry had created a fire condominium that oversaw 80 percent of the province and almost all of its commercial woods. Dr. C.D. Howe, dean of the University of Toronto School of Forestry, observed that "in no province of Canada" were lumbermen more disposed toward conservation by forestry or was there a friendlier spirit of co-operation between industry and government. "Opportunity and necessity walk amicably together."[24]

Over the next forty years, New Brunswick steadily implemented that agenda. Where it could install the uncompromised precepts of forestry in the service of forest industry and the state, it wrung fire from the land. Where it faltered, fires persisted, like a rash of blister rust or stubborn pockets of insect infestation. What is striking is not simply the tempo but also the thoroughness of the endeavour. The province documented its fire hazards, real and imagined, with a rigour unprecedented elsewhere in Canada. Little was overlooked; little went unrecorded; almost nothing went undone, within the limits of what was possible. What professional forestry demanded, with reservations and occasional setbacks, it eventually achieved. The School of Forestry meant that its woods got studied more often than elsewhere (save perhaps Ontario) and that it hosted an exceptional number of national trials, experiments, and conferences. A province with 1 percent of Canada's landmass and a dwindling population of fires became a national paragon of fire protection. The Dominion Meteorological Service here implanted the first of its network of fire weather stations; the Dominion Forest Service established the Acadian Forest Experiment Station outside Fredericton, and Herbert Beall expanded fire-hazard rating and undertook the "most comprehensive forest-fire report analysis" yet seen in Canada. By the 1960s, the University of New Brunswick had, uniquely among Canadian universities, a Fire Science Centre. In the 1980s, it added another forestry faculty at the University of Moncton. New Brunswick consistently exerted an influence far out of proportion to its measurable fire problem, for which it could thank its hard weld to forestry and the forest industry.[25]

At heart, this was a forester's system applied through a forester's vision and with a forester's techniques. It worked because New Brunswick was a commercial woodlot. In 1945, some 81 percent of the province remained forest, although virtually no place had not been logged at least once, and of that amount the crown controlled 7 million acres, 97 percent of which was under licence, 63 percent to three companies, while another 2.5 million acres resided in the private hands of five owners. The belief prevailed that progress only demanded more of the same, that decade by decade there should appear more roads, more towers, improved communication, less volatile slash, better prevention, all of it wrested to yield maximum revenue. (Alone, New Brunswick recorded its fire statistics not through burned area but through dollar losses.) Still, the condominium between state and private foresters remained a marriage of convenience, and not until the 1950s was the system built out sufficiently that it had to confront questions of diminishing returns, which it solved by reaching out to Canada overall and then to the United States for additional firefighting resources. The core issue, however, was not insufficient means but uncertain ends. By 1970, the province resolved the intramural competition between its foresters by asserting the ultimate power of the state.[26]

The deep conundrum, however, remained those lands that did not fall under forestry's bailiwick. Historically, New Brunswick had experienced a kind of fire bipartism. It was an awkward tossed salad of two forest types, two ethnicities, two patterns of land use – one rural and agricultural, the other a forest-based industry – that resisted a singular authority. The northern forests had lightning fire, the rural counties a stubborn legacy of spring burning. The vexing fires flourished in those cracks and nooks still beyond the reach of formal forestry and its capacity for fire control, places yet dominated by indifferently regulated settler burning, sites only thinly laced with roads or lacking in fire pumps and brigades, scenes subject to irrational fire causes such as lightning and children. So long as these circumstances persisted, so could bad fires, including such aftershocks of 1923 as the outbreaks of 1934 and 1946-47.

The Forest Service grappled with these eruptions in three ways. It placed its greatest hope in education and propaganda, although in practice results were disappointing. A firmer institutional arrangement was to expand what had become known as the Westmorland model, by which county officials' status as fire wardens empowered them to conscript men to fight fires on private lands (without pay) and allowed the county to tax all owners of forest land greater than fifty acres, with the money collected by the county council and applied to fire protection. By 1948, six of the province's fifteen counties had signed on, and then eight, but with mixed results. (A 1957 report noted sardonically that, "in fact, seven out of the eight counties with protection agreements have the worst fire records in the Province – one or two of them being very bad indeed." Other counties cynically assumed that the province would aid them during a crisis whether they had formal fire institutions or not.) A third strategy was the boldest. It proposed to expand the practice, inaugurated in 1924, by which the Forest Service elected to assist settlers in burning their slash, much as Nova Scotia's foresters had opted to help blueberry pickers burn their barrens. By such means, despite Westmorland's waffling, the Forest Service began to contain rural fire, until it eventually withered along with rural populations and the further end of forest colonization, while municipalities extended the range of their urban fire services.[27]

In 1957, the New Brunswick Forest Development Commission reported that New Brunswick had proportionately more forest land than any other province, got significantly more value out of those lands, and remained particularly dependent on its wooded economy, which was also, however, why annual cash income was only two-thirds that of the average Canadian and why the province needed to double its value "within half a lifetime." That outcome demanded better management of what already existed. And while the commission determined that, "on the whole," fire protection was "very good indeed as compared with the national average," the old problems persisted. There was still no "unified control" over forested land, efforts to contain rural fire seemed perversely counterproductive, and the logic of improvement was approaching the point of diminishing returns. In twenty years, outlays had tripled, even allowing that aircraft expenses were shared with an endless aerial spraying program. The commission concluded that the time for further reformations "*at materially higher cost*" was "past."[28]

Within a decade, those issues were nearly solved. Between 1967 and 1969, the department reorganized, at mid-point changing its name to Natural Resources. The legislature abolished county governments, and the resulting gap in fire services was plugged, as the Forest Service received the jurisdiction it had so long clamoured for. With a few minor exceptions, the department had come close to achieving its formative agenda. What the founders had sought they now had, and only, it seemed, the crushing, once-a-decade, big-fire year remained. For that, the Forest Service would require a level of staffing and equipment that the province alone could not justify. But it did not have to. Amendments to the Canada Forestry Act extended modest assistance for forest inventories, regeneration, and eventually fire protection. The service looked, too, to the United States through the Northeast States Fire Protection Compact. This was an American response to the horrific 1947 fires, encouraging the northeastern states, which lacked much federal land, to form a consortium among themselves. But Congress also allowed, with the approval of both national governments, that Quebec and New Brunswick might subscribe as well. After a period of bureaucratic negotiations, a 1952 order-in-council authorized New Brunswick to join, subject to approval by Ottawa. In 1970, the province officially enrolled. In 1983, the United States and Canada signed a mutual aid treaty, and the Canadian Interagency Forest Fire Centre opened, together assuring New Brunswick access to fire suppression aircraft, crews, and equipment from across North America. Little New Brunswick had once again found a way to leverage its influence. The old, good fight could continue.[29]

The real issue for the future, however, was not a lack of means but a change of ends. The founding problems morphed into more modern variants, one challenging forestry from within and one challenging it from without. The challenge within came from a slow-combustion epidemic of spruce budworm. Open flames New Brunswick could beat down; insects it could not. It had endured one mass outbreak between 1916 and 1922. By 1950, the defoliation had become chronic and, if uncontained, potentially menaced most of the province. The department confessed that "no successful method of control is known." The Forest Service responded, as it would against fire, by direct attack, in this case aerial spraying. That commenced in 1952. The budworm propagated regardless. Year after year, the same scenario replayed: more spraying, more budworms, more spraying. By 1961, while fire swept 14,735 acres, and most of that from the 12,000-acre Lakeland fire, the department was spraying 2.2 million acres with DDT to control spruce budworm. The historical move from sawlogs to pulp, and from pine to spruce, had its parallel in a biotic shift from fire to insects. Before long, a menagerie of hostile bugs swarmed over the province: European beech bark louse, birch sawfly leaf miner, white pine weevil, larch sawfly, Dutch elm disease, balsam woody aphid. There were fungi as well, white pine blister rust and birch dieback, which, between 1937 and 1950, had levelled 80 percent of New Brunswick's mature yellow birch. An ecological insurgency was under way and would not respond simply to better roading, power pumps, and aerial reconnaissance. However much foresters might obsess over fire, their historical nemesis, nature had coughed up new rivals. At some point, instead of imagining insects as fire, foresters would have to reimagine fire as an ecological agent, not unlike insects. As it deepened, the crisis questioned not only forestry's practices but also its legitimacy as an authoritative guild. Yet forestry's only response, it seemed, was to call for more of the same.[30]

The challenge from without followed changes in settlement that argued for values other than forestry. In 1950, the province acquired its first national park, Fundy. (Fittingly the fires of that year documented an unusual number associated with recreational use, and twice forests had to be closed to travel.) Rural "colonization," long fading, officially ended as the province ceased to dispose of crown land and in fact gave way to a reversal, signified by the Park Act, through which the province began to buy back once-granted lands to support industry or recreational sites such as Mactaquac Provincial Park or helped to arrange for Kouchibouguac National Park. A slow recolonization, as it were, gathered momentum as urbanites interested in amenities and nature preservation took renewed interest in the forest. Old branches of the department dedicated to parks and tourism split off to become a separate ministry. These reclassified lands competed with forestry, even as industrial demands intensified. Another commission, the Forest Resources Study, reported in 1974 that "there is now no available surplus of spruce, fir, or pine to be had for the taking." While there was greater volume of growing timber than forty years previous, more of it was younger, the demands made upon it were heavier, and the competition from parks, fires, and insects was fiercer. The suggested solution, the only option the study group could imagine, was more meticulous silviculture. A new federal-provincial cost-sharing agreement made some implementation feasible. The new colonization would be met by similar means used on the old.[31]

The study lauded the fire organization. "The record of New Brunswick in forest-fire prevention and suppression is impressive and enviable – as it should be." Although the numbers of fires had increased, partly due to improved detection and mostly because of escalating recreational use, their average size had shrunk. Research done through the University of New Brunswick put a number to that achievement; from 1920 to 1975, the mean size of fires had plunged from twenty hectares to about four hectares. There were fewer years with big fires and fewer big fires altogether. Paradoxically, its success meant that fire protection was a mature enterprise. It could not – would not – claim priority or experience bold initiatives for bureaucratic growth. Its rise would be measured, proportional, in sync with any rise in the values being protected. National Forest Week was no longer oriented to fire prevention since the greatest natural threat to standing timber was spruce budworm and its entomological cousins. Fire protection shrank proportionally as a bureaucratic entity within the department. Yet for all the administrative shuffling and shouting, the forest remained, the forest industry still dominated the provincial economy, and foresters claimed pride of place as its overseers and protectors against flame.[32]

Those trends continued into the early 1980s. There were more reorganizations, more adjustments in tenure licensing, more task forces. The competition for timber (or, more broadly, for forest land) sharpened. Timber had to argue against other values, which were unlikely to bring in substantial revenues; forestry had to answer, if tepidly, to ecology as well as economics; conservation could no longer be a synonym for controlled logging. In 1976, an Ecological Reserve Act resulted in gazetting sixty-five sites for special preservation. In 1977, the department moved fire control into a general Forest Protection Branch, for which two years later a new federal-provincial General Development Agreement promised funding under co-operative programs.

It was unclear, however, whether forestry, however construed, could contain all the contemporary issues as it could free-burning fire, for too many were rooted in cultural values. As attempted legislative and bureaucratic fixes quickened, some conclusions seemed broadly apparent. There was not enough wooded land for every purpose, the intensification of old practices would prove insufficient to overcome that crush, and the province could never match national norms of wealth unless it diversified out of its corporatist and fiberholic economy. The forestry that had so shaped and energized New Brunswick's extraordinary fire establishment was also the measure of its limitations. Fire protection, not fire's pluralistic management, survived as the official ambition. The province remained a woodlot, ever more dependent on fire control to protect that timber on its way to the mill.

Quebec

All these themes coalesced in Quebec. The fishing village, the farm, the woodlot – Quebec had them in abundance, all converging, like the St. Lawrence itself, on the Québécois hearth; and to this suite it added a boreal outback. It differed from the western provinces in its bond to the gulf and the absence of dominion lands. It differed from the gulf provinces by its immense hinterland and an exquisite equilibrium among its parts. Unlike Nova Scotia, it had scads of crown land; unlike New Brunswick, logging could not dominate; unlike Prince Edward Island, agriculture could not consume every landscape. In Quebec, the state, farming, and logging were rudely balanced, with any two parts checking the third, resembling the child's game of rock-scissors-paper. All in all, its fire problems were like those of the others, only more so, exaggerated by the politics of identity.

So, while many places celebrated Confederation with bonfires, it was perhaps apropos that Quebec should greet it with a wave of wildfires. In August 1867, with provincial elections on the horizon, settler slash fires broke free and swept large chunks of the Gaspé Peninsula. In July 1868, an abandoned campfire near the mouth of the Wash-Shee-Shoe River blew up and over an eight-day period blasted east for sixty kilometres and north for twenty. Other blazes joined it, turning vast swaths of the Lower North Shore into ash and smoke. The timing was providential, for fire in Quebec was, from the onset, political. What made the province distinctive was the way in which the three great actors in Canadian fire – loggers, settlers, and the state – played out that politics.[33]

The timber industry, still rattled by the termination of the Reciprocity Treaty, struggled to find markets, convert from sawtimber to pulp, and pump up revenues. (The economics mattered since the industry filled a third of the provincial coffers, with subsidies from Ottawa contributing nearly half.) Fire and axe cut through the accessible woods like scissors through paper. Loggers reckoned that flame took ten times more timber than felling, that reburns led not to regeneration but to barrens, and that since 1850 wildfires had burned a third of the rich white pineries of the Saint-Maurice. The cost of burning had become an unacceptable burden. Industry clamoured to government for protection, which, for the state, also meant the protection of crucial revenues.

At the same time, the province sought to spur settlement by establishing a Colonization Societies Act (1869). The scheme went beyond simple pioneering. It envisioned a permanent settlement of farms and small villages, and as such it became an ideological axiom of both church and state, an idée fixe of provincial politics. Colonization meant internal colonization, a search for patches of tillable soil along riverbanks and lakeshores, agricultural niches within the grim scoured rock of the Laurentian Shield. It meant both building up and keeping *habitants* within Quebec, not letting them leach into the United States or flow in settlement tributaries to the prairies. It was a means to sustain a traditional society, although variants could graft to that rootstock minor factories. Revealingly the colonization movement was promoted heavily by the clergy and ultimately directed by the Catholic Church. Yet settlement, too, slashed the woods and sparked self-devouring fires that could consume whole communities.

The two, cutting and colonizing, often competed openly for the same sites and by equally mincing up the woods led to fires that threatened one another. There were places where they could syncopate practices into an agro-forestry regime in which farmers helped to log in the winter, or in which small woods owners contributed to the stream of timber to the mills, but provincial politics tended to polarize and pit one against the other. Logging companies wanted exclusive access to timber and colonists well removed from the scene, while settlers wanted to convert the forest to farms without inhibitions from loggers. Yet too often, for both, the axe proved subordinate to the torch, and flames melded their selfish alarms into a collective conflagration.

The state actively promoted both colonization and logging – the one guaranteed its fiscal solvency and the other its Québécois character, and because fire threatened both, often one to the other, it could not evade intervention. In 1869, it empowered a special committee to investigate the rash of post-Confederation wildfires, boosting the committee's charge to include the question of fires "in any part of the country" and the status

of the province's forests generally. Its recommendations were encoded in
a February 1870 law that prescribed how, when, and where people could
and could not set fire. Three months later *le grand feu* rampaged around
Lac-Saint-Jean, a colossal burn that was to Quebec what the 1871 fires were
to the United States. In its wake, nearly a fourth of the regional population
required immediate aid. In December, the provincial legislature upgraded
its February forest fires act with a more stringent version.[34]

For nearly a century, this political ménage à trois defined the institutional
character of fire protection. Each side sought protection, each defined
protection differently, each wanted the others to pay, and each, at different
times, temporarily dominated. The timber industry wanted fires eliminated.
Settlers wanted fires controlled but not at the expense of land clearing,
fallow fires, or pastoral burning. The government, trying to appease both,
found itself paralyzed and wanted the problem to go away. Its solution, by
default, was to outsource. As it deferred to the church to oversee much of
the colonization movement, so it allowed lease holders to organize against
fire. The resulting timber protective associations became an eerie echo of
the colonization societies. What made the issue both unique and implacable
was that fire was not strictly under the control of any one party or even of
them all together. It stood outside the traditional dialectics of Québécois
identity politics, a third solitude that claimed its own sovereignty. Yet it
could not be ignored: it demanded that something be done. And so, for the
remainder of the century, fire protection remained highly public, politically
toxic, institutionally unstable, and occasionally lethal.

The outcome was often an earnest farce as the government tried to
appease both sides, then one or the other, each party manoeuvring to get
the other to pay for the job. Industry got its say in 1883 with a new Fire
Act that proposed stricter controls over ignitions from both land clearing
and locomotives and that authorized "fire districts," each with a "fire
superintendent" and a complement of fire rangers, one group hired by
the government to patrol unlicensed crown land and the other supplied
by industry to shield their limits. As an initial gesture, the government
announced fifteen fire districts, allocated $5,000, and awaited payments-
in-kind from an industry publicly avid to insure itself against fire. It waited
in vain. The scheme could work only with industry support, and industry,
when the time came, picked up its axes instead of its chequebooks; few
even responded to Commissioner W.W. Lynch's petition; others were
reluctant to contribute unless competitors did, and the rest were content
with a free ride. After two years of frustration, with only a token corps,

Commissioner Lynch reported ruefully that, although the system had foundered in Quebec, it had been adopted successfully in Ontario.[35]

The government then reversed its emphasis and sought to shelter the settler from the logger's axe and fire. When the National Party came to power in 1887, Premier Honoré Mercier openly supported colonization and, as a gesture, abolished the fire districts, which had checked the encroachment of settlers and their torches. If the timber industry was unhappy, it had only itself to blame. Settlers no less than lumber companies deserved the protection of the state. The railway used by the Société de Colonisation du Témiscamingue, for example, ran over a rudimentary four-to-five-mile track set on tree trunks, over which the engine scattered an endless spray of sparks and soot.[36]

So it went. Small steps were taken, sound ideas hammered out, bold gestures proclaimed, with permits mandated for burning, fire rangers posted along critical locales, fire acts amended, a model protection system established with department oversight. But none could find a solid institutional home, making impossible the application of suitable techniques, which all parties accepted in principle, and the steady incrementalism so characteristic of Canadian institutions, without which reform could not gain traction. Accordingly, reforms slid back as well as forward. Officials were inclined to mistake good luck for good practices such that one successful season was enough to prove a point, while unsuccessful ones only argued for more staff and funding. That Ontario adopted and then transferred to the west the concept of dual-sponsored fire ranging is symptomatic of what Quebec could imagine yet not implement.

Serious reform required a crisis, which an outbreak of savage fires duly supplied. Premier Simon-Napoleon Parent convened a committee, appropriately named the Commission on Colonization, to review the scene. In April 1904, it concluded that, for practical purposes, "the care of the forests [should] be restricted to its protection from fire." No one gained from wildfire. Simultaneously, having created two demonstration fire-protection units in the Outouais and Saint-Maurice regions, the Department of Crown Lands was eager to expand that model throughout the major timber holdings by raising the fire tax and increasing staff. Even limit holders acceded that, as District No. 1 Steward Norman McCuaig put it, "it is the only system of assurance or protection in the form of practical cooperation that they can adopt." But co-operation had bounds. The department wanted industry to pay for fire suppression; the Quebec Limit Holders Association wanted to scrap the system altogether, arguing that the state merely supply inspectors and that both state and industry split costs evenly. The fires of 1905 decimated the government's western model but spared the Gaspé, then outside the regimen. Meanwhile, the Parent government imploded, its ambitious reforms deflated.[37]

Between the Commission on Colonization's recommendations and the breakdown of 1905, the government sought a wholesale reorganization. In December, it established the Quebec Forest Protection Service, with W.C.J. Hall as head, and announced abolition of the fire tax and devolution of responsibility to industry, which would hire rangers and prepare monthly reports. The department would retain responsibility for railways and roads, split the cost of actual firefighting, and issue insignias and posters. If companies failed to provide adequate protection, the government would do it and charge them. Meanwhile, it created two new forest reserves and dispatched two students, Avila Bédard and Gustave Piché, to the School of Forestry at Yale University to receive master's degrees (and later conduct a study tour of France). Upon their return, they inserted modern concepts of forest conservation into the debate and subsequently founded the first French-language forestry journal in North America, *La vie forestière et rurale*. Hall's instructions to his *garde-feux*, written with B.L. O'Hara, *Traité de la protection des forêts contre le feu*, became the first handbook for fire control in French. Once more, massive fires followed major reforms.[38]

The service stabilized the scene on unleased crown lands. Colonization was more difficult to contain, although Hall pursued settlers who violated slash-burning laws and enlisted Msgr. J.-C.K. Laflamme, dean of Université Laval, to rally the clergy to promote fire protection and conservation generally. But in 1911 the population of Quebec remained 62 percent rural and was actively colonizing. Momentum transferred to the third party, industry, and as often in Canadian experience the defibrillating jolt came from the United States. When Quebec forbade the export of logs in 1910, American manufacturers moved north and brought ideas as well as capital.

The limit holders thus acquired the responsibility for fire protection they had sought, but they appreciated that each company alone could never do all that was required. In 1908, Ellwood Wilson of the Laurentide Pulp and Paper Company proposed to complement the co-operative log driving that had emerged within the Maurice River Valley with co-operative firefighting. For this he also appealed to a fast-evolving American concept of "co-operative fire protection" that had emerged first among timber companies in Idaho and then propagated throughout the north, including New England. In the spring of 1912, Wilson convened sixteen owners in

Montreal to "exploit, establish and put into operation a complete and efficient fire protection system for all the woodlands of the St. Maurice Valley." A dual resident of Quebec and New Hampshire, W.R. Brown, familiar with the timber protective associations in the United States, served as vice president and helped to draft the articles of agreement. The provincial minister of lands and forests appeared and expressed his approval. The outcome was the St. Maurice Forest Protective Association.[39]

The scheme was a sensation. Henri Sorgius, formerly of the Protection Service and a protégé of Piché, assumed the role of general manager and outlined a "working plan" to beat down the fire menace. The railway companies assisted with railway patrols. The Quebec government contributed funds to bring unlicensed crown lands into the scheme, agreed to pay half the cost of lookout towers, and funded half the expenses of actual firefighting. The *Canadian Forestry Journal* boasted that this "pioneer work" of institution building would "soon be widely copied throughout Canada." It was not, but it did propagate in Quebec. In 1914, the Ottawa Forest Protective Association received letters patent; by 1917, other associations appeared (the Laurentian and the Southern St. Lawrence); and the proliferating groups, in turn, banded together to form the Quebec Forest Protective Association. In March 1919, the government made compulsory what logic and convenience were urging and required all timber companies to join an association or otherwise contribute funds. Five years later the law broadened from large landowners and limit holders to those with private forests of more than 800 hectares. Two more associations joined in 1924 and 1927. At least in principle, there would be no difference in standards between state- and industry-sponsored protection. Wilson insisted that fire protection was "a business by itself," that it would not work with part timers, and that, "if we cannot conquer the fires," everything else in forest conservation was "wasted." The Quebec Forest Protection Service, doing duty on unleased lands, became in effect one more association, although as *primus inter pares*. The Quebec strategy was now complete.[40]

It was an odd institutional arrangement, peculiar to provincial politics, as was true throughout Canada, but it allowed the standard techniques of fire protection to be applied – how well would depend on whether consistent leadership was present and how often bad fires rekindled political enthusiasms. The associations proved remarkably stable and in some regards innovative. It was the St. Maurice Association under the direction of Ellwood Wilson that arranged for a young war veteran, Stuart Graham, accompanied by his wife and a mechanic, to fly a Curtiss HS-2L hydroplane, christened *La Vigilance,* from Halifax to Trois-Rivières in 1919 for an experiment in aerial fire surveillance. It was a romantic gesture, not a little daring for taking a seaplane over land, as the crew stopped at Saint John for an opera and spent another, unplanned evening at a logging camp at Eagle Lake, Maine, when weather forced them to land. They saluted Quebec City with an overflight, dropped leaflets over Trois-Rivières, and generally created a sensation. Then the crew returned to Halifax to deliver a second plane. Wilson subsequently arranged for company directors and the scheme's promoters to take a joy ride, but dollars overcame dreams, and the program shut down.[41]

Meanwhile, the Quebec Forest Protection Service acquired its patriarch, following the charismatic W.C.J. Hall and the savvy Gustave Piché, in the person of Henry Kieffer. A professional forester, first hired in 1908, Kieffer remained head of the Protection Service until 1962, seeing it through depression and world war, dry spells and wet, *colons* (settlers) and *gardes-feux* (patrolling fire fighters), and coping with an ever more dominant pulp industry and its protective associations. Foreshorten those decades and the outcome seems little less than heroic. But to those on the ground, it was all a ceaseless slog, year by year, berth by berth, always refracted through institutions far from ideal for the purpose.

And while fires diminished, the bad years remained a cautionary tale and a prod to do better. Even as Piché explained to the British Imperial Forestry Conference about Quebec's progress, having scaled up the Protection Service's annual budget from $10,000 to $415,000, some three million acres burned, the worst on record and comparable to the Miramichi burn a century previous. Piché argued that such fires were particularly damaging (worse than "wasteful lumbering," "useless settlement," and insect epidemics) because they ruined the soil; especially horrific were recurring fires in *brûlés;* here, in its forests and barrens was the real record of Quebec's baleful fire history. In musing over reforms, Piché noted the enduring problem of slash, the need to render the staff of the Protection Service more permanent, and the blind insistence that Quebec was a "pays essentiellement agricole" when any rational mind would declare it a "pays essentiellement forestière." At the 1924 conference, however, New Brunswick's minister made an equally telling point when he voiced his opinion that it was "remarkable" that, after all its investments, experience, and "increased protection," Quebec should get "the worst fires on record." That was not a paradox limited to Quebec.[42]

Until the 1960s, the parties of this triumvirate evolved with a mix of autonomy and synchronization, and while bad years broke free on a roughly decadal cadence, the general trend was downward. (The question of truly remote fires vanished by declaring a rough line of control at the fifty-first parallel.) Then Quebec fire underwent its "quiet revolution." The rural fire scene withered away, no longer resuscitated by periodic colonization. Between 1941 and 1971, Quebec lost two-thirds of its farms; as remote rural sites sank into poverty, *colon* became a term of derision; and by 1955 slash burning had plummeted from a dominant cause of wildfire to a negligible one. The colonization movement of the future lay in the north, not with agricultural villages but with hydropower. The James Bay scheme replaced Témiscamingue. The new reality was that Quebec was neither a farm nor a woodlot. It was urban; its economic future lay in industry and services. Fire protection would have to project those values.[43]

That left the contest for control between the Protection Service and the associations. In 1962, the *longue durée* of Henry Kieffer ended with retirement; soon afterward, the Service reorganized its increasingly archaic institutional structure into ten regions and modernized its apparatus, for which aerial fire control was both an emblem and a prime mover. Aircraft became common, then mandatory. In 1962, lookout towers still formed the backbone of the provincial detection system; by 1970, the towers were gone, replaced by aerial observers. In 1961, the service tested two Canso PBY-5As for waterbombing; by 1971, it was flying three Canadair CL-215s, the only aircraft designed specifically for firefighting and one conveniently manufactured in Quebec, the first of a fleet of fifteen.

As the old arrangement collapsed, Quebec sought new ones. Within the province, the government asserted its rule over industry and, in April 1970, pushed through an agreement that restructured the institutional fundamentals. In effect, Quebec nationalized fire protection, as it did hydropower. It created a Conservation Branch within the department, dissolved the thirty-nine associations and reorganized them into seven regional "conservation societies," and assumed responsibility for fire over even small private holdings. The system no longer had excuses due to confused jurisdictions or incomplete coverage.[44]

So, too, there were readjustments in Quebec's relationships beyond its provincial borders. In 1970, it joined the Northeastern Forest Fire Compact, thus gaining access to American resources and countering pressures to ally with Canadian ones. Where it sought alliances with other provinces, it did so through arrangements that in no way compromised its claims, overt or implied, to sovereignty, a stance that merged readily with the insistence of all the provinces that they, and they alone, had jurisdiction over natural resources. It adopted, for example, the Fire Weather Index devised by the Canadian Forest Service as a national fire danger rating system, adapting it to Quebec circumstances; however, unlike most grants from Ottawa, this one came with no political strings, even as it latently acted as a nationalizing force by quietly synchronizing the provinces under a common regimen of terminology, procedures, and standards. A similar political calculation applied to joining the Canadian Interagency Forest Fire Centre in the early 1980s, which Quebec did hesitantly and then because CIFFC was a corporation, not an organ of the dominion, and because like other provinces Quebec preferred to meet the United States through a collective Canadian institution rather than confront it alone. In the end, it preferred the historical dialectic it understood, and assumed that it could, as in the past, direct that process to its own goals.

But that dialectic itself was changing. An exurban colonization was replacing an agrarian one; the thrust of fire institutions included protection of nature reserves as well as raw timber; the contest for control had to involve agencies outside the province since Quebec had to admit that it could not, through its own resources, respond to the exceptional year. In this, Quebec more resembled the rest of Canada than it cared to admit. It conceived of fire through an identical instrumental and commercial lens, accepted efficiency of operation as a goal in itself, and struggled inconclusively to imagine fire as something perhaps indispensable as well as inevitable. Here lay the real challenge. Prescribed fire for habitat might replace slash burning for timber, free-burning fire might be left to roam in remote lands and nature reserves. Such practices, however, had been, since the earliest forester, anathema. The apparatus that Quebec had for more than a century wrestled finally into a disciplined and coherent form might no longer apply because the purposes that inspired it were shifting.

In this evolution lay fire's true quiet revolution, one barely acknowledged, much less accepted. Fire had not been a signatory to reforms governing its administration; it obeyed no logic save lightning, drought, wind, and combustibles suitably arrayed; it claimed its own sovereignty, as ecologically insistent by its absence as by its presence. Worse, fires were compounding with other disturbances such as insects, disease, ice and wind storms, a witch's brew of wrecked forests. Then came the summer of 2005, the worst since 1932, and smoke again spread wide palls across the land. The question posed after the 1923 outbreak – why, after all the proper reforms had been enacted, fire still rampaged – returned. An answer required a reconceptualization of fire management beyond the customary demand for more pumps, planes, and plans for reorganization. It required an admission of fire's complex autonomy, which stood outside the historical dialectic that had defined Quebec's understanding of itself, a third solitude. Admitted or not, Quebec remained a country of fire, with a natural memory far deeper than that of any of its occupying societies.

Ontario

With no direct outlet to the gulf yet without entree into the plains, Ontario was the odd man out. It was part of the founding two Canadas, still clinging to the rapids of the St. Lawrence and its tributary lakes, yet it swelled with a raw hinterland acquired from Hudson's Bay Company, the one tethering it to old Canada and the other tugging it west to a new Canada. It held eastern Canada's best agriculture sites yet burst with raw boreal bush. It was terrestrial Canada at its narrowest and longest, with its least and most fire-prone woods. It was middle Canada, the geographical and historical transition between the two regions and two eras. It was crucible Canada, where the fire institutions of the east metamorphosed into those of the west. It was the forge, the conduit, and the propellant that created the strategy, the model, and the means by which to cope with fire in the boreal backcountry.

Ontario, too, greeted Confederation with fires, which raged on both sides of the Ottawa River, the two solitudes being for fire only two banks of the same river. But Ontario dodged the 1870 fires that clustered amid the force-fed colonization around Lac St.-Jean. Instead, it got smashed by the 1871 fires that scoured the newly unsettled landscapes around the upper Great Lakes. While million-acre burns ripped Wisconsin and roared through Michigan, an estimated 2,000 square miles burned from the French River to the Kaministiquia River around Lake Superior, not a few of the fires along the route being explored for the Canadian Pacific Railway. Six packers from a CPR survey party, in fact, died in the main conflagration.[45]

The difference between Quebec's 1870 *grand feu* and Ontario's 1871 Superior burn suggests the differences between the two provinces' styles of settlement, forestry, fire, and governmental responses. The railway was national, trending to the Great West, not to arable nooks in provincial hinterlands; settlement followed the rails, not the rails settlement; the rail surveys led to mines, not farms, the "New Ontario" of Sudbury. The ideology of colonization was one of commerce, not culture. To such large fires, the government responded sluggishly, unconvinced that its fire scene was chronic rather than fitful. Both provinces endured the same storm-surge of flame that swept the region from 1908 to 1923, sending one giant fire breaker after another crashing into its woods, burning Cobalt as well as Porcupine, Haileybury as fully as Témiscamingue. When Ontario finally responded, however, it acted with uncompromised authority. It behaved like a nation-state unto itself. It, rather than Quebec, first implemented the fire-rangering program that the Ottawa loggers had devised and then held to that original design. The model that the western provinces would follow, building on the wreckage of the Dominion Forestry Branch, was the one that rode the rails out of Ontario.

A Fire Act went on the books in 1878. It had the usual provisions for a restricted burning season, penalties for careless use of fire or its abandonment, and spark arrestors for locomotives. It also provided for the establishment of fire districts, in which the provisions of the Fire Act would apply, the first such legislation in Canada. Two districts were promptly proclaimed, centred on areas bustling with settlement, and not much happened on the ground. These were the circumstances prevailing at the time of the Montreal Forestry Congress, which prompted proposals from the timber industry for surer fire protection. Quebec's ministry embraced them but could not convince industry to follow through. In Ontario, the commissioner deputed Aubrey White to report on the prospects, the inaugural of a distinguished train of inquiries.[46]

In March 1885, White submitted his findings, sketching a "plan or system" that focused on a Fire Ranging Service, a corps of rangers jointly appointed and funded by government and industry, distributed where most needed on both licensed and unlicensed crown land. Success would demand co-operation from both settlers and loggers, for "should ill blood between the two classes be created" the scheme would collapse, but White assumed all parties could see the logic of fire protection, and the government agreed. The commissioner solicited the opinions of licensees at the end of the season, then concluded that "the experiment having proved such a success, it was thought right to continue and extend it." Mostly the chief fire problems centred on the settled, eastern lands of the province; the principal causes were settlers burning slash, small fires left by river drivers, sparks from locomotives, "careless hunters, fishermen, tourists and explorers" negligently sloughing off fires, tossing matches, and leaving "smouldering gun wadding." For such tasks, the Fire Ranging Service was ideally suited.[47]

A decade's record seemed to confirm the commissioner's assertion that "close supervision" and "systematic organization" could triumph over formidable weather and continued public profligacy. "All seem to think that the service is admirably adapted to accomplish the object for which it was established." The following year, 1896, brought big fires, big expenses, big losses, and, despite the previous note of triumphalism from the province's politicians, an alarming "general disbelief in the future of the timber industry in Ontario," as Clerk of Forestry Thomas Southworth bluntly expressed it. Much of Ontario – a growing fraction – was now cut over and abandoned, unfit for farming and bristling with "weed" trees. The future of the timber industry thus demanded that it keep moving to uncut frontiers, a flaming front of axe-fed fire. Southworth called for a committee of inquiry, to which the commissioner acceded, having himself pondered for some time what action the province might take "without at present incurring any large expenditure." In time-honoured fashion, the government empowered a royal commission, with Southworth as secretary, which reaffirmed what Southworth as clerk had asserted, that the future of the timber industry depended on new timber and an adequate regrowth of white pine, and both were impossible without fire protection. Bad cutting made for bad fires, and bad fires encouraged reburns, which instead of birthing a new forest spawned barrens. All that Ontario required to practise forest conservation and scientific forestry was better fire control. If fire ranging had not so far stopped the flames, the solution was more fire ranging. That was the preliminary conclusion.[48]

The full report, issued in 1899, amplified its reasoning, asserting that the restoration of "fire swept tracts of land" to productivity and the prevention of other tracts from being burned comprised "the forestry problem awaiting solution in Ontario." Accordingly the commission divided the province into three parts. The southern division, mostly cleared for farms, stood in need of replanting to support agriculture. The central division, habitat of "that most valuable of all trees in North America," the white pine, much of it slashed and burned, required fire protection to allow regeneration. The northern division argued for preservation, again through the control of wildfire, to permit a later harvest. (Along routes of travel, the forests were all young, due to the fire "carelessness" of canoeists and indigenes.) The commission's conclusion: Make the fire-rangering service compulsory on both licensed berths and adjacent crown land. Place all fire rangers under the Department of Crown Lands and enlist the Hudson's Bay Company to help distribute fire proclamations to the indifferent "Indians of the Northern Districts." Make felling selective. And create permanent forest reserves from the berths of defaulted licences and forested land otherwise unsuited for settlement.[49]

It was a dazzling vision, a sirens' call. The solution was breathtakingly simple. All that was needed was to stop fires, and nature would do the rest. The costs of fire protection the province would split with, or extract altogether from, industry, which also paid licence rents. Complicated and politically touchy questions of silviculture, logging methods, land tenure, exploitative mining, and reckless settlement all collapsed into the single proposition that sound fire protection would encourage loggers to behave better, fire-wielding settlers to display prudence instead of promiscuity, nature to profligately restore white pine, and the province to avoid messy expenses. The argument became an axiom of Ontario forest administration. Fire, not the axe, was to blame for Ontario's forest ills; overburning, not overcutting, was the root problem; fire control could not merely substitute for but subsume forestry (and avoid those "intensive and expensive systems of Germany or France," which all observers, not least the royal commission, dismissed as "quite out of the question" for Ontario). Technique could substitute for deeper policy. The thrust of fiscal investment, and of intellectual inquiry, could point to wider effectiveness and greater efficiencies. Instead of regulating industrial logging, the province sought to remove the checks against it, including those voiced by conservation.[50]

When other provinces looked to Ontario, this was the vision that rose like a mist out of the Canadian taiga. They saw a robust organization for fighting fire, one that was highly mechanized, ideologically uncompromised, and bureaucratically secure. They saw state forestry as a controlling authority for fire in the province. They saw a sufficient answer to conservationist critics, for even parks and forest reserves existed primarily to shield those sites from flame. And they saw that, however costly fire protection might be, it exerted a far lesser claim against the provincial treasury than a full-service program of forestry, while its failures could be shunted aside as due to insufficient coverage or extraordinary weather.

How it happened in detail is a story that depended, in Ontario as elsewhere, on political determination, ingenuity in the field, persistent and long-tenured leadership. No network of lookouts, telephones, trails, and tool caches sprang up spontaneously like mushrooms. Political approval did not, by itself, send a corps of fire-ranging canoeists over portages and across lakes. A tough bureaucracy did not guarantee that tough men would battle flames throughout the boreal Shield with grit and resolve.

The institutional framework advanced in 1898 with passage of the Forest Reserves Act, and then in 1900, acting on the royal commission's recommendations, fire rangering became compulsory on all licensed lands, the cost split between the department and the licensee. Rangers could impress citizens as needed, paying them local wages. But the department quickly appreciated the fundamental geography of fire protection that argued for three zones of different intensities. There were remote sites, often kindled by lightning, beyond the height of land and beyond both reach and concern. There were wild timber berths, leased but removed from settlement and mining, for which fire was a matter of endless "anxiety," but whose practical risk careful fire ranging could, if suitably conducted, make "almost non-existent." The volatile scenes were those along the frontier, where settlers, miners, railways, or recreational hunters, fishermen, or tourists tramped, cut, burned, or fire littered. The scheme boomed. After twenty years, the province boasted 425 rangers.[51]

Another twenty years would pass before the system fully congealed. Within that period, Ontario suffered through a sickening succession of holocausts. Each outbreak, by itself, had echoes elsewhere in Canada or across the Great Lakes. Their causes were nauseatingly familiar. A land scabrous with drying slash, settlers negligently if not homicidally reckless with their torches, railways hacking through wildlands and casting embers, too-feeble fire protection, these were common everywhere. Ontario added a few lethal particulars. Prospectors, treating the Shield like a colossal outcrop, applied flame to scrape off its biotic cover. Colonizers were scattered and fire feckless; Ontario's settlement was as laissez-faire as Quebec's was *dirigiste*. The railways punched through the boreal Shield, their surveyors as undisciplined as the most cavalier trapper, their rights-of-way unbuffered by agriculture. In most places, colonization meant farming eventually. In New Ontario, it meant a rawer form of industrial capital, at most a smattering of farms around mill, factory, or mine. There would be no Quebec compromise by which industry could regulate itself, with government subsidies to assist. The government of Ontario would see that industry did the job, and charge industry for it, and after a burn it would harvest for its "money value" whatever timber could be salvaged. Under all this, the big fires kept the institutional pot boiling.[52]

The system hardened amid a fifteen-year fugue of rogue fires and fire reforms. These were the most notorious serial holocausts in Canadian history, and they were fought in the Toronto legislature as well as the little clay belt around Cochrane and the dishevelled wilds north of Lake Nipissing. The roster began in 1908, rippling along the border from Puget Sound to the Bay of Fundy; in 1909, the reserves were hit; in 1910, lands around Lake Superior suffered, as the Fire Act was amended to compel fire protection by licensees, and amended again in 1912 and 1913 to compel patrols by the province on unlicensed crown lands. Between those codicils the Porcupine and Cochrane fires raged through the clay belt. In 1912, E.J. Zavitz became director of the Dominion Forestry Branch, thus installing the obligatory patriarch. The next year Ontario organized for railway fire protection under the national board and compelled patrols on unlicensed crown lands. In 1914, the department began keeping systematic fire records, while flames again struck around Superior. Two years later the Matheson fire blasted the clay belt. In 1917, Zavitz became provincial forester, and a new Fire Act replaced the patchy old one. But until settlers burned under permit and loggers disposed of their debris as rapidly as they created it, the department concluded that "our forests will burn." Ontario's fire arms race quickened: the province pitted practices that produced revenue (but sparked fires) against those that spent revenue (to quell those fires). The province, in effect, bet that fire rangering could hold the flames in check. It was right, but only after further reforms strengthened its hand and another rash of holocausts. In 1919, the department underwent a postwar expansion and suffered a near-record year for area burned and timber lost. In 1920, a co-operative program in aerial reconnaissance commenced with the assistance of the Dominion Air Board, while a timber commission launched inquiries into the Crown Timber Act. Its report, issued in 1922, urged stronger fire protection measures, including firmer methods to reduce that enduring scourge, slash. The first steel lookout towers appeared, along with the first proposal for a ranger school; the next two years suffered record drought and fire. The October 1922 Haileybury fire furnished an unwanted prelude to the British Empire Forestry Conference, while two million scorched acres preceded Ontario to the national Forest Fire Conference.[53]

The province became a veritable empire in miniature. The Toronto office was a thousand miles away from outlying satraps, some thirty-five districts, each under the charge of a chief fire ranger. The districts were in turn subdivided into sections under deputy chief rangers, who supervised ten to twelve fire rangers. Both chiefs and deputies were permanent staff, assigned to other forest duties during the winter. There were "forest engineers" who oversaw six district offices, assisted by graduate foresters; two special officers for railway inspections; and a chief flying officer, stationed at Sudbury, for aerial reconnaissance. Zavitz acknowledged that, to imperial foresters, the "prominence of forest fire protection" in Canada must be "very noticeable," declared his envy for those foresters who found their careers full of "the peaceful fields of forest investigation or reforestation," a luxury not allowed Canadians, and concluded with the glossy statistics for 1922, from which the Haileybury conflagration was neatly expunged.[54]

Ontario's problems were those common everywhere in Canada, but the department recognized early that, while burned settlements got public attention, it was the outliers that mattered. It was the small number of fires that became large that, as Zavitz explained, "really created our big burned-over acreage." Some clustered along the railways (one along the Algoma Central ran for twenty miles in a day before men could be mustered to fight it and then transported from Port Arthur, a hundred miles distant). But most were in remote timber berths or berths-to-be. So while it amended the Fire Act in 1924 to better regulate slash burning, it also turned to machinery, introducing the portable hand pump and especially the "aeroplane," which became instantly axiomatic as a "factor in reaching a solution of forest protection." Within two years after their introduction, aerial patrols were soaring over thirty million acres and had become "imperative."[55]

Aerial fire control – that was where Ontario would place its bets. The province had distilled forestry into fire protection and now distilled fire protection into aerial attack. On the eve of the experiment, the Department confessed that "the outstanding feature" of forest administration, not only in Ontario but also throughout Canada, was the "inability to control the losses from forest fires," before which "all other phases of administration are comparatively minor matters." Aerial fire protection offered a technological fix. When the Dominion Air Board ended its subsidy, nearly all the other provinces, if reluctantly, withdrew. Ontario elected to create its own air service. It was a bold move, rightly honoured in memory, and one justified only because fire protection commanded the intellectual no less than institutional enthusiasms of the province. (The choice sharpens the contrast with Quebec, whose experiment in aerial reconnaissance rose and fell with the ledger books of the St. Maurice Association.)[56]

The provincial air service began as the dominion's did, with surplus planes, in this case Curtiss HS-2Ls from the United States. For the 1922 and 1923 seasons, Ontario ran the program co-operatively with the Air Board, through a contract with the Laurentide Air Service. The main base was at Whitney, where the Grand Trunk Railway crossed Algonquin Park, with a secondary base at Parry Sound. The next season added bases at Ramsay Lake near Sudbury and Trout Lake near North Bay. The experiment "clearly demonstrated" a set of related facts: that for reconnaissance aircraft had "no equal"; that where ground detection was prohibitive, as in the western reaches, aerial surveillance was the "best solution"; that aircraft would not reduce ground personnel; that efficient patrols required special aircraft; and that the "moral effect" was immense on both the public and the rangering staff. But if Ontario wanted aerial fire control, it would have to pay for it. Minister of Lands and Forests James W. Lyons argued for outright purchase rather than leasing. It would provide a permanent organization, complementing the various reforms that had jelled since 1917. And Lyons believed that "undoubtedly" the bulk of protection would depend on aircraft "in the course of a very few years." Ontario's Department of Lands and Forests required planes for its northwest outback for the same reason that the Dominion Forestry Branch required them for its Northwest Territories. There was no other practical option.[57]

The particulars became sticky when it came time to actually acquire the planes. Initially the scheme called for purchase through a jobber from surplus stocks in the United States, until President Harding issued an executive order prohibiting sales of such military planes to foreign countries. The province then turned to the Laurentide Air Service, which sold fifteen Curtiss HS-2Ls and then had its vice president and general manager, Roy Maxwell, resign and transfer to the Department of Lands and Forests as director of the Ontario Provincial Air Service (OPAS). The high cost of the aircraft – the purchase forced a 25 percent reduction in fire-ranging staff – compelled the protection branch to use them everywhere imaginable for patrolling, surveying, sketching, photographing, and general hauling. The purchase of fifty pumps assured the basic alliance that would govern fire control in the backcountry, a combination of aerial detection and pump-and-hose suppression. It was, Minister Lyons asserted, an "important advance" in the "policy of forest protection," even if it occasionally killed people, as it did a co-pilot and observer when a plane crashed that inaugural season.[58]

Thereafter, the Ontario Provincial Air Service took on a life of its own. The patrols operated in two districts, east at Sudbury and west at Sioux Lookout, with Lake Nipigon as the divide. Providentially the next five years were subpar for fires, as damp as the preceding five had been droughty. The province could absorb the start-up cost of the OPAS and could experiment with tasks, even subcontracting for services to mines, the Hudson's Bay Company, Indian treaty supplies, prospectors, and Ontario Hydro. The operation resembled, in effect, a kind of crown corporation. The planes vaporized the distance that had made fire ranging by paddle and portage as hopeless as it was heroic. Throughout, fire protection remained the OPAS's indelible raison d'être. The province would never have purchased its own fleet without the needs of fire control, and fire control had already become unthinkable without aircraft at the ready.[59]

Ontario now commenced a long trek through the swings of climate and politics, the peculiar cadence of bureaucratic tedium and conflagrating terror that beat through a maturing fire agency. Fire protection flourished or famished as the provincial economy feasted or starved, through boom, war, depression, recovery, and stagnation. Statistically it fell into the familiar rhythms of Canadian fire overall. Background burning steadily subsided, while most burning occurred from a handful of big fires that burst forth, roughly every decade or so. Institutionally, it underwent the usual cavalcade of reorganizations, amended fire acts, infrastructure improvements, and equipment upgrades. What did not change were the bred traits of Ontario fire protection, notably its pushiness, its persistence, its reliance on mechanical power, particularly aircraft, and its rationale. Firefighting remained not merely a supplement to forestry but all too often a surrogate for it. Looking back from the mid-1960s, T.E. Mackey pondered the department's chronicle of sometimes fitful but ultimately resolute progress. Improvement had been neither trivial nor inevitable: it had occurred because determined people, acting through long tenures under a consistent vision, had made it happen. The Ontario story was one not of brooding and hand-wringing, of pondering the ecological and conceptual limits of fire protection and the implacable fury of boreal conflagrations, but of acting, of applying practical technology to push the limits of its ambition ever further.[60]

The greatest crisis occurred when drought colluded with Depression. Fires sorely tested it in 1929, when it got hammered by the second greatest number of fires (1,550) under conditions more severe than in 1923, yet the resulting firefight "proved beyond a doubt" that the province could control fires, and the experience had an "immeasurable" effect on departmental "morale." More insidious was the Depression-induced attrition of staff. By 1931, numbers were below those of 1923, and reductions continued into 1932. Big fires came regardless. But in a familiar scenario, the sources of fires were changing, and the worst burning fled to ever-farther reaches. A report from Trent (1932) outlined a typical slate of causes, which collectively contributed 37 percent of the year's fire load. Some fires were set so locals could be hired to fight them, some to burn off deer pastures, to renew blueberry patches, to retaliate for grievances, "to place an enemy under suspicion," and, given changes in the game laws that prohibited the use of dogs, "to create open hunting grounds." Campers, recreationists, and incendiarists of various ilks replaced railways and colonizers, while lightning increasingly dominated remote landscapes. Partly this was an artefact of pushing fire protection ever farther outward and partly of finding more fires to report. In 1936, lightning in the backcountry kindled the most intractable burns, accounting for 80 percent of the 1.2 million acres burned and straining the OPAS to the breaking point. Planes became more valuable for transportation than detection, as firefighting morphed into a kind of aerial pioneering and the OPAS had to enlist outside help. A more permanent solution required either that the department pull back from such hinterlands or that it fully "settle" them with advanced technologies, notably aircraft and radio. The last hurrah for the era of settler holocausts came two years later when October fires in the Fort Frances District burned 92,400 acres and killed twenty people.[61]

Following a select committee in 1939 and a royal commission in 1946, the department experienced what T.E. Mackey considered a "virtual rebirth." An institutional renaissance, perhaps, but not an intellectual one, for the future promised to revive the past. A vision of comprehensive forestry succumbed to recurring reorganizations for greater efficiency; the task for which the Department of Lands and Forests had achieved its greatest efficiencies, fire protection, became the model for whatever else it did. As Director Mackey noted approvingly, fire protection provided the model for forest administration overall, extending its methods to "biological" concerns such as insect infestations, and had become "generally accepted as the nerve center of all activity." Even as the latest royal commission urged "Total Forestry," the default setting remained fire protection.[62]

Aerial operations retained pride of place, and the spectacle of the recent war suggested scores of ways that modern machinery might be redirected from the fight against fascism to the fight against flame. Radios, aircraft, helicopters, power pumps, bulldozers, paracargo, and, that enduring *fata morgana* of firefighting, waterbombing – all could supply added mechanical muscle to an unwavering goal. In 1946, the department experimented with helicopters; in 1950, it tried waterbombing; by 1959, waterbombing by Otter and Beaver floatplanes went operational. Its air service was now fully enfolded with fire protection like the twin strands of a DNA molecule. Even outbreaks such as the 1961 season confirmed rather than challenged the axiomatic premises that the big acreage resulted from a handful of big fires and that every big fire began as a small fire that another waterbomber or helitack crew could have caught. All in all, Ontario was doing, with more might, what other provinces did or wished to do. An outside observer might aptly have characterized the Division of Forest Protection as an empire within.[63]

Throughout, the founding dialectics endured. It was fire versus machine, and nature versus institutions. By the early 1970s, the flow favoured fire protection. More land was protected more intensively; burned area, and area per fire, shrank; a few rogue fires in the untamed bush did nearly all the damage. Then the tide turned in 1974. Even amid the festivities celebrating the fiftieth anniversary of the OPAS, wildfires walloped Ontario with 1,625 starts that burned 1,294,800 acres, the largest outbreak since 1923. Some fifty years of modern fire control had, by the raw standard of burned area, with a cynic's glazed eye, accomplished nothing. That, of course, was not the gloss put on the eruption by the Division of Forest Protection, which quickly noted that two fires had burned outside the normal season and that seventy-one had broken free beyond the zone of intensive protection, and these had ripped through 79 percent of the total area scorched; the Red Lake No. 78 fire alone blew through 302,848 acres. The next year fire starts reached a statistical high, although burned acreage remained low. The following year shredded those statistics and leaped over the 1974 acreage with 1,344,517 blackened acres. Records fell like jackstrawed pine. The seemingly self-evident lesson was to extend the forces of suppression when needed and to absorb within the pale of protection those lands that traditionally had stood beyond them, or else accept that fires left uncontrolled would, in fact, burn uncontrollably. All this recycled the classic logic of fire protection. Two years later, after a return to more "normal" seasons, the province opened a modern Aviation and Fire Management Centre, and another familiar logic of Canadian fire asserted itself, as disaster followed reform.[64]

The subsequent two seasons dealt a double blow. The first came in 1979, an otherwise "average year." On 22 August, outside Geraldton, a prescribed fire in slash (site PB-3) turned feral. Such burns had become routine since 1966, yet another effort to stimulate regeneration and in keeping with provincial predilections to have fire management substitute for more intensive silviculture. The Geraldton district had become a program leader, ready to respond to a 1978 ministerial conference to pressure foresters to get in their burning as well as to get out their timber, with the control-burned area for that year more than double the average. The burnout went bad, the crews became disoriented in the smoke and wind, and a clutch of junior rangers, seventeen-year-old interns, five boys and two girls, enlisted for the project died in the flames. The entire area enclosed by the fatal fire amounted to 2.5 hectares. The second blow followed a year later, a season that was, as even the official report confessed, "one of the worst ever suffered in Ontario." An estimated 1.38 million acres burned; one fire, Thunder Bay 46, romped over 313,200 acres. The ministry poured out $56.9 million in fighting that tide, mustering forty of its own aircraft and contracting for an additional ninety-three helicopters and thirty-five other aircraft from private sources and even the United States. Two firefighters died in a helicopter crash.[65]

Still, what it meant remained a matter of perspective. One perspective was this: for all of the twentieth century, Ontario had pinned its forestry hopes on fire protection, that fire control would protect uncut berths, shield regrowth from reburns, abate slash, and stimulate regeneration and that Ontario unaided could handle the task. Those assumptions had now suffered massive breakdowns, in 1979 with the ability to light fires and in 1980 with the ability to fight them. The reality was that, when the weather turned sour, Ontario could no longer pretend that it could muster enough counterforce to match a massive outbreak of conflagrations. The reality was that under such circumstances Ontario's fire problems, as Ontario defined them, were beyond the province's capacity to contain them. What rendered reality into politics, however, was the begrudging admission that what happened to Ontario was happening to other provinces as well, that none could build up staff, stock tool caches, and service air fleets sufficient to fight the worst outbreaks, and none could dismiss those crisis years as statistical anomalies or outliers because they were the years that mattered, the fires that broke records, busted budgets, and did the real ecological work. This realization is what made the big fires of 1980 revolutionary. But whether the revolution was one of institutions or of ideas remained unsettled.

Another perspective was that the issue was a familiar one of money and materiel. If Ontario couldn't muster the staff and planes for the blowout year, it might cultivate alliances that could. It was still possible to imagine that with access to a larger (a national or even international) cache of pumps and fleet of waterbombers and with slicker methods of pre-positioning and dispatching the old ways might continue. With that understanding, Ontario switched from balker to booster for a national fire centre. Yet this was a profoundly conservative revolution. Instead of a debate over goals, discussion shunted onto familiar political side rails such as provincial prerogatives in administering natural resources and deeply rutted fire-strategy tracks such as the power of initial attack. This of course had long been Ontario's historical role, the soft weld between east and west.

Yet in pushing it, Ontario was also reaffirming its default fire philosophy, formally announced by the report of its 1899 royal commission, the precept that fire protection was the essence of forestry, with the hard-learned codicil that initial attack was the essence of fire protection. Both CIFFC and the Canada-US mutual aid treaty put more gas in the tank and allowed that old strategy to fly on without having to check the map and maybe ponder a new route. Those monster caches substituted a debate over means for one over ends, such that, even as mass fires swept over the founding precepts, the old verities reseeded in the ash, like a jack pine forest regrowing en masse after immolation.

Fire's Lesser Dominion

The DFS Implodes

The transfer of natural resources to the provinces did not happen instantaneously. A 1929 conference of dominion and provincial forest authorities laid a foundation for a national forest inventory. The transfer itself did not occur until after the 1930 season and, for British Columbia, not until 1933. It was an odd affair, all in all. The provinces wanted the minerals, from which they could derive maximum revenue with minimal expenditures, not the woods, which were costly to protect and for which there was no real forest industry. The dominion insisted they take it all, partly on constitutional grounds and partly out of administrative and fiscal concerns. The forests were a revenue sink.[1]

A scheme to ease the dislocation took the form of a proposed fire conference of ministers and fire officers, modelled on that of 1924. Conservation gadfly Frank J.D. Barnjum had badgered Prime Minister King on forestry matters, especially slash. This nagging evolved into the ambition to replay the majestic 1924 convocation, updating reports and focusing on the altered administrative landscapes. King, however, thought the time "inopportune" for a fire conference and no doubt worried that the provinces would this time, as last, renew pleas for funds, so the conference was deferred until late spring or summer 1930. That timing brought it into conflict with elections, which argued for postponement. The resulting change of government made the proposal's subsequent burial all that easier. What degree of national cohesion the Dominion Forest Service had achieved now disaggregated.[2]

The scrappy E.H. Finlayson went down swinging. In a final memo, Finn argued that forest devastation especially by fire was a national problem, that the federal government needed to assert leadership, and that palming off responsibility to the provinces did not solve the serious depletion of Canada's forests by axe and fire. And while the transfer would reduce "temporarily" the fiscal pressures on the national treasury, "it is only a question of time until the federal government will have to financially aid the provinces in their forestry programs." That forecast proved true. In 1930, however, the dominion was more interested in reducing its costs than in sparring with the provinces over theirs. The transfer went through without the bother of ameliorative conferences.[3]

Finlayson put on a bold front. The move would, he announced, "relieve" the Dominion Forest Service of its expansive administrative functions and allow it to concentrate "on investigation, research, and experiment," while providing "leadership" to the provinces and industry. The agency had retained its research, the national forestry inventory, and the Forest Products Labs. In principle, the reconstituted (and renamed) Dominion Forest Service could do for national forestry what other bureaus did for agriculture and mining. Abruptly reversing his earlier exhortations, Finlayson announced that the agency's "dominion-wide" duties would prove, "in the long run," of "much greater importance" than its founding tasks.[4]

The Bennett regime did not agree. By fiscal year 1932-33, the Forest Service budget had plummeted 83 percent, its staffing slashed, its morale gutted, its mission vague. A review of the realignment estimated that formal responsibilities had been halved but funding reduced to a sixth. Actually the situation was worse, for Finlayson had only grudgingly allotted space for research during the late 1920s. The Dominion Forest Service was a shambles. It had less in the field than on paper and more on paper than in its labs. As if to symbolize its disorientation, an overworked Finlayson began suffering "nervous collapses" and bouts of amnesia. The bureau, too, unsure where to house its records, had chunks of its archives pulped. On 26 February 1936, Director of Forestry Finlayson simply vanished.[5]

A month later a reorganization removed the Forest Service from the Department of the Interior and transplanted it to the Department of Mines and Resources. But that did not change the fundamental fact: the agency had lost its hard bond to the land and did not have an equivalent valence to science. In general, the provinces wanted money, not advice, while government research belonged under the auspices of the National Research Council. The Dominion Forest Service became a minor bureau with a cluster of legacy tasks that didn't seem to fit anywhere else. It did forest economics, sought to collect essential forestry statistics, studied insects and fire, advised the dominion regarding its territories, oversaw two forest products labs, and conducted silviculture experiments at Petawawa. While impressive, the tasks did not add up to a compelling national presence. Its director confessed that it was "primarily a fact-finding and advisory organization." The only legal authority for the Forest Service did not even mention the research that had become its primary duty. The agency could neither stand on its own nor fit tidily into other bureaus. Reorganizations followed. Reorganizations always followed; they came as often as sunspot cycles.[6]

The near future jostled into order in 1936. Roy Cameron replaced the vanished Finlayson as director. Meanwhile, beginning in 1933, the imperative for unemployment relief had encouraged the federal government to establish experimental stations in New Brunswick, Quebec, Manitoba, and Alberta (Kananaskis); they were in place by 1936, miniature versions of Petawawa, primarily devoted to silvics and fire protection. The agency's reorientation into research got boosts at the dominion level that year from the National Research Council, which created a Subcommittee on Forest Fire Research, and the Canadian Society of Forest Engineers, which likewise authorized a Fire Research Committee. Clearly fire remained a vital if forlorn driver of national interest. During its administration of the forest reserves, much of what the DFS did, and how it justified its existence, had been dictated by fire. Now that research had supplanted the reserves, fire continued as its most commanding purpose.[7]

Sometimes the two could combine. Petawawa could only conduct its silvic experiments if fire could be kept from the sites, which pushed it to devise a model fire protection system. In August 1936, outside Kananaskis, a fire was spotted on Mount Galatea. The Alberta Forest Service packed in crews. The fire continued, and prevailing winds suggested that the burn might threaten the experimental forest, so the DFS took to the field as well, with forester Harry Holman assuming charge of some crews. On 9 August, the "whole country blew up," trapping some forty men along with their horses and equipment. A wild flight carried the crews to river bars and beaver ponds, where they weathered the firestorm. With its trivial land base, such firefights had become uncommon for the agency, but that a province might turn to it was emblematic, for that, in a sense far deeper than a shovel-wielding crew boss, would be the agency's anointed role. When, after the Second World War, the federal government inquired about fire protection in its suddenly interesting Northwest and Yukon Territories, it dispatched Holman to assess the scene.[8]

But such calls were few during the Depression. Another boost came with the National Forestry Program, although it had barely begun when the war derailed it and alternative service workers partially replaced them. The same might be said of the Forest Service overall. Hardly had it realigned from doing to studying than the war stripped away its funding and staff, leaving a caretaker regime; even at Petawawa, research came "to a virtual end." Its premier topic, fire science, became a simple holding action against fires on experimental plots. Although weather stations sprouted up to expand the data for fire hazard tables under the Wright-Beall System, with particular note in the western national parks, the war years all but swatted out the last flickering flames.[9]

The most dramatic innovation was yet another attempt at a national forestry policy, this one anticipating dramatic reforms after the war concluded. The Wallace Report of 1943 stumbled, as had its predecessors, but it appealed strenuously for serious silviculture and argued that the greatest check against good administration was wildfire. In that, it embodied a general consensus. Fire would continue to inform the character of Canadian forestry and of those institutions, however hapless, that sought to oversee, investigate, or even tabulate Canada's woods.

Fire by Committee

So, if it seemed intuitively self-evident that Ottawa should have an interest in fire (after all, forestry was a major industry and wildfire a relentless threat), after 1930 no one seemed able to state exactly what that interest was or how it should express itself. Forestry was a provincial responsibility; the federal government had little means, other than public shaming and political bribery, to exact reforms or even information. There was no standard method to report fire, no databank of national statistics. There were no norms for the level of protection. The provinces could not, individually, support much research and could only rarely agree on what kinds of questions might interest them all. In brief, fire got sucked into the maelstrom of provincial-federal relations. Matters boiled down to who should pay and who should say.

Yet Ottawa could not bring itself to withdraw completely. There were some legitimate national needs; by the mid-1930s, a shaky consensus emerged. Predictably, perhaps, it was a corporatist third party that prompted action. In July 1935, the Woodlands Section of the Canadian Pulp and Paper Association and the Canadian Society of Forest Engineers met jointly at Petawawa and passed a resolution that the National Research Council convene a conference on forest research. The well-attended conference proceeded that November in Ottawa. The committee writing the final report for the inaugural meeting included E.H. Finlayson, P.Z. Caverhill, G.C. Piché, and E.J. Zavitz, a roster of the major personalities in forest protection. At its conclusion, the NRC agreed to establish an Associate Committee on Forest Research that would sponsor annual meetings at which researchers could review topics and methods. Its creation lent some status to fire research and helped the downsized DFS, no longer reeling, to regain its balance. The Petawawa group quickly bonded with the committee.[10]

A national perspective could now walk on two legs. The solution extracted no money from industry or provinces and exercised no coercion. It was a self-described "forum" for discussing mutual problems. The

Subcommittee on Forest Fire Protection did "not undertake the solution of problems" but only attempted "to identify them, and to analyse their importance and refer them to the attention of competent authorities." In sum, the committee furnished a neutral setting, independent of political authorities, where all could speak and no one had to listen. For the next fifty years, the Associate Committee and its avatars provided the only collective council for Canadian fire, the closest approximation to a national organ. Here, rather than through the DFS, the Canadian fire community could describe their year's activities, ambitions, and alarms.[11]

The DFS, however, quickly grasped the significance of the committee, became a dominant member, and used the collective recommendations to reinforce its value as a research institution. At the first committee meeting, D.A. Macdonald, then DFS deputy, submitted a long paper that surveyed research needs from the "lack of balance" between prevention and suppression to the spectacular promise of fire hazard prediction, the pressing need for better detection and communication, and to the mechanization of fire control. All these were rehearsed, with special attention given to topics such as chemical retardants and radio, where collaboration with the National Research Council's in-house programs might be possible. In particular, there was an "urgent need" for a "Fire Research Field Laboratory" to "investigate, improve, design, and standardize fire fighting equipment and methods at some centrally located proving grounds." That of course did not happen – was unlikely to happen granted the grim political economy of the Depression. But Petawawa promised an approximate alternative. Jim Wright soon retooled his facilities to examine pumps, measure nozzles, test hoses, and sample chemical retardants with the same meticulous energy he had applied to the moisture content of duff. Some of the trials were divided between Petawawa and the NRC laboratories, culminating in a joint report in 1938. By the next year, the collaboration had produced the design for a self-priming centrifugal pump and a "light portable one-man hose-reel for picking up wet hose."[12]

The fire group rapidly distinguished itself and after the war became sufficiently vigorous that it split off informally in 1947 as a separate Subcommittee on Forest Fire Protection, chaired by Herb Beall; within a year, that status had become formalized. Here, where the best minds in Canadian fire convened under the rubric of the National Research Council, was surely the place to ponder the larger purposes of fire management. Here one could transcend the mundane bureaucracy of paper shuffling and the seasonal rounds of equipment cleaning, crew training, and fire extinguishing. But nothing of the sort happened. The title told all: this was a program concerned not with the science or political economy of fire but with the technology of fire control. Page after page, contribution after contribution, year after year, the subcommittee obsessed over techniques, not ideas; tools, not concepts. It accumulated hundreds of pages on hoses and pumps, on radios, retardants, and fire camp rations. With nothing truly important at stake, nothing truly important was discussed. What Canadian fire organizations craved were more tools, more machines, longer-lasting hoses, and ultimately dominion-sponsored aircraft. Their goal was efficiency, and they did not wish to discuss whether they were efficient to the wrong ends, only how to improve the means at hand. They themselves became tools, institutional instruments, so mesmerized by the free range of fire across Canada that they did not pause to wonder if the tools available were themselves determining the uses to which they might be put. They chose to focus on gadgets rather than goals.[13]

What the subcommittee did offer was something perhaps more fundamental. Each year there was an "exchange of information." Each province and every institution told the others what it experienced, what it hoped to do in the year ahead, what it thought the critical problems were. In effect, the subcommittee institutionalized the 1924 Forest Fire Conference into an annual affair. It amassed the raw data and coarse circumstances of Canadian fire without the worrisome implications of political obligation, and in so doing it created a Canadian community for fire protection. It did what the political fabric of the Canadian Confederation prohibited the federal government from doing. It did something everyone wanted, and so persisted, although in typical Canadian fashion it survived by reorganizing, adapting, finding new institutional handholds on the slick rock of governance by confederation. In 1952, the Associate Committee on Forestry dissolved, its tasks absorbed by other organs, save those connected with fire. That subcommittee reconstituted itself as an Associate Committee on Forest Fire Research, while T.E. Mackey replaced Herb Beall, then consumed with other administrative duties, as chair.[14]

For the next thirty years, the Associate Committee did what no other body could, renaming itself the Canadian Committee on Forest Fire Control in 1971 before undergoing a final chrysalis in 1983. The minutes of its annual meetings are the fullest register of Canadian fire from a national perspective. If they sometimes seem tedious, if not tendentious, if the discussions too often appear mired in the metrification of couplings and the abrasion characteristics of linen hose, if fire management obsessively identified itself with infrared cameras, fog nozzles, and water bombers, that was still no small achievement. The committee remained true to its founding charter. It was a forum, unique and irreplaceable. Revealingly, during the dismal Duplessis regime, it was the only national organization in which Quebec's forestry department was allowed to participate.[15]

Tracer Index: James G. Wright and Herbert W. Beall

If fire protection had defined the Dominion Forest Service's mission before 1930, fire research determined its future. Its silvicultural experiments could well be overseen by another organ of government from the National Research Council to the Department of Agriculture; its statistics could go to the Census Bureau or to Treasury; the Forest Products Lab could be a stand-alone institute. But free-burning fire belonged nowhere scientifically, even as it bonded field and lab weld. It seemed only natural that the Forest Service, whatever its avatar, should continue the investigation.

That it should have done research at all was a near-run thing. Finlayson had been hostile until the repeated fire crises that plagued a thinly spread Forestry Branch had convinced him that field officers needed better forecasts of wind and relative humidity, which had become the simplest direct measure of the daily fire hazard. He himself had dabbled with such a system while district inspector of Alberta reserves, an interest that led to the establishment of weather stations, including hygrothermographs, which inspired, in turn, co-operation with the Dominion Meteorological Service in Victoria. The foresters sent in weather data; the forecasters returned predictions of wind and humidity. Scribbled correlations between local weather and observed fire behaviour lent some credence to warnings of high hazard. But good quantitative data, experimental control, and consistent predictions over large areas – these were absent. A strict science of fire danger rating was a good idea. It was good for line officers who needed to know when to place forces on alert, good for an industry that wanted a reliable system for shutting down operations if the hazard became too great, good for administrators who sought an objective index against which to measure performance. It was, in sum, a good idea that no one quite knew how to wrestle into scientific shape.

Revealingly the process began not with foresters but with meteorologists and a civil engineer. The meteorologists were Dr. John Paterson and Sir Robert Stupart of the Dominion Meteorological Service; the engineer was James G. Wright, hired by the Department of the Interior in 1918 as a surveyor but transferred in 1922 to the DFB. In 1925, Wright discussed with the Meteorological Service the prospects for issuing fire weather forecasts for dominion lands as it was doing for British Columbia and Ontario. The following year a network of weather stations was installed, and forecasts commenced for Alberta. But while a measurable improvement, an understanding of the mechanics by which weather got transmuted into fire was obscure. The question intrigued Wright; there had to be a way to translate forecast weather into forecast fire behaviour. In principle, if the relationships were understood quantitatively, one could devise an index to do just that. As a concept, the idea was not new, for the US Forest Service, which had formally established a research branch in 1916, was rapidly investigating the same phenomena. The trick was to make it happen.[1]

Wright sketched out a proposal and took it to Finlayson, who disapproved on general grounds, despite (or perhaps because of) his own early dabblings. Wright himself proposed another explanation. "My method required the setting of experimental fires," a practice that irked Finn and that was "one of the reasons, I think, why he refused to allow me to undertake forest fire research." Fortunately his deputy, Roy Cameron, was enthusiastic. Still, another three years passed before Wright initiated work at Petawawa, which had its own demands for practical fire protection and hence shared common cause to understand fire more precisely. That summer, 1928, Herbert W. Beall joined Wright as a student assistant. All in all, the collaboration was coincidence of a high order. The director had acceded to the project grudgingly, Wright had stumbled onto fire from other duties, and Beall was an arts major at Queen's whose uncle knew Finlayson sufficiently well to get him posted for a summer job. Beall was assigned to Wright since the important (that is, silvicultural) research went to forestry students. Money was scarce, equipment was primitive, and a successful outcome was far from foreordained. Within two years, the DFS was in freefall.[2]

For the next twenty years, however, the collaboration between Wright and Beall defined Canadian fire science. The "tracer index" that summed up the fire hazard of a site was one of the outstanding achievements of the Forest Service and one retained in every future iteration of the system. As much as anything the agency did, the Wright-Beall index confirmed the significance of Petawawa as a research institution and a model forest and established the agency's continued relevance to the provinces. The tracer index held together not merely duff and humidity but also dominion and province; it tracked the evolution of what became a great institution of fire research.

The two men made an ideal tag team: Jim Wright, the astute engineer and deft administrator, and Herb Beall, bright and affable, a newly minted forester, having transferred to the forestry program at the University of Toronto before joining the DFS full time in 1932. Cam Macleod, who later headed fire research for the DFS and directed Petawawa, recalled

Wright as "an absolute power of a man – the first fire researcher in Canada and one of the first in the world. He was loaded with ideas of things to do and how to do them, but he had the gift of being able to concentrate on the main objective." He was disciplined, indefatigable, inventive. These were traits he "instilled" in the young Beall, whom Macleod characterized as having "by far the most brilliant mind I have come across, either in or outside the Service, for pure logic and absolutely uninhibited thought." Like Wright, he overflowed with ideas, and like his mentor he worked relentlessly. Both men, moreover, had a knack – not common in either of their chosen professions – for working with people.[3]

But what mattered most in those early years was their ability to work with each other. The cold fact was that forestry had repeatedly failed to render fire into a robust science. Time and again, foresters, for all their insistence that theirs was a species of engineering, stumbled in the actual conduct of research. Too often the rush of doing – the need to respond, the obsession with efficiency of operations – drove what they wanted to know and how they proposed to study it; too often fire was an administrative problem, or a question of forest economics, not a matter for natural science. What the scene required was the imagination of an engineer, the mind of someone who could identify the critical quantitative features, who could devise instruments to measure those components, who could factor those data into a mathematical model, who could approach the question of what kind of conditions yielded what kind of fire as he would the question of erecting a bridge or digging a canal. The need was to define fire as a phenomenological puzzle to be solved, not an enemy to be fought, an engineering problem to be broken down into researchable units – this was Jim Wright's achievement. It took a forester's imagination to insert that science back into field operations – this was the particular accomplishment of Herb Beall.

From the onset, it was Wright who defined the core problem and the methodology to address it. (Ever after, despite his own innovative modifications, Beall always and graciously referred to the outcome as the "Wright System." Wright, he stated unequivocally, supplied the inspiration and he, Beall, the "perspiration.") Over that first winter, Wright completed plans for an intensified research program. He recognized that the critical component of the Petawawa pine forests was their surface litter, notably the upper layer of duff. The greater the duff, the drier the duff, the more vigorous the fire. In the summer of 1929, he and Beall installed instruments to assess ambient moisture, both precipitation and relative humidity; to

The grand pair of Canadian fire research. *Top*, J.G. Wright, third from right. *Bottom*, Herb Beall in Banff, 1940.

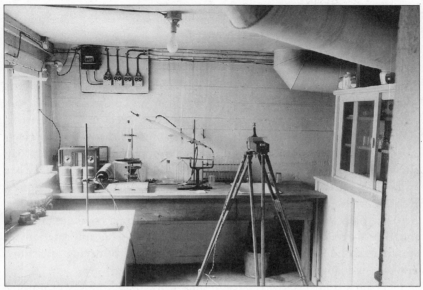

The Petawawa lab, 1938.

determine the rate of drying, through temperature and wind, assisted by a newly contrived evaporimeter; to measure the duff directly with a special hygrometer; and to correlate the derived indices with actual fires. Initially the latter were inadvertent burns that occurred over the course of the season. Later it became standard practice to kindle small test fires in the field under rudely controlled conditions. All in all, Wright reckoned that he had "started, or arranged the starting through subordinates, or more experimental forest fires ... than any other human being." Supplementing the field trials, Wright contracted with the Forest Products Lab to run controlled experiments on pine duff combustibility, demonstrating the variability of ignition temperatures with moisture content.[4]

Fire research at last entered the consciousness of the DFS. In his annual report, Finlayson noted that 1929 had been a "busy season" for fire control at Petawawa but also one that had allowed "the collection of most interesting and valuable data." Within a year, reports, both published and unpublished, began spilling out, and despite the deprivations of the Depression and the hiatus of the war, those reports flowed until Beall resigned from active research in 1953. They were, in the truest sense, definitive. As C.E. Van Wagner observed sixty years later, Wright and Beall covered "such a wide range of subject matter that it is hard to find an important aspect of physical forest fire science on which they left no mark." In the coming years, the startling disjunction between the plummeting status of the DFS and its soaring fire science went beyond irony.[5]

The first results were published in 1930. Wright quickly dismissed the journalistic trope that fires "just happen like Spanish influenza." Rather, it could be seen that "the moisture content of a fuel determines its behaviour in the presence of a potential source of ignition, and if the weather factors which influence this moisture content can be isolated and measured, it should be possible to determine the inflammability of the fuel under given weather conditions; in other words, to build up a chart from day to day showing the cumulative effect of the weather upon the fire hazard." That chart required hard data, the empiricism of engineering, which he acquired by establishing plots, recording the weather, cutting patches of duff that he twice daily weighed, and fine-tuning duff hygrometers acquired from the Forest Products Lab in Madison, Wisconsin. This information he summarized into three charts: effect of rainfall, rate of drying after rain, and rate of change of inflammability.[6]

His conclusion was that the techniques worked and that by exploiting the curves it should be possible "to compute from the weather records with a reasonable degree of accuracy, the degree of fire hazard." That determination came with two qualifiers. The first was that a robust index demanded moisture measurements from more than the surface duff, and the second that the curves applied only to the red and white pine woodlands of Petawawa. Annually, as more data accrued, reports, published and unpublished, poured out. In 1932, Wright wrote "Forest Fire Hazard Research," which amplified his annunciatory essay and proclaimed the rationale behind a program of systematic study. Fire was a prominent, "some authorities say … *the most* important, phase of forestry in Canada." Yet, puzzlingly, no attempt, "until recent years," had been made to unravel the laws that governed it, and while "we have standards, or units of measurement for practically everything," none existed for measuring fire hazard. The breakthrough publication came in 1933. Belying its banal title, "Forest Fire Hazard Tables for Mixed Red and White Pine Forests" was a revolutionary document and, along with its 1932 antecedent, the foundation for all future Canadian projects in fire hazard rating. It introduced the tracer index as a means of correlating recorded weather with fuel flammability, and it codified the results into working tables that foresters could take into the field. Those tables were the intellectual equivalent of a portable power pump. Fire officers immediately recognized their value, for they showed where best to position those pumps and point their nozzles. "It caught on like nobody's business," Beall recalled. "Everyone was enthused about it."[7]

Between them, the two papers established the next decade of Canadian fire science, during which the concepts were refined and the range of data expanded. Each feature of the system underwent close scrutiny, from instruments such as drying ovens, evaporation pans, and sling psychrometers to the creation of means by which to estimate wind velocity in mixed woods (the Beall wind scale). The realization quickly arrived, too, that the tracer index needed to absorb more than the volatile surface duff, that the "sluggish" realm of heavy downed wood and deeper litter in which it was embedded was also a crucial factor, that a parameter for long-term drying was needed. The incorporation of drought was one of Beall's particular contributions to the grand project. His other intellectual achievement, about which he was especially proud, was to devise graphical means to integrate and display the multiple correlations that the tracer index summed.[8]

But if the Wright System deepened, it also broadened. Every region and climate required its own unique tables. Wright had gingerly tested his preliminary conclusions in western Quebec in 1931; firmer tables appeared with his 1933 paper. But to go further, the Wright-Beall team would need field plots, and the dominion had divested itself of the lands that would ideally serve. Here the increasingly irascible Finlayson came to the rescue. He had, as Beall recalled, "good contacts with the army." Again, Petawawa provided a precedent. Finn parlayed his influence to get access to army lands outside Quebec City and Fredericton, what evolved into the Valcartier and Acadia Forest Experiment Stations established respectively in 1935 and 1937. There were plans to expand into Manitoba, but "a fire wiped out the whole of the Duck Mountain Forest Reserve the next year," ending the scheme. In 1934, stations took root at Prince Albert and Riding Mountain National Parks. Finn succeeded at Kananaskis, where twenty years previously he had tinkered with the rudiments of hazard rating, although the project did not take tangible form until 1939 with the labour supplied by the National Forestry Program. For all these sites, Herb Beall did the fieldwork – installed instruments, platted sites, trained observers, assembled the data into preliminary tables. By 1939, the Wright System was "in practical use" in three Canadian provinces and the national parks of the west.[9]

There was more. After the National Research Council took an interest in fire, Wright worked out a research program in pumps, hoses, and chemical retardants. Moreover, his extraordinary experience with experimental fires led him to promote controlled burning for slash disposal and regeneration.

"Any of these things," he explained, "can be done under control; the whole thing is a matter of control, and the control is hinged on our fire-hazard index." Meanwhile, Beall, who had to deal with park and provincial fire officers, evolved into an accomplished diplomat of fire, the point man between the provinces and the federal government.[10]

By then the tag-team was broken. Beall had enlisted in the Royal Air Force in 1941; Wright left fire research in 1943. The war years put the program into suspended animation. After Beall returned in 1945, he and Wright co-authored a final summary of their work, but that was more a clerical exercise, a digest of work accomplished for an audience outside Canada, than an announcement of new initiatives. Nonetheless, Beall picked up the pieces, revived the field projects, and in 1946 published a "provisional" summary of the tables that nearly spanned the country. (A political spate had kept British Columbia out of the program until after the war.) The scrimped circumstances had allowed not only fire research to slide but fire protection as well; Beall estimated that operational effectiveness had dropped 20 percent since 1929. A forester to his marrow, he believed the tables only as good as their impact in the field, which is to say, the final measure of the tracer index was its capacity to reduce the burned area. To achieve this, however, the Wright System needed help to translate its forecasts into operations, and Beall again looked first to the United States, which was leaping ahead with the planning that had to underwrite its vigorous expansion of fire protection into the backcountry. Thus, in addition to updating and publishing his composite tables, he orchestrated a model fire plan for Petawawa, both published in 1948.[11]

That suggested to his pragmatic mind that, if the diverse fuels of Canada could be subjected to systematic analysis by standard methods, so, too, could the various practices that characterized the country's fire agencies. What Canada needed was a Wright System for fire control, and the way to do that was to fashion some standards for protection. In 1946, the Canadian Society of Forest Engineers (CSFE) had passed a resolution urging the adoption of at least "minimum standards of forest-fire protection for all defined forest zones in Canada," a project then passed along to the DFS. It was exactly what Beall believed was needed, and, if anyone could attempt to evoke or cajole a common system out of Canada's cacophonous fire agencies, it was he. So in 1947 he began adapting to Canadian conditions some core concepts that the US Forest Service had developed over the past thirty years, notably the least-cost-plus-loss theory of fire economics and the hour-control schema for fire planning, especially as Lloyd Hornby and Harry Gisborne had revised them for the northern Rockies. It was a piece of work he regarded as his "most original" contribution.[12]

The tracer index could register the hazard. What was needed to complement it was an index that could tell how much effort fire agencies should expend to counter that hazard. Like its model, Beall determined that the data should be quantitative, the analysis mathematical, and the final product a kind of tracer index that should establish the level of protection required. Just as different forests responded differently to weather, so too protection agencies should adjust their efforts to the values that they sought to protect. Before the Wright System, fire officers could broadly agree that certain conditions made for more troublesome fires, but they could not do so with rigour or with an objective basis for comparison. So, too, they could agree that some places required more intensive protection, but they could not argue with much pretence of quantitative logic or with any good basis for comparing places and efforts. Beall hoped to achieve for this problem what Wright had done for hazard forecasting.

The antithesis of the isolated genius scribbling in his garret, Herb Beall circulated his ideas widely. He talked, he travelled, he corresponded, he mailed out drafts for review; he sent out drafts along with the criticisms he had received for others to comment upon. He toured the United States with the DFS's new chief, D.A. Macdonald. Gradually he crafted a formula that could establish how much area any particular agency could allow to burn, what he called "standards" for fire protection, ultimately aspiring to derive a suite of standards for all of Canada. As the dominion and provinces debated what kind of collaboration they might accept for forestry, Beall laboured to furnish some criteria for determining where co-operation and funds might be most effective, a general formula that could replace raw politics.[13]

His "Outline of Forest Fire Protection Standards," published in 1949, thus complemented the Canada Forestry Act. But while there was widespread admiration for his intellectual achievements, there was only wary enthusiasm for what might be termed the Beall System. Its mathematics were complicated; the determination of values and damages was often arbitrary; the data were inadequate, particularly considering the extreme variability of burning in the boreal forest. Every agency thought that it knew better than any formula what it needed. Provincial particulars mattered more than national norms. Unlike the Wright System, which told local officers the nature of the hazard they faced, the Beall System implicitly told them what they should do about it. That made it a political project, and, while the Dominion of Canada might consider the scheme exemplary, the Confederation of Canada did not. Federal standards could look suspiciously like federal control. To provincials, it seemed that Ottawa might reclaim by stealth what it had openly disbursed in 1930. Standards – any standards – were a tough sell.[14]

Perhaps inevitably it fell to Herb Beall to administer the agreements that the Canada Forestry Act produced, to achieve by personality what he could not instil through formulas. He confessed himself "heartbroken" that the Act had not made fire protection a centrepiece. The fire-prone provinces, too, howled in protest; almost no province could truly justify aerial suppression, yet none could do without it, and those like British Columbia that contributed disproportionately to the national timber trade insisted that they performed a national service that deserved a national subsidy. Beall agreed and believed that, with the right persuasion, he could wangle it into the agreements, and he did when the program came up for renewal in 1956. When he accepted that administrative post in 1952, however, he left research for good.[15]

For most of Canada, and for most of the world, Herb Beall had become the face of Canadian fire. With each year since his return from active duty in 1945, his administrative duties had swelled, not only within the DFS but also for the NRC's Associate Committee and even Canada's External Aid Office, which sought his advice regarding an Agroforestry Centre in Nairobi. Moreover, it was the courtly Beall who delivered the story of Canadian fire hazard research to the Fifth British Empire Forestry Conference in 1947, Beall who authored the essay on forest fire research for the Imperial Forestry Bureau, and Beall who represented Canada at the 1949 UN Scientific Conference on the Conservation and Utilization of Resources. When he retired in 1969, he was serving on several national advisory councils regarding forestry, and after his retirement he continued as a consultant and as a member of the 1970 Special Task Force on Forestry. He had become a diplomat and emissary of Canadian fire, always reaching out to the provinces, to the national parks, to the territories, to the Commonwealth, the United States, the United Nations. His successor, Cam Macleod, fulminated that "it was a crime against humanity to make a good researcher like him an administrator." But it is hard to see how it could have been otherwise.[16]

Jim Wright, too, had veered into administration. In 1943, the department seconded him to the Northwest Territories to help administer an economic survey of the Canadian Eastern Arctic. A year later he became executive assistant for the National Parks Bureau. In 1946, he received an appointment as superintendent for the eastern Arctic and as secretary of the Northwest

Territories Council. Retiring in 1952, he moved to Sackville, New Brunswick, where for some years he taught engineering at Mount Allison University before entering local politics as an alderman and eventually becoming mayor in 1960. Beall had marvelled over Wright's ability to work with people, to get people to like to do what they had to do, but the same might be said of Beall, that his was a genius of common sense, courtesy, thoroughness, not of raw intellectual brilliance. He had, as Wright did, that Canadian ability to work within a broad confederation of narrow interests.[17]

That the two founders of fire research left both fire and research for administrative posts says something powerful, and ominous, about the parlous state of the dominion's presence in fire protection. Political support was meagre, and there was little mechanism to move research into operations. Until the Canada Forestry Act, Ottawa had feeble leverage to influence provincial practices, and then the task called more on the art of political engineering than on the science of engineering research. The federal presence was too unstable, the institutional dynamics too restless.

Yet the Wright-Beall legacy was real enough. The tracer index revived after the war; it flourished, propagated, and evolved. Modestly Beall dismissed his own contributions as but "one link in the chain." Others knew better. In nominating him for the Order of Canada, C.E. Van Wagner, himself long the doyen of Canadian fire science, confirmed that Canada had the only national system "that has been adopted successfully and without question by all the forest fire agencies in the country" and that the core of that enterprise was the tracer index of the "Wright-Beall System." More broadly the collaboration between Wright and Beall had produced "a unique Canadian school," with results "not exceeded in scientific value and practical usefulness anywhere in the world."[18]

Herb Beall regarded himself as "lucky," shunted as he had been into a job as a student that no one valued but that then became indispensable. He and Jim Wright were simply the right men at the right time, he insisted. Yet it might more aptly be said that it was the times that were lucky to have found the right men. No one had told Wright to invent his method. He did that work with a touch of defiance, against the overt wishes of his director, with paltry support and jerry-rigged equipment. And no one compelled Beall to learn that method, or to alter his college major, or to seek to amplify its lessons. They did those tasks because they were necessary, interesting, and right. Beall once reminisced about his first summer at Petawawa. Finlayson had visited and told him that this profession was "self-denying. It's for the future, for the benefit of other people. It's something that you go into not for your own benefit so much as for the good of the country."[19]

That is not a bad collective epitaph. If their fate was like that of many Canadian intellectuals to have their identity subsumed by the instruments and institutions they inspired and birthed, they had asked for nothing more. Their colleagues knew. Their data endured. Their character persisted in that far more complex tracer index that was Canadian history.

Plain and Mountain: Fire Provinces of Western Canada

The west was different. Geographically it replaced the Precambrian Shield with the Great Plains, the worn Appalachians with the densely ranged Cordillera, and a dominantly humid climate with a chronically semi-arid one. The plains were grassy to the south and woody to the north, and both were prone to burn, broken only by rivers, empty of the Shield's watery matrix, each biota in its own way among the most flammable fire regimes in North America. Historically European settlement came late, not really transforming the land until rails and aircraft made transportation routine. By then, Confederation and conservation could converge to match the special character of the western setting with a special politics. Save for the Red River Settlement, these were from the onset crown lands that existed "for the purposes of the Dominion." Large chunks across the plains Ottawa bestowed as a subsidy on the railways; much of the arable land it sold to settlers; but the vast hinterland remained its own, governed, as much as a tiny staff could oversee so immense an estate, by the Dominion Forestry Branch. Even British Columbia retained its public domain almost wholly intact. From the onset, the state loomed large in fashioning fire institutions, and excepting British Columbia forestry lagged. The provincial fire establishments evolved out of a federal template.[1]

Manitoba, Saskatchewan, Alberta – these were the geopolitical links that secured British Columbia to Old Canada. Although prairie, or rather the conversion of wild grass to wheat, defined their post-Confederation settlement and economy, the provinces were mostly wooded. Here, again, east and west diverged. The western provinces had to weld together strikingly different political economies. The emerging Canadian nation ran east and west, arcing roughly along the lines of its great biomes. But the western provinces ran north and south, against that geographic grain, forcing prairie to link with taiga, and woodland with tundra, and doing so on an immense scale. Until recent decades, only Ontario among the eastern provinces had to grapple with such challenges. What worked in one landscape would not work in another. The fires on their prairies they could snuff out by further settlement; the fires in the boreal bush they could not. The assumption, so fundamental to eastern Canada as to be unconscious, that water was always handy to haul, pump, or scoop from the air was not the case in the west. As tactics varied, so did strategies.

The complications went beyond the geographical realm into the political one. Most of their nominal estate the western provinces did not themselves administer; Ottawa did. The politics between province and dominion were fundamentally different from elsewhere in Canada. The dominion drove land use decisions by its promotion of prairie farms along the Canadian Pacific Railway, by its sale or grant of lands to private owners and railway companies, by its control over the immense hinterlands of boreal forest. Save (as always) the Red River Settlement and British Columbia, the provinces had no prior colonial status from which to negotiate entry into Confederation. They came in as a colossal block of the North-West Territory. That changed, of course, as the provinces evolved into their present configuration, and it saltated abruptly in 1930 when the dominion ceded its crown lands to the provinces. This was a redefinition of responsibilities without precedent elsewhere in Canada, a continental divide between the institutional fire histories of east and west. The defining struggles, for half a century or more, by which eastern provinces cobbled together institutions for fire protection were absent in the west, along with their often paralyzing politics. The western provinces simply took over the apparatus the Dominion Forestry Branch had left them, together with its justification. The provinces would do the same, only better. But if they avoided a discourse of doubt at their origins, they had to endure one later. By the time most celebrated their fiftieth anniversaries, they were frequently convulsed by reorganizations behind which were uncertainties about what these fire agencies, now powerful, were doing and why.

British Columbia evolved differently still, at the time of Confederation a separate colony in its own right. A strong dominion presence along the railway belt stiffened fire institutions, like rebar in concrete. But the province did not stabilize beyond gold strikes and fur-trading posts until the conservation era, by which time foresters could command the dominant industry and thus could shape a state forestry bureau that here, as everywhere, became the bulwark of fire protection over a land mass almost wholly crown land. The provincial government itself did what the dominion government did for the others. In this, British Columbia resembled Ontario, and between them they held the fire practices of the intervening provinces within their force field.

Manitoba

Beyond the Great Lakes and the Shield lay the prairie, and along the banks of the Red River lay the improbable colony established by Selkirk, a supreme irritant to the way of life that had washed seasonally over the grasses but one that could transmute into something majestic, like a grain of sand into an oyster pearl. After Confederation, that anomalous presence forced a political crisis, a muted rebellion, and the formation of the first of the great western provinces. The way west, whether by Hudson's Bay Company or the Canadian Pacific, went through Winnipeg. For forty years, Manitoba remained a grassland gate to the great west.

Manitoba was the pioneer: the first province carved out of Rupert's Land, the first to balance prairie farm with logged forest, the first to thrash out a metastable reconciliation between aboriginal culture and industrial capital, between an economy of pemmican and pelt and one of steam, wheat, and timber, the first to track a new politics between province and dominion, between those older provinces that had evolved independently and then confederated with the suite of provinces invented *de novo* out of the raw wilds of the North-West. It began as a prairie province little bigger than New Brunswick. With its expansion northward in 1912, following completion of the railway from The Pas to Churchill, the province swelled beyond its grassy nucleus to incorporate swaths of woodland, boreal forest, and tundra, a vast hinterland that both tempted and unbalanced. Some 60 percent of its land now rested on the Shield. A third of its landscape was, in fact, lake.

Through Winnipeg were channelled not merely goods but ideas. The forest farming typical of Canada from the Great Lakes to the Atlantic here had to adapt to the largely treeless prairies; the railways made that possible. Here, too, a province had to cope with fires on the forested Shield, which at first involved, as in Old Canada, an adaptation of voyageur culture. But as the urge to control flame intensified, so did the need for sterner, more mechanical, technologies. What rails did for the prairie, aircraft did for the taiga. Accordingly Manitoba needed to look no further than the neighbour with whom it shared some of the most fire-prone landscapes on the continent. The Ontario strategy, filtered through an apprenticeship with the Dominion Forestry Branch, served nicely.

Manitoba's prairie fires were as fundamental as seasonal thunderstorms. The old cycle, however, described not merely a rhythm of seasons but also a rhythm of human itinerancy, of hunting, trapping, trekking, and burning. That itinerancy withered when the hunters and bison died out or slunk off elsewhere. The scene Henry Hind so vividly described along the Assiniboine and Paul Kane painted along the South Saskatchewan vanished as a tide of farms washed over the plains, rippling out from the railways. The wildfires went the way of the wild grasses that fed them. The faster the settlement – the quicker the pace of roads, ploughed fields, homesteads, intensive grazing, and firebreaks – the faster prairie fires faded. The wheat shock replaced the bunchgrass, and the milk cow the red buffalo.

There was often a period of wild excess during the transition. Some old burning persisted, now untethered from its historical context, no longer greening up hunting grounds but threatening unharvested wheat or winter forage. Newcomers proved often careless with fire, uncertain how it might behave and when one could burn prudently, so transients littered the land with untended campfires; locomotives cast sparks with reckless promiscuity, and ranchers often burned in the spring, seeking a flush greenup, but not always with care or on lands buffered with firebreaks. Improvident farmers, threatened with wildfire, set backfires, which then bolted across the countryside. Elsewhere lightning and locomotive linked the pristine with the industrial.

A year after Manitoba acquired provincial standing, an inspector with the Dominion Lands Branch, Lindsay Russell, wrote how his surveys were "most seriously retarded" by extensive fires. Smoke prevented sightings; flames threatened encampments, and field parties suffered narrow escapes "from suffocation and burning." Unsurprisingly fire codes seeking to regulate burning were among the earliest laws passed; the North West Mounted Police soon found itself fighting fires. (One 1879 report singled out a particularly egregious autumn fire, "generally believed to have been the work of Indians when leaving for the southern country to hunt.") The Northwest Territories Council, first meeting in 1877, promptly promulgated An Ordinance Respecting the Prevention of Prairie and Forest Fires. Where settlements thickened into towns or colonies (such as the Mormon Settlements in Alberta), organized fire brigades or at least the possibility of rallying neighbours appeared. Until then, as the Department of the Interior declaimed in 1890, prairie fires were "a matter which is probably at present of more importance to the Territories than any other."[2]

It was the unsettled lands, or the border between the feral and the domesticated, that caused alarm. By their nature, until sold, these were crown lands, subject to dominion administration. The Department of the Interior began addressing the issue seriously during the mid-1880s as the Canadian Pacific neared completion. "Too great care cannot be exercised in respect to prairie fires," its annual report intoned. Citing "Manitoba and portions of the North West," the secretary concluded that "very serious losses have been occasioned by these fires" and would continue, and in places, "never an autumn passes" that they are not "run over by fires." Without intervention, some districts would remain "perfectly valueless." Yet settlers too often neglected fires, trusting to wind and luck. While further settlement would ultimately resolve the problem, the current scene demanded action in the form of artificial firebreaks, enforcement of fire codes, and fines for those who refused to render assistance when called.[3]

For such fires often could be fought. Wet blankets and volunteers could halt even extensive burns, particularly if applied at night. "Four men on horse back, accompanied by a team, driver, and two barrels of water have frequently put out ten miles of fire." It was possible. There was no excuse for fatalism, or laissez-faire procrastination, or outright shirking. Too often settlers left the problem to the Mounties, as though unwanted fires were a criminal matter over which ordinary citizens had little responsibility. The RCMP on the prairies found its seasonal routine driven by fires, by frequent requests for assistance to fight them, by fire patrols, by the need to board men and horses at farms "during the dangerous seasons." None of this it deemed necessary. Oddly, some thinly settled districts, where each colonist had to rely on others, were better at fire control than some more densely settled ones, which deferred any action to a constabulary. Forage-hungry ranchers, worried about loss of winter range, often organized better than townsfolk. And at a time when colonists fretted over the absence of trees for fuel wood and timber, and as the dominion geared up to help plant the prairies to woods, a casual attitude toward free-burning fire was counterproductive and apathy a form of hostility.[4]

All in all, the prairie conflagration was a serious problem. But it was one that, unlike thunderstorms or drought, would go away as landscapes matured. Fires more resembled the threat from wolves or marauding Natives. All parties understood this. They recognized that, as settlement spread, free-burning flame would recede, like wetlands drained and ploughed. This perception, essentially correct, was a major reason for the seeming indifference of the population. They assumed that the solution to fire was to quicken settlement. Against this view stood officials charged with maintaining public order, for whom a tsunami of flame rolling through an ocean of grass constituted a breakdown of social order.

In the meantime, fires happened, fires broke free, fires overran range and field and occasionally house and hamlet. The saga of settlement burst with gripping tales of harrowing escapes, of horizons aglow with rampaging flames, of heroic rescues, brazen arsons, bold dashes to safety, desperate stands along ploughed furrows with wet burlap bags. The encounter with a full-blown prairie fire was one of the acknowledged hazards of pioneering. But once vanquished, it vanished, along with the long-stemmed flowers, the locusts, and the wolves. Like them, the flaming prairie was one of the burdens of the first-contact prairie, eagerly shed, but also among its special glories, often recalled and not readily reclaimed.

The circumstances were different for the forested Shield. It would not be farmed, or cleaved by roads, ditches, and cultivated fields. Ploughed fireguards would not break the momentum of a crown fire; neighbours would not gather to face down the flames. There was a vague supposition that, at some indefinite future, in principle, forestry might subdue the wild woods with aggressive silviculture. But that remained a forester's fantasy. The dense conifers existed as timber, to be mined, and their fires – bold, remorseless, undeniable – would not submit to silvic cultivation. The laissez-faire fire protection that served on a plains rolling with bunchgrass and forbs would not work on a Precambrian Shield bristling with jack pine and black spruce.

For decades, the issue remained hypothetical. Not until Manitoba expanded, first in 1905 and then in 1912, did it absorb within its provincial borders the untameable taiga. A primary incentive for enlargement was the Hudson Bay Railway, which linked wheat fields with seasonal shipping through Churchill. Even so, those lands remained crown property, subject to administration by the Dominion Forestry Branch. In 1912, it assumed responsibility for fire control throughout the province, both within and beyond the forest reserves. For another two decades, whatever fire protection existed the DFB furnished. Its fire rangers concentrated their efforts on the major reserves that clothed that chain of forested highlands fringing the Shield, notably, Porcupine Hills, Duck Mountain, and Riding Mountain. Between the farmed prairies and the unfarmable taiga, a swath of immense lakes, dominated by Lake Winnipeg, served as a fire-impermeable barrier.

"The fire loss and danger are appalling," observed J.R. Dickson, surveying the proposed railway route. "Within the past century, two great general fires along with numerous intermediate ones have reached every part of the region." That was a good cross-section of the backcountry fire hazard. "The Indians, the constant winds, the severe electrical storms, the enormous area of the region, the lack of any means of rapid communication, and the highly inflammable nature of the dense stands of small coniferous timber which prevail," he lamented, "combine to make the problem a very difficult one." About all one could do was patrol the few canoe routes and discourage carelessness. The railway would open the country to some access but probably kindle more fires than it would help to extinguish. Beyond its right-of-way, "no protection is possible."[5]

That put most of the northern forests off limits. Instead, rangers focused on the borders between the forests and the grasslands, adapting some techniques of prairie fire protection. Mostly they graded roads, ploughed and burned fireguards, sought to limit reckless burning in the slash from logging and land clearing along the border, and posted notices. Ideally, the grassy fireguards would be burned early in the season, but doing so did not always prove necessary. In places, "sloughs covered with reeds, bushes and long grass" and "higher grounds" clothed in hay and peavine could be burned easily in the spring, between the weeks of melting snow and drying woods. Such fireguards did not, they noted, work in dense woods. What made conflagrations somewhat self-limiting was the extensive matrix of lakes, bogs, and streams, the physical texture of the Shield, which also restricted the kind of human traffic possible and encouraged the use of local indigenes and "half-breeds" for fire duty.[6]

Still, fire ranging outside the reserves improved, lookout towers sprang up along the Hudson Bay Railway, and extensive canoe patrols became an annual ritual. The reality remained, however, that only aerial reconnaissance and transport could install a serious fire protection system. When the British Empire Forestry Conference assembled to hear about DFB activities, and the subsequent Forest Fire Conference convened in Ottawa, Manitoba's aerial network had become a showcase. It did for the dominion what the Provincial Air Service did for Ontario. Unlike crown holdings farther west, where the mountains ruled or the boreal forest was full of bogs but not pocked with lakes suitable for water landings, the Forestry Branch could depend on aircraft to counter fire and came to demand them. The federal government could deliver because it could direct the Royal Canadian Air Force to furnish planes and pilots "without charge."

That idyll ended with the transfer of land from the dominion to Manitoba on 15 July 1930. In anticipation, the province had promulgated in March a Forestry Act that established a Forest Service under the Department of Mines and Natural Resources. The restructuring yielded one immediate result in that it ended the contest that had so crippled the Department of the Interior between the Forestry Branch, which spent money, and the Crown Timber Branch, which collected it. One unified organization emerged, quickly parsed into four districts. The Manitoba Forest Service retained the forest reserve system along with the fire-ranging districts. Most of what had been progressive about DFB fire practices and codes it could adapt and even expand, and not a little of the former staff remained on duty, transferring along with the land. In fact, while admitting the significance of long cycles of drought, the provincial progeny prided itself that its efficiency compared "very favorably with earlier years during which Dominion authorities had control." Unlike 1929, "the worst fire year" since the DFB had organized, 1930 proved mild, and the institutional handover avoided stalling thanks to an arrangement by which Manitoba agreed to pay the DFB to continue fire protection on a reimbursement basis until 15 September.[7]

Manitoba now had open claim to minerals, waters, game, and woods, equal to that of the eastern provinces. The wrench in the machinery was that the transfer coincided with the onset of the Great Depression and a cycle of drought. Whatever efficiencies and wealth Manitoba had gained through acquiring political control it lost through fixed administrative expenses and plummeting revenue. By 1932, the crunch was serious. The province decided it could no longer afford the kind of aerial fire protection that had evolved over the past decade, and "it therefore became necessary to reconsider the whole policy of fire protection in the forested area outside the Forest Reserves." Fire officers knew precisely what this meant. They would have to "withdraw all fire protection from northern and eastern Manitoba" except for the "limited area" that could be reached from the northern railways and from Lake Winnipeg. Since unsupervised rangers were not worth hiring, and canoe-borne rangers were comically ineffective, the circumstances might argue that the "ultimate expense" of such economizing would probably be greater than an air service, but this was the enduring logic of fire efficiency speaking; there was no serious thought that perhaps there was little reason to fight fires in the hinterland. What had been utopian the aircraft had made possible, and what once could be made to happen now became mandatory. The compromise was to withdraw from all but the most rudimentary operations on the reserves proper and to segregate aerial reconnaissance from transportation. To compensate for the first, the Manitoba Forest Service would expand a tower network and ground patrols, and for the second, would limit aircraft usage to "a contract basis by a private company." (For communications, it continued with carrier pigeons, breeding a nucleus from four birds donated by the RCAF.)[8]

Here luck favoured the bold. Government economies forced the RCAF to reduce personnel and to mothball planes. Negotiations between the dominion and the province allowed the transfer to Manitoba of five Vickers-Vedette flying boats with two spare Lynx engines and a cache of spare parts. Thus was born the Manitoba Government Air Service. The Ontario model had indeed flown west and, after moulting its federal feathers, had grown provincial replacements. Even so, the force was never enough. Big fires continued to break out, to which the inevitable response was, if enough airpower had been on hand, those fires could have been hammered when small and halted. Meanwhile, an improvement in revenues – less than the flow prior to 1930 but more than what a minimal staff and small fleet of aircraft required – promised a brighter future.[9]

Unsettled, however, was the reason for fire control. The DFS had fought fires because it seemed to be a means of establishing a federal presence and exercising a duty of government, and it did not expect an immediate return of revenue. But Manitoba did. It had inherited an instrument in search of a justification. While commercial forestry seemed a self-evident goal to the foresters who still ran the fire program, the province's legacy of past fires and current conflagrations made the prospect of a pulp and paper industry illusory. In 1934, J.D.B. Harrison of the DFS analyzed the forest estate and concluded that the fire scene could "only be described as appalling." Unchecked, that roster of wildfires would do away with any prospective mills by burning away their supply of wood. If Manitoba wanted a forest industry, it had to either reduce the harvest ("undoubtedly ... impracticable") or battle fire, which by default alone became "the correct line of attack." Without quick action, the forests of Manitoba were "doomed to something approaching total destruction." That argument gave its fire agency a cause, even if it was one that was only hypothetical.[10]

So while Manitoba had its peculiarities, it confronted in its boreal forests a similar suite of fires to those known to the eastern provinces, it met those flames with a similar suite of counterforces, and it understood that fire protection "overshadowed" all its other activities, for if it failed all else would fail as well. Particularly intractable were three ignition sources. There was lightning, about which one could do little except spot new smokes and attack them quickly, there were chronic bouts of incendiarism, and there was reckless land clearing. Permits could quell slovenly slash burning, but incendiarism by its nature resisted appeals. It could only be met by criminal prosecution. Moreover, there was the intractable problem of "neglected Indian camp fires." Before spring breakup, patrols by dogsled or airplane could identify camps and issue warnings, but sometimes breakup came suddenly or late, and during breakup itself nothing could be done. In bad years, those smouldering hearths dashed across the countryside. (In 1959, for example, they accounted for 60 percent of the area burned.) Registering traplines could, like issuing travel permits, dampen some carelessness. The Forest Service, however, found it "extremely difficult" to communicate the seriousness of the situation to the Natives. Appointing honorary fire guardians, enlisting the RCMP, posting polyglot notices – foresters were desperate to find "some approach that will bring results."[11]

Mostly the Forest Service continued to do what it had been doing and understood was necessary. It built out its infrastructure, including roaded fireguards into the interior of reserves; beefed up staff; modernized equipment; expanded the use of permits for burning, trapping, and travelling; and declared outright fire bans during extreme conditions. In 1948, it began experiments with paracargo drops. When 1951 offered an especially hazardous spring, crews pre-emptively burned along roadsides, hay meadows, and open swamps to eliminate the threat. After a period of postwar adjustments, it commenced detailed fire control planning for every district. In 1950, it arranged a mutual assistance pact with Ontario; in 1956, it crafted a similar agreement with Minnesota; and later (1963) it did so with Saskatchewan. It experimented with waterbombing (1958) and subsequently determined that helicopters and aircraft in tandem were the ideal. It staged special training courses at The Pas to create a cadre of "Indian fire foremen" capable of leading First Nations crews. And once an apparatus existed to fight fire almost everywhere, the pressures built to make it a universal fire service, protecting land outside reserves, including provincial parks, Indian reservations, unorganized territory, and even unincorporated municipalities. The Forest Service appreciated keenly that the only way to protect valued places was to protect their less valued peripheries as well, especially since so many vital sites were scattered, and like ancient Rome it found itself pushing new frontiers outward, each to better shield the last. Overseeing this miniature empire was J.G. Somers, another of Canada's long-tenure administrators, only retiring in 1963.[12]

The shakeup came not with the episodic cadence of big-fire seasons, even one of the magnitude of 1961, which burned 2.75 million acres, but with the atonal beat of politics. With Somers' retirement as director of forestry, the Forest Service fissioned into two branches, Forest Management and Forest Protection. That meant little in the field. In 1970, however, the department reorganized and then kept reorganizing. This shook the bureaucracy. The deputy minister admitted that "some of these changes" were of a "pioneering nature in the overall history of resource management agencies." A memorial history published on the occasion of the department's sixtieth anniversary quoted, a touch facetiously, from Petronius Arbiter (AD 66): "I was to learn later in life that we tend to meet any new situation by reorganizing; and a wonderful method it can be for creating the illusion of progress while producing confusion, inefficiency and demoralization." The reorganizations kept coming as the movers and shakers intended to stimulate resource development, to smooth out interdepartmental co-ordination, and to consider "social and aesthetic values" along with economics. After two decades of institutional "wandering," a critic wryly observed that "the department is almost back to where it started."[13]

Here was the dark side of its origins. Fire protection in Manitoba had never questioned its legitimacy: it simply sought to do its job more broadly and more briskly. It had adapted shrewdly from others and pioneered techniques such as aerial ignition, long-distance water delivery, and the use of single-engine aircraft on early-season fires when ice prevented scooping by waterbombers. Studies repeatedly showed that Manitoba stood nearly unchallenged in measures of efficiency. The Forest Service had apparently driven its fire problem into the hinterlands, where lightning ruled and fires grew large because they were observed rather than attacked, although eventually these too would succumb. But bad fires did not slink quietly away, and reorganizations questioned the unchallenged premises that had allowed the Forest Service, from its origins, to proceed with such ruthless single-mindedness.[14]

The fires of reference remained 1929 and 1961. The agency had regarded the former as prehistory and the latter as a freak. Now the plague of reorganizations matched a plague of bad fire seasons, not severe by numbers of fires alone or in burned area but by expense; the aerial program that made firefighting effective also made it costly. The 1973 season set records for aircraft use; the 1976 and 1977 seasons blew up both area burned and expenses, and a departmental post mortem declared them "the most severe in the recorded history of Manitoba"; and, as yet another reorganization became operational for the 1980-81 fiscal year, the 1980 fire bust blew away 1.25 million acres and any effort at cost containment, while the 1981 season scorched another 900,000 acres. It became evident to even the most ardent partisan that Manitoba could not, by itself, especially with its lean staffing, cope with such outbursts and that, since its neighbours were equally strained, it would have to seek a national pool of planes and pumps to draft from during the crisis years. Like the others, it turned to the newly chartered Canadian Interagency Forest Fire Centre, which granted to Manitoba the mechanized force to fight whatever fires it might choose. CIFFC's goals were those of Manitoba's Forest Service: more tools to fight more fires with greater efficiency. The old logic continued. Appropriately CIFFC was headquartered in Winnipeg.

What remained unanswered was a deeper examination of why and how to fight fire, to what extent economics might have to accommodate ecology, and how fire agencies had to answer to the changing values of a society moving beyond commodity production and agrarian values. Investigating the 1980 outbreak, the Canadian Forest Service concluded that the environmental consequences of the burns were probably "neutral" and urged that "economic activity in the north strike a rational compromise with fire rather than regard it simply as an enemy that can and should be eliminated." But that was the logic of science, not of politics or bureaucracies. Manitoba Forest Protection saw the scene differently, saw those flames through the prism of its founding premises, which is to say, the need to control fire, the validity of suppression, the primacy of rapid initial attack, the necessity for greater efficiency. It identified the problem as one of limited resources: insufficient crews and pumps, too few aircraft, too little money. In August, its chief used the baleful crisis to reaffirm that the old 10 a.m. policy – to control every fire by 10 a.m. the morning following its report – was "the one in which all other fire management policies should rest." And, he might have added, on which all other crown land activities depended.[15]

Saskatchewan

Saskatchewan's fire scene was a curious inverse of Manitoba's. Its defining feature was a great swath of grassy plains, with a wedge of forested Shield to the north. Hay meadows replaced barrens; settlement scattered across ploughed steppes rather than clustering around a metropolitan entrepôt. Conservationists saw their challenge as planting trees more than guarding woody patches on prairie hills or salvaging remote taiga. Forestry found itself squeezed between a northern economy of hunting, trapping, and mining and a southern one based on wheat farming. It lay between two fires, the semi-domesticated flames of the prairie and the feral fires of the taiga. Prairie wildfire was a known hazard and was met by traditional means. Conflagrations deep in the taiga could, at first, be ignored. But how to protect the land between became the special duty of Saskatchewan.

The Dominion Forestry Branch bequeathed both an assessment of the problem and a raw infrastructure to cope with it. A survey under H.R. MacMillan at Turtle Mountain, in southwest Manitoba ("similar"

conditions prevailed in Saskatchewan, he noted), identified the problem as
people. Some flame got into the woods because it came from squatters, some
because it breached the border from land clearing around the perimeter.
A few farmers leased hay meadows within the reserve and burned them in
the spring, without adequate regard for control. "Half-breeds and Indians"
left campfires as they passed through. Backfiring and surreptitious burns
by ranchers added to the load. Inevitably there were bouts of lightning.
And prairie wildfires crashed through lines drawn on maps. In 1885, one
such fire "swept over almost the whole" of Moose Mountain, sparing only
pockets of trees. Thereafter "traces" could be found of "some fire nearly
every year," until in 1897 another storm surge of flame had swept "over a
large area of the same country and destroyed the reproduction which was
then eleven years old." *Brûlés* abounded, "a constant menace to the young
forest." The northern forests (which the prairie settlers would "imperatively
require" soon) were no better off. Barring some "comprehensive scheme of
protection," Saskatchewan's forests would join so many others in Canada
as a "blackened and almost barren waste."[16]

The Commission of Conservation sponsored an inquiry into Saskatchewan's forests between 1913 and 1915, and although J.C. Blumer never
completed his task he found plenty of objectionable burning from seasonal transients and new settlements, railways and prospectors, hay meadows
and a vogue for fox hunting. The contrast with islands, which enjoyed a
"natural protection" from fire, was striking. A report in 1910 noted that
the southern portion of a studied lake, crossed by the main boat route,
had been "repeatedly swept by fires," while the northern portion survived
"well wooded." With mineral discoveries in 1914, fires promptly took out
many of the remaining forests, including those on previously immune
islands. But what distinguished the report was Blumer's understanding
that fire overall was "not merely artificial or incidental, or belonging to
the present," but that it was "a great phytogeographic force that has been
operative for long ages past." Like a forestry Paracelsus, he argued that the
pyric poison lay not in its substance but in its dosage. "If fire intervenes
at the right time, the spruce is thereby perpetuated; if it is repeated too
often, the forest is destroyed." The boreal fire could renew as well as destroy. In fact, fire "must intervene at a certain period" or the forest would
fade, a principle common to "coniferous forests the world over." Still, as
an agent of conservation, Blumer argued that the ultimate development of
the north would require its raw materials intact and that "fire prevention
should begin now."[17]

The DFS considered its Saskatchewan reserves "in very poor shape."

Worse, they were relatively few and scattered, dispersing what sound administration would have concentrated. Dominion foresters reckoned they could offer less than half the protection they ought to offer, considered the Fire Act "a dead letter," and watched a surge of prairie settlement hack and burn into the woodland belt. Inspector C.A. MacFaydon concluded that "it is a hard thing to preach fire protection in a country where eight out of ten men are doing their best to get rid of the standing timber." Beyond the reserves, the strategy was to prevent fires, since they could never be fought, and to segregate, as long as possible, the two worlds, to prevent the fires of one from overrunning the other. Patrols were the practice of choice for the former and fireguards for the latter. Fire rangers trekked over the traditional routes each spring (with dog sleds in snow and canoes after breakup) to search for abandoned campfires and to post warnings. They fought what fires they could. During the Great War, even that capability shrank as the war effort siphoned off money and staff. By the time of the 1930 transfer, Saskatchewan fire protection stood roughly comparable to those in other western provinces. What distinguished the program, though, was the relative lack of aircraft or, more properly, a protection program built around planes. Although the DFS operated seven planes, the province lacked the lake-saturating landscape that made Manitoba inviting for float planes, or the open plains along mountain flanks that put aircraft adjacent to fire problems in Alberta, and the planes supplemented on-ground efforts rather than informed them.[18]

What Saskatchewan excelled at instead was fireguards, a physical barrier between grass and forest and farmer and forester. A provincial manual explained the matter squarely: "Undoubtedly the most effective method of reducing fire hazard along forest boundaries is by strip burning very early in the spring as the snow is disappearing. Spring burning should keep pace with the vanishing snow and should be completed before snow is gone from the woods." In some places, this might require, or be integrated with, roads or ploughed fireguards, but mostly skilled practitioners could cobble fireguards together by burning along natural wetlands and sloughs and patch firing between receding snow banks. The practice required an organization both ready and fit, for the opportunities to burn early might last only five to six days. Too early and the fires would fizzle; too late and they could gallop across the countryside. Spring firing promised a frenzied week, but on it was premised the strategy of Saskatchewan fire protection, a scheme that adapted the methods of prairie farmers to the goals of boreal foresters.[19]

With cession from the dominion in 1930, a Saskatchewan Forest Act (1931) placed the administration of forest reserves under a Department of Natural Resources (DNR). Mostly the DNR took over the apparatus of the DFS but immediately found itself downsizing to accommodate the economic crisis. With drought, Depression, crop failure, and threatened foreclosures, the provincial finances were a shambles, and provincial priorities looked to relief for farmers rather than schemes for foresters. The province's wealth lay in its harvested wheat, not in its uncut spruce. Where the DFS had flown seven planes, Saskatchewan contracted with a commercial operator for four, one (a Stinson) equipped with skis to patrol for "moss fires" and to transport rangers for early duty. It placed its bets, however, on spring burning.[20]

This became the core strategy on and around the forest reserves. In 1932, for example, despite a wet April, rangers attributed their successful season more to their "spring strip burning" than to favourable weather. The magnitude of the burning unburdened the department from a wildfire load that "would otherwise have been felt and the force could give their whole time to the suppression of fires within forest boundaries as fires in settlements were in the main isolated." In 1934, its agents burned over a thousand miles, and in 1936 they burned over 2,000 miles. The practice of contracting for "agricultural fireguards" further evolved as well. Until the time when the department concluded its strip burning, settlers were allowed to burn as they wished. Thereafter they became subject to burning permits. Even railway fires were contained through spark arrestors and right-of-way burning in the spring.[21]

Its forests of interest – those of commercial prospects, those gazetted as parks or forest reserves – lay in a broad band between the Shield and the Plains. To the south, prairie fires rolled over the hills, and land-clearing burns crowded against reserve boundaries. Year after year, officials cited "settlers, as usual," as responsible "for the greatest number of fires." The friction of that frontier would continue to abrade into flame until thickening settlement choked those flames from the scene. To the north, the coarse matrix of the Shield sputtered with a tight mosaic of boreal burning. The department defended against the farmer with fireguards, adapting aboriginal burning to its own purposes. It defended against the trapper and prospector with fire-ranging patrols, notices, and lectures.[22]

Practical results were mixed, as transients from elsewhere ignored warnings and prospectors often set fires to scour off the vegetation and soil that hid outcrops. In 1928, for example, Indian Agent J.W. Waddy observed along the Churchill River that the newcomers had "stripped a 250-mile

district and the fires were going strong when we came through." The scene
worsened when a combination of Depression, high prices for precious
minerals, provincial-sponsored exploring parties, and regular air service to
La Ronge inspired a fresh surge of prospectors. In 1937, fires again swept the
major thoroughfares and moved north with the feverish mineral foragers.
The geography and scale of burning through old regimes stirred the land
into turmoil. It especially upset the arrangement of traditional hunting
and trapping grounds, and where a lichen-feeding, migratory species such
as caribou was involved it could deflect the seasonal movement of herds.
This alteration could ripple through Native economies with devastating
effects. The department concluded in 1940, for example, that fire had
become "the single greatest agency on the destruction of wildlife, and
impoverishment" of the northern peoples. What the province gained from
mineral exploitation it lost from traditional economies. (Saskatchewan's
"caribou crisis" thus anticipated the politically charged fire controversy
in the Northwest Territories that emerged in the 1960s.) Although free-
roaming fires were not the whole of the cause, they were a notoriously easy
one to identify.[23]

Yet what emerged was a complex fire narrative in which the scrambled
regime was not simply the outcome of wildfires let loose by newcomers
but equally the result of breakdowns in customary practices. In its *Annual
Report* for 1936, the department reported, to its disgust, one telling,
anecdotal consequence. Some "misguided seer" argued that a shortage of
muskrats was due to poisoning by the decaying rushes and vegetation in the
big flats around Cumberland. Remediation called for burning "these grass
and rush areas." Although dense smoke caused a scare, the fires burned
themselves out "without doing any damage other than exterminating large
numbers of the weasel and duck population." Probably the rotting rushes
had not poisoned the muskrats, only helped to starve them; probably the
delta had been routinely burned in the past, and the new spring fires did
what they were supposed to do. That is not, of course, how foresters saw
the scene.[24]

The next year, 1937, confirmed this creed, as large fires ripped widely
and in places that could record them. Even so, over the next few years, even
as fire-casting prospectors plunged into the backcountry, as new settlers
desperately cleared uneconomical farmland, and as job-seeking citizens
kindled fires in the hope of being hired to fight them, fire statistics dropped
noticeably. Number of fires, area burned, losses, and expenditures, every
category declined. How much was attributable to favourable weather, how
much to aggressive fire control, how much to simple reporting is unclear.

Beyond the pale of protection, certainly north of the Churchill River that fringed the Shield, the department kept scant records, as it did for the farmed prairie. What mattered was the productive forest belt it sought to protect in between. Here the statistics seemed to show improvement, as expected. Here the department concluded, reasonably, that it saw no reason to radically alter either its methods or its personnel.

As finances slowly improved, the department applied, with ever more power, the tried and true methods of Canadian fire protection. These methods included a small fleet of flying boats, and the department eventually contracted for other aircraft (after a brief bout of experimentation, it determined there was no cost advantage in provincial ownership), as well as spring-burnt fireguards. The outcome was striking. Despite short staffing and funds, and spring wildfires in 1942, the system held. The postwar era began with a sombre admission that its forests were in bad shape and that inadequate fire protection over them was a "gigantic problem." So recklessly had Saskatchewan overcut its forests, first from the urgency of prairie settlement and then from the exigencies of war, that its "forest capital stock" was in a state of "complete exhaustion of supply." An all-out collapse might occur as early as 1950. Better forest management was one solution, symbolized by the establishment of a Timber Board, a crown corporation rudely modelled on the Wheat Board. But every proposed reform would only prove as good as the protection the diminished forest enjoyed from fire, and the existing program was too feeble to withstand the stress. The department awaited eagerly the conclusions of a royal commission that, it believed, would urge "an increase in firefighting power and other preventative services."[25]

Saskatchewan's Royal Commission on Forestry convened in October 1945. Less than a month later, so urgent seemed the issues that it released an interim report on the fire scene. The reasoning was simple: "We are of the opinion that unless the forest fire situation is seriously faced, as in our opinion it had not been up to the time of our sittings, it is useless to discuss further the problems of forest development and improvement that merit attention." It acknowledged uncertainty about how to cope with lightning fires, for the commission had received "no good suggestions," there was not "much of value in the literature," and the prevailing conviction seemed to be that while lightning-kindled fires could burn large areas, they did so remote from commercial stocks. But on the question of human-caused fire, the commission was unyielding. Forest fires from "any human cause whatsoever must be stamped out."[26]

Beyond this pyrophobia lay an understanding of Saskatchewan's potential wealth in wood. Although the public, crowded onto the farmed grasslands, believed that Saskatchewan was the definitive "prairie province," in fact it held extensive forests and excelled as a habitat for white spruce, valuable as sawtimber. Decades of wreckage by axe and fire, however, had both reduced this natural legacy and distorted its future. What had not burned up outright regenerated into stands of landscape-sized patches that were less than thirty-three years in age; the merchantable timber that yet survived was too paltry to sustain continued logging, and the timber that could replace it would need several decades to mature, and that was possible only if fires were shut down. Like so many royal commissions before it, and so many that would follow, this one concluded that the forestry problem was, in the end, a fire problem: "Shall we conquer the fire or allow it to continue as it has in the past?" Over and again the commission reiterated, and made no apologies for its repetitions, that "the most extraordinary precautions are necessary to put a stop to forest fires." There could never be any lapse in vigilance. So extreme was the threat that it warranted immediate measures, "no matter how apparently spectacular." While the commission admitted that Saskatchewan laboured under "special handicaps," they in no way lessened the charge laid to it or absolved it of apathy. In fact, if the province acted boldly on its advice, Saskatchewan could "take the lead among the provinces of Canada."[27]

Here was a daring vision, the most audacious royal commission pronouncement on fire since 1899 in Ontario, and it was avidly seized upon by the Department of Natural Resources. The interim report had been enough to spark the purchase of two aircraft, destined to evolve into an air fleet for fire patrol and other administrative duties in the far north. Since logging would have to push north in pursuit of mature timber, opened by roads, fire protection would have to precede it, borne on wings. Immediately reforms tumbled forward as Saskatchewan endowed a forestry school for technical staff, amended the Forest Act and the Prairie and Forest Fires Act, sought tougher enforcement against settler burning (enlisting the RCMP for aid), and, most dramatically, in the spring of 1947 established a smokejumper squad, the first in Canada and, for decades, the only one. Within another year, the department had launched a modernization program that scrutinized fire detection, fire weather forecasting, communications, and planning.[28]

It was the eight jumpers housed at Prince Albert, however, that symbolized Saskatchewan's reply to the royal commission's challenge. Serious fire protection in Canada meant aircraft, but the relative dryness that accounted for its prairies also meant that the province's commercial forests had more hay meadows than lakes. This allowed smokejumping to do for Saskatchewan what waterbombing did in Manitoba. (Even so, the cadre relied on a float-equipped Norseman, which allowed for amphibious attacks.) The department did not record any smokejumper dispatches over the 1947 season; for 1948, it enlarged the corps, although they were not used for firefighting at all. The next year recruitment expanded the program to "full strength." On some fires, they jumped, while on others, they worked as a regular fire crew. Mostly their mere presence made a public declaration that Saskatchewan was, with respect to fire protection, both committed and modern.[29]

In 1951, the department celebrated its coming of age, the twenty-first anniversary since the transfer from the DFS. For the most part, the province had achieved below what it wished. There was less development (and revenue) and less informed conservation. The Depression had so crippled administration that, "in fact, for a time Saskatchewan was probably disappointed in the birth right of resources it had fought so hard to obtain from the Government of Canada." The war years accelerated exploitation but left systematic conservation wanting for lack of staff and funds. But now the province was prepared to do what it should have done from the beginning. That meant a reinvigorated fire protection program, the "essential basis for all other forest conservation programs." Forest Fire Control became a separate branch and later a functional division. Soon it acquired all the apparatus of modern firefighting, including access to aircraft from the Saskatchewan Government Airways and co-operative arrangements with Manitoba and Alberta for mutual assistance. So rapidly did the branch build up its store of power tools, acquire motorized vehicles and bulldozers, erect towers, and cut new roads that its administrators believed the time had come to shift attention from fire suppression to fire prevention, "ultimately the most important phase of forest fire control," since people started 90-95 percent of fires, and in principle these fires could be throttled before they began. For this ambition, new and old could find common cause, so when not fighting fires, the smokejumper corps provided public exhibitions to promote fire's prevention.[30]

Yet a more fundamental shift was under way. In purpose and practice, Saskatchewan was coming to resemble the other provinces, with a dash of special spice from its smokejumpers and Native crews. It was more accepting of industrial forestry as a goal and more reliant on mechanical power as a method. There was more fire fighting and less fire lighting: smokejumping replaced the spring burning of fireguards as a provincial talisman. Increasingly fireguards meant graded roads, not agile burning between bog and snow bank. Even the indigenes were further weaned away from traditional burning, not with missionary exhortations and honorary fire wardenships but with intensive training in fire suppression, as northern Natives and Métis became a source of seasonal fire crews. Trapping and hunting that had once relied on selective burning to sculpt a suitable habitat were replaced by piece-work firefighting. During the Third National Forest Fire Research Conference, sponsored by the Canadian Pulp and Paper Association, a demonstration by smokejumpers and Native fire crews "stole the show." In 1955, the branch formally divided the province into two zones, a southern swath of intensive fire protection and a northern belt "of little [timber] value commercially," for the branch would protect only mining communities and the "occasional block" of merchantable timber; that season's fires, held to average in the southern zone, overran vast acreages in the north, probably in excess of a million acres, mostly in caribou range. In 1957, the province again revised its Prairie and Forest Fires Act. By the late 1950s, the department openly scorned its heritage of spring burning and disparaged it as potentially compromising the clarity of its fire prevention propaganda.[31]

Gradually the postwar euphoria, the war-stimulated demands for provincial commodities, and a run of benign weather wore off. Since 1940, the province had not experienced a major fire crisis, and its remarkable reforms had proceeded against a backdrop of benevolent weather, lessened pressure from settler burning, and a bulking up of mechanical muscle. Since 1930, save for 1937 and 1940, the trends had ratcheted downward. Then flame revived. The 1958 season was aggravated by smoke palls drifting from the west, which obscured new ignitions and let fires build some momentum prior to initial attack. The 1960 season, the "lightning fire year," brought a massive outbreak of burning that rippled across the Shield from Alberta to Manitoba, to which Saskatchewan replied with waterbombing and helicopters. But it was the 1961 blowout that bodychecked any illusions about adequate control. Over a long season, opening in March and shuttering only in November, 507 fires burned some two million acres. Direct losses went beyond merchantable timber, which was considerable, to include two bulldozers, caches of pumps and hoses, a saw mill, and several fire camps ("complete with personal belongings"); the burns sharply reduced forestry revenue; suppression expenses were stratospheric ("four times greater than the cost of suppressing fires in 1937, the worst previous year"); and fire-salvage timber dumped on the market only drove down stumpage value. The fire bust confirmed what observers had long understood, that averages meant little in the boreal forest. The 1961 season single-handedly reversed all statistical trends, although it is a measure of how much the organization had matured that a burned area of 140,000 acres seemed huge and unacceptable. Then the 1964 season, during a brief but ferocious outbreak, trampled those records.[32]

The Division of Forest Fire Control once again found itself between two fires. The old narrative worked toward its denouement. The steady litany of improvements had, by bureaucratic reasoning, eliminated the need for the spectacular gestures urged by the royal commission, and in 1967, with helicopters cheaper and a reasonable infrastructure in place, the division disbanded its increasingly ceremonial smokejumper corps. The new narrative was one in which burning became unstable; the light years were very light, the heavy years very heavy, and they kept coming. A study of fire history from 1918 to 1979 identified the 1960s and 1970s as having "the highest burned area of any decades in this period." Campfires and lightning competed as causes, accounting between them for over half of all ignitions, with incendiary fires a distant third. Equally unsettling, the 1970s commenced a wave of serial reorganizations. Fire control could stand by itself as a service available on command. But it was unclear just whom it should serve. The 1947 royal commission had endorsed intensive fire protection because it wanted a forest industry; forty years later it was apparent that forestry would not command that kind of provincial attention, and the fire agency created to support it found itself combined in assorted ways and even soldered to the Department of Tourism. It threatened to become a masterless man, wandering about the bureaucratic landscape.[33]

In all this, Saskatchewan marched in rough alignment with its neighbours and with Canadian fire protection generally. What thirty years previous had been deemed indispensable for the province's economic vitality, and which had dominated administrative attention, had now become but one of a congested suite of government services for a resident population whose livelihood depended less and less on simple commodities, whether of wheat, gold, or wood, and instead was slowly morphing into a service economy overall and saw forest usage steadily inflecting into amenities rather than raw cellulose. The apparent decline of fire protection was only relative. It seemed to have shrunk only because other duties of government now commanded the attention of the electorate and had swelled to embrace recreation as well as revenue from its crown lands. It appeared lesser, too, because the crisis of big fires seemed to strike as a force of nature, like an early frost or a dry winter, over which even government could exert little influence.

Not until the 1990s would the full transformation become undeniable. But while similar trends swept all of Canada, Saskatchewan had its peculiarities. The character of its prairie and far north frontier had dispersed settlement; alone among the western provinces, it lacked a commanding metropolis, an urban centre that could concentrate the forces of the emerging new economy. Instead, it commenced a slow haemorrhage of people and wealth. The prairies began to depopulate, while the northern Shield began to repopulate with small First Nations villages. The two groups had different perceptions of what constituted their fire problems. In the south, urbanites fretted over recreational parks and nature preserves. (Even urban fire services segued from firefighting as a primary duty into all-purpose emergency response, typically by ambulance, thus reflecting the population's obsession with government-supplied medical care.) In the remote north, fire concerns were likely to focus on habitats for game and fur. Large fires, or the legacy of old burns, on barren-land caribou range became politically volatile. And while Saskatchewan could ill afford to shed the jobs and revenue its wood industry represented, and, in fact, inaugurated a program of extensive forest planting, the deep waters flowed elsewhere.

The prospect was for the branch to do in the future what it had done in the past. It would redouble its search for greater efficiencies, leaving large fires, sparked by lightning, to retreat to the fringe, along with the muskrats and caribou. But fires refused to acknowledge the new provincial realities. The 1977 and 1978 seasons boosted burned area; then came the fire tsunami of 1980, the worst year in the province's recorded history. The fires that clobbered Manitoba also blasted Saskatchewan, although most soared through the Shield. A record 742 fires burned a record 3,313,032 acres, roughly 25 percent of which belonged in the zone of intensive protection. The Canadian Armed Forces dispatched ground troops, vehicles, and helicopters to relieve "exhausted provincial" fire crews. Neighbouring provinces were too overwhelmed with their own fires to lend serious assistance.[34]

The fires shocked the two governing bureaus, the Department of Tourism and Renewable Resources and the Department of Northern Saskatchewan, into commissioning a review by a consultant, John S. Mactavish, who submitted his report in early May 1981. All in all, he concluded that Saskatchewan's agencies had proved themselves "to be highly competent and effective." As hockey was a game of inches, he observed, so fire control was a matter of minutes; had initial attack succeeded in two cases, the wreckage among the merchantable woods would have been manageable. Mostly Mactavish confirmed the received wisdom of Canadian fire.

Concentrate on areas of commercial value. Emphasize initial attack. Establish clear objectives and lines of authority. Invest in special crews and power machinery, particularly aircraft, without which fire control was a chimera. Meanwhile, the installation of a lightning-detection network promised to chip away at the unbanishable spectre of fire prevention, the dry lightning storm.[35]

But Mactavish also noted that a kind of dry rot was eating away at Saskatchewan's suppression capabilities. There was a decay in facilities, a deterioration of equipment and caches, a drop in morale. A decade of reorganizations had replaced mission clarity with confusion; staff were overextended, staff were confused. The Forest Fire Centre at Prince Albert, for example, was, depending on opinion, a site to give orders or one to take them, a place of centralized dispatching or a warehouse to ship out supplies. The policy manual had not been revised since 1974. Fire prevention was pro forma. The fire lookout network was an anachronism. The great reforms of 1947 had built on an unshakable conviction that fire protection was a sine qua non; forty years later it was just something the province did, while the real political energies lay elsewhere. Saskatchewan was living off its inheritance, an institutional trust fund whose capital was being fast depleted. Mactavish recommended a further dose of received wisdom in a prescription for "measures designed to improve an already sound initial attack system."[36]

It was not sound enough. The fires of 1981 exceeded those of 1980. The reforms had interbred, each spawning another, but so had big fires, each monster seemingly worse than the last. Every time the department killed off a Grendel, it had to face another Grendel's dam. It was as though nature's economy had changed as profoundly as Saskatchewan's human economy, accompanied by an inverse demography that saw the population of people decline and that of fires swell. The instinct of its fire organization was to meet those challenges by becoming more like the other provinces – to muster more resources, to excel at those practices and score high on those indices that most mattered to the Canadian fire community. Even as it integrated via CIFFC into a national confederation of fire services, it seemed to yearn for another royal commission to rekindle the postwar boom.[37]

Yet Saskatchewan had historically brought distinction to itself by being different and nowhere more so than when it had reconciled prairie burning with forest protection. As the provincial fire service approached its golden anniversary, it might have pondered whether its future lay with bigger planes and more pumps, a lesser version of an emerging national model, or with somehow reconciling the goals of its protected woods with the practices of its contemporary citizens, finding new equivalents for early burning. Its defining fires were as much in the mind as on the ground, or perhaps between what its citizens believed possible and its fire officers considered mandatory, or perhaps truer still between what people wished and nature willed. Between those two fires it yet remained.

Alberta

Alberta ran cross-grained to the great fire rings of Canada. It held the Rockies to the southwest and the Shield to the northeast; its plains waved with prairie grass to the south and bristled with boreal forest to the north. Above loomed the Cordillera, its bulk deforming fire's geography, as a massive star might bend space, and it was along the eastern slope of the Rockies that Alberta defined a model system for fire protection, while below lay ancient landscapes, long lithified into petroleum and tar sands, that allowed Alberta to impose that paragon throughout its varied firescapes. That fossil biomass powered the machines behind modern fire suppression by fuelling and financing them and dissolving the old dialectics in a pool of postwar oil. It allowed Alberta to yoke its combustion regimes under a single administration. That ambition required cleverness or muscle or both, and the outcome was one of the purest firefights in Canadian history.[38]

Its prairie fires went the way of those farther east. Here, as there, the shock of settlement could be brutal, and the earliest years, the most harrowing. The country was awash with transients, with what the Mounties characterized as "thriftless farmers" too lazy or indifferent to the future to practise normal precautions, and with immigrants, often from countries where conflagrating prairies were unknown. That was the scene around Bardo, for example, flush with new settlers from Norway.[39]

In 1895, a wet spring and early summer had fluffed the landscape with grasses, no longer cropped by the migrating herds and not guarded by ploughed fireguards so great had been the rush of breaking land, haying, and erecting shacks. Fires kindled, their origins unclear. Men hastened with horses and ploughs to scratch firebreaks around hayfields and houses until, confronted with galloping flames and high winds, they broke and fled, scattering to save their residences and families. Some succeeded, some failed. Before the ashes cooled, the fabled Big Fire burned "from Fort Pitt to north of Beaver Lake and up to the North Saskatchewan River; and two hundred and fifty miles from the south to Beaver Lake west."[40]

The pattern repeated itself in 1896 and again in 1897, though on smaller scales. This time the newcomers appreciated the hazard and succeeded in ploughing "a great fireguard around the whole settlement." As Ragna Steen and Magda Hendrickson recalled, three furrows were ploughed close together with a strip of land left untouched between each row and "the grass burnt off between the rows." Sod and roots could smoulder for days, which demanded constant patrol. But the guards held, and in time the whole countryside itself, latticed with roads and ploughed strips and cultivated fields, became a gigantic fireguard. Statutes for organized fire districts and proposals for "Fire Day," modelled on Arbor Day, proved unnecessary. Chain drags – logging chains pulled between two horses over the flames – became rare, and the beef drag, using a split steer, rarer. The last outbreak of regional fires appeared in 1906. By then, settlement was thickening rapidly; between 1901 and 1906, for example, homesteading entries on the prairies had increased fivefold. "Prairie fires disappeared," the pioneers recalled. "Now they are only a memory."[41]

The enduring fight was in the forest. The DFB minced no words regarding the menace it faced there. The 1910 fires savaged an estimated 3.6 million acres in the Canadian Rockies, while the fire scene in the north was unspeakable. The manual of instructions for the Bow River Forest Reserve declared that "the protection of the woods from fire is the chief reason for the Dominion Forest Reserve Organization. It is the first requisite of proper forest management. No other work must be allowed to crowd it out." At that time its Alberta-based staff then totalled one inspector, eleven supervisors, five forest assistants, fifty-six forest rangers, six clerks, and eighty-six labourers – this for 9,691,000 acres of reserves.[42]

The usual primitive techniques were applied with the usual results to the region of reserves, on which the DFB concentrated its efforts, and to two immense fire-ranging districts in the north, over which it could do little save patrol, post notices, and douse campfires. The future, however, lay not with administrative shufflings but with mechanical power. This was the experience throughout North America, insisted DFB Director R.H. Campbell. The 1910 season alone "demonstrated the absolute necessity both of a sufficient number of rangers and of all the mechanical aids that can be provided." For a landscape with few navigable rivers and fewer roads, the future of fire protection meant rails, graded tracks and pump-mounted vehicles, and aircraft. The future required motor cars, paddle-wheeled boats along the Athabasca, Slave, and Peace Rivers, tractor ploughs, pumps, wireless, telephones, and of course airplanes.[43]

The western provinces were as dazzled by aerial fire control as those farther east. The first patrols commenced officially in September 1920 but allowed for only a few token flights to patrol mostly the Crowsnest and Bow River reserves, the only reserves with "decent communications." Western Canadians might well have looked covetously on their eastern brethren, whose planes could hop and dart from lake to fire, while they, at the end of their feeble roads, packed mules and trekked over mountains; however, for the airplane to apply its full power in the mountainous west (or even on the little-laked boreal plain), it had to attack fires directly. In the early 1920s, it could not. Still, if the planes went, C.H. Morse informed the 1924 conference, "we have nothing left." The region would have to implant a network of lookouts, and while aircraft were expensive a system of lookouts, requiring structures, staffing, maintenance, and supply, was even more formidable. When the Air Board experiment folded, that, however, is exactly what the Rockies acquired. For Alberta, there would be no flying *deus ex machina*.[44]

Still, the program advanced, step by step, year by year, and as settlement sprawled across the province, prevention and rapid attack did change the geography and dynamics of burning. More and more, the bad fires originated with lightning and transients, neither amenable to social engineering and both pushed to the (still immense) margins, especially the northern bush. As the 1930 handover approached, E.H. Finlayson objected bitterly that the "wholesale transfer" was a "retrograde step," that the provinces could never "finance the intensive administration required," and that any current federal savings would be offset by the inevitable need in the future to subsidize the provinces. All mostly true and all more or less irrelevant. The transfer proceeded, after a bad fire season, with Alberta accepting responsibility on 1 October 1930. What Finlayson failed to recognize (or admit) was the shared vision among Canada's fire officers, a collective ambition reinforced by the guild of foresters and particularly by the role of long-serving chiefs, which meant that the transfer did not, on the ground, change the purpose of fire protection or even its personnel. The province simply absorbed many of the DFS fire rangers into its newly constituted Alberta Forest Service (AFS) as it did tool caches, trails, and manuals. The old agenda persisted. What it lacked, as Finlayson did clearly understand, was a potential claim on the federal treasury, the means to put purpose into practice.[45]

The transfer brought both continuity and change. Among the substantial stabilities was the lengthy reign of T.F. Blefgen as director, originally hired by the DFB in 1911 and retiring only in 1948 because of illness. Among the reforms were some eagerly sought by government foresters and others forced upon them by provincial poverty. A new Prairie Fires Act in May

1932 rendered the entire province one gigantic fire district, over which
the Alberta Forest Service assumed responsibility, save for municipalities
and villages. All this simplified co-operation since there was, in practical
terms, only one fire service outside incorporated towns. (Alberta thus early
acquired that holy grail of Canadian fire agencies, a unified command. It
came late, however, to appreciate the downside, that a common authority
might mistakenly attempt to apply a common regime to wildly different
landscapes.) Overall, for the next fifteen years, the Alberta Forest Service
struggled to put into practice the purposes it inherited from the dominion
and the new order prescribed to it by the province. During the Depression,
it lacked money; during the war, it lacked manpower. Reorganization
meant, in reality, retrenchment.

The AFS believed it knew what had to be done, and it had the resolve
to do it properly. But its thin staff oversaw a vast domain, with poor
access, whose main economic wealth derived from a destitute prairie farm
economy. Director Blefgen declared simply, "from the point of view of
forest protection the situation is not satisfactory, but cannot be greatly
remedied until funds for organization, improvements and equipment are
made available." One ranger put it more directly, that during fire busts
no one could cope "even if he had more legs than a centipede." What
evolved was an administrative fire triangle. There were the prairies, their
internal fires quelled by settlement; there were the forest reserves, clustered
along the Rockies (and Cypress Hills), that received intensive protection;
and there was a vast dominion of fire ranging, the Northern Alberta Fire
District (NAFD), over which seasonal guards patrolled by paddle-wheeler,
horse, canoe, and speeder where rails existed and for which there were
virtually no communications. Fire rangers vanished for weeks, like hunters
of old. While the reserves underwent consolidation, the NAFD could
barely be visited as part of an annual circuit. Between them, the difference
in scale of land was an order of magnitude; the reserves embraced nearly
14.4 million square miles, the NAFD almost 148 million. A greater gulf lay
with their ecological dynamics, one controllable largely through people,
the other powered by lightning, oblivious to posted warnings and fines.[46]

The fire organization faced a future of frustration. The AFS needed to
pump up its staff, not deflate it. It needed an infrastructure to detect fires,
report them, and move crews quickly to them for initial attack. Only along
the Rockies and a patch around Lesser Slave Lake, where the DFS had
laboured steadily, did it have even a modest array of lookouts. Everywhere
it needed mechanical equipment, although machines were more costly than
hand labour. At a time when neighbouring provinces, also wrestling with

crimped budgets, had air fleets at their disposal, the Alberta Forest Service could hardly stock its caches with pumps and motor cars. As late as 1951, Deputy Minister John Harvie stipulated that only the director or assistant director of forestry could authorize hiring a bulldozer, and two dozers would require ministerial approval. When then-Director Eric Huestis argued that machines actually reduced the efficiency of hand labour, he was making a departmental virtue out of an Albertan necessity.[47]

The AFS understood only too well its circumstances. Over some conditions – lightning, the country of the far north, mass outbreaks of fire – it had little control. But campers, settlers, and border burns it could address. The emerging narrative was the familiar tale of relative control along the eastern slopes and scant control in the northern bush. It was possible to contain recreationists by establishing campgrounds, by issuing temporary fire bans or even closing the reserves during periods of extreme hazard, by education and propaganda, and by concentrating protection on sites of likely risk. That was not true in the north. New settlers were more stubborn, indifferent to the woods that the AFS was charged with protecting, avid to slash and sell what they could and to burn and plough what remained. Instead of calming the scene, as on the prairies, settlement enflamed it. Blefgen observed that the "history of settlement shows that the settler, with the fire hazard, arrives first and the roads later." Meanwhile, traditional sources persisted, such as trappers "burning the grass around lakes and sloughs in order to more readily find the muskrat runs," as well as abandoned winter campfires that could smoulder into spring flame. Perhaps most galling were the blowups that roared out of British Columbia. The BC Forest Branch had also retrenched and was unable to tackle fires that subsequently blew over the summit. In 1936, two whopping fires blasted across the border, one into Castle River Valley and the other into Highwood River Valley. The AFS stationed crews at both passes to check any advance but discovered that "instead of being an asset" they had become "almost a liability for the fire passed over them and trapped them." What was true for settlers was proving true for fire agencies. They were only as safe as their neighbours.[48]

There matters remained. Year after year, the AFS hectored its political masters to protect better the "forests of this province." Year after year, funds failed to match needs, particularly the scourge of settlement and the vast terrain of the north. Yet year after year, the Forest Service managed to add to its lookouts, upgrade its communication net with wireless, improve trails, acquire tools, and fight fires. Although its staff confronted "almost insurmountable obstacles," they showed themselves "to be extremely loyal, putting in long hours of work during the fire season, and they have been extremely successful in fire suppression work in spite of their handicaps." While no fire organization has ever been satisfied with its funding or political standing, Blefgen's chronic lament had substance. The barriers were formidable, the fires relentless. The lookout established at Mayberne in 1938, for example, required that the parts be trucked fourteen miles by road from Edson, then hauled sixteen miles by wagon, and over the last three-quarters of a mile dragged two or three pieces at a time by "stone-boat" since the parts were too large and heavy for transport by pack horse. Meanwhile, stoked by drought, crushing fires ran nearly at will from 1936 to 1939. Against such outbreaks, the development of twenty-three-pound radiophones for field officers and rain gauges for lookouts seemed technologically quaint.[49]

By then, Canada had plunged into another world war. The good news was that the demand for forest products soared and provincial revenues with it. The bad news was that there was scant increase in operating funds and a serious drain on manpower either for government service or for industry. Within three years, lumber production had tripled, and the entry of the United States into the war immediately stimulated additional demand, and interest in the Alaska Highway, the Canol Project at Fort Norman, and associated air bases added to local requisitions. The effect multiplied on itself. Coal production rose to help ship lumber, which encouraged a harvest in mine props, which further stimulated fuel levies. Throughout the war years, from a shortage of labour and a feeble infrastructure, Alberta's forest industry never met that swelling demand with supply.

Staff shortages struck the fire organization hard, but there was a shortfall in equipment as well. The 1941 season scattered efforts to contain it, but there were helpful revisions to the Prairie and Forest Fires Act and the Land Act, and war demands had so jolted a moribund forest industry to life that Blefgen warned that the extraordinary rates of depletion from axe and fire would strip the province of its gains if it did not seize control over both after an armistice; and while wildfires no longer scourged the prairies or routinely rambled over the Rocky Mountain parks and reserves, the threat remained undiminished, and the NAFD was, as ever, a festering wound, inflamed by feckless citizens and an indifferent politics. Alberta's future seemingly depended on the vigour of its forests. Its forests' future depended on their protection from fire.[50]

The war ended not in the forecasted recession but in a boom. Logging accelerated, stimulated by demand for building materials, hitting its highest rates ever. Director Huestis noted that in 1931 the annual lumber cut had been 51 million board feet; in 1948, it was 390 million, and the pulp and paper industry was about to arrive as well, along with a customary train of slash fires as the province found itself "over-cutting." Having spent years boosting up a timber industry, the AFS now needed to restrain it. Besides, the real wealth of Alberta lay not in its forest biomass but in its fossil biomass. On 13 February 1947, the Leduc Well No. 1 southwest of Edmonton struck an oilfield of 200 million barrels. A swarm of high-tech prospectors probed the province's geological basins, as earlier gangs had for placer gold, watersheds, and homesteads, and the economy shifted from grain to petroleum as the smoke from the burning clearings of settlers was replaced by the gas flares and oil smoke rings of derricks. The provincial population boomed, building boomed, logging boomed. Within a decade, oil revenue made possible the firefight provincial foresters had long hungered for, and oil distilled into diesel and aviation gas made possible the suppression of free-burning fire by the instruments of internal combustion.[51]

The boom extended to the Alberta Forest Service. Reforms cascaded, one after another; the apparatus for fire protection was effectively re-chartered and restaffed. The Alberta Post War Reconstruction Committee identified forestry, watershed protection, and fire control as priorities. Soon afterward, the Eastern Rockies Forest Conservation Board (ERFCB), constituted in April 1948, assumed direction for the reserved lands along the east slope, promising to pump considerable monies into development and protection and render the eastern slopes into a model forest, an exercise in co-operative administration and a kind of Canadian Tennessee Valley Authority. (The experience left a bitter memory in provincial politics, however, as it seemed that Ottawa was reclaiming the presence it had ceded in 1930.) By an order-in-council, the province then established what became known as the Green Area, which restricted settlement on the timbered lands of the province, almost two-thirds of its land mass, ending an era of laissez-faire pioneering and broadcast (and often brutal) burning. The Canada Forestry Act stimulated a cost-shared forest inventory, which fed into a forest industry (the survey also served petroleum prospecting). The Department of Mines and Lands promptly fissioned into two bureaus, one devoted to Mines and Minerals, the other to Lands and Forests. A revised Forests Act followed in 1949 and a new Forest Reserves Act in 1950; administrative responsibility for provincial parks came in 1951. A new assertiveness abolished the long-standing "10 mile firefighting limit" that had prohibited any suppression efforts in the north unless the fire burned within ten miles of a navigable river, road, or settlement. It had been adopted originally, Director Huestis admitted, because "we didn't have much to fight" with, "so nothing was done." Now the decision to attack lay with the AFS, and as its capacity improved so did its will to act. Meanwhile, Blefgen retired; his long-serving assistant, J.A. Hutchison, resigned to become superintendent of Banff National Park; and a copse of foresters freshly graduated from the University of British Columbia, class of 1949, arrived to ride the next wave. Two of them, R.G. Steele and S.R. Hughes, became directors of forestry and forest protection respectively.[52]

While all this was welcome, of course, and the money put quickly to use, it further strengthened the protection of Alberta's already best-protected lands. The crisis had always been the northern forests, either deemed too vague in value or too remote for action. They were now finding an industrial purpose, a destiny other than as ash for agriculture, the provincial finances were overflowing, and outside critics began hammering Alberta to upgrade its fire services to modern standards. There were surveys by the ERFCB and a begrudged forest inventory that laid out the magnitude of provincial wood stocks and the threats that might reduce them. There was an administrative review commissioned by the minister in 1949 that fell to Wallace Delahey of Toronto, which, although the director promised to receive it "with a great deal of interest," when delivered a year later, met with thunderous silence. A year later the consulting firm of Stevenson-Kellogg undertook an exhaustive survey of the Department of Lands and Forests that argued for more staffing and better fire protection in the north. This review was circulated widely and became the basis for planning over the next fiscal year.[53]

The breakthrough study, however, came unsolicited, at least officially. Seeking to shatter any provincial complacency, the Rocky Mountain Section of the Canadian Institute of Forestry conducted its own survey and in 1953 presented its findings, "Forest Fire Protection in Alberta: A Review and Recommendations," what became generally known as the "Fire Brief." The Rocky Mountain foresters chose to focus on fire as "the greatest single problem" and laid out a detailed analysis, "based exclusively on facts and opinions published by various governments." It pulled no punches. Alberta, it announced, had "by far the poorest record of any province in Canada in the matter of forest fire protection." The reasons were insufficient personnel and insufficient infrastructure, which is to say "not enough money," to establish forest fire protection by modern standards. Comparisons easily confirmed Albert's abysmal standing. Alberta had 5 percent of mainland

fires yet 29 percent of burned area, and the contrast within Alberta reinforced what contemporary fire protection could accomplish. The eastern
slopes had more or less contained their fire problem; the NAFD had not;
the task before the AFS was to carry the standards of the former to the
latter. When the minister, Ivan Casey, responded by letter in July 1953, he
quickly explained that the department had independently come to many of
the same conclusions and that most of the twenty-two recommendations
the IFC had nailed to his ministerial door were, in fact, either under way
or accepted "in principle."[54]

In truth, with or without the prod of professional foresters, the Big
Buildup was underway. Reorganizations unfolded; the province, either
from shame or economic sense or fiscal euphoria, was prepared to
funnel monies into fire protection. Between 1947 and 1956, fire funding
doubled, then tripled. The AFS purchased light tools and stocked caches,
then heavy equipment from bulldozers to graders to pumpers; it began
a construction program that fleshed out its lookout network, punched
roads and trails into the bush, and erected suitable ranger stations; it
hired new staff, both permanent and seasonal. In 1952, it experimented
with aircraft in support of fires near lakes. It promoted research with
the federal Forestry Service; it worked up modern fire control plans.
But the study phase was over and the boom was on. It got temporarily
lowered in 1956 when two large fires burned through the berths of North
Western Pulp and Paper, which had begun construction of Alberta's first
pulp mill (at Hinton) and which required an assured flow of cellulose.
Worse, the lands operated under a co-operative arrangement whereby
the company oversaw forest management and regeneration, and the AFS
undertook fire protection, for which the company was assessed an annual
fee. The company was furious at what it regarded as deficient firefighting,
and even apart from such rebukes the savagery of the fires shocked the
minister of lands and forests. Embarrassment and economics converged
to pour yet more funds into fire protection. Wisely the AFS spent two
years planning as well as buying, before the splurge. The boom leaped
into another phase, more than tripling fire-related costs over the next
decade and installing the infrastructure of which Albertan foresters had
long dreamed.[55]

The Big Buildup stepped from one bureaucratic terrace to another
roughly every ten years. There was that initial reformation in 1947-
48, another boost around 1957, a smaller reorganization and plateau in
1966 (not completed until 1969), a major reorganization in 1975. Each

had accompanied the passage of a bureaucratic generation: the Blefgen pioneers in 1948, Eric Huestis in 1966, Stan Hughes (the last of the UBC '49ers) in 1974. Then came a massive infusion, the largest of all in absolute (though not relative) terms in the early 1980s. Not coincidentally, the final two shuffles followed international oil crises that saw the world price for crude triple overnight. On cue, nature's combustion economy also suffered inflation, with record wildfires.

Yet those swells were only stages of a larger narrative arc, for once begun the AFS had expanded briskly if sometimes by lurches. There were no retrenchments, no troughs to balance the crests, as fire protection went from strength to strength; annually it expanded its domain of both legal responsibility and practical reach. In 1958, it attacked two border fires in British Columbia and one in Saskatchewan. It acquired fire protection responsibilities over provincial parks, over a number of Indian reserves under a federal-provincial agreement, and over the Air Weapons Range at Cold Lake for the Department of National Defence. It received authorization to control fires when municipalities were unable to protect themselves and on private lands if wildfires on them posed a threat to crown land. It devised proposals to extend coverage to rural lands unable to field a firefighting force equal to the task. In 1964, a new Forest Reserves Act was passed. In 1969, the department opened a Fire Control Depot, a central facility for dispatching and logistically supporting firefights, the first such institution in Canada. In 1971, a new Forest and Prairie Protection Act allowed the cost of rehabilitating burned lands to be charged against suppression expenses. In 1973, the province reclaimed responsibility for the eastern slopes from the ERFCB. A Forest Development Research Trust Fund (1974) ensured a degree of provincial investment in science and planning. (Even as the CFS located its Northern Forestry Centre to Edmonton, A.D. Kiil observed that the AFS's "increased protection effort has outstripped fire research and there is now a lack of research information" to assist "judgment and experience.") By then, the AFS had accomplished what its founders had set as their daunting ambition. It could fight fire everywhere. The gross disparity in administrative capabilities between the eastern slopes and the NAFD at last dissolved into a common system through the brute power of money and machinery.[56]

Inevitably the Big Buildup took to the air. Every large province relied on air power – had long insisted that without aerial suppression fire protection was impossible. But Alberta, after participating (through the DFB) with the Air Board experiments, had withdrawn, unable to justify the costs, not without a leap into the remote north, which was beyond both provincial capacity and ambition. Not until 1957 did the AFS purchase a plane, a fixed-wing Fleet Courier, while also renting a Bell helicopter. They became the nucleus for a small fleet, quickly integrated into suppression operations. During the 1961 fire bust, the leased and departmental aircraft flew reconnaissance, helped to open and close towers, moved crews and gear, and even dropped bentonite on spot fires. All in all, Albertan aircraft assisted on more than 25 percent of reported fires. Yet Alberta recognized that its aerial fire requirements were different and that it needed to shape aerial support to fire plans, not vice versa. Light planes and helicopters replaced pack trains and trucks and long-suffering lookouts, fitting into an existing infrastructure rather than seizing centre stage and wrapping all else around them. By 1960, planners had devised a system in which fixed-wing aircraft hauled crews and equipment to the nearest airstrip, from which helicopters ferried them as close to the fire as possible, while a second and more heavily equipped crew moved overland and released the initial attack crew for new assignments. The AFS's fire program had grown out of the Rockies, not the Shield; it would remain fundamentally ground based; its preferred aircraft differed from those best suited on the Shield and in the Maritimes. With its wings, Alberta now had, as for so long it had not, the means to pursue whatever ends it wished.[57]

Yet even the Big Buildup could not shut down big fires. They came in 1956, 1958, 1961, 1967, and with special ferocity in 1968. Each failure to smash or strangle such fires could be explained by, as yet, incomplete infrastructure and equipment. There had been worse seasons in the decades before the Big Buildup, but the fires of 1939, 1941, and 1949 belonged to a patriarchal generation, like biblical plagues. The 1968 outbreak, however, rightly shocked those who had just recently assumed authority, and worse, the conflagration had stemmed from an explosive rash of spring brush burning that accounted for 71 percent of the total area. Alberta's Seven Days in May seemed to be a massive holdover fire, as though primeval practices had smouldered for years before breaking free. Yet careful analysis by both the AFS and the CFS concluded that the blowup was the outcome of a rare concatenation, unlikely to repeat itself, which left the 1968 fires as a freak of nature. More worrisome were inquiries that noted that costs, as though in obedience to Parkinson's Law, were rising without regard to actual conditions in the field. The Big Buildup looked like a fiscal Blowup.[58]

The 1968 season, which had seemed anomalous, soon became the norm, not in damages but in costs. Bad seasons came and went, but the fixed costs of suppression, particularly reliant on aircraft and auxiliary bases, were high and unyielding. Such considerations had not mattered much when the boom was on, when there had been so much – everything – to do. A forest industry was promised, environmental values were becoming more prominent, and expenses seemed high now only because the agency had scrimped for funds for so long. Yet gradually the discourse began to shift from how to fight fire to where and when fires ought to be fought, and whether Alberta could do the job or ought to try, and maybe whether a universal suppression standard could span montane Douglas fir and black spruce. Here was the downside to the Big Buildup. It had come so quickly and with such exaggeration that Alberta had avoided the hard slog of debating, the give and take, year after year, of what it wanted and what it could afford. Ultimately, booms end in busts.[59]

The crash came just as the Alberta Forest Service was readying for its fiftieth anniversary. There were economic factors; the oil shocks, while inflating the petroleum interests, had stalled Alberta's still fledgling forest industry. The argument that almost all forest land was worth protecting came into question, and the premise that fire control was ecologically better than free-burning fire shifted from an unquestioned axiom, as certain as a postulate from Euclid, to a hypothesis in need of proof. Clearly fire protection had reached a point of diminishing returns, with the entire apparatus pivoting on a policy of aggressive initial attack, an adaptation of the 10 a.m. policy enunciated by the US Forest Service in 1935 and formally abandoned between 1968 and 1978 by all the US federal agencies. On the eve of the anniversary, Deputy Minister F.W. McDougall observed that, "since its inception," the Alberta Forest Service had been "primarily a forest fire control agency" and was now a superb machine for fighting fires. But the logic of a program committed to a strategy of initial attack argued in only one direction. Every fire that escaped might have been caught had better facilities and warnings been available, and, while pricey, the costs of fighting big fires justified the endless investment to catch every fire while small. Sooner or later the economics of such programs end in excess.[60]

However mighty, the AFS was less powerful than boreal nature. Drought struck during 1979, and then lightning, and before it ended the AFS grappled with a record number of 1,000 fires, some 480,000 burned acres, and suppression costs that, at $9 million, nearly doubled the previous high. The crisis rolled into 1980 with 1,300 fires burning 1.6 million acres and suppression costs blasting to a ballistic $26 million. The 1981 season was worse yet: 1,556 fires, 3.12 million acres, and $60 million exhausted fighting them. Then came 1982: 1,285 fires and 1.63 million acres, with

$75 million in total suppression costs. Historically the AFS had answered every crisis by building out; now it had to consider the question of cutting back. In the past, the AFS had been unable to fight remote fires because it lacked the means. In the future, having the means, it would have to limit its ambitions or seek allies. The AFS did both.[61]

The department had been edging toward a more nuanced policy as it felt the first effects of diminishing returns throughout the 1970s. In 1976, it explained to the Canadian Council of Resource and Environment Ministers that it appreciated that, despite granting "the highest priority" to fire protection, the province could not yet cope with multiple large fires during extreme conditions. It thus trimmed its stated objective to keep annual losses at one-tenth of 1 percent of the forested land. By 1980, ecology and economics, and citizen concern over both, were pushing the agency toward a policy of variable suppression, adjusted to four priority zones according to population centres, the eastern slopes, areas of commercial timber or petroleum, and the rest. No longer, in principle, would the AFS have to mass against remote fires kindled by lightning with the same ferocity that it battled fires around communities or timber berths. But it still needed more mechanical muscle than it could muster and a better sense of how to apply it, and for that it would have to look beyond the "Alberta advantage."[62]

Yet if it had to search outside itself, Alberta was also particularly well placed to broker a national strategy. Its experience trying to yoke diverse fire regimes under a common policy potentially sensitized it to the fact that no single standard could encompass Canada, and its long legacy with the Eastern Rockies Forest Conservation Board made co-operation a plausible solution, particularly if it brought federal money without federal control. The CIFFC could do for fire what the ERFCB had done for the eastern slopes. But it was a hard choice for an organization barely past a robust adolescence, whose director of fire operations could liken his organization to the US Marine Corps and whose instincts were to fight. Even as it joined CIFFC and as it, like so many other provinces, began to spin amid a vortex of mission redirections and reorganizations, the Alberta Forest Service had plenty of fight left in it.[63]

British Columbia

It was an oddity: a far west colony confederated to the rest by rails. British Columbia was all mountainous, virtually all wooded, almost wholly crown land. A coarse geography of rainfall divided its ranges and rumpled plateaus into wet west and drier east; that set the pattern of its fires. A peculiar political economy set the pattern of its fire institutions. Timber replaced furs and minerals, logging created the slash that fuelled settlement fires, and more loggers, not settlers, replaced the first wave of land clearing. Fire programs evolved not, as elsewhere, in competition with farming or fur trapping but in close collaboration with the one factor that decided everything else, a timber industry fostered on public land. British Columbia became a colossal timber mill. Like western Canada overall, economics pushed the province into commodities, politics into corporatism, and timing into conservationist ideals. What made it distinctive was how these kneaded into the peculiarities of its land ownership. Private holdings were slight (4 percent) and the presence of the dominion limited, for its oversight of the railway belt and Peace River block from 1871 to 1930 was a useful inspiration, not the basis for permanent bureaus. From nearly the origins of its timber industry, the province recognized it needed fire protection and knew it had to do the job on its own.[64]

In 1868, the first of a series of historical Great Fires preceded the colony's decision to join Canada. From Oregon to the Skeena River, a summer of fire ended with dark days in September, leaving North America's northwest under a pall of smoke. British Columbia joined Confederation three years later in 1871, granted the carrot of a railway that would link it with Ontario and threatened with the stick of American absorption. Three years after that, in 1874, the provincial legislature enacted its first, limited Bush Fire Act.

Thereafter big fires and Bush Fire Acts came in familiar Canadian counterpoint. Vancouver burned, mining camps burned, the backcountry burned. The usual culprits were those identified by Robert Bell as fur traders, missionaries, surveyors, explorers, prospectors, etc. and, nearer to civilization, railway builders, common-road markers, lumbermen, bush-rangers, and settlers and singled out for special scorn as "travellers who are not Canadians, who do not place any value upon the preservation of our timber and who are too ignorant or careless to bother to put their fires out" (although he offered little evidence that Canadians and Natives behaved any differently). Edward Whymper, advertising British Columbia as a frontier for climbers, raged about impassable *brûlé* and "range after range" obscured by smoke. In 1915, H.R. MacMillan summarized the scene since Confederation. British Columbia, he thundered, "has lost by fire about seven hundred billion feet of merchantable timber, more than now exists in the whole of Canada, enough to supply the whole Canadian domestic and export demand for over one hundred years." History offered no comparable catastrophe.[65]

Still, it took more than smoke and the occasional holocaust to shake the political establishment beyond rhetoric and hollow statutes. There was no serious agency for fire protection because there was no serious political will, and there was no will because there was no sufficient economic interest. The fire scene was inchoate, not unlike the province, then sparsely settled, its last easy flush of revenue exhausted, its institutions embryonic. What changed this dynamic was a timber boom early in the twentieth century. The putative fire scalping of its forests mattered because it promised to strip British Columbia's green gold as recklessly as miners had its placers. The CPR had linked the interior forests to the prairies, a hive of settlement, rabid for wood; American demand on the West Coast (after the San Francisco earthquake) now boosted its coastal forests. The effect was galvanic, a veritable timber rush amid a speculative fever. Timber now mattered, which meant that smoke was no longer simply an urban nuisance or wildfire a phenomenon of its mountain hinterland, like grizzlies, nor was fire protection a utopian scheme of the conservation movement. Fire competed openly with the axe.

Thoughtful observers parsed British Columbia as a fire province, like Caesar's Gaul, into three parts. There was, first, the problem of railway fires. The Railway Act of 1911 allotted this issue to the Board of Railway Commissioners, which worked toward a national strategy. Like other provinces, British Columbia assisted with co-operative fire plans. Unlike them, it pushed hard for locomotives to switch to oil, which was far less prone to disgorge firebrands than wood or coal. Its mountains explain the reason. Locomotives so struggled on ascents that engineers removed spark arrestors, which led to clouds of cinders; either that, they insisted, or they could not make the grade, literally. Oil tamed the menace.[66]

The second realm was the broader railway belt itself. This was a four million hectare strip of land along the route of the CPR that the province had ceded to the dominion as its contribution to the continental railway, along with a block of land in the Peace River region. The Dominion Forestry Branch inherited this responsibility, its only duties in British Columbia. Once organized, it contemplated a primitive program of fire control similar to that in dominion lands to the east. After 1911, it gazetted forest reserves, administering them in the same way (and through a common headquarters at Calgary) as the Rocky Mountain reserves. For the remainder of the belt, it relied on fire ranging. Since the only logging or settlement of any significance demanded a rail link, the DFB thus contained most of the province's economically important fire problems. Here was a source of inspiration and practical innovation that reached beyond provincial borders. It created a template of modern fire protection. What remained was to devise a means to expand that model across a vast hinterland.[67]

That left, for administrative purposes, provincial crown land. What kind of fire protection might be suitable depended entirely on what kind of use the land might have and how the province chose to oversee it. As always, the immediate concern was money. Minister of Lands William R. Ross put the matter directly: "Each annual Budget was a nightmare." Public revenue was insufficient to promote development, and without surveys and roads, there was no investment, which stalled settlement. Yet British Columbia had assets or at least collateral in its timber, which American capital was eager to unlock. This moment of opportunity was also, as Ross confessed, "a moment of danger." History was full of "sad examples" of countries that stripped their natural estates for quick cash and ended with only debt and ruined land. The province's response determined its fire protection apparatus for most of the twentieth century.[68]

The solution began with "public ownership of the forests," a concept rooted in the tradition of Canadian corporatism, now burnished by conservation, and embodied in a Forest Act of 1905. It guaranteed (in principle) both maximum revenue and careful stewardship. The money would flow now while demand for sawtimber was high and provincial need desperate, and it would continue at some predictable rate into the future. Defending a revised Forest Bill in 1912, Minister Ross glowingly described the ripe results of that strategy to mint woods into money as a "success without a shadow of a doubt." British Columbia boomed as money poured into roads, surveys, settlement, and prospecting. But the scheme also committed the province to a "very heavy responsibility," for it stood as trustee of the public interest and guarantor to licensees. That meant fire protection. The state alone could insure the existing forest and assure its regeneration, for without that warranty, a "permanent" timber industry and revenue flow were fantasies. Using Ontario as a rude template, fire districts were created and fire wardens appointed.[69]

Problems quickly surfaced with both leasing and fire control. The particulars of licensing encouraged a speculative bubble that burst in 1907; the belief that a handful of broadsheet-posting wardens could cope with fire went up in the smoke columns of the 1908 season. Within three years, the Department of Lands was compelled to suspend the old tenure grants and to increase dramatically both the number of wardens and the expenditures in fighting fires. A similar expansion followed the 1910 season, which "completely wiped out" the town of Whitewater, "destroyed" the

Kaslo and Slocan Railway, and "retarded" mining throughout the west Kootenays. Even so, the apparatus was laughably short of what the situation required. The more the province promoted logging, the greater the volumes of logging slash; the buildup of protection forces would never equal the buildup of hazards. As the department itself admitted in 1911, its "wandering patrolmen" were "hard to find in any emergency," although later critics noted that, given their tasks, it could hardly be otherwise. The problems, and their political toxicity, of course went deeper.[70]

In time-honoured fashion, the government appointed a royal commission. Few inquiries have had such profound influence. Chaired by Frederick J. Fulton and convened in 1909, the commission travelled extensively, heard endless testimony, issued its report in 1910, and watched its recommendations inform a new Forest Law in 1912 that defined the pattern of forestry and fire protection in British Columbia until 1979. But the commission started with an assay of what was wrong. Alfred Flumerfelt, a Victoria businessman (and commissioner), scorned a forest policy that he dismissed as "like some wild story of a commercial fairy-land." In effect, the government had told investors, "here ... are immense forests that will be put to no use for many years. They produce no revenue, they are in constant danger of destruction by fire, and it is beyond our power, financially, to give them any efficient protection. Moreover, the Province needs the revenue now in its growing-time and youth." Whatever the fallacies of tenure, that forest wealth meant nothing without practical protection from flame, and as the commission trekked not only to Ontario, Quebec, and Ottawa but also to Idaho, Michigan, Wisconsin, and Washington, DC, all agreed on the indispensability of fire protection. Dr. Carl Schenk spoke for professional foresters when he said that, if given five million dollars to devote "to the good of forests," he would "spend every cent of it on fire patrol." Almost all observers denounced British Columbia's creaking warden system as inadequate; there were too few wardens, with too little power, and too little co-operation from limit holders or the public. A Kaslo lumberman, A.A. Carney, bluntly dismissed it altogether: "The present fire system is a perfect failure."[71]

The commission was more generous. It affirmed fire protection as the "supreme need," believed the province had made a "good beginning," accepted that the necessary public support would evolve slowly, and reasoned that because British Columbia's forests rested on public land their protection was a responsibility of "the Government." The duty should fall to a "permanent forest organization," and the costs should be "shared" between the public and the private sectors. Forestry might not require an agency, but fire control did. The commission secretary, Martin Grainger, subsequently argued that the government did deserve some credit, that any organization would at first be "somewhat rough and ready." What fire protection needed was what the province needed, "development." In its final report, the commission noted "with pleasure" that the province was already acting on its recommendations. Grainger then wrote the new Forest Law.[72]

That exercise reflected two perceptions gleaned from the long harvest of the Fulton Commission's travels. One was the model of Ontario, which the Commission had visited, probably at the recommendation of Judson Clark, Canada's first home-grown professional forester and until 1906 Ontario's provincial forester, but at the time a resident of Vancouver, where he ran a consulting firm. The commission liked the proposition that fire protection could subsume forestry, that the state should command the program, and that a Forest Protection Fund, separate from the general budget, could establish a permanent endowment with which to erect an infrastructure for fire control, pay for fire rangers, and "solve that greatest problem of all forestry, the disposal of logging slash." (All this British Columbia could achieve, its minister later proclaimed, "without imposing any serious burden on either the Government or the operators," an argument that met with "prolonged applause.") The second prism was the US Forest Service, which had inherited America's forest reserves in 1905. The Americans had quickly sprinted to the vanguard of North American forestry, and they were rabid about fire protection, particularly after the 1910 conflagrations had savaged the northern Rockies across the border. Gifford Pinchot spoke at the commission hearings; after the 1912 Forest Act created the British Columbia Forest Branch, he seconded two of his own adjutants, Overton Price and R.E. Benedict, for duty in British Columbia. For the remainder of the century, Ontario and the US Forest Service remained the two peers against which the BC Forest Branch measured itself.[73]

The Forest Act passed in February; by June, the Forest Branch had established headquarters in Victoria and founded eleven regional offices throughout the province. Foresters, not political hacks, dominated staff and field. Wisely the act had consolidated and granted to the new service most of the land use powers that might fall to its administration, from grazing to wildlife to timber. As chief stood H.R. MacMillan, a native Ontarian, valedictorian of the Yale School of Forestry (1908), and former assistant inspector with the Dominion Forestry Branch who had surveyed perceptively and indefatigably along the Rocky Mountains. At its core mission stood fire protection, for without security from flames it would be "most unwise" to pursue an "active policy" of timber sales, and there was "even less justification for letting public property burn up than there is for failing to use it wisely." The goal that the Forest Branch set for itself – an "entirely practicable goal" if granted the proper means – was that British Columbia should experience "no material damage done by forest fires at all."[74]

That utopian declaration might stand as an emblem for all that was bold, progressive, and fanciful about the government's vision and the instrument chosen to grasp it. The events of 1905-7 had been, as William Ross assessed them, a true crisis, both a hope and a hazard. Like a chronometer with bimetallic strips, a timber boom and conservationist enthusiasm counterbalanced one another. British Columbia could plausibly claim that it had adopted the most advanced precepts of forest administration. It had taken the best features (as it understood them) of Canadian experience and the best from the United States and combined the lot in an inchoate setting, a just-developing province relatively unburdened by a bureaucratic past. Conservation, commerce, and good government could all converge.

But in taking the best of everything it had also assumed the best of all possible outcomes. A cynic might recycle Flumerfelt's sardonic assessment of the act's predecessor, that it was a fantasy. It assumed an outcome both painless and profitable. The forest wealth of British Columbia could only increase to unimaginable heights, while "heavy taxation need never fall." Success demanded only the proper form of land tenure and its administration. The Forest Act resolved the first by entrusting provincial land to public ownership in perpetuity, while fire protection resolved the second. Most observers interpreted the proposition that conservation meant good business to mean that it made good sense over the long run, what today might be termed sustainability; British Columbia finagled that doctrine to read that it should pay immediately. The corollary that conservation was good for business typically meant that it should stabilize the market and reduce risks; for the BC forest industry, however, it meant that the government assured business of a steady supply of timber and assumed for itself the moral hazard, for it, not the lease holders, was the final guarantor of the land should industry fail in its tasks. The argument that conservation meant good government proposed that public lands could be run as a public utility, avoiding problems of monopoly, waste, and private exploitation; in reality, disinterested experts had their own agendas, as did bureaucracies. Foresters became a constituency unto themselves, and government foresters were habitually more attuned to their professional colleagues in industry than to the public at large. (In passing years, such an agency might behave less as a public steward than as a royal monopoly, like the Spanish *mesta,* with trees instead of sheep.) The belief that forestry was a suitable instrument for the management of public forests tended to mean, in practice, that protection was sufficient to satisfy the dictates of "scientific" management.[75]

In practice, the apparatus bent to favour revenue. In 1907, as boom turned to bust, the government scrambled to stimulate the timber trade further and would continue to intervene as political circumstances encouraged. The means were never quite enough to match ends. There was always a reason to upgrade the harvest and pare staff, patrols, or infrastructure. There was always a fiscal crisis or an economic opportunity, a war, a depression, a political scandal, a surge in export markets. The timber industry was always in arrears. The province was always desperate for revenue. There was always a reason to quicken the cut now in order to invest, at some indefinite time, in the future. What decades later a provincial forester described as a "chronic deficit" was present at the creation. Provincial forestry, and hence provincial fire protection, would always be in chronic deficit of money, of remedial measures, of the practical means to enact its noble ideas and good intentions. In reality, its origins lay not with the Fulton Commission but with the economic crisis that had precipitated the commission. The BC Forest Branch habitually prefaced its annual report with a summary of the export market. As if to personify those strains, shortly after he researched the problem in 1915, H.R. MacMillan resigned as head of the service to open his own timber export company, what eventually evolved into MacMillan Bloedel, one of the giants of Canadian industry.[76]

From its creation, the BC Forest Branch understood clearly the systemic task before it and undertook its mission with zealous efficiency. It appreciated the political economy behind its fire protection service: what was lost to fire was lost to logging, and what wasn't logged was wasted. Its receipts were the "mainstay of the Provincial Treasury." Likewise, it understood thoroughly the basics of fire protection. The service might need to adapt, but it did not need to invent. Its leaders were bright, committed, energetic, and eager to grapple with a "fire hazard that has been the despair of every forest service on the continent." From the beginning, the Forest Branch saw itself as exemplary, and not a few others agreed.[77]

For the next thirty-five years, the two economies, nature and bureaucracy, played against each other. With astonishing good fortune, they were often countercyclical; only when the weather turned droughty and the monies soured simultaneously did the organization verge on collapse. Two reforms in 1917 markedly strengthened the apparatus. One was an amendment to the Forest Act that legally allowed for overdrafts to fight fire, provided the monies were later repaid. The second created two oversight committees for the Forest Protection Fund, one for the interior and one for the coast. Both consisted of five members, including the chief and assistant forester, the deputy minister of lands, and two representatives from the limit holders and operators. Their specific charge was to allocate the monies of the fund, an ever more onerous chore as expenditures consistently exceeded income. Any doubts about the value of the project were eased by the publication of a special survey under the Commission of Conservation's Committee on Forests. The *Forests of British Columbia,* written by H.N. Whitford and Roland D. Craig, instantly became a Canadian classic. They noted the obvious: British Columbia had a lot of wood, perhaps half of all the sawtimber in the dominion, which translated into a larger tributary of revenue than for any other province. And after documenting the infinite ways fire affected virtually every landscape, they concluded that fire protection was the "first and most important duty" of forest administration, that the Forest Branch had rightly devoted "the major portion of its efforts" toward this end, and that probably no agency had ever confronted "a more difficult problem." All in all, the report was a sturdy endorsement that confirmed the Forest Branch as the vanguard of Canadian conservation.[78]

Even in the trough of the Great War, the department soldiered on. A conversation with an air service vet "inspired" Minister of Lands T.D. Pattullo to push a contract with a Vancouver company to build an H-2L, which the Forest Branch would lease with an option to buy. Although assured that the "machine" would "fly herself," a test flight on 4 September 1918 ended when the engine stalled and the plane augered into a Vancouver house, dumping the pilot, a military flight instructor, into an upstairs bathtub. That episode dampened the euphoria until the Dominion Air Board arrived and granted Vancouver an air station in 1920. A few experimental flights followed, and showing political acumen they included joy rides for the prime minister and his wife. Aerial fire protection arrived the next summer, but the breakout came with the rough fire season of 1922. There were surveillance flights, an airlift of men and pumps to a fire at Buttle Lake, and, tragically, a fatal crash in September. By then, the liabilities of the resident H-2Ls and F-3s were apparent, notably their incapacity in the mountains and their increasing decrepitude. When the

Air Board dissolved, the Forest Branch was scraping for funds and retreated from aerial attack. When it required aircraft, which was not often, it contracted with the Department of National Defence. The campaign against fire would be won on the ground, a program that received a boost from the DFB when at Kamloops it contrived an exemplary program that featured a new-standard mountain lookout cabin, a fire-control plan with much greater detail and sophistication than any before it, and an inaugural ranger school for seasonals.[79]

When it profiled its program for the British Empire Forestry Conference and 1924 Forest Fire Conference, British Columbia retained the glow of its origins, the joined-at-the-hip prospects for forest wealth and forest security. Chief Forester P.Z. Caverhill explained that the "arrangement for fire control [was] almost ideal." There was no political hesitation about the value of protection, one organization had comprehensive responsibility, and the Fire Protection Fund forced government and industry to co-operate. The chief concerns were the urgency to build infrastructure and to cope with a frontier of slash and flame moving briskly northward with the axe. Visually, the scene was appalling: "Most people from the East, especially people from Europe, when they see the operations in our woods throw up their hands in holy horror at the waste that is remaining." The question was whether to "protect" through burning that slash deliberately or whether to beef up fire control for the eight to ten years of maximum hazard. The choice was largely a matter of practicality and cost. To date, the odds favoured that fire of some kind would enter, unless very intensive patrols were in place, and the department preferred that those flames be deliberate rather than accidental. But whether or not this was the right policy was something "upon which we have not yet made up our minds."[80]

The conferences had revealed British Columbia as an international presence in timber and a North American force in fire. Already, however, it was entering a dismal spiral that saw it more often scrambling to make up overdrafts than plunging into new projects. In good years, the program held; in bad years, it faltered. The dual premises – that timber would boom and that the cost of protection would plunge – had both gone bust. Remarkably the core work went on, not merely the emergency firefighting but also the building of an organization, an infrastructure, a public persona, everything possible to shape the bureau into "an efficient fire-fighting machine."[81]

But when drought and Depression interbred, the premises underlying the system collapsed, and the Forest Protection Fund plummeted $576,000 in the red. More fires, more duties, less money – not the shining formula forestry's founders had envisioned. It got a lot worse. For the 1930 annual report, Chief Forester Caverhill addressed the matter openly: "The large number of fires occurring each year, the continuing fire losses, and the drain for control expenditures, naturally raise the question of the efficiency of fire-control. Are the results obtained compatible with the moneys expended?" He had to answer yes; then he gave the conventional answer, that such events were beyond the agency's control, that damages would have been worse without its heroic labours. Like an organism in shock, the Branch siphoned its energies from the periphery to the centre, restricting what fires it would fight. In 1932 and 1933, with the economic conditions gangrenous, the Forest Protection Fund was, by statute, abolished, "without making any other provision for protection." Instead, the agency would rely on the "energies" of its permanent staff and on gangs of the unemployed to tackle fires, as temporary staff plummeted from 360 to 40. The seasons were mild, and the Forest Branch slid through. And so it continued, this atonal dance between nature's weather and a bureaucracy's will. In 1934, the Forest Protection Fund returned, although, as always, in arrears. Then the 1938 season cruelly stripped away the temporizing patches. The Campbell River fire in central Vancouver Island immediately became a Canadian classic, and the fund sank into a sea of red ink (over $328,000). Instead of a jointly funded program between industry and government, fire protection became a steady drain on the provincial treasury. Chief Forester E.C. Manning openly confessed that it was the bad year that had to drive planning and that the episodic cadence of bad years made rational planning impossible. Construction of the Alaska Highway and wartime stringencies further boosted big burns and dampened the capacities to attack them. Benevolent weather, however, crowded the monster fires into the north, and in 1945 the US Forest Service dispatched smokejumpers over the border and "assisted materially" in what threatened to become a "disastrous conflagration." The Forest Branch again escaped.[82]

The logjam broke for British Columbia, as it had for Alberta, in the postwar boom. A 1945 royal commission under Chief Justice Gordon Sloan sparked a redefinition of policy, a new Forest Act (1948), and a departmental reorganization (1951) as the timber industry reached the levels that eager politicians had long forecast for it, with the interior especially boosting output. Fire protection at last acquired the means to pursue flames to the farthest reaches. In practice, the BC Forestry Branch did what the other provincial agencies did or wished to do. It had the advantage (and burden) of its times. It had emerged early enough in provincial history that government and forest industry could together shape a program at its origins and late enough in national history that it captured the reformist zeal of conservation. It seemed to gather into one agency the best and brightest ideas of its age. The one brake on its endeavours had simply been that of funding. The postwar commission confirmed the logic of its founding premises, and the postwar boom granted it the means to enact them. When resources became available, notably with aircraft, the agency rapidly swelled to fill, and even overflow, the provincial estate. Once fully engaged, it confronted two decades of relatively benign conditions, further removing checks on its drive. A subsequent royal commission, also headed by Sloan, reconfirmed these developments in 1956. The wartime Sloan Commission set off an era that persisted as long as the one unleashed by the Fulton Commission.[83]

The first Sloan Commission had forestry policy, not fire protection, as its charge. Its terms of reference were to inquire into the state of British Columbia's forest resources and to assess their "conservation, management, and protection." The outcome was to move policy away from simple development into an explicitly multiple-use scheme that would assure a "sustained yield" of wood. But fire control seemed an obvious requirement and its current degraded condition a blight. The commission noted with only mild sarcasm the state of the branch's tool caches: "To protect 100 million acres of land and our forest resources, present and potential, worth untold millions of dollars, the Forest Service is the proud possessor of 3 fire-line ploughs, 11 bulldozers, and 253 fire pumps. It must also be recorded that its firefighting equipment includes 154 rowboats and canoes, some of which are equipped with outboard motors." This "grossly inadequate" state of affairs the commission attributed to lack of funding. While money could usually be found for emergency firefighting, the province habitually scrimped on presuppression and improvements, which ran counter to the doctrine of rapid initial attack that still seemed the surest guarantor of success, however defined. There was no apparent downside to bolstering forest fire protection. Accordingly, of the commission's nine major recommendations, fire control claimed priority. "Fire-protection must be greatly increased."[84]

That was the good news. The deepest reform of the commission, and its reason for having been called into being, was to replace the faltering system of leases with a new arrangement for tenure, embodied in Public Sustained Yield Units and Forest Management Licences. In his testimony, Chief Forester C.D. Orchard, the primary architect of the scheme, admitted that he thought the "greatest benefit for the most people" would occur if half the crown lands were in private hands. "I don't think we could do it," he confessed, however. "We've got ourselves involved, we've sold the idea of Government ownership so thoroughly, we have such a strong minority element of socialism, I don't think the people will ever let us sell the land." H.R. MacMillan then forecast, in the words of Ken Drushka, that "the new tenure system would lead to monopoly control of the province's forest lands by companies that in the end would fail to manage the forests properly." An increasingly corporatist arrangement was exactly what occurred. The British Columbia Forest Branch (renamed as the Forest Service) would have special responsibility for all timber-related issues on the 96 percent of British Columbia that remained crown land. Several senior members of the department resigned in protest, alarmed at both the policy and Orchard's autocratic and cabalistic style.[85]

None of this immediately affected fire protection. Its mission remained unchanged, while its means allowed it, at last, to fulfill them. The problem fires hid in the inaccessible north, although some were monsters; five of the top twenty largest known occurred between 1948 and 1951, all in the north. The program became an ever more industrial firefighting machine. "Actually," the chief forester confessed, "fire-suppression technique is gradually developing into a mechanical project, supported and aided by man-power if and when necessary." The future was pumps, bulldozers, engines, and especially aircraft. A fleet of fixed-wing planes and helicopters was a means so powerful that it could define ends; it could make the most secluded landscape accessible; it could equally shred budgets. Fire protection became both more expansive and more expensive. The Forest Service had begun chartering planes in 1945, and it experimented with helicopters in 1946. The real takeoff, however, occurred after the successor Sloan Commission in 1956. Each subsequent year marked another milestone: the first operational use of helicopters (1957); the first waterbombing (1958); the conversion of the mammoth Martin Mars flying boat (1959). On the occasion of its fiftieth anniversary in 1962, the Forest Service contemplated with pride, and perhaps awe, a de facto provincial air force. While greater firepower came with much greater costs, a self-analysis submitted to the second Sloan Commission affirmed that "'extravagance' in attacking a spot fire, or a fire of small dimension, is the ultimate in economy when contrasted with the cost of fighting a large fire out of control."[86]

The Sloan Commission agreed and went further. While acknowledging "very marked improvement" in fire control, Sloan concluded that genuine success meant the capacity to cope with the exceptional years, not the average years, and that the BC Forest Service was far from achieving that goal. In the mid-1950s, it was plausible that it had not done so because of feeble funding. The crown had to contribute more, Sloan decided, and in 1956, as his report went to the lieutenant governor-in-council, the Forest Protection Fund was abolished by statute. Industry still contributed, but everything now went through the ministry, along with revenue from logging, which sluiced through the department in record flow. A programmed ten-year plan for increased appropriations to fire protection followed, even as the proportion of expenditures devoted to fire control shrank from 42 percent in 1943 to 20 percent by 1956. With such funds, aerial fire control was possible, and the application of a 10 a.m. suppression policy throughout the province became plausible. The ancient limitations of money and machinery were more or less gone. By 1961, the firefighting bill was escalating at a dizzy rate. There were fewer big fires, lesser damages, and greater costs – and still the fires came. The 1970 season set (another) new record for costs.[87]

Soon afterward, a professor at the University of British Columbia, J.H.G. Smith, asked, how much protection was really needed? Wretched statistics made an answer "impossible," but clearly something was out of whack. Looking over the fifty-year record, Smith observed that the number of fires reported annually had doubled, that reported damage to forest cover had increased "24 times," and that suppression costs had swollen to "480 times" the founding fund, not including support from other co-operating agencies. Greater efficiency, which is to say, a sharper initial attack, had allowed the agency to halve the average fire size, but total damages per fire had risen five times and direct suppression costs per fire twenty-one times. Smith sardonically concluded that "protection costs have increased 250 times, B.C. Forest Service revenues 17 times, total timber cut 6 times, and population 4 times." For every dollar spent, the BC Forest Service pruned damages by less than fifty cents. This could not continue.[88]

Historically the Forest Service had seen its mission as expansionary. It had to install fire protection where none existed, and that investment in infrastructure drove great expenses. Beyond that first-order infrastructure, the agency sought to knock down those few fires that escaped initial attack and ran up damages and costs, and for this it looked to technology. But the automated detection of lightning did not prevent strikes; shuffling crews could reduce the cost per fire but not the overall fixed costs of having the crews; adding aircraft added, also, to annual expenses regardless of whether many fires occurred or only a few, or whether they broke out in slash or bush, during drought or drizzle. The 1970 season had a record number of fires (4,003), less than the ten-year average burned, and more than double the ten-year average of costs per fire. The logic of initial attack finally met the logic of diminishing returns.[89]

What happened to fire protection was happening to the Forest Service overall. Each had become an empire unto itself. MacMillan's predictions had come true as more and more leases were hoarded by fewer and fewer companies, which yielded less and less revenue, while the bureaucracy, not the legislature, made the crucial decisions about the timber industry. In 1975, the government reverted to its usual strategy and appointed a royal commission, this time under Peter Pearse. The Pearse Commission released its findings in 1976, most of which dealt with breaking up the tendency toward industrial monopoly and redefining the department's mission from sustained yield to multiple use, with an emphasis on the larger "health" of the forest. In 1978, with assistance from the Council of Forest Industries, a revised Forest Act was adopted that demanded a full two years to work through its prescribed restructuring. Meanwhile, fire control had become more and more a stand-alone service, answering to its internal dynamics, unmoored from land management other than timber production. On cue, a Zeus-like nature hurled enough lightning to stress the 10 a.m. strategy to the breaking point and run suppression costs to double the new ten-year average.[90]

By now, provincial fire problems had settled down to three. There was lightning fire in the remote bush. There was slash, sprawling not only along the wet coast but also throughout the more volatile interior. And there was the expense of building up sufficient forces for the exceptional year. All these had to operate within the context of the Ministry of Forests, now in reformation; all stirred concerns and aroused ardent constituencies outside the bureaucracy; and all questioned the reigning strategy in a different way. Lightning fire questioned the value of universal suppression. The big-fire year challenged the ability of a province to cope with the defining catastrophes. Slash burning queried the automatic supremacy granted to timber over any other land use. Fire's economics was not only pushing against its internal limits but also colliding with ecology and urban-based values. Not all of the public dismissed the untouched forests, as the chief forester did, as simply "old decadent timber stands," a source of wood and waste. Nor did they agree that slash burning was benign and a topic for technical experts to weigh costs against benefits. An increasingly metropolitan public disliked it. They disliked its looks, they disliked its cloying smoke. Ever vaster clear-cuts seemed to be environmentally ruinous, a woody cancer and an international embarrassment, and smouldering slash appeared less as a seasonal nuisance than a chronic threat to public health. Fire protection's swelling costs made it a dubious alternative, leaving what had been a defining issue at the agency's birth still festering in its maturity. As cutting quickened and planting lagged, the old instinct remained to have fire protection plug the gap. That option was becoming both more expensive and less effective.[91]

What really tore at the agency's fabric was the increasingly unanswerable question of the big-fire and the bad-fire year. The past two decades of fire had, in truth, been modest. Of the twenty largest fires recorded, six had come in the 1950s but only one each during the 1960s and 1970s. In 1980, British Columbia dispatched crews and planes to assist with the large fires in the Northwest Territories, Ontario, and Alberta. At some point, British Columbia knew, it would have to ask them to reciprocate. Then the hammer hit. The 1981 season set records for suppression costs ($39.2 million), and the 1982 season bested that ($42.9 million) while contributing two burns to the province's top twenty. Its fire organization, like its timber industry, had to confront the logic of a commodity economy, either to seek new markets or to merge. Public ownership of the provincial estate did not change that calculation, and the agency's first reaction was the traditional one. It searched out further resources – that stray airtanker, that extra rapattack crew – to hurl against the flames and that just might stop a giant fire before it built up steam. A passage in the 1982 annual report pointed out how this might happen when it noted that staff had devoted "three man months" to "developing the Canadian Interagency Forest Fire Centre at Winnipeg." A boom of materiel could spare the agency from a bust of ideas.

Prosperity and Peril

Department of Forestry

No less than its provincial colleagues, the Dominion Forest Service caught the postwar boom. The 33 percent of its staff that had gone to war marched proudly home. In D.A. Macdonald, appointed dominion forester in 1948, it had a director of conviction and talent, with the vision that now was the time "to re-state the contribution which the Federal Government can make in the application of scientific forestry in the Dominion of Canada" and the political savvy to make it happen. Herb Beall, as director of forest fire research, resuscitated the program of fire hazard rating, plunged smartly into his research on standards, and chaired the newly chartered NRC Subcommittee on Forest Fire Protection.[1]

As its fiftieth anniversary approached, the DFS expanded its staff, transformed Petawawa from a place for summer fieldwork into a permanent facility for research, re-established its experimental stations and installed new ones, and linked with half a dozen fire-interested institutions. It issued revised tables for the Wright System. It commenced publishing an annual summary of *Forest Fire Losses* and, on behalf of the NRC, *Forest Fire Abstracts,* a digest of research projects. It dispatched consultants to the Yukon and Northwest Territories, to Indian reserves, and to Newfoundland, soon to join Confederation. It signed on to the Eastern Rockies Forest Conservation Board. It cultivated connections with the Department of National Defence, with which it shared land and with whom it co-operated on fire-related questions of civil defence. It represented Canada on international matters, from the 1947 British Empire Forestry Conference to the freshly chartered UN Food and Agriculture Organization to the International Union of Forest Research Organizations. The climax came with the Canada Forestry Act of 1949, which granted the organization the statutory authority it had lacked for almost twenty years and which promised, by means of provincial-dominion agreements, to kindle a national forest inventory that would restore some operational duties to complement its research mission; implementation began in 1951. In the second phase, beginning in 1956, the federal government agreed to help fund equipment and presuppression but left the provinces to pay for outright suppression. In brief, the federal fire establishment was rechartered and reinvigorated.

There was a departmental realignment in 1950, stuffing the DFS into the Department of Resources and Development, and another in 1953, subsuming it within a Department of Northern Affairs and National Resources. The Forest Research Division underwent an internal reorganization that year as well. The practical consequences were meagre; reorganizations had become a kind of background disturbance, almost required as well as expected. Kenneth Johnstone even mused that the organization seemed "to have somehow acquired that quality of survival and regeneration that the forests themselves often manifest after the ravages of insect, disease, fire, and man."[2]

As the new director of Forest Fire Protection, J.C. Macleod avidly continued the themes of his predecessors. Under his supervision, the Wright-Beall System strengthened its store of data, expanded into new territory, and became simplified, its complex calculations hidden within more accessible tables and eventually a pocket-sized meter. New fire hazard field stations sprang up at Whiteshell Forest Reserve, Manitoba; Grand

Falls, Newfoundland; Bittern Creek, Saskatchewan; and Whitecourt, Alberta. But there were targeted projects on every aspect of fire protection, from assessing fire season severity to fuel-type classifications and to the design of slip-on tankers. What excited Macleod most, however, was the search, conducted with NRC labs, for a preservative that would shield linen hoses from mildew. "Any province in Canada, except PEI or possibly Newfoundland, bought more unlined hose than the whole U.S.," he observed. Pumps, hoses, and airplanes – these drove the costs of fire control. Accordingly, they blazed the paths of fire research.[3]

The transformation had been astonishing. Within a handful of years, DFS fire research had progressed from Jim Wright baking duff samples in a campstove to a sophisticated establishment that could address, with modern scientific apparatus, nearly every aspect of fire control and even produce training films on proper firefighting. Although Petawawa served as the dominant site for field tests, the primary staff remained in Ottawa. The process of revising data and calculations continued, absorbing "the greater part" of the group's collective effort. Gradually the new tables appeared, those for the older, longer-studied provinces first, the laggard provinces later. By 1957, even British Columbia had field parties at Vancouver Island and Cariboo, and preliminary work was underway in Yukon and the Northwest Territories. That year the agreement system by which the dominion could contribute to the provinces was renewed with provisions for five-year terms, which this time allowed "the hiring of aircraft and vessels." When Quebec finally enrolled, completing the sweep of provinces, the Canada Forestry Act succeeded in erecting a rude scaffolding for a national agenda in forestry for the first time.[4]

It was a heady moment, a long time in coming. In 1960, nearly a century after Confederation, Canada at last seemingly recognized the national significance of forestry and granted it both autonomy and authority. The Department of Forestry Act combined the DFS with the Forest Biology Division from the Department of Agriculture to become a Department of Forestry. The new institution would administer the federal-provincial agreements, thus superseding the Canada Forestry Act. In 1963, the department convened the first Federal-Provincial Forest Ministers' Conference. This shifting of bureaucratic plates triggered aftershocks that yielded a proposed internal reorganization in 1963 and a full-dress one in 1965. The department erected regional centres and thematic institutes. The core fact appeared to be this: no longer was forestry the foster child of Ottawa, handed off to the temporary care of one or another ever-changing departments. It could – it needed to – stand alone.[5]

As one of forestry's founding missions, fire research feasted on these developments. It was completing the third iteration of the Wright System, with major revisions released in 1956, the tables for Saskatchewan and Alberta printed in 1959, and research underway that would culminate in publication for the Northwest Territories (1962) and British Columbia (1965). It had data from some 14,000 test fires, now ready for punch cards, and the hazard tables were being configured into a more portable pocket meter. It hired new staff, among them two prominent figures for fire research's future, A.J. Kayll and C.E. Van Wagner. It had begun an internal redistribution of researchers. Until now, the staff had concentrated in Ottawa and dispersed for summer fieldwork. Under the new scheme, a small core would remain in Ottawa, with connections to Petawawa, while others fanned out to regional centres. The move would strengthen provincial links, particularly vital since the freshly gazetted department oversaw federal programs for co-operative forestry. It had published the first directory of Canadian forest fire research, a register of scientists, facilities, and ongoing projects. Federal fire research was leaving its Ottawa Valley habitat to forage more widely and establish permanent dens across the country.[6]

The boom continued. In 1965, the department underwent a full reorganization, a process of both co-ordinating its statutory duties and consolidating its rapid expansion. With the third iteration of the revised Wright System completed, fire research sketched the parameters for a fourth, one that would encompass a broader range of fire behaviour and claim a national reach. At the same time, it declined invitations to join a similar American effort; Canada had its own traditions, better suited to its circumstances. It was active internationally, principally through the International Union of Forest Research Organizations (IUFRO) and the Food and Agriculture Organization (FAO), especially the North American Forestry Commission, which nurtured a special committee on fire protection. It floated plans to hire a hundred new staffers. The Ottawa group, no longer migrating to the provinces for field seasons, became one of a cluster of departmental institutes. The Forest Fire Research Institute addressed questions that transcended strictly regional interest with a charter specifying investigations "on fire hazard forecasting, fire behaviour, danger rating in different forest fuel types, detection and suppression equipment."[7]

A new generation was storming onto the scene. The wreckage of the 1930 transfer, the organizational ruins like black trunks amid fireweed, had ripened into a majestic regrowth. But like a maturing forest of jack pine, it was inevitably being readied for the next crown fire. Had the agency devised a Wright System for rating institutional hazard, it might have watched a tracer index of political danger rise ominously, awaiting only a spark. Ignition came in 1969.

Reburn

To commemorate the sixtieth anniversary of the formative 1906 Canadian Forestry Convention and Dominion Forest Reserves Act, the Department of Forestry hosted a National Forestry Conference and, with support from both industry and the provinces, boosted a six-year plan for aggressive expansion. Yet the rot that would topple that ambition was already at work. Even as he negotiated the Department of Forestry Act, J.D.B. Harrison, then director of the Forestry Branch, recalled how "the whole approach to this Committee [of Cabinet] was not to talk research: it was to talk economics." The only acceptable argument was that Canada needed forest science to maintain its standard of living. At present, only four provinces earned revenue from their forest operations, and only two of those earned substantial revenues; the only way to add value was through research; and the sole mechanism for research was the federal government since "there was nobody else in Canada to do it." With the treasury full, there was little reason to object.[8]

When those coffers drained, however, parliamentary support went with it. Parsimony could instantly follow opulence. The immutable political fact was that the provinces controlled the natural resources on their lands, including forests. The fledgling Department of Forestry lacked authority over the management of even those forests that remained under dominion jurisdiction, those of the Yukon and Northwest Territories, national parks, and military and Indian reserves. What it had instead was its administration of the federal-provincial agreements. In 1962, before the department got properly organized, the first wave of austerity hit; the second followed in 1966, when another Government Reorganization Act forced a hostile merger of Forestry with Rural Development. Even as the institution boosted an ambitious six-year plan, Minister Maurice Sauvé observed that the original Department of Forestry was "unreal: it had no weight, no serious budget"; the money was in "ARDA [Agricultural Rehabilitation and Development Administration] and Feed Grains." A year later the federal-provincial agreements, with provisions for cost sharing, ended, replaced by outright grants without any requirements to meet national standards. Or without any need for an agency of the federal government to establish standards and ensure compliance with them. When Ottawa gave freely away any leverage over the provinces by chucking national standards, the sacrifice fell upon the Department of Forestry.[9]

C. Northcote Parkinson once observed how often grand edifices, even capital cities (he cited New Delhi), were erected even as the foundations for their existence were being simultaneously eroded away. "It is now known," he lectured, tongue-in-cheek, "that a perfection of planned layout is achieved only by institutions on the point of collapse." That is not a bad description of the curious chronicle of Canadian fire research. Every bold flight of an initiative had a weighted string that pulled it down; Ottawa put one foot on the accelerator and the other on the brake. In 1968, as the department planned another round of expansion, and as Forest Fire Research, under J.C. Macleod, plotted out the contours of a spectacular new iteration of fire danger rating, recession set in, a national election brought in the Trudeau administration with a landslide, and an order-in-council combined the Department of Forestry and Rural Development with the Department of Fisheries, effective March 1969. Another department: Fisheries and Forestry. Another name change: Canadian Forestry Service. Another downsizing: this one the most draconian since the 1930 debacle. While plans called for dramatic new hiring and upgraded facilities, reality demanded staff reductions and the merging of institutes in Winnipeg and Calgary into one at Edmonton that would serve all the prairie provinces and the territories. Programs slowed, projects vanished; within a decade, staff was halved; morale suffered a "blow" that was "brutal and long-lasting." Even Petawawa felt the strain, surviving by merging in 1979 with the two Ottawa-based institutes, Forest Management and Forest Fire Research.[10]

In truth, it was an old story and one that did not cease with the 1969-70 "bloodletting." Less than two years later, federal forestry was amalgamated with a Department of Environment (what D.E. Williams sourly called the "Department of Everything"). Then it went to Fisheries and Environment (1978); back to Environment (1980); then to Agriculture (1986). In the years between the Department of Forestry Act of 1960 and its absorption into Agriculture, Forestry had been whip-sawed into and out of seven departments (and since 1950 nine). Its average tenure in each was shrinking to something under five years and was doomed to an even shorter cycle, by 1990 roughly two years. Every reorganization inevitably shook the institution. Fire research felt every tremor.[11]

There was thus, at the heart of this enterprise, a vast incongruity, which federal forestry and fire research shared with Canada overall. The success of scientific inquiry occurred amid a chronic institutional instability. Yet this, one could argue, was Canada in cameo: the vigour of everyday

life contrasting with the wobbliness of its larger organs of government.
That, perhaps, was how it should be, for Canada could be conceived as a
confederation of convenience to shield its inhabitants from the uncontrollable vagaries of outside forces from climate to geopolitics and global business cycles. Those institutions, so often aquiver and shapeless, were the
buffer between a harsh outer world and daily life. They took the blows;
they creaked and warped and sometimes broke so that the routine of quotidian life might continue. For an institution such as the Forest Service,
unmoored from the critical piers of Canadian politics and economics,
the buffetings could be severe. When the postwar boom turned bust, the
trough into which it plunged was as intense as the crest that had lifted it
so precipitously.

What the federal government failed to do for forestry overall, however, it
did achieve for fire danger forecasting. During the early days of the buildup,
in 1965, a cadre of department researchers assembled into a working group,
housed in the newly established Forest Fire Research Institute in Ottawa,
to review the status of the tracer index and plan for a next generation.
The past two decades had witnessed both the dissemination of the index
and its distortion as it adapted, province by province. In good Canadian
fashion, the indices continued to share a common ideal but had assumed
local shapes to such an extent that they tugged and warped that ideal into
barely recognizable forms; the third iteration of the Wright System had
evolved into nine species of indices. The time had come, readied both
by the temporary politics of affluence and by a sharpening science, to
reassert a national standard. By 1967, the contours of that scheme were
announced in the form of a "modular" strategy, with rough kinship to
systems engineering, that would retain a collective structure yet allow
for regional variability. The upshot was the Canadian Forest Fire Danger
Rating System (CFFDRS), arguably the outstanding accomplishment of
Canadian fire science and one of Canada's most extraordinary cultural
achievements.[12]

The scheme had two components, addressed in sequence. The first was a
Fire Weather Index (FWI). This was the tracer index upgraded and parsed
into three subindices or moisture codes (for fine fuel, duff, and drought).
It derived from weather observations recorded at noon but recalibrated
with mid-afternoon fine fuel moisture and fire behaviour, as correlated
with test fires. Specifically, the FWI built out of temperature, relative
humidity, wind speed, and composite twenty-four-hour precipitation,
as they affected those surface combustibles that most power fires. It was

"decided early on," C.E. Van Wagner recalled, "that the main goal was a new fire danger index based solely on weather that could be used to give uniform results throughout Canada." The eccentricities of fire behaviour were deferred for a second, later index.[13]

The core group – and it was emphatically a collective enterprise – consisted of S.J. Muraro and J.A. Turner from the Pacific Research Centre, A.J. Simard and D.E. Williams (who served as overall co-ordinator) of the Forest Fire Research Institute in Ottawa, and C.E. Van Wagner at the Petawawa Forest Experiment Station, but a dozen others swarmed usefully around the periphery. Discussions and delegated tasks quickly identified the critical questions. In its full scope, the scheme had four tasks: basic science, fire data collection, system design, and technology transfer. Although an implicit assumption existed that anyone could do any job, reality quickly sorted out people and projects. While Muraro proposed the scheme's modular structure, Van Wagner became, if by default, the principal designer and did the bulk of the background science. He devised the six components of the FWI, save for the drought code, which J.A. Turner completed. He wrote the core equations, tested their internal logic, and conducted some laboratory inquiries and experimental field fires from Petawawa. Others contributed to the critical 400-odd test fires and the investigated wildfires that made up the data set, bartered with the provinces for experimental sites and support, and ensured that the final product assumed a form that fire agencies could understand and use. While Van Wagner became the program's public face, the details of who did what were often lost in an extraordinary outpouring and give-and-take of ideas and institutions. Always there was the need to reconcile the abstract with the concrete, to accommodate what Van Wagner called "the immense range in fire weather throughout Canada" with the particulars of places, from coastal rainforests to mountain krumholz to grassy groves of aspen, and the peculiarities of institutions, that gaggle of provincial and federal agencies charged with overseeing Canadian fire.[14]

All, however, agreed on the project's pedigree. The genealogy of the FWI wended back to the tracer index, particularly as modified by Beall in 1948. In particular, the fine fuel moisture code absorbed the old tables, recasting them on a new scale with suitable mathematics. This was a deliberate choice. The assembled group valued not only the simplicity and directness of the old concept but also a continuity of data and methodology and, with no little whiff of nationalism, the distinctiveness of the approach vis-à-vis a parallel project in the United States. In 1970, after four hard years of investigation, the group issued their initial findings as a new series of tables suitable for use in the field, specifically as an initial spread index and burning index adjusted to critical fuel types. Updates began immediately. In 1974, Van Wagner published a formal summary of the project.[15]

The second component was a Fire Behaviour Prediction (FBP) system intended to strengthen the linkage between the observed weather and fire dynamics, that is, between the predicted "hazard" and actual fire behaviour. Again the strategy continued the founding traditions of Wright and Beall, grounding forecasts in experimental fires in the field, supplemented by intensively documented wildfires that flared well beyond the limits for what might be done with semi-controlled test fires. While allowing for some laboratory research on the physics of fuel moisture and heat transfer, the endeavour was, fundamentally, a vast exercise in correlation. Given a handful of simple measurements in the field, it would be possible to forecast the kind of fire that might occur along with rates of spread, fuel consumption, and head fire intensity. Later the program added features such as head fire spread distance, fire shape, flanking and backing fire spread, and fireline intensities.

Over the course of the 1970s, the project bred this suite of indices out of the coarse burning index, originally intending that they would serve as regionally based guides. With the FWI as a strong nuclear force to bind them together, these proliferating supplements formed, in the words of the Fire Danger Group, "the first truly national system of fire danger rating in Canada." In the early 1980s, proposals circulated for a major revision, what became the Canadian Forest Fire Behaviour Prediction System. In 1984, an interim edition diffused among field agencies that focused only on the rate of spread component for some fourteen fuel types. These, and the range of inquiries, continued to expand. By 1992, the FBP bulked out to its intended dimensions, embracing a robust range of Canadian fuels, a roster of predictions for fire behaviour, and computerization of the underlying equations. Not only did the CFFDRS absorb the vagaries of Canadian landscapes into a confederation of indices, but it also was poised to become the dominant method for fire danger rating throughout the Earth's boreal forests.[16]

Its remarkable continuity came not only through inherited ideas but also through personalities. Some members of the FWI group had dropped out by the time the FBP module was under development; others, such as Bruce Lawson and Brian Stocks, made the transition; newcomers such as Marty Alexander were eager to join yet wanted to steep the project in their own personalities. But unquestionably the most trenchant force was the persistence and intellectual personality of C.E. Van Wagner. From 1961, when he joined the Forestry Service, until his full retirement in 1991, Van

The Canadian Forest Service fire research staff at Porter Lake for experimental burns, Northwest Territories, 1982. *Front row, left to right:* Gyula Péch, Brad Hawkes, Marty Alexander, Brian Stocks, Bruce Lawson, Gary Hartley, Mike Weber. *Back row left to right:* Jack Bell, Tim Lynham, John Mason, Charlie Van Wagner, Wybo Vanderschuit, Dennis Dubé, Kelvin Hirsch, Murray Maffey, Gilles Delisle, Pat Golec.

Wagner, rightly or wrongly, personified Canadian fire research. While no one person dominated Canadian fire during this era – Van Wagner would be the first to protest his iconic stature – the story refracts through him as through no one else.

Two Solitudes: C.E. Van Wagner and Donald Stedman
Charlie Van Wagner, like Herb Beall before him, considered himself "lucky," the right man at the right time. For thirty years – "the only three decades" possible, in his opinion – he had been able "to roam freely over the whole range of forest fire science." His predecessors had either dabbled in fire as an intellectual hobby or wrestled with it as an adjunct to their real task, or they had been shunted into administration as institutional incentives for fire research waned. Van Wagner spent his whole career, a calling extraordinary in its output and originality, in fire science at a time when it became fundamental to the identity of the Canadian Forestry Service. No one had done that before, and even Van Wagner doubted someone could do that now, not with the same freedom. When he joined in 1961, the agency was poised to undertake its great leap forward; when

he left in 1991, the CFS was again shuffling between directorates and downsizing and within a few years would shutter its flagship facility, the Petawawa National Forestry Institute, where Van Wagner had worked so prodigiously.[1]

Van Wagner came into that career indirectly. Born in December 1924, he had been raised in Montreal and lands north, the heart of old Canada. He took a degree in chemical engineering from McGill in 1946, then worked in the paint and varnish industry for a dozen years, migrating between Montreal and Toronto, until the tug of "the forest and lakes" he had known as a youth pulled him back to school for a degree in forestry from the University of Toronto. Like Beall, he commenced work at Petawawa a year before he graduated (1960), with the then-director for fire research, Cam Macleod, instantly impressed with the seriousness, talent, and commitment of this older-than-normal student. Once at Petawawa, Van Wagner never left.[2]

The pith of Canadian fire science was the layered surface of fine fuels – their arrangement, their ability to wet and dry, their capacity to absorb heat, and the effects of that heating as woody solids dissolved into gases. That was the focus of the tracer index, and these were topics not wholly alien in principle to a chemical engineer with experience in varnished and painted surfaces. Like Wright before him, Van Wagner brought an engineer's vision to the task, isolating the essential components, matching select laboratory experiments to the dynamics of real-world wildlands, content to solve the problem within the limits established without demanding a universal solution based on first principles. Early, too, Van Wagner came to agree with the Wrightian philosophy, that "the answers to predicting fuel moisture and fire behaviour would never be found in expensive laboratories or through sophisticated complex maths and physics." They would come through intensive fieldwork, supplemented with studies informed by "basic physics and mathematical design," or they would not come at all. "Pretty presumptuous stuff," he admitted, from someone who was "mainly an engineer rather than a proper scientist." Yet that perspective placed him squarely within Canadian tradition.[3]

The man who published a foundational study of crown fire propagation began his public career with the slightly comical assignment to determine the flammability of Christmas trees and the effect of placing the cut trees in a bowl of water. Moisture, fine fuels, heat transfer – the essentials of combustion physics were all here. The resulting publication, and TV broadcast, became an annual, public staple. His real work commenced in 1964 with the formation of the Fire Danger Group. This was always a collective enterprise, a "visible example," to Van Wagner's mind, "of *successful cooperation*," although, in truth, the co-operation was hard won. Members disagreed over designs, suitable tests, appropriate measures. Even more, they displayed wildly different temperaments and mixed uneasily as a group, ever poised to fly apart, yet forced to mingle one with another and concoct some working confederation of interests. Always a trifle formal, lacking the affability of Jim Wright and the social ease of Herb Beall, Van Wagner's was an intellectual contribution.[4]

It was he who best identified the critical choke points of fire science and was willing to grasp and express them directly as few others were. Time and again he worked out the basic mathematics and then wrote up the results in crystal prose. Only George Byram in the United States, a physicist improbably working with the US Forest Service during the 1940s and 1950s, could compete with him for breakthrough insights. He worked particularly on the fine fuel moisture code, perpetuating the Wrightian creed, by publishing a clutch of fundamental papers that substantiated the revised indices released in 1970. Over the years, as soft patches were identified, he helped to stiffen them with critical experimentation, data collection, and analysis. Steadily, too, he expanded the scope of themes, including a 1977 study on the dynamics of crown fires, a topic most researchers had dismissed as beyond reach, and a second equally seminal work a year later that plotted crown fire history through the boreal forest, which went to the core of how agencies should think about fire and what they might, and might not, do about it. A codicil correlated the "cycle" of fires not with age per se but with the evolution of fuels. All that remained was to translate those analyses into economics, which he began in 1983. No one else could approximate his range and depth. Whether he wanted the role or not, whether his colleagues liked the outcome or not, Canadian fire science had found its champion.[5]

This mattered, among other reasons because the Canadian strategy had American challengers. The undefended border proved porous to data but impervious to founding philosophies. For all the collegial friendliness, the approaches were constitutionally different and incommensurable. In the postwar era, American fire science sought to erect itself on the first-principle hard pilings of physics, chemistry, and math. As money poured into the system, particularly after civil defence and military interest kindled, the fire literature from America became a "flood" compared with Canada's "trickle." Beginning in the 1950s, Americans had proposed a collaboration, but Canadians balked, worried that they would become mere hewers of woody tests and drawers of data. Eventually Charlie Van Wagner was called upon to evaluate alternative approaches, particularly the big-science enterprise launched by the US Forest Service in the 1950s and revitalized in the mid-1960s to create a National Fire-Danger Rating System (NFDRS). It was a task that he performed over and again as perhaps the only Canadian fire scientist with sufficient international stature to make a countercase.[6]

The US Forest Service had published in 1964 a new fire spread index, part of its first national system. Even then Van Wagner wrote up a systematic comparison, observing with characteristic fairness that "each system has apparent weaknesses" and with diplomatic understatement that, "wherever in Canada the two indexes are compared, poor correlation between them can be expected." The reason was structural, so fundamental that both approaches "can hardly be valid for the same forest and fuel types." Beyond that, he offered no conclusion, but then none was needed. The two systems might co-exist; they could not merge. Van Wagner saw no reason to abandon the Wrightian tradition, and by the time he circulated his comparison the Canadian Forest Service had committed, with an investment of major resources, to upgrade the tracer index into the Canadian Forest Fire Danger Rating System (CFFDRS). The prospect of de facto absorption into the American system if Canada did not devise a powerful alternative was surely part of that calculation and helped to account for the phrasing of its title.[7]

As the Canadian version went public, Van Wagner wrote up a more serious comparison, revealingly titled "Two Solitudes in Forest Fire Research," an allusion to Hugh MacLennan's novel *Two Solitudes* about the seemingly immiscible characters of French and English Canada. For fire science, the two solitudes were the American predilection for the lab and the Canadian preference for the field. The former sought to explain fire's behaviour by means of controlled experiments and physical (and mathematical) models erected from first principles, the latter by rough-hewn test fires in the open, with a degree of rasping and sanding by select experiments and physical modelling. Similarly the language with which Van Wagner couched the choices could be read differently by both tribes of North American fire researchers. He did not presume to conclude that "fire behaviour research should be done one way or another," only urging that both sides confess openly to their limitations. In this way, the "barrier" might be broken down, adding parenthetically "(if indeed any exists)."[8]

Of course, that conceptual border did exist, and as the Americans scaled up their publications, dominating the international literature of fire science, and as the NFDRS swept internal rivals aside, their Canadian colleagues worried that perhaps they were in truth laggards, that theirs was a "stopgap" science, that perhaps they should accept the invitation to create a universal system for North America, subordinating Canadian contributions in much the way that the Canadian military did for North American defence. Charlie Van Wagner thought otherwise. He remained sceptical of the American strategy – thought its ambition to reduce free-burning fire to formulas delusional; worried lest his colleagues give away more than they gained; believed that, if tested in its own boreal settings, the CFFDRS would triumph. If his formal declarations were "circumspect," as he admitted, disguising a "good deal of scientific and technical fault" he had excavated from the design, his inner conviction told him Canadians should hold to their own, time-tested traditions.[9]

The contrast in national styles was a theme that ran "strongly all through" his career, as it did through the Canadian fire establishment. From the onset, the United States, far more than Britain, had been a dominant influence. Canadians had studied in America, had adopted common definitions, had seized upon potentially useful instruments from pumps to duff hygrometers, had read America's fire literature. Beall's efforts to orchestrate a national standard looked to the United States for concepts of control standards and co-operative fire protection. Yet there were limits. The Canadian political system resisted national models, regardless of their institutional origin. Equally there was the vexing matter of Canadian identity, a debate curiously undergoing one of its periodic bouts of renewal at precisely the time the CFFDRS was being promulgated. If the American NFDRS stands as a contrast, Margaret Atwood's inquiry into Canadian literature, *Survival,* serves as a comparison.

Published a year after Van Wagner argued for his "two solitudes" of fire research, Atwood's "thematic guide to Canadian literature" asserted that the "central symbol for Canada" was "undoubtedly Survival, *la Survivance.*" The term encompassed many subthemes: sheer physical endurance, survival after a disaster, the "hanging on" of a people and their traditions amid hostile surroundings, the lingering of a vanished order. Over the centuries, Canadian literature had shifted from the ordeal of surviving a bleak and unyielding land to that of surviving "obstacles" to identity, a "spiritual survival." Revealingly Atwood launched her survey with a study of "nature the monster" and segued directly into a chapter on "animal victims." The natural world was the archetype for all those untameable threats to Canadians, as the frightened creature was the exemplar for the innumerable victims that nature threatens.[10]

Yet these were precisely the circumstances the CFFDRS addressed and what distinguished its approach from that of the Americans, and they are the questions Charlie Van Wagner, the chemical engineer turned forest-fire scientist, posed with regard to the choices open to Canadians. The issue was not simply the lab versus the field, or physical models versus empirical ones; it had to do with differing cultural contexts. The Canadian strategy assumed, as Atwood did, an outside world that was hostile, immutable in its core properties, and threatening. In response, the CFFDRS offered a simple way to assess the threat posed by sampling the weather and correlating those measurements with actual fires. While fire agencies could not alter those fundamental conditions, they could prepare to resist or rebound from the forecasted blows.

The American strategy assumed otherwise. It was premised on an understanding of fire fundamentals, encoded into a fire behaviour model that grew out of lab experiments and mathematical-physical principles. It had ample flaws – its devisers, particularly Richard Rothermel, were frank about its limitations and aghast at the reckless extrapolations made from it – but the fire model was the core. Into it were fed the typical parameters that affected open combustion, and from it came a forecast of fire behaviour. Implicit in this arrangement was the assumption that one can change the outputs by altering the inputs, tinkering with the mechanics of fire so that America's fire agencies were not simply victims of environmental circumstances. In principle, they could intervene and alter the outcome. The best Canadians could do was to predict events over which they had scant control; Americans assumed they could influence those outside forces. The world existed to be shaped.

The two solitudes of fire science, as encoded into national fire-danger rating systems, thus conveyed not only two distinctive national traditions of research but also two very different national understandings of how cultures and their intellectuals related to their surroundings. The world Margaret Atwood depicted aligned tidily with that which Charlie Van Wagner had long scrutinized; but where Atwood tracked a literary litany of losers, victims, and hobbled artists, Van Wagner spoke to another Canada, a Canada of practical science, technology, and applied politics, a world in which potential victims might move smartly to counter the anticipated blows of a hostile world, in which success was measured not by winners and losers but by levels of efficiency, a Canada that could stand eye to eye with America and stare down a system whose science was suspect and did not suit its circumstances.

Atwood, and those who followed her line of cultural inquiry, and they were legion, would have done well to look beyond their literary texts and toward the world of woods, waters, and rocks that Canadians inhabited and from which they extracted their economy. The Canadian answer to identity lay not in the country's art but in its artifice. In retrospect, the truer manifesto of Canadian nationalism may not be *Survival* but the awkwardly named, cobbled-together, and unquestionably effective Canadian Forest Fire Danger Rating System. In discriminating between the literature of Quebec and that of English Canada, Atwood pivoted her analysis on a Jacques Ferron story about an "ambiguous" house fire. "Whereas Quebec authors may have trouble imagining the world after the fire," she argued, "English Canadian ones are just beginning to imagine the fire itself." That might hold for its littérateurs, but Canada's scientists, from Newfoundland to the Yukon, had spent several generations contemplating fire and had published a literature as competent and necessary as any in the world. When in 1972 Robertson Davies spoke on what Canada might expect of its writers, he argued that they should create a sense of national character, uphold intellectual freedom and moral vigour, and depict life as it is in Canada. Whether or not its writers had done that was a matter of public discourse. But its fire scientists had achieved precisely those goals, even if they did so in the red pine forests of Petawawa rather than in the seminar rooms and libraries of Toronto.[11]

There is another way, moreover, in which C.E. Van Wagner differed from the usual roster of Canadian intelligentsia. He rarely worked alone; always he was part of a group, always he had to talk and argue with others, nearly always he laboured to answer questions that were not entirely his own to select. Compared to fire colleagues, he enjoyed an unusual degree of independence. Compared to the typical cultural templates for the creative mind – the isolation, whether self- or socially imposed, of the genius – he had to operate as a relentlessly social creature. Neither outcome was inevitable. There were alternative histories possible for Canadian fire research, one in which no formidable personality managed to struggle to the fore and impress his distinctive wit on the subject, and another in which the genius might have turned inward and sunk into solipsism, talking to no one but himself. That alternative history did, in fact, happen with the saga of another chemist-turned-fire-scientist, Donald F. Stedman.

Born in England but raised in British Columbia, the young Stedman was the bright lad from the provinces, full of curiosity, ambition, and tenacity; he educated himself with correspondence courses, then worked through a BSc from the University of British Columbia and, still driven, returned to Britain for a doctorate in chemistry from the University of London. By 1924, he was back in Canada, working for industry and universities until the National Research Council, eager to boost Canadian science, recognized his promise, hired him to its permanent staff, and dispatched him to Alberta to solve problems with troublesome gas deposits in the Turner Valley. There he made his name with the Stedman fractionating column, an enormously successful device to assist fractional distillation. It showed Stedman at his best: a scientist-inventor, able to translate theory into practice and express it in a machine.[12]

Within the NRC, Stedman became "legendary" for his versatility, a brilliant tinkerer, a craftsman with a deep understanding of chemical concepts and a special attraction to instrumentation. He worked on photometers, vulcanization, de-icing and defrosting, indelible markers for furs, furnace design, ski waxes, and glass cements. He devised better means of candling eggs. He proposed means to automate postal services. He even fashioned a "sea-walker suit" for marine rescues. Shortly after Beall published in 1948 his tables, Stedman, already recognized as an "eccentric loner," turned his restless imagination to the question of fire hazard rating. He wrote to Beall regarding the mathematical analysis behind the tables and described his epiphanous insight that it should be possible to subsume the entire process into a "continuous integrating recorder."[13]

Since the mid-1930s, liaisons had developed between the Petawawa fire group and the National Research Council. An engineer, Jim Wright had turned to other engineers to help with instrumentation, which his crude facilities could not create adequately. The NRC thus experimented with specialty devices by which to measure directly the moisture content of surface fuels; these were, in effect, Canadian alternatives to the flawed American duff hygrometer. In the summer of 1936, D.C. Rose visited Petawawa and ran trials with electrical resistance through wet and dry particles, with heated copper plates to measure heat capacity and transfer through duff, and thermopile recordings of radiant heat flux from test fires. None worked; the instruments, cobbled together from materials at hand, were primitive and the outcomes extremely variable. While "further trials" would be conducted at Chalk River, the experiment did not recommend these as a venue to the "prediction of fire hazard." Here and there other instruments sprouted, like seedlings, most of which withered in the shade.[14]

From time to time, matters pertinent to these themes came to Stedman's attention, until eventually he proposed a composite machine that would do all the tasks required to predict fire hazard. It would take the weather, measure fine fuel moisture, and perform the calculations behind the Beall tables. The Stedman forest fire hazard recorder would be, in effect, a mechanical analogue of a forest at risk from fire. Meanwhile, other matters began to distract him. He came to believe, on the basis of "spectroscopic evidence," that the speed of light was not constant and that "time is actually a field, in many ways very similar to electric and magnetic fields." When the *Physical Review* rejected his submission, he wrote to the US National Bureau of Standards to warn that the wobbly nature of light made its measurements insecure. He plotted out electron shells and quantitized j values into geometrical forms that were almost Keplerian in their nesting of one shape into another. He quested after a category of heavy inert gases, hitherto undiscovered, until forced to abandon the search because of sabotage by "supernatural forces." And he became drawn to what Charlie Van Wagner had termed the "fascinating but exasperating" science of free-burning fire. Like Van Wagner, he approached the problem through the physical chemistry of wetting and drying, about which he knew a great deal. Unlike Van Wagner, he assumed that, with enough experimentation, the proper instrumentation, and a sound model, he could break the problem down into its minutiae and then reassemble those shards into a functional whole, a literal machine. By the early 1960s, the task had become an obsession.[15]

The NRC tolerated Stedman's quest, allowing office space and shop technicians, but the real momentum remained with the Forest Fire Research Institute under Cam Macleod, who was fascinated by the scheme after Stedman had written and elaborated his proposal in 1960 and exclaimed that "it should not be too difficult to turn this analysis into an actual instrument." A colleague at the NRC explained that the point of "Dr. Stedman's device" was to eliminate "the human element" in making the calculations. The prospects mesmerized Macleod. In 1964, Stedman submitted a two- (in another version, three-) volume progress report, a wad of dense pages on a "Design Analysis of Forest and Grass Fire Hazard Recorders." Macleod handed it to Van Wagner for comments. While full of "admiration and awe" for Stedman's analysis of the tables, Van Wagner found the overall manuscript "very difficult to read and comprehend," less a blueprint than "an entire history of all his deliberations over a number of years, assembled in a very haphazard manner," which left the forester searching for a "concise description of the instrument and how it works" lodged "somewhere in the report." He couldn't find one. What the scheme needed was a genuine prototype.[16]

The NRC Associate Committee on Forest Fire Protection was "only too happy" to support that effort; so, too, was Cam Macleod on behalf of the Forest Fire Research Institute. Still, time was running out as, shortly afterward, Stedman "retired on age." The NRC allotted him an office and lab space, and its technicians continued, after a year's labour, to work through a prototype, and Stedman, toiling feverishly from 5 a.m. to 11 p.m. daily, had scribbled 4,300 pages of handwritten manuscript. Yet the project limped along, taking more time, snagging on more obstacles, and convincing Stedman that he ought to be paid beyond his superannuation. Macleod agreed to contract for Stedman's services, with the hope bright that another six months would yield a working device ready for field testing. Macleod believed that, depending on cost, several hundred units could sell in Canada and that the gadget might well find a world market. Another year, further delays, more hope and hype, and then in early 1967 the prototype was in hand shortly before Donald Stedman died. So much had been invested, however, that like a spring tightly coiled the momentum unwound to a second prototype and field trials during the 1970 season. Three years later the *Forestry Chronicle* published an account of those experiments, and the Stedman Forest Fire Hazard Recorder sank into oblivion.[17]

The enterprise died from any number of reasons. Its gearing mechanism remained cued to the 1948 tables, while two generations of new tables had supplanted them. It flopped because it operated with a machine calculator when the age was rapidly shifting toward digital computers. It failed because it proposed a mechanical model of fire that ultimately derived from a vision of a clockwork universe at a time when the computer was replacing the clock as a ruling metaphor. It assumed that the natural world, even the phenomenon of fire, could be resolved by the reductionism of endless experiments that could then be recomposed into a functional whole for which the gleaming gears of the Stedman machine were a material analogue.

All this happened, in fact, precisely as the Department of Forestry was boldly devising a new national fire danger rating system founded on an alternative approach, which was a modern restatement of the Wrightian strategy. Van Wagner repeatedly explained the informing rationale, that free-burning fire was too complex for a thorough mechanistic analysis, that the only practical approach was through select experimentation, swarms of field fires, and correlation, a mixed economy of empiricism, logic, and experiment, in which "the researcher had better be something of an artist as well as a scientist," in which output was both reasonably accurate and immediately useful, and in which the guiding intelligence required "a liberal dose of philosophy" as well as combustion physics. Doubting even the possibility of a "comprehensive model," Van Wagner believed that the best one might hope for was to "put logic and numbers to a few key features." There would be no Grand Unified Theory of fire, and none was necessary. Rather than attack too formidable topics directly, it was better to work around them, a philosophy of science that mimicked Canada's political philosophy of negotiated confederation. By method and metaphor, Stedman's machine argued otherwise, which made his contraption not only cumbersome but also antiquated before the first NRC machinist ever soldered a joint.[18]

That observation, however, prompts the question of why it ever got built – how it got conceived, how it got funded, how such a flawed project could have persisted. Or, to state the issue another way, why did C.E. Van Wagner, seated in his office at Petawawa, well above the fray of provincial firefighting, not follow the trajectory of Stedman's career? At issue were two models of nature but also two models of doing science, and the answers are several, not least in the realm of personality. Donald Stedman represented the tradition of the lone genius, a John Harrison furiously focused on a machine peculiarly tied to his own character. Macleod admitted as much when, on accepting Stedman's proposal, he observed that "no one else on this continent, or elsewhere, has the knowledge, ability and tenacity to complete the task." The more Stedman pored over the work, however, the more eccentric and less applicable the project became, and the more institutions, trusting to his isolated insights, were compelled to let him continue. While the machine's posthumous publication testified to a weird genius, it also bore witness to a false path, a road not taken by others for good and sensible reasons. When he died in his traces, Stedman was still pulling along a trail to a rainbow where the speed of light varied and a lab-based machine of gears and springs replicated the boisterous world of duff, wind, drought, and organic soil.[19]

Whether or not Charlie Van Wagner had any such inclinations, he had no such opportunities. The CFFDRS was a far better product for his labours, yet it would have happened without him. Constantly his ideas were checked by others; interminably he had to talk, correspond, meet with, and explain to the rest of the Fire Danger Group. He pulled in harness with others who were only too ready to snap at his heels or jerk him back if he veered far. The group was an odd squad, a herd of temperamental cats, with little to connect them outside the intellectual puzzle they shared.

Over the years, their differences became tensions, which imposed strains and ended in a fraying that looked like a rupture. By the time he semi-retired in 1988, Van Wagner acknowledged the social shearing and abrading personalities, the jealousies of diverse careers and goals, the philosophical disputes over theory and design. In particular, many colleagues began to yearn for something like the sense of conceptual closure offered by the American system, having a feeling that theirs was only a stopgap or transitional undertaking, and they resented what to their minds was often the inordinate acclaim given to Van Wagner as public spokesperson for their collective efforts. They began to mutter and quarrel and eventually unravel, like all groups, while the CFS itself was collapsing like a long-scorched snag. Until then, Van Wagner had helped to lift the enterprise beyond the drudgery of normal science, and the Fire Danger Group had granted Van Wagner a place where his talents could uniquely flourish without degenerating into obsession, blather, and hallucination.[20]

Van Wagner eased into retirement in two phases, a partial withdrawal in 1988 and a final parting in 1991. Before leaving, he wrote a summary publication on the development and structure of the Canadian Forest Fire Weather Index System and a retrospective of Canadian fire science since Wright, reaffirming the validity of that tradition. Then he sanded down some rough edges in his oeuvre with reviews on prescribed burning, an analysis of crown fire behaviour from new data, and an obituary of Cam Macleod, who had first hired him and whom he "admired greatly." Significantly Van Wagner turned to some contract work with Parks Canada, which was quickly becoming the most intellectually vibrant institution on the Canadian fire scene. Reconstituted, the Fire Danger Group moved on, the FBP system got published, there were renewed discussions with the Americans about a common North American model, and there was unease about the Canadian output not having the same scientific heft as that pouring out south of the border. On such matters, Van Wagner – no longer in harness, left to fade away in his residence at Chalk River amid the landscape he had grown up in and on which he had expended his career – had no voice.[21]

Yet Charlie Van Wagner returned to the fight once. Shortly after he retired, he deposited an exposition on the logic behind the FBP system and its equations with his colleagues. The group subsequently published the results but, to his mind, deleted one "crucial function." He wrote letters to no effect and eventually, "after considerable soul-searching," went public by publishing a statement in the *Forestry Chronicle* in 1998 so that "at least" he might "hold up" his head again. At issue was a lapse of logic, the removal of an equation that might seem to the uninitiated a minor matter that concerned the persistence of foliar moisture content in conifers.[22]

In a practical sense, it was uncertain that the factor would matter much. But it mattered to Van Wagner because the internal logic of the system was what made the Canadian strategy work, because the absence of the factor refuted the FBP system's claim to provide a "comprehensive crown-fire model," and because, ever the traditionalist, ever pleading that looking backward was necessary before leaping ahead, he recognized that the topic harked back to his own beginnings in fire science. It was a vast arc indeed – no torching spruce ever hurled an ember further – from the flammability of drying Christmas trees to the propagation of flame through the closely packed crowns of parching forests, yet the link was there, as similar links were there to join the makeshift instruments of Jim Wright and the ruler-drawn graphs of Herb Beall to the automated weather stations and computer models of the CFFDRS. Charlie Van Wagner knew that – knew it in his bones, knew it from his personal history. Even in retirement he tried to communicate to his colleagues why that mattered and how that fact made Canada both right and different.

Revanchism and Federalism

The Feds Take Flight

Amid all the squabbling among all the contestants, federal and provincial, public and private, region and region, there remained one shared proposition, as constant as a postulate from Euclid: commercial timber needed protection from fire. This collective wisdom was, in the words of historian Richard Rajala, the "glue" for early conservation, the "inspiration" for much state-sponsored fire science and technology, and a "central" core to policy debates today. And no issue summed up the prospects and perils better than aircraft. Planes and later helicopters made fire protection expansive, effective, costly, and political. Before the Second World War, they were indispensable for reconnaissance and transportation; after the war, they became sharp instruments for direct attack by waterbombing. Without aircraft, the Canadian way of fire protection could not exist, but few provinces could afford their own fleet, and none could staff at a level to accommodate the occasional blowout season. This was the issue that wouldn't go away, the living dead of Canadian fire policy. The political economy of aerial fire protection thus mimicked that of the railways earlier, and like them the new machines forced mergers.[1]

The prospects for federal aid for aircraft had been the climax to the 1924 Forest Fire Conference, branding collective memory for decades.

When the feds declined, only those provinces rich enough and desperately dependent enough on the forest industry kept up an in-house air service. The two models that emerged were state-owned fleets, as in Ontario, or industry-financed fleets, notably in British Columbia. The issue regrew, hardier and knottier than ever, in the postwar era. Aircraft were cheaper and pilots abundant, new models, such as the DeHavilland Beaver (1947) and Otter (1951), met more precisely the needs of backcountry administration, war-surplus planes became available, and experiments in the United States, USSR, and Australia, as well as Canada, suggested that waterbombing was feasible. In late 1948, Alexander Koroleff, director of woodlands research for the Pulp and Paper Research Institute of Canada, circulated a bold proposal to recharter Canadian fire protection with a comprehensive commitment to aerial methods. After first extracting a resolution from the Canadian Pulp and Paper Association, and then from the Canadian Society of Forest Engineers, he carried the crusade to the National Research Council, arguing for a major campaign jointly sponsored by the NRC and the Department of National Defence. The existing fire scene was deplorable, he exclaimed. The agencies "badly lack[ed] control over the situation" and more or less depended on "luck." The recent outbreak at Chapleau-Mississagi only confirmed the "rather ineffectual" means available, with massed crews, at enormous expense, left waiting for rains.[2]

There were some dissenters to the scheme. Major General Howard Kennedy believed that the lofty "Course of Action" was bloated with "generalities," which in his opinion (one shared by "every other member of the Associated Committee, except yourself," he bluntly informed Koroleff) "doomed to failure" the proposed line of research. Better, he insisted, to concentrate on improving ground forces and a "comprehensive road system." Worse, publicizing a chimera like "airborne attack" would "deflect attention from these stubborn facts and delay the solid solution of the problem another decade or two." In rebuttal, Koroleff argued that control efforts, ground and air, should be "parallel, not competitive," yet conceded that publicity should be constrained until it had translated into "definite improvement on our practice." The NRC Associate Committee duly filed the reports.[3]

But with or without aircraft, improvement was vital. Herb Beall was at that time pursuing his grail quest for national standards; provincial fire agencies rebounded, some riding postwar booms in oil, minerals, and timber; yet few could absorb the escalating costs of upgrading fire protection, much less indulge in opulent initiatives such as aerial fire suppression. When the initial round of federal-provincial agreements failed to include fire control, J.R. Johnston of British Columbia spoke for all when he bluntly declared that, "without federal financial assistance, the burden of adequate protection of fire of any one province's share of the Canadian forest is too great for that province alone to carry." Still, air superiority was becoming as fundamental to fire strategies as to military doctrine. Those provinces that lacked aircraft got them, and those that had them expanded their fleets. Meanwhile, US fire agencies rapidly took to the air.[4]

Aerial attack added to its lustre when chemical retardants appeared. They swelled the domain of possible use because those provinces that did not have the Shield could now bomb as well. The classic waterbombing strategy relied on a rapid turnaround from nearby lakes such that small planes could muster large effects. Now western provinces, in particular, could add punch to their drops because durable retardants could persist on the land after the watery matrix had evaporated; fewer drops with retardant could have a cumulative blow equivalent to multiple water deliveries, which meant landing fields could substitute for lakes. In 1958, the Canadian Pulp and Paper Association organized a full-blown conference on fire research around demonstration drops at Charlo, New Brunswick.[5]

The provinces continued to add to their fleets, each according to its needs, abilities, and opportunities. By 1962, the Department of Forestry was surveying the use of aircraft for fire control, trying to impose some conceptual order on the proliferation. By the mid-1960s, this collective air armada, both planes and helicopters, tallied more than 150 aircraft, including Cansos, Snow Commanders, Grumman AG-Cats, Avengers, Beavers, Otters, P2V7 Neptunes, Douglas A26 Invaders, Stearmans, B25s, B26s, and even the Martin Mars flying boat. As the aircraft aged, spare parts became a problem, and as provinces began sending planes to help neighbours under mutual-aid agreements, the mix of aircraft became unwieldy. Even by 1963, a general sense was emerging that some degree of order might be essential. All sides looked to Ottawa.[6]

Ottawa looked to the NRC for advice. The process commenced in January when the Associate Committee passed a motion that nudged the National Aeronautical Establishment, an NRC division, to sponsor a two-day convocation. Adding waterbombing to reconnaissance and transportation had expanded the range of aircraft usage, complicated the choice of planes or helicopters, and confused the economics. Many observers regarded the airtanker as a flying fire truck or airborne bucket brigade and doubted that such a single purpose, however impressive, could justify the exorbitant costs. Others fretted over the relative merits of large and small airtankers. Every province had peculiar needs and would refuse to support any program that did not contribute pointedly to its particular specifications. The workshop concluded that no one aircraft could "meet all of the requirements of every fire control organization in Canada." The conflict of opinion was too intense, probably impossible to resolve since it was "a reflection of differing economics and fire control philosophies." What all did share was anxiety over the inflating expenses; aircraft were gobbling up 10-55 percent of provincial fire budgets. The session ended with a list of research projects intended to improve various technical aspects of waterbombing. The deeper question – whether existing budgets were "economically correct" and hence whether agencies could afford more aircraft, as they wished, or were already using their existing fleets beyond their fiscal limits – was dismissed as "unanswerable," since it resided in the realm of politics, which lay outside the "scope of this meeting."[7]

While compromise assumed the traditional appeal to more research, that research probed into the possibility of creating an airtanker from scratch that might serve most purposes. The task of polling the provincial fire services fell to S.G. Chester at the Department of Forestry's Richmond Hill Regional Office, where he surveyed more systematically the various national needs and the proposed ideal airtanker traits filtered from the workshop. The prospect intrigued the Ministry of Industry, keen to boost Canadian manufacturing; nor did it hurt that the likely company, Canadair, would build its machines in then-restive Quebec. As all participants observed, and as the more bold stated openly, the issue was really not the technical specifications but the costs – the cost of development, the cost of purchase, the political costs of association.[8]

The outcome was the Canadair CL-215, the only airplane ever manufactured specifically for firefighting. By 1965, its design was sufficiently advanced to appeal for government subsidies under the Program for the Advancement of Industrial Technology. When that program asked the Forestry Service to validate the virtue of the plane, or at least its mission, D.E. Williams referred to ongoing studies, especially by D.G. Fraser, that noted the ineffable ambiguities of fire economics, compounded by the expensive but apparently "indispensable" value of planes, particularly as waterbombers. The decision deferred back to politics, which assented in early 1966 after Quebec promised to buy twenty planes and France ten. The CL-215 moved toward a prototype, the C-FEU-X, which flew October 1967.[9]

From the outset, the project had said all the right things: it would be simple, inexpensive to manufacture, rugged, modern. "It didn't turn out

A national fleet for aerial firefighting, a sixty-year project. *Top,* the DFB's aerial reconnaissance over the Rockies, 1922, placed the sand grain in the political oyster. *Bottom,* the CL-215, Canadair's classic and a Canadian icon, the only plane designed specifically for waterbombing.

that way," as a historian of the program wryly observed. Costs kept bolting out of control, as though the economics of firefighting had infected even the production of firefighting machinery. In fact, some of the design features made the new plane "something of an anachronism"; one friendly critic quipped that "it set the aviation industry back 50 years." Once flying, there were problems with rudder control, which delayed certification until 1969. A change of government in Quebec dampened its order to fifteen, although Spain and Greece picked up some of the excess, Spain bartering surplus wine for planes. The French CL-215s quickly suffered three accidents, including a fatal crash. Overall, nonetheless, those who used it were content. The CL-215 became the flying image of Canadian fire control.[10]

The most striking twist, however, may have been the refusal of this made-in-Canada marvel to propagate within Canada. Sales remained stuck in the province that made the plane and in France, ever eager to promote *la francophonie,* and through France other Mediterranean countries. The reasons were as varied as the provinces but boiled down to the fact that they were content with what they had. What they wanted was to upgrade and expand their existing fleets, preferably with federal support. Or, failing that, they would consent to alternatives, again if Ottawa subsidized the transition or underwrote a national fleet. The latter interested various ministries, such that by 1967 a bustle of meetings inquired into the prospect. Evaluations fell to the Department of Forestry, which noted that, compared with other options, the CL-215 was "prohibitively expensive" and would require a "drastic revision in fire control budgets" of most provinces or federal subvention and concluded that any decision about a national fleet "would seem to be premature." (That was equally true for schemes to convert to another aircraft. Thus, Ontario was also willing to adopt military-surplus Trackers, but the Treasury Board refused to finance the switch.) Worse, just as Canadair was soliciting sales, the federal-provincial agreements pact dissolved, and just as the Department of Industry was keen to justify production, the Department of Forestry was embroiled in fierce downsizing. The prototype CL-215 was not the only thing Canadian with rudder problems.[11]

Still, the research went on, prompted by ministerial memos requesting analysis of a hypothetical "Reserve Water Bomber Fleet" while Canadair aggressively marketed its hypothetical planes to the provinces. The Forest Fire Research Institute released a careful study on existing and projected airtanker use, which Director M.L. Prebble forwarded with extensive commentary. The conclusion was that there seemed to be "no evidence of forces lining up *against* a mobile fleet." Concerns were partly over the influence that a "*Canada-owned and operated*" fleet might wield over provincial prerogatives in forestry and the potential spoiler role that Quebec might exert if it possessed its own fleet that it would contract out, thus extorting from the other provinces the monies it needed to subsidize its aerial aspirations. The scheme boiled down to money, and money to politics, and politics to the bottom-line reality of federal-provincial turf wars. The research went on.[12]

The quest for a national fleet metamorphosed into the query about the value of such a fleet; airtanker studies joined fire danger rating as a distinctive, permanent feature of the FFRI, with reports annually renewed like birch putting out new buds. The arena for synthesis, however, remained the NRC Associate Committee, which in October 1970 sponsored a National Forest Fire Seminar on Aircraft Management at Petawawa. The meeting was a rousing success, ending with a dozen resolutions pleading for more meetings, more money, and more research. The uncontested consensus, however, was that aircraft had been indispensable and that the way to control costs was to improve efficiency through better operations and techniques. Of special note were demonstrations of helicopter deployments, including rappelling, a reminder that the issue of aircraft ranged far beyond the quirks of the CL-215.[13]

This time the studies culminated in political action of a sort. The Privy Council Office established an interdepartmental committee, and the Canadian Council of Resource Ministers resolved on a task force to consider a national airtanker fleet, wrapped in the language of "federal government assistance in dealing with forest fire control emergencies." The group convened in December 1970. Some matters were dispensed with easily (e.g., questionnaires). The sticking point was the character of proposed federal assistance – what form it might take, what liabilities it might impose, what power it might grab from the provinces. In particular, "fears were expressed that the CL-215 would be foisted on fire control agencies as supplementary support in spite of the considered judgment of Task Force members." The plane was simply too expensive: too expensive to buy, too expensive to operate, too expensive in what it could not do and so required other aircraft to supplement it; it was a Concorde among airtankers. Ontario led the opposition. There were enough heavy airtankers in Canada, it insisted; what was needed was a mechanism to pay for their transfer during emergencies. If more planes were required, fire agencies could look to surplus military aircraft, as Ontario was doing with the

Tracker. Similarly, the apparatus for mutual aid already existed. If Ottawa wanted to help, it could plump up the money to pay for an enlargement of the current interprovincial agreements into a national system.[14]

The task force reconvened in January 1971. But it could not reconfigure the exquisite balancing of suspicions, the universal perception that more financial assistance was needed and that the federal government was alone capable of supplying that aid, and the worry that each party would surrender more than it might gain. The pressure from fires, too, faded. Before the year ended, the task force disbanded, unable to overcome the interlocking resistances, expressed in the assertion that a national fleet would be "uneconomical." Translated, that meant it cost too much politically. Ottawa had needed to sell fifty CL-215s in all to break even, and Canadair began pressuring the provinces to buy their own apart from any hypothetical national fleet. Briefly the Atlantic provinces considered a regional alliance, perhaps to acquire a CL-215 to be used collectively. But if any such arrangement were to emerge, they preferred the aircraft they knew to a Quebec interloper. From Nova Scotia, John Gass decided that "basically it appears that Canadair is trying to either (1) sell airplanes or (2) find work for the ten aircraft to be manufactured for the Federal Government," an order solely justified to warrant a manufacturing run for planes for Spain. Save for Quebec, the provinces found the CL-215 too pricy and too specialized.[15]

The research went on. Increasingly sophisticated fire behaviour models along with clever computer programming allowed for simulations, matching projected fires against possible fire control technologies. Annually CFS researchers swelled the understanding of how airtankers worked, what tank configurations belonged with what aircraft, what mix of planes and practices would yield the most efficient outcome. When Al Simard published a summary in 1979, he could appeal to two decades of active waterbombing. But while usage thrived and matured, the romantic quest for a national fleet seemed more illusory than ever. Research only led, it seemed, to more research. When in 1979 the Canadian Committee once again resurrected the idea of a Canada-wide program, D.H. Owen of British Columbia observed that, while the "concept is great," there was little possibility of a Canadian counterpart to America's national fire centre, the obstacles to overcome under the "different circumstances in Canada" being simply "too great." He then pointed out that it seemed "incongruous" to argue for a national forest fire centre given the "recent demise of the Forest Fire Research Institute." Something would have to jar the current arrangement out of its meticulously balanced mutual suspicions.[16]

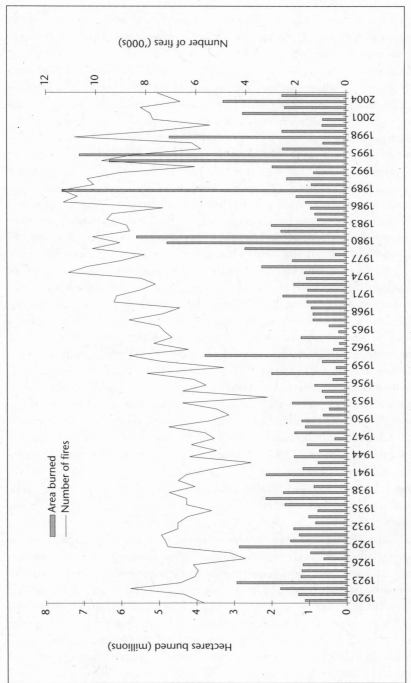

Historical fire statistics, 1920–2005. Note the apparent surge between 1979 and 1981.

That something was fire. Big fires returned, not once but over several years, not striking one unlucky province but smashing through a row of them, as immense blazes rolled over the boreal backcountry. Aircraft shortages became acute, and ad hoc agreements broke down as neighbouring provinces were themselves overwhelmed. There weren't enough planes or a mechanism adequate to shunt them around. Fire officers also looked longingly across the border, where American colleagues operated under the government-funded Boise (later, National) Interagency Fire Center (NIFC), opened in 1969, that sought precisely to allocate the firefighting resources of various agencies on a country-wide basis when crises struck. But like a national airtanker fleet, a Canadian version had foundered on traditional concerns over who would pay and who would control. Weirdly there was a better chance of the provinces getting aid from the United States than there was from elsewhere in Canada; a formal treaty between the countries was more imminent than an agreement within the·Confederation. After the 1981 season, however, the bloodied provinces were ready to agree to a national fleet, which also meant some intergovernmental organ to coordinate its deployment. But the federal government was also keen on the proposal. It still looked worryingly at a CL-215 program that had stalled, a trickle of planes flogged off mostly to countries along the Mediterranean rim. Suddenly interests converged, and wildfires catalyzed action.

Ontario brought the matter to the Canadian Council of Resource and Environment Ministers (CCREM) in July 1980 as its worst fire season flared, and by September it was arguing for a Canadian analogue of the American model. It then submitted in February 1981 a proposal for a "federal presence in forest fire control in Canada," which led to a discussion paper to the deputy ministers in March. Although thinking along similar lines, British Columbia agreed to table its own proposal, and Ontario then led a task force to review the national scene. By August, that Task Force on Forest Fire Control presented its conclusions. At its December meeting, the CCREM approved the concept of a national fire centre as part of a "forest fire information/intelligence system," directed that it be established "with the utmost dispatch," that its governance structure take the form of a non-profit corporation owned by the participating governments, that it be sited in Winnipeg as a central locale, and that it be operational by the 1982 season. A complex formula determined who would pay what percentage of contribution, with Ottawa providing a third of the costs in all. (Quebec declined to join until 1984.) On the acquisition of additional or replacement aircraft, there were some reservations, deferred until the members could consult with their respective deputy ministers.

Amid a remarkable sense of urgency, the Canadian Interagency Forest Fire Centre (CIFFC) opened on 2 June 1982. Legal incorporation followed in September 1983.[17]

The Centre, however, still needed its institutional software and something to share beyond the existing stockpiles in provincial caches. The two issues were related: a spoonful of new airtankers would make the political medicine required for co-operation go down easier. The drive for formal co-operation actually ran on two parallel tracks, one internal to Canada, the other between Canada and the United States, with the international agreement moving more quickly than the internal one. Both addressed the worsening situation in that agreements for mutual aid were ad hoc, cumbersome, and without legal foundation. For a number of years, Canadian provinces had negotiated arrangements with American states, in the case of Quebec and New Brunswick with the Northeastern Forest Fire Protection Compact. Later other provinces joined the Lake States Fire Protection Compact.[18]

By 1975, however, the US State Department "perceived a need" for a more robust and comprehensive agreement between America and Canada to cover the range of activities, particularly as Canadian agencies were tapping into the resources at BIFC. The US proposal, however, seemed too "centralist" for Canada, since it rendered the Government of Canada responsible for what the Government of Canada considered the responsibility of the provinces. The US State Department wanted an agreement between sovereign states; the Canadian Department of External Affairs wanted the provinces and territories to request aid directly as, in effect, delegated agents. Ottawa could not speak for Canada as Washington, DC, could for the United States, and the provinces did not want any national agreement that might compromise their ability to cut deals with the states across the border. New drafts were exchanged that highlighted differences in matters of liability and reimbursement practices as well as formal procedures agreed upon in advance for exchanges. In the end, the United States accepted in principle that requests for aid could come from any Canadian institution directly. An exchange of drafts continued through 1976 and into 1977.[19]

What finally allowed agreement was, indirectly, the creation of CIFFC, which provided a cognate institution to NIFC. Requests for assistance, from one country to the other, could now go through equivalent national institutions by formal channels and with mechanisms for compensation. While provinces might initiate a request, CIFFC would "co-ordinate."

What drove the provinces into alliance was the realization that, under the treaty, NIFC would now decide which Canadian requests to honour in what priority, that NIFC would "be the collector and disseminator of information and intelligence on the status of the Canadian forest fire situation." NIFC would become for fire protection what NORAD was for air defence. While the existing arrangements might be shaky, the provinces at least understood how they worked and had internalized the politics behind their compromises. None of that would apply if, during crises, NIFC had the jurisdiction to determine which Canadian fires got American help and which did not. Even Ontario preferred some "centralized mechanism" within Canada to "provincial dependence on the United States." The obvious solution was a Canadian version of NIFC, though as a corporation not an agency of government. This satisfied all parties. The Canada/United States Forest Fire Fighting Assistance Agreement was ratified on 7 May 1982 through an exchange of diplomatic notes. Two months later, CIFFC became operational.[20]

As it had from time to time in the past, Washington achieved what Ottawa could not: a reassertion of Canadian nationalism. An internal threat (from fires) combined with an external one (the perceived threats to Canadian pride if not sovereignty) to break the logjam of provincial politics. What the United States had compelled, Canada more cautiously cajoled with a replacement of informal arrangements by legal instruments, culminating in the adoption of the Mutual Aid Resources Sharing Agreement (MARS), formally signed in September 1983. Providing for the transfer of personnel, equipment, and aircraft, MARS became the heart of CIFFC, the operating system that ran all its other programs. Still, its fractious members expected something extra to share, and while the CL-215 had a certain national cachet, it cost $7 million to purchase, while a refurbished Tracker could be bought for $350,000. Ottawa wanted the provinces to agree to buy a quantity of CL-215s as replacements, particularly for aging Cansos. The provinces insisted that the federal government purchase a goodly number as a dowry for CIFFC.[21]

At its September 1982 meeting, CCREM constituted yet another task force to examine the issue. What emerged was a Co-operative Supply Agreement that led to the purchase of twenty-nine CL-215s as the nucleus of an air armada available for use throughout Canada, with costs borne by the federal government and provinces through a Special Capital Recovery Assistance Program. In the end, the provinces got their planes, Ottawa got to boost Canadair, and the costs fell largely on the feds. Sixty years after deputy ministers and fire officers convened in Ottawa to campaign for the idea, Canada had a federally sponsored program of aerial fire protection. The first planes arrived in September 1985 and the last in May 1988, just in time to assist the Americans wrestling with conflagrations in Yellowstone National Park – and barely a season ahead of a flood tide of fires that washed over Canada even more seriously than those that had prodded the country into collective action a decade earlier.[22]

Banff, Buffalo, and Burning: Parks Canada

There remained, however, one arena where the federal government could influence fire directly on the ground without having to refract every proposal through the provinces. For decades, the national parks were an afterthought in the administration of Canadian fire, either too small in area or too fragile in capacity to exert a distinctive national presence. But as more parks were added to the network, their aggregate land mass began to equal that of the smaller provinces, and as they sharpened their charter into a more robust commitment to the preservation of natural biotas they began to diverge in policy and practice from other fire institutions. Nonetheless, for fifty years after the National Park Act, the system remained caught between its two models, like filings between two charged poles of a magnet. Those poles were Banff and Wood Buffalo.

The Banff scenario continued to play out during the 1930s. Two years, 1934 and 1936, defined most of the burned area, with the Flints Park fire capturing more than half the recorded 8,000 hectares burned. In 1940, a similarly sized fire swept the North Saskatchewan River valley along the Banff-Jasper highway, at one point trapping a crew of thirty, who escaped with their lives but lost their equipment. A smaller fire started in the Goat Range, possibly by lightning. Although the war stripped Banff of its traditional manpower, the park gained another source with camps for Alternative Service Work (ASW), which immediately began to upgrade its infrastructure for fire protection. More roads, more lookouts, more fireguards, more forest thinning, all strengthened the forces for suppression, while a war-induced decline in tourism lessened ignitions. The 1940 outbreak was the park's last.[23]

The program of fire exclusion continued. Even despite "prevailing shortages" caused by the war, "every possible effort was made to maintain and increase the efficiency of the fire-fighting organization in all phases, including personnel, fire-detection and suppression, transportation, and communication." The Rocky Mountain parks became a site for weather studies by the DFS, they entered into interagency agreements, and Banff devised a written "fire control plan for the Park." The Eastern Rockies Forest Conservation Board reinforced these developments, even as it punched a new road along the border. The Trans-Canada Highway laid a thick ribbon of asphalt alongside the CPR right-of-way. Thinning of infected lodgepole stands and selective logging persisted. A change in the character of tourism meant fewer escaped campfires. Even as occasional large fires struck parks to the west, Banff escaped. The one exception came in 1968, when a fire spilled over from Kootenay Park and threatened Storm Mountain Lodge.[24]

The Vermilion Pass fire was not a happy experience. The park had not had a major fire for twenty-eight years and was unprepared, unskilled, and ill equipped. Compared with the surging Alberta Forest Service, called in to help, Banff, the flagship of Parks Canada, looked amateurish. Perhaps not fortuitously the fiasco coincided with the imperative for other reforms, all of which resulted in a major reorganization in 1969 and, in 1971, a consolidation of fire equipment and expertise to Lake Louise and Banff village along with a twenty-five-person Native trail crew available for large fires. But expectations had also changed. In 1940, a large fire might rage over 4,000 hectares; now a "large" fire was 40 hectares. Banff had become a victim of its own success: fire seemed unimportant and fire protection an archaic art. There were few backcountry fires, for which the park could turn to the Alberta Forest Service for assistance, while the rare threats to settlements at Lake Louise and Banff could be met by local brigades. The park's problems seemed elsewhere, especially as Parks Canada began to reform its general management policies for natural areas.[25]

After the adrenaline washed out, the park reverted to type. The new fire crew worked trails, the lookouts were dismantled, and the level of readiness sank to parity with the sinking presence of fires. In 1976, Banff devoted 600 person hours to training, of which fire protection claimed nine. As one observer wryly noted, "the lack of fires" did not encourage Banff's managers "to continue a high level of readiness." Banff had become a fire sink – a sink for fires, a sink for fire management. Paradoxically it was that very *absence* of fire that epitomized Banff's crisis.[26]

Wood Buffalo followed a very different evolution, more typical for a forest reserve, which was reasonable since for most of its existence it was overseen by government foresters. Since 1908, fire rangers had patrolled the Peace and Slave rivers; a special force, the Buffalo Rangers, was established in 1911, whose core duties were to protect the bison and fight fires. After Inspector of Fire Ranging E.M. Finlayson toured Fort Smith in 1914, the DFB concluded that "the most serious possibility of danger might be a general conflagration in the district, and the patrol of fire rangers, made as effective as the appropriation will permit, is designed to prevent the occurrence of such a catastrophe, as well as to assist otherwise in the protection of the bison herds." The 1919 season hinted at what such a megafire might do. In 1921, Finlayson reorganized the patrol system in the North-West, leaving it with dual administrative outposts at Fort Simpson and Fort Smith.[27]

The creation of the national park in 1922 strengthened those duties, muddled the actual chain of command between three interior bureaus (the newly organized Northwest and Yukon Branch, the DFB, and Dominion Parks), and left Wood Buffalo with overlapping patrols. Eventually those duties settled onto the NYB, and in 1924 responsibility for the Mackenzie fire-ranging district formally relocated from Calgary to Fort Smith. Soon afterward, the district's chief fire ranger decided that far-flung patrols were a "waste of money" and dismantled the organization north of Great Slave Lake. What remained was Wood Buffalo National Park, which officials at Fort Smith treated as another forest reserve, even to the point of leasing timber berths. Unlike Banff, a side rail to the CPR, Wood Buffalo was too remote for mass tourism.[28]

The economies that Fort Smith officials expected to garner by collapsing its patrols were overwhelmed by a string of bad seasons. Campaign fires broke out in 1925, 1927, and 1929, when conflagrations reached a crescendo with some 200,000 acres burned. Observers reported that fires – coming "like hell" – had scorched most of the park's southern end. Inevitably the inexorable logic of fire suppression began to unfold. The best way to stop big fires was to stop small ones, the only way to catch small ones was to detect and attack them early, and the only way to shield the protected sites was to expand the perimeter of control into an ever larger protectorate. Without the park, officials could have dismissed the region's ceaseless conflagrations as a natural scourge, like its black flies and mosquitoes, about which one could do little. The park, however, demanded protection, and there fire control would not come cheap or easy. Unlike Banff, lightning was an ample source of ignition, so fires flared and subsided with the synoptic rhythms of weather, not the comings and goings of people. At Banff, fire protection meant fire prevention, and its effects could be cumulative; at Wood Buffalo, fire protection meant fire suppression and had to be renewed each season.[29]

The fires kept up their boreal beat, and fire officers fought them with the resources at hand and lamented their sparse cache. An influx of trappers and prospectors, and later the massive movement of military personnel associated with the Alaska Highway, kept the Mackenzie District frequently aboil, particularly from 1936 onward. What happened throughout the region was funnelled through Fort Smith. Officials defended their administration by attributing outbreaks to lightning and bad behaviour by inhabitants and by concentrating on the vast park at their elbow. They were undoubtedly correct in noting the disparity between the region's rapid, not to say chaotic, development, which sparked fires everywhere, and the government's reluctance to invest in an infrastructure to protect those lands, most ostentatiously from fire. The one partial exception was the park, which not incidentally, and unlike most of the Northwest Territories, had merchantable timber that it happily logged. (By 1959, three companies were milling 1.5 million board feet yearly.)[30]

Regional reorganizations came and went in the postwar era, along with a rising tide of funds; from 1950 to 1960, federal monies increased by an order of magnitude. Usefully, the early 1950s witnessed several major fire seasons. After the 1950 crisis, Harry Holman, advising the federal government about fire protection needs, announced at Fort Smith that the "fire suppression set-up here will eventually become as efficient as anywhere." The 1953 outbreak then rambled over 261,253 hectares and threatened Fort Smith itself. By the end of the decade, the protection bureau had evolved into the Mackenzie Forest Service (MFS) and emulated its provincial counterparts, including the Alberta Forest Service, with which it had a mutual aid agreement. By now, the park entered a fifteen-year period of relative fire somnolence. The MFS used the Fort Smith facilities as a base for operations elsewhere.[31]

Wood Buffalo more and more resembled a provincial forest, not even listed in annual reports from Parks Canada. Its exceptionalism quickly lost its charm as the early tremors of a more ecologically founded conservation began to shake the national organization. In 1962, J.S. Rowe could declaim on behalf of foresters the "special responsibility" they had as professionals to enlighten the public regarding "wilderness and natural areas," a "phase of land use so closely related to forestry." But most wilderness enthusiasts felt a growing distrust, soon to be visceral, about state-sponsored forestry as a custodian and interpreter of such lands. In 1964, as the US Congress passed a Wilderness Act, Parks Canada adopted new policies about park protection and visitor use and moved to reclaim Wood Buffalo. The administrative transfer was not completed until the 1969 season, when the park was hit by forty-one fires that burned a modest 3,200 hectares.[32]

Yet much survived the transfer. Parks Canada was committed to fire exclusion as an ultimate goal; a firefighting infrastructure, and equally an institutional memory, remained at Fort Smith; rapid detection and initial attack defined the limits of strategic thinking. But with the transfer the park was no longer covered under the fiscal regimen of the MFS, while the 1970 season blew up into the largest since 1953, racking up forty-nine fires, 58,000 hectares, and five dead firefighters. That catastrophe inspired both special funding and a search for a priority system for dispatch. The park needed all that and more, as the 1971 season became a full-immersion baptism by fire, with eighty-three ignitions and 164,000 hectares burned, while army bulldozers, called in for assistance, ploughed a fire line through the whooping crane nesting habitat. A "priority system" came online in the midst of the rolling outbreak, sent to the park by the regional director on 22 June and confirmed by the director on 6 July. A postseason review estimated that it took two weeks "before a regrouping of [already committed] forces was achieved." The review also identified the liabilities: "Fires actioned and extinguished when resources were available could and would be overrun by later fires in periods of limited resources. Decisions to let fires burn opened the strong possibility of continuation in the next year. Moreover, the Zone boundaries were schematic, unrelated to fuel, topography and other factors such as wind and moisture." They might also have mentioned that the prioritizing project was enormously complicated by the presence of extensive logging berths licensed until 2000. They did note, however, that fire duties absorbed all the energies of the park's staff, leaving many "important functions" undone. In brief, a change in park administration did not mean a change in fire behaviour.[33]

Wood Buffalo responded as fire organizations throughout Canada did. It sought to bolster its capacity to fight fire. It quickly recapitulated within itself the organization that the MFS was projecting over the Northwest Territories, becoming a province in miniature, with its Fort Smith headquarters functioning as a provincial fire centre. It hired specialty crews, commenced a doubling of its lookouts, and contracted for helicopters and fixed-wing aircraft. Beginning in 1978, it boasted a small fleet of airtankers "solely for park use." In typical Canadian style, the reforms came just in time to be flattened by a rising wave of mass fire – 66,000 hectares in 1979; 258,000 hectares in 1980; 652,000 hectares in 1981. Not only did the buildup seem ineffectual, but also the anomaly of an enormous nature preserve, a unique home to North American wood bison and whooping cranes, fighting lightning-kindled flame with bombers and bulldozers became more intolerable. Just as that fire quake struck, Parks Canada was adopting a new policy that intended to allow more fire on the preserves under its stewardship.[34]

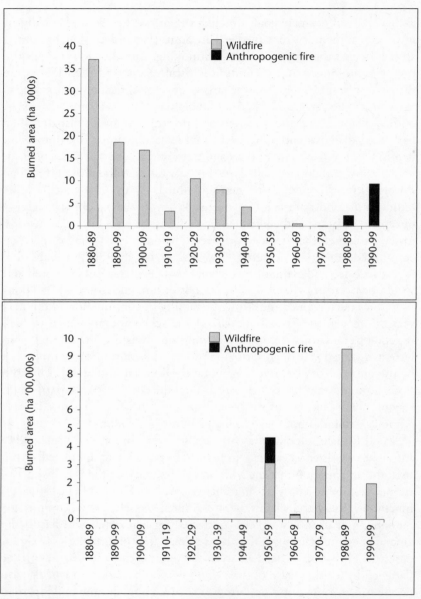

Park polarities, as manifest by amount and type of burning. Banff, *top,* shows a reduction in burning from all sources until a revival in the 1980s that is almost wholly anthropogenic. Wood Buffalo, *bottom,* obeys a more boreal rhythm, sharply etched by a regime change when Parks Canada assumed full control such that anthropogenic fire almost disappears while lightning-kindled flames are allowed to roam, supplemented by aerial backburning.

By the late 1970s, Parks Canada had three models of fire administration, a kind of fire triangle for policy. There was Banff, Wood Buffalo, and a bold American alternative that had emerged during the 1960s. Overall, Banff remained the gold standard, and what happened there happened generally throughout the system. Wardens happily intervened to shut down fire by patrolling, preventing, felling for in-house timber needs and "sanitation," and developing access by road and trail. The big prairie-province parks, Riding Mountain and Prince Albert, occasionally did some burning along their perimeters. But mostly the parks resembled forest reserves, and unsurprisingly they relied on co-operative agreements with local towns and the provincial foresters to provide fire protection if and when fires blew up or threatened facilities. Their own capabilities steadily deteriorated. Their success in reducing burned area they celebrated as the gradual elimination of a problem, like vaccinations against polio, rather than a measure of ecological imbalance.

But Banff was, by one critical criterion, exceptional, for lightning fires were minor, even trivial. That was often not true for the Rocky Mountains west of the divide or the big parks in the boreal belt, of which the newly absorbed Wood Buffalo was exemplary. There fire protection committed administrators to a high-maintenance program of suppression, although practical considerations argued for a priority system for dispatching, which weakened the system just when it most demanded aggressive initial attack. The prospect of outfitting each such park with a stand-alone suppression system was daunting. In practice, it meant co-operative agreements with the beefier fire organizations, typically provincial, within which the park was embedded. Even so, there seemed little evidence that the investment at Wood Buffalo had dented overall burned area.

The third model migrated from the United States. During the 1960s, a popular enthusiasm in America for wilderness, along with advances in ecological science, began to argue in favour of fire's restoration rather than its continued exclusion. The Tall Timbers Fire Ecology Conferences begun in 1962, the Leopold Report of 1963, the Wilderness Act of 1964, new policies encoded into a suite of administrative handbooks issued in 1968, all sought to reinstate fire – free-burning natural fire where possible, controlled burning where necessary. The reformed directives for the Canadian Parks System (CPS) paralleled these developments and often echoed their language, except for fire. While Americans began to burn in sequoia groves, sawgrass, and the understoreys of montane forests, their Canadian counterparts were struggling to keep the Fort Smith airtanker fleet aloft and to wrestle the Vermilion Pass fire into containment. While the example of the National Park Service began to force the US Forest Service into similar reforms, even allowing long-burning, occasionally high-intensity fires to roam in wilderness, Banff was unable to find enough fire-related tasks to keep its twenty-five-person crew busy. Wilderness fire, and by association prescribed burning, dominated the fire conferences of the era, as they did policy. In 1978, in a historic reversal, the US Forest Service finally and fully repudiated its 10 a.m. policy in favour of a strategy of fire pluralism. Even the most hard-bitten Canadian fire officer could not ignore those developments.

Only Parks Canada, however, responded in kind. It began to appreciate that there were systemic problems with its two model fire parks. Banff had too little fire, and Wood Buffalo had too much fire control; neither offered a suitable template for the rest of the system. Moreover, Banff's career as a recreational resort seemed increasingly inappropriate in an age of environmentalism and of ardour for the wild that sought to leave lands "unimpaired" for future generations. In this reconceptualization, the CFS became a silent partner, particularly in the person of Dennis Dubé at the Northern Forestry Centre, who commissioned fire studies for half a dozen prime parks. This support lent intellectual heft to a thinly staffed organization then struggling to imagine its estate as something other than resorts and outdoor zoos and for which fire management demanded genuine and arduous research, not merely annual inspections of building fire extinguishers. The agency commissioned a literature review of fire ecology, published in 1978, and staged, with help from the CFS and with mixed results, a prescribed fire in the deteriorating grasslands of Elk Island National Park. The next year it promulgated a new policy that read much like that for the American parks, expressing a preference for the "natural" but allowing for anthropogenic burning where the ecological evidence argued that human meddling had too thoroughly upset the natural order. Intervention, however, required adequate monitoring before it could be justified.[35]

Like a dislodged boulder, the tumbled policy set off an administrative avalanche. Any thought that the transitional period might proceed with bureaucratic reason and leisure was disabused by the great plague of fires that infected Canada in those years. Among the 1980 outbreaks, the Rolling River fire at Riding Mountain National Park, probably of anthropogenic origin, scorched 20,400 hectares and demonstrated with brutal candour the incapacities of the CFS program nationally. Although the new policy urged a more natural scene (while allowing for interventions to reset the landscape to receive "natural processes"), it also mandated certain research projects and monitoring before acting. As a review politely expressed it,

Riding Mountain remained in transition "until the knowledge, expertise and the resources become available for implementing the full intent of the corporate policy." That meant the park had tried to suppress fire, and it had failed. Its preplanning was appalling; its detection and initial attack capabilities were inferior to common standards; its subsequent efforts were "mainly undirected" and conducted on an "ad hoc day to day basis"; it launched aerial attacks "against clearly insurmountable odds"; three times crews were nearly trapped by the flames. That said, the park's actions were also now out of sync with national policy.[36]

The breakdown was systemic and total on the fireline, at headquarters, and at Ottawa. The expertise did not even exist to staff a competent review, and what was true for Riding Mountain was true for Canada's parks generally. The crisis extended even to Wood Buffalo, which found itself overwhelmed in 1980 and was subject to a board of review, two of whose members had sat on Riding Mountain's board. The crisis affected attempts at controlled burning, which, despite agency enthusiasms and eager assistance from the CFS, faltered because "in almost all cases the CPS could not sustain" the programs. Parks Canada was simply not equipped to manage fire, certainly not a major suppression campaign and, by implication, not the prescribed or natural fires its new policy urged upon it. In effect, Parks Canada had two policies – one promoting fire's exclusion, one promoting its necessary presence. As the board of review for the Rolling River fire concluded, while this arrangement might be "philosophically acceptable and desirable," the reality was that a park had to "implement one or the other."[37]

There was, then, an urgent need for upgrading on-the-ground fire organization, for completing a conceptual transition in policy, and for educating the Warden Service about what was happening and why. The rebuilding of a trained cadre of fire-dedicated staff centred on Banff. Slowly but shrewdly administrators recognized that they could not generate the necessary national expertise within the context of a single park, or else the experience at Banff after the 1968 season would repeat itself and a sudden buildup would lead to a rapid decline. The parks had to nurture a cadre of fire professionals, and that cadre had to service the entire network, and while housed at Banff it had also to cope with the recurring conflagrations at Wood Buffalo. With unexpected synergy, the two tasks found a common ground in the commitment, one born of necessity as much as conviction, that what the two scenes shared was a demand for deliberate burning. At Wood Buffalo, only wholesale backfiring, typically aerial, could counter the wild flames without scarifying the preserve, while at Banff the urgent requirement was a program of fire restoration. In that novitiate corps, the two experiences bonded. In 1983, they conducted their first prescribed burn in Banff. Over the next two decades, the Banff brood left its aerie to colonize the entire parks system.[38]

The 1980 season went further by forcing open fissures in CPS policy and the philosophy behind it. Even a transitional system, like a temporary bridge, had to carry all traffic that needed to cross it, and for all its bold declarations the 1979 policy did not allow that. It left the parks with fire suppression as the only practical response, even as it undercut the conviction that fire control was the right choice. That confusion needed correction, quickly. As the Wood Buffalo review noted, the organic act for the parks did not address fire directly and hence failed to furnish "a legal authority for the development of Regional and Park Fire Management Programs." If new plans required research into fire history and ecology, then that research needed to happen rapidly. If policy directives did not mention fire specifically, then administrators needed to revise them accordingly.[39]

Behind this confusion, however, lay another, the conundrum of "naturalness." The 1979 policy consolidated thinking that had developed primarily in the United States and hence encoded cultural concepts about wilderness and pristine nature. Yet discriminating between fires originating from people and those from lightning compromised both planning and field operations. The solution came by redefining the goal as one of ecosystem-wide management grounded in vegetation and by dismissing differences in the source of ignition. What cracked this code was a commissioned paper authored by C.E. Van Wagner and I.R. Methven on "Fire in the Management of Canada's National Parks: Philosophy and Strategy," published in January 1980 and destined to become one of the foundational documents for Parks Canada and contemporary Canadian fire management.

At its core were two axioms: first, that much of what the parks protected was a fire-dependent biota; second, that fire management "implies nothing short of complete vegetation management." There was a perfect circularity between fire and land. Fire management meant vegetation management, and vegetation management meant fire management, because "of all possible techniques and tools" fire is the "only one that is compatible with national park policy." Excluding fire, even if that were possible, would produce disastrous results. Yet a "totally natural fire regime" was "neither possible nor desirable; some "planned fire regime" would have to substitute, and Van Wagner and Methven reasoned that "certainly the amount of fire required for managing park vegetation under pseudo-natural fire regimes would be many times what the national parks are presently used to."[40]

At a stroke, concerns over "naturalness" or the transcendence of nature, so vital to the imagination of the wilderness ethos, vanished. What mattered was the "vegetation" or, in the language of Parks Canada directives, the "ecological integrity" of the land. One could achieve that goal by either axe or torch. Behind this prescription lay the forestry training of its authors. Here was an ecological equivalent to silviculture, with fire cycles substituting for a rotation cycle and prescribed burning for planting, pruning, and harvesting. The authors dismissed the question of fire origins as irrelevant – as metaphysical, in a logical-positivist sense – in favour of fire outcomes as recorded by the vegetation. The Canadian genius for applied knowledge could now apply itself to the protection of nature as it had previously done for the protection of timber. Adherence to the announced doctrine instantly dispelled philosophical mists and liberated a program of targeted scientific research and calculated intervention. The paper became the cornerstone for the revised directives, of which the 1986 version became seminal.

Still, it would take time, effort, and institution building to translate these ideas and experiences into the field. Later that year a series of high-level workshops commenced to prepare the agency for a reformation beyond what anyone probably believed possible. The fire history inquiries, the core science, the creation of a corps of fire specialists, the alliances with the CFS, select universities, the hard-won experience – all this was yet to come, and another decade would pass before Parks Canada could claim a working program to match its vision. But unlike the CFS, it had lands to manage, and unlike the provinces it had a national constituency and the national treasury that could allow it the space to stand back from the iron logic of fire's suppression and ponder the metalogic of fire's restoration. Nature's economy could, within limits, determine fire's economy. Other Canadian fire reforms obeyed the imperative to make more efficient the existing institutions and practices. Parks Canada could imagine an alternative future.

Under Review

At a Forest Fire Control Conference held at Petawawa in 1962, J.C. Macleod sketched the question posed directly or indirectly to his organization: "When are you going to find a way to stop those *big* fires?" Breakthroughs, Macleod reminded his audience, didn't happen that way. His department wasn't expecting any. "Instead," he summarized, "the staff is working on a program of studies aimed at finding answers to recognizable problems that show a reasonable chance of being solved." Fire research was decentralizing in theme as well as geography; the cluster housed in Ottawa was dispersing to the provinces. Research was assembling a glossary of fire control terms, evaluating power pumps and hoses, studying radio communication, testing techniques for burning out, measuring slash flammability. A year after reorganization into a Department of Forestry, the ambitions of the past for a truly national program of fire protection organized under the auspices of the federal government had long dimmed.[41]

A decade had passed since the last major reorganization. Then the Forestry Service had denounced fire as "the chief natural enemy of the forests of Canada," consuming 50 percent of the expenditures by provincial forestry departments, and had promoted research as a means to improve protection. A revision of the Wright tables was under way, along with a new laboratory at Petawawa. But it was the decade that followed Macleod's modest pronouncements that promised something more. In 1965, the boom was on; by 1968, a "bleeding" Cam Macleod was writing its obituary. The department staffing favoured entomology over fire, and the brutal reductions under way slashed overall positions by 6-7 percent but those in fire by 25-30 percent. Appeals from the NRC to boost fire research went nowhere. In July 1968, Macleod drafted an in-house review.[42]

He totted up the ways in which fire research differed from other programs, explaining its various disadvantages. Identifying "national" fire problems was like creating an "average man"; the regional differences mattered more than the commonalities, however opaque and illegible those realities seemed to home-office bureaucrats. In particular, Macleod spoke about the "long-range, often frustrating task of training staff to be fire scientists." Salaries were too low to attract qualified researchers from outside Canada; the solution was to send promising Canadians to the United States and then initiate them into the department. This approach took time, reflected in what might appear as reduced productivity. Paradoxically, the CFFDRS, perhaps the outstanding achievement in federal fire research, was advancing briskly. All of these arguments were reasonable but irrelevant. Forestry was not a priority for the national government, nor research within the confederation of provincial fire agencies, nor fire within the reorganized Department of Forestry and Rural Development; the core facts had been decided in 1930. So, even as the Fire Danger Group in particular poured out world-class science, the larger program was being flushed.[43]

In 1975, A.D. Kiil, having completed a two-year tour as a "special advisor" on program co-ordination and evaluation, summarized the status of Canadian fire research. Apart from the CFS, fire science bubbled up at the NRC, the Arctic Land Use Research Program, and several universities, particularly the Fire Science Centre at the University of New Brunswick. The strengths of the CFS program were its nimbleness – its capacity to respond to "client agencies" with directed research, the close contacts enjoyed with the fire community, its ability to serve as a consultancy. Yet it remained modest in size, with some twenty-five researchers and forty support staff throughout the country. Probably in the coming years it would move into more operations research; probably, though, the near future would look like the near past. Two years later Kiil updated his survey, ending with the more downbeat observation that the CFS had been "unable to respond meaningfully to requests from provincial and federal fire management for increased emphasis on fire research." Canada invested in fire research less than 2 percent of what it spent annually on fire protection. That year Charlie Van Wagner published his seminal study on crown fires. A year later further fiscal economizing forced the Ottawa-based institutes into a merger with the Petawawa facility.[44]

The position paper on fire research had become an art form, a genre in itself, elegant, perceptive, and politically negligible. It could describe, it could not move. Its artistry tended to be indirectly proportional to the urgency of the matter at hand, for institutions in times of turmoil, whether in reform or collapse, lack the leisure to craft careful syntheses. They scramble to catch up with the rush of events. Something else – an exogenous force, as the economists might phrase it – has to move the apparatus. The old engines of fire politics, timber and wildfire, did that. By 1981, the CCREM proclaimed its alarm over a flaccid timber supply as three years of explosive burning razed the national woodpile. While the council endorsed a 40 percent escalation in wood harvest by 2000, that timber supply could exist only if protected, and increasingly protection demanded research. On this cause, the major professional and political organizations could rally.[45]

The Canadian Committee's Subcommittee on Fire Research was unusually blunt. The national effort was "totally inadequate." Even within the CFS, fire science had shrunk by 60 percent since 1968, while reorganizations intended to link researchers with provincial clients had only diluted a lethally underfunded program to the point that it was "puny" relative to the task at hand. There were, in brief, "problems with respect to funding, structure and focus." What the subcommittee urged was a research equivalent to CIFFC, housed within the CFS, with interagency "coordination and focus" provided through the Canadian Committee on Forest Fire Management. The CFS called upon Van Wagner to survey the history and status of its fire research program, while J.F. Goodman spoke for Ontario (and by implication for other provinces) and the subcommittee continued its deliberations. By 1986, the subcommittee had isolated four priorities, each of which dealt with a traditional strength of the CFS in fire danger forecasting, fire behaviour prediction, and fireline operations and urged that this agenda become the foundation for a reinvigorated fire research establishment.[46]

The facts remained, however, that science mattered more to researchers than to practitioners and that the provinces were sceptical of surrendering any control over their natural estate, however inferentially. The CFS made some internal adjustments; the prospects for a national system withered. One reason was the very presence of CIFFC, which caused a slow metamorphosis in the dynamics of Canadian fire politics. Instead of the Canadian Committee's Subcommittee on Forest Fire Research being absorbed into the CFS, the entire Canadian Committee became ultimately absorbed by CIFFC. The lesson was that power resided in the field. The CFFDRS succeeded as a conceptual construct because of the calibre of its intellectual brilliance, and it succeeded as a political construct because it compelled the fire agencies, notably the provinces, to do nothing. It gave them something they wanted without extracting any costs. By comparison, the CFS's meticulous studies of airtankers remained grounded because they had no power to move the critical political levers. They were advisory. And that, increasingly, inevitably, became the fate of the CFS. It advised Ottawa and where possible continued to inhabit a niche that by patient trial and error it had learned it could occupy without threatening rivals, which meant without exercising significant power.

As the aftershocks from the 1979-81 seasons faded, Canadian fire protection (or fire management as it had come to call itself, prematurely) jostled into new arrangements. In truth, it had undergone a quiet chrysalis. There were national models that had not existed before, each proposing a way to pack more punch into the vital tasks before fire management. A CIFFC model boosted fire suppression, leveraging the clout of each province by allying it with the others. A Parks Canada model, still embryonic, proposed a complementary program of fire reintroduction, able to float the discussion to a national level above the political muskeg of provincial self-interests. A CFS model urged a strengthened commitment to research, again seeking to leverage what the individual institutions could not do themselves and even forging mutual projects with colleagues from other countries.

Yet the question posed to Macleod in 1962 persisted. A frontier of exurban settlement was sparking fires as agricultural settlement had a century before; nature preserves, with their imperative for intense burns, were challenging timber berths in the environmental calculus of an urban citizenry; and wildfires were savaging deep bush and urban fringe both. The big fires continued.

Fire's Outer Limits: Fire Provinces on the Fringe

The provinces on the fringe are fire's outer limits, but for political, not pyrological, reasons. Here, as throughout Canada, fire shapes the landscape, fire forces a response, fire becomes a charge of government. The lands have fire aplenty. Wildfires washing over the battered hills of the Yukon have done biologically what hydraulicking did geologically in previous times. The boreal belt of the Northwest Territories erupts in flame like a geyser basin, and fires in the barren lands have sparked controversy by warping the migration and size of caribou herds. The contrast between interior woods and offshore gas defines the emerging economy of Newfoundland. The politics of Native claims for the one and provincial claims for the other – these drove the process of Confederation to its final frontiers. Inevitably fire entered into those negotiations. Fire protection had to find a justification not grounded in timber, an institution not overseen by foresters, and an expression not grossly at odds with the rest of the country. In pushing to its fire fringe, Canada completed the chronicle of Confederation and, in the case of Newfoundland, retold its fire saga in miniature. All in all, a fire cycle as profound as any scorching its woods.

Northwest Territories

There has always been plenty of fire in the Northwest Territories: free-burning fires were as much a seasonal phenomenon as spring breakup. Robert Bell had penned his paean to inextinguishable boreal flame from the banks of the Mackenzie. Surveyors fretted under palls of summer smoke. The situation only got worse as steamers began to ply the Athabasca, Slave, and Peace rivers in the 1880s. They belched cinders as fully as locomotives, and any quickening of human traffic soon translated not only into shoreline fires but also a bush dappled with the abandoned camp and smudge fires of transients interested only in ore or fur, and particularly to those searching for minerals a forest-stripping burn was more asset than liability. Surveying around Fort Smith, Charles Camsell found himself endlessly in "an area of burnt rolling country." Elihu Stewart himself toured the region in 1906, impressed equally by its riverine spruce and its bottomless burns. Canada's last frontiers might repeat the shambles wrought by axe and fire in its earlier frontiers. But what exactly to do and who should do it were more troubling. If its fires were among the vastest on the continent, its politics were among the fiercest within the Confederation.[1]

It was not the northwest's forests, however, that inspired the earliest efforts at conservation; they were too remote. The inspiration was its wildlife. Its animals could be converted to fur, meat, and trophies in ways its trees could not be hewn into timber, but expansive burns were a fast-spreading blot, peeling away prime habitat like an acid. In 1894, the government responded with the Unorganized Territories' Game Preservation Act, aimed at protecting the charismatic wood bison and muskox but without much practical policing power to enforce its provisions. The 1906 Northwest Game Act was little better. The fact was that, lying beyond the limits of forestry, the Northwest Territories lay beyond the limits of organized forest fire protection. The region's fauna, not its forests, would structure the institutions for managing its fires. Bison, not white pine, and lichens, not spruce pulp, would sculpt fire's politics. The loss of wildlife, not the loss of woods (overhunting and lack of habitat, not overcutting and lack of regeneration), formed the debate. Significantly the first of the Northwest Territories' reserves was for game, not forest, and to protect the game "for the inhabitants of that country." Instead of settlers demanding unbridled rights to burn slash, First Nations insisted on the free exercise of their claimed rights to traditional hunting and trapping and ignored efforts to restrain their burning.[2]

Thus evolved a peculiar three-body problem between foresters, wildlife and park officials, and indigenes for control over fire. With the 1911 Dominion Forest Reserves and Parks Act, the Dominion Forestry Branch assumed responsibility for wildlife (including the wood bison herd acquired in 1906) with the argument that it was the proper repository for the administration of all forest-related resources. The Parks Branch thought differently, insisting that it could more suitably oversee the animals, and in 1917 it acquired that responsibility. Over the next thirty years, some seven game reserves came into existence. Thus foresters, who dominated the theory and practice of fire protection, did not control the primary resource and would not use fire protection as a means to extend their dominion.

In truth, survey after survey reached the same conclusion, that there were patches of merchantable timber, and perhaps someday a local market, if by that someday the fires, thick as black flies and vast as the midnight sun, had not stripped the land bare. If the economic argument was tepid, there remained an appeal to fire protection as an administrative duty and as something that civilized countries did as an expression of conservation. Fire rangers were the emissaries of the metropole, and other than the overextended Mounties they were often the only government presence.[3]

In 1911, the Dominion Forestry Branch pushed its patrols north of sixty degrees latitude. Like other travellers, it followed the rivers, paddling the Great Slave in the region ceded under Treaty Number Eight. Inspector H.A. Conroy mused over the character of his staff, for it was "no small difficulty to select suitable men to act as fire-rangers," since the requirements were many and the pool of local candidates few. The fire ranger required the same skills as the fur trader. Yet it was, in some respects, a mock heroic era. A scant five rangers patrolled the Northwest Territories. River patrols – there were no other options – were arduous, laughably overextended, and almost wholly ineffective aside from dousing abandoned campfires along the routes and inspiring (or shaming) some degree of fire carefulness among the resident population. Mostly rangers posted notices in a polyglot of languages and handed them to the RCMP and Hudson's Bay Company men for further distribution. They showed the flag. Steamers improved the velocity of their tours – when they worked. Over one summer, the SS *Rey* plied fifteen trips and 5,000 miles "without accident." Unfortunately no detailed log was kept since the engineer, McClennan, "while capable in other ways," could "barely write his name." The SS *Hope,* chugging along Great Slave Lake, suffered so many breakdowns it scarcely made port, while the inspector allowed the ranger's wife to accompany him, "otherwise there would probably have been no log kept." The boats themselves worsened the fire scene because they lacked proper spark arrestors and left ranger John Connor convinced that the fire patrol boats were themselves "responsible for a lot of fires."[4]

In 1912, E.H. Finlayson, as inspector for fire ranging, reorganized the patrol system outside the western reserves into eight districts. The Great Slave District, however, lagged, overseen by an employee of the Indian department. This made sense since the majority of fires, along well-trafficked routes, were attributed to travellers and "wandering Indians." The foresters thus proselytized among the indigenes, spreading a gospel of fire prevention, missionizing with posters and medals for good behaviour. While officially reporting admirable results, ranger Henry Jones lamented that most of the Natives were "very careless, and speaking to them about this does no good, they say they can do as they like about fires, and I cannot get them punished."[5]

The 1914 season gave the fledgling organization its first real test, which it fumbled. Finlayson, while not surprised, was dismayed. "It is impossible," he observed, stating the obvious, "to arrange for organization in a fire-ranging district on the same basis which applies to reserves." The indefatigable Finlayson pressed on; that fall he toured the region. Meanwhile, in addition to their normal duties, the rangers were also responsible for two prized bovids, the bison that had been reintroduced in 1906 and a herd of obstreperous reindeer brought down from Alaska. Already its game more than its fires were the object of administrative interest, for there was some hope of promoting the game and little of preventing the burns. A fire ranger along the Mackenzie River, T.W. Harris, observed that, "when a fire has got well under way, it appears to me a waste of money to try and control it as can be done in civilization."[6]

That was not the official position. The official line was that this frontier, like others to the south, would evolve along traditional patterns, for which fire protection would inevitably intensify. For the present, it was necessary, "in order to avoid serious conflagrations," to patrol the entire region extensively. As forest reserves arose, Finlayson predicted, fire protection would adjust to make them "just as fire-proof as possible." The preferred means, it seems, were inspection and reorganization. The region thus commenced its career as a serial reorganizer, chronically readjusting rather than evolving, because it didn't mature economically or politically as the others had, because there were never sufficient funds or staff to install serious fire protection, and because the justification for forestry-based fire control was unsettled. Fire protection had no stable matrix within which to evolve: no consistent bureaucracy, no long-serving chief, no immutable goals, only a ceaseless colonial churn. In 1917, the Dominion Parks Branch claimed responsibility for wildlife, and with a revised Northwest Game Act an Advisory Board for Wildlife Protection assumed oversight. That left the Forestry Branch with little more than fire control but a fire organization that was dissociated from the primary economic (and political) concerns of the Northwest Territories. It had authorization only to protect "*the timber resources of the country.*" Fire patrols remained under the direction of the government agent at Fort Smith, while blistering fire seasons in the Rockies drained DFB resources away from the outer territories.[7]

More reorganizations. In 1921, Finlayson shifted responsibility for fire ranging around the Slave River and Great Slave Lake to rangers in northern Alberta, leaving the Mackenzie River valley under control of the agent at Fort Simpson, apparently agreeing with the Fort McMurray-based ranger that they could not depend on patrols "by the Buffalo Rangers." The next year the Department of the Interior revamped all its regional operations by placing them under a new bureaucracy, the Northwest Territories and Yukon Branch. It also established Wood Buffalo Park, which absorbed the bulk of the lands most actively patrolled. All this confused rather than clarified which agency actually had responsibility for fire ranging – or, more precisely, which had to pay for it. Patrols overlapped, firefights were compromised, invoices shunted from one office to another. Parks, Forestry, the new Northwest Territories and Yukon Branch, all could claim jurisdiction. Officials worried less about ineffective fire control, however, than about duplicate patrols and hence duplicate costs. The template devised elsewhere simply didn't fit. The patrol system remained awkward in execution and ambiguous in goals, in practice little more than a glorified circuit riding. The chief fire ranger for the Mackenzie District, John A. McDougal, scorned the far-flung operation as "a waste of money." Either rangers could not get to fires in time to douse them while they were small, or, if large, they could not rally sufficient forces to fight them.[8]

The future of the DFB lay elsewhere. So, in 1924, E.H. Finlayson arranged to transfer responsibility outright to the Northwest Territories and Yukon Branch. In principle, game wardens would take over patrols, particularly around the Slave River; in practice, McDougal quickly dismantled the entire apparatus. The Dominion Forestry Branch disappeared from the scene, while the Dominion Parks Branch found itself with fire duties for which it was ill prepared. Big fires walloped its fiefdom in 1925, 1927, and 1929. For almost fifty years, Wood Buffalo was, with minor exceptions, the fire program of Canada's national parks; no other site commanded anything like its involvement, a commitment that grew out of its inheritance from the DFB. To the extent that fire codes applied, the RCMP sought to enforce them. Otherwise, fire ranging in the Northwest Territories withered away, ending not with a flash but with a smudge.[9]

Not until national interest revived during the Second World War did fire protection return. Mineral development, road construction, corridors for aircraft, troop movement, all caused fires and this time seemed to imperil national security and could not be ignored. Extensive burns stalled construction projects, gigantic smoke palls shut down air traffic. If only as a wartime emergency, something had to be done. In 1943, the dominion turned to its rump of a Forest Service for advice, and the DFS handed the problem to H.L. Holman, who eyed the fires as only a forester could. He commenced surveys, appreciated the urgency of the problem, and promptly dismissed schemes for blanket coverage. His assessment agreed with those of other experts, that as much as half the Mackenzie District had burned during the war years. But fire protection for its own sake or as a cultural endeavour like opera did not impress Ottawa administrators or propose an institutional medium.[10]

That came with postwar reorganizations. The dominion's Department of Mines and Resources spawned a Forest and Wildlife Division, chartered to protect the Northwest Territories' renewable resources, its woods as well as its wildlife. The new division accepted a "substantial appropriation" to organize a protection service more adequate to the "serious conflagrations" that had begun to infest the Mackenzie District, although its charge ranged over the Northwest Territories generally and even included patrol for Wood Buffalo. A former BC forester, E.G. Oldham, headed the project. Early in 1946, he toured the region by airplane, conferred with everyone from government officers to trappers, and placed orders for equipment, including pumps, new boats, and charter aircraft such that the new organization could begin at the same technological level as the older provincial services. Oldham transferred from forestry to game the ancient, unanswerable argument for aggressive fire control, that unless fires no longer swept the country, there would be "little to conserve or manage." State-sponsored fire protection had returned.[11]

As officials planned for systematic development of the north, the Forest Protection Service assumed a role akin to that of the Mounties during the Yukon gold rush, assuring that the scramble would not succumb to an environmental vigilantism. Even fire science was brought to bear. J.G. Wright, now an official in the eastern Northwest Territories, solicited advice from his old colleague Herb Beall, thus conscripting to the cause the two doyens of Canadian fire research. Quickly the institution ordered more equipment; trained RCMP officers and seasonal wardens; laid out a chain of river and road patrols, complete with resident cabins; enacted co-operative arrangements with the military; experimented with radio; established a major supply depot at Fort Smith; and fought fires. In its inaugural year, almost a million and a half acres burned.[12]

Reorganizations rolled on, as frequent as big snows and hard droughts. In 1950, the Department of Mines and Resources became the Department of Resources and Development, with a special Northern Administration and Lands Branch. The territorial council enacted a special fire ordinance in 1951. In 1953, the branch metamorphosed into a full-blown Department of Northern Affairs and Natural Resources. Money began to pour into the Northwest Territories, not a little siphoning into forest protection, followed, it seemed, by conflagrations. Immense fires broke out in 1950. In 1952, a single 113,024-acre burn, the Point Ennuyeuse fire, blew away several seasons of improving fire statistics. Still, Holman declared that fire suppression would "eventually become as efficient as anywhere."[13]

Efficiency, however, required clarity of purpose. A professional forester, Holman never doubted that the goal was the protection of merchantable timber and fretted when the young organization, awash with fresh gear and vehicles, attacked fires away from the harvestable stands along the Slave, Mackenzie, and Liard Rivers. He gave no consideration to wildlife, dismissing, for example, a request for fire control around Lac La Martre, a 50,000-square-mile sweep of barren land habitat favoured by caribou. The organization that emerged in the Northwest Territories was an adaptation of fire control as practised throughout Canada, modified to accommodate the region's vast distances and limited timber values. Holman repeatedly cautioned against trying too much, by which he meant not sinking suppression efforts into the bottomless muskegs of fires in "wastelands" abundant only in caribou, foxes, and muskrats. But Chief Fire Warden R.T. Flanagan knew well the limitations of his operation. Once, flying down the Mackenzie River with his Ottawa boss on tour, they spotted a "goddam big smoke" to the west. His boss asked, "What're you gonna do with that fire?" Flanagan replied, "I'm gonna take a picture of it." That, he insisted, was "all we could do."[14]

The exception was Wood Buffalo, the traditional centre for fire operations, but the reason was less its bison than the three logging companies that held leases within it. Strategists such as Holman treated the park as, in effect, a forest reserve, overseen by the ever-morphing Department of Northern Affairs and National Resources. Year by year, its suppression capabilities improved with lookout towers and patrol cabins, suppression crews and equipment caches at Fort Smith and Yellowknife, airplanes and a helicopter under contract. To promote a keener sense of fire prevention, the service broadcast two films throughout the Northwest Territories, *Timagami Ranger* and *Forest Commandos,* and even enlisted the tuberculosis survey to show them "at outlying settlements." And year by year, while the organization strengthened, big fires continued to ramble. In 1953, more than two million acres burned, and a monster fire, bursting out of Wood Buffalo, threatened Fort Smith and was only contained with help from the Alberta Forest Service. Two years later another giant fire repeated the experience. This one led to negotiations with Alberta that culminated in a formal mutual aid agreement in 1956.[15]

All this moved the Northwest Territories along a familiar narrative of expanded service and increased efficiency. In 1959, the forest protection operation became, formally, the Mackenzie Forest Service (MFS), with responsibility for both the Northwest and Yukon Territories as well as Wood Buffalo. A comprehensive fire plan soon followed, grounded in larger visions of state-sponsored development. Protection commenced by strengthening existing arrangements to control fire around towns, major thoroughfares, and the Wood Buffalo timber berths. The logic was familiar. Adequate fire protection would boost development, development would improve protection, and the soaring economy that resulted would painlessly cover the costs. It was a common chimera. A critic might point out that there had been an expansion of means, fire control, to promote an end, forestry, that didn't really exist and wasn't wanted by the indigenous population.[16]

And that was the crux. What seemed reasonable to Ottawa bureaucrats and émigré foresters could seem otherwise to the Northwest Territories' indigenes. They lived not by devising technocratic plans or harvesting timber but by pursuing the traditional economies of fishing, hunting, and trapping. The fires that mattered to them were not those that sent potential board feet up in smoke but those that gutted grazing lands and ruined traplines. The industrial "development" of the north had brought more fires but not improved fire control, save where the flames threatened forests or towns. By official reckoning, timber-based fire protection could pay for the service, at least at some future time, while a subsistence economy could not. Local leaders considered the fire campaign not only misdirected but also ineffective even on its own terms. Instead of resolving these differences, administrators reorganized. Departmental sections changed names seemingly as often as their chiefs did clothes. The critical tension remained, like the electrical charge between the Earth and its atmosphere, and from time to time it discharged.[17]

Not yet a crisis, yet without an easy compromise – the administrative response was to develop two parallel tracks in the hope that they might someday meet. One was that erstwhile bureaucratic reply to awkward criticism: sponsor research. Such studies had begun in 1952 with a query into caribou habitat and burns in the barren lands. The Canadian Wildlife Service added its own appeal, targeting the winter range for special consideration. The Canadian Conservation Association passed a resolution in 1953 promoting fire protection in the tundra, an attempt to shield some pristine landscapes from reckless use. A decade later several scientific agencies, including the NWT Wildlife Service, commenced studies on the ecology of fire and fur-bearing and meat-bearing wildlife, particularly caribou, and a decade after that national enthusiasms for pipelines spawned regional-scale surveys. Inevitably, however, the results were inconclusive. In the far north, science could answer scientific questions (maybe, granted more funds) but stood dumb before political questions. Worse, ecologists might introduce another set of values that, while challenging forestry, would only replace it in the triangular whirl of provincial politics. The second track was to adopt, as a working policy, the strategy of fighting non-timber fires where and when possible, assuming that such endeavours did not crimp the agency's truly important assignments, for the foresters in charge of the fire service were deeply wary of foreign adventures of dubious merit that would divert limited resources away from towns and timber. While the chief of the MFS, Rory Flanagan, recognized that the "frontier" of fire protection needed to go beyond forest inventories, for example, he balked at the costs, as he no doubt knew his political minders in Ottawa would. The finesse was symbolic, a political gesture, not a guide to practical administration. The studies could not satisfy Native demands for better protection of habitat (i.e., an improved harvest of fur and meat); nor, granted that big fires, and big-fire seasons, accounted for almost all the burned area, could fire agencies control with any pretence of precision how much might burn any year. Big fires blasted away in 1961, 1964, and 1966.[18]

With no resolution, both tracks continued. The research conducted by the Canadian Wildlife Service proved inconclusive. Intuitively, burned area, game habitat, and herd size had to be linked, but very little could be stated with much confidence. A general sense had grown that, since the 1920s, an influx of outsiders – white "bushmen" in the guise of trappers, prospectors, and sport hunters – had created a scorched earth that had effectively contracted the range accessible to caribou. Historical estimates of herd size suggested a significant reduction over the previous decades; reconnaissances for minerals and timber reported immense swaths of burned land; First Nations trappers and hunters complained about dwindling game populations. (And to the shrinking caribou were added other concerns about apparent diminution of prime fur bearers.) Yet all this was typical of northern phenomena in which large swings were normal and nineteenth-century estimates unreliable. Still, it seemed plausible that fire protection could promote game as it could timber, which inspired a five-year exercise in fire control, from 1965 to 1972, on the winter range of the Beverly herd around Porter and Sandy Lakes. Expenses were high, outcomes were marginal, and ecological arguments arose that leaving it all to "nature" would be best. These were not conclusions that the indigenous hunters wanted to hear. They had been an active agent in this putative wilderness for millennia and were prepared to shape it to their own ends. They demanded the same attention for caribou, marten, and fox that the government had traditionally extended to loggers, who were no more inclined to let "natural" fire harvest their berths.[19]

While the science stuttered, the institutional build-out continued apace, with the ontogeny of the MFS recapitulating the phylogeny of Canadian fire services. It erected more towers, linked them with modern communications, trained Indian firefighting crews, arranged with the CFS to establish a fire danger index for Fort Smith, and accepted, on the model of the southern provinces, that initial attack was the unalterable core of fire protection. On the 1961 fire ("one of the worst ... on record"), the MFS called in waterbombers, with good effect. The next year the Forest Service proudly announced that, while fire protection necessarily remained the core of its administration, it was expanding into a full-service forest management agency, not unlike those in other provinces.

But the Northwest Territories was not like the others, and it lacked one of the most striking traits of provincial agencies: a steady administration by a long-reigning chief. Instead, decisions depended on a shape-shifting bureaucracy to which it was bound, worsened by a relentless churn of personnel, particularly senior administrators. A 1961 metamorphosis changed it into the Department of Indian Affairs and Northern Development (DIAND). In 1964, administrative responsibility for Wood Buffalo National Park transferred to Parks Canada, although a final handover of fire management occurred only in 1968, a delay during which the 1964 fires ripped through the park. This kind of divestment appealed to the federal bureaucracy and made even more inscrutable the Caribou Range experiment in fire protection, about which officials began to mutter openly that the money went to sites "of little or no value." More fundamental was a slow devolution of power from Ottawa to the Northwest Territories. On the recommendations of the Carrothers Commission, offices relocated from Ottawa to Yellowknife in 1967, along with some responsibilities and a sudden population influx that created small Brasilias in Canada's Amazonia.[20]

Importantly, DIAND retained control over natural resources, whose offices it left in Fort Smith. The fire program still answered to Ottawa, although now to the Treasury Board rather than to the mandarins of development. This left operations unscathed. The agency continued to do what it had always done. But the change of overseers also left it isolated from the political ferment that was bubbling in the Northwest Territories, to which, ultimately, it had to answer. Specifically the locals wanted control over fire's administration – wanted its funds, wanted its capacity to hire local crews and contractors, wanted its efforts directed toward the fast-declining economies of hunting and trapping that were, nonetheless, integral to the ethnic identities of First Nations and subject to their political ambitions. The Treasury Board worried less about uncontrolled fires in barren grounds than about their uncontrolled costs. Increasingly fire, economics, identity politics, devolution, and climate became linked in a tightening choreography that resembled the atonal rhythms and wild swings that bonded snowshoe hares with lynxes.

It became difficult to hold them together. The 1967 restructuring yielded a formal fire policy, the first made explicitly for the Northwest Territories. Basically it refined the widespread practice of demarking which zones to protect and which not to protect. In this case, the agency, or its Ottawa minders, tried to rank landscapes by their values, both the potential revenues they might yield to the Treasury Board and the likely costs they would impose. Not everything could be protected; not everything warranted protection; and, since the dominion was paying, it would decide which lands were worth protecting at what price. Life and property ranked highest, followed by those "natural resources" useful to an industrial society, namely those traditionally assessed by foresters, who not coincidentally oversaw the fire program. The year previous, in fact, Ottawa had instructed the Mackenzie Forest Service to classify the lands under its jurisdiction by their cash values; these assessments now served to determine the level of service. Free-burning fire, however, is not a bureaucratic category. In 1971, fires blasted some 2.5 million acres and caused this hastily improvised political shack to tumble, collapsing like the burned roof of a bear's den.[21]

There had been big fires before and a few scares. A 1968 fire had even threatened Inuvik with an imminent evacuation. From the beginning, all of the provinces had devised internal lines of control, beyond which they did not attempt all-out suppression or even patrol; the Northwest Territories pushed fire protection past that line of control for Canada overall. Beyond corridors of travel, villages, and Wood Buffalo, fire control was tenuous, only possible by aircraft and the exorbitant expenses that kept that air force aloft. The 1971 outbreak pushed the fire organization past its limits. Some 322 fires scorched some 2.5 million acres, killed six firefighters, crashed a helicopter and two Canso waterbombers, nearly destroyed the Village of Pine Point, and isolated Yellowknife, severing its sole highway and electrical power. Costs went to a ballistic $5 million. The experience was, in the words of Stephen Janzen, a "complete disaster."[22]

Everyone was astonished and furious. Fire officers struggled to explain how an apparently model organization, although young, could be so badly blindsided. Treasury officials blanched at the expense and sent analysts for a de facto audit. Ecologists converged, fascinated not simply by the fire ecology of caribou habitat but also by flame's pervasive presence in an environment they considered fire driven. And local residents, organized into hunter and trapper councils, harassed the colonial authorities, unhappy not merely that fires had burned so much but also that they had burned areas Ottawa had not deemed significant and hence hadn't tried to protect at all. The whole political porridge soon came to a boil.[23]

The official response, unsurprisingly, was to sponsor research, issue reports, and ... reorganize. Fire science kneaded easily into the broadcast surveys that more aggressive northern development, including prospective pipelines, was funding. Science, however, is long, while the art of politics is short. Policy reform could not wait for publication, which would not begin seriously until mid-decade, so, while research called for more research, administrators reorganized the MFS into the Northwest Lands and Forest Service, added a staff policy expert, trained personnel at Alberta's Forest Training School, hired more Native fire crews, and promulgated a revised policy that did not lash protection solely to timber. Its gist was to identify four "priority" zones. Zones 1 and 2 embraced the obvious: towns first, then villages and critical components of the north's industrial infrastructure such as highways, mines, and tourist sites. Zone 3 targeted prime areas for wildlife and trapping. Zone 4 included all the rest. These classifications contained instructions for responding to fire. Zone 1 called for full suppression. Zones 2 and 3 also called for active control, but, if crews and aircraft were inadequate to the full fire load, then they would go to the zones in order of ranking. Thus, Zone 1 fires could command everything the organization could throw at it. The others could call up what remained. This might be quite a lot if Zone 1 was not threatened or very little if fires swarmed over both Zones 1 and 2. Zone 4 got action only if little was happening elsewhere and a fire could bust out into a higher-ranking zone.[24]

The exercise had the value of making public and explicit what had been implicit in the bureaucracy. But that also exacerbated the conflict in values that had underwritten the designation of priority zones, for a ranking could only work if people agreed on the criteria behind it. What mattered most to the indigenous communities, Zone 3, might not qualify for much protection during a mass fire bust – exactly the time when the rankings would come into play. It also underscored the vulnerability of a strategy based solely on initial attack. If that attack failed, and the woods were dry and the winds high, there was no way to stop the fire's further spread. The zones, that is, were porous. Classic Canadian fire experience, however, could only urge more initial attack. Until every fire everywhere was hit hard and quickly, control could stall. The policy of zoning by priorities not only failed to defuse quarrels over what should be protected but also could not guarantee protection even over the zones of highest priority, and it could not staunch a fiscal haemorrhage during a blowup year, which quickly followed. The 1973 season added 163 fires and 70,000 acres to the dimensions of the 1971 holocaust, even as official reports noted with satisfaction that aerial tankers had become "an effective fire-suppression tool in the North." Whatever effect they had on fire lines, they sent fiscal flames soaring, mocking assumptions about the prospects for planned, rational development in the north.[25]

All the elements now began a rapid spiral of convergence. Treasury bureaucrats panicked, funding faltered, and policy, instead of firming up, turned to jelly. An officer with the Northern Lands and Forest Service (NLFS), as a reorganized MFS was called, put it simply: the agency went "from 'fight all fires' to fight 'as few fires as possible.'" Almost immediately Zone 3, constituting the bulk of game habitats, fell off the charts. By 1976, federal officials directed the NLFS not to respond to Zone 3 fires unless they actively threatened settlements. A year later the zone was officially scrapped; protection again collapsed to towns and roads. Meanwhile, ecology began to compete with economics as an informer of policy, although with science, as with everything else in the north, there were several sponsors, and they disagreed on fundamentals. DIAND funded the biggest effort, the Arctic Land Use Program, a four-year broad-spectrum agenda tied to oil development and the Mackenzie Valley Pipeline. Usefully, Americans had scrutinized Alaska as an arena for fire management, with the politics likewise marinated in Native claims, pressures for local development, and a giant pipeline. Syntheses were published in 1974 and 1975. One group could still see the northern lands as a matrix of natural resources from hydropower and minerals to wood and fur. They proposed a familiar dialectic between development and protection. Another group, however, unmoored themselves from timber and game alone and argued that, as an ecosystem, the north's preferred state might be wilderness. Instead of resolving political turmoil, the research freshened it. In a classic technocratic response, the department sponsored a literature review of fire and wildlife as a means of calibrating its priority system and ... reorganized.[26]

Yet something had changed. Ecologists were replacing foresters as the principal investigators of fire and injecting a novel set of values into the discourse. Their research suggested that wildfire could not be expunged, that there was no good reason to try to do so, that "natural" fire might be the preferred management option. These conclusions merged with concepts of wilderness to argue that, with respect to wildlife, the ideal strategy was to do as little as possible. The only reason to intervene might be to shore up populations of threatened or endangered species, and the treatment of choice should be prescribed burning to mimic missing wildfire or restore fire-dependent habitat to a condition where natural processes could reclaim control. One study concluded that effective fire suppression, "if implemented over a large area of the Northwest Territories," would constitute "an inadvertent ecological experiment on a scale unprecedented in North America" – and not a welcome one. Thus, a valence of convenience emerged that bonded Ottawa bureaucrats with territorial wildlife biologists to argue that, where fire management was concerned, less was more. In the Northwest Territories, it seemed that state-sponsored ecology might replace state-sponsored forestry.[27]

But neither of these logics, government economics or ecological science, led inexorably to political choices. Field research could establish the tenacity of boreal fire, but administrative conclusions clearly derived from environmental philosophies, not environmental sciences. The First Nations disagreed. Animals were not simply "wildlife" but also meat, hide, and fur, the sinews and barter of an ancient life. They had to fight government economists to create space for a traditional lifestyle, one that would lead not to modern development but to self-perpetuation, and they had to fight an emerging environmentalism to argue for the continuance of their presence, that wilderness was a misreading of their habitat, that human hunting, fishing, trapping, and burning deserved to persist. By the mid-1970s, a back-to-the-land movement reinforced those demands, not merely as symbol but also as practical necessity. The political economics was further complicated because, in the name of conservation, trappers and hunters had had to register their traplines and sites, which denied them the loose-jointed mobility that had made their compact with the boreal forest possible. Previously, if a fire burned one site, they could move to another; now, like open-range ranchers faced with barbed-wire fencing, they could not and could ill afford to have their assigned plats burned. Like ranching, too, trapping became demonized; what practitioners considered a working business and an honourable lifestyle outsiders dismissed as state-subsidized welfare and ecological vandalism. As Native populations ratcheted up and markets tanked for furs, economic distress became acute. The indigenes had as little control over the business cycle as they did over the climatic cycle.

But they did have a growing political voice. The territorial council, established in 1966, steadily expanded such that by 1974 it was wholly elected. The federal government, however, retained control over natural resources and economic development, for the Mackenzie Valley held something the rest of Canada wanted: the route of a pipeline for Arctic oil. From 1974 to 1977, a royal commission headed by Justice Thomas Berger inquired into the controversy, vividly highlighting Native claims. In 1975, the Dene Assembly even issued a declaration that asserted sovereignty. Inevitably fire entered into this intensifying discourse. It mattered enormously in the dynamics of those habitats vital to traditional economies, and it mattered symbolically. "Fire control" referred less to control of fire in the landscape than to control over the apparatus of fire administration.[28]

What happened next was fire. The fires of 1979 to 1982 had rumbled across Canada like a rolling thunder, shaking institutions into new patterns. In the Northwest Territories, they came like a *Götterdämmerung*. However inclusive the Berger Commission, it had not brought fire before the commissioners, had not recorded fire's claim to the land, had no way to devolve responsibility for fire to fire itself. Instead, people argued between people over its control. In 1979, fire ignored humanity's bombast and pretensions and, submitting its own testimony, soared across the Northwest Territories. Some 380 fires scorched nearly five million acres. Resistance crumbled. Almost two-thirds of the area burned lay in the Fort Smith District, long the centrepiece of territorial fire protection. The fires burned through timber, through park, through caribou habitat, through traplines, across learned texts, ethnic declarations, bureaucratic policies, commission reports, through money dumped into their suppression. The fires inflamed all the passions invested in the Northwest Territories' tenuous politics. The Hunters and Trappers Association complained about the lack of action on areas of greatest interest to it; the Native Council of Canada fielded a crew and attacked a fire ignored under the priority tables; the NLFS scrambled to spare communities such as Pine Point. Critics screamed for a political inquiry – and got one.

The fires seemed to confirm whatever assumptions people brought to them. They convinced the NLFS that it needed a more robust initial attack force, with the capacity to pre-position for maximum effect. They affirmed the belief of the Treasury Board that fire protection in the region was a bottomless fiscal pit, that anything much beyond an urban fire service was an extravagance. They seemingly supported the conclusions of fire scientists that fire here was untameable, that wildlife was best served by a laissez-faire fire policy, and that, inevitably, much more research was needed. They nurtured the resentments of Natives that the fire program was misdirected and that nothing less than its total governance by the Northwest Territories' indigenous residents could redeem it. All this a Ministerial Fire Review Panel, hastily convened after the fire season, absorbed and tried to reconcile.[29]

The Fire Review Panel was a model exercise, which in five short months emulated the Berger Commission, matched the fire program of the Northwest Territories against comparable agencies in Canada and Alaska, and wrote a comprehensive report, complete with ninety-six recommendations. But it was, not unexpectedly, a technocratic document from a select committee of three fire specialists, addressing the extent to which policy was suitable and implementation adequate to that policy, while the core issues lay elsewhere. Efficiency, that talisman of Canadian fire strategy, assumed that an agency knew what to do and how to do it. For the Northwest Territories, the science was insufficient and disputed, and the objectives of fire management were unsettled and disputed. It did little good to improve efficiency when there was no consensus where the agency should be more efficient.

Big fires become important when they interact with society; then they become galvanic, even great. The 1979 eruption was followed by a 3-million-acre outbreak in 1980, the second largest on record, and by 2.4 million burned acres in 1981. The upshot was that the spiral of converging forces tightened. There was more research; the Canadian Forestry Service, in particular, found the Northwest Territories an ideal arena, demonstrating again the critical link between state-sponsored research with state-administered lands. There was more politics; the 1980 Drury Report kept alive the momentum for devolution, nudging toward a transfer of authority over natural resources. There was more Native activism, much of it now funnelled through one of the innovative recommendations of the Fire Review Panel, that a NWT Fire Management Program Committee be established that could represent local opinions. But what the department characterized as advisory, Native groups deemed mandatory. To their minds, the committee, to which they sent representatives, should itself decide policies and determine priorities. There was a reorganization, a new policy, a significantly ramped-up funding, a committee designed to quell a political insurgency, detailed policy reviews, and the first official whispers about a wholesale transfer of the program to the Northwest Territories.[30]

The revised policy scrapped the contentious hierarchy of priorities and parsed the Northwest Territories into two zones: a fire action zone (about 20 percent of the land) and an observation zone. Fires in the action zone would be fought, for which the tried-and-true strategy of a powerful initial attack offered the best solution, made effective by a doubled budget and a Territorial Forest Fire Centre at Fort Smith, now linked to the Canadian Interagency Forest Fire Centre. But the politics stalled. The Dene Nation and Métis Association had regarded the "awesome destruction" of the 1979 season as "unnecessary," the outcome of bad policy badly applied. No fix was possible save through an outright transfer of authority; the Dene Nation had "never accepted" either the Fire Review Panel's recommendations or the response to them by DIAND. The Fire Management Committee stumbled through its first year and then imploded. When reconvened, P.H. Beaubier, director of the NWT Region, recorded his opinion "that when issues become 'political' it is not always productive to dwell on them." This of course missed the point entirely and deliberately. Keeping discussions to technological concerns about aircraft and remote weather stations avoided the very essence of the problem. The Dene and Métis representatives made a "united stand" to have the entire program transferred to their control by April 1982. They scorned the priority zones as a reification of what they considered their subordinate status. The government's policy they dismissed as one intended "to support the systematic burning off of the land." Instead, on the unanimous instructions of their "people," they insisted that "all fires must be fought in all areas until out. All the land is a priority." No round of study on the fire behaviour of spruce-lichens at Porter Lake or the fractal migration habits of barren-ground caribou would change that perception.[31]

The spiral tightened without mixing. Fire research seemed to say that fire was uncontrollable and classic fire suppression impossible. Fire management insisted that nothing could be done until control was possible at some level, which demanded serious initial attack capabilities, and those in a landscape well beyond the pale of protection for the southern provinces. Foresters wanted suppression only where timber or towns were at risk. Ecologists urged a long-term, evolutionary perspective on fire and wildlife, observing critically that "acceptance of fire as a natural expression" of ecosystem dynamics was hampered "by the short planning horizon of resource users." Those users – trappers and hunters – wanted fire protection to help stabilize their livelihoods, increasingly buffeted and marginalized by beyond-control cycles of climate, economics, and public fashion. In a weird, historic reversal, environmentally attuned officials campaigned for fire's accommodation, while Native groups argued for fire's exclusion. Federal planners demanded some consensus among goals, while local groups largely insisted that consensus was impossible. They wanted to oversee the program, not simply advise it. The 1979 Fire Review Panel that the authorities had considered, rightly, as exemplary, staffed by leaders in fire science and management, local residents dismissed, with equal conviction, as more southern colonialism, overseen by people ignorant of traditional life. Amid this vortex of identity politics, fire continued to burn, indifferent to all their nuances of language and gesture. Political discourse was so much vapour to be sucked into the next firestorm.[32]

One by one the separate issues worked out their destinies. When the CIFFC came on line, it quelled the need to staff locally for the worst year. Parks Canada wrestled Wood Buffalo, for decades the pivot for fire protection in the region, into conformity with an enlightened 1979 policy that accommodated burning for ecological purposes. Devolution quickened in 1985 and went to full term in 1987, followed by ... reorganization. The Northwest Territories had become a province in all but name. But no one, not the Berger Commission, not the Dene Nation, not the NLFS, not the Treasury Board, had invited fire into the discourse. It should have surprised no one, then, that the new policies, sophisticated initial attack plans, alliances across borders, and sharper technology ended in more fire. In 1989, nearly 1.4 million acres burned.

Yukon Territory

Within the Yukon fire protection thinned to a thread. The Northwest Territories had extended the fire protection strategy of Alberta northward, pivoting around Wood Buffalo National Park. The long trek north caused that strategy to shed and replace parts: substituting game for timber, restricting more rigorously the geography of places in which to fight or observe fire, transferring decisions to local communities. The Yukon was too remote even for this. It served mostly as a conduit between British Columbia and Alaska, and that fact aptly characterizes its fire system: it was forever a program in transit. Yet if its institutions seemed recent and transient, its fires were ancient. The Yukon Valley sucked in thunderstorms that occasionally sparked fire busts, and by remaining unglaciated it had known anthropogenic fire for longer than anywhere else in Canada. If its geography made fire urgent, its history made fire unique.

Those facts combined into a land of two fire geographies, one hard and one soft. There is a hard matrix of deep structure and long rhythms, a tough template of terrain and climate that extends back into the Pleistocene by which lightning concentrates in the central valley where summer moisture plies up the long reach of the Yukon River, with a particularly heavy focus around the Klondike River. Fires clump like placers with the difference between sites varying as much as a hundredfold. Big fires rage and vanish with the peculiar lumpiness of boreal burning. The second geography is a soft pattern shaped by people. It is a mobile matrix of sudden shakings and abrupt restructurings, a land of tight fire corridors and sprawling fire rushes as people change how and why they come and go and how they release and hold fire. Both the hard and the soft matrices are regimes of boom and bust; they can co-exist, each in its own realm, but they can also clash with explosive violence. By the end of the twentieth century, fires were about equally divided in their cause between people and lightning, which is to say the two geographies enjoyed a rough balance.[33]

The great shockwave after Confederation was the Klondike gold rush, unleashed in 1896. The stampede of Klondikers forced the government's hand: some political entity was required, and the 1898 Yukon Territory Act provided that patina of governance and assured a source of revenue. The Mounties famously stood for order, contrasting brilliantly with the riotous sprawl in Alaska. Ten years later amendments allowed for a wholly elected governing council. Thus, the Yukon acquired formal status before the organization of the Dominion Forestry Branch. Minister of the Interior Clifford Sifton visited the region at the height of the boom (August 1897) and concluded that the place was "good for nothing except mining, which in all probability will be temporary."[34]

As Sifton observed, it was gold, not timber, that drove the economy. The point of woods was to furnish fuel and local construction timber. The fires that rambled over the bush were useful in exposing outcrops and, by deadening patches of forest, in stacking fuel to stoke the fires that turned paddlewheelers, heated cabins, and melted permafrost into soil fit for sluicing. The rush itself passed over the landscape like a fire, not simply as a metaphor but as fact. By deliberation or accident, from insight or ignorance, fires accompanied the miners, a stampede of flame. Much of the wooded landscape fell to axe and fire, which became a prelude to gouging, dredging, and hydraulicking the very ground itself. Hastily erected railways flung sparks over the diggings. Campfires abandoned by the stampeders, after smouldering through the spring, swept forests around mining camps during the hot summer of 1898. What accident missed intent hit. Permafrost interfered with a tunnel at Dease Creek, for example, until "the woods and moss" were "burnt off," after which there were "no further complaints" of frozen ground.[35]

As with forestry, industrial capital soon replaced individual miners, and a system evolved that was both corporatist and colonial. Population ebbed as rapidly as it had flooded; vast chunks of the landscape were wrecked, overturned and burned, and depopulated by disease. The idea of controlling free-burning flame in such a context was a mirage. The security of Yukon mining royalties, not the sustainability of its woods, guided the early scramble to impose order. The DFB hardly dared to probe beyond the shores of Great Slave Lake.

The rhythm of rush and recession continued. A few ephemeral booms followed in the form of scattered ore discoveries, a patch of petroleum over the Mackenzie Mountains, and a fur frenzy during the 1920s. Paradoxically its residual minerals, hard won by dredgers, helped to sustain the territory during the Depression, gold being one commodity not overproduced. A new order of fire likewise stabilized. The rush of fire, rather like the wholesale hydraulicking that shrank into dredges, shrivelled into discrete patches and established routes of transit, while deep burning gradually recovered along with the return of woods. The next, the defining, boom commenced when, during the early crisis of the Second World War, the American military platted out a highway to Alaska, running through Whitehorse. The Alaska Highway replaced the Yukon River as the defining corridor of fire. The motor vehicle succeeded the steamboat and the narrow-gauge railway. The new stampede let fire loose widely and then channelled it within the broad levees of the highway. Instantly the geography of Yukon fire realigned. Construction across some 6,700 miles cast off fires with all the abandon of railways and steamers in earlier times. The road was slashed, hastily and often crudely, through hills and woods; soldiers were ignorant of the land, and frequently calloused in their treatment of it, and indifferent to fires they might kindle. They were, after all, only passing through. Roadside slash burned often. South of the BC border, the highway tracked two of the largest twenty fires in provincial history; how far the fires rambled to the north is unknown. They quickly became, however, more than a nuisance, or graffiti scrawled on the land, by threatening some operations while a smoke pall obscured the sky and prevented surveying and aerial traffic.[36]

In 1943, the burns had become sufficiently burdensome that the territory established a Forest Protective Service. Its charge was the lands of transit: the Alaska Highway, the Haines Cut-Off, the Lewes-Yukon River systems, and those tributary roads that branched from them. The officer in charge liaised with the US Army, which maintained the highway, and the crown agent for land and timber. Housed in Whitehorse, the program quickly gathered "considerable fire-fighting equipment." Abandoned construction buildings became patrol cabins. The service promoted co-operative arrangements with the military. In April 1946, authority transferred from the United States to the Canadian Department of National Defence. When a fire burned some structures around Carmacks, equipment had to be shipped by sternwheeler from Whitehorse and "took three days to arrive." But that was the old era.[37]

The new era evolved a protection apparatus superficially similar to that in the Northwest Territories. That is, it was remote from the centre of political control, it operated on a short funding leash tied to tangible benefits, and its capacity was always in danger of being overwhelmed by an explosion of boreal burning. Where the NWT fire program spread from Wood Buffalo, the Yukon's clung to the Alaska Highway. For fire protection, the land divided into a sharpening relief, with fields of fire in the backcountry and lines of fire along corridors of travel. Abandoned campfires, careless Natives while on their "muskrat and beaver hunts," residents firing green timber to make fuel wood, and lightning, against these there was little the fledgling agency could do. But along the highway and fresh tributary roads such as the North Klondike to Dawson, it could act. Patrols prowled the highways; prevention programs sprouted along the roadsides like morel mushrooms; designed campgrounds and picnic grounds boxed in recreational burning; and the RCAF provided aerial reconnaissance.[38]

Then the postwar lull broke in 1951 when reported fires increased from thirty-eight to sixty and burned area swelled from 29,000 to 463,000 acres. The saving grace, of course, was that the bulk of the burning occurred from a handful of fires in areas of "almost complete inaccessibility." But some fires, with malicious irony, blitzed along the newly hacked corridors, the "windrows of tinder-dry debris on either side of the road" acting "as a torch." While fire authorities battled those blazes near settlements, which made sense, fire protection remained, anomalously, within the context of forestry, which did not (a "forest engineer" oversaw town-based wardens). The arrangement addressed neither the territory's legacy economy nor its emerging service industry. The fires that threatened Dawson resulted when the Yukon Consolidated Gold Corporation burned the slash it had stripped away from creek bottoms it intended to dredge, yet already tourism mattered far more than timber.[39]

Forestry nonetheless remained the erstwhile Canadian engine of fire control. H.L. Holman, who had performed a similar task for the Northwest Territories, now the Yukon's "forestry liaison officer," submitted a report in November 1951 that laid out a ten-year program for firmer protection. He fretted, in particular, over the Whitehorse area, richer in fires, subject to drier conditions, even prone to chinook winds, and, he did not need to add, the newly designated territorial capital. The "only practical way" to improve access to the interior, Holman insisted, was by aircraft based at Whitehorse and Mayo. For this, he advanced the classic argument that with aircraft, initial attack might succeed. And he advanced the classic justification that the region's timber would soon become important. On his fears for Whitehorse and his forecasts for aircraft, Holman proved prescient; on the future of forestry, he did not. Its roads, not its woods, were the future of Yukon fire.[40]

The crash came in 1958. A hundred fires burned 1.8 million acres, "the worst fire season in living memory." The terrifying news was that these fires had not remained deep in the bush. Two of them, driven by winds of forty miles per hour, exploded almost instantaneously over 32,000 acres and converged on Whitehorse. Authorities immediately responded "to enlarge the fire suppression organization."[41]

That ambition extended beyond the days of crisis, for the basic apparatus of Canadian fire administration had begun to travel the Alaska Highway and the newly bladed roads that fed into it. The long trek northwest meant that not everything survived the transit; like the baggage of Klondike prospectors, non-essential goods got dropped by the wayside. And while the government had no desire to see the 1958 conflagration repeated, it had equally no intention of pursuing wildfire into the backcountry or financing a program of extermination. Instead, the core infrastructure continued to bulk out as temporary shacks became permanent, war-surplus vehicles gave way to new models, a network of lookouts supplemented fire sightings by the travelling public, and makeshift patrols evolved into rigorous reconnaissance. There was a self-limiting quality to the program since it lacked both the commercial forestry subsidy available to the provinces and the urgency that linked fire to politically volatile local lifestyles in the Northwest Territories.

The timing of the buildup was ideal. The five years that followed the eruption of 1958 were perhaps the lightest in the formal record. Rapidly, the agency hired staff, leaping from eighteen to ninety-nine; more cautiously the agency left the road for the air with an inaugural aerial reconnaissance in 1961 and experiments with helicopters in 1963. In 1965, the department formally redefined the focus of both the Yukon and the Mackenzie Forest Services to embrace overall forest management, not simply fire protection. But there would be little forestry in the Yukon. The defining duty remained fire control. On cue, fires returned, roughly at the level of the 1951 season. They prompted the first call for airtankers. The next year was marginally better.

The cycle of fire violence – big fires leading to bigger firefighting forces followed by more big fires – could not continue indefinitely. After 1958, the organization had fought every fire it could reach with whatever it had. By 1967, it was clear that this had to end. The Forest Service identified zones that it would protect and not protect. Protection embraced a quarter of the territory, tracing the matrix of roads and settlements. While this decision "simplified planning" and relieved "pressure during extreme periods," social values, not fire behaviour, inscribed the geography of zones. The cycle of federal funds was as vital as that of drought. Extreme seasons still ruled the statistics of how much burned. Tough fires sparked calls for better aerial suppression, and in 1968 two Snow Commanders joined the fleet under charter, dousing flames with retardant, but their contribution was "definitely limited" in comparison with the versatility of the helicopter. Yukon required precision fire control along the paved waterways of an industrial folk, the seasonal migrations of tourists, not blanket protection of remote timber berths or caribou ranges. Even when the program soared, it remained tethered to asphalt and bladed gravel. Aircraft did for the highway what velocipedes and speeders had done for the fire corridors of the railways elsewhere.[42]

The lid blew off in 1969. In the protected zone, 111 fires burned 910,000 acres, and in the non-protected zone another 26 fires scorched 319,000 acres, all in all an outburst second only to 1958 and one not readily discounted as a by-product of remoteness. One fire incinerated the new town of Faro, others forced evacuations of Pelly Crossing and Crestview, while smoke palls made difficult the detection of new starts.[43]

Inevitably the government moved to bolster its fire control forces; predictably this involved an escalation in aircraft use and hence in costs. The 1971 season recommended that even the pared protected zone was too vast, that protected lands too had to be ranked. Meanwhile, the trends pointed to more fires, equally divided, on average, between human and natural origins. The number of anthropogenic starts levelled off in the early 1970s as the road network stabilized. The number of reported lightning fires rose steadily and accounted for most of the big-burn acres; this was probably an artefact of better (that is, aerial) surveillance. The only solution seemed to be a more robust initial attack, which meant a fuller system of reconnaissance and a brisker response, thus inviting initial attack crews along with more helicopters and A-26 airtankers.

The readjustment of priorities, congealed as a fire dispatch hierarchy, occurred in the midst of a larger departmental reorganization prompted by revisions in territorial land use regulations. In 1972, the Yukon Lands and Forest Service (YLFS) took to the field with a four-priority strategy much like that in the Northwest Territories. The protected zone fractured into three groups: towns, roads and recreation sites, timber berths and wildlife habitats. Accordingly nine of its ten lookouts oversaw settlements, that is, the nodes of its roads. And since the "KEY to a successful fire control program" was "good headquarters control," the Forest Service established a strict line of authority with a central dispatcher who reported to the territorial fire control officer. For the 1974 season (again modelled on the Northwest Territories), the YLFS got additional funds to bolster crews and aircraft for a more vigorous initial attack; by 1975, it had at its disposal nine helicopters, two patrol planes, a crew of contract smokejumpers (who came with their own aircraft), and two A-26 airtankers with a lead plane (and a third tanker on casual contract) operating out of five retardant-equipped air bases. Faced with a large bust – in June the agency was fighting sixty fires – the two bombers and lead plane were acting as "a team" with the third "lone-wolfing." The bomber group worked thirty-one fires in the Yukon and another in British Columbia. The year before the YLFS had crossed into Alaska to extinguish a fire, and in 1975 the Americans reciprocated by attacking four Yukon burns. The exchange of information across the border was "continuous." Superintendent Edo Nyland proudly declared the Yukon Lands and Forest Service a "modern, however small, fire fighting organization."[44]

That was true. The YLFS looked like most Canadian fire agencies. It accepted the same principles, operated according to much the same protocol, flew the same aircraft and relied on the same pumps and hand tools, attended the same conferences; staff could easily transfer to and from other provinces. It wanted to do what the others did. What distinguished it was its disconnection from industrial logging and its singular patrol of the highway network. Elsewhere commercial discoveries of minerals, soils, and timber had allowed the provincial fire agency to send its tendrils into the evolving latticework of development. No such opportunities appeared in the Yukon. The YLFS would remain on the road, even if it patrolled that road by air. Like the territory itself, the agency seemed to be unable to sprawl much beyond the highway's penumbral right-of-way.

Instead, it devised sharper, more precise techniques to achieve that goal, replacing the blunt-force methods favoured by the major provincial fire powers. One such innovation was smokejumping, an idea probably borrowed from Alaska, although the contract jumpers themselves migrated seasonally from British Columbia. Another technique, borrowed from Australia, was aerial ignition. With a small staff and immense lands to protect, the YLFS needed a way to ignite backfires rapidly and safely, and after the CFS helped to adapt the techniques aerial ignition did just that. Superintendent Nyland believed that, under northern conditions, aerial ignition was "far more desirable" than bulldozers and "far cheaper" than airtankers and mass helicopter attacks. While the generic concept had originated elsewhere, the Yukon offered its "first practical application as a fire control tool."[45]

That still left two critical issues, both analogues of Canada-wide problems but both with Yukon-distinctive qualities. One was stable funding. An average year, that statistical mirage beloved of administrators, especially Ottawa bureaucrats, meant little. "One year we spend $4,000 and another we might spend $3,000,000." The other issue was actually protecting the priority sites away from the main highway, especially those old mining settlements embedded in the regrown woods. It simply wasn't possible to mass counterforces along their fringe to halt a full-bore crown fire. That meant that those potential fires had to be caught while small (hence smokejumping) or blocked by burnouts before they encroached on the villages (hence aerial ignition). But big seasons would overwhelm the suppression organization, as they did budgets; unstoppable conflagrations could roar in from the unprotected zones. The towns themselves had to become less fire prone.[46]

If possible. After the 1969 debacle, the agency had surveyed "key" problems with the hope that it might find "a practical solution to the annually repeated wildfire threat" to communities. The prospect for serious destruction by wildfire, it announced, was "very real," stoked by "forest fuel buildup" around settlements. Communities were being hacked out of a restored and even-aged boreal forest such that woods and towns glowered at each other across a border without so much as a stone wall to separate them. Each side needed modification, which suggested a program of systematic mitigation. In 1974, the Forest Service contracted with a consultant from Vancouver to recommend measures for Whitehorse. The following year the agency reached for advice to the US Forest Service. New communities needed planning, as did Whitehorse, which was beginning to sprawl with the mindless vigour of other capital metropolises. One outcome was the cutting of fireguards to the windward side of villages strung along the Alaska Highway. In principle, suppression forces could aerially ignite backfires on the outside of the guard. In principle, the various reforms – conceptual, technological, bureaucratic – could converge into a distinctive Yukon model.[47]

That was too much to expect, but the program did improve, broaden, and narrow. It improved thanks to fresh funds for better detection and aerial suppression. More lookout towers sprang up near communities, an automated lightning detection network (introduced in 1981) provided inexpensive coverage of the hinterlands, and aerial firefighting, while small by the standards of western provinces, was focused, trained, and versatile, outfitted for reconnaissance, helicopter rappelling, airtankers, and a tiny corps of smokejumpers. It broadened when it became caught in the outer vortex of territorial politics in which the resolution of Native land claims, proposed pipelines, and "constitutional development" meant, in practical terms, devolution. While controversies flared with less ferocity than in the Northwest Territories, the restated policy applied to both proto-provinces, and the YLFS had its budget for 1981-82 increased by nearly 30 percent. But even as the program moved inexorably, if tediously, toward devolution, it widened its range through co-operative agreements with British Columbia and Alaska, the latter extending to a shared lightning detection system. And, finally, the program narrowed by reasserting its customary priorities: the highway, its tributaries, and the villages that were the nodes of the network. In the Northwest Territories, the politics of Native claims had compelled fire authorities to upgrade the status of lands away from settlements if they had value to traditional economies and ethnic identities. The Yukon held to its traditional ranking on settlements and on the corridors that trafficked between them. Territorial economics depended on travel and tourism, not forestry, fur, or fish. In the Yukon, unlike the Northwest Territories, a fire management committee authorized by the 1981 reforms did not immediately materialize, act as a lightning rod for protest, or catalyze an unseemly scramble for federal monies.

The dual geography of fire in the Yukon had a startling clarity. Compared with most provinces, the Yukon faced a simpler task in principle and a harder one in practice. The principle was to keep each fire to its assigned place, to let the long rhythm of the hard matrix beat as it would and to contain the fires of the soft matrix within the fire-suppression levees thrown around the corridors of human traffic and habitation. The crunch came in practice, for no institution could hold big fires to a predestined place any more than it could hold a thunderstorm to a single hill. Boreal fires could not be turned up and down like the flames of a gas stove by twisting a bureaucratic dial. What mattered most were the bad seasons and the big fires that could conceivably obliterate small communities nestled like nuggets amid the flammable placers of the boreal forest. Those fires continued, often, as in 1982, after policy reform and reorganization.

What mattered was their larger setting, and that was the problem on the horizon, the glowing spark in the deep duff. With each year, it became harder to separate the two realms. The deep matrix was regrowing its coniferous coating and so recovering its ancient capacity for expansive boreal fire, even as the soft matrix of roads and settlements proliferated, forcing proportionally more of the land into higher protection status, gerrymandering the landscape into more borders and less bulk, developing exurban burls and sending out new branches. Each border crowded against the other, and each pushed back. The two geographies blurred and, if unchecked, would require near-blanket coverage of the backcountry to protect the fractal borders thrown up by a new-character colonization.

The big fire was a fundamental fact of fire's boreal economy, and the Yukon Land and Forest Service temporized around it as the other provincial agencies did, by enrolling more firefighting forces. By the early 1980s, it bulked up its fire power with access to a national airtanker fleet, a fire treaty with the United States, accords with the Alaska Fire Service, and high-tech environmental monitoring. When it could, the YLFS pursued fires into the backcountry; when it couldn't, it withdrew. Meanwhile, an agreement with the Council for Yukon Indians promised to quell confusion over jurisdictions, and the prospects for devolution dissipated senseless squabbles over policy. The future depended on whether the soft matrix could hold, for if its borders blurred too deeply, no fire agency could contain wildfire except by a forward strategy that would prove ruinously expensive and hopelessly insufficient when the Big One came. No Canadian agency could face down such a fire, and no other had such need to hope it wouldn't have to.

Newfoundland and Labrador

In trait after trait, Newfoundland's fire saga stands both uniquely and at times inversely as a cameo for Canada generally. Here tundra lies to the south and boreal forest to the north, the result of hard use and a harsh climate. Here an island controls a mainland, a bonding of metropole with mainland fractured across the gulf. Here, a place where chrome rusts, surveys have repeatedly reported fire as "a dominant factor" in the composition and arrangement of its forests. Where, as elsewhere, torch and lightning mingle in often complex ways, here they inform separate geographies, of eastern island and western, and of island and Labrador. In its quest for fire protection, it recapitulates the struggle among the provinces generally to reconcile bureaucracy with the boreal woods, though with' exaggerated stress and insular quirkiness. The first of Canada's lands to be colonized by Europe, it was the last to be absorbed by Confederation and thus brings closure to the country's historical geography by completing control over the Gulf of St. Lawrence, the ancient entry into Canada.[48]

As elsewhere, the prospects for Confederation accompanied an outbreak of wildfires. "Extensive" fires swept the Avalon Peninsula, St. John's, and the aptly named Fogo Island in 1867, but monster fires, as reported by the Geological Survey of Newfoundland, swept over Gander Lake and inland of the Terra Nova River in million-acre gulps. Two years later the population rejected Confederation. The island had no prospect for a rail link with the mainland and hence no willingness to finance the transcontinental railway, whose economic necessity finally coerced the other colonies. What it needed, instead, was a transinsular railway, which it had authorized in 1868. Two years later another wave of flame crashed over settlements. Miscellaneous fires merged with "alarming rapidity" and "immense injury and destruction." One account insisted that, for sixty to seventy miles along that coast, "there is one continual fire." While most residents ignored the fires, leaving them to the inland barrens while they faced the sea, critics feared that forests would someday have to supplement, if not replace, fish in the island's economy. They fretted that the great woods might be burned out as the Grand Banks were being fished out.[49]

The hammer that shattered this ancient rhythm was the long-delayed railway. The House of Assembly finally passed the Newfoundland Railway Act in 1881. Two contractors failed before a successful award in 1890, a project lubricated lavishly with grants of land and timber licences. That summer large fires raged against the horizon and socked in bays with fog-like banks of smoke, the full sweep only apparent to coasting ships. While survey crews hacked and burned a swath through the interior, the old pattern persisted among the settlements. In 1892, "raging with unequalled and continued violence for over a month," woods fires laid waste "hundreds of square miles" in the eastern island. The rampage climaxed on 8 July, when the winds drove a barn fire through St. John's and reduced three-quarters of the colony's capital to a smoking ruin. The costs of rebuilding, along with a subsequent financial crisis, were enough to force a reconsideration of Confederation with Canada. This option was again rejected in 1896. On cue, a fire wiped out Pilley's Island, obliterating forty-five to fifty houses, two churches, and the courthouse and sending the residents to their boats to ride out the firestorm at sea. When the rails successfully crossed the island in 1898, they exposed no mineral wealth but did identify a large patch of white pine suitable for sawtimber and black spruce eventually amenable for pulp. Instead, they exposed the island to regular and explosive fires. The right-of-way became a blackened wasteland. "For several decades," as fire historians W.C. Wilton and C.H. Evans report, "the region was swept by a number of conflagrations until there was scarcely any land that had not been burned on at least one occasion." The 1904 scourge was the worst recorded in Newfoundland's history, as fires ripped from coast to coast, around hamlet, across barrens, and through bush, more than two million acres in all.[50]

A big fire concentrates the mind. The 1904 outbreak spared few. By boat, by train, by telegraph – the news poured in of fires bolting into villages, sweeping away outlying settlements, racing locomotives along the rails, devouring the projected timber wealth of the colony. One "vast conflagration" seemingly followed another. Telegraph lines burned down. A schooner captain reported the smoke too thick along the north shores to run at night. Trains hauled refugees before themselves halting where fires had burned away sleepers and twisted rails. But what makes for great fires is not how much land they burn but how deeply they brand the society inhabiting that land. Context is all, and timing is the greatest part of context. The 1904 fires had impeccable timing. Within a handful of years, loggers had scalped off the premier white pine; the sawtimber business peaked the same years as the conflagrations; axe and fire converged to threaten the next-wave economy of the island. Fires obliterated the mill at Sop's Arm and the Terra Nova Milling Company, and only blackened ruins remained of the New Lands Company's "railway station, lumber stocks, sectionmen's houses, outhouses and big mill." The next year the legislature moved to promote a pulp and paper industry by encouraging the Anglo-Newfoundland Development Company (ANDC). But such gestures were meaningless without an assured reserve of wood. The island had fewer productive lands than it wished. If it wanted a forest industry, it would have to shield those precious stocks from fire.[51]

Thus, fire and axe, with government sponsorship, began their corporatist alliance with the simultaneous passage in 1905 of the Forest Fires Act and the Pulp and Paper Act. The pairing was, in the words of one historian, "obviously more than just coincidence." The Pulp and Paper Act, which prompted the ANDC, catalyzed a process of consolidation and near monopoly fed by the vast timber licences lavished on the railway. Over the years, promotional schemes typically stumbled, but the new timber berths, along with those long-tenure leases granted to the railway, passed to already established companies. By 1939, the forest industry had become a duopoly between the Anglo-Newfoundland Power and Paper Company and Bowater Newfoundland, which together controlled half the total area of the island. The consolidation that characterized Canadian forestry overall was here exaggerated and crystallized.[52]

Something analogous happened with fire protection. The 1905 act applied the common wisdom of the day. It made the railway company responsible for certain fire practices and preventative measures. It appointed a chief woods ranger, Thomas Howe, who served primarily as a fire warden, overseeing a soon-created forest fire patrol. Howe's uncompromising stance was that Newfoundlanders could not afford "to waste one acre of our forest," since the land yielded almost nothing else of value, and that fire had destroyed more timber "than could be sawn into lumber in a hundred years." Once stripped, the land would never restock to anything like its presettlement level. Here, as throughout Canada, forestry meant mills and fire control. The Government Fire Patrol, as it became known, was responsible for railway protection in the eastern island and over those crown lands not yet under lease, an archipelago almost impossible to survey much less shield from fire. Together these reforms granted Newfoundland the vital necessities for a fire program: a controlling economic interest by the railway and timber industry; an institution, however ramshackle; a patriarch, whose thirty-year reign assured a steady hand and consistent vision; and paltry origins. Howe had three assistants.[53]

The Government Fire Patrol was inadequate: it could hardly be otherwise. Moreover, the transfer of tenure management from the public sector to the private sector complicated the duties of the state. The large timber companies did not wait for the intricacies of political attention, but moved to protect their most valued holdings. They organized prevention programs, restricted travel, erected lookouts, strung phone lines, and fought fires. They even imposed a no-smoking rule, much disliked by loggers. Their reforms, however, applied solely to company lands. Unlike the major timber provinces, there was no provision for joint fire protection through a fire levy or industry-sponsored fire rangers. Systematic fire protection was no better realized than systematic economic development. Newfoundland lacked the political heft of the large provinces and the connections to Confederation enjoyed by the small ones.[54]

Across the island, coverage was patchy and uneven in the power it could apply. In 1909, the Government Fire Patrol fielded six men. The obvious solution was a co-operative venture that could unite public and private firefighters, and it came from the small timber companies that the patrol could not protect and that could not themselves afford a private fire service. The upshot was a self-organizing movement that led in the spring of 1910 to a consolidated Newfoundland Fire Patrol (NFP) to oversee the railway. The hastily organized consortium extinguished 718 fires that summer. The legislature responded by formally authorizing a Fire Patrol Act in 1911, which allowed the governor-in-council to enter into agreements with private companies and persons for purposes of fire control. All parties would contribute to the cost.[55]

Even a colony could not evade the curse of confederated Canada, that bad fires often followed big reorganizations. The Newfoundland Fire Patrol focused on the railway; the rest of the island remained under the purview of the companies or the crown, and however indomitable the determination of its chief the Government Fire Patrol was flimsy on the ground, and in 1912 nature hammered it to shards. While the total acreage burned, at least as registered, was not immense, Howe brooded over the cumulative weight of the losses: "The dissipation of the forest is going on every year with no let-up." Before long, Newfoundland would be all white stumps and black snags. Thereafter, the broken rhythm of boreal burning set in. The 1920 season quickly exceeded 1904 and 1912 to establish itself as the year of reference. Conditions were "most fitting in every way for the encouragement of forest fires" and were "much alike all over the Island." The burned area exceeded a million acres, "much greater than all which has been burnt since the summer of 1912."[56]

Over the coming decades, fires came and went, some large, most small, the abundance of burns swarming around settlements and roads, the greatest burned acreage hidden in the hinterlands. So, too, institutions swelled in good times and shrank in bad. The Bowater mill established at Corner Brook in 1925 practically doubled the presence of the forest industry, but expansion also led to consolidation, and as more land came into production fewer companies held those acres. The Government Fire Patrol, the Newfoundland Fire Patrol, the company fire patrols – each held to its separate fiefdom, although the chief woods ranger had nominal authority over all the island's woodlands and authored an annual report to the House of Assembly.[57]

The colony thus had echoes of Canadian institutions but mixed in a curious way that made its search for order almost a parody of the Canadian fire establishment generally. It left big companies to run fire protection in their leased lands, somewhat as in New Brunswick and Quebec. It oversaw the railway with a special commission, not unlike that devised for the CPR. Its premier institution, the NFP, was an organ jointly financed by the state and industry, with a Controlling Committee chaired by an executive from the ANDC. It fielded a public fire service for those areas of densest settlement. There were pleas during the mid-1920s to expand forest protection beyond fire to include insects, since outbreaks were being recorded for the first time, but the cabinet declined to change either the Fire Patrol's charge or its name. In part, this refusal reflected Newfoundland's intrinsic conservatism, in part its shaky finances, and in good measure the fact that fires did not stress the island's institutions sufficiently to force mergers.[58]

The galvanizing crisis, perhaps appropriately, was financial. The Depression caused Newfoundland's economy to implode. Between 1928 and 1932, state revenues shrank by 21 percent, while expenditures rose 7 percent (with a quarter of the population on relief), and debt servicing commanded over 60 percent of the budget. Amid charges of corruption, demonstrations turned to riots. The colony even sought to sell off Labrador, over which it had formally acquired title in 1927, for $110 million. With default likely, a royal commission reported in October 1933 that bad government had transformed a fiscal crunch into a political crisis. Britain agreed to reschedule and guarantee Newfoundland's debt but at the cost of self-governance. A commission of government replaced the existing elected government and oversaw the colony from 1934 to 1949.[59]

While fire protection survived, justified as mandatory for industry and as a public service, it felt the shock. The loss of authority was Newfoundland's inverted image of the transfer to the western provinces of control over their natural resources. Reorganization meant not so much devolution as diminution. The old legislation was rescinded and then restated as a Revised Forest Fire Act (1933); the Government Fire Patrol was absorbed into a reorganized Department of Natural Resources; Thomas Howe's tenure ended. The government's contribution to the Fire Patrol dwindled, even as a fire at Rattling Brook convinced the department that "a more comprehensive system is necessary." That meant opening negotiations with the paper companies "and other interested parties with a view to amalgamation." Still, a bad outbreak of settlement blazes in 1933 convinced the authorities that they could slash services only so much.[60]

That didn't happen. Instead, each part of the mixed-economy system continued to do what it had to do. Often this was not much, and there was a clear disparity among the three entities. The industry took care of its own and was not eager to sink funds outside its holdings. The government oversaw the mostly settled eastern peninsulas and had little control over or co-operation from industry. Where they converged was with the Newfoundland Fire Patrol along the railway. The NFP was not, in truth, a full-bore firefighting outfit but a publicity campaign and a first-response network, equipped to swat out fires along the right-of-way. If a fire escaped, then the patrolman reported it and left its suppression (and damages) to the landowner. The system worked because of close watch and the tight valence between the rails and fires. Many of its patrolmen still tramped the rails on foot or by velocipede.[61]

Then matters got worse. The commissioner of natural resources worried that the department had "very little influence in the affairs of the patrol." In February 1936, the commission of government repealed the 1911 organic act that had established the Fire Patrol. It continued to contribute but through the budget of the Department of Natural Resources, and it denied, at least officially, that the NFP had any statutory authority. Still, patrolmen trod on. In 1935, the association erected its first lookouts. The situation displeased Chief Ranger Edgar Baird in particular. He saw the government's capacity deteriorating, as its caches depleted, its élan eroded, and its legitimate role in governance sloughed off in the mistaken guise of bogus economies. Field personnel confirmed the daily confusions caused by split responsibilities, the indifference of industry to fires that did not immediately threaten their leases, and the dry rot within the infrastructure. Critics urged a firmer merger of government and industry, though under some chartered committee, not simply by state fiat. The commission of government, still hounded by the colony's fiscal malaise, declined to amalgamate what it had just disaggregated. When Baird argued to adopt aircraft, at a time when the island's firefighting caches held barely half a dozen power pumps, the proposal seemed hallucinatory and met with derision. The commission did, however, sink funds into equipment, more in 1938 than it had altogether during the previous six years. The NFP expanded its coverage from rails to roads.[62]

But most observers agreed that what Newfoundland needed was not more hardware but the software to smooth out its dysfunctional organization. Government foresters, particularly, could not see how the anomalies, especially the Fire Patrol, served the public interest and forestalled a full and legitimate takeover by the government. Of the 375 railway miles patrolled, only 50 passed through crown timber, yet the government contributed a third of the annual budget and, as of 1938, sustained a subvention for highway patrol. The state was, in effect, subsidizing the paper companies, which held long-term leases, paid "low rents, practically no stumpage, and no fire protection taxes." Meanwhile, large fractions of crown land went unprotected altogether. Abolishing the NFP outright might compel a more rational realignment. Meanwhile, in 1939 the NFP celebrated a momentous statistical turning point: more timber fell to axe than to flame.[63]

For the bulk of Newfoundlanders, the year meant the return of a worse scourge, war. The Second World War both magnified the strains and stiffened the resolve to hold fire at bay. Wartime demands boosted production, while American money began to sluice through the island and Labrador, where a major base evolved at Goose Bay. In 1942, the NFP instituted an annual four-day inspection tour prior to fire season; the military added its co-operation. In 1944, a revised Fire Control Act helped to adjust the law to realities on the ground. Among amendments were changes in titles; the chief woods ranger became chief fire warden, and the Fire Patrol of Newfoundland became the Newfoundland Forest Protection Association (NFPA). Ambitions expanded, while duties contracted. Blissfully the war years had not bludgeoned the land with fire and were among the mildest on record. In fact, the span from 1921 to 1945 was the longest chronicle without a major blowup. The economic crisis had yielded a political crisis but avoided an environmental crisis that might, by cumulative weight, have fatally broken the institutions.[64]

That period of grace ended in 1946. The fires returned, some 846 in all, overrunning almost 100,000 acres mostly in the eastern island. Losses were greater than the scorched area alone might indicate, for one fire savaged Gloverton, razing forty-six houses, two schools, two business buildings, and a sawmill, besides lesser structures. In keeping with the pattern of Newfoundland fire, the next year was still more massive, consuming in excess of 474,000 acres, much of it around the island's northern timber region; the Anglo-Newfoundland Development Company especially suffered losses. Unnerving, too, was the discovery that some of the worst fires had been deliberately set because the confused jurisdictions had created "a premium" on "labour for fighting fires," and men had kindled the fires in order to be hired to fight them. The fires got the attention of politicians.[65]

All parties became alarmed. The fires had exposed the fragility of every firefighting institution and with particular vehemence had revealed their incapacity to co-ordinate. None had sufficient men and materiel to battle a serious fire, and none had adequate organization, while "overlap," in the words of the chief fire warden (who was also the NFPA field manager), was becoming "an issue which is about impossible to deal with." The NFPA did not even have legal standing. Simply pouring money into the existing arrangement would not solve the critical issues, notably "overlap of organization, discontent, inefficiency, and lack of co-operation." The consensus was that only a "unified Patrol" would work. The drive to merge was inherent in the northern economy of fire, but everywhere that logic was resisted, and Newfoundland's political circumstances further exacerbated that imperative. Its core co-operative institution, the NFPA, was a legal anomaly, which technically had no authority to do what it was doing. But then Newfoundland was itself a political anomaly, a colony that had reverted from responsible government to an appointed commission. What kind of merger its fire institutions should craft would demand a kind of internal confederation, not unlike the external confederation Newfoundland had to confront.[66]

The concerned parties converged in November 1947. The commission dismissed the NFPA as untenable and considered withdrawing altogether. At a minimum, it wanted to separate the fusion of chief fire warden with the NFPA's field manager. It preferred a two-state solution in which the "two paper companies" could look to their lands while the government would protect the rest. The strategy that characterized much of eastern Canada, a fire tax to underwrite a collective system, could not apply because, in its desire to encourage industry, Newfoundland had granted tax-exempt status to the Anglo-Newfoundland Development Company. The strains could only worsen with the prospect of aerial fire control, which seemed imminent even as its practical worth appeared "little known." So while all parties sought a unified system, none wanted to pay for it, and none wanted to surrender control over its own special interests. The commission balked. In the revealing words of the minutes, "the first step towards unification should be separation." Or, to complete the paradox, there was no entity sufficiently large enough within Newfoundland to make a merger work.[67]

In the end, granted the conditions that existed, the old order was reinstated. A new Fire Patrol Act appeared in June 1948 that was almost a carbon copy of the repealed act but that fixed the government's financial contribution and that reinstated the fire patrol, not general forest protection, as the purpose of the state's interest. The new charter authorized aircraft, which Edgar Baird, now a veteran pilot returned from the war, quickly pushed. A change from coal to oil as primary fuel for locomotives promised to slash dramatically the number of fires along the rails and boost a more efficient patrol. Meanwhile, the NFPA sponsored an inspection tour by Herb Beall of the Dominion Forestry Service, who recommended measures that had become standard across Canada – more lookout towers, aerial patrols, modern communications, and (his specialty) an upgraded fire danger rating system. The next year, in what critics considered a forced merger, the Colony of Newfoundland joined the Confederation of Canada.[68]

The island celebrated Confederation with forest fireworks. The 1949 and 1950 seasons were not top-tier fire years, but they belonged to Newfoundland's second tier, and they were troublesome enough for an organization that was scarcely able to do what it was charged to do and was now entangled in the confusion of Confederation. The NFPA breathlessly reported the ordeal of 1949's big fires kindled by lightning in the Upper Humber Valley and lower Notre Dame Peninsula; they burned for weeks, discouraged firefighters "because of the apparent uselessness of the task," and raised the question "as to whether or not fire fighting was worthwhile." The NFPA's chairman cited explorers from 1876 and 1878 who had reported similarly massive blazes in much the same places, the Gander River conflagrations of a magnitude not less "than 2,000 square miles." Yet in 1949 suppression had checked the fires at key bottlenecks. It was an arduous task, "detested by everybody," but there was "no doubt," he concluded, "that fire fighting pays." The larger 1950 outbreak affected crown lands and the paper companies.[69]

The tougher trial was institutional. While political merger had brought greater resources, as promised, it also coerced change, as feared. The early years were especially bumpy, as the organization tried both to grow and to integrate not only within the island and Labrador but also with Canada. The federal government worked like a giant flywheel, smoothing out Newfoundland's quirks and irregularities and bringing it into sync with Canadian practices generally. The Dominion Forestry Service was a notable presence. Its director, D.A. Macdonald, toured in 1950, and J.C. Macleod established a fire hazard rating station, trying to adapt eastern Canada's codes to Newfoundland's peculiarities. Eventually the need for technical information led to a Research Committee (1954). The companies sponsored a reciprocal study tour to the Maritimes and Quebec. Annual conferences brought together the various agencies to debrief and plan.

Meanwhile, aircraft became an established presence; by 1950, officials were even contemplating helicopters to sharpen initial attack. But the trickiest question was the one at the core of the island's idiosyncratic evolution, the Newfoundland Forest Protection Association. Even as the Newfoundland railway was absorbed by the Canadian National Railways, the NFPA continued fire patrols, its ancient ritual on rails.[70]

Inevitably a royal commission was called upon to analyze the scene. Its historical review was largely a litany of wanton and destructive fire, although it confessed to the "strange" circumstances in which the riotous fires kindled by the construction of the transinsular railway had regenerated black spruce of an age exactly right for an expanded pulp industry. Silviculture by serendipity was not, however, the commission's preferred solution. The future of Newfoundland forestry lay with pulp – the more the better – and the productivity of the industry depended on the security of its supplies. The commission appreciated that its recommendations for fire control constituted "perhaps its greatest single responsibility." It found the contemporary fire scene mixed, both lagging and rapidly advancing (among its "most stimulating" impressions). It requisitioned an intensive report by J.A. Brodie, a fire specialist from the Ontario Department of Lands and Forests, who both complimented the "efficiency of the present fire protection forces" and dismissed the "myth, still present in some quarters, that fire protection is a lesser problem in Newfoundland than elsewhere in Eastern Canada." The core recommendation reiterated what critics had urged for decades, that what Newfoundland required was a way to link its parts into a whole. Specifically the commission proposed to establish a new Newfoundland Forest Protection Association, to be authorized as a crown corporation, that could serve as the long-wished-for central authority. Industry would levy a "voluntary contribution" for a Forest Protection Fund. The CNR would assume patrol over the railways, as it was obligated to do throughout Canada. Newfoundland would morph into something akin to the other provinces.[71]

The proposition stalled, as had all its predecessors, and for all the familiar reasons. Industry was reluctant to surrender control to government and saw no reasons to "voluntarily" tax itself to pay for fire control beyond its own lands. The old NFPA had little desire to dismiss itself and considered the predicted federal financial aid "hopelessly short" of what the commission's proposals would demand. The government paused over the prospect of extending protection to crown lands of marginal economic value or subsidizing company berths that yielded no taxes. With attitudes typical of provincial brethren, they wanted the existing arrangements to persist, although with a lot more money dumped into the system and tinkering to improve fireline "efficiency." Many of the commission's minor recommendations were adopted. But its bold reorganization proved too revolutionary.[72]

Instead, the quadripartite rule continued, both pushed and pulled into more modern forms. An invigorating economy liberated more funds to build up facilities and upgrade equipment, the federal government commenced joint programs to inventory forests and install a research capability, and closer linkages with colleagues on the mainland silently nudged the Newfoundlanders into like-mindedness. Industry bolstered its internal capacities. The Government Fire Patrol evolved into a provincial Forest Service and began to assert a presence where none had existed previously, pushing its "control further west and north over the island than ever before," and probing into Labrador with a depot at Lake Hamilton, "hoping for quite a lot of cooperation from the Armed Services, both Canadian and American." To finance these initiatives, the government proposed to draw down its subsidies to the NFPA.[73]

That led to a critical moment in 1958 as the Controlling Committee decided, amid a year of few fires but serious budgetary deficits, to cease its railway patrol. The CNR assumed that job, while the NFPA scouted the highways, manned lookouts, and staged its elaborate propaganda campaigns. Yet the decision was momentous. The rail patrol had been the founding task, the administrative ceremony that gave meaning to all the others. Cutting that thread allowed momentum to transfer to the Government Fire Patrol, now a Forest Service embedded within the Department of Mines and Resources. With railway fires more or less contained, with a freshly mechanized force, and with aircraft to provide access, the scene shifted to the crown backcountry, not only on the island but also in Labrador. A fire geography once defined by rails and roads became one defined by planes and helicopters. Fires that previously no one might have even reported were now recorded and often fought.[74]

The curious obverse was a flourishing, simultaneous debate over controlled burning, "a subject of considerable discussion" that became the theme of a dedicated conference in 1957. Traditionally, observers had condemned the burning of heath and barrens while applauding the burning of blueberry patches. In the decade since Confederation, Newfoundland had in fact "successfully" burned over 80,000 acres of blueberries. The interesting question was whether similar techniques could be applied to silviculture. Certainly slash burning reduced hazard but stimulated reproduction, and some researchers believed that controlled burning in areas infested with balsam woolly aphid, followed by sowing spruce seed, was the "cheapest and surest way" of getting back productive soil. Wildlife specialists recognized the value of *brûlé* for browse and heath as habitat. And there was the indubitable example all around of spontaneous black spruce regeneration after wildfires, the regrowth of which was fuelling the province's pulp industry. Might not the same results come from deliberate, cost-effective prescribed burning? The Dominion Forest Service pitched in with some sponsored research.[75]

The flurry of questioning makes for interesting speculation. Throughout Canada, as fire agencies stockpiled their caches and added to their air fleets, the thrust was to combat fire and to project ever further the old lines of control. By the late 1950s, slash burning was beginning to wobble in favour of direct protection, more intensive utilization, and scarification; Saskatchewan was ceding its spring rite of burning fireguards; barrens were being restocked with trees, not berries. A postwar generation was enamoured with machines and aerial fire suppression and had the affluent wherewithal to challenge firefighting's inherited frontiers. Newfoundland's query thus ran cross-grained to Canadian enthusiasms, but the colony-turned-province was still enough of an outlier to be willing to pursue the question of prescribed burning. Had it persisted, it might have helped to reform Canadian fire practices; instead, that task fell to Parks Canada. By the end of the decade, the climate mandala turned, and Newfoundland obsessed over wildfire, not controlled, and abandoned semi-domesticated berry burning for the flaming wilds of Labrador.

The move into Labrador carried an organization nurtured along rails, roads, and villages into an immense bush as raw as any in North America. Fire-control plans called for the Forest Service to fly in crews and supplies from the island's cache at Gander during emergencies in the expectation that any fires would cluster around the military base at Goose Bay or the valleys being probed for timber and minerals. In 1959, a mix of seven fires, some from construction, most from lightning, scorched almost 600,000 acres. Despite float planes, helicopters, radio telephones, and a force of firefighters, it "was not found possible" to contain the flames. The fact that the agency might even contemplate suppression was a sign of both growing might and alarming hubris; the following year it established its first formal facilities on the mainland. Still, crown fires on the Labradorian plateau remained hidden from public scrutiny. The island, it was assumed, was reasonably well protected, with the fire services becoming more proficient each year.[76]

That presumption was challenged in 1960 and then crushed in 1961. It was not simply that the latter fires were big, though at over a million acres, they exceeded the burns of 1920 and harked back to the earliest records in 1904. More than big, they were damaging. One fire in the Bonavista North area blew up over 493,000 acres. They forced the evacuation of 9,000 people from thirty-one settlements, and Gander nearly found itself among them. They blasted prime productive forests, essential to an industry that now claimed 30-50 percent of the island's economy. Firefighting equipment losses were "fantastic"; then two airplanes and a helicopter crashed. Ontario and Quebec dispatched waterbombers; the New Brunswick Forest Service, the Dominion Forest Service, and Parks Canada sent crews. The Canadian military furnished helicopters, and the Canadian army flew in over 1,200 troops from Camp Gagetown to assist.[77]

One response was to be expected. The province immediately commenced a crash program to build up its stocks of equipment, to convert additional government-owned aircraft to waterbombing, to improve radio communications, and to establish a Fire Control Centre at Gander. The centre suggested that the fires had demonstrated with unblinking clarity that Newfoundland fire protection needed institutional reform, not simply more crews and Cansos, and that only the government could exercise that ultimate authority, which was not solely a question of efficiencies but also one of public safety. The NFPA was more and more an anachronism. A year before the blowup, it had celebrated its fiftieth anniversary; a year after the blowup, it staged its last inspection tour. Thereafter, it rapidly ebbed as a field force. The centre of power for Newfoundland's fire protection flowed from the power to fight fire, which flowed, increasingly, from aircraft. Immediately following the conflagrations, the Forest Service purchased six aircraft and added more waterbombers through shared payments from industry. With a calamity still cooling and the political punch conveyed by being a Canadian province, the Ministry of Mines, Agriculture, and Resources was prepared to claim that centre for the Forest Service. Amid the ashes of 1961, the Forest Service announced that, "barring unforeseen circumstances," it could cope "with any outbreak that may occur during future fire seasons."[78]

The Newfoundland Forest Service quickly acquired the trappings and capabilities of the Maritime provinces. It hosted a research centre for the Canadian Forestry Service; it sent staff to the Maritime Forest Ranger School and then instigated its own training in St. John's; when a lightning bust kindled twenty fires in western Labrador in July 1964, it hurried suppression forces into the "far northern lichen forests of Labrador" for the first time, asserting that, if protected, those woods would yield pulp. The next year the service dispatched a Canso to Nova Scotia to assist with firefighting. In 1965, Minister of Mines, Agriculture, and Resources W.J. Keough announced to a startled NFPA the province's readiness to reclaim timber limits and take responsibility for protection over all forested lands; once the shock wore off, companies accepted the logic of a government fire service. Their firefighting capabilities, they confessed, had become "somewhat puny" compared with the mechanical muscle of its rivals. In December 1966, the Controlling Committee notified the ministry that it would cease its patrols and lookouts and disposed of its equipment, determined instead to concentrate on its publicity campaigns for fire prevention and forest conservation and to serve as a neutral forum for the remaining agencies to meet and discuss common problems. Although the Newfoundland and Labrador Forest Protection Act confirmed its legal status, two years later the government withdrew its contributions, leaving industry to finance the organization. Manned lookouts plummeted from thirty-nine to seven; the NFPA's principal project remained the annual forest queen contest. Then, in 1972, the government reconsidered and rejoined. In the meanwhile, reflecting its new duties, the NFPA sought, and received, formal affiliation with the Canadian Forestry Association, which allowed it to become a conduit for a variety of national fire prevention programs. By then, everyone recognized that building incombustible fire pits for recreational users was more effective in reducing roadside fires than exhortations and essay contests.[79]

Meanwhile, the reorganized fire services dealt with a redefined geography. Fires on the island were many but small; fires in Labrador were few but large. In 1967, after assuming responsibility from the NFPA, the Forest Service swatted out 136 fires on the island (654 acres) while campaigning for several weeks in Labrador, where 95 fires scorched 610,179 acres. The firefight absorbed every Forest Service staffer that could be spared, along with 600 troops from Camp Gagetown and personnel from industry. In less than twenty years since Confederation, Newfoundland had gone from a mixed force cobbled together largely under the aegis of the NFPA to a modern fire suppression brigade with a fleet of Cansos and float-equipped Sikorsky S-55s and borrowed Otters and from a solitary weather station to experiments with aerial rainmaking. The Forest Service resolved never to allow a repetition of 1961.[80]

When another royal commission reviewed forestry in 1970, it found a mature industry, and a mechanized one, with the two companies holding 60 percent of the island's productive forests. But it worried, as all such commissions did, about future stocks and believed that losses from fire, insects, and disease "may exceed the annual cut." In general, the commission concluded that fire protection was adequate only for "normal" years, which made it inadequate for the dynamics of boreal burning. Meanwhile, industry's role made fire protection confusing, Labrador made it complicated, and reliance on aircraft made it costly. All pushed for an increasing presence by the Forest Service, which had expanded into Labrador, taken over the field chores of the NFPA, was considering a fire tax on private lands, and, the commission proposed, needed to provide the requisite "back-up assistance in emergencies." The expansion of government services in the province, however, depended on the relationship between the province and the federal government.[81]

That fed into a special committee for the Federal-Provincial Task Force on Forestry in 1972. Carefully summarizing the province's peculiar history, environmental and institutional, it documented profound changes. At the time of the Fire Patrol Act (1910), the railways caused more than 90 percent of all fires, protection was a confederation of convenience, and the firefighting services barely looked beyond those corridors of travel and the village peripheries. By 1970, the railways accounted for roughly 10 percent of all fires, the government Forest Service dominated fire control, and lightning fires in Labrador drove statistics and suppression costs. There was no extra-colonial presence when the Fire Patrol was inaugurated; now the CFS sponsored research, Parks Canada contributed to fire expertise, the CNR oversaw the railways, and federal funds were a necessary if not sufficient contribution to the enterprise. The pivot, however, was aircraft. Its "air service," while "extremely effective," was also "costly" and likely to escalate as retardants supplemented water. Whether those planes also kept down burned area was moot. Since waterbombing had become the treatment of choice, no conflagration had swept the island, although the committee qualified (and convoluted) that observation with a double negative, that it "should not be concluded that the situation would have been greatly different without them."[82]

The upshot was a reorganization that did "more to influence forest management" in Newfoundland than any other. The task force strengthened the hand of the government, which forced management plans from all the landowners, thus breaking down the strict segregation between private and public tenure. Smoothing the transition was a whopping Forestry Subsidiary Agreement with Ottawa. Yet there were oddities aplenty, not least the absence of a province-wide fire protection system under a unified command. The links between the companies and the Forest Service were unstable during big outbreaks; the province had not filled the vacuum left by the imploded NFPA, particularly its network of lookouts; its air fleet was unbalanced and aging; protection of private land was still unsure. Nonetheless, Newfoundland looked liked the other provinces. Fire control dominated its Forest Service, claiming 85 percent of its staff, and nearly all of its budget, while projected demands of the forest industry argued for a further expansion of that mission, an enlargement of authority as well as an amplification of funding. Its Labrador hinterlands required a better definition of purpose and practice, preferably with some system of priority zoning. It needed to address, as all Canada did, the problem of the big fire. The 1975 season, the "worst year on the Island since 1961 and for Labrador since 1967," led to an amended Forest Fire Act to empower the minister's reach to extend to all lands in the province, not simply crown lands. Meanwhile, spruce budworm raged, and "aerial protection" referred not simply to firefighting but also to chemical spraying.[83]

In all this, Newfoundland looked more like New Brunswick than the colony of Thomas Howe. Its system had plenty of kinks and imbalances, but so, each in its own way, did those of all the other provinces. Surveying the challenging 1979 season, the chair of the NFPA sadly confessed that, even with "all modern forest fire suppression aids," wildfires would still burn beyond control. It was time to reorganize, and time for another royal commission. Thus, all the parts came together, as well as they ever did, in 1981. The NFPA admitted that its methods no longer suited modern times. The Royal Commission on Forest Protection and Management argued that forestry required silviculture and a strategy for insects, not just fire control, that having finally built up a fire organization the province needed to move beyond it. (The department conceded that approximately 50 percent of disturbed forest land was "not regenerating satisfactorily."[84])

Yet the commission affirmed some founding verities. It concluded that forest fires had had "a dominating influence" on the geography and composition of the province's forests, save on the western island. Some effects had been devastating, sparking a downward spiral to barrens; some had been helpful, stimulating the spruce that made the pulp industry possible. Yet the defining fact remained that fire had always been there, sculpting institutions as fully as landscapes. In its efforts to link metropole and hinterland, and its struggle to forge institutions adequate for a boreal biota, Newfoundland's chronicle could stand as a cockeyed synecdoche for Canada's.

Internal Combustions

The era of the engine, too, had its characteristic fires, its prodigious paragons. Like earlier exemplary fires, they were large, damaging, sometimes lethal, and ever challenging. But what made them definitive was not their size and statistics but the ways in which they interacted with their sustaining society. They commanded attention; they focused minds, elicited commentaries, and rallied politics. As the decades rolled past, they morphed into new monsters. The conflagrations that savaged raw bush settlements at the beginning of the twentieth century had a different character from those that forced aerial evacuations of exurban enclaves at that century's end; the prism for interpreting those flames evolved with economies, sciences, and heavy technology; and the institutional machinery for responding to them went from fire ranging in canoes to waterbombers. But these were the fires that mattered, the fires that symbolize the rest.

"The Most Outstanding Problem"

The 1908 wave of fires rode the rails east from British Columbia to Ontario. As a powerful cold front rushed over the slashed and simmering landscape, it fanned embers into flames and flames into conflagrations, one after the other, incinerating along the way the odd adjacent town, from Fernie to Rainy River. Something similar characterizes the fire history of that time. For fifteen years, from 1908 to 1923, serial holocausts blasted settlements. Again Fernie makes a prologue for this dreadful narrative; Haileybury, Ontario, offers an epilogue. Between them lie Porcupine, New Liskeard, Charlton, Engelhart, Earlton, Milberta, Cochrane, Matheson, Porquis Junction, Timmins, and scores of lesser villages, an exceptional number clustered in the new-lands little clay belt of northern Ontario. This was the period when the full onslaught of Canadian industrialization slammed against the land: the constellation of bush fringe settlements bore the brunt. Usefully, this was also the era when Canadian conservation reached its high-water mark. For those who sought to plunder and those who wished to preserve, wildfires were, in the words of Ontario's fire marshal, the "most outstanding problem."[1]

While the flame-wracked towns were a disparate bunch, they were also variants on a theme. They were new settlements, hewn from the woods, linked by rail; for some, like Fernie, the rails were the source of fire as well as its corridor. But these conditions soon dampened through the steady discipline of the Railway Commission, such that, while numbers of starts remained high, their capacity to spread dwindled. For the rest, the rails shaped them indirectly by channelling the flow of newcomers and connecting towns to markets. The settlers bred fires – they had to. In the opening up of "New Ontario," as Fire Marshal E.P. Heaton declared, "the early settlers must meet conditions peculiar to the territory" and had "to clear his land by the only feasible method of fire without this necessary act uniting and combining into a destructive force."[2]

It was the sudden, violent mingling of two worlds that sparked and powered the burns. It was the geographical slamming together of slash, field, and woods, the temporal collision of two ways of living, each with its own peculiar fire practices. Wild bush presented one circumstance, agrarian landscape another, and it was the frontier of contact between that posed the danger. For rail towns such as Fernie, shuffling lumber from the hills to the depot, the life cycle was brief, and it was partly a matter of luck whether spark and wind caught the slash heaps (of which the wooden town was one). For communities like those around Lake Temiskaming, the period of transition was more prolonged. In 1900, a survey laid out the rail right-of-way; by 1908, the rails reached Cochrane; by 1922, Haileybury, the county seat, lay in ashes.

That the bad fires came serially was significant. One fire could be dismissed as a freak of nature, or a glitch in frontier settlement, or just bad luck; three could not. They occurred, moreover, against a backdrop of conservation enthusiasms, an era of environmental reforms unmatched until the 1990s. They commanded public attention, for these were not simply big fires, which Canada had in abundance, though remote like grizzlies, conflagrations known by their sun-discolouring palls. They incinerated towns, they killed, they brought the issue of fire – fire of all kinds – before the public. They could not be ignored. They also baffled the Department of Lands, Forests, and Mines because technically they stood outside its script. Reporting on the 1911 conflagration that obliterated Porcupine and Cochrane, the minister noted that "these fires were practically the only forest fires of any moment occurring last year." The fire-ranging service had done its job. The fatal failures, "still fresh in the public mind," had not been its doing.[3]

The 1911 fires involved a tangle of tiny towns, hastily erected along recent railways that linked mines with metropolises. The whole Témiscamingue region was in upheaval as loggers, miners, settlers, shopkeepers, and the catalytic rails chewed up large chunks of the clay belt. A spur rail line to Porcupine opened only on 7 June and was still crunching west in a rush, villages sprouting like berries on a steep vine; the region was a veritable sea of slash. Even the towns, from Timmins to Porquis Junction to Cochrane, were heaps of logs and planks, joined with corduroy roads and wooden sidewalks, barely distinguishable from the red slash that surrounded them. Inevitably open fires littered the landscape as well. When the weather turned brutally hot and dry, sparks and smouldering campfires flared and roamed over the countryside. Here and there crews mustered to drive them back into the woods. Then on 11 July a "gale" blew over the whole cluster. That afternoon a conflagration razed virtually all of them.[4]

A bad fire was neither unprecedented nor unexpected. Most of the town sites had burned, in part or in whole, before. Cochrane had turned to ash in August 1910. For nine-year-old John Campsall of Porcupine, this was the third such burn he had lived through. Most townsfolk had seen fires, or fought them, and many were doing so on the 11th. But the quickening wind caused the scattered flames to merge into a vast arc twenty miles long. Crown fires soared through jack pine and spruce, billowing into towering smoke clouds that showered sparks like a macabre fire thunderstorm. No one at first appreciated the immensity of the fire front or the punch it packed. Some people took the usual measures to protect themselves and their shops, gathering families and rain barrels. Some fled, seeking shelter across lakes or in them, or in mine reservoirs, or in the timbered mineshafts: walking, paddling, swimming, wading, riding rails to the next town. Some fought back. The mines, in particular, had fire brigades, pumps, hoses, and some sense of organized labour.[5]

The main drama centred on the West Dome mine in Porcupine. It had firefighting equipment and men, and the manager decided to make a stand. Smoke had been sighted about two miles distant at noon; the fire whistle sounded, pumps were started, hoses were strung out, and the ground was wetted. At 1 p.m., "a tornado like those passing over Kansas," its winds 80-100 miles per hour, struck, accompanied "by great clouds of flames." The gale blew down trees and buildings, and soon everything at all combustible was aflame. The assembled crews fled, save ten men who perished. Like so many embers caught in the vortex, stories swirled of those who lived, died, panicked, stood heroically against the flames, survived, and suffered. It does no disservice to note that the themes and even many of the particulars had become almost ritualistic over the past forty years since the inaugural holocaust of the era, the 1871 fires that savaged Wisconsin and even caught Chicago in their gyre. Some fifty-seven men survived by crowding into the West Dome mine's pond. Mine manager Bob Weiss gathered his wife, daughter, and seventeen miners to weather the storm in the West Dome mineshaft, his wife announcing, as they entered the bucket, "if we're going to die, we'll all die together." They did, asphyxiated, as fire gorged on the mine's timbers, sucking oxygen from the shaft. People burned, people choked, people drowned. Officially seventy-three people died in all.[6]

Yet, typically, too, a few events stood out. The accounts of those miraculously, capriciously spared, like the fleeing miner who wrenched his ankle, then lay down stoically to await his cremation, only to have the flames pass to both sides of him, leaving him untouched. The account of a boxcar of dynamite and blasting powder, 350 cases and 50 kegs in all, that blew a crater fifteen by forty-seven feet and caused waves on the lake to fibrillate, only to have arise from the cavity a spring that would supply water for survivors. And essentially, accounts of unselfish courage. Of all those narratives, the one that best survived was the saga of Edward Bell of South Porcupine.[7]

The story was simple enough. The fire "tornado" had struck without warning. At the "dwelling house" on the hill, the general manager's residence, nine persons had taken refuge, H.C. Meek (the manager) and his wife, their two children, four other male workers, and a sixty-six-year-old woman retiree, Mrs. Meek's mother. One man dashed out to the west before collapsing 200 feet away; another fled eastward to a pond but faltered and died a few days later. When the house caught fire, the remaining seven staggered to some half-full rain barrels. They were exhausted, nearly done in by the ordeal of fighting, unsuccessfully, to keep the fire from the house. The smoke and heat were terrible. They lay on the ground, "without any strength to reach up to the barrels for water to put out the showers of sparks, which continually dropped from the air." Manager Meek recalled, "all of us were more or less in an unconscious condition, and unable to do anything ourselves, or care for anything." The end could not be long in coming.[8]

Then, "from somewhere out of the smoke," like a mysterious folk hero of legend, appeared Edward Bell. He stood at the barrels, "with great courage and abnormal strength," and swatted out the sparks that threatened the prostrate party. Mrs. Meek's ankle was burning from a blazing scrap of birch bark, and her mother's dress was on fire. Bell quenched the flames, brushed away the firebrands, and splashed water. The party passed out. When they came to, after the conflagration had passed, "he was still there, doing what was possible for their comfort under the circumstances." An awed Meek noted that Bell could have passed the party by, seeking his own survival, but did not. The mine manager wrote to A.P. Turner, president of the Canadian Copper Company, to urge that Bell be awarded "in some way," such as a medal from the Carnegie Hero Fund. Turner passed the recommendation along to the national Parliament.[9]

The man who had come "out of the smoke and flames" and stood so majestically over the Meek party was identified variously as a mill worker and foreman carpenter, aged fifty or sixty, a resident of South Porcupine or Sudbury, as vague as the smoke was impenetrable. He was both particular and generic. Revealing, too, was his size. The Meeks were a tall family; the husband stood at six foot two, his wife at five foot eleven. Their looming rescuer was four foot eleven and 190 pounds, probably not very distinguishable from the rain barrels. But the Meeks lay flat, and Bell stood over them and must have seemed as tall as the uncut spruce, his stature determined by his soaring character and "great heart." Horrors like the Porcupine fire require heroes, and in Edward Bell, and in scores of others, the community found them.[10]

Investigating the fires, the Department of Lands, Forests, and Mines determined that it was "impossible to fix the responsibility upon any one in particular." The causes were generic, environmental, structural; such conflagrations were the cost of how Ontario chose to settle its hinterlands. The plight of the homeless aroused a storm of public sympathy, and funds to rebuild the towns, which quickly rose from the ash and became again "active business centres." They were scrub towns, which regrew like boreal woods or blueberries. The department noted further that the burned forests had consisted of jack pine and spruce and hence suffered little commercial loss.[11]

The reburn was the incubus of Ontario forestry, for one burn, even through slash, did not devastate a site; on the contrary, it often improved regeneration. It was the ghoulish cycle of reburning that stripped off the soil, gutted the seed trees, and ground down the capacity of a place to return to productivity. The ruinous reburn, however, seemingly did not apply to towns. They burned, and reburned, and as long as the mines produced precious metals they regrew, larger than before. The flush of relief money, like nutrients liberated in the ash, stimulated an immediate recovery. The cycle would continue until the mines played out and the clearings became permanent. The recurring settlement fire was simply a fact of frontier violence. In 1916, rogue fires returned to the clay belt. Their devastation traced with relentless fidelity the route of the Temiskaming and Northern Ontario Railway, which connected to the National Transcontinental Railway at Cochrane (they had linked only in 1908), which is to say, it tracked the industrial savagery that had settled and unsettled the region. And while deadly and thereby lamentable, the fires had paradoxically done in a matter of hours what would have taken small-farm pioneers years of grinding labour. The minister of lands, forests, and mines observed, without a whimper of irony, that "large sections of country in place have been almost completely denuded of timber and made ready for the plow."[12]

The 1916 outbreak had two parts, a serious but containable fire at Cochrane and a more immense and ferocious fire west of Lake Abitibi in which the rail town of Matheson, whose surroundings had three times in recent years partly burned, was obliterated. The Cochrane crisis blew up on 29 July from small settlers burning off their choppings. The town fire brigade had proved unable to extinguish the stubborn flames, and a southwesterly gale, quickening ahead of a front, pushed the fire through the centre of town and then to the limits beyond, where it died out. But the "Cochrane fire" was actually a complex, a matrix of burns, some of which remained small, a few of which galloped with the wind. The scattered settlements and broken forest both boosted and checked their spread. Along the transcontinental, serious fires ranged for 130 miles west. In particular, dry moss and slash left from harvesting pulpwood carried the fire "from point to point." Ten people died trying to scramble to a small lake. The flames devoured buildings, crops, culverts, corduroy roads, and small bridges, all the accoutrements of land conversion. Nonetheless, nature's labour by fast combustion substituted for the slow-combusting muscles of humans. The vast clearings that resulted proved subsequently "in many instances of very great assistance to the settlers."[13]

The second fire had Matheson as ground zero. The fire started everywhere and spread at will; kindlings flared "at almost every point of the compass." What the axe had spared fires and storms had levelled into windfalls around the dry swamps. "The flames swept from one farm clearing to another; fields of grain and swamps formed no barriers or protection. Township after township was burned over and even the virgin forest in places was left practically ready for the plow." Village after village, clearing after clearing, bridge after bridge fell to the flames throughout the watershed of the Abitibi River. The flames blew into Matheson like "a howling tornado"; the wood-framed village, despite broad streets, was aflame within a matter of minutes. Throughout the day, trains had hauled evacuees south, and those who understood the magnitude of the threat had sought shelter in the usual places. But the toll was staggering; on-the-scene estimates ran to 500 dead; official records tallied 224.[14]

The Northern Ontario Fire Relief Committee, with funds still remaining from the Porcupine fire, retooled. This time the province insisted it would co-ordinate the operation. The Temiskaming and Northern Ontario Railway operated under a provincial charter, and fire protection was thus its obligation. The rails ensured relatively prompt aid, once the line could be restored. Beyond that, the government insisted there was little it could do. It had helped the Northern Development Branch fight fire. "No further action on the part of the Government could have saved the situation." The settlers were determined to burn, for only a good fire could put land into agricultural production, and since the past few years had been too wet, they crowded that backlog into one season. Although their fires escaped, some good had yet come from them, for they boosted clearing by wiping out forests, greatly assisted drainage by stripping away the insulating moss, and generally improved the "climatic conditions of the country." The department noted gratuitously that the area burned was "much exaggerated" and that, apart from the "tremendous loss of life," the fire could not compare with the really large fires over the past fifty years, like those of 1864, 1871, 1877, 1891, 1896, or the 1894 fires in the Rainy River district that killed 140. Those lands had likewise been considered unfit for cultivation but now boasted "one of the best agricultural sections in Northern Ontario." The Abitibi pulpmill had survived. Much of the land regrew to blueberries, which were exported by the carload.[15]

A war-weary country, however, having endured the burning of the Parliament building barely six months earlier, displayed greater generosity. The outpouring of aid was spontaneous and immediate. The residents of the clay belt responded with a stoic alloy of resolve and fatalism. As it happened, they would need more of both. The great fires had not yet vanished.[16]

Fire and sword – conflagrations and the Great War – had stalled the settlement of the north. The government transferred its Colonization Branch out of the Department of Agriculture and into the Department of Lands, Forests, and Mines. After the war, assisted colonization, with recruiting in Britain, rebounded, while the economy picked up, keeping slash strewn across the countryside. In 1920, the department confessed

Conservation and conflagration, the cycle of great fires in New Ontario. *Top,* Porcupine fire, 1911. *Bottom,* aftermath at Haileybury, 1922.

that "the outstanding feature" of forest administration in Ontario, as elsewhere in eastern Canada, was the "inability to control the losses from forest fires." So overweening was the charge that all "other phases of administrative work are comparatively minor matters."[17]

The last of the Great Three struck on 4 October 1922. This time the fire overran the south clay belt, the rail lines west of Lake Temiskaming. The towns of Charlton, North Cobalt, and Haileybury vanished in the flames. Land clearing and town erecting made a dark dynamo, each worsening for a while the other. Incorporated in 1904, for example, Haileybury had burned in 1906 and burned again in 1911, before becoming the indelible symbol of the 1922 holocaust.

When those flames struck, Haileybury, with a population of 5,000, was still a boomtown, a self-proclaimed "millionaire town," with three movie theatres, a newspaper, a school of music, and an elevator-equipped hospital. Around its perimeter, settlers were actively expanding a thick fringe of fields and pastures, cutting, drying, and burning as circumstances allowed. At the beginning of October 1922, conditions were ideal, and in the words of Fire Marshal Heaton "the whole of the area over which the fire burned was literally and practically a hot bed of hundreds of different fires." Settlers were promiscuous with their burns; "everybody was doing it." The townsfolk, however, felt some satisfaction at the rising smoke, a symbol of progress in the north as smokestacks were in the urban south; they felt, too, some smugness in the thought that the expanding ring of cultivation provided an impregnable barrier to any onslaught of wildfire. But vast swaths of land to the south were not yet colonized. They, too, smouldered with fires, not "set out" but "purely accidental from the natural hazards invariably found in this class of territory," probably from the abandoned campfires of sportsmen and travellers. The upshot was that "certain townships were surrounded by fires," and it only required a wind "from any quarter" to drive the flames through field and street.[18]

On 4 October, those winds rose, first from the south and west in the sun-dried afternoon, then around 5 p.m., shifting to the north (the signature of a cold front) and stiffening to gale force, sent a blizzard of embers over clearings and roads, kindling outlying structures; with malicious irony, they included the rail station. The blustering winds then stampeded the flames "with irresistible fury" on a front two blocks wide the length of the town, from the railhead to the docks. Only when the fire struck the perimeter did the townsfolk take alarm, while the destruction of the rails severed their last, best hope of flight. They herded to the lake front. Save for one building, Haileybury was a smoking ruin. Forty-three people died.[19]

It had all happened within an afternoon. The winds ran before a front, and when the blitz had passed snow snuffed out the flames. Yet the scene was different, as though the three fires had tracked an evolution from raw mining camp to settled agricultural countryside. Of the burned area, some 90 percent had passed into private hands, thanks to the generous provisions of the Homestead Act and promotion by the province. "This fire," the Department of Lands and Forests concluded, "could scarcely be designated as a forest fire." Much of the land had been "cleared and partly under cultivation for over twenty years." The still incomplete conversion, however, had helped to kick the fire along, as pockets of forest and new slashings had kindled and catalyzed the fire front. When the smoke cleared, some eighteen townships had incinerated, approximately 6,000 people were homeless, and forty residents had died. The Northern Ontario Fire Relief Committee swung back into action, the legislature incorporating it outright. The department, considering the conflagration as a rural rather than a forest fire, deferred commentary to the provincial fire marshal.[20]

Haileybury was the last and worst of the era's holocausts. Afterward, fire protection strengthened around clusters of settlement; colonization ceased its furious pace; the frontier reached an equilibrium that neither side could breach. The problem fires migrated elsewhere.

"A Good Rain Is ... the Only Salvation"

The fires moved into a logging frontier no longer bonded to agricultural settlement. The Bloedel or Campbell River fire of 1938 is a grim paragon of such a burn, as is the Mississagi fire of 1948. The first was among a liberal sprinkling of large fires throughout the North American west, this one centred on Vancouver Island, where temperature and dryness reached record levels, needing only ignition and wind. The spark arrived on 5 July, emanating from a pile of cold-decked logs about 300 feet from a rail line. It was spotted around 4 p.m. and attacked vigorously on Bloedel, Stewart, and Welch timber berths. By 8 p.m. it had bumped up to five acres, and when a gusting wind struck it, embers carried the fire half a mile across Gosling Lake. For the next forty-three days, the Bloedel fire scoured out a blackened cavity in the Campbell River region.[21]

There were patches of private land, and even some agrarian communities (notably Mennonite) amid the scene, but mostly the fire ripped through crown land, and almost exclusively it burned on land owned, leased, shaped, or run by and for logging companies. The burn was a geography of logging, particularly of high-lead cutting with its extravagant debris fields. The fire commenced in cold-decked logs; it ripped through lands laden with slash or bristling with the young reproduction and struggling second growth that sprouted after cutting or burning; the firefights went from cold-deck to cold-deck, from slash field to slash field, along the roads and railways of logging companies, making stands around camps and communities that housed loggers. Of the 75,000 acres burned, some 80 were grazing or pasture land; 30,000 were logged and burned; 8,300 were immature timber; and 15,690 were merchantable timber. Logging companies furnished most of the labourers and equipment, leaving the Forestry Branch, while nominally in charge as a matter of public order, to supplement. Companies such as Bloedel could field forest workers, bulldozers, trucks, pumps, and hoses and lease airplanes and buses; the BC Forestry Branch could hire from the ranks of the unemployed in Vancouver and requisition assistance from the Royal Canadian Navy, which stationed two destroyers, the HMS *Fraser* and the HMS *St. Laurent,* by the Campbell River to assist.

The suppression buildup was rapid. The fire commanded almost 200 men on the first day; by day twelve, at 8,000 acres, it held 800; by day sixteen, swollen to 30,000 acres, some 1,200 firefighters were on the lines, along with all the mechanical supplements the island could muster; by day seventeen, blowing up to 50,000 acres, there were some 1,700 men, with more requisitioned and every able-bodied man not on the line being impressed into service; by day twenty-two, with the burn close to its maximum, the fire held 2,500 men, thirty pumps, sixty-seven miles of hose, twelve tractors, twelve bulldozers, railway trains, along with assorted aircraft for reconnaissance and transportation, and more were expected. On 17 July, the minister of lands ordered the lower two-thirds of Vancouver Island closed to logging and open fires. The next day, Black Friday, saw the fire's size jump by a third, amid rumours of sabotage and arson. As evacuations escalated, the two naval destroyers became a calming presence. By 25 July, the closure extended throughout the island and included travel. (The one exception was for tourists, who were also exempt from impressment as firefighters and assured that sport fishing was at its prime.) Collapse came when the winds stalled for four days; then came light rains and then a hard rain. By day thirty, 4 August, demobilization was under way. By day forty-three, 17 August, torrential rains knocked down the last embers, and the fire was officially declared out.

If far from world class, these were serious numbers, and, worse, the firefight occurred in the backyard of British Columbia's capital, amid some of the prime timber of North America. Economic damages were extensive.

Suppression costs exceeded $211,000, sixty million board feet of felled and bucked timber burned, along with 75,000 acres, fourteen million board feet of cold-decked timber, $75,000 worth of destroyed equipment, twenty bridges, and a hotel. Political costs were no less serious. Amid the Great Depression, the fire consumed an estimated "50,000 years worth of employment" and paradoxically made restrictions on high-lead logging and its flammable residue more difficult. As Chief Forester Manning remarked, it would not do to shut down this admittedly wasteful method if it meant companies could not operate at a profit, "thereby adding to our unemployment problem." Salvage logging helped to recover some costs and kept loggers in the woods but further swamped an already glutted market.[22]

"It all depends on the weather." That was the Forestry Branch's official comment on when the fire might be contained. So long as weather and fuels remained extreme, the fire remained uncontrollable. The winds were asynchronous – blustery at night, calm during the day, forcing backfires during evening and smothering the scene under a dense pall during daylight. But even when the winds were slight, if the slash and new growth were dense, fire defied attempts to quench it. There were two seemingly contradictory lessons for fire protection. One might stand in awe of what was accomplished amid this vast mobilization, the army of men and machines, and the power of mechanization. Even if in relentless retreat, the crews had surrendered lines reluctantly and re-established new ones with zest. As the superintendent of the Comox Logging and Railway Company crowed, "it would take nearly all the manpower in Canada to accomplish in one week by the old methods what we have done." Another perspective was that the larger forces behind the burn were too vast. Pumps could not counter droughts, dozers could not overcome slash, railways could not resist wind. As Manning himself confessed near the midpoint, "the only things that will help us now are rain and a favourable wind."[23]

As fire protection pushed beyond the fringe of settlement, that was the competition: the grand forces of nature against the burgeoning counterforces of industrial civilization. In 1938, nature still commanded the tide. But some fire officers were coming to believe that that might not always be the case.

The escalation of power and ambition broke against nature next on 25 May 1948 when carelessness, probably from a poacher, kindled a fire in the Mississagi Provincial Forest. The circumstances pumped that spark into an instant crown fire from a spell of intense, pre-greenup desiccation in mature boreal forest, overrun by a train of dry spring cold fronts, full of blustering, shifty winds and unstable air, an unholy mix of careless humanity and indifferent lightning. An aerial observer spotted the initial fire near Rocky Island Lake around 1 p.m.; a second reconnaissance at 3:20 p.m. reported the fire at 50 acres and at 4 p.m., 100 acres.[24]

The authorities immediately moved to match what promised to become a conflagration. By ten o'clock the next morning, the fire had roared to 2,000 acres and the following afternoon leaped over the Mississagi River in three places; 137 men and eleven pumps, hauled to the front lines by aircraft, confronted a fire of 7,000 acres and quickly accelerating. A light rain burned off like morning mist. By 28 May, the fire had consumed 29,000 acres despite a doubling of firefighters. A long-range firebrand started what became a separate fire. That was the rhythm: more fire, more firefighters. Then matters became complicated. A slash burn for road construction bolted out of control in the Chapleau District after crews left it unattended while they took lunch. On 5 June, a lightning bust kindled three fires that quickly ramped up. Fire suppression forces were split and split again as they rushed to make an initial attack on four new fires and hold the Mississagi and its spawn, all under a deepening pall that made aerial reconnaissance difficult and transportation dangerous. Any pretence at control disintegrated, however, while crews struggled to save lumber camps, tourist facilities, the Peshu Lake Ranger Station, and, not infrequently, themselves. A litany of near misses and desperate dives into lakes to avoid entrapment became part of the Mississagi legend.

It got worse again. The fast-spreading fires, already huge, threatened to merge. Fire officers pulled out crews between the Mississagi and Chapleau burns, allowing their merger to proceed, which occurred on 12 June. The effect probably tripled the overall size; the Mississagi-Chapleau fire was a monster, growing until 20 June, when weather began to abate. On 22 June, a good rain knocked the burn into patches of smouldering organic soil or "smudges." Crews then tackled the fire from the perimeter in, extinguishing smudges as they went. Officials declared the fire controlled on 23 July, and out on 31 July, although aerial surveillance persisted for another month.

When the last embers expired, the Mississagi totalled 323,520 acres, and the Chapleau 424,000 acres, a staggering complex of 747,520 acres, a fire of reference for the Ontario Department of Lands and Forests. Suppression costs tallied $240,048.73. Officers had drafted hundreds of men from wherever they could get them. They imported forty-three power pumps, twenty miles of hose, bulldozers, and a small fleet of aircraft, both departmental and commercial. The effort gave added meaning to the expression "campaign fire."

In the end, as officials freely admitted, rain, not dogged firefighting, had contained the fires. But not everyone accepted that this circumstance would always hold. It was the Mississagi-Chapleau burn that Alex Koroleff used to urge before the NRC a national commitment to aircraft. Others also thought that improved technology might tip the balance. Reviews pointed to the prospects for helicopters, more effective waterbombing, and even cloud seeding by dry ice (which was attempted several times on the fire). The most remarkable fact may be that Ontario even fought the fire at all or that, once having attacked and failed, it continued to pour men and machines into the fight. These were fires far removed from settlements, remote from the centres of commercial timber harvest, a region stricken with massive bug kill and blowdown, well beyond the field of vision of Toronto politicians. Although logging had already begun its assault, with some 50,000 acres of slash to feed the flames, and logging crews were the backbone of the workforce, the "lack of roads" was cited as a prime cause of the lack of suppression punch. Rather, the fire opened the land by encouraging salvage logging.

A "striking change" in the forest followed the burn. Mature white, red, and jack pine along with balsam fir and white spruce regenerated to vast stands of jack pine, white birch, and poplar. The Mississagi fire, one reviewer concluded twenty-eight years later, was "just nature's way to renew a forest that had reached too old an age." Whether the outcome was good or bad depended on "personal opinion." Indisputable was that "now we must manage the forest that [the Mississagi fire] gave." Also clear was a determination not to let commercial timber reach too old an age and to be ready for the next outburst of flame. Fifty years after the Bloedel fire, a historian noted that "only a trained eye" could detect what had happened. Where the fires persisted was in the institutional memory of agencies that would have to stand before the flames again and judge what to do based in part on what had happened before. Those scars healed more slowly.[25]

Red Lake #14: Ontario, 1980

The fire was large, but there were lots of big fires in 1980, and for that matter the preceding decade had witnessed a startling rise in big burns. Partly this was an outcome of better detection and a more aggressive forward strategy in fire control. But mostly it was the product of droughty weather and suitable woods, with the right mixture of ignitions. What shocked, however, was not the reality of large fires but the openly confessed inability of fire agencies to contain them. The long wave of burning reached a crescendo in 1980, although there were sharp tremors in 1979 and thunderous aftershocks in 1981 and for some places in 1982. The 1979 season was the fourth most severe on record; 1980 was the worst, period. Especially hard hit was the vast arc of boreal forest from northwestern Ontario to the Northwest Territories, so widely and intensively burned that it resembled a red Milky Way.[26]

When what became known as Red Lake #14 began on 20 May, the season in the northwestern region of Ontario was already well advanced. Early burns had broken out in April, followed by a blitz of railway fires and a rash of ignitions from people (forty-three) and lightning (seventy-five). By 12 May, a dozen large fires burned, some six classified as project fires. On the 20th, one of them, Kenora #23, broke loose, while the Red Lake #14 fire kindled in fresh slash from an unidentified human source. A review later declared that "the spread potential of the fire was unlimited." It was reported at 7:06 p.m. at 25 acres; attacked at 7:40 p.m., having doubled in size; and evaluated at 10 p.m., now at 3,000 acres. Its horizon indeed seemed unlimited.[27]

The fire spread at will, crossing Highway 105, burning out the hydro line, severing radio and television communications, threatening a cluster of small communities. By 6 a.m. on 22 May, the fire had bloated to 60,000 acres. Both waterbombing and backfiring had failed to slow it. Now, with the fire six to seven miles south of Red Lake, communities and officials began discussing the prospects for evacuation. At 6:30 a.m., the minister of natural resources declared an emergency, and the Provincial Fire Centre assessed which aircraft might be available since the fire had overrun the sole highway to the town. Two military C-130 Hercules and three commercial 748s were already removing residents from Fort Hope and could be redirected if called upon, and the Canadian Armed Forces had another four C-130s that could be dispatched. When the fire reached a mile from Red Lake, evacuations commenced at 7 p.m. on 22 May. Some 3,550 residents in all were flown to a reception centre at Winnipeg.[28]

By the 28th, the fire's perimeter had stabilized at 107,900 acres. Winds had weakened sufficiently for fire suppression to hold its lines, including one only three-quarters of a mile from Red Lake. The return of residents commenced on 31 May, and shortly afterward the Ministry of Northern Affairs took up claims for compensation. The rolling thunder that was the 1980 season continued. And while the stand at Red Lake was outwardly successful, the season impressed Ontario and the other savaged provinces that something had to change. Amid the embers, a handful of reviews scrutinized every aspect of the fire organization, a process that led, among other things, to the Ontario proposal that sparked CIFFC.[29]

The aperture began to close on a great era of provincial fire protection. The contrast between 1980 Red Lake and 1922 Haileybury is instructive. Both towns began as mining camps, and both at the times of the fires numbered about 5,000 inhabitants. But Haileybury looked back to an era of colonizing burns, for which the prescribed policy was to help settlers get it right, while Red Lake anticipated an age of amenity, in which residents had little enthusiasm for free-burning fire or smoke and policy was steadily committed to a program of suppression to the point, in principle, of fire's exclusion. In 1922, there was still ample room to expand the domain of fire control; in 1980, Ontario, and in time the other provinces, recognized that it had come "close to total commitment in fighting fires," not to mention its "heavy reliance" on crews and equipment from outside its own caches and the worrisome suggestion that the organization might have discovered that its "tremendous resources are being committed to hopeless causes." The future required something different.[30]

For more than a century, the political borders of province and territory had defined the geography of Canadian fire. They had fashioned the critical institutions, defined policy, shaped the image of fire; they did so in the name of economic development, to protect timber and agricultural colonization. Now, it appeared, fire management had to transcend those boundaries. Fire protection had to leap across provincial borders and even the national state; it had to support an increasingly service-oriented economy, amenity communities, and urban perceptions of the Canadian landscape; and, accepting that all fire might never in principle be controlled, or that, in principle, it might be unwise even to try, it had to accommodate a range of fire practices.

In the aftermath of the 1980 season, the Board of Review noted that "significantly there is no umbrella policy incorporating goals and objectives and enunciating what Ontario's fire management policy is or should be." It had always been enough to muster more men and machines and attack whatever fires one could reach. Efficiency had substituted for policy. While the board identified a positive "spirit" to the organization, despite its drubbing, a willingness "to face the fire challenges of the future with renewed vigour and confidence," the issues were grander, and they could not be staunched indefinitely by a national airtanker fleet or CIFFC. They, in truth, went beyond scrounging more waterbombers during the next crisis or restating a sole-source strategy of initial attack. The issue was more like that tiny smoke spotted beyond Red Lake whose opportunity to spread was almost unlimited.[31]

EPILOGUE

GREEN CANADA

Continental Drift and
Global Warming

A full century after the last spike, driven at Craigellachie, completed the Canadian Pacific Railway and bonded nationalism with industrialization, the Canadian experience had confirmed the transformative power of industrial combustion but left shaky the political welds of Confederation. In politics, economics, military and cultural concerns, and, yes, fire management, the old centre wobbled, and new alignments evolved; political Canada resembled less and less the deepening nationalism of the United States and more a European Union in reverse. Meanwhile, continentalism drifted onward, and the Earth warmed. Journalist Peter Newman intriguingly characterized the decade between 1985 and 1995 as a "revolution," the "greening of our discontent."[1]

By the new millennium, that greenery was everywhere but especially in Canada's lands and in its mind. The Canadian landscape continued to shed ice from its peaks and arctic seas; its forests spread north into tundra and south across grasslands. While logging and land clearing no longer had the proportional influence of old, the axe was as restless as ever, and softwood poured south despite episodic American tariffs. Yet the population, increasingly urban (or suburban or exurban), looked at their wooded estate in greener terms, as places for recreation and nature protection, and sought more pristine reserves amid crown lands. Officially Canada adopted the Brundtland Commission standard for protected lands and accepted sustainability as a national goal, particularly for its boundless forests. How such conventions translated into the provinces, which actually controlled the land, was problematic. But the direction was clear. The future promised an ever-greening Canada.

But a green Canada would also be a black Canada. There were fires aplenty, and more to come. There were wildfires deep in the boreal belt and along the urban fringe, controlled burns in national parks and experimental plots, and behind them both the big burn of industrial combustion, so pervasive as to be invisible, so powerful as to be nearly ineffable, and so implacable that it has begun to nudge and disrupt even climate, that archetypal shaper of the Canadian scene. These were not the fires for which Canada's fire agencies had been created. To address them would require a veritable reconfederation of Canadian institutions.

Fire Geography of Green Canada

There were some features that endured unchanged. The Shield remained as immutable as ever. Snows fell in the winter, lakes and rivers froze and flowed, the tread of the Hudson Bay High trailed drought and lightning. People slashed and shoved combustibles around and kindled fires. But the details were different, so much so that they apparently altered even the very axioms of Canadian fire. The escalation of fossil fuel burning refigured the fundamental calculus of combustion. It affected what burned or didn't burn; how fires were started and suppressed; how the Earth's fire agent, the one creature endowed to manage fire, lived and did in fact apply and withhold flame. The outcome could be so radically different that it hardly seemed the same landscape. It was as though fire geography had been recast into non-Euclidean geometry.

Fire's Reconfederation
The Quest for a National Model, Continued

The shock of the 1979-81 fires, and their aftertremors through 1983, broke the autarky of the provincial fire agencies. They could only cope if they shared, and they could only share through some national mechanism. Yet paradoxically, while they began to converge in policy and practice, the federal government continued to recede as an informing presence. Arguably, Washington had as much leverage as Ottawa. The federal institutions were lesser participants and greater sponsors but, with only minor land holdings, could not shape the agenda. This was, after all, the same decade that saw the repudiation of both the Meech Lake and the Charlottetown Accords, a widening gulf between what the elites believed wise and what the public wished. The outcome for fire management was a kind of reconfederation of Canadian institutions that left the provinces stronger than ever.

The choices for a national presence were several. There was a CIFFC model, a "Strategic Plan for the Renewal of Canadian Forest Fire Program," expressed as a five-point plan that clamoured for more waterbombers, more pumps, more money, a stronger suppression force, yet through an agency that was not itself an organ of the federal government. There was a CFS model, conveyed in a "Canadian Wildland Fire Strategy" that argued for expanding fire suppression into the format of all-hazard emergency services, proposed a mitigation model of presuppression, and begged for more instruments, more data, more money, and a more powerful research agenda that could transcend pumps, hoses, planes, and the often gearhead fantasies of provincial fire services. There was a Parks Canada model, encoded in Directive 2.4.4, which promoted more, not less, fire (more wildfires left to roam in the far bush, more kindled fires along borders and patches within nature preserves), a program made possible by the fact that the parks controlled an archipelago of lands. And there was what might be called a Confederation model, which asked for more of the present arrangement: more negotiations, more of Ottawa proposing and provinces disposing, more federal money and fewer federal constraints.

There had of course been another presence, the venerable Canadian Committee for Forest Fire Control (CCFFC) under the aegis of the National Research Council. But after CIFFC came on line, qualms surfaced about how the two related. Initially each insisted that it had a separate charter, even as CIFFC began to sponsor research into equipment technologies and other practical affairs. The Canadian Committee agreed that CIFFC should emphasize operational matters and the CCFFC, fire research. In 1984, the committee officially renamed itself the Canadian Committee for Forest Fire Management (CCFFM), aligning its title better with contemporary trends but not altering one iota the core issues.

The question of who would do what would not go away, yet money inevitably flowed to practice, to field applications as flames soared, and away from research, save that which directly assisted field operations. With a quickening tempo, the applied research into machinery, the exchange of information among the dozen Canadian fire institutions dedicated to fire, the nationalizing power that the CCFFM had brought to Canadian fire management shifted to CIFFC. This happened during mild fire years, the result of the steady gravitational power of doing compared with studying.

A record fire year in 1989 did nothing to alter that balance of power. A year later the NRC announced that it would suspend its associate committees, including that on fire. In 1993, the Canadian Committee sponsored its last gathering.[1]

Its dissolution stranded fire research. The other tasks of the committee could be scooped up by various institutions, notably CIFFC and the Canadian Council of Forest and Environment Ministers (CCFEM), formed in the aftermath of the 1980 fire season. But the CFS lost an essential anchor and drifted, whether out to sea or onto rocks was unclear. The NRC had granted a legitimacy to fire science as science and as applied knowledge vital to Canadian interests. Now only the CFS funded fire research, and within the CFS fire was withering as a proportion of effort; even those shattering fire years did not alter the equation. The provinces wanted waterbombers, not scientific studies, or would accede to science if it helped the dispatch and efficiency of those bombers. Still, the CCREM Forest Fire Task Force chartered after the big fires had prepared a study on fire science that called for a National Forest Fire Research Agency with a "funding formula similar" to that used for CIFFC. The problem was to mass sufficient science without concentrating it within an organ of the federal government. This would be Canada's equivalent to America's Joint Fire Science Program or Australia's Bushfire Cooperative Research Centre. In effect, the CIFFC model would be applied to research.[2]

This was a clear critique of how Canada treated the CFS. The subcommittee headed by I.R. Methven expressed outrage at the indifference to research shown by Canada overall and conveyed dismay at the failure of the CFS to address this. Canada's research effort was "totally inadequate, the funding bearing no relation to the importance of fire in the protection effort or to its importance in meeting Canada's forest management goals." The CFS had worsened this state of affairs by "regional fragmentation," by a "matrix management" that shorted a national focus, and by simple starvation. Over the past fifteen years, the CFS commitment to fire research had been reduced by 60 percent, leaving only twenty "active professionals," about half at Petawawa, to cover the six major research areas, namely, "fire behaviour, fire ecology, fire suppression, prescribed fire, fire economics, and fire management systems." University staffing was feeble. There was no alternative to the CFS, and it was almost no alternative at all. The agency needed a radical overhaul in "funding, structure, and focus."[3]

It did not come. While the dismay was general among the fire community, none of the agencies was willing to put real money – its own money

– into the effort, instead urging the federal government to do so. Ottawa had more intractable problems, however, from free-trade agreements to separatist movements, and although it funded another round of five-year agreements on "forest resource development" (i.e., replanting programs) with the provinces beginning in 1982, it did not have responsibility for those lands and woods and was not willing to invest in research. It had once again bailed out provinces that had cut beyond their capacity to replant, and when that particular crisis seemed to pass so did the political will to promulgate something like a Forest Sector Strategy. Untethered to the public estate, the CFS bounced about in the political winds, pooling its resources to what it understood to be its most vital organs, which did not include fire. Canada's exalted international standing in fire science flourished largely through the residual glamour of Van Wagner and the CFFDRS. Canada's fire science, like its military, lived off a past tradition that Canadians seemed unwilling to fund further.

Yet the work went on despite the erosion of staff and money and attention. The trauma, the forced merger that had transferred the FFRI to Petawawa, lingered. The institutional itinerancy of the CFS continued, along with its subsequent mendicancy. (With the Canada Forestry Act of 1989, it became a department until 1993, when it was inserted into Natural Resources Canada and retitled the Canadian Forest Service.) By 1994, a successor generation began redefining and enlarging the Wright tradition by publishing a Fire Behaviour Prediction System for the CFFDRS, while others worked on operations software, fire ecology, suppression technologies, and automated detection, an astonishing achievement for a dwindling staff that seemed at times on life support.

Then in 1995 Ottawa pulled the plug. The CFS budget collapsed from $221 million to $96 million; the Petawawa National Forestry Institute shut down, with some 40 percent of its staff offered reassignments and the rest declared redundant. Most of the fire personnel moved to the Northern Forestry Centre and the Great Lakes Forestry Centre, while a small handful remained at the Pacific Forestry Centre. This occurred even as record fires blasted the boreal forest in 1994 and 1995.[4]

Globally Canada remained a major presence in fire research. But that was largely because several rivals had suffered an even greater implosion, notably South Africa and especially the Soviet Union. Increasingly, however, Canadian fire science would exist to serve operations more closely, or to help promote Canadian fire suppression technologies for sale, or as part of multinational projects such as the International Crown Fire Modelling Experiment. The Canadian presence came less from direct sponsorship than by participation in FAO study tours, the North American Forestry Commission, and an inexhaustible stream of American-sponsored symposiums to which Canadians were always welcome. These relationships, especially with the United States, often allowed Canada to do internationally what it could not do internally. The one magnificent exception was the CFFDRS, which exported widely.

The CFS became an advisor to the federal government, a trusted if lesser vizier on topics such as global warming, model forests, sustainability, forest protection, and forest sector foreign aid, and because of that standing it became the voice of Canadian fire management before the world. Through the indefatigable Dennis Dubé and similar colleagues, it prompted and prodded Canadians to think smarter and more broadly about fire, and when the occasion came to write a general fire history, the CFS stepped in to sponsor it. After the 2003 and 2004 fire seasons, as it had done so often in the past, it spearheaded efforts to reform Canada's response to fire, trying to direct the thrust of new initiatives in ways that made intellectual sense, to float the discussion beyond the close-to-the-bone calculations of the provincial fire services, to make knowledge mean something more than data banks and nifty software programs for initial attack dispatching. The Canadian Wildland Fire Strategy (CWFS), announced in 2005, was the latest in a long chronicle of thoughtful submissions, a bid for Canadians to imagine fire as something more than simply a menace to fight with ever more powerful machines, that fire was in truth an inextricable part of the northern lands they inhabited, that it demanded more than brute force and deserved more than shudders.

Yet the CWFS was another volume in the library of shrewd initiatives that would take flight or fall depending on whether Ottawa could pay the provinces to do what it calculated was in the collective best interest. The emerging consensus, however, promised to cherry pick what the provinces most wanted – help with protecting exurban landscapes and federal subsidies – while shedding the larger research program that would sustain the CFS. The likely outcome was one that would bring the provinces the most revenue with the fewest controls. Still, this was progress, and while it might seem like a glass half empty in comparison with the mustered science of a powerful nation-state, it could well seem a glass half full in comparison with other political confederations such as the European Union. This was an old role and an honourable one, even if other institutions treated the CFS less as a counsellor than as a *consiglière*. Prestige followed power, and since 1930 the dominion had ceded that power to the provinces.

Part of the CFS's burden was its pedigree in forestry, which by the late 1970s seemed as empty of intellectual excitement and cultural ferment as it was full of pompous professionalism and machines. The real action lay not in attempts to revive silviculture as "new forestry" or "sustainable forestry" or similar noises that sought to drown the rattle of chain saws. The real future lay in nature protection.

The mantle of reform fell to Parks Canada. Its 1979 policy sparked a move to novel thinking and practice; the 1980 paper by Van Wagner and Methven clarified the intellectual arguments; the 1980 fires revealed the hard complexities of implementation. In 1985, the Alberta Forest Service listed the rudiments of fire protection that it believed were lacking in the mountain parks and that it assumed it would, in times of crisis, have to plug. The restatement of policy contained in Management Directive 2.4.4, issued January 1986, became the working text for what followed. It turned to advantage features of Parks Canada that had seemed liabilities. Its smallness allowed for innovation and nimbleness; its fragmented estate encouraged fire teams to assist throughout the system and promoted transfers among fire specialists, which spread ideas, techniques, and enthusiasm rapidly; its scientific foundations in wildlife rather than forestry made it simple to segue into concepts of ecological integrity. Equally, it belonged to CIFFC and hence submitted to national standards for training.[5]

Yet these devices were not what most distinguished the national parks. What made them distinctive was their determination to keep fire on the land rather than to abolish it. Policy recognized fire "as a natural process which under ideal circumstances will be allowed to run its course." Yet it also appreciated that "active management" might be necessary; management by fire suppression, management by manipulating fuels around towns and habitations, management by lighting fires. Here was prescribed burning tied not to logging but to the administration of preserved landscapes, burning that would emulate the historical conditions under which the biota had evolved with a goal to "duplicate nature as closely as possible." Thus, prescribed fire was preferable to other alternatives of vegetation management, and burning out was preferable to direct attack in suppression. In brief, the primary instrument for managing fire would be fire itself.[6]

This was an ambitious agenda. It demanded considerable administrative commitment to secure the funds, to train a cadre of fire experts, to sponsor the requisite research, to insist on compliance, and to defend the inevitable failures as the system learned how to do what it must. Moreover, controlled burning had to build upon fire control. The parks needed a fire protection force that they lacked, save in anomalous Wood Buffalo.

The fundamental mechanism would be individual park fire management plans, but recognizing that few parks were equipped to do that level of analysis, the 1986 directive (which was considered an "interim" measure) provided for a two-year exercise during which preliminary fire plans would "identify inadequacies" and thus detail how they could be eliminated. Accompanying (and informing) Directive 2.4.4 was a commissioned analysis of issues, and included with the directive was a generic fire management plan for use as a template. Headquarters believed the entire system could be brought to specifications within a decade.[7]

When the two years concluded, two reviews evaluated the results. For one, the CPS contracted with R/EMS Research, a consulting agency headed by Ian Methven, to study the dozen major "fire parks." Its conclusion: the park system had a long way to go. While there were "pockets of expertise" that were "second to none," there were pockets of incompetence, scepticism, and indifference. The overall project was as likely to crash as to thrive. The second survey, headed by Cliff White from Banff, summarized national meetings within the CPS in July 1988 and June 1989 that reviewed the program direction in the light of experience and the R/EMS critique and led to an extraordinary document titled "Keepers of the Flame: Implementing Fire Management in the Canadian Parks Service." It also concluded that few units had succeeded in integrating fire into management, and even those that had still lacked the capabilities a robust program demanded. Most parks remained at least ten years away from comprehensive plans.[8]

"Keepers" laid out options, costs, scenarios. Of various strategies to advance the agenda, it elected a commitment to "good fire control and a phased approach to fire use." The key was to upgrade all aspects of fire control capability as a basis to expand into new bureaucratic territory. The CPS had to be as good a fire organization as any in Canada, and it would have to excel at both lighting and fighting fires. All in all, "Keepers of the Flame" proposed a breathtaking vision that would succeed only if granted "senior management support" and "additional funding." Without that administrative stiffening, fire management was "poised for failure."[9]

Yet the timing was dreadful, as pressures of all sorts intensified: fiscal, philosophical, political, practical. The federal government was cutting budgets, not inflating them. Traditionally the CPS had relied on the CFS to provide some services. Now, not only was the CFS on life support but the CPS was requesting significant dollops of dollars. The situation was likely to worsen as the parks continued to move out of a recreational mode and into genuine nature protection, from Banff as a hot-springs resort to Banff as a genuine preserve for elk, wolves, grizzlies, and other fauna and flora both charismatic and mundane. So extensive had development become in the Bow Valley that Banff even faced potential delisting as a World Heritage Site. Staunching those trends and healing their scars required considerable political will, and there was no constituency for free-burning fire as there was for bighorn sheep.

Even the conceptual infrastructure became shaky, as one paper by Van Wagner seemingly undercut another. The seminal paper was the one co-authored by Van Wagner and Methven that had redefined fire management as vegetation management. Revisions to the National Parks Act in 1988 bolstered that premise by making "ecological integrity," not naturalness, wildness, or recreation, the primary goal of park management. This made a case for managerial activism. It encouraged, in particular, programs of prescribed fire. Banff began to burn. But critics immediately appealed to another Van Wagner study to forge a counterargument. In 1978 Van Wagner had characterized the chronicle of Canadian fire history as a negative exponential distribution of forest age classes, coded into an iconic graph. Critics interpreted that observation to mean that fire management was ineffective altogether. What mattered – *all* that mattered – was the gross ensembles of climate that drove big fires. Against such gargantuan forces humans were helpless; neither their fire fighting nor their fire lighting made the slightest difference; the best one could do was nothing. There was no justification for the CPS to engage in fire management.[10]

All these trends converged by the mid-1990s, and instead of reaching a climax, stalled. In 1995, Banff failed to do any burning at all. Then the logjam broke. Biodiversity offered an index of ecological integrity that could not be left to coarse climatic forces, an orientation that justified intervention and one subsequently sanctified by the Panel on the Ecological Integrity of Canada's National Parks. The larger delisting crisis at Banff passed; the parks got new funding and found new political energies; fire management matured. The CPS fielded fire command teams for suppression as good as any in Canada, while administrators set as an unofficial "soft management" goal that parks should ensure that 50 percent of their annual average burned area, as determined from fire history, did in fact burn. Although funding could not yet match that goal, the 2005 National Fire Management Strategy committed the country to a national target of 20 percent of historical annual area burned, an extraordinary reversal of the traditional thrust to suppress all and any fires. A Banff diaspora, the dispersion of its hardcore fire practitioners, carried the torch to park after park. The promised decade arrived, if a decade late.[11]

The Banff model, or vision, or ambition, or simple élan, however it might be seen, spread also to the provinces as they began converting crown land into parks and preserves. The inherited model that fire protection meant timber protection, and that efficiency was a sufficient index of success, would not serve such landscapes, and it was unlikely that forestry-based fire agencies could make the transition to a new order without help, not merely in practice but also in philosophy. Parks Canada promised to midwife that birthing. Here, rather than in model forests, lay perhaps the most exhilarating future for Canadian fire. While forestry services could add more mechanical muscle, mustering the forces of industrial combustion to counter those of free-burning fire, the parks were learning to turn those flames against themselves or to tame them to further the ends of biodiversity. Banff routinely kindled crown fires that ripped up the slopes of the Great Divide, an act and an idea far more audacious and powerful than any turbo-charger slapped onto a CL-215.

Still, in the early 1980s, an institutional void had emerged. The CFS was in free fall, the Canadian Committee was headed to a bureaucratic hospice, and Parks Canada was barely fire sentient. The Canadian Interagency Forest Fire Center filled that vacuum. It provided a national focus without imposing a national policy. As a practical matter, it took over the technical committees from the CCFFM, became the clearinghouse for the annual "exchange of information" among the various fire agencies, hosted conferences, oversaw the creation of manuals and guidelines, and moved a national airtanker fleet from mirage to reality. Above all, it *did*. It acted. That it moved along directions long familiar to fire bureaus made the provinces tolerant of its fledgling stage. It co-ordinated, took money from Ottawa, and left the power with the provinces. That its innovations were essentially calls for more of the same made its cause theirs. Eventually it convinced even sceptics such as Prince Edward Island and Quebec.

At its core were two complementary agreements: the Canadian Interagency Resources Sharing Agreement, which established a national pool of planes, equipment, and personnel, and the Canada-US Reciprocal Forest Fire Fighting Accord, which allowed CIFFC to co-ordinate with its American counterpart to do the same across the international border. The first serious trial came in 1988, when fires threatened to overwhelm northern Ontario, and the United States dispatched kits of pumps, hoses, and radios along with crews to assist. Later that year CIFFC reciprocated tenfold as it shipped south resources from British Columbia, Alberta, Saskatchewan, Manitoba, Ontario, Yukon, and the Northwest Territories to assist with the blowup at

Yellowstone National Park. The following year Canada experienced "an all time record of 12,118 forest fires and a record loss of over 7.5 million hectares of forested land." The costs reached what were for Canada a staggering $400 million. CIFFC was where the action was.[12]

Big fire years that had previously affected one or a handful of provinces now seemed to affect them all, as bad fires in one region prompted help from others, with CIFFC co-ordinating. In 1986 it passed a management audit by an outside consultant and boasted, with cause, about the extraordinary savings and efficiencies it was bringing to the Canadian fire community. Increasingly requests for international assistance, whether from the World Bank or the Canadian International Development Agency, were routed through CIFFC. When the Second International Wildland Fire Conference was held in Vancouver in 1997, CIFFC assisted and provided "seed money." Yet as nation-wide fire control became more effective, it also became more expensive. The 1998 season burned 63 percent as much area as the 1989 season but cost 185 percent more. That, too, was possible because interprovincial transfers were simple.[13]

By the onset of the new millennium, the promise glowed of still greater efficiencies through ever larger investments. All the fire institutions of Canada, it seemed, admitted that circumstances had changed and zealously prepared "strategic plans" for the future. In 1997, the CFS hosted a national workshop to review the "policy implications" of the evolving fire scene, both the apparent escalation in fires and the uncertainties about the agencies responsible for their management. In 2000, the United States, after a long span of media-saturated fire seasons, adopted a bold National Fire Plan to correct deficiencies. That spring CIFFC, under the energetic leadership of C. Allan Jeffrey, assembled the "directors of Canada's wildland fire agencies" to discuss and ultimately hammer out an analogous scheme to present to the CCFEM. The "Strategic Plan for the Renewal of the Canadian Forest Fire Program" identified eight areas for "immediate action," among them an equipment test facility, Native community protection, and upgrading of suppression infrastructure and aerial fleets. By September 2001, CIFFC was ready with a five-point plan of implementation.[14]

It was vintage Canadian fire politics. To its credit, the plan recognized that fire exclusion was neither economically nor ecologically justifiable. But the provincial fire services existed for fire protection; the emphasis, inevitably, was on more planes, more pumps, more applied knowledge, more money. The provinces approved of the scheme but unsurprisingly balked at the costs and proposed timetable. The likelihood was that

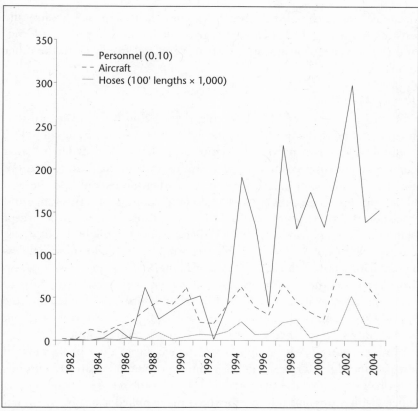

The CIFFC effect, the nationalization of fire protection through the interprovincial transfer of planes, pumps, and personnel.

each would pursue what it most wanted and ignore the rest, waiting for the federal government to make up the deficit. But Ottawa was more sensitized to human health care than to forest health. The political calculus of expenses and returns argued for at most a modest contribution, particularly as Canadair ceased production of CL-415s, which left CIFFC struggling between what it could implement and what it could initiate. In the end, it acted as a distributor and flywheel that helped to keep the pistons synchronized and the flow of power smooth. It could not say where to drive; it could only do what its members wanted. And what they wanted was help to go on doing what they had traditionally done.

By the time CIFFC matured, the institutional scene looked strikingly familiar, like an old building sandblasted clean and outfitted with modern wiring. The institutional cratons that defined the contours of Canadian fire remained unchanged. If there was renewal, it happened because the existing mountains had risen a bit higher, the basins dropped a bit lower, and the movement of bureaucratic water and soil from one to the other quickened.

Provincial Pastiche

The provinces guarded their prerogatives jealously, as ever wary of inequities among themselves as of federal encroachments. Each ran a close audit of what it gained from association and what it yielded. Their shared core strategy, suppression, drove them to institutional confederation, for, as with financing railways a century earlier, none could do the task alone. But just as the rails compelled them to adopt a collective gauge and common practices, so mechanized fire control meant they had to accept standards, or exchanges would fail. Otherwise, nozzles might not fit hoses, aircraft might not be able to land, imported crews could stand helpless before flames unlike those they knew at home, waiting, perhaps, to pump from lakes that didn't exist. Paradoxically, even as they rejected efforts to establish federal standards, their self-interests compelled them to converge quickly to a universal template. An ironist might note further that, in repudiating Ottawa, they might effectively be accepting Boise.

Still, the early 1980s brought a sea change. From their birth, most of the provincial fire services had been joined at the hip to forestry bureaus; most had developed in the early decades under the tenure of long-serving chiefs, with a singular mission to which they applied a steady, consistent vision, with success measured by efficiency in reducing area burned. The agencies might suffer from (what was to their minds) a deprivation of funds and staff, but they held an unwavering compass about where they wished to go and little internal dissent about how to get there. A pervasive professional identity as foresters gave them common cause and bound them to a global project. There were striking differences of course. Quebec had its *société,* Nova Scotia struggled to move beyond niche forestry amid farms and fishing villages, the prairie provinces had scrambled to make the transition from dominion forests to their own, the Northwest Territories hardly had a forestry presence at all. Yet the larger story is one of a general blueprint applied to local materials, substituting indigenous limestone or river cobbles for the prescribed bricks.

The old regimes typically persisted into the postwar period, during which they commenced a several-decade modernization as fresh money and hardware and bold ambitions overhauled them all. Yet even as they lengthened their stride, as aircraft and staffing allowed them to press fires harder, they began to draw inward, like a gaseous red giant starting to collapse. The global project that had cast forestry bureaus to every colony now went into reverse. The lands they oversaw, the goals they proclaimed, the methods by which they sought to install those ends, all were challenged. Once the vanguard of international conservation, state-sponsored forestry now found itself in forced retreat.

The reasons were many and varied, no less within Canada than elsewhere. Perhaps most fundamentally the political economy underwriting the enterprise was changing. Population was becoming urban, business was driven more to services than to commodities, and cultural preferences no longer saw the burnt stump as a sign of social progress. By the 1980s, even industrial Ontario found that tourism had become its largest source of wealth. The shift struck particularly those provinces that had struggled, after sometimes mammoth investments, to create a forest products economy. There were now groups eager to see crown lands put to different purposes, or at least to have logging done differently, and green certification was even forcing a silvicultural monolith such as Sweden to incorporate some prescribed fire. So even as state-sponsored forestry appeared to triumph, it was dying on its feet. As an apt symbol of the transformation, the lengthy narratives that had traditionally sustained the annual reports of provincial forest departments shrank to business-school snippets with little more than mission statements, costs and "investments" – the lineaments, at once timorous and blatant, of a shareholders' report.

Other issues affected land ownership, or how lands were governed or to what purpose, and hence affected traditional institutions and policies. The federal government, for example, committed Canada to the ambitions of the Brundtland report, which recommended that 12 percent of a national land base have formal protection. At the time of accession, Canada had roughly a third of that, of which a good fraction was in rock and stone, scenic attractions rather than ecological preserves. A lot of professional angst was to follow, for foresters considered lands under their administration as already "protected," along with hard political controversies since the provinces controlled resources other than the national parks. Equally at issue were First Nations land claims, particularly where the colonizing powers had not bothered with treaties. Meanwhile, devolution transferred responsibility for natural resources to the Northwest Territories in 1986 and the Yukon in 2004. Paradoxically, as a national system built out, it became more secure in its means and less stable in its ends.

Beginning in the 1960s, quickening in the 1980s, the tremors had begun to shake the agencies into new patterns or, at least initially, new titles. Reorganizing and rechartering became chronic, and in the worst cases left agencies shell shocked, ambiguous in name, uncertain in tasks, and confident only that fire still needed control. Out of this political jostling, two trends emerged. One isolated fire agencies within provincial departments, and the other integrated them nationally. Increasingly, they became fire services, disconnected from general land management, even as they found ways to join together as a guild among themselves on a national level.

Such matters had not been an issue previously because everyone assumed that fire protection was the foundation for land management and that removing fire suppression would cause the institutional plywood to delaminate. But new public enthusiasms pushed agency attention away from firefighting, which was left to continue its assigned task, one that could not be reorganized or legislated away since fires never ceased. Logging could be slowed or stopped, replanting might be scuppered or boosted, recreational facilities could be scattered like seed, but the fires would come regardless. Whatever else a department of resources, land, tourism, sustainability, or the environment might or might not do, it had to manage fire, and as the mission of land agencies became spongier, their fire assignments hardened. Fire protection became a stand-alone service, like road building or garbage collection, a module that could fit into any bureaucratic flowchart. The larger matrix and mission might change; the fires would still be fought. Fire specialists became a guild with their own training, skills, lore, and values, such that, while forestry still claimed fire for itself, the guild no longer required forestry.

Fire ceased to be a job done by fire specialists as a seasonal afterthought and became their core identity. They were more likely to look to other members of the fire guild than to the civil servants of unstable provincial politics. This trend was strengthened by the national sharing of resources such as an airtanker fleet. The instincts of the fire guild looked to CIFFC (or NIFC) for guidance as much as to their home provinces. They and their equipment had become mobile, a service for hire. In extreme forms such as that which emerged in British Columbia around 2000, the government could contemplate outright privatization. It might contract for fire crews as it did for airtankers; it could outsource the entire service in the spirit that it could back-office paperwork. The 2003 and 2004 fires broke that trend, ensuring that fire protection became a matter of public safety that no provincial politician could afford to nudge aside in the name of greater efficiencies. But re-embedding fire protection within the civil service was not the same as entwining it within land management. Rather, integration to achieve access to more pumps might, in fact, work against integration into genuine land stewardship.

The years that followed CIFFC's founding showed an astonishing ferment among the provinces. The turmoil was weaker in the Maritimes, where there was less crown land or where fire agencies had emerged after long decades of painful debate over their purpose and reach, where the provinces had struggled to patch together coherent institutions. Those places had in a sense undergone a political vaccination. It was worse in the western provinces, particularly where both an apparatus and a rationale had been inherited from the DFB. There the controversies struck hard, like measles deferred until adulthood. It was as though the old dialectics had passed through a century's looking glass and been reversed. Yet an answer, if any, would probably come out of the provinces, which soon bubbled and fizzed with management studies, another attempt to render nature's economy more entrepreneurial, hinting that the day was fast approaching when fire might claim its MBAs.

Beyond Confederation

Canada's fire interests went beyond Confederation. This should surprise no one. Canada had always been a global nation. It was discovered, explored, and settled within a context of European geopolitics, and its extraction economy depended on international commerce in furs, fish, and forests. With so much to burn, Canada also entered the global economy of combustion.

In the first half of the twentieth century, Canada was moored to two offshore piers. One was the British empire. Canada became Britain's prime woodlot, and in 1923 the host for the second British Empire Forestry Conference. Although India remained the hearth of imperial forestry and the model for African and Australian colonies, it began to recede, particularly after the Great War. Closer Canada, not Greater India, would have to supply Britain's woods; Canada's fire scene mattered more than Uttar Pradesh's. But India and its African analogues had never mattered much to Canada; the boreal forest was too different in its fire ecology, human biology, and politics. Besides, Canada was in near orbit with the United States. That country, not empire forestry, had trained its foresters, become its principal market for sawtimber and pulp, and shaped the dominion's attempts at a national network of forest reserves. Canada was vital to the empire for its exported wood but not for its fire expertise. The United States was indispensable to Canada for both its market and its fire philosophy. Canada found it convenient, where possible, to play one off against the other.

The postwar era prompted a realignment. Even as Britain hosted the 1947 conference, India became independent, the empire morphed into a commonwealth, and the major fire powers shifted to the Big Four: America, Australia, Canada, and the USSR, with South Africa a secondary contributor in the arena of fire ecology. In 1952, Canada again hosted the gathering, a last hurrah. Replacing the empire was the United Nations, notably the Food and Agriculture Organization (FAO), and Canada's foreign assistance programs. Through them, Canada began to project its influence in the global imperium of fire. Yet even here it could not avoid the politics of Confederation or the geopolitics of proximity to the United States. Except for matters of research, it had to enlist the provinces to staff overseas projects, and it found itself in ever-closer bonds to the Americans, even through the medium of international organs. Paradoxically it benefited from anti-Americanism (its own and others') by providing a conduit to "North American" technology without the onus or opprobrium of dealing with America directly.

Some of the exchanges, study tours, and contract efforts were in lands that had merit both diplomatically and environmentally. Thus, External Affairs arranged for fire study tours of the USSR in 1968 and 1985 and China in 1982. The China contact evolved into a major technology transfer program, staffed by fire specialists from Ontario, which put Canadian observers on the scene of the 1987 Black Dragon fire that swept Manchuria's Hinggan Forest. At the request of the World Bank, Canada, along with the United States, dispatched a team of observers to Belarus in 1993. Later the bank requisitioned a study to help it establish "purchasing standards" for fire equipment.[15]

But assistance soon leaped beyond the boreal belt. In 1973, the Canadian International Development Agency (CIDA) responded to a plea from Colombia for aid and dispatched a fire team from Alberta. From 1978 to 1982, New Brunswick sent fire specialists to Honduras under CIDA auspices. In 1988, first Peru and then Brazil requested aid through the Canadian embassies; CIFFC dispatched teams from British Columbia to the former and from Quebec to the latter. In 1992, Indonesia asked for aid in establishing fire programs, which CIDA agreed to support, first with a team from Saskatchewan, then with training cadres from Alberta, British Columbia, Saskatchewan, and Parks Canada, supported by research on fire danger rating by the CFS. In 1994, an emergency request came from Ecuador that sent specialists from British Columbia and Saskatchewan hurrying to fires in the Galapagos. As part of its Southern Cone Project, CIDA sponsored a fire assistance mission to Argentina, Chile, and Uruguay · in 1996. And with the CANUS Treaty in place, Canadian fire forces began "exporting," in the revealing language of their dispatchers, to the United States, spectacularly so during the 2000 blowout.[16]

Programs went beyond simple hotspotting by consultancies, the most prominent medium being the FAO, which expanded the fire study tours that had begun in 1952 between the United States and Australia to include all of North America. And in 1961, it established the North American Forestry Commission (NAFC) as part of a global network of regional bodies. With American prodding, the NAFC adopted a Forest Fire Control Working Group that soon became its most active component. The fire guild again found that it had more in common with colleagues across the border than with compatriots in other specialties. Fire research, in particular, often struggled to find a niche even in forestry organizations such as the Society of American Foresters or the International Union of Forest Research Organizations.[17]

The complicating factor for Canada was the ever-vexing question of just which Canadian institution should speak for the country. While the CFS might have assumed the mantle, the provinces insisted that they did the heavy lifting and deserved standing. In fact, there were murmurs that they should serve in the rotating chair, thus claiming for each province a status equivalent to Mexico and the United States. Eventually the CFS had to seek clarification from the Department of External Affairs, which replied that it had "no objection in principle," it being official policy to include "where possible" provincial officials in Canadian delegations to international conferences. The issue was whether the provinces had "demonstrable interest" in the topic. L.H. Amyhot, director of the Federal-Provincial Co-Ordination Division, thought that perhaps the provinces were "satisfied" with present arrangements. What decided the matter was that the CFS could obtain funding to participate in overseas conferences; the provinces, to the chagrin of the most ardent advocates, could not.[18]

Programs in fire science were simpler. Here Canada spoke with one voice, that of the CFS, whose hard-wrought experience negotiating with the provinces tempered it into an ideal partner for international consortiums. Canadian scientists became active in the International Geosphere-Biosphere Programme (IGBP) agenda in Global Change, especially atmospheric chemistry with its interest in emissions from biomass burning. They were prominent in climate change and carbon cycling research that suggested the boreal realms of the Earth would feel the earliest destabilizations from global warming. They helped to design and execute large experimental burns in Siberia and Alaska as well as the Northwest Territories. They exported the CFFDRS to an increasing number of countries that liked its pragmatic blend of field and lab, even as they joined efforts to abstract more generic models by close work with American and Australian colleagues under a tripartite Agreement on Wildland Fire Science Research. They hosted the spectacular 1995-2001 International Crown Fire Modelling Experiment. Only Australia's Project Vesta approximated this scale of high-intensity experimental fire, but the CFS, long accustomed to co-operative endeavours, was able to bring the United States, Russia, and other countries into the matrix. And the CFS was everywhere at international fire conferences. At such settings, Canadian fire researchers discovered a welcome, a recognition, and a stability unlike the ceaseless sparring and turmoil of their quotidian bureaucratic existence.

Nonetheless, the United States dominated its foreign relations and at all levels. Save for Prince Edward Island, Newfoundland, and Nunavut, every province or territory belonged to some kind of border agreement or fire council talk-shop. The Northeastern Forest Fire Protection Compact, a regional consortium capable of fighting fire as well as exchanging information about it, embraced Nova Scotia, New Brunswick, and Quebec. The Great Lakes Forest Fire Compact included Manitoba and Ontario. The Interior West Fire Council, a forum that amalgamated the Interior and Rocky Mountain Fire Councils in 1988, reached across the border to Alberta, Saskatchewan, and the Northwest Territories. The Northwest Wildland Fire Protection Compact extended to British Columbia and the Yukon (which had a separate agreement with Alaska). Transcending all these was the Canadian-US Accord governing mutual aid through NIFC and CIFFC. But the practical contacts were far denser because of the annual cavalcade of fire conferences that, while largely staged in the United States, had ample Canadian representatives. It would be no exaggeration to speak of a NAFTA for fire.[19]

Canada's international status was curious, and as with so many things Canadian the United States was a prominent reason. Its fire alliance with America gave Canada far greater leverage than it could have had on its own, a collective "North American" presence unparalleled elsewhere. Without the Americans, Canadian fire science would be on par with that of South Africa and its fire technology on a developmental level with that of Russia. Yet its ability to distance itself from the United States gave it access denied to the Americans. It was in many respects an ideal formula.

Unclear, however, was the extent to which the Canadian public would support fire institutions to sustain the alliance. Other than the immediate protection of life and property, Canadians had never invested seriously in fire's management; fire control had been an insurance premium, grudgingly paid. There was no sense that fire might bond to something like Canadian nationalism, that fire's management was a cause to which Canadians might devote special enthusiasms.

There is almost no Canadian art of fire, no poems, no paintings of flames, few novels. The firefight is not, as it is in Australia and America, a set-piece of national literature. Rather, as a new millennium dawned, the Canadian public was far more exercised about the state of public health care, in which they differed from Americans, than on fire in unhealthy public forests, on which they had much in common. It was entirely possible that the Canadian citizenry would choose to pull back from fire administration, as it had from its military, and let fire's science become ceremonial and fire's management merge into a North American protectorate.

Yet if the level of its global involvement was wobbly, the character of its contributions was predictable. Canada did best internationally what it did best at home, excelling at technology and negotiated politics. But its success at both came because it overlooked the cultural fundamentals. It could make efficiency of operation its measure of achievement because it needed only to find better means – superior machines, sharper methods of dispatching – to advance clear-cut ends, notably suppression or suppression ranked by economic priorities. When called upon to probe deeper, it struggled. Its experience in Confederation had honed its skills at compromising, at keeping the secessionist and seemingly incompatible parts together, at tolerating interminable discourses and rhetorical blather. But it achieved that metastable state by largely ignoring the core disputes on philosophy, social values, and identity politics that were intractable to technology and science and whose pressures caused the fissures. In disseminating a Canadian model, the Canadian fire community exported techniques and tools, literally equipment and instructions on how to use it. That rendered Canadian products highly exportable, ready to fit into any number of systems.

The world, however, needed to know how to establish ends as well as how to outfit means. It needed precisely that discourse about essentials. Which policies were suitable? Which institutions? What sort of knowledge was required? From what species of scholarship? Not the *hows* but the *whys*. On this, with the exception of its national parks, Canadian fire authorities stood mute and left the metaphysics to the Americans while they operated

(and sold) their pumps. All of which made Canada a strong partner but a
weak leader, and to that extent Canadian fire was unable to move beyond
Confederation.

Settlement Symmetries: Then and Now

A century after Ontario fielded its first fire rangers, Canada's institutions
were still wrestling with settlers and protecting forests. But the scene
had inverted, as though having passed through a historical looking glass.
Institutions created for one suite of problems and purposes had to cope
with quite another suite.

Instead of agricultural colonizers, urbanites were sprawling over the
landscape. They pushed the suburbs of cities ever deeper into what had
been fields and forests; they flung exurbs into mountain valleys and
bush lakeshores. A century after the Riel rebellions, Métis and Native
communities, instead of withering, began to propagate and dapple the
boreal belt with villages. Such communities were as much at risk as the
often feckless farmers of the old frontier. From 1986 to 2003, every province
save the territory of Nunavut had towns threatened by wildfire, with the
tempo of urbanization and burning both quickening. Some events such
as Chisholm, Alberta, in 2001 and Kelowna, British Columbia, in 2003
grabbed national attention, the twenty-first century's echo of Matheson
and Haileybury. The prospects argued for more of the same: more urban
sprawl and splash, more savage fires on the fringe, more expansive fire
protectorates around them.[20]

The old settlements had spawned fires because agriculturalists chewed
up woods and scattered slash, and then torched the residue, deliberately
and accidentally. The early cabins were wooden, often stacked logs chinked
with moss, an ideal fuel bed. Firefighting forces were few; defence often
meant backfires along tracks or fence lines. Eventually widening fields,
denser roads, and mature houses banished fire to the backcountry. The
new settlements attracted fires precisely because urbanites declined to clear
around their plots, often allowing a thickening bush to crowd their lots and
press against their houses, and while rarely using fire their prohibition paradoxically meant that nothing culled the combustibles and left (especially)
exurban enclaves vulnerable to feral fire when, inevitably, it arrived. Fire
control was industrialized. It was mechanized, sophisticated, and powerful,
and hoarded as though it were a monopoly of the state. Local residents had
no role; the official response was to evacuate whole communities.

Still, there was a countervailing determination to "empower" communities at risk and thus to make them accountable for reducing the hazards.

The strategy (dubbed FireSmart) promised to be both cheaper and less politically contentious and became that part of the CFS Canadian Wildland Fire Strategy that the provinces were willing to accept and Ottawa to finance. Eerily it echoed the scene from the era of agrarian colonization and suggested analogous remedies in the form of some gross zoning to segregate the worst clashings and active assistance to help the settlers do what was necessary. Exhortations, edicts, threats – none had helped to quell the settler slash issue. What dampened it was a system of permits that brought rangers personally to the scene to assist. The social forces driving these colonizing waves were (and are) well beyond the provenance of fire agencies. Raging against them or denouncing the settlers does not the slightest good. What matters now (as then) is tangible help.

More dramatic, however, was the steady proliferation of nature preserves of one sort or another. Protecting biotas imposed very different goals and protocols than protecting timber berths. Certainly fire exclusion could no longer serve as a goal, however utopian, for preventing bad fires was only half the equation. It was equally necessary to promote good ones, and to establish criteria for judging which fires were good and which bad, and whether prescribed fires had performed their task or not. With timber berths, there were clear economic measures and a demonstrable return on investment. With nature protection, however, there was neither. The charge was cultural rather than commercial, a duty of care. There might be financial returns from recreation and a cost-accounting for "ecological services," but they did not enter into the budgetary ledgers of fire institutions. Certainly they did not tally in the reckonings of the provinces, even as they began, whether ardently or reluctantly, under pressure from urban constituencies, to set larger fractions of crown land aside as protected nature.

Only Parks Canada had made that transition, and while inspirational its example testified to a hard slog of policy, practice, and bureaucratic manoeuvring. Almost twenty years passed from the enactment of policy in 1979 to a self-sustaining suite of programs on the ground. Concepts such as ecological integrity could make budget claims, through sponsored research, as great as that an earlier age had consumed as pumps and hoses. Within limits, knowledge was indeed power, and information could replace horsepower by determining where (and whether) to place those pumps. But a service economy of fire substituted one form of intensive administration for another; its costs could be substantial. The country struggled to cover the expenses of Parks Canada. How the provinces would pay for internal equivalents was not at all obvious.

Nor was it apparent how fire agencies, grown mighty in the context against wildfire, could be retrofitted to accommodate the new order. Most had spent the past two decades torqued, hammered, and warped as the provinces struggled to fit the square-peg bureaus that housed them into the round-hole tasks the public sought. By the early twenty-first century, it seemed likely that fire agencies would trend toward all-hazard emergency services, organized strategically around principles of risk management, a track well rutted by urban fire services. Yet while this was a proven means to cope with fires society didn't want, the strategy had never demonstrated that it could promote those fires society did want.

Integration with land management of the sort required for nature preserves would be difficult, expensive, controversial. America's example was here ambiguous because the agencies that transformed themselves were federal, and American states, with few exceptions, had not undergone such a metamorphosis, and would not. The one prediction possible was that the provinces could not, for long, continue to reclassify crown land into preserves without devising a program of active management to cope with fire. Those lands could not be left alone; suppression was insufficient; prescribed fire would prove tricky and more costly than the public was likely to wish or tolerate. There might be ways to apply FireSmart concepts to landscapes, although it was doubtful that Canadians would accept an extension of their modified welfare state to their landed estates.[21]

Counting Carbon

What linked all these trends was a new chain of combustion. Over and again, in place after place, the confined combustion of fossil biomass was supplementing the open burning of grass, leaves, woods, and peat. To most observers, that connection seemed unobvious, if not impertinent, and to most fire scientists the dynamic weld seemed irrelevant. What they failed to appreciate was the power of humanity as a fire agent, a fire broker, direct and indirect, whose control over burning was a power to restructure the planet. Startlingly, its fire practices had begun to perturb even the cadences of climate that had for so long epitomized those natural forces beyond humanity's reach.

In this new economy of combustion, carbon was fast becoming the common currency, and Canada rose to a prominence equivalent to that it earned for free-burning fires. The dual realms of combustion etched a new geography of burning on Canada and created an alternative dynamic of fire ecology, as sources and sinks connected in novel ways. By scale, only Russia rivalled Canada's standing as a power in both realms, for the boreal biota was the largest living reservoir of stored carbon on earth. Begin with free-burning fires. From 1959 to 1999, these burned an average of 2 million hectares per year, although varying from 300,000 to 7.5 million hectares. The average direct quantity of emission was 27±6 teragrams (Tg) of carbon per year or roughly 18 percent of the current carbon dioxide emissions from the "Canadian energy sector." In reality, the carbon release was greater because postfire decomposition added to the load, and the gross impact was worsened because the burn, at least temporarily, reduced the forest sink available to soak up or store carbon. A significant fraction consisted not of trees but of peat, the stockpiled organics cached in soils. Smoke from large fires affected air quality in the United States, nicely reversing Canadian complaints about acid deposition from American coal-fired power plants.[22]

Canada boasted an equivalent stature as a source and sink for fossil biomass, becoming one of the most energy-intensive countries in the world – this despite an enormous investment in hydropower (56 percent of national electrical power). Its energy intensity exceeded that of Germany by a factor of two and of the United States by a third. By 2001, its per capita energy consumption was 18 percent greater than America's. That consumption helped it claim global leadership in carbon emissions, spewing some 156.2 million metric tonnes annually. Yet it produced more than it consumed and stood as the fifth greatest producer of energy in the world. It possessed enormous crude oil reserves (180 billion barrels), including tar sands; it had proven reserves of natural gas totalling 60.1 trillion cubic feet; it held reserves of coal on the order of 7.2 billion short tons. The rates of both production and consumption were increasing. In the decade following 1990, Canada boosted its use of crude oil by 20 percent, of natural gas by 28 percent, and of coal by 23 percent. By 2001, it ranked eighth in the world for carbon emissions from fossil fuels (a non-trivial fraction was due simply to the production of such fuels themselves, especially oil tars). In justifying itself to a world concerned about greenhouse gas emissions and global warming, Canada could shrug that it was merely passing many of these fuels along to the United States as the end user and that its inexhaustible forests constituted a carbon sponge that yielded a positive carbon cost accounting of planetary significance. For the public, the combustion crisis of 1979-81 was an OPEC oil embargo, not flames in the Manitoba backcountry.[23]

Carbon counting showed how radically the geography of Canadian burning had changed. The old geography of open fire had resided mostly on

the prairies and boreal belt and across the Cordillera. Through technological substitution and outright suppression, some of those landscapes no
longer held flame, and others had less flame or flame in very different arrangements. The new geography of industrial combustion redesigned that
pyric cartography to highlight Alberta, Nova Scotia, the offshore banks
of Newfoundland, and patches of coal in Yukon and the Northwest Territories. Sources centred on Alberta (to produce the stuff) and sinks on
Ontario, for transportation and manufacturing, with secondary arenas in
Quebec and British Columbia around major metropolitan clusters. Only
in Alberta did the dual geographies overlap. Caches of buried hydrocarbons deformed the landscape of Canadian combustion as massive bodies
did interstellar space.

But while the two realms competed, they also complemented one another in a dark cycle by which each stimulated the other, with the atmosphere as a shared medium. Between 1990 and 2000, six fire seasons
exceeded in carbon emissions the output from fossil fuels; not until 1987
did the rise in industrial combustion break beyond the most extreme fire
season. Those fires, of course, burst forth and crashed with enormous variability from year to year. In 1978, emissions amounted to 3 Tg carbon,
while in 1989 they rose to 115 Tg. Industrial fire burned without such wild
swings. It burned remorselessly through winter and summer, decade after
decade. It might wobble for a year or two, even dip (as it did in the worst
energy crunch and recession), but the curve moved implacably upward
and left the forest fire component as a shrinking if still substantial fraction.
Similarly, industrial combustion put nothing back into the Earth. Forest
burning did as, over decades, the woods regrew and restocked their carbon
reservoirs.[24]

Still, those vast fires mattered in two ways. One, their carbon contribution was not trivial, and it was unlikely that suppression could dampen it
substantially. On the contrary, evidence pointed to a future of more fire,
both wild and prescribed. It might be possible through innovative technologies to reduce emissions from fossil fuels; it would not be possible in a
sustainable way to reduce by much those from free-burning fires, and both
ecology and economics argued persuasively against even an attempt. Two,
the same reasoning compromised assertions that Canada's immense stocks
of living hydrocarbons could absorb the effluent released by combusting its
fossil hydrocarbons. Along with other disturbances, it was implausible that
Canada's woods could be stocked more densely. Fire would crop off the addition, and, if anything, magnifying the wild woodpile would only add fuel
to those free-burning flames.

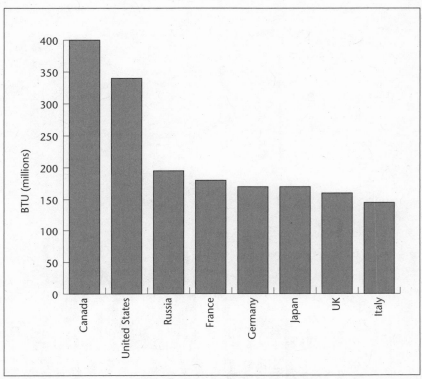

Comparative per capita energy consumption, 2001. While consumption is high, much of Canada's energy comes from hydropower.

Pumping carbon into the atmosphere, where it got picked up by plants, meant that it was stored in forms that could inflate the amount burned by flaming and smouldering. It meant that geologically sequestered carbon was now available for an accelerated and perhaps intensified regimen of burning on the surface. Much of the rest of that carbon lofted into the atmosphere, where it performed as expected for a greenhouse gas and ratcheted up the planetary warming that became documented over the course of the 1990s. That warming was expected to aggravate the conditions propelling big fires, especially in high-latitude lands since they felt such changes first and most acutely, amplifying the signals, and in continental interiors, particularly prone to drought and heat. Some argued that the record fires from 1980 onward were a hard signature that global warming had arrived. That assertion was awkward to prove because the provinces had recorded statistics by different methods and at different times. An approximation of consistent records only commences around

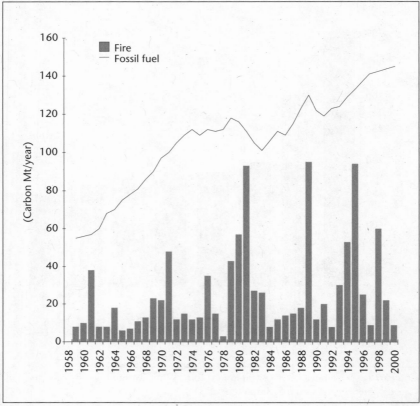

Canadian direct carbon emissions, 1958-2000. Fossil-fuel emissions have risen steadily, while forest-fire emissions are more irregular, in keeping with the rhythms of boreal burning. Still, the contribution is high and probably rising for both.

1975, which suspiciously aligns with the modern advent of recorded big fires. And careful recalibrations from old reports and age-stand data argue powerfully that similar outbreaks have occurred in the past. Forests had burned even when no one had been around to see the fires.[25]

All this has policy implications for Canada, the global carbon budget, and fire management. Canada ratified the Kyoto Protocol in December 2002, obligating the country to reduce GHG emissions by 6 percent from 2008 to 2012, relative to 1990 output. (A year later the prime minister admitted that no practical plan existed and that open resistance from energy-rich provinces – "distinctive carbon societies," as it were – would complicate implementation.) Integral to accession, however, was the belief that Canada could make up the difference by magnifying its sinks rather than diminishing its sources. Canada turned, once again, to its forests to make up the shortfall. As always, cutting was accelerating, replanting was falling behind, and despite national agreement on "sustainable forestry," schemes were floated like the one from Ontario to push the frontier of logging farther north under the bogus claim that cutting "emulated" natural disturbances such as fire. (It doesn't.) Canada's forests were already overcommitted, and even if the axe were stayed, the prospects were good that disturbances were on the upswing. Everywhere, an insect insurgency of some kind seemed to be maturing.

The cost of shutting down forest fires to make room for fossil fuel fires was staggering. Suppression was beyond the limits of diminishing returns – was contemplating withdrawals from more lands, letting them free burn under observation. When proposals floated to substitute the revenue-enhancing axe for the revenue-draining fire, researchers commented blandly that it would be "virtually impossible to treat the whole Canadian forest." Even a modest network of fuel breaks would demand swaths over fifteen million hectares, when the annual timber harvest approximated one million hectares. Besides, peat, not trees, constituted the dominant carbon reservoir, and slashing the woods to save them would undercut conventions on biodiversity, provisions for more nature preserves, and ecological sustainability overall. So the fires would stay; probably they would become larger. At most, the CFS concluded, Canada's forests were probably "a small carbon source, or at best, a small carbon sink." Fire meant they would not serve as a reserve carbon mine or a Fort Knox for carbon bullion. Fire was not an exogenous event or a tax on forests that wiser policy could revoke. It was what made that forest work.[26]

In the beginning, fire policy had been a simple matter of protecting commercial assets. Institutions sought more money to bring greater protection, which would yield more revenue and hence justify further investment in protection. A carbon economy introduced a new accounting, linking the two realms of combustion and unsettling the old formulas. Fire's geography had to include tar sands and offshore gas and the engines of industrial combustion; fire's ecology had to study the dynamics that joined carbon source to carbon sink, indifferent to which realm the carbon derived from; fire's policy had to determine which fires, in which realm, to promote and which to prevent. As they scanned the future, members of the Canadian fire community saw more fire and less certainty about how to respond.

Virtual Fire

The issue, if truth be known, was increasingly not even about real fires or the actuarial registry of past burns. More and more the dynamics of Canadian fire was what computerized simulacrums said it was. Plans referred to scenarios, proclaimed future desired conditions, projected regimes under the assumption of various possible climates. These computer-manufactured data fed the software behind model forests, model fires, preferred practices, and policies. Fire agencies tested themselves against virtual fires.

Knowledge had always meant power. But as fire management shifted into something like a service economy, not only folklore but also empirical science was being overwhelmed by simulated understanding – not even information, certainly not knowledge, but simply digitally generated data. The implications were curious and potentially immense. They suggested that change was so rapid and humanity's awkward agency so potent that the past offered only limited insight. Over such a scale was humanity reshaping the planet, from the structure of woods and the composition of biotas to the chemistry of the atmosphere, that history, whether human or natural, mattered less than what people were doing now and what they ought to be doing.

At best, simulations could act as a self-fulfilling prophecy. They could guide actions in ways favourable to people and land, reconciling cultural ambitions with ecological imperatives. That assumed, of course, that the models were accurate, that they understood how society and the biosphere worked. To the extent that the models drove policy, they would become truer over time simply because, by directing behaviour, what they described would come to be. At worst, they were expressions of high-tech hubris. People might (or might not) be compelled to conform to their prescriptions. It was not at all clear that nature would. For all their dazzling graphics, they might be little better than just-so scenarios and technological fairy tales. Nature might be watching the monitors; almost certainly fire was not.

Slow Burns, Fast Flames

Like all those previous eras since the land had shed its ice, contemporary Canada has its characteristic fires. Combustion's deep driver, swallowing everything around it like a black hole, and growing as it did so, was industrial fire. Little existed beyond its touch, and more would fall within its grasp. That realm lay beyond the purview of fire agencies. They coped instead with the flames and smoke that people saw – those of the wildfires they sought to protect against, those of the prescribed fires they wished to promote.

Big Burns: Wild

The oft-mauled but still intact boreal belt remained one of the world's great landscapes for high-intensity fire. The flames beat to their ancient rhythms on a scale suitable for largely unbroken bush. The 1989 season set a historical record of 7.5 million hectares blackened, from Manitoba to Yukon; 1994 and 1995 reached 6.5 and over 7 million hectares; 1998 overran 4.6 million hectares; and 2002 spread over 3 million hectares. The flames of 1995 were, in the words of CIFFC, "truly national," branding boreal Canada in a continental-sized triangle from Quebec to Alberta to Yukon. But every province had some year or years that exceeded its capacity. Thanks to CIFFC, all fires had become, in a sense, national. The movement of pumps, planes, and personnel rose, year by year, spiking during those extraordinary seasons.

Still, authorities recognized that, while they had the capacity with aircraft and satellites to survey those burns, they had neither the resources nor the political resolve to fight them. An effective line of control still existed, beyond which the fires would be observed but otherwise left unmolested.

There had been a period when Ontario and Quebec, emboldened by the CL-215, had tried to confront those remote burns; they soon withdrew as they appreciated that effectiveness was slight, costs exorbitant, and ecological justification nil. While in principle the logic of initial attack remained, it endured as an axiom of fire metaphysics. Fire protection would have to contract, and it would probably be subsumed within an all-hazard emergency service that would concentrate on commercial assets and public safety.

The fires of consequence were those that threatened towns. There were ever more exurban enclaves and no lessening of flames to strike them. Province after province felt their blows, whether glancing or full, from Badger, Newfoundland, to Burwash Landing, Yukon, to Chisholm, Alberta. The most explosive, however, broke out in the Cordillera. There were two premonitory burns in British Columbia, the Garnet fire in 1994 and the Salmon Arm fire in 1998. But the 2003 crisis stunned all of Canada. Gripped by the worst drought in a century, amid a backdrop of massive pine beetle infestations that threatened to hollow out the interior of the province, dry lightning, human carelessness, and high winds sent 2,500 fires rumbling over 260,000 hectares to menace the suburban fringes of McLure, Barriere, and Kelowna. Some 334 homes perished in the flames; 45,000 people were evacuated; three pilots died; and the costs of the "firestorm" soared to $700 million. It was, simply, the "worst ever" fire year for British Columbia.[1]

A provincial review identified multiple causes. The largest – "forces of nature," such as drought and dry lightning – were "beyond anyone's control." In similarly generic, non-accusatory fashion, the review rang up a roster of contributing factors, from slack attention to community protection to confused lines of authority to various slippages and breakdowns in operations. For all these conditions, technical fixes existed, and various efficiencies could be pursued. None of these observations suggested that the outbreak might demand a serious reformation. Rather, the fires were larger due to exogenous forces, and they fell upon houses as well as slash. The proper response required more of the same, a change in scale, not in kind.[2]

A more profound insight concerned the proliferation of fuels, much of which followed from human land use. Four million hectares and metastasizing, promising to kill 80 percent of merchantable timber, the bark beetle infestation fed on mature lodgepole pine, which over the past century, in the aftermath of logging, grazing, and fire control, had grown denser, more expansive, and more uniform. Logging slash was no longer burned at a rate commensurate with cutting. In the late 1980s, some 90,000 hectares a year had burned, by 2000 only 10,000 hectares, and the pressures were strong to shrink even that figure. Urban fringe communities added combustibles with wood structures and a longing for thick woods. Provincial parks were proliferating almost as promiscuously, a breeding sanctuary for fires. The worst admission, however, was that suppression, or more properly fire exclusion, had encouraged a "buildup" of forest fuels that made future fire control more difficult and dangerous. The effect was especially pronounced in the montane belt favoured by exurbanites.

Here was a critique of fire control that went beyond upgrading radios and pumps. It proposed that there were limits to suppression, that the logic of fire exclusion was flawed. For ninety years, the BC Forest Service had proudly declared a "formula" for fire protection: find fast, hit hard, attack where the need was greatest. Now it was proposed that the endless pursuit of initial attack could not, even in principle, succeed, not for lack of resources but because it could never abolish flame from fire-prone public lands, and the fires that did occur would simply become fiercer and huger.

The review concluded that the provincial parks needed more cutting and the managed forests more burning. While legislation prohibited commercial logging in the parklands, in late 2003 BC parks revised policies to allow the "removal of trees" for various purposes and hoped to emulate Parks Canada in allowing the sale of harvested timber to subsidize the costs of non-commercial practices such as thinning, chipping, and burning. Similarly the instinctive reaction to the beetle-killed woods was to "harvest" them, for the timber was otherwise "wasted" and would only add to the provincial fuel load. The commercial logic was clear.

Whether such provisions, enacted after the crisis, set the province back on its slippery slope, allowing re-entry by BC forest industries into protected areas and permitting (once again) cutting to sprint ahead of planting, was unclear. BC forest history had been one of good intentions gone awry. Cutting would get out of hand; proposals would be floated, backed by "scientific" studies, to reform and rehabilitate; but the costs were such that only more cutting could enable them; so the cutting continued while the restoration never quite got done; and the cycle would begin anew. The reforms assumed a world as orderly as the ministry's bureaucracy. Instead, there was always a crisis, to which the only "reasonable" response was to hasten the cut.

Likewise, prescribed burning still orbited around logging. While broadly accepted in principle, it was becoming harder to enact in practice.

Burning opportunities were few, liabilities serious, smoke and escaped fires not merely a nuisance but also a public menace, and skills and funding scarce. Most burning targeted slash, bonding the torch to the axe, and to burn outside such patches was trickier. Parks Canada could push burning because policy stipulated a standard of ecological integrity; the standards for provinces such as British Columbia were far more likely to focus on public health and safety. An emphasis on "fuel reduction" would inexorably argue for the axe (or engine) over the torch and for treating the new slash (e.g., woodchips) by burning it in biomass energy plants rather than in situ.

Left unresolved was the institutional arrangement that had, in 1995, segregated BC fire protection from land management. That move, while introducing various economies, had unmoored fire control – had made it an urban fire service in the woods. It divorced fire protection from decisions that affected what fuels would feed the flames it would have to confront and nudged it on a path that pointed to outsourcing. The 2003 firestorm killed the prospect of outright privatization, but the review was unwilling to force a bureaucratic remarriage. In this, British Columbia, for all its peculiarities, could stand for much of Canada, which seemed content not to have its left hand know its right, for the one brought in money and the other spent it, and a close coupling would probably mean less coming in and more going out.

The big burns continued. In 2004, British Columbia suffered through 2,400 fires, 220,000 burned hectares, and $164 million in suppression costs alone.

Big Burns: Prescribed

The barriers were high and the institutional caltrops many, but controlled burning continued its revival in the various guises of prescribed fire. These burns took three forms: scientific research, ecological burning, and slash fires.

Since Jim Wright first lit patches of Petawawa pine, Canadian fire science has favoured field fires as a source of data. Researchers understood well the intellectual limitations of this method, that they were not isolating and analyzing the physical processes behind free-burning fire in the classic reductionist style of modern science but only establishing a real-world data set against which to run correlations. That, however, was what they had the means to do; it satisfied their principal end, a fire danger rating system; it avoided the painful conceptual gridlock that came to characterize the American commitment to fire models based on first principles, supplemented by small-scale laboratory trials. And it lay behind some of the most impressive fire experiments in the world as the new millennium approached: the International Crown Fire Modelling Experiment (ICFME).[3]

The ICFME proposed to escalate the experimental tradition into full-bore crown fires. Between 1994 and 2001, the consortium kindled eighteen high-intensity fires in mature jack pine northeast of Fort Providence, Northwest Territories. As it evolved, the project gathered 100 participants from thirty organizations in fourteen countries. But the critical partnership was with the United States. Americans needed Canadian data; Canadians needed help in the intricacies of physical and mathematical modelling. CFS researchers realized that it was "physically and logistically impossible to develop empirically based fire behaviour models for all major Canadian fuel types," while their American counterparts appreciated the limitations of their prevailing paradigms (especially the Rothermel model) "in the prediction of high-intensity crown fire behaviour." They needed each other.[4]

The opportunity was extraordinary: only the Project Vesta burns in Western Australia offered anything comparable. Other research projects attached themselves to the core program. There were auxiliary experiments in protective fire shelters, in the ignition of houses from radiant heat, in aerosol emissions, in the fire behaviour consequences of management "treatments" such as thinning, pruning, and hardwood patches on fire properties, on regeneration, on radiant emissive power and temperatures, on charcoal creation and deposition. The outcome was a bazaar of specialized fire research. In the end, although a behaviour model still proved delicate, and the vital circumstances necessary to escalate a surface fire into the crowns remained elusive, the data were abundant and substantive. Perhaps the real model to emerge was how to run a global confederation of fire scientists.

The ICFME was a one-off enterprise, not likely to be repeated. Increasingly the momentum for routine burning lay with Parks Canada and the indispensable Banff. An interim fire plan synthesized preliminary studies in fire history, weather, biomass, and disturbance. It identified four zones: one for experimental burns, one for mechanical fuel treatments, one for suppression, and one where "random ignitions" might be allowed to roam.

The program commenced firing in 1983 with a 7-hectare burn, and two others followed leading to a 400-hectare burn in 1987. From them, Banff quickly learned several facts. It learned that a prescribed fire program could not overdrive the headlights of fire protection; the park needed to upgrade its fire capacities overall, not simply hand out drip torches. It learned that small-area fires were harder to control than well-designed large ones. In big burns, there was more area relative to perimeter, and prescriptions could incorporate natural fuel breaks. Banff learned that experience counted more than simulations, that fire management could only be learned by doing it, that reintroducing fire was arduous, complicated, and serendipitous. It would take time. The 1986 directive reflected that experience.[5]

In spring 1988, the Minnewanka 1 Burn swelled to 1,050 hectares. The program then paused as drought throttled much of the Rockies and an extravaganza of flame at Yellowstone National Park, Banff's American rival, mesmerized the media and forced Banff to field public questions about how its program resembled Yellowstone's (or not). A practical upshot was to relocate burning out of the Bow Valley and into the backcountry and to allow more "mechanical" surrogates. Meanwhile, the "Keeper of the Flame" and a national strategy brought some rigour and stiffened bureaucratic spines. In 1990, the Panther Burn racked up 1,400 hectares, while the Palliser 2 reached 1,000 hectares. There followed a slate of smaller burns, many tied to the construction of fireguards along the mountains flanking the Bow Valley. Cliff White and Ian Pengelly announced at a fire symposium that, in firing around Banff town site, they had been "lucky so far." All it would take to compromise the program was a "thick blanket of smoke on a key facility." That came with the Sawback Burns in 1993. The fires stayed within prescription; public furor, however, blew up. The next year some 1,600 hectares burned. It proved too much. From 1995 to 1997, the burn program was suspended. Not only fire but also other ecological crises, mostly centred in the Bow Valley, boiled over.[6]

When it revived, the program set six fires in 1998 and never looked back. The next year it crossed a threshold, over 2,100 hectares burned. It was well on target to meet its rough goals, 1,500 hectares a year. While this was less than the estimated 2,000 hectares a year in historical times, it was a far cry from the 1 percent load to which the park had succumbed by 1980. Even more, it hatched a brood of burners who dispersed throughout Parks Canada. By 2004, every park had a fire plan and stipulated goals for restored fire. A few stood out, recovering ancient fire practices. Elk Island fired grass to promote elk habitat; Prince Albert burned fireguards along its border and internally; Wood Buffalo allowed lightning fires free reign away from major developments.

The lessons were, again, several. Fire management was not a let-burn program. Rather, it was a voracious consumer of research, money, labour, and administrative attention. Prescribed burning required prescribed burners; it had to enlist supporters in the field, at park offices, at national headquarters; it demanded, as it were, affirmative action. It could rally public support where, as at Banff and Elk Island, the fires could link clearly with powerful ecological talismans, especially with charismatic species. Banff boasted grizzlies, wolves, elk, bighorn sheep, all of which feasted on fresh browse or on fauna that fed on such fodder and would expire in homogeneous swaths of old-growth forest. In rejuvenating patches of woods, Banff's burn program was feeding those creatures. It learned, too, that the public liked fire best in someone else's backyard, where the flames could not escape and the smoke would stay in box canyons.

For the most part, the parks met these criteria. As urban Canada recolonized rural Canada, however, the clashes would come, and multiply, as they had at Banff. The Banff paradigm had propagated throughout the Canadian national parks. Whether it could leap over that institutional fireguard was one of the fundamental questions before the Canadian fire community.

It was not obvious how, or whether, the provinces could manage. From time to time, here and there, they had control-burned. They had burned fireguards amid snow-fenced prairies and along the ploughed borders, they had regulated the firing of blueberries and fallow fields, and especially they had assisted the burning of slash. But as fire protection agencies had strengthened their presence and applied more and more mechanical power, they steadily turned from open burning to chemicals and machines, much as modern agriculture had.

By the 1970s, Canadian foresters were willing to call their old practices by a new name, prescribed fire, but prescribed fire meant different things, and it particularly meant different things across the international border. Until Parks Canada announced an alternative, controlled burning had existed in Canada to support forestry. It swept away combustibles from some of the most dangerous fuels on the planet, prepared the site for planting, and promoted new growth, notably in jack pine. Typically fire assisted other techniques such as scarifying, herbicides, aerial seeding, or hand-planted tubes of seedlings. Some provinces were casual about its use; some closely bonded it to silviculture. For a while in the 1960s, New Brunswick, for example, relied on early spring burning as part of a larger regimen. On sites of "recent clear cuts with heavy brush," burning was done as soon as the snow melted off the cut-over but still remained in the surrounding woods. This was done "solely to make planting easier." Another variant was to follow this burn with a second, "when the hazard is high," to "purge the place of fine fuel and duff and expose the mineral soil." A co-operative program between provincial and private foresters, dubbed the Miramichi Fire Project, attempted to rekindle some further enthusiasm. (It didn't.) Timing the burns with snowmelt also characterized the protective border burns characteristic for a while in Saskatchewan.[7]

The justification for fire as a silvicultural "tool" was a formula for fire's ultimate expulsion, for eventually another tool could replace it without fire's awkward side effects, unpredictability, and dependence on extraneous factors such as weather. This process was well under way even as provincial foresters began speaking of prescribed fire. In the United States, the new term signified a determination to reintroduce fire not merely for fuel reduction but also for ecological enhancement – and this despite reservations by foresters. In Canada, it became a euphemism for a dying art, a technique justified by the support it lent industrial forestry. The most interesting challenge emanated from Newfoundland. Closer to a rural heritage, not yet baptized fully into the orthodoxies of Canadian forestry, in the late 1950s Newfoundland pursued efforts to expand agricultural burning into the woods. The CFS was enlisted for advice; a conference was held; field trials were conducted. The experiment ended with the 1961 wildfires, which pushed provincial authorities into a commitment to serious suppression. The future lay with Canso waterbombers, not with prescriptions for burning. In 1967, J.H. Cayford of the CFS observed that, "with the exception of slash burning in British Columbia as a fire prevention measure and which has been carried out for more than 50 years, relatively little prescribed burning has been done in Canada." He noted, however, that over the past decade an "accelerating interest" had developed and that the CFS could integrate some experiments within its traditional field trials for the CFFDRS, but elsewhere controlled burning always nestled securely within the confines of timber production and fire protection. Increasingly the bulk of Canadian burning resided within the massive logging industry of British Columbia.[8]

And that burning was fast shrinking. Wildfires in slash had of course been the nemesis of early forestry and conservation. For British Columbia, legislation in 1912 had required that slash be treated, and most was fired, as one might burn garbage or an infected carcass. But generally participants believed that fire was only an expedient, and a poor one that too often required that rangers not only issue permits but also assist on the ground. The practice thus remained, as Protection Officer C.D. Haddon observed, "the centre of a great deal of controversy," rekindled with each wave of revived logging and escaped conflagration. Writing in

1962, Haddon could declare that it was accepted "almost without question as good, sound Forestry practice." A careful 1970 study confirmed that "benefits can exceed costs many times." But these were the voices of foresters. As cutting escalated, so did slash burning, and as with replanting the remedial measures lagged such that there was, before the public, both a lot of smoke and a lot of still-festering slash. When the economy shifted to more metropolitan services and environmental concerns became more prominent, criticism mounted, then morphed into protest about the management of BC forests. The dense palls that spread from ever-widening clear-cuts were a vivid, ugly, and, for urban residents, unhealthy reminder. The smoke made the cutting impossible to ignore yet gave credence to the idea that shutting down the smoke might equally shut down an industry run amok.[9]

Critics received inspiration from the northwestern United States. There slash burning had been tolerated as a necessary evil, its escapes at least marginally better than wildfires. (This led to the famous retort that slash burning resembled a man who commits suicide for fear that he might have a fatal accident.) During the 1960s, the old arguments revived. As more slash burned, more fires escaped, and more smoke contaminated critical airsheds, now subject to federal air-quality standards. To those objections, the push into higher cuts (and into old-growth woods) further alarmed environmental sensibilities. By the 1980s, controversy was escalating into crisis. A decade later logging on the public lands was being strangled and burning shut down. Even ancient agricultural burning for grass-seed production in the Willamette Valley and around Spokane was banned. With a customary delay, such concerns migrated north and interbred with other anxieties of forest mismanagement, with fire, once again, a cipher for them all.[10]

Prescribed fire in British Columbia pursued two countervailing trends. The BC Forest Service continued to demand that hazardous slash be treated (preferably burned), and beginning in 1965-73 it co-operated with the Provincial Wildlife Branch to broadcast burn in the northeast for habitat, primarily for elk, bighorn sheep, deer, and moose. A revised Wildlife Act (1981) created a Habitat Conservation Fund that helped to underwrite various treatments, prescribed fire among them, and a protocol agreement made the program co-operative between the Ministries of Forests and Environment. A 1986 review found problems with both programs. CFS researchers unveiled possible uses of prescribed fire to control beetles and dwarf mistletoe and to thin overstocked stands. Still, by 1987 the area burned for habitat increased 40 percent; by 1991, it had tripled. Meanwhile, slash burning declined. The ministry convened a task force.[11]

During the 1990s, the two trends accelerated. There was less slash burned on the assumption that fuller utilization and better suppression could compensate. And there was, at the same time, an expansion of burning but for purposes other than silviculture and by agencies other than the Forest Service. Yet here, in miniature, was the troubled future of prescribed fire. Whatever the professional judgment, public opinion disliked slash burning and trusted other burns only when remote from settlements. It was doubtful that the case for aggressive burning could be made solely from arguments of fuel reduction and for habitat; to be compelling, it had to be linked, as at Banff, with charismatic creatures and monumental settings. If, as foresters insisted, prescribed fire was another tool in the kit, then the public was prepared to tell them to find another tool. That, after all, was the whole thrust of industrial fire. Writing for the BC Forest Service, John Parminter pondered the unhappy political irony by which, just at the time "our knowledge of ecosystem functioning" and "our level of expertise in using prescribed fire" had converged with professional consensus, other factors were "limiting or overruling" its use. At the beginning of the twentieth century, the public had favoured burning, and professional foresters had condemned it; now forestry and wildlife management wanted it, and the public was hostile to it. Whether the provincial parks and forestry bureaus could overcome that suspicion would determine the coming character of Canadian fire.[12]

What happened in British Columbia is a synecdoche for Canada overall. With regard to prescribed fire, British Columbia (like Alberta) had some advantages in the form of lots of montane forest and steppe that could be underburned. This was not true for the boreal forest, where burning had to be in unwooded openings or along borders or in patches. The two provinces also had established fire agencies, technologically capable of applying force to start and stop fires; they had the example and co-operation of Parks Canada, especially at Banff; they had relatively wealthy provinces to fund them. But state-sponsored forestry had become a flawed vessel, as unstable as sunspots; suppression organizations found it difficult to retool for prescribed burning; agency momentum lay elsewhere. The BC record was ambiguous. Two decades after the ministerial review, it could not assemble, from the two responsible agencies, even a base table of area burned under prescription. After the 2003 "firestorm," although official doctrine pleaded for more controlled fire, the money went into sparkling new suppression tools.

The prospects for open fire resided on lands and under agencies that saw flame as an ecological process that did biological work that nothing else could replicate. Classic fire protection had at least enhanced timber revenue, while ecological burning had overt costs and yielded largely covert biotic services. If anything, the choices would get murkier, for fire, as always, could be good and bad and be both at the same time. It could enhance biodiversity and release greenhouse gases, it could destroy old-growth forest and rejuvenate habitat, it could threaten human health and boost that of biotas. Political discourse does not, however, thrive on ambiguity. A betting man would predict that prescribed fire was not likely to happen beyond a few ceremonial sites. It was more plausible that agencies would fuss with ever grander studies over technical issues, while politicians put public money where the voters would see it. The land might be green; the society was not.

In its confusions and in its instinct to substitute technique for idea and its wish to do what it could instead of what it could not, Canada was far from unique. Among boreal firefighting nations, it was supreme by virtue of its vast estate, its power to suppress, and its research establishment. Boreal Europe had sought, with genuine success, to cultivate fire from the land and then found that, having converted its woods into tree farms, environmental concerns such as biodiversity demanded that it put some fire back. Russia had attempted to squash flame in proximate lands of economic value and otherwise banish it east of the Urals, a heavy and clumsy strategy of suppression and ecological exile, most often overwhelmed by the sheer immensity of the ambition compared with the means at hand. America had put much of its boreal lands into nature protection, where it sought, with earnest yet sometimes ineffective and often expensive tactics, to allow it range to roam. In comparison, Canada made little attempt to intensify silviculture, restricted the scope of fire exclusion for economic rather than ecological reasons, and when it chose to fight fire did so with a sophisticated system of real mechanical punch. In research, thanks to the CFS, it remained among the top three nations by volume of publications and dominant within the boreal biota.

Yet it did not reach the top tier of fire powers. That honour belonged to Australia and America. The reason is that both nations, while well endowed in firefighting and fire science capabilities, could address the more fundamental questions of fire and country. For each, fire management had intertwined with land management in ways that made questions about what to do with fire of importance to its national culture. Whether wildland fire was attacked or kindled or left to free burn, and the means by which these ends might be achieved, tapped into issues of land stewardship that in turn spliced into the genetic memory and aspirations of these countries' peoples. Although they identified, in particular, with outback and wilderness, fire anywhere in their wildlands and along their exurban frontiers could spark similar discourses about who they were and how they should behave. In quirky, powerful, and exasperating ways, fire bonded with their national identities. So, while they often chattered about abstract values and intangible meanings in ways nonsensical to hardnosed pump operators, and while the intensity of their ambiguities about what bushfire meant and how to cope with it made a singular strategy impossible, tactics awkward, and efficiency as a measurement of achievement hopeless, fire mattered to Australians and Americans in ways that it did not matter to Canadians.

Canada's awful splendour inspired no real cultural engagement across scholarship, the arts, and politics. Among the Earth's fire powers, Canada was more big than important. It was content to sell its pumps and planes and the software to run them but not to determine when and why to apply those instruments. Its ancient fear, that it would be a mere hewer of wood and drawer of water, had, ironically, come true for fire. It was a partner, not a leader, a supplier of goods and techniques, not an originator of new ways to live on a fire-prone land.

Yet Canada's ferment was real, and something new might bubble up out of it. The one constant was fire itself. It could not be bought off, legislated away, carbon-traded into insignificance, or badgered into obedience. A warming Earth could only enhance the habitat for fire. However Canadians might wish to conceive their relationship to fire, the future promised more flame, not less.

Fire and Ice

No creature so symbolizes the Arctic as the polar bear. The only maritime species of *Ursus*, it found on the frozen Arctic and its shores a remarkable prey, the seal. More and more it took to the pack ice, where paradoxically food was constant, and dispensed with seasonal hibernation. Only pregnant females resided temporarily on shore, where they holed up in dens to give birth and shelter their fragile cubs. It was their last link with terra firma. The refrigerated Pleistocene had been a world of ice, broken by interglacial droughts or warm spells, and the emergence and dissemination of the polar bear around the Arctic was as emblematic of those cold epochs as *Homo sapiens* was of the warm.[1]

But the ice receded; the land burned rather than froze. The Holocene (or Anthropocene, as some propose) was a Long Summer and an era of fire resurgent over ice. In November 2002, the Canadian Wildlife Service reported from Churchill on the western shore of Hudson Bay, ripe with the world's densest population of white bears, that extensive fires were causing dens to collapse. Flames had burned the willows; smouldering purged away the insulating organic mat, allowing the ground to melt. Roots, soils, the mortaring frost, all gave way. The bears had to flee to their floes.[2]

These, however, were proving a transient ark. The trapped effluent of fossil fuel combustion was turning the Earth into a colossal crock pot. Global warming was eroding away the edges of the arctic pack, and simulations predicted the ultimate disintegration of the arctic ice-ocean. If so, the polar bear might go the way of so many other relic megafauna of the Pleistocene, driven over the evolutionary edge by humanity's remorseless expansion. The ice world would yield to a fire world. And that was precisely the habitat that favoured *Homo*. However threatened by wildfire, a world that burned, a combustible biota, would select for and favour a creature whose whole existence and whose power were defined by fire.

So the immemorial rivalry between fire and ice continued. The forces behind both were global, genetic, celestial, climatic; they would not fade away. This time they were also cultural. In this turn of the wheel, with humanity to assist it, fire was triumphant. But whether these events foretold an end or a beginning or only another pause was ambiguous. The struggle would persist, an archetype of so many elemental forces that, with awful splendour, had contested over this land. So long as it engaged that struggle, so would Canada.

Yet Canada was more than the transcendent dialectic between the tidal tugs of freezing and firing. Such primordial struggles did not define Canada: Canadians did. It was their capacity – too rarely admitted – to choose that shaped the outcome. It was asking too much of Canadians that they embrace fire in the bush, but they could engage it, and they would have to, whether they wished to or not. That engagement would not take the form of a grand national strategy – Canadian geography and history and politics argued against such a solution. Rather, they would meet it with pragmatic means that satisfied their instrumental vision of fire and its landscapes. They would invent and adapt and tinker with tools and institutions that would shelter them from the vagaries and occasional terror of boreal flame and perhaps, here and there, allow them to exploit it.

By the sum of their separate decisions, they would define a collective strategy, and those choices would come with a very human bias because people could not freeze landscapes as they could burn them, could not hurl waterbombers against an ice front as they could against flame, could not kindle the ice against itself. Long ago they had instinctively turned to fire, and they could not now lightly turn away.

Notes

Foreword: Mon pays c'est le feu

1 The most useful, accessible assessment is the British Columbia 2003 Firestorm Provincial Review, conducted by Gary Filmon, which provides the appraisal reported in the last sentence of this paragraph. http://www.2003firestorm.gov.bc.ca.

2 Transcribed from Dinwoodie's version of "Put the Fire Out," www.firewatch.net/music.

3 Jeremy Hainsworth, "Over 30,000 Flee Blazes in Western Canada," 23 August 2003,http://cms.firehouse.com; CTV News, "1,000 Homes Evacuated near Kelowna Fire Scene," 22 August 2003, http://www.ctv.ca. Perhaps the best encapsulation of what the fire meant to residents can be found on the Okanagan Mountain Firewatch website at "Firewatch Archive," http://www.firewatch.net.

4 Environment Canada data cited in British Columbia 2003 Firestorm Provincial Review.

5 Center for Public Integrity, *City Adrift: New Orleans Before and After Katrina, A Center for Public Integrity Investigation* (Baton Rouge: Louisiana State University Press, 2007)

6 The allusions here are to Stephen Pyne, *Fire in America: A Cultural History of Wildland and Rural Fire* (Princeton, NJ: Princeton University Press 1982); *World Fire: The Culture of Fire on Earth* (New York: Holt, 1995); *Vestal Fire: An Environmental History, Told through Fire, of Europe and Europe's Encounter with the World* (Seattle: University of Washington Press, 1997); *Fire: A Brief History* (Seattle: University of Washington Press and British Museum, 2001); *Burning Bush: A Fire History of Australia* (New York: Holt, 1991); *Fire on the Rim: A Firefighter's Season at the Grand Canyon* (Seattle: University of Washington Press, 1995); *Year of the Fires: The Story of the Great Fires of 1910* (New York: Viking, 2001).

7 In Stephen Pyne, "History with Fire in Its Eye: An Introduction to Fire in America," *Nature Transformed: The Environment in American History,* Use of the Land, National Humanities Center, TeacherServe http://www.nhc.rtp.nc.us/tserve/nattrans/nattrans.htm.

8 Quoted in Ken Drushka, *Canada's Forests. A History,* Forest History Society, Issues Series (Montreal and Kingston: McGill-Queen's University Press, 2003), 37.

9 Robert Cooney, *A Compendious History of the Northern Part of the Province of New Brunswick, and of the District of Gaspé, in Lower Canada* (Halifax: Joseph Howe, 1832), 79.

10 R. Peter Gillis and Thomas R. Roach, *Lost Initiatives: Canada's Forest Industries, Forest*

Policy and Forest Conservation (Westport, CT: Greenwood Press, 1986); Richard S. Lambert and Paul Pross, *Renewing Nature's Wealth: A Centennial History of the Public Management of Lands, Forests & Wildlife in Ontario 1763-1867* (Toronto: Ontario Department of Lands and Forests, 1967); John V. Parminter, "An Historical Review of Forest Fire Management in British Columbia" (M.F. thesis, University of British Columbia, 1978).

11 Richard A. Rajala, *Feds, Forests, and Fire: A Century of Canadian Forestry Innovation* (Ottawa: Canadian Science and Technology Museum, 2005), 15.

12 Arthur R.M. Lower, *My First Seventy-five Years* (Toronto: Macmillan of Canada, 1967), 61-64.

13 See National Atlas of Canada, http://atlas.nrcan.gc.ca/site/english/maps/environment/naturalhazards/forest_fires/1, and for a collection of pictures of and news articles about the Porcupine Fire, Library and Archives Canada, "SOS! Canadian Disasters" http://www.collectionscanada.ca/sos/002028-4100-e.html.

14 Natural Resources Canada, "Suppression at All Costs," *The State of Canada's Forests, 2003-04*, http://cfs.nrcan.gc.ca/sof/sofo4/feature05_e.html .

15 Rajala, *Feds, Forests, and Fire* is a very useful brief summary on which this paragraph depends substantially (see especially pp. 18-19, 85).

16 Natural Resources Canada, "Suppression at All Costs,"

17 Natural Resources Canada, "Managing Forest Fires: The Path to Sustainability," *The State of Canada's Forests, 2003-04*, http://cfs.nrcan.gc.ca/sof/sofo4/feature09_e.html.

18 Goldwin Smith, *Canada and the Canadian Question* (London: Macmillan, 1891), ch. 1.

Prologue: White Canada

1 My major source of information on post-ice reconstruction is E.C. Pielou, *After the Ice Age: The Return of Life to Glaciated North America* (Chicago: University of Chicago Press, 1991).

2 See Edward A. Johnson, *Fire and Vegetation Dynamics: Studies from the North American Boreal Forest* (Cambridge, UK: Cambridge University Press, 1992), especially 11-21. See also M.J. Newark, "The Relationship between Forest Fire Occurrence and 500 mb Longwave Ridging," *Atmosphere* 3 (1975): 26-33; M.D. Flannigan and J.B. Harrington, "A Study of the Relation of Meteorological Variables to Monthly Provincial Area Burned by Wildfire in Canada (1953-80)," *Journal of Applied Meteorology* 27 (1988): 441-52; and B.J. Stocks and R.B. Street, "Forest Fire Weather and Wildfire Occurrence in the Boreal Forest of Northwestern Ontario," in *Resources and Dynamics of the Boreal Zone,* ed. Ross W. Wein, Roderick R. Riewe, and Ian R. Methven (Ottawa: Association of Canadian Universities Northern Studies, 1983), 249-65.

3 Again, my primary source is Pielou, *After the Ice Age.*

4 The most comprehensive study remains Paul Martin and Richard Klein, eds., *Quaternary Extinctions: A Prehistoric Revolution* (Tucson: University of Arizona Press, 1989; reprint).

5 The debate over causes continues unabated; references are legion. The core argument, however, remains with Martin and Klein, eds., *Quaternary Extinctions.* For a somewhat acerbic survey of pre-Columbian impacts, which goes beyond the megafauna controversy, see Charles E. Kay, *Wilderness and Political Ecology* (Salt Lake City: University of Utah Press, 2002). The evidence does seem to mount in favour of extensive, and locally intensive, modifications by people through means both direct and indirect.

6 See, for example, A.M. Swain, "Environmental Changes during the Past 2000 Years in North-Central Wisconsin: Analysis of Pollen, Charcoal, and Seeds from Varved Lake Sediments," *Quaternary Research* 10 (1978): 55-68. On fire frequency shift in the Rockies, Mark Heathcott, letter to the author, 12 July 2005, in which before 1760 the mountain

fire cycle was about 60 years and afterward jumped to 175 years.

Kindling

1 See Edward A. Johnson, *Fire and Vegetation Dynamics: Studies from the North American Boreal Forest* (Cambridge, UK: Cambridge University Press, 1992), 7-11; R.A. Bryson, "Airmasses, Streamlines, and the Boreal Forest," *Geographical Bulletin* (Canada) 8, 3 (1966): 228-69; and Serge Payette et al., "Recent Fire History of the Northern Quebec Biomes," *Ecology* 70, 3 (1989): 656-73.
2 James George Frazer, *Myths of the Origin of Fire* (London: Macmillan, 1930), 151, 159-89.

Fire Rings of Indigenous Canada

1 Reid A. Bryson, W.N. Irving, and J.A. Larsen, "Radiocarbon and Soil Evidence of Former Forest in the Southern Canadian Tundra," *Science* 147, 3,653 (1965): 46-48; Leslie A. Viereck and Linda A. Schandelmeier, "Effects of Fire in Alaska and Adjacent Canada: A Literature Review," BLM-Alaska Technical Report 6 (November 1980), 63. For an excellent summary of the shifting borders across Canada, see Deborah L. Elliott-Fisk, "The Stability of the Northern Canadian Tree Limit," *Annals of the Association of American Geographers* 73, 4 (1983): 560-76.
2 J. Stan Rowe et al., "Fire Studies in the Upper Mackenzie Valley and Adjacent Precambrian Uplands," ALUR 1974-75 (Ottawa, 1975), 37; Ross W. Wein, "Frequency and Characteristics of Arctic Tundra Fires," *Arctic* 29 (1976): 213-22. See also Richard J. Barney and Albert Comiskey, "Wildfires and Thunderstorms on Alaska's North Slope," US Forest Service, Research Note PNW-212 (1973).
3 Henry Lewis, personal communication re Inuit burning, ca. 1985.
4 Randi R. Jandt and C. Randy Meyers, "Recovery of Lichen in Tussock Tundra Following Fire in Northwestern Alaska," Alaska Open File Report 82, BLM/AK/ST-01/001+9217+20 (October 2000), 1.
5 For general ecology, see Jandt and Meyers, "Recovery"; A.N.D. Auclair, "The Role of Fire in Lichen-Dominated Tundra and Forest-Tundra," in *The Role of Fire in Northern Circumpolar Ecosystems*, ed. Ross W. Wein and David A. MacLean, SCOPE 18 (New York: John Wiley and Sons, 1983), 235-56; and R.W. Wein, "Recovery of Vegetation in Arctic Regions after Burning," Task Force on Northern Oil Development, Report 74-6 (May 1974).
6 An excellent summary of boreal fire is Serge Payette, "Fire as a Controlling Process in the North American Boreal Forest," in *A Systems Analysis of the Global Boreal Forest*, ed. Herman Shugart, Rik Leeman, and Gordon B. Bonan (Cambridge, UK: Cambridge University Press, 1992), 144-69.
7 There is a large literature on jack pine, but a good summary is J.H. Cayford and D.J. McRae, "The Ecological Role of Fire in Jack Pine Forests," in Wein and MacLean, eds., *The Role of Fire*, 183-99. Again, black spruce could support a library by itself, but see L.A. Viereck, "The Effects of Fire in Black Spruce Ecosystems of Alaska and Northern Canada," in Wein and MacLean, eds., *The Role of Fire*, 201-20.
8 M.D. Flannigan and B.M. Wotton, "Lightning-Ignited Forest Fires in Northwestern Ontario," *Canadian Journal of Forest Research* 21 (1991): 277-87, contains a good review of factors leading to lightning kindling; C.H. Nash and E.A. Johnson, "Synoptic Climatology of Lightning-Caused Forest Fires in Subalpine and Boreal Forests," *Canadian Journal of Forest Research* 26 (1996): 1859-74, aligns lightning fires with fine fuel moistures and the weather conditions that make them possible. For a thorough introduction to lightning as an ignition mechanism, see Don Lathan and Earle Williams, "Lightning and Forest

Fires," in *Forest Fires: Behavior and Ecological Effects,* ed. Edward A. Johnson and Kiyoko Miyanishi (San Diego, CA: Academic Press, 2001), 375-418. On estimates of magnitude, see Edward A. Johnson, *Fire and Vegetation Dynamics: Studies from the North American Boreal Forest* (Cambridge, UK: Cambridge University Press, 1992), 6. Information on doubling a burned area has come from C.E. Van Wagner, personal communication, 2002.

9 See Payette, "Fire as a Controlling Process," 149. See also P.C. Ward and A.G. Tithecott, "The Impact of Fire Management on the Boreal Landscape of Ontario," Aviation, Flood, and Fire Management Branch Publication 305, Ontario Ministry of Natural Resources (April 1993), 2-4.

10 On anthropogenic fire, see Henry T. Lewis, *A Time for Burning,* Occasional Publication 17, Boreal Institute for Northern Studies (Edmonton: University of Alberta, 1982); and Henry T. Lewis and Theresa A. Ferguson, "Yards, Corridors, and Mosaics: How to Burn a Boreal Forest," *Human Ecology* 16, 1 (1988): 57-77.

11 Quotation in Sidney Stephen Janzen, "The Burning North: A History of Fire and Fire Protection in the NWT" (MA thesis, University of Alberta, 1990), 18.

12 Quotation in Lewis, *A Time for Burning,* 20.

13 Ibid., 40.

14 Ibid., 50.

15 Ibid., 43.

16 Ibid., 1, 50.

17 Richard Glover, ed., *David Thompson's Narrative 1784-1812* (Toronto: Champlain Society, 1962), 110.

18 Lewis, *A Time for Burning,* 1.

19 The literature on prairie fires is immense. I've relied in particular on two general texts: Henry A. Wright and Arthur W. Bailey, Jr., *Fire Ecology: United States and Southern Canada* (New York: John Wiley, 1982) and Scott L. Collins and Linda L. Wallace, eds., *Fire in North American Tallgrass Prairies* (Norman: University of Oklahoma Press, 1990).

20 J.S. Rowe, "Lightning Fires in Saskatchewan Grassland," *Canadian Field-Naturalist* 83 (1969): 317-24; quotations from George W. Arthur, *An Introduction to the Ecology of Early Historic Communal Bison Hunting among the Northern Plains Indians,* Archaeological Survey of Canada Paper 37 (Ottawa: National Museums of Canada, 1975), 21-22.

21 Washington Irving, *A Tour of the Prairies,* ed. John Francis McDermott (Norman: University of Oklahoma Press, 1956), 15; John Palliser, quoted from Kenneth F. Higgins, "Interpretation and Compendium of Historical Fire Accounts in the Northern Great Plains," in US Fish and Wildlife Service, *Resource Publication 161* (Washington, DC: US Fish and Wildlife Service, 1986), 26.

22 B. La Potherie, *The Indian Tribes of the Upper Mississippi Valley and Region of the Great Lakes,* vol. 1, trans. and ed. E.H. Blair (New York: Kraus Reprint, 1969), 366, quoted from Higgins, "Interpretation and Compendium," 10.

23 Louis Hennepin, quoted from Higgins, "Interpretation and Compendium," 9. For a counter opinion, see Edwin T. Denig, who argued against fire "to facilitate hunting"; "nothing they desire less," he insisted, "and their laws to prevent it are severe in the extreme"; quoted from ibid., 21. Denig attributed the burning, instead, to travellers and war parties.

24 Quotation in Arthur, *Introduction,* 23-24; Palliser, quoted from Higgins, "Interpretation and Compendium," 25; La Potherie and Perrot, quoted from ibid., 10; Lewis and Clark, quoted from Stephen Pyne, *Fire in America* (Princeton: Princeton University Press, 1982), 75.

25 Waheenee, quoted from Higgins, "Interpretation and Compendium," 28; Palliser, quoted from ibid., 26.

26 The best judgment for northern plains is Higgins, "Interpretation and Compendium," 7; see also Arthur, *Introduction*, 29-30. Dodge cited in Higgins, "Interpretation and Compendium," 28. On herding behaviour, see Tim Flannery, *The Eternal Frontier: An Ecological History of North America and Its Peoples* (New York: Grove Press, 2002).

27 J. Russell Harper, ed., *Paul Kane's Frontier* (Austin: University of Texas Press, 1971), 83. See also, for more examples, Higgins, "Interpretation and Compendium," 22, 21 (which includes quotation from Ross). The escape fire is a common set-piece of prairie travel. It was the subject of a famous Currier and Ives print, *The Trapper's Defense,* and even appears in James Fenimore Cooper's *The Prairie.*

28 E.H. Findlayson, "Report of the Director of Forestry," in *Report of the Department of the Interior, 1914-15* (Ottawa: Government Printing Bureau, 1915), 79.

29 Macoun and Palliser, quoted from Higgins, "Interpretation and Compendium," 23, 33, 26; Ernest Thompson Seton, "Prairie Fires," *Manitoba Historical Society Transactions,* series 1, no. 16, 8 January 1885.

30 A.R.C. Selwyn, quoted from Higgins, "Interpretation and Compendium," 35.

31 Miller Christy, "Why Are the Prairies Treeless?" *Proceedings of the Royal Geographical Society* 14, 2 (1892): 98.

32 Ibid., 79-80.

33 Henry A. Wright and Arthur W. Bailey, *Fire Ecology: United States and Canada* (New York: Wiley and Sons, 1982), 328-40; C.E. Ahlgren, "Effects of Fires on Temperate Forests: North Central United States," in *Fire and Ecosystems,* ed. T.T. Kozlowski and C.E. Ahlgren (New York: Academic Press, 1974), 195-224. See also Eric A. Bourdo, Jr., "The Forest the Settlers Saw," and Charles E. Cleland, "Indians in a Changing Environment," in *The Great Lakes Forest: An Environmental and Social History,* ed. Susan Flader (Minneapolis: University of Minnesota Press, 1983), 3-16, 83-95.

34 J. Terasmae and N.C. Weeks, "Natural Fires as an Index of Paleoclimate," *Canadian Field-Naturalist* 93, 2 (1979): 120.

35 L.J. Chapman and M.K. Thomas, "The Climate of Northern Ontario," in *Climatological Studies No. 6* (Toronto: Department of Transport, Meteorological Branch, 1968); M.D. Flannigan and B.M. Wotton, "Lightning-Ignited Forest Fires in Northwestern Ontario," *Canadian Journal of Forest Research* 21 (1991): 277-87.

36 See, for example, Walter L. Loope and John B. Anderton, "Human vs. Lightning Ignition of Presettlement Surface Fires in Coastal Pine Forests of the Upper Great Lakes," *American Midland Naturalist* 140 (1998): 206-18.

37 Thaddeus Harris, *The Journal of a Tour into the Territory Northwest of the Alleghany Mountains (1805),* reprinted in *Early Western Travels, 1748-1846,* vol. 3, ed. Reuben Gold Thwaites (Cleveland: A.H. Clark, 1904), 327; Peter Kalm, *Travels into North America,* trans. John Reinhold Forster (Barre, MA: Imprint Society, 1972; reprint), 210, 361; Timothy Dwight, *Travels in New England and New York,* ed. Barbara Miller Solomon (Cambridge, MA: Harvard University Press, 1969), 1, 72.

38 See D.G. Green, "Fire and Stability in the Postglacial Forests of Southwest Nova Scotia," *Journal of Biogeography* 9 (1982): 29-40.

39 See Ross W. Wein et al., "Bog Profile Evidence of Fire and Vegetation Dynamics Since 3000 Years BP in the Acadian Forest," *Canadian Journal of Botany* 65 (1987): 1180-86; and Sean Basquill et al., *The History and Ecology of Fire in Kejimkujik National Park,* Parks Canada Technical Reports in Ecosystem Science, Report 029 (Parks Canada, 2001), especially 98-100.

40 Ross W. Wein and Janice M. Moore, "Fire History and Recent Fire Rotation Periods in the

Nova Scotia Acadian Forest," *Canadian Journal of Forest Research* 9, 2 (1979): 170; Ross W. Wein and Janice M. Moore, "Fire History and Rotations in the New Brunswick Acadian Forest," *Canadian Journal of Forest Research* 7 (1977): 287-90. Nicholas Denys, *Description and Natural History of the Coasts of North America (Acadia) 1672*, trans. W.F. Ganong (Toronto: Champlain Society, 1908), 395-96. Christien LeClercq, quoted from Ruth Holmes Whitehead, *The Old Man Told Us: Excerpts from Micmac History 1500-1950* (Halifax: Nimbus, 1991), 56-57.

41 Maillard quotes from Whitehead, *The Old Man Told Us*, 10-11.

42 See Basquill, Woodley, and Pardy, "History and Ecology," 40-43. The authors conclude that there is little evidence for anthropogenic burning, but this is true only if compared with such extravagantly burned sites as the prairies. For a thoughtful survey of their neighbours, see William A. Patterson III and Kenneth E. Sassaman, "Indian Fires in the Prehistory of New England," in *Holocene Human Ecology in Northeastern North America*, ed. George Nichols (New York: Plenum Press, 1988), 107-35.

43 For general surveys, see Henry A. Wright and Arthur W. Bailey, *Fire Ecology: United States and Canada* (New York: Wiley and Sons, 1982), especially 267-93.

44 See the graph in Wright and Bailey, *Fire Ecology*, 275; and see, especially, S.J. Muraro, "The Lodgepole Pine Fuel Complex," *Canadian Forest Service Information Report BC-X-53* (Victoria: Canadian Forest Service, 1971). Chilcotin plateau figures from Wright and Bailey, *Fire Ecology*, 275-76, on which see Muraro, "The Lodgepole Pine Fuel Complex"; and R.M. Strang and J.V. Parminter, "Conifer Encroachment on the Chilcotin Grasslands of British Columbia," *Forest Chronicle* 56 (1980): 13-18.

45 See Cliff White, *Wildland Fires in Banff National Park 1880-1980*, Occasional Paper 3 (Parks Canada, 1985); and Jack Wierzchowski, Mark Heathcott, and Michael Flannigan, "Lightning and Lightning Fire, Central Cordillera, Canada," *International Journal of Wildland Fire* 11, 2 (2002): 41-51.

46 Mary T.S. Schaeffer, *A Hunter of Peace: Mary T.S. Schaeffer's Old Indian Trails of the Canadian Rockies*, ed. E.J. Hart (Banff: Whyte Museum of the Canadian Rockies, 1980), 68.

47 Pierre deSmet, quoted from Stephen W. Barrett and Stephen F. Arno, "Indian Fires in the Northern Rockies: Ethnohistory and Ecology," in *Indians, Fire, and the Land in the Pacific Northwest*, ed. Robert Boyd (Corvallis: Oregon State University Press, 1999), 51.

48 Quotations in Barrett and Arno, "Indian Fires," 52; R.M. Rylatt, *Surveying the Canadian Pacific: Memoir of a Railroad Pioneer* (Salt Lake City: University of Utah Press, 1991), 162-64.

49 The indispensable references include Nancy J. Turner, "'Time to Burn': Traditional Use of Fire to Enhance Resource Production by Aboriginal Peoples in British Columbia," in Boyd, ed., *Indians, Fire, and the Land*, 185-218; Sandra L. Peacock and Nancy J. Turner, "'Just like a Garden': Traditional Resource Management and Biodiversity Conservation on the Interior Plateau of British Columbia," in *Biodiversity and Native America*, ed. Paul E. Minnis and Wayne J. Elisens (Norman: University of Oklahoma Press, 2000), 133-79; and Shirley Mah, "Ktunaxa Ethnobotany and Fire Ecology," FRBC Project KB96095-RE, Final Report and Literature Review (BC Ministry of Forests, 2002).

50 Quoted from Peacock and Turner, "Just like a Garden," 188-89.

51 Barrett and Arno, "Indian Fires," 50-64; Stephen Barrett, "Relationship of Indian-Caused Fires to the Ecology of Western Montana Forests" (MSc thesis, University of Montana, 1980).

52 On Garry oak, see Boyd, ed., *Indians, Fire, and the Land*, 1 and passim.

53 For a survey of Douglas fir and fire, see Wright and Bailey, *Fire Ecology*, 250-51, 255-56.

54 See Leslie Main Johnson, "Aboriginal Burning for Vegetation Management in Northwest British Columbia," in Boyd, ed., *Indians, Fire, and the Land*, 238-54; on the Haida, see Nancy J. Turner, "'Burning Mountain Sides for Better Crops': Aboriginal Landscape Burning in British Columbia," *Archeology in Montana* 32, 2 (1991): 57-73, especially 67.

55 On Sitka spruce, see Wright and Bailey, *Fire Ecology*, 312-16; and Fire Effects Information System, http://www.fs.fed.us/database/feis.

56 The best summary is Gyula Péch, "Fire Hazard in Budworm-Killed Balsam Fir Stands on Cape Breton Highlands," *Forestry Chronicle* 69, 2 (1993): 178-86. Parks Canada, alarmed over the potential fire threat, commissioned two earlier studies that failed to appreciate the true fuel dynamics of this particular forest; see A.J. Kayll, "Fire Management Requirements for the Plateau of Cape Breton Highlands National Park," Fire Science Centre, University of New Brunswick (1978); and Ross W. Wein and Janice M. Moore, "Role of Fire in Cape Breton Highlands National Park" (unpublished report, 1979).

57 Reference to the 2001 lightning fire comes from Raymond Quenniville of Parks Canada. I'm grateful for his information.

Tongues of Fire: Black Spruce and High Plains

1 Again, black spruce could support a library by itself, but see L.A. Viereck, "The Effects of Fire in Black Spruce Ecosystems of Alaska and Northern Canada," in Wein and MacLean, eds., *The Role of Fire*, 201-20. Regarding the inevitable origin of black spruce stands from fire, I am indebted to C.E. Van Wagner, personal communication, 2002, relating the collective experience of the Canadian Forest Service.

2 Ibid., 1, 336, 208-9.

3 Bruce Haig, ed., *A Look at Peter Fidler's Journal: Journal of a Journey over Land from Buckingham House to the Rocky Mountains in 1792 & [179]3* (Lethbridge: HRC Limited Edition Series, 1991), 36.

4 Ibid., 13, 25, 36.

5 Ibid., 41, 58, 59.

6 Ibid., 60, 62, 69-71, 75, 82, 88-91, 93.

Conflagration and Complex

1 The best summary is Peter J. Murphy and Cordy Tymstra, "The 1950 Chinchaga River Fire in the Peace River Region of British Columbia/Alberta: Preliminary Results of Simulating Forward Spread Distances," in *Proceedings of the Third Western Region Fire Weather Committee Scientific and Technical Seminar*, 4 February 1986, ed. M.E. Alexander, Canadian Forest Service NOR-5-06 (Edmonton: Minister of Supply and Services Canada, 1986), 20-30. A comparable fire swept the Horn Plateau more recently in the Northwest Territories, reaching about 1.1 million hectares.

2 N. Nimchuk, "Wildfire Behavior Associated with Upper Ridge Breakdown," Alberta Forest Service, ENR Report Number T/50 (1983). On the dispersing smoke, see C.D. Smith, "The Widespread Smoke Layer from Canadian Forest Fires during Late September 1950," *Monthly Weather Review* 78, 9 (1950): 180-84; and H. Wexler, "The Great Smoke Pall – September 24-30, 1950," *Weatherwise* 3, 12 (1950): 129-34, 142.

3 My primary source here is B.J. Stocks and R.B. Street, "Forest Fire Weather and Wildfire Occurrence in the Boreal Forest of Northwestern Ontario," in *Resources and Dynamics of the Boreal Zone*, proceedings of a conference held in Thunder Bay, August 1982, ed. Ross W. Wein, Roderick R. Riewe, and Ian R. Methven (Ottawa: Association of Canadian Universities for Northern Studies, 1983), 249-65.

4 Stocks and Street, "Forest Fire Weather and Wildfire Occurrence," 255.

Creating Fuel

1 The Manitoba references are in E.C. Pielou, *After the Ice Age: The Return of Life to Glaciated North America* (Chicago: University of Chicago Press, 1991), 296; the Great Lakes comparison is from James S. Clark, "Fire and Climate Change during the Last 750 [Years] in Northwestern Minnesota," *Ecological Monographs* 60, 2 (1990): 135-59, and J.S. Clark and P.D. Royall, "Transformation of a Northern Hardwood Forest by Aboriginal (Iroquois) Fire: Charcoal Evidence from Crawford Lake, Ontario, Canada," *Holocene* 5 (1995): 1-9.

Fire Frontiers of Imperial Canada

1 Stephen Parmenius to Richard Hakluyt, 6 August 1583, in *By Great Waters: A Newfoundland and Labrador Anthology,* ed. Peter Neary (Toronto: University of Toronto Press, 1974), 9.
2 Ibid., 10.
3 Quoted from W.C. Wilton and C.H. Evans, "Newfoundland Forest Fire History 1619-1960," Newfoundland Forest Research Centre, Information Report N-X-116 (April 1974), 93.
4 Quoted from ibid., 93-94.
5 W.E. Cormack, "Report of Mr. W.E. Cormack's Journey in Search of the Red Indians in Newfoundland: Read before the Boeothick Institution of St. John's, Newfoundland" (1828?), 9; W.E. Cormack, *Narrative of a Journey across the Island of Newfoundland in 1822,* ed. F.A. Bruton (Toronto: Longmans, Green, 1928), 24; Cormack, "Report," 10.
6 Cormack, "Report," 5; Cormack, *Narrative,* 49, 48.
7 Cited in Wilton and Evans, "Newfoundland," 95-96.
8 Ibid., 94-95.
9 Nicholas Denys, *The Description and Natural History of the Coasts of North America (Acadia),* trans. and ed. William F. Ganong (Toronto: The Champlain Society, 1908), 426-37.
10 Ibid., 435-36.
11 Ibid., 437, 396.
12 Sieur de Diereville, quoted from Andrew Hill Clark, *Acadia: The Geography of Early Nova Scotia to 1760* (Madison: University of Wisconsin Press, 1968), 160.
13 Clark, *Acadia,* 330.
14 Ralph S. Johnson, *Forests of Nova Scotia: A History* (Halifax: Department of Lands of Forests, 1986), 26, 39-40, 42.
15 Ibid., 43.
16 This process is described in ibid., 51.
17 I follow closely and, for Perkins, paraphrase ibid., 51-52.
18 The percentage of white spruce – and the farming cycle overall – come, with modifications, from ibid., 52.
19 All material on and quotations from Smith are from ibid., 59-60; the observations from Burke are closely paraphrased from ibid., 60.
20 Smith paraphrased from ibid., 60.
21 The figures here are from Andrew Hill Clark, *Three Centuries and the Island* (Toronto: University of Toronto Press, 1959), 30-31.
22 Jean-Pierre Roma, quoted from Douglas Sobey, *Early Descriptions of the Forests of Prince Edward Island: A Source Book, Part I: The French Period – 1534-1758* (Charlottetown: Prince Edward Island Department of Agriculture and Forestry and author, 2002), 90. The two dominant methods of forest clearing are described in Clark, *Three Centuries,* 63.

23 Sébastien-François-Ange Le Normant de Mézy, quoted from Sobey, *Early Descriptions,* 93; Louis Duchambon Du Pont, quoted from ibid., 96 (see also François Bigot in ibid., 97); Louis Franquet, quoted from ibid., 102; Joseph de La Roque, quoted from ibid., 106; blueberry barrens quoted from Clark, *Three Centuries,* 33; Franquet, quoted from Sobey, *Early Descriptions,* 101-2; La Roque, quoted from ibid., 106; Pichon, quoted from ibid., 115. Captain Holland, quoted from J.F. Gaudet, *Forestry Past and Present on Prince Edward Island* (Charlottetown: Department of Agriculture and Forestry, 1979), 25.

24 William Cobbett, quoted from Clark, *Three Centuries,* 65.

25 The figures are from ibid., 66, 76, 125.

26 Thomas Curtis, "Voyage to the Island of St. John's," in *Journeys to the Island of St. John or Prince Edward Island 1775-1832,* ed. D.C. Harvey (Toronto: Macmillan, 1955), 28-29, 34, 46-47.

27 Walter Johnstone, "Letter Fourth: Charlotte Town, Nov. 29th, 1820," in Harvey, ed., *Journeys,* 111, 108. A handy distillation of fire references is available in Gaudet, *Forestry Past and Present,* 10-28.

28 Johnstone, "Letter Fourth," 108-11. On smudge fires, see Walter Johnstone, "Letter Sixth: Charlotte Town, Sept. 13th, 1821," in Harvey, ed., *Journeys,* 134.

29 Johnstone, "Letter Sixth," 157; J.L. Lewellin, *Emigration: Prince Edward Island: A Brief but Faithful Account of This Fine Colony* (Charlotte-Town: James D. Haszard, 1832), 193, 196.

30 Walter Johnstone, "Letter Third: Charlotte Town, Oct. 20th, 1820," in Harvey, ed., *Journeys,* 104.

31 Johnstone, "Letter Third," 105-7.

32 On the 1821 fire, see Gaudet, *Forestry,* 27; Alexander Warburton, cited in ibid., 26-27.

33 The figures are from C. Bruce Fergusson, quoted from Johnson, *Forests of Nova Scotia,* 63. See Graeme Wynn, *Timber Colony: A Historical Geography of Early Nineteenth Century New Brunswick* (Toronto: University of Toronto Press, 1981). Anyone familiar with this book will recognize my debt to a marvellous piece of scholarship.

34 The figures are from Wynn, *Timber Colony,* 3, 29. A.R.M. Lower, *The North American Assault on the Canadian Forest* (Toronto: Ryerson Press, 1938).

35 For details, see Wynn, *Timber Colony.*

36 Details, again, are from ibid. For a larger context, see Harold Innis, *Essays in Canadian Economic History* (Toronto: University of Toronto Press, 1956).

37 The "monopoly" quotation is from Wynn, *Timber Colony,* 147.

38 Charles Morris, quoted from W.F. Ganong, "Great Fires in New Brunswick," *Bulletin of Natural History Society of New Brunswick* 20 (1902): xx. For a good digest, see Janice Moore, "Forest Fire History in New Brunswick" (unpublished paper on file with the New Brunswick Forest Service). Other references are summarized in Wynn, *Timber Colony,* 15. For a tight distillation, see also Ross W. Wein and Janice M. Moore, "Fire History and Rotations in the New Brunswick Acadian Forest," *Canadian Journal of Forest Research* 7 (1977): 286.

39 R.A. Cooney, *A Compendious History of the Northern Part of the Province of New Brunswick and of the District of Gaspé in Lower Canada* ... (Halifax: J. Howe, 1832), 65-72; Wynn, *Timber Colony,* 47; for a graph summarizing logging quantities, see 34.

40 James Johnston, *Notes on North America,* vol. 2 (London: W. Blackwood and Sons, 1851), 12.

41 John A. Dickinson and Brian Young, *A Short History of Quebec,* 2nd ed. (Toronto: Copp Clark Pitman, 1993), 4-5; Peter A. Baskerville, *Ontario: Image, Identity, and Power* (Don Mills, ON: Oxford University Press, 2002), 5-6.

42 The most comprehensive summary is Conrad Heidenreich, *Huronia: A History and Geography of the Huron Indians 1600-1650* (Toronto: McClelland and Stewart, 1971); see, for agriculture, 174, 175. The case that indigenous effects were trivial is made by I.D. Campbell and Celina Campbell, "The Impact of Late Woodland Land Use on the Forest Landscape of Southern Ontario," *Great Lakes Geographer* 1, 1 (1994): 21-29, part of a vaster literature, deeply embedded in Canadian scholarship, that intends to demonstrate that humans have had, and can have, no significant effects on the Canadian environment.

43 On village abandonment, see Heidenreich, *Huronia*, 213-16. Returning reclamation is my supposition but is universal among swidden societies. On the weed problem, see Robert Leslie Jones, *History of Agriculture in Ontario 1613-1880* (Toronto: University of Toronto Press, 1946), 7.

44 The swidden estimate is from Heidenreich, *Huronia*, 198.

45 Samuel de Champlain, *The Works of Samuel de Champlain*, vol. 3, ed. H.P. Biggar et al. (Toronto: Champlain Society, 1932), 122; Gabriel Sagard, quoted from *Sagard: The Long Journey to the Hurons*, ed. G.M. Wrong (Toronto: Champlain Society, 1939), 90; Catharine Parr Traill, *The Backwoods of Canada* (Toronto: McClelland and Stewart, 1989; reprint), 59, 95.

46 Traill, *The Backwoods of Canada*, 109.

47 Dickinson and Young, *A Short History of Quebec*, 17.

48 Jones, *History of Agriculture in Ontario*, 8. On fallow and rough pasture, see 13-14.

49 See Daniel C. Dey and Richard Guyette, "Anthropogenic Fire History and Red Oak Forests in South-Central Ontario," *Forestry Chronicle* 76, 2 (2000): 339-47, for a marvellous summary. On the various lightning fire rates, see also D. Strickland, "Why Fire Is like Rain," *Raven* 31, 9 (1990): 1-2; and Walter L. Loope and John B. Anderton, "Human vs. Lightning Ignition of Presettlement Surface Fires in Coastal Pine Forests of the Upper Great Lakes," *American Midland Naturalist* 140 (1998): 206-18.

50 Fire frequencies are from Dey and Guyette, "Anthropogenic Fire History," 345.

51 Daniel C. Dey and Richard Guyette, "Fire History Near an Historic Travel Corridor in Ontario," Forest Research Report 140 (Sault Ste. Marie: Ontario Forest Research Institute, 1996).

52 Richard Guyette, Daniel C. Dey, and Chris McDonell, "Determining Fire History from Old White Pine Stumps in an Oak-Pine Forest in Bracebridge, Ontario," Forest Research Report 133 (Sault Ste. Marie: Ontario Forest Research Institute, 1995); Richard Guyette and Daniel C. Dey, "A Dendrochronological Fire History of Opeongo Lookout in Algonquin Park, Ontario," Forest Research Report 134 (Sault Ste. Marie: Ontario Forest Research Institute, 1995).

53 Richard Guyette and Daniel C. Dey, "A Presettlement Fire History in an Oak-Pine Forest Near Basin Lake, Algonquin Park, Ontario," Forest Research Report 132 (Sault Ste. Marie: Ontario Forest Research Institute, 1995), 5; and Dey and Guyette, "Anthropogenic Fire History," 343.

54 James Wolfe and George Scott, quoted from Dickinson and Young, *A Short History of Quebec*, 48. The quotations on the fireships are from Francis Parkman, *France and England in North America*, vol. 2 (New York: Library of America, 1983), 1342-43.

55 Traill, *The Backwoods of Canada*, 110, 112. On the two methods, see Jones, *History of Agriculture*, 71, and on windrow-firing see 70.

56 Traill, *The Backwoods of Canada*, 158-59. An excellent original account of a logging bee is given in Jones, *History of Agriculture*, 70.

57 Traill, *The Backwoods of Canada*, 158-59.

58 Ibid., 159.

59 Ibid., 158.

60 Susanna Moodie, *Roughing It in the Bush* (Toronto: McClelland and Stewart, 1989; reprint), 305.

61 Ibid., 307.

62 Ibid., 308-9.

63 Ibid., 311.

64 Ibid., 389-90.

65 Ibid., 394-95.

66 Ibid.

67 R. Peter Gillis and Thomas R. Roach, *Lost Initiatives: Canada's Forest Industries, Forest Policy, and Forest Conservation* (Westport, CT: Greenwood Press, 1986), 6. On the agro-forestier system, see Baskerville, *Ontario,* 73-74.

68 Several excellent summaries of the system exist: see Lower, *The North American Assault on the Canadian Forest;* and Gillis and Roach, *Lost Initiatives.*

69 I follow closely Gillis and Roach, *Lost Initiatives,* 18-23.

70 On the 1851 fires, see Arthur H. Richardson, *Forestry in Ontario* (Ontario Department of Forestry, n.d.), 20.

71 W.H. Withrow, quoted from Lower, *North American Assault,* v.

72 Again I follow closely Gillis and Roach, *Lost Initiatives;* "in one way or another" is quoted from 1. For revenue, see H.V. Nelles, *The Politics of Development: Forests, Mines, and Hydro-Power in Ontario 1849-1941* (Montreal and Kingston: McGill-Queen's University Press, 2005; reprint), 17-19; the Bronson quotation is from 18.

73 George Head, *Forest Scenes and Incidents, in the Wilds of North America* (Toronto: Coles Publishing, 1980; reprint), 314-15.

74 Elizabeth Simcoe, *Mrs. Simcoe's Diary,* ed. Mary Quayle Innis (Toronto: Macmillan of Canada, 1966), 72.

75 The first conviction date is from Donald MacKay, *The Lumberjacks* (Toronto: McGraw-Hill Ryerson, 1978), 269. The quotations are from Jones, *History of Agriculture,* 85-86, and the fallow estimates from 91. Moodie is quoted from Baskerville, *Ontario,* 71. The comparative estimates on wood cut are from J. David Wood, *Making Ontario: Agricultural Colonization and Landscape Re-Creation before the Railway* (Montreal and Kingston: McGill-Queen's University Press, 2000), 13-14.

76 The urban information is from Dickinson and Young, *A Short History of Quebec,* 142.

77 For general discussion, though centred on Europe, see Stephen Pyne, *Vestal Fire: An Environmental History, Told through Fire, of Europe and Europe's Encounter with the World* (Seattle: University of Washington Press, 1997).

78 Robson quoted in William H. Goetzmann and Glyndwr Williams, *The Atlas of North American Exploration* (New York: Prentice-Hall General Reference, 1992), 106. On the larger setting, see John S. Galbraith, *The Hudson's Bay Company as an Imperial Factor 1821-1869* (New York: Octagon Books, 1977; reprint).

79 For a distilled summary of exploration, see William H. Goetzmann and Glyndwr Williams, *The Atlas of North American Exploration* (New York: Prentice Hall, 1992). The quotations are from Samuel Hearne, *A Journey from Prince of Wales's Fort, in Hudson's Bay, to the Northern Ocean ...* (Dublin: Printed for Byrne, 1796), 283, 19, 184, 146.

80 Hearne, *Journey from Prince of Wales's Fort,* 454.

81 Alexander Mackenzie, *Voyages from Montreal ... in the Years 1789 and 1793* (London: Printed for T. Cadell, Jr., and W. Davies ..., 1801), 38, 103, xliii, 241.

82 Ibid., 24, 170, 179, 300, 185.
83 Alexander Henry and David Thompson, *New Light on the Early History of the Greater Northwest: The Manuscript Journals of Alexander Henry and David Thompson 1799-1814*, ed. Elliot Coues (Minneapolis: Ross and Haines, 1965; reprint), 1, 180, 176, 229, 265, 519, 229.
84 David Thompson, *David Thompson's Narrative of His Explorations in Western America*, ed. J.B. Tyrrell (Toronto: Champlain Society, 1916), 241, 248; David Thompson, *Columbia Journals*, ed. Barbara Belyea (Montreal and Kingston: McGill-Queen's University Press, 1993), 221 (25 July 1807).
85 For the treatment of HBC posts, I'm obligated to Gregory Thomas, "Fire and the Fur Trade: The Saskatchewan District: 1790-1840," *Beaver* 24 (1983?): 32-39; quotations from 34.
86 Ibid., 34, 37.
87 Ibid.
88 E.C. Pielou, *After the Ice Age* (Chicago: University of Chicago Press, 1991), 309.
89 John Macoun, *Manitoba and the Great North-West* (Guelph, ON: World Publishing, 1882), 651-52, 296.
90 James Douglas, quoted from Robin Fisher, "Contact and Trade, 1774-1849," in *The Pacific Province: A History of British Columbia*, ed. Hugh J.M. Johnston (Vancouver: Douglas and McIntyre, 1996), 63.
91 J.I. Little, "The Foundations of Government," in Johnston, ed., *Pacific Province*, 68-69. I follow closely Little's text.

With Fire in Their Eyes: Gabriel Sagard and Henry Hind
1 John Palliser, *The Papers of the Palliser Expedition 1857-1860*, ed. I.M. Spry (Toronto: Champlain Society, 1968), 9, 159; John Palliser, *Solitary Rambles and Adventures of a Hunter in the Prairies* (Tokyo: Charles Tuttle, 1969), 89-95. On fires set on purpose, see Palliser, *Papers of the Palliser Expedition*, 204.
2 Gabriel Sagard-Théodat, *Sagard's Long Journey to the Country of the Hurons*, ed. Georg M. Wrong, trans. H.H. Langton (New York: Greenwood Press, 1968; reprint), 2.
3 Ibid., 61, 59, 109; 186, 149 (smoking); 156 (war); 161 (torture); 163 (escape); 187 (superstition); 197 (sweat); 200 (disease); 205 (feast); 209 (cemetery); 228 (fleas).
4 Ibid., 103-4.
5 Ibid., 269.
6 Information on Hind comes from W.L. Morton, *Henry Youle Hind 1823-1908* (Toronto: University of Toronto Press, 1980), quotation from 35. Also useful is Richard A. Jarrell, "Hind, Henry Youle," in *Dictionary of Canadian Biography (Online)*, http://www.biography.ca.
7 Henry Youle Hind, *Narrative of the Canadian Red River Exploring Expedition of 1857 and of the Assiniboine and Saskatchewan Exploring Expedition of 1858*, vol. 1 (New York: Greenwood Press, 1969; reprint), 256, 292, 336.
8 Ibid., 317, 337, 348 (sterility); 340 (aridity); 405 (remarkable); 372 (river); 405-6 (lamentable); 337 (reclamation). A good summary of Hind's opinions is in vol. 2, 376.
9 Henry Youle Hind, *Explorations in the Interior of the Labrador Peninsula*, vol. 1 (London: Longman et al., 1863), 203-4.
10 Ibid., 237, 206-8.
11 Ibid., 205, 207, 250.
12 Ibid., 221-22, 226, 225.

13 Hind, *Narrative*, vol. 1, 336; Hind, *Explorations*, 208-9.

14 H.Y. Hind, *The Dominion of Canada* (Toronto: L. Stebbins, 1869), 65, 70.

15 Morton, *Henry Youle Hind,* 122.

"Burning Most Furiously"

1 Captain Thomas James, *The Strange and Dangerous Voyage of Captaine Thomas James ...* (London: Theatrum Orbis Terrarum and DaCapo Press, 1968; reprint), 83-84.

2 Ibid., 84.

3 Ibid., 84-85.

4 Ibid., 85.

5 Henry Youle Hind, *Explorations in the Interior of the Labrador Peninsula,* 2 vols. (London: Longman et al., 1863), 250. I follow Hind's account unless otherwise stated. Since my text was written, a new study has appeared that tracks the origins of the 1780 Dark Day to drought and burning; see Erin R. McMurry et al., "Fire Scars Reveal Source of New England's 1780 Dark Day," *International Journal of Wildland Fire* 16, 3 (2007): 266-70.

6 Fred G. Plummer, *Forest Fires,* US Forest Service Bulletin 117 (Washington, DC: Government Printing Office, 1912), provides both a cross-section of a large fire as it thins downwind, indicating the region of dark days, and recycles Hind's accounts.

7 Hind, *Explorations,* 251-52, 257.

8 Quoted in ibid., 254-55.

9 Ibid.

10 Ibid., 257-59, 261.

11 Ibid., 261-63.

12 For the Miramichi fire, I have relied particularly on Alan MacEachern, "The Meaning of the Miramichi Fire," an unpublished manuscript the author generously shared with me that tallies all sources and analyzes their content and reliability. It is a rare model of careful fire scholarship. Most of my quotations come from the original sources, but my appreciation of the context was shaped by MacEachern's important essay.

13 Major Samuel Strickland, *Twenty-Seven Years in Canada West* (London: Richard Bentley, 1853), 1, 20-21. Other quotations ("fires in the woods" and "raged") are from Beamish Murdoch, *A Narrative of the Late Fires in Miramichi, New Brunswick ...* (Halifax: Holland, 1825), 5-6.

14 Robert Cooney, *A Compendious History of the Northern Part of the Province of New Brunswick ...* (Halifax: Joseph Howe, 1832), 65-66.

15 The most thorough examination of evidence is W.F. Ganong, "On the Limits of the Great Fire of Miramichi of 1825," *New Brunswick Natural History Society Bulletin* 24, 5, Part 4 (1906): 410-18. Other quotations and the Maine references are from *Narrative of the Late Fires,* 5, 8.

16 Cooney, *Compendious History,* 76; the best summary (and the source for the burned-body quotation) is *Narrative of the Late Fires,* 9.

17 The summary is in *Narrative of the Late Fires,* quotation from 12; the Douglas address is from 38-43, quotations from 39. For the committee, see William Stewart Wallace, compiler, *Report of the Commissioners for the Ascertaining the Losses Occasioned by the Late Fires in New-Brunswick* (Fredericton: G.K. Lugrin, 1826). A detailed summary of Douglas' performance in the crisis is given in Murray Young, "The Great Fires of 1825," *Officers' Quarterly* 13, 1 (1997): 7-11, which quotes the account given in S.W. Fullom's *Life of Sir Howard Douglas.*

18 James Pierce, Chatham *Mercury,* 27 June 1826, quoted from MacEachern, "The Meaning

of the Miramichi Fire," 32-33. The story of fading ceremonies is from MacEachern, 40-41. James E. Alexander, *L'Acadie: Or, Seven Years' Explorations in British America*, vol. 2 (London: Henry Colburn, 1849), 142.

19 The quotations are from the *Journal of the Legislative Council of the Province of New-Brunswick*, Sixtieth Session of the Eighth General Assembly, 19 January 1826, 796.

20 The ship's master quotation is from *Narrative of the Late Fires*, 8n; Cooney, *Compendious History*, 10.

Reconnaissance by Fire: Robert Bell and Bernhard Fernow

1 George Perkins Marsh, *Man and Nature* (Cambridge, MA: Harvard University Press, 1965; reprint), has many references to fire and forest destruction, but Miramichi is highlighted on 30n28.

2 John A. Macdonald, quoted from Kenneth Johnstone, *Timber and Trauma: 75 Years with the Federal Forestry Service 1899-1974* (Ottawa: Minister of Supply and Services, 1991), 11-13.

3 A good summary of political evolution, as it affected fire protection, is in Peter Murphy, *History of Forest and Prairie Fire Control Policy in Alberta* (Edmonton: Alberta Energy and Natural Resources, 1985).

4 R. Peter Gillis and Thomas R. Roach, *Lost Initiatives: Canada's Forest Industries, Forest Policy, and Forest Conservation* (New York: Greenwood Press, 1986), 34.

5 Ibid., 37-38.

6 A.T. Drummond, "Canadian Timber Trees: Their Destruction and Preservation," in *Fourth Report of the Montreal Horticultural Society* (Montreal: Witness Printing House, 1879), 17, 24-26.

7 Gillis and Roach, *Lost Initiatives*, 39-41; Johnstone, *Timber and Trauma*, 14-15.

8 H.G. Joly de Lotbinière, quoted from Murphy, *History of Forest and Prairie Fire Control*, 72.

9 Quotation from Gillis and Roach, *Lost Initiatives*, 45.

10 On Burgess, see Johnstone, *Timber and Trauma*, 15.

11 Cited in *Annual Report of the Department of the Interior for the Year 1897* (Ottawa: S.E. Dawson, 1898), 61; A.O. Wheeler, *Annual Report of the Department of the Interior for 1899* (Ottawa: S.E. Dawson, 1900), 7.

12 H.M. Ami, "Memorial of Robert Bell," *Bulletin of the Geological Society of America* 38, 1 (1927): 27. I am the beneficiary of early research done by Marty Alexander, who assembled a general collection of materials on Bell and then generously made them available to me. I needed only to supplement his work with a few items in the archives.

13 On the properties of the Second Age, see William H. Goetzmann, *New Lands, New Men: The United States and the Second Great Age of Discovery* (New York: Viking, 1986).

14 Sources for a Bell biography include Library and Archives Canada (hereafter LAC), Robert Bell Papers, MG 29, B15 1, which include major biographies, both published and unpublished; "The Official Career of Dr. Robert Bell, F.R.S., of the Geological Survey of Canada," *Ottawa Free Press*, 1907; Ami, "Memorial of Robert Bell," 18-34; "Biographical Notice with Portrait of Dr. Robert Bell," in *Transactions of the Royal Society of Canada*, 3rd series 12 (Ottawa: Royal Society of Canada, 1918), 11-14; and Charles Hallock, *One of Canada's Explorers* (Washington, DC: Gibson Brothers, 1901), reprinted from *Forest and Stream*.

15 Robert Bell, "The Geographical Distribution of the Forest Trees of Canada," Montreal Horticultural Society Report 7 (Montreal: Gazette Printing, 1882), 15, reprinted from "The Northern Limit of the Principal Forest Trees of Canada East of the Rocky Mountains," in

"Report on Hudson's Bay and Some of the Lakes and Rivers Lying to the West," in *Geological Survey of Canada, Report of Progress 1879-80,* Part C (Montreal: Dawson Brothers, 1881), 38-56. Quotations from 1884 come from Robert Bell, "The Forests of Canada," *Canadian Record of Science* 2, 2 (1886): 71-72.

16 Bell, "The Forests of Canada," 72-73.

17 Ibid., 77, 73.

18 Ibid., 71-72.

19 Robert Bell, "Forest Fires in Northern Canada," *Proceedings of American Forestry Congress* 7 (1889): 50.

20 Ibid., 52.

21 Ibid., 54. The story of the burned cache is in Douglas Leechman, "The Father of Place Names," *Beaver* 34 (1954): 28. The "scenes of destruction" quotation is from Robert Bell, "The Geographical Distribution of Forest Trees in Canada," *Scottish Geographical Magazine* 13 (1897): 294.

22 Bell, "Forest Fires in Northern Canada," 55; the "turpentine" and "stopping for fires" quotations are from Robert Bell, "The Alarming Destruction of Our Forests by Fire," in *Report of the Canadian Forestry Convention* (Ottawa: Government Printing, 1906), 31-32.

23 Bell, "Alarming Destruction," 32.

24 Ibid.

25 For details of the dispute, see Morris Zaslow, *Reading the Rocks: The Story of the Geological Survey of Canada* (Toronto: Macmillan, 1975), 136-38.

26 For biographical facts, see Andrew Denny Rodgers III, *Bernhard Eduard Fernow: A Story of North American Forestry* (New York: Hafner, 1968; reprint).

27 Quoted from ibid., 476. I'm indebted to Peter Murphy for reminding me of the differences between the American and Canadian strategies, particularly the commitment of Canadian foresters to protection outside reserves.

28 Heinrich Cotta, quoted from Bernhard Fernow, editor's preface, *Forestry Quarterly* 1 (1902-3): 3; the conservation as business quotation is from Rodgers, *Fernow,* 526.

29 Rodgers, *Fernow,* 535, 167.

30 Ibid., 535.

Fire Provinces of Industrial Canada
Dominion of Fire: Canada's Quest for Fire Conservancy

1 Elihu Stewart, "Report of the Chief Inspector of Timber and Forestry for Canada," Part 9 of *Annual Report of the Department of the Interior for the Year 1899* (Ottawa: S.E. Dawson, 1900), 19-20.

2 Ibid., 5, 12, 20.

3 *First Annual Meeting of the Canadian Forestry Association,* Ottawa, 8 March 1900 (Ottawa: Government Printing Bureau, 1900), 19 (Southward), 24 (Pearce).

4 Stewart, "Report," *Annual Report ... 1899,* 3; Elihu Stewart, "Report of the Superintendent of Forestry," in *Annual Report for the Department of the Interior for the Year 1900-1901* (Ottawa: S.E. Dawson, 1901), 3-4 (rangers), xii (deputy minister).

5 Elihu Stewart, "Report of the Superintendent of Forestry," in *Annual Report of the Department of the Interior for the Year 1901-1902* (Ottawa: S.E. Dawson, 1903), 3; Elihu Stewart, "Report of the Superintendent of Forestry," Appendix 1, "Report of Norman M. Ross," in *Annual Report of the Department of the Interior for the Year 1906* (Ottawa: S.E. Dawson, 1907), 15, 18; Elihu Stewart, "Report of the Superintendent of Forestry," Appendix 8, "Report of James Leamy," in *Annual Report of the Department of the Interior for the Year*

1903-1904 (Ottawa: S.E. Dawson, 1905), 25; Stewart, "Report," Appendix 10, "Report of Jos. E. Stauffer," *Annual Report ... 1906*, 30. On American burning, see also Stewart, "Report," Appendix 11, "Report of C.A. Walkinshaw," in *Annual Report ... 1906*, 31.

6 Elihu Stewart, "Report of the Superintendent of Forestry," *Annual Report ... 1903-1904*, 8; Elihu Stewart, "Report of the Superintendent of Forestry," in *Annual Report of the Department of the Interior for the Year 1905* (Ottawa: S.E. Dawson, 1906), 3.

7 Wilfrid Laurier, quoted from Johnstone, *Timber and Trauma*, 38.

8 On Petawawa, see I.C.M. Place, *75 Years of Research in the Woods: A History of Petawawa Forest Experiment Station and Petawawa National Forestry Institute* (Burnstown, ON: General Store Publishing House, 2002), 61.

9 Robert Campbell, "Report of the Superintendent of Forestry and Irrigation," in *Annual Report of the Department of the Interior for the Year 1908* (Ottawa: S.E. Dawson, 1909), 8; Robert Campbell, "Report of the Superintendent of Forestry and Irrigation," Appendix 1, "Report of the Inspector of Forest Reserves," in *Annual Report of the Department of the Interior for the Year 1910* (Ottawa: S.E. Dawson, 1911), 13; the statistics are from Campbell, "Report," *Annual Report ... 1908*, 3.

10 Robert Campbell, "Report of the Superintendent of Forestry and Irrigation," Appendix 2, "Report of R.H. MacMillan," in *Annual Report of the Department of the Interior for the Year 1909* (Ottawa: S.E. Dawson, 1910), 41.

11 Campbell, "Report," Appendix 1, "Report of the Inspector of Forest Reserves," and Appendix 2, "Report of R.H. MacMillan," *Annual Report ... 1909*, 28, 36; Robert Campbell, "Report of the Superintendent of Forestry," Appendix 3, "Report of A. Knechtel," in *Annual Report of the Department of the Interior for the Year 1911* (Ottawa: S.E. Dawson, 1912), 40.

12 Campbell, "Report," Appendix 16, "Report of W.R. McLeod," *Annual Report ... 1909*, 81; Campbell, "Report," Appendix 3, "Report of A. Knechtel," *Annual Report ... 1911*, 39.

13 Campbell, "Report," *Annual Report ... 1910*, 7; Campbell, "Report," *Annual Report ... 1911*, 11.

14 Campbell, "Report," *Annual Report ... 1910*, 17; Robert Campbell, "Report of the Director of Forestry for the Year 1914," Part 6, Appendix 6, "Report of the Inspector of Fire-Ranging," in *Annual Report, Department of the Interior, 1914* (Ottawa: Government Printing Office, 1915), 115.

15 The Nelson River quotation is from Robert Campbell, "Report of the Director of Forestry for the Year 1912," Part 6, Appendix 28, "Report of Frank M. Beard," in *Annual Report, Department of the Interior, 1912* (Ottawa: Government Printing Bureau, 1912), 130; the final quotation is from Campbell, "Report of the Superintendent of Forestry and Irrigation," Appendix 6, "Report of Peter Z. Caverhill," *Annual Report ... 1910*, 71.

16 Campbell, "Report," *Annual Report ... 1910*, 18. For a survey of qualifications, see Campbell, "Report," *Annual Report ... 1912*, 12-13. For a register of duties for rangers on reserves, see Knechtel's instructions in Albert Helmer to Director of Forestry, 1911, LAC, RG 39 249, file 130590.

17 Robert Campbell, "Report of the Director of Forestry for the Year 1913," Part 6, in *Annual Report, Department of the Interior, 1913* (Ottawa: Government Printing Office, 1914), 19.

18 Campbell, "Report," *Annual Report ... 1914*, 74 (staff); 79 (India burning); E.H. Finlayson, quoted from Robert Campbell, "Report of the Director of Forestry for the Year 1915," Part 6, in *Annual Report, Department of the Interior, 1915* (Ottawa: Government Printing Office, 1916), 66.

19 Robert Campbell, "Report of the Director of Forestry for the Year 1916," Part 6, Appendix 4, E.H. Finlayson, in *Annual Report, Department of the Interior, 1916* (Ottawa: J. de L.

Taché, 1916), 77. The quotations on staffing are from Clyde Leavitt, "Report of Committee on Forests," in Commission of Conservation, *Report of the Eighth Annual Meeting* (Montreal: Federated Press, 1917), 193.

20 The remote patrols were reorganized in 1916. For a description, see H.J. Bury, Memorandum, to R.H. Campbell, 11 November 1916, LAC, RG 39, vol. 862, file 39112.

21 On railways, see Robert Campbell, "Report of the Director of Forestry for the Year 1917," Part 6, in *Annual Report, Department of the Interior, 1917* (Ottawa: J. de L. Taché, 1918), 19; Robert Campbell, "Report of the Director of Forestry for the Year 1918," Appendix 4, "Report of the District Inspector of Forest Reserves for Alberta," Part 3, in *Annual Report, Department of the Interior, 1918* (Ottawa: J. de L. Taché, 1919), 54.

22 Robert Campbell, "Report of the Director of Forestry for the Fiscal Year Ended March 31, 1920," Appendix 3, "Report of the District Inspector of Forest Reserves for Saskatchewan," in *Department of the Interior, Canada* (Ottawa: Thomas Mulvey, 1921), 23.

23 Campbell, "Report," *Annual Report ... 1918,* 7-8.

24 Robert Campbell, "Report of the Director of Forestry for the Fiscal Year Ended March 31, 1921," Appendix 5, "Report of the District Forest Inspector for British Columbia," in *Department of the Interior, Canada* (Ottawa: F.A. Acland, 1922), 7-8, 40.

25 Robert Campbell, "Report of the Director," in *Report of the Director of Forestry for the Fiscal Year Ended March 31, 1922* (Ottawa: F.A. Acland, 1923), 7.

26 Appendix 2, "Report of the District Forest Inspector for Manitoba, H.I. Stevenson," Appendix 3, "Report of the District Forest Inspector for Saskatchewan, C. MacFayden," in Campbell, *Report for ... March 31, 1922,* 23, 28-29; Johnstone, *Timber and Trauma,* 56; but see also Appendix 5, "Report of the District Forest Inspector for British Columbia, D. Roy Cameron," in Campbell, *Report for ... March 31, 1922,* 37-41.

27 Progress Reports, May to September 1927, Department of the Interior – Forestry Branch, LAC, RG 39 263, file 39440-1, O/Salmon Arm Fire RG – Supervision – Reports.

28 The quotations are from Cliff White, *Wildland Fires in Banff National Park 1880-1980,* Occasional Paper 3 (Parks Canada, 1985), 27-28.

29 Ibid., 30, 35-36.

30 H.R. MacMillan, "Report on Proposed National Park" (unpublished report, Parks Canada, 1909), 7-8.

31 White, *Wildland Fires,* 47. W.W. Cory, Deputy Minister, "Report of the Department of the Interior, 1914-15," *Annual Report of the Department of the Interior of Canada, for the Year 1914-15* (Ottawa: J. de le Tache, 1916), xlv.

32 White, *Wildland Fires,* 54-57.

33 "1924 Forest Fire Conference," LAC, RG 39, vol. 597, (J.B. Harkin) 69-70.

34 Ibid., 70-72.

35 "Forest Fire Conference, 1924," (N.C. Sparks) 73-74.

36 "Forest Fire Conference, 1924," (J.B. Harkin) 221, 72-73, 222.

37 White, *Wildland Fires,* 58-60.

38 The quotation is from Gillis and Roach, *Lost Initiatives,* 74; the summary of reliance is from 72-78, 189-98.

39 J.H. White, "Memorandum Regarding the Country between Sudbury and Port Arthur," in Clyde Leavitt, *Forest Protection in Canada, 1912* (Toronto: Bryant Press, 1913), 155.

40 The Fernow quotation is from Rodgers, *Fernow,* 480. See too, B.E. Fernow et al., "Report of Committee on Forest Fires, Canadian Forestry Association," *Forestry Quarterly* 9 (1911): 577-88.

41 On Leavitt's background, particularly his relationship to Fernow, see Rodgers, *Fernow,*

340-41, 481, and 502-3; the Fernow quotation is on 503. Leavitt, *Forest Protection in Canada, 1912;* Clyde Leavitt, comp., *Forest Protection in Canada, 1913-14* (Toronto: William Briggs, 1915).

42 C.D. Howe, "The Effect of Repeated Forest Fires upon the Reproduction of Commercial Species in Peterborough County, Ontario," in Leavitt, *Forest Protection in Canada 1913-1914,* 201; C.D. Howe, "How Shall We Make Our Forests Safe for Trees?" in Commission of Conservation, *Report of the Tenth Annual Meeting, 1919* (Ottawa: Mortimer, 1919), 177.

43 J.H. White, "Forestry on Dominion Lands," in Leavitt, *Forest Protection in Canada 1913-1914,* 274.

44 Commission of Conservation, *Report of the First Annual Meeting* (Ottawa: Mortimer, 1910), 19.

45 J. Grove Smith, "Fire Prevention," in Commission of Conservation, *Report of the Seventh Annual Meeting, 1916* (Montreal: Federated Press, 1916), 185. This analysis was later expanded into a separate publication by the commission: J. Grove Smith, *Fire Waste in Canada* (Ottawa: Commission of Conservation, 1918).

46 Smith, "Fire Prevention," 186.

47 B.E. Fernow, "Scientific Forestry in Europe: Its Value and Applicability in Canada," and "Co-Operation in Forestry," in Commission of Conservation, *Report of the Sixth Annual Meeting, 1915* (Ottawa: Bryant Press, 1915), 40, 121, 126.

48 The quotation is from Gillis and Roach, *Lost Initiatives,* 196.

49 The best summary of the macroeconomics of Canada's "northern economy" remains Harold Innis, *Essays in Canadian Economic History,* ed. Mary Q. Innis (Toronto: University of Toronto Press, 1956). All that is required is to insert fire into the ranks of forests, fish, furs, and farms. Worster's comments from Donald A. Worster, "Two Faces West: The Development Myth in Canada and the United States," in *Terra Pacifica: People and Place in the Northwestern States and Western Canada,* ed. Paul Hirt (Pullman, WA: Washington State University Press, 1998), 71-91.

50 A concise summary of developments is available in Richard A. Rajala, "Feds, Forests, and Fire: A Century of Federal Forestry Innovation in Canada" (manuscript, National Museum of Science and Technology, 2000), 47-53.

51 H.C. Johnson, "Better Apparatus for Forest Fire Fighting," *Canadian Journal of Forestry* 13 (1917): 899.

52 *Report of Forest Branch of the Dept. of Lands for Year Ending Dec. 31, 1921* (Victoria: King's Printer, 1922), 37. For interesting insight into the impact of portable pumps, see H.C. Johnson's paper read before the Board of Railway Commissioners in Toronto, January 1925, "Fighting Forest Fires with Mechanical Equipment," reprinted by Watson, Jack, and Company.

53 See Rajala, "Feds, Forests, and Fire," and Gillis and Roach, *Lost Initiatives,* for thumbnail summaries of early research; see also H.W. Beall, "Forest Fire Danger Rating: The Early Years" (unpublished report included with papers collected to support the nomination of Beall for the Order of Canada, now housed at the Northern Forestry Centre, hereafter known as the Beall file). The Finlayson quotation is from E.H. Finlayson, *Report of the Director of Forestry 1927-28* (Ottawa: F.A. Acland, 1929), 5. On Petawawa and early Dominion Forest Service research, see Johnstone, *Timber and Trauma,* 51-52; and Place, *75 Years.*

54 Again see Rajala, "Feds, Forests, and Fires"; and Gillis and Roach, *Lost Initiatives.* The Finlayson quotation is from *Report of the Director of Forestry 1929-30* (Ottawa: F.A. Acland, 1931), 12. See also C.E. Van Wagner, "Six Decades of Forest Fire Science in Canada," *Forest Chronicle* 66 (1990): 133-37.

55 "Forest Fire Conference, 1924," (P.Z. Caverhill) 326. But see Rajala, "Feds, Forests, and Fires," 58-59, for the alternative.

56 On pre-armistice advocacy, see, for example, Major K.E. Kennedy, "Guarding Forests by Airplanes," *Canadian Forestry Journal* 14, 2 (1918): 1521-24; on the Commission of Conservation and Quebec interest, see Hy Sorgius, "Hydroaeroplane for Forest Protection," *Canadian Forestry Journal* 14 (1918): 1970; on zeppelins, see "'Zeps' and Forest Patrolling," *Canadian Forestry Journal* 15 (1919), 4: 155-56; on the St. Maurice experiment, see Stuart Graham, "The First Flying Patrol of Forests," *Canadian Forestry Journal* 15, 5 (1919): 243-44. The best summaries are the submissions to the "Forest Fire Conference, 1924," 336-90; Bruce West, *The Firebirds* (Ministry of Natural Resources, 1974); and Rajala, "Feds, Forests, and Fires," 57-74. The details are available in annual reports of the agencies and an interminable stream of journal articles.

57 For a thorough summary of the early institutions and trials, see D.G. Fraser, "Aircraft for Forest Fire Control in Canada" (Ottawa: Forest Research Branch, 1964); a quick synopsis is available in Rajala, "Feds, Forests, and Fires," 60-61.

58 Fraser, "Aircraft for Forest Fire Control in Canada"; Rajala, "Feds, Forests, and Fires," 62-63, 65, 72.

59 "Forest Fire Conference, 1924," (E.J. Zavitz) 365. For a complete history of early Ontario fire patrols, see West, *The Firebirds*.

60 "Forest Fire Conference, 1924," (H.I. Stevenson) 344-45; (Gustave Piché) 367.

61 "Forest Fire Conference, 1924," (H.I. Stevenson) 348.

62 "Forest Fire Conference, 1924," (J.L. Gordon) 368.

63 Ibid., 369.

64 "Forest Fire Conference, 1924," (T.D. Pattullo) 382.

65 "Forest Fire Conference, 1924," (J.L. Gordon) 379, (R. Cameron) 381.

66 "Forest Fire Conference, 1924," (J.L. Gordon) 382; (J.J. Lyons and T.D. Pattullo) 379.

67 See, for example, "Transportation as a Factor in Canadian Economic History" and "Government Ownership and the Canadian Scene," in Innis, *Essays in Canadian Economic History*, 220-32, 78-96.

68 Brandis, particularly, became a global emblem of state-sponsored forestry; see as an influence, Gifford Pinchot, *Breaking New Ground* (Seattle: University of Washington Press, 1972; reprint), 9; on Algeria, see Theodore S. Woolsey, Jr., and William B. Greeley, *Studies in French Forestry* (New York: John Wiley and Sons, 1920), vi. For the larger setting, see Stephen Pyne, *Vestal Fire* (Seattle: University of Washington Press, 1997), 484-99.

69 Background information is from Gillis and Roach, *Lost Initiatives*, 194.

70 D.R. Cameron, "Forest Fire Protection in Canada," in Second British Empire Forestry Conference, *Proceedings and Resolution* (Ottawa: F.A. Acland, 1927), 178-79.

71 Ibid., 178, 182.

72 Ibid., 184.

73 Ibid., 186-87.

74 Second British Empire Forestry Conference, *Proceedings and Resolution*, (McLachlin) 208, 207; (Schierbeck) 209; (Cubitt) 206.

75 Ibid., (Cameron) 178; (Lovat) 211.

76 "Forest Fire Conference, 1924," 4.

77 Ibid., (Stewart) 6-7. For a concise summary of this combustible era, see Janet Looker, *Disaster Canada* (Toronto: Lynx Images, 2000), 101-33, and Donal Baird, *The Story of Firefighting in Canada* (Erin, ON: Boston Mills Press, 1986), passim.

78 "Forest Fire Conference, 1924," (Stewart) 6-8; (Cameron) 9; (Pattullo) 13; (Stewart) 16.

79 "Forest Fire Conference, 1924," 413-14.

80 See the exchange between Robinson and Piché in ibid., 31; (Zavitz) 34; (Cameron) 36; (Pattullo) 19.

81 Ibid., (Stewart and Cameron) 413; (Pattullo) 414.

82 D. Roy Cameron, "Forest Fire Protection in Canada: Progress since 1923," *Papers Presented, Third British Empire Forestry Conference, Australia and New Zealand 1928* (Ottawa: F.A. Acland, 1928), 3.

83 Ibid., 9-13.

84 Ibid., 9-10; the Saskatchewan quotation is from J. Smart, in Finlayson, *Report ... 1927-28*, 25.

85 W.L.M. King, quoted from Cameron, "Forest Fire Protection," 14.

86 Finlayson, *Report ... 1929-30*, 9.

87 For the Conference on the National Inventory of Forest Resources, see Gillis and Roach, *Lost Initiatives*, 210-13.

Sea and Shield: Fire Provinces of Eastern Canada

1 The most ready source for early history and fires is Ralph S. Johnson, *Forests of Nova Scotia: A History* (Halifax: Department of Lands and Forests; Four East Publications, 1986). The Daniel Moody story is on 123.

2 Ibid., 89-90, 106.

3 Ibid., 108-9, 159, 92, 104.

4 Otto Schierbeck, "Report of the Chief Forester," in *Report of the Department of Lands and Forests 1927* (Halifax: King's Printer, 1928), 20.

5 For a list of fires, see Johnson, *Forests of Nova Scotia*, 159. For a list of legislation, see Dr. Wilfrid Creighton, *Forestkeeping: A History of the Department of Lands and Forests in Nova Scotia 1926-1969* (Department of Government Services, 1988), 20-23. B.E. Fernow, C.D. Howe, and J.H. White, *Forest Conditions of Nova Scotia* (Ottawa: Commission of Conservation, 1912), Howe on 77 for detailed surveys of burned area and on 93 for quotation, and Fernow on 14-21 for statistics and on 38 for recommendations.

6 J.A. Knight, "Organization for Fire Protection," LAC, RG 39, vol. 597, file "1924 Forest Fire Conference," 66-67. The statistics on fire starts are from Brian Stocks, Jen Beverly, and Mike Wooton, "Fire Management Policy in Canada," paper presented at the Northern Forestry Centre workshop, April 2004.

7 Otto Schierbeck, "Report of the Chief Forester," in *Report of the Department of Lands and Forests, 1928* (Halifax: King's Printer, 1929), 10, 14-15, 19. For the details, see the annual reports of the relevant department (commissioner of forests and game, then Department of Lands and Forests) and the official memoir of Creighton, *Forestkeeping*.

8 Owen Barr, "Forest Fire Fighting in Nova Scotia" (manuscript on file with Department of Natural Resources), 7. The quotation on meals is from Creighton, *Forestkeeping*, 44.

9 For the 1933-34 reforms, see Creighton, *Forestkeeping*, 40-43.

10 Ibid., 142, 138; Nova Scotia Department of Lands and Forests, *Annual Report 1969* (Halifax: Queen's Printer, 1969), 21-23; Creighton, *Forestkeeping*, 132, 150.

11 Daniel W. Bower, "Spring Burning," 16 December 1974, newspaper scrapbooks, Provincial Fire Centre, Shubenacadie. For a sample of large fires sprouting on the residue of industrial forestry, see Randall S. Tattrie, "The Porcupine Lake Fire: A Case Study" (BS thesis, University of New Brunswick, 1978).

12 The best summaries are J.F. Gaudet, *Forestry Past and Present on Prince Edward Island*

(Department of Agriculture and Forestry, 1979), and J. Dan McAskill, "The People's Forest" (photocopy of original publication, in holdings at Forestry Branch office, Charlottetown), 88-96. The reference to smoke is from McAskill, "The People's Forest," 95. Sample fires are from the Department of Energy and Forestry, Management Notes, "Controlling the Burn," a handout from the Forestry Branch.

13 The quotation is from McAskill, "The People's Forest," 95; on farm abandonment, see Gaudet, *Forestry,* 46-47.

14 The quotation is from *Report of the Department of Agriculture and Forestry 1970*, 105. The statistics are from Margaret R. Conrad and James K. Hiller, *Atlantic Canada: A Region in the Making* (Don Mills, ON: Oxford University Press, 2001), 198.

15 Gaudet, *Forestry,* 52-55, 59, 48.

16 Ibid., 27-28; *Department of Industry and Natural Resources: Annual Report 1960*, 11.

17 *Annual Report of the Department of Agriculture and Forestry of the Province of Prince Edward Island for the Financial Year Ending March 31st 1971* (Summerside, PE: Williams and Crue, 1972), 109; *Department of Agriculture and Forestry: Annual Report 1977*, 40; *Department of Agriculture and Forestry: Annual Report 1978*, 45. See also references in LAC, RG 39, Accession 1995-96, box 16, file 1165-36/C279, which surveys the 1986 season, including the PEI outbreaks.

18 See Department of Energy and Forestry, "Prince Edward Island: Forest Fire Policy and Procedures" (c. 1986), 1-2, 4; Prince Edward Island Department of Energy and Forestry, *Annual Report 1986/87*, 28. The department has also produced a video about the fires titled *Seven Days in May,* which is full of useful information. A graphic summary of fires from 1958-1993 is available in Department of Agriculture, Fisheries and Forestry, *Annual Report 1994*, 26.

19 On the propane-fuelled blueberry burners, see Department of Energy and Forestry, "Controlling the Burn," 5. For an assessment of the larger forestry context, including the escalation of work around 1980, see Department of Agriculture, Fisheries, and Forestry, Forestry Division, "Prince Edward Island: State of the Forest Report 1980-1990" (1993).

20 The 1875 quotation is from B.R. Stevenson, *Fifteenth Annual Report of the Crown Land Department of the Province of New Brunswick for the Year Ended 31st October 1875* (Fredericton: Reporter Office, 1876), viii; surveyor general, quoted from Edward S. Fellows, "New Brunswick's Natural Resources: 150 Years of Stewardship" (Fredericton: Department of Natural Resources and Energy, n.d.), 51; James Mitchell, *Twenty-Third Annual Report of the Crown Land Department 1883* (Saint Stephen, NB: Courier Steam Printing House, 1884), ix, 7. For fuller accounts of events mentioned, see the annual reports, especially *Forty-Third Annual Report of the Crown Land Department, 1903* (Fredericton, 1904), xxii; *Forty-Fourth Annual Report of the Crown Land Department, 1904* (Fredericton, 1905), 17; and *Forty-Sixth Annual Report of the Crown Land Department, 1906* (Fredericton, 1907), xiv.

21 *Forty-Seventh Annual Report of the Crown Land Department, 1907* (Fredericton, 1908), xxi-xxii; *Forty-Eighth Annual Report of the Crown Land Department, 1908* (Fredericton, 1909), ix-x. See also "New Brunswick Forestry Convention Held at Fredericton, N.B., February 21st and 22nd" (1907).

22 *57th Annual Report of the Crown Land Department, 1917* (Fredericton, 1918), 10; Fellows, "New Brunswick's Natural Resources," 88-89; *60th Annual Report of the Crown Land Department, 1920* (Fredericton, 1921), 11.

23 *63rd Annual Report of the Crown Land Department, 1923* (Fredericton, 1924), 64-65; G.H. Prince, "Organization for Fire Protection in New Brunswick," in "Forest Fire Conference, 1924," LAC, RG 39, vol. 597, 40-41.

24 G.H. Prince, "New Brunswick," in *Second British Empire Forestry Conference: Proceedings and Resolutions* (Ottawa: F.A. Acland, 1927), 199, 198; Prince, "Organization for Fire Protection," 39; C.D. Howe, quoted from Fellows, "New Brunswick's Natural Resources," 89.

25 *67th Annual Report of the Department of Lands and Mines, 1927* (Fredericton, 1928), 65. On the Acadian Forest Experiment Station, see *76th Annual Report of the Department of Lands and Mines, 1936* (Fredericton, 1937), 14-15. H.W. Beall and C.J. Lowe, "Forest Fires in New Brunswick, 1938-1946," Forest Fire Research Note 15 (Ottawa: Department of Resources and Development, Forestry Branch, 1950), 3.

26 The statistics are from J. Miles Gibson, "The History of Forest Management in New Brunswick," H.R. MacMillan Lectureship address, University of British Columbia, 7 April 1953 (Vancouver: University of British Columbia, 1953), 8.

27 See *64th Annual Report of the Crown Land Department, 1924* (Fredericton, 1925), 65. The quotation is from Murray B. Morison, "The Evolution of Forest Policy in New Brunswick" (manuscript, Dominion Forest Service, 30 January 1936), 22. *Report of the New Brunswick Forest Development Commission* (Fredericton, 1957), 44-45, 50-51. On the problem of municipalities, see also R.G. McCullogh, "A Study of Fire Suppression on Granted Lands and Municipal-Provincial Fire Fighting Agreements" (unpublished report, February 1964).

28 *Report of the New Brunswick Forest Development Commission*, 5; other quotations are from Fellows, "New Brunswick's Natural Resources," 121. *Report of the New Brunswick Forest Development Commission*, 50-51, 85.

29 Fellows, "New Brunswick's Natural Resources," 127; on the counties, see *112th Annual Report of Department of Lands and Mines, 1948* (Fredericton, 1949), 83; *114th Annual Report of the Department of Lands and Mines, 1950* (Fredericton, 1951), 60-61.

30 The quotation is from *114th Annual Report ... 1950*, 9; the 1965 statistics are from *125th Annual Report of the Department of Lands and Mines, 1962* (Fredericton, 1962), 6; on birch dieback, see Gibson, "History of Forest Management," 9.

31 See Fellows, "New Brunswick's Natural Resources," 121; R.E. Tweeddale, "Report of the Forest Resources Study" (Fredericton, 1974), 62 for growth statement.

32 Tweeddale, "Report of the Forest Resources Study," 234; Ross W. Wein and Janice M. Moore, "Fire History and Rotations in the New Brunswick Acadian Forest," *Canadian Journal of Forest Research 7* (1977): 287.

33 See Patrick Blanchet, *Forest Fires: The Story of a War* (Montreal: Cantos International, 2003), 25. A longer, earlier version of my account was published as "Mon pays, c'est le feu. Le Québec, le Canada, les forêts et le feu," trans. Pier Courville, *Revue internationale d'études québécoises* 9, 1 (2006): 142-75. As will be obvious, I rely on Blanchet's conscientious study for the main chronicle of fire in Quebec and on the research accumulated during Blanchet's inquiry under the direction of Julie Fortin, documentation now held by the ministry, for much of the background sources. All I can claim to add is a comparative perspective and the judgments to which understanding leads me. As usual, I relied heavily on annual reports from both the ministry and the timber protective associations.

34 For accounts of the 1870 fires, see Blanchet, *Forest Fires,* 30-32, and Claude Cauchon Godfroy Lamarche, "Le grand feu de 1870 au Lac Saint-Jean" (BAS thesis, Laval University, 1971).

35 Blanchet, *Forest Fires,* 39-41; on Lynch's references to Ontario, see W.W. Lynch, *Rapport du commissaire des Terres de la Couronne de la Province de Quebec, 1885* (Quebec: Charles-François Langlois, 1886), vi-vii.

36 On the railway, see Blanchet, *Forest Fires,* 44-45.

37 Ibid., 60, 54-55, 64-65.

38 W.C.J. Hall and B.L. O'Hara, *Traité de la protection des forêts contre le feu* (Québec: Telegraph Printing, 1912). For a summary of the early era, see G.C. Piché, "L'histoire de l'administration des forêts dans la province de Quebec," *Canadian Forestry Journal* 7, 1 (1911): 20-21. For the best summary of Hall's reforms, see Blanchet, *Forest Fires,* 68-78. A good summary of the forest reserve movement is available in Bruce W. Hodgins, Jamie Benidickson, and Peter Gillis, "The Ontario and Quebec Experiments in Forest Reserves 1883-1930," *Journal of Forest History* (1982): 20-33.

39 See Blanchet, *Forest Fires,* 84-85; George E. Bothwell, "Co-Operative Forest Fire Protection," *Forestry Branch Bulletin 42* (Ottawa: Government Printing Office, 1914); and Ellwood Wilson, "Forest Fire and Forest Protection," *Canadian Forestry Journal* 4, 1 (1908): 102-5. It is worth quoting Bothwell on this topic: "Although in Canada the original idea of co-operative protection among lumbermen was conceived independently of American influence," and although it emulated some features of French forest protection *syndicates,* once instituted it "followed closely in the steps of the older fire-protection associations" in the United States (16).

40 See Henry Sorgius, "The Working Plan of the St. Maurice Protective Association," *Canadian Forestry Journal* 11, 11 (1915): 247-49; "St. Maurice Forest Protective Association," *Canadian Forestry Journal* 9, 3 (1913): 37; "Four Fire Associations Now Blanket Quebec," *Canadian Forestry Journal* 13, 5 (1917): 1098; and S. Jensen, "Organisation of Forest Protection in the St. Maurice Valley," *La forêt québécoise* 6, 5 (December 1943): 274-90. Wilson quotes from Ellwood Wilson, "Fire Protection from the Private Timber Owners' Viewpoint," in Commission of Conservation, *Report of the Seventh Annual Meeting Held at Ottawa January 18-19 1916* (Montreal: Federated Press, 1917), 16.

See also Henry Sorgius, "Co-Operative Forest Protection," in Commission of Conservation, *Report of the Eighth Annual Meeting Held at Ottawa January 16-17 1917* (Montreal: Federated Press, 1918), 75-80, which gives a detailed account of how the system worked. Also valuable are the annual reports from the associations, especially from their first, formative years.

41 Stuart Graham, "The First Flying Patrol of Forests," *Canadian Forestry Journal* 15, 5 (1919): 243-44. For the preliminaries, see Major K.E. Kennedy, "Guarding Forests by Airplane," *Canadian Forestry Journal* 14, 2 (1918): 1521-24.

42 See G.C. Piché, "Quebec," in *Second British Empire Forestry Conference, 1923: Proceedings and Resolutions* (Ottawa: F.A. Acland, 1927), 188-95. For the 1924 quotation, see Oscar Desjardins, "De l'organisation du service de protection contre l'incendie dans la région du Témiscamingue," *La vie forestière* 6, 1 (June 1931): 7. The New Brunswick quotation is from W. Robinson, "Forest Fire Conference, 1924," LAC, RG 39 597, 31.

See also G.C. Piché, *Notes on the Forests of Quebec* (Quebec: Telegraph Printing, 1923), and G.C. Piché, "Rapport sur la protection des forêts par G.C. Piché, chef du service forestières, 27 septembre 1923," Appendice 14, in Département des Terres et Forêts, *Rapport de la province de Québec pour les 12 mois expirés le 30 juin 1923* (Quebec: Ls-A Proulx, 1924).

43 Statistics are from John A. Dickinson and Brian Young, *A Short History of Quebec,* 2nd ed. (Toronto: Copp Clark Pitman, 1993), 283.

44 A concise summary is in Blanchet, *Forest Fires,* 164-66.

45 T.E. Mackey, "One Hundred Years of History: Forest Protection – After 1878" (manuscript, 1965), Bushplane Museum, Sault Ste. Marie, 4-5.

46 A summary of developments is contained in *Annual Report of the Clerk of Forestry for the Province of Ontario 1899* (Toronto: Warwick Brothers and Rutter, 1899), 126-33.

47 See *Report of the Commissioner of Crown Lands of the Province of Ontario for the Year 1886* (Toronto: Warwick and Sons, 1887), vi-viii; *Report of the Commissioner of Crown Lands of the Province of Ontario for the Year 1887* (Toronto: Warwick and Sons, 1888), vii-xi; Aubrey White, "Forest Fires and Fire Ranging" (Toronto: Warwick and Sons, 1886), 3, 5, 8; and *Report of the Commissioner of Crown Lands of the Province of Ontario for the Year 1894* (Toronto: Warwick Brothers and Rutter, 1895), viii.

48 *Annual Report of the Clerk of Forestry for the Province of Ontario 1897* (Toronto: Legislative Assembly of Ontario, n.d.), 4, 9; Commissioner, Royal Commission on Forestry in Ontario, *Preliminary Report* (Toronto: Warwick Brothers and Rutter, 1898), 6-7, 9, 11; *Report of the Royal Commission on Forestry Protection in Ontario 1899* (Toronto: L.K. Cameron, 1900), especially 10, 13, 20.

49 *Report of the Royal Commission ... 1899,* 11.

50 *Annual Report of the Director of Forestry for the Province of Ontario 1900-1901* (Toronto: L.K. Cameron, 1902), 5.

51 *Report of the Minister of Lands, Forests, and Mines of the Province of Ontario for the Year 1908* (Toronto: L.K. Cameron, 1909), xi. For a thorough review of the fire-ranging system, see the annual report published in 1908, ix-xii. A good summary of the forest reserve movement is available in Hodgins, Benidickson, and Gillis, "The Ontario and Quebec Experiments in Forest Reserves 1883-1930," 20-33.

52 See *Report of the Minister of Lands, Forests, and Mines for the Province of Ontario 1910* (Toronto: L.K. Cameron, 1911), ix.

53 The quotation is from *Report of the Minister of Lands and Forests of the Province of Ontario for the Year Ending 31st October 1923* (Toronto: Clarkson W. James, 1924), 177-78. Other data are from the annual reports. *Report of the Minister of Lands, Forests, and Mines of the Province of Ontario for the Year Ending 31st October 1916* (Toronto: A.T. Wilgress, 1917), xviii. For a good summary, see E.J. Zavitz, "Forest Fire Protection in Ontario," in Commission of Conservation, *Report of the Ninth Annual Meeting Held at Ottawa November 27-28, 1917* (Ottawa: A.T. Wilgress, 1918), 50-54.

54 E.J. Zavitz, "Organization for Fire Protection in Ontario," LAC, RG 39, vol. 597, file "Forest Fire Conference, 1924," 52-55, 196-97.

55 Ibid., 195; *Report of the Minister of Lands and Forests of the Province of Ontario for the Year Ending 31st October 1922* (Toronto: Clarkson W. James, 1923), 221.
        A comprehensive but undocumented source for the history of the Ontario Provincial Air Service is Bruce West, *The Firebirds* (Toronto: Ministry of Natural Resources, 1974). See also J.C. Dillon, *Early Days: A Record of the Early Days of the Provincial Air Service of Ontario, of the Men and the Ships They Flew* (Toronto: Department of Lands and Forests, 1961).

56 *Report ... 1920,* 207-8.

57 The first quotations are from J.W. Lyons, cited in West, *Firebirds,* 18; *Report of the Minister of Lands and Forests of the Province of Ontario for the Year Ending 31st October 1924* (Toronto: Clarkson W. James, 1925), 13.

58 *Report of the Minister of Lands and Forests of the Province of Ontario for the Year Ending 31st October 1925* (Toronto: Clarkson W. James, 1926), 84.

59 *Report of the Minister of Lands and Forests of the Province of Ontario for the Year Ending 31st October 1927* (Toronto: Printer to the King's Most Excellent Majesty, 1928), 7.

60 Mackey, "One Hundred Year History," 49.

61 *Report of the Minister of Lands and Forests of the Province of Ontario for the Fiscal Year Ending*

March 31st, 1929 (Toronto: Herbert H. Ball, 1930), 116-17, 97. The material on incendiarism is from "Report from the District Forester, Trent, 1932," Ontario Provincial Archives, RG 1-316, 22-23. *Report of the Minister of Lands and Forests of the Province of Ontario for the Fiscal Year Ending March 31st, 1937* (Toronto: T.E. Bowman, 1937), 110. *Report of the Minister of Lands and Forests of the Province of Ontario for the Fiscal Year Ending March 31st, 1939* (Toronto: T.E. Bowman, 1940), 87.

62 Mackey, "One Hundred Year History," 67. See *Report of the Ontario Royal Commission on Forestry 1947* (Toronto: Baptist Johnston, 1947), especially 9, 12, 130-31.

63 On helicopters, see Dillon, *Early Days;* Archives of Ontario, Pamphlet 1961 No. 36, 27. On waterbombing, see "'Water Bomb' Conference" and Q.F. Hess, letter of 13 September 1950, both in Archives of Ontario, RG 1-210, box 1. See also *The Detailed Annual Report of the Minister of Lands and Forests of the Province of Ontario for the Year Ending March 31st, 1962* (Toronto, 1962), 134-35.

64 *Annual Report of the Minister of Natural Resources of the Province of Ontario for the Fiscal Year Ending March 31, 1975* (Toronto, 1975), 19-20. *Annual Report of the Minister of Natural Resources of the Province of Ontario for the Fiscal Year Ending March 31, 1977*, 24. For an internal analysis, see "Problem Areas and Opportunities for Improvement" and J. Drysdale, compiler, "Problem Identification Exercise, 1975-1976," 26 February 1976, unpublished reports, Archives of Ontario, RG 1.

65 *Annual Report of the Minister of Natural Resources of the Province of Ontario for the Fiscal Year Ending March 31, 1980* (Toronto, 1980), 37; for a detailed analysis of the tragedy, see G.A. McCormack et al., "Geraldton PB-3/79. Board of Review Report. September 1979" (Toronto: Ministry of Natural Resources, 1979). *Annual Report of the Minister of Natural Resources of the Province of Ontario, Fiscal Year Ending March 31, 1981* (Toronto, 1981), 7-9.

Fire's Lesser Dominion

1 The observation on provincial interest in minerals is from Peter J. Murphy, conductor, "Interview with Herb Beall in Ottawa, Ontario, July 27, 1989" (transcript, December 1989), Beall file, Northern Forestry Centre.

2 See multiple memoranda, R.A. Gibson and E.H. Finlayson, 10 March to 23 May 1930, and a memorandum, R.A. Gibson to E.H. Finlayson, 21 January 1930, containing detailed replies to Barnjum's inquiries, LAC, RG 39 24, file U9897.

3 E.H. Finlayson, quoted from Kenneth Johnstone, *Timber and Trauma: 75 Years with the Federal Forestry Service 1899-1974* (Ottawa: Minister of Supply and Services Canada, 1991), 71.

4 E.H. Finlayson, *Report of the Director of Forestry 1931-32* (Ottawa: F.A. Acland, 1932), 3.

5 E.H. Finlayson, *Report of the Director of Forestry 1929-30* (Ottawa: F.A. Acland, 1931), 5. Statistics are from Johnstone, *Timber and Trauma*, 72, and Finlayson amnesia is from 75. On the reluctance of provinces to take forestry, see H.W. Beall, quoted from I.C.M. Place, *75 Years of Research in the Woods: A History of Petawawa Forest Experiment Station and Petawawa National Forestry Institute* (Burnstown, ON: General Store Publishing House, 2002), 45.

6 On absent legal authority, see Place, *75 Years*, 45. The quotation on "fact-finding" is from Department of Mines and Resources, *Report of the Lands, Parks, and Forests Branch for the Fiscal Year Ended March 31, 1938* (Ottawa: J.O. Patenaude, 1939), 110.

7 Johnstone, *Timber and Trauma*, 88.

8 Ibid., 90-92.

9 The quotation on Petawawa is from Place, *75 Years*, 63. On expansion of the stations, see Department of Mines and Resources, *Report of Lands, Parks, and Forests Branch for the Fiscal Year Ended March 31, 1943* (Ottawa: Edmond Cloutier, 1944), 96.

10 The story of origins is a close paraphrase from Place, *75 Years*, 54.

11 Quotations are from Department of Mines and Resources, *Report of Lands, Parks, and Forests Branch for the Year Ended March 31, 1937* (Ottawa: J.O. Patenaude, 1938), 108.

    An overview of the NRC committee system, including a thumbnail sketch of those committees relevant to fire, is available in D.J.C. Phillipson, *Associate Committees of the National Research Council of Canada 1917-1975*, rev. ed. (Ottawa: National Research Council, 1983).

12 D.A. Macdonald, "Forest Fire Protection," Appendix C, in National Research Council, "Proceedings of the Conference on Forestry Research, Ottawa," 26-27 November 1935, mimeograph; quotations are from C-5 and C-10. Department of Mines and Resources, *Report of the Lands, Parks, and Forests Branch for the Fiscal Year Ended March 31, 1939* (Ottawa: J.O. Patenaude, 1940), 143. On pumps and hoses, see Department of Mines and Resources, *Report of the Department of Mines and Resources Including Report of Soldier Settlement of Canada for the Fiscal Year Ended March 31, 1940* (Ottawa: Edmond Cloutier, 1941), 121.

13 See Phillipson, *Associate Committees*, 48, and Associate Committee on Forestry, "Proceedings of the First Meeting of the Subcommittee on Forest Fire Research, 5 March 1948," LAC, RG 39 212, file 50536-1, Subcommittee on Forest Fire Record (August 1947-March 1949).

    For a survey of topics through 1960, see D.G. Fraser, "Index to Minutes of Annual Meetings, Associate Committee on Forest Fire Protection, National Research Council," Forestry Branch, Department of Northern Affairs and National Resources.

14 National Research Council of Canada, "Proceedings of the First Meeting of the Associate Committee on Forest Fire Protection" mimeograph (Ottawa, 1953), especially 2-3.

15 Associate Committee on Forest Fire Protection, "Proceedings of the Nineteenth Meeting, Ottawa, January 26, 27, 28, 1971," 44; National Research Council of Canada, "Proceedings of the Thirty-Ninth Meeting of the Canadian Committee on Forest Fire Management, Victoria, British Columbia, January 22-24, 1991."

Tracer Index: James G. Wright and Herbert W. Beall

1 Johnstone, *Timber and Trauma*, 57.

2 The general surveys are from C.E. Van Wagner, "Six Decades of Forest Fire Science in Canada," *Forestry Chronicle* 66 (1990): 133-37, and Richard A. Rajala, "Feds, Forests, and Fire: A Century of Federal Forestry Innovation in Canada" (manuscript, National Museum of Science and Technology, June 2000), 96-100, 124-25 (for early years).

    On Finlayson's hostility, see Johnstone, *Timber and Trauma*, 103, and for quotation from J.G. Wright, 88. An alternative view comes from Beall, in Murphy, "Interview with Herb Beall," 35-36. See also Wright's graceful compliment in J.G. Wright, "The Influence of Weather on the Inflammability of Forest Fire Fuels," *Forestry Chronicle* 6, 1 (1930): 40. On Beall's employment, see "Making History," *Forestry Chronicle* 76 (2000): 598-600.

3 Cam Macleod, quoted from Place, *75 Years*, 59.

4 J.G. Wright, quoted from Johnstone, *Timber and Trauma*, 88. The "perspiration" quotation is from Herbert W. Beall, "Fire Research in Canada's Forestry Service – The Formative Years," in *The Art and Science of Fire Management*, ed. M.E. Alexander and G.F. Bisgrove, Information Report NOR-X-309 (Edmonton: Forestry Canada, 1990), 18.

5 Quotations on data are from E.H. Finlayson, *Report of the Director of Forestry 1929-30* (Ottawa: F.A. Acland, 1931), 7; Van Wagner, "Six Decades of Forest Fire Science in Canada," 134. An oft-cited summary and chronicle of the evolution is available in H.W. Beall, "Research in the Measurement of Forest Fire Danger," paper presented at the Fifth British Empire Forestry Conference, 1947, reprinted as Information Report FF-X-8 (Ottawa: Forest Fire Research Institute, 1967).

6 Wright, "Influence of Weather," 40-55; quotation on 40.

7 Ibid., 55. The 1932 paper was released in two forms: J.G. Wright, "Forest-Fire Hazard Research as Developed and Conducted at the Petawawa Forest Experiment Station," reprinted as Information Report FF-X-5 (Ottawa: Forest Fire Research Institute, 1967); J.G. Wright, "Forest Fire Hazard Research," *Forestry Chronicle* 8, 3 (1932): 133-51; quotations are from 133-34. See also J.G. Wright, "Forest Fire Hazard Tables for Mixed Red and White Pine Forests: Eastern Ontario and Western Quebec Regions," (Ottawa: Dominion Forest Service, 1933). Beall quotes from Murphy, "Interview with Herb Beall," 35.

8 H.W. Beall, "A Graphic Correlation Method for Four-Variable Problems Involving Complex Joint Functional Relationships," Forest Fire Research Note 3 (Ottawa: Dominion Forest Service, 1938); H.W. Beall, "Outline of a Proposed Short Method of Solving Correlation Problems When Three or More Variables Are Involved," Forest Fire Research Note 2 (Ottawa: Dominion Forest Service, 1938).

9 On Finlayson's role, see Murphy, "Interview with Herb Beall," 38. The creation of experimental forests is tabulated in E.H. Finlayson, *Report of the Director of Forestry 1933-34* (Ottawa: J.O. Patenaude, 1934), 10-12.

For the chronicle and summary of stations, see Rajala, "Feds, Forests, and Fire," 99-100; Johnstone, *Timber and Trauma*, 87-88; and Beall, "Research in the Measurement of Forest Fire Danger," 8. And of course there are the annual reports of the DFS, which catalogue the successive phases.

On the particular papers and published tables, see Forest Protection Service, "Preliminary Tables for the Determination of the Index of Inflammability of Forest Stands Following the Wright System" (Quebec: Department of Lands and Forests, 1939); Forest Protection Service, "Forest Fire Danger" (Fredericton: Department of Lands and Mines, 1941); J.G. Wright, "Preliminary Fire Hazard Tables for Cut-Over Lands of Eastern Canada" (Ottawa: Dominion Forest Service, 1939); J.G. Wright and H.W. Beall, "Preliminary Improved Forest Fire Hazard Tables for Eastern Canada" (Ottawa: Dominion Forest Service, 1938; reprinted, 1940, with supplements); J.G. Wright and H.W. Beall, "Grass Fire Hazard Tables for Eastern Canada" (Ottawa: Dominion Forest Service, 1938); H.W. Beall, "Forecasting Weather and Forest-Fire Hazard from Local Observations," Forest Fire Research Note 10 (Ottawa: Dominion Forest Service, 1940); H.W. Beall, "An Investigation of the Reliability of Eastern Forest-Fire Hazard Tables in Manitoba and Saskatchewan," Forest Fire Research Note 9 (Ottawa: Dominion Forest Service, 1939); H.W. Beall, "Preliminary Forest-Fire Danger Tables and Fire Control Administration Plans for the New Brunswick Limits of the Bathurst Power and Paper Company," Forest Fire Research Note 8 (Ottawa: Dominion Forest Service, 1939); H.W. Beall, "Tables for Estimating the Tracer Index from Early Afternoon Weather Readings: Table for Diurnal Hazard Variation: Lists of Forest Types of Eastern Canada Showing the Fire-Hazard Table to Be Used for Each Type," supplement to Forest Fire Research Note 5 (Ottawa: Dominion Forest Service, 1939); H.W. Beall, "Fire Hazard Investigations in Riding Mountain and Prince Albert National Parks," Fire Hazard Note, Miscellaneous Paper (Ottawa: Dominion Forest Service, 1940); H.W. Beall, "What the Forest-Fire Hazard Index Means in Terms of Actual Fire Conditions in Riding Mountain and Prince Albert National Parks" (unpublished report, Dominion Forest Service, Ottawa, 1941); H.W. Beall, "Forest Fires and Fire-Hazard Records in the Mid-West National Parks," *Forestry Chronicle* 22, 2 (1946): 135-37. Also useful are the unpublished annual summaries of data and techniques; a set is housed at the Northern Forestry Centre. The quotation "in practical use" is from Beall, "Research in the Measurement of Forest Fire Danger," 3.

10 The Wright quotation is from Johnstone, *Timber and Trauma*, 88.

11 J.G. Wright and H.W. Beall, "The Application of Meteorology to Forest Fire Protection," Technical Communication 4 (Oxford: Imperial Forestry Bureau, 1945), reprinted as Information Report FF-X-11 (Ottawa: Dominion Forest Service, 1968). H.W. Beall, "Wartime Influence on Forest Fires in Canada," *Forestry Chronicle* 22 (1946): 25-29.

See H.W. Beall, "Forest Fire Danger Tables (Provisional)," Forest Fire Research Note 12 (Ottawa: Dominion Forest Service, 1946); H.W. Beall, "Forest Fire Danger Tables (Provisional)," 2nd ed., Forest Fire Research Note 12 (Ottawa: Dominion Forest Service, 1948); and Dominion Forest Service, *Forest Fire Control Plan for the Petawawa Forest Experiment Station, Chalk River, Ontario* (Ottawa: Edmond Cloutier, 1948).

12 The best source of biographical information is the Beall file, Northern Forestry Centre, which was assembled to nominate Beall for the Order of Canada. On the CSFE resolution and its impact on the DFS, see D.A. Macdonald to P.W. MacKay, 3 February 1947, LAC, RG 39 879, file 32-11-9, part 1. The file includes much of the original correspondence relevant to Beall's study. The quotation on "most original" work is from Place, *75 Years*, 60.

13 The quotation is from H.W. Beall to R.M. Brown, 17 December 1946, LAC, RG 39 379, file 32-11-9, part 1. The file contains a rich correspondence between Beall and others as he sought to hammer out a suitable statement.

14 H.W. Beall, "An Outline of Forest Fire Protection Standards," *Forestry Chronicle* 25 (1949): 82-106.

15 The "heartbroken" quotation is from Murphy, "Interview with Herb Beall," 13. On provincial responses, see J.R. Johnston, "The Situation with Respect to Fire Protection," *Forestry Chronicle* 30 (1954): 24.

16 The Macleod quotation is from Place, *75 Years*, 59.

17 Beall on Wright is from "Making History," 599.

18 C.E. Van Wagner to Richard Boily, 9 March 2000, Beall file, Northern Forestry Centre.

19 H.W. Beall to Dennis Dubé, 23 April 1989, Beall file, Northern Forestry Centre; the Finlayson quotation is from "Making History," 600.

Plain and Mountain: Fire Provinces of Western Canada

1 Quoted from Peter J. Murphy, *History of Forest and Prairie Fire Control Policy in Alberta* (Edmonton: Alberta Energy and Natural Resources, 1985), 57.

2 Ibid., 59 (Russell); 66 (RCMP quotation); 64 (1877 act); *Annual Report for the Department of the Interior for the Year 1890*, part 1 (Ottawa: S.E. Dawson, 1891), 12.

3 *Annual Report for the Department of the Interior for the Year 1887*, quoted from Murphy, *History*, 74-75.

4 RCMP, quoted from Murphy, *History*, 89-90.

5 J.R. Dickson, "Report of J.R. Dickson," Department of the Interior, in *Report of the Director of Forestry, Annual Report 1910-1911* (Ottawa: Government Printing Bureau, 1912), 59-60.

6 See, for example, W.A. Davis, "Report of W.A. Davis, Chief Forest Ranger," Appendix 9, Department of the Interior, in *Report of the Director of Forestry, Annual Report 1908*

(Ottawa: Government Printing Bureau, 1909), 40; "Report of the Inspector of Forest Reserves," Appendix 1, Department of the Interior, in *Report of the Director of Forestry, Annual Report 1910* (Ottawa: Government Printing Bureau, 1911), 14; and A. Knechtel, "Report of A. Knechtel, Inspector of Forest Reserves," Department of the Interior, in *Report of the Director of Forestry, Annual Report 1910*, 40.

7 *Annual Report of the Forest Service for Fiscal Year Ending April 30th, 1933*, 34.

8 *First Annual Report of the Forest Service, Department of Mines and Natural Resources, Manitoba, 1930-1931*, 4-6; on pigeons, see *Second Annual Report of the Forest Service, Department of Mines and Natural Resources, Manitoba, 1931-1932*, 11; *Annual Report of the Forest Service for the Fiscal Year Ending April 30th, 1933*, 34, 37.

9 Ibid., 37.

10 J.D.B. Harrison, "The Forests of Manitoba," Forest Service Bulletin 85 (Ottawa: J.O. Patenaude, 1934), 41-42, 47-48.

11 *Annual Report of the Forest Service, Fiscal Year Ending April 30th, 1938*, 31-32; *Annual Report of the Forest Service, Fiscal Year Ending April 30th, 1940*, 10, 19; Department of Mines and Natural Resources, *Annual Report for Period Ending March 31st, 1959*, 49.

12 See annual reports for exfoliation techniques. For the spring burning episode, see Department of Mines and Natural Resources, *Annual Report for the Period Ending March 31st, 1952*, 44; Department of Mines and Natural Resources, Forest Service, *Annual Report for the Period Ending March 31st, 1943-1944*, 16. See Department of Mines and Natural Resources, *Annual Report for Period Ending March 31st, 1949*, 44, which records that formal fire protection extended over 93,000 square miles, of which only 30,500 yielded productive timber.

13 Allan Murray, ed., "Manitoba Natural Resources, 1930-1990" (Department of Natural Resources, 1990), 1-3; Department of Mines, Resources, and Environmental Management, *Annual Report, Year Ending March 31st, 1974*, 1; Department of Mines, Resources, and Environmental Management, *Annual Report, Year Ending March 31st, 1975*, 6; Murray, ed., "Manitoba Natural Resources," 4.

14 R.E. Capel and A.G. Teskey, "Efficiency in Suppressing Forest Fires: A Study of the South East Area of Manitoba," Information Report MS-X-24 (Canadian Forestry Service, 1970). See also Forestry Team, "The Forests of Manitoba" (unpublished report, Department of Mines, Resources, and Environmental Management, July 1973), later updated and published as *The Forests of Manitoba (1974)* (Department of Mines, Resources, and Environmental Management, 1975), with statistics from 1963-72 listed on page 36.

15 B.J. Stocks et al., "The 1980 Forest Fire Season in West-Central Canada: Social, Economic, and Environmental Impacts" (unpublished information report, Canadian Forest Service, March 1981), i, 23; A. Briggs, "Forest Fire Management in Manitoba: A Proposal" (unpublished report, 15 August 1980, Department of Conservation library), 21.

16 "Report of Roland D. Craig," Appendix 2, in Department of the Interior, *Report of the Director of Forestry, Part X, Annual Report, 1905* (Ottawa: Government Printing Bureau, 1906), 15-16; "Report of Norman M. Ross," Appendix 1, in Department of the Interior, *Report of the Director of Forestry, Annual Report 1906* (Ottawa: Government Printing Bureau, 1907), 18; Department of the Interior, *Report of the Director of Forestry, Annual Report 1908* (Ottawa: Government Printing Bureau, 1909), 8-9.

17 J.C. Blumer, "Forest Resources of Saskatchewan Commission of Conservation 1913-15" (unpublished report, c. 1916), 33, 101-2, 61, 84-85, 7-8, 21, 85-85a, 102.

18 G.A. Gutches, Appendix 3, in Department of the Interior, *Report of the Director of Forestry for the Year 1917* (Ottawa: J. de Labroquerie Tache, 1918), 54; E.H. Finlayson, "Report of Inspector of Fire Ranging," Appendix 5, in Department of the Interior, *Report of the*

Director of Forestry for the Year 1913 (Ottawa: Government Printing Bureau, 1914), 96-97; C.A. MacFaydon, "Forest Fire Conference, 1924," LAC, RG 39 597, file "1924 Forest Fire Conference," 103-4.

19 "Fire Protection Manual," Archives of Saskatchewan, NR 5.B.5x, "Fire Fighting, 1938-39," 3.

20 "Report of the Director of Forests, Department of Natural Resources, 1930-1931" (Department of Natural Resources, 1931), 1, 5.

21 "Report of the Director of Forests, Department of Natural Resources, 1932-1933," 9; "Report of the Director of Forests, Department of Natural Resources, 1933-1934," 5.

22 Department of Natural Resources, *Annual Report for Year Ending April 30th, 1936*, 16.

23 Quotations are from Anthony G. Gulig, "'Determined to Burn Off the Entire Country': Prospectors, Caribou, and the Denesuliné in Northern Saskatchewan, 1900-1940" (unpublished essay), 7, 18.

24 *Annual Report ... 1936*, 16.

25 *Annual Report of the Department of Natural Resources of the Province of Saskatchewan for the Fiscal Year Ended April 30, 1943* (Regina: Thos. H. McConica, 1944), 22-25; *Annual Report of the Department of Natural Resources and Industrial Development of the Province of Saskatchewan for the Fiscal Year Ended April 30, 1946* (Regina: Thos. H. McConica, 1947), 9.

26 Royal Commission on Forestry, *Report of the Royal Commission on Forestry Relating to the Forest Resources and Industries of Saskatchewan, Canada* (Regina: Thos. H. McConica, 1947), 9, 32, 31.

27 Ibid., 10, 23, 26, 36.

28 *Annual Report of the Department of Natural Resources and Industrial Development of the Province of Saskatchewan for the Fiscal Year Ended March 31, 1947* (Regina: Thos. H. McConica, 1947), 10-12, 23; *Annual Report of the Department of Natural Resources and Industrial Development of the Province of Saskatchewan for the Fiscal Year Ended March 31, 1948* (Regina: Thos. H. McConica, 1949), 16.

29 *Annual Report ... 1948*, 16; *Annual Report of the Department of Natural Resources and Industrial Development of the Province of Saskatchewan for the Fiscal Year Ended March 31, 1949* (Regina: Thos. H. McConica, 1950), 14; *Annual Report of the Department of Natural Resources of the Province of Saskatchewan for the Fiscal Year Ended March 31, 1950* (Regina: Thos. H. McConica, 1950), 54.

30 *Annual Report of the Department of Natural Resources of the Province of Saskatchewan for the Fiscal Year Ended March 31, 1952* (Regina: Thos. H. McConica, 1952), 3, 69, 72, 71.

31 *Annual Report of the Department of Natural Resources of the Province of Saskatchewan for the Fiscal Year Ended March 31, 1956* (Regina: Lawrence Amon, 1957), 82-83.

32 *Annual Report of the Forestry Branch for the Fiscal Year Ended March 31, 1960*, 22-23; *Annual Report of the Department of Natural Resources of the Province of Saskatchewan for the Fiscal Year Ended March 31, 1959* (Regina: Lawrence Amon, 1959), 11; *Annual Report of the Department of Natural Resources, Province of Saskatchewan, for the Fiscal Year Ended March 31, 1961* (Regina: Lawrence Amon, 1961), 19, 21; *Annual Report of the Department of Natural Resources, Province of Saskatchewan, for the Fiscal Year Ended March 31, 1962* (Regina: Lawrence Amon, 1962), 16-17; *Annual Report of the Department of Natural Resources, Province of Saskatchewan, for the Fiscal Year Ended March 3, 1965*, 6, 8.

33 *Annual Report of the Department of Natural Resources, Province of Saskatchewan, for the Fiscal Year Ended March 3, 1967-1968*, 7; Jeffrey Thorpe, "Fire History and Its Application to Management of Saskatchewan Forests," Saskatchewan Environment and Resource Management, SRC Publication E-2500-2-E-96 (February 1996), 15. See annual reports for details of the reorganization.

34 Stocks et al., "The 1980 Forest Fire Season in West-Central Canada."

35 John S. Mactavish, "Saskatchewan: Forest Fire Control Program Review" (unpublished report, 7 May 1981), 1.

36 John S. Mactavish, "Forest Fire Control," cover letter to L.G. Lensen and W.A. Klassen, 7 May 1981, within report.

37 For the impacts of the 1980 and 1981 seasons, see the annual reports, especially Saskatchewan Tourism and Renewable Resources, *Annual Report 1981-82*, 10.

38 For basic sources for Albertan fire history, see Peter J. Murphy, *History of Forest and Prairie Fire Control Policy in Alberta* (Edmonton: Alberta Energy and Natural Resources, 1985), and P.J. Murphy et al., *The Alberta Forest Service, 1930-2005: Protection and Management of Alberta's Forests* (Edmonton: Alberta Sustainable Resource Development, 2006).

39 The quotation is from Murphy, *History*, 97.

40 Ragna Steen and Magda Hendrickson, *Pioneer Days in Bardo, Alberta* (Tofield, AB: Historical Society of Beaver Hills Lake, 1944), 66.

41 Ibid., 64, 67. Statistics on homesteading are from Murphy, *History*, 125. Murphy is the best single source of information about prairie fires and their control throughout the prairie provinces. Chain and beef drag is described by Eric Huestis, cited in Murphy, *History*, 230. The implement was used throughout the plains; Frederic Remington drew a picture of one, and Theodore Roosevelt described its use in North Dakota.

42 G.H. Edgecombe and P.Z. Caverhill, "Rocky Mountains Forest Reserve: Report of Boundary Survey Parties," Bulletin 18 (Ottawa: Dominion Forestry Branch, 1911), quoted in the 1913 annual report from Murphy, *History*, 181; the manual is quoted in ibid., 199; ibid., 180. *Annual Report, 1911*, quoted in ibid., 161. On early burning, see Superintendent of Forestry and Irrigation, Department of the Interior, *Annual Report for Fiscal Year Ending March 31, 1909* (Ottawa: Government Printing Bureau, 1909), 28. During the 1910 fire season, probably 3.6 million acres burned; see Murphy, *History*, 149.

43 On the 1919 fires, see Murphy, *History*, 206-7. The size estimate is from Rocky Mountain Section, Canadian Institute of Forestry, *Forest Fire Protection in Alberta*, pamphlet (Canadian Institute of Forestry, January 1954).

44 C.H. Morse, "Forest Fire Conference, 1924," LAC, RG 39 597, 357-60. For a different account of communications problems, see Murphy, *History*, 209.

45 E.H. Finlayson, "Memorandum to R.A. Gibson, Re: Transfer of Natural Resources, 6 December 1929," quoted in Murphy, *History*, 223-25.

46 T.F. Blefgen, "Report of the Director of Forestry, T.F. Blefgen," in *Annual Report of the Department of Lands and Mines of the Province of Alberta for the Year Ended March 31st 1942* (Edmonton: A. Shnitka, 1943), 31.

47 T.F. Blefgen, "Report of the Director of Forestry, T.F. Blefgen," in *Annual Report of the Department of Lands and Mines of the Province of Alberta for the Year Ended March 31st 1933* (Edmonton: W.D. McLean, 1934), 82-83. Huestis is cited in Murphy, *History*, 256.

48 T.F. Blefgen, "Report of the Director of Forestry, T.F. Blefgen," in *Annual Report of the Department of Lands and Mines of the Province of Alberta for the Year Ended March 31st 1940* (Edmonton: A. Shnitka, 1941), 32; T.F. Blefgen, "Report of the Director of Forestry, T.F. Blefgen," in *Annual Report of the Department of Lands and Mines of the Province of Alberta for the Year Ended March 31st 1941* (Edmonton: A. Shnitka, 1942), 30; T.F. Blefgen, "Report of the Director of Forestry, T.F. Blefgen," in *Annual Report of the Department of Lands and Mines of the Province of Alberta for the Year Ended March 31st 1937* (Edmonton: A. Shnitka, 1937), 49, 53-54.

49 T.F. Blefgen, "Report of the Director of Forestry, T.F. Blefgen," in *Annual Report of the*

Department of Lands and Mines of the Province of Alberta for the Year Ended March 31st 1938 (Edmonton: A. Shnitka, 1939), 63; Blefgen, "Report," in *Annual Report ... 1940*, 33; T.F. Blefgen, "Report of the Director of Forestry, T.F. Blefgen," in *Annual Report of the Department of Lands and Mines of the Province of Alberta for the Year Ended March 31st 1939* (Edmonton: A. Shnitka, 1940), 77-78; Blefgen, "Report," in *Annual Report ... 1940*, 39.

50 T.F. Blefgen, "Report of the Director of Forestry, T.F. Blefgen," in *Annual Report of the Department of Lands and Mines of the Province of Alberta for the Year Ended March 31st 1945* (Edmonton: A. Shnitka, 1946), 33; E.S. Huestis, "Report of the Assistant Director of Forestry, E.S. Huestis," in *Annual Report of the Department of Lands and Mines of the Province of Alberta for the Year Ended March 31st 1948*, 31.

51 E.S. Huestis, "Report of the Director of Forestry, E.S. Huestis," in *Annual Report of the Department of Lands and Mines of the Province of Alberta for the Year Ended March 31st 1949* (Edmonton: A. Shnitka, 1950), 19; the overcutting remark is quoted from Murphy, *History*, 250. On oil exploration, see James G. MacGregor, *A History of Alberta* (Edmonton: Hurtig, 1972), 287.

52 For an overview of investments and their significance for fire protection, see Murphy, *History*, 243-58, 267-69. See also W.R. Hanson, "History of the Eastern Rockies Forest Conservation Board, 1947-1973" (unpublished report, 1973), and of course the annual reports of both the AFS and the ERFCB, beginning in 1948; on Huestis and the ten-mile policy, see Murphy, *History*, 258, 260.

53 On Delahey, see E.S. Huestis, "Report of the Director of Forestry, E.S. Huestis," in *Annual Report ... 1949*, 19; E.S. Huestis, "Report of the Director of Forestry, E.S. Huestis," in *Annual Report of the Department of Lands and Mines of the Province of Alberta for the Year Ended March 31st 1950* (Edmonton: A. Shnitka, 1951), 27; E.S. Huestis, "Report of the Director of Forestry, E.S. Huestis," in *Annual Report of the Department of Lands and Mines of the Province of Alberta for the Year Ended March 31st 1951* (Edmonton: A. Shnitka, 1952), 26. On Stevenson-Kellogg, see E.S. Huestis, "Report of the Director of Forstry, E.S. Huestis," in *Annual Report of the Department of Lands and Mines of the Province of Alberta for the Year Ended March 31st 1953* (Edmonton: A. Shnitka, 1953), 26.

54 Rocky Mountain Section, Canadian Institute of Forestry, *Summary of: "Forest Fire Protection in Alberta: A Review and Recommendations"* (Canadian Institute of Forestry, 1954), 1; quotations from full text of Fire Brief are cited in Murphy, *History*, 258; comparisons are from Rocky Mountain Section, *Summary*, 4-6.

55 E.S. Huestis, "Report of the Director of Forestry, E.S. Huestis," in *Annual Report of the Department of Lands and Mines of the Province of Alberta for the Year Ended March 31st 1957* (Edmonton: L.S. Wall, 1957), 29-30; the response by the minister and North Western Pulp and Paper is in Murphy, *History*, 264-65.

56 A.D. Kiil, "A Problem Analysis of Forest Fire Research in Alberta (Revised)" (unpublished report, Forest Research Branch 65-A02, Calgary, 1965), 1.

57 E.S. Huestis, "Report of the Director, E.S. Huestis," in *Annual Report of the Department of Lands and Mines of the Province of Alberta for the Year Ended March 31st 1958* (Edmonton: L.S. Wall, 1959), 32; E.S. Huestis, "Report of the Director of Forestry, E.S. Huestis," in *Annual Report of the Department of Lands and Mines of the Province of Alberta for the Year Ended March 31st 1960* (Edmonton: L.S. Wall, 1960), 30. Murphy, *History*, 265. On fixed and helo strategy, see E.S. Huestis, "Report of the Director of Forestry, E.S. Huestis," in *Annual Report of the Department of Lands and Mines of the Province of Alberta for the Year Ended March 31st 1961* (Edmonton: L.S. Wall, 1961), 28. On air tankers, see Alberta Energy and Natural Resources, "Forest Services Division," in *Annual Report, March 31st 1977*, 25.

58 R.G. Steele, "Report of the Director, R.G. Steele," in *Nineteenth Annual Report of the Department of Lands and Forests of the Province of Alberta for the Fiscal Year Ended March 31st 1968* (Edmonton: L.S. Wall, 1968), 32, 48; A.D. Kiil and J.E. Grigel, "The May 1968 Forest Conflagrations in Central Alberta: A Review of Fire Weather, Fuels, and Fire Behavior," Forest Research Laboratory Information Report A-X-24 (Ottawa: Forestry Branch, 1969); Jack McLean and Blane Coulcher, "'Seven Days in May': Meteorological Factors Associated with the Alberta Forest Fires of May 18-25, 1968" (Edmonton: Alberta Forest Service, 1968).

59 On economic reviews, see, for example, R.S. Miyagawa, "Legislative and Economic Realities: An Alberta Viewpoint," in *Proceedings, Fire Control in the '80s: Symposium, Intermountain Fire Council* (Missoula, MT: Intermountain Fire Council, 1979), 53-62; R.S. Miyagawa and E.V. Stashko, "Fire Size and Cost," (Albert Forest Service, 1971); A.D. Kiil, "Fire Research Programs and Issues in Mid-Canada," in *Proceedings of International Fire Management Workshop,* comp. D. Quintilio, Information Report NOR-X-15 (Edmonton: Canadian Forest Service, 1979), 5-14.

60 The statistics are from F.W. McDougall, quoted from Murphy, *History,* 294, and the quotations are from 295. For an analysis of fire trends, see Kiil, "Fire Research Programs and Issues in Mid-Canada."

61 For statistics, see J.A. Brennan, "Alberta Forest Service, Report of the Assistant Deputy Minister, J.A. Brennan," in Alberta Energy and Natural Resources, *Annual Report, March 31st 1980,* 30, 86-88; J.A. Brennan, "Alberta Forest Service, Report of the Assistant Deputy Minister, J.A. Brennan," in Alberta Energy and Natural Resources, *Annual Report, March 31st 1981,* 29, 93-95; J.A. Brennan, "Alberta Forest Service, Report of the Assistant Deputy Minister, J.A. Brennan," in Alberta Energy and Natural Resources, *Annual Report, March 31st 1982,* 34, 102-3; J.A. Brennan, "Alberta Forest Service," in Alberta Energy and Natural Resources, *Annual Report, March 31st 1984,* 36 and Table 22. A summary of Alberta fires from the DFS era to the Big Bust is available in G.P. Delisle and R.J. Hall, "Forest Fire History Maps of Alberta, 1931-1983" (Northern Forestry Centre, Canadian Forestry Service, 1987).

62 Quoted in Murphy, *History,* 285; the priority zones are described in ibid., 291. For a distillation of duties as of 1981, see Alberta Energy and Natural Resources, "Alberta Public Lands" (Edmonton: Alberta and Natural Resources, 1981).

63 Allusion to the Marine Corps was made to the author during conversation at the provincial fire centre.

64 British Columbia is blessed with many superb studies of its forest industry. Of special interest are Ken Drushka, *In the Bight: The BC Forest Industry Today* (Madeira, BC: Harbour Publishing, 1999), and two overlapping studies by John Parminter, which remain the foundation of any introduction to fire history: "Protection as Conservation: Safeguarding British Columbia's Forests from Fire, 1874-1921" (unpublished report, Ministry of Forests, 1980), and "An Historical Review of Forest Fire Management in British Columbia" (MSc thesis, University of British Columbia, 1978). See also Thomas R. Roach, "Stewards of the People's Wealth: The Founding of British Columbia's Forest Branch," *Journal of Forest History* 28, 1 (1984): 14-23.

65 For the 1868 outbreak, see Parminter, "Protection as Conservation," 4. Robert Bell, "Comments," *Report of the Ninth Annual Meeting of the Canadian Forestry Association Held at Montreal, March 12 and 13, 1908* (Toronto: Imrie Printing, 1908), 53; Edward Whymper, "A New Playground in the New World," *Scribner's Magazine* 33, 6 (1905): 646, 658; H.R. MacMillan, "The Forest Fire, a National Danger and Its Remedy," *Canadian*

Magazine 44, 6 (1915): 549.

66 Parminter, "Protection as Conservation," 22-23. See also Clyde Leavitt's reports, *Forest Protection in Canada, 1912* (Toronto: The Bryant Press, 1913).

67 On the DFB and its federal successors, see S.W. Taylor, "100 Years of Federal Forestry in British Columbia," *Forestry History Newsletter* 57 (1999): 1-7.

68 William R. Ross, *British Columbia Forest Policy: Speech by the Hon. William R. Ross, Minister of Lands on the Second Reading of the Forest Bill,* pamphlet, Legislative Session 1912, 3-4.

69 Ross, "British Columbia's Forest Policy," 8-9, 16, 18, 20. For reactions, see Parminter, "Protection as Conservation," 11.

70 Parminter, "Protection as Conservation," 24; the quotations on "patrolmen" are from 25. On the impacts of the 1910 fires in British Columbia, see E.E. Chipman, "Ainsworth, Slocan, and Slocan City Mining Divisions"; Angus McInnes, "Slocan Mining Division"; and Fleet Robinson, "Slocan Mining Division," in *Report of the Bureau of Mines* (Victoria: King's Printer, 1911), 96, 98, 136. I'm indebted to John Parminter for bringing these references to my attention.

71 Alfred Flumerfelt, quoted from David J. Climenhaga, "Early History of the British Columbia Forest Service" (unpublished report, 1981), British Columbia Archives (hereafter BCA), GR 1366, box 1/1, file 3. See compilation of fire-related statements in Timber and Forestry Commission, "Abstracts of Testimonies," BCA, GR 271, box 1, file 8, F1 (Schenk) and F9 (Carney).

72 *Final Report of the Royal Commission of Inquiry on Timber and Forestry 1909-1910* (Victoria: Richard Wolfenden, 1910), 59-61; Ross, "British Columbia Forest Policy," 16-21; "Report on Forest Protection," in *Report of the Minister of Lands for the Province of British Columbia for the Year Ending December 31st 1911* (Victoria: William H. Cullin, 1912), G 23.

73 Ross, "British Columbia Forest Policy," 24.

74 *Report of the Forest Branch of the Department of Lands for the Year Ending December 31st 1912* (Victoria: William H. Cullin, 1913), 6.

75 Ross, "British Columbia Forest Policy," 11.

76 The quotation is from C.D. Orchard, cited in Parminter, "Historical Review," 64.

77 The "fire hazard" quotation is from *Report of the Forest Branch of the Department of Lands for the Year Ending December 31st 1912* (Victoria: William H. Cullin, 1913), D 34, and "mainstay" from *Report of the Forest Branch of the Department of Lands for the Year Ending December 31st 1913* (Victoria: William H. Cullin, 1914), 47.

78 Parminter, "Historical Review," 36; H.N. Whitford and Roland D. Craig, *Forests of British Columbia* (Ottawa: Commission of Conservation, 1918), 125.

79 There are several accounts in print; see John Parminter, "Guardians in the Sky: Aircraft and Their Use in Forestry in B.C.: 1918-1926," *Whistle Punk* 1, 4 (1986): 3-10; for details of the 1918 crash, see Betty C. Keller, "British Columbia's Annual Ash Heap," *Beaver* 68 (1988): 36-37; on Kamloops, see Murphy, *History,* 211.

80 P.Z. Caverhill, "British Columbia," in *Proceedings and Resolution,* Second British Empire Forestry Conference (Ottawa: F.A. Acland, 1927), 200-2; P.Z. Caverhill, "Forest Fire Conference, 1924," LAC, RG 39 597, 257-58, 261-62.

81 Parminter, "Historical Review," 38-39; on the 1920 season, see *Report of the Forest Branch of the Department of Lands for the Year Ending December 31st 1920* (Victoria: William H. Cullin, 1921), 20; the "machine" quotation is from *Report of the Forest Branch of the Department of Lands for the Year Ending December 31st 1925* (Victoria: Charles F. Banfield, 1926), E40-41.

82 *Report of the Forest Branch of the Department of Lands for the Year Ending December 31st 1931* (Victoria: Charles F. Banfield, 1932), V 36; *Report of the Forest Branch of the Department of Lands for the Year Ending December 31st 1932,* T 28; *Report of the Forest Branch of the Department of Lands for the Year Ending December 31st 1938,* N 49-50; *Report of the Forest Branch of the Department of Lands for the Year Ending December 31st 1945,* 75.

83 For a political overview, see Mary L. Roberts, "When Good Intentions Fail: A Case of Forest Policy in the British Columbia Interior, 1945-56," *Journal of Forest History* 32 (1988): 138-49.

84 Parminter, "Historical Review," 63-64. See *Report of the Commissioner Relating to the Forest Resources of British Columbia 1945* (Victoria: Charles F. Banfield, 1945), especially 129-33.

85 I've relied on Ken Drushka's very informative *In the Bight* for context; the quotations are from 46-47.

86 *Report of the Forest Service Year Ended December 31st 1951* (Victoria: Don McDiarmid, 1952), 69; *Report of the Forest Service Year Ended December 31st 1952* (Victoria: Don McDiarmid, 1953), 79. For fire sizes, see John Parminter, "Largest 20 Known Fires in B.C., 1920-2001" (unpublished paper, July 2002). On aircraft development, see the annual reports. The "extravagance" quotation is from I.T. Cameron, "Report to Royal Commission on Forests and Forestry, British Columbia, 1955" (Protection Division, British Columbia Forest Service, 1955), 12-13.

87 Gordon Sloan, cited in Parminter, "Historical Review," 69-71.

88 J. Harry G. Smith, "How Much Forest Protection Is Needed?" *Forestry Chronicle* 46 (1971): 23-24.

89 *Report of the Forest Service Year Ended December 31st 1970* (Victoria: K.M. MacDonald, 1971), 63.

90 I have followed Drushka, *In the Bight,* 51-52; *Report of the Ministry of Forests, Year Ended December 31, 1978* (Victoria, 1979), 31.

91 The "decadent" quotation is from *Report of the Forest Service Year Ended December 31st 1974* (Victoria: K.K. MacDonald, 1975), 37.

Prosperity and Peril

1   *Report of Lands, Parks, and Forests Branch for the Fiscal Year Ended March 31, 1946* (Ottawa: Edmond Cloutier, 1947), 113-14.

2   Johnstone, *Timber and Trauma,* 101.

3   The quotation on hoses is from Place, *75 Years,* 85. Reports from each of the field stations are held in file cabinets at the Northern Forestry Centre.

4   "Seventh Annual Report on Active Forest Research Projects, Year Ended March 31, 1956," Forest Research Division, Department of Northern Affairs and National Resources, Ottawa (1956), 27.

5   Johnstone, *Timber and Trauma,* 152-56.

6   The evolution of this process is nicely tracked through the annual reports of the agency.

7   Department of Forestry of Canada, *Annual Report: Fiscal Year 1965-66* (Ottawa, 1966), 3.

8   J.D.B. Harrison, quoted from Kenneth Johnstone, *Timber and Trauma: 75 Years of the Federal Forestry Service, 1899-1974* (Ottawa: Ministry of Supply and Services, 1991), 148.

9   Maurice Sauvé, quoted from Johnstone, *Timber and Trauma,* 156, 163.

10 C. Northcote Parkinson, *Parkinson's Law and Other Studies in Administration* (Cutchogue, NY: Buccaneer Books, 1957), 60; other quotations are from Johnstone, *Timber and Trauma,* 170. On Macleod's projected ambitions for fire research, see J.C. Macleod, "Forest Fire Research: A Position Paper" (in-house document, 1968). I.C.M. Place, *75*

Years of Research in the Woods: A History of the Petawawa Forest Experiment Station and Petawawa National Forestry Institute (Burnstown, ON: General Store Publishing House, 2002), 125.

11 D.E. Williams, quoted in Peter J. Murphy, "Interview with Herb Beall in Ottawa, Ontario. July 27, 1989" (transcript, December 1989), Northern Forestry Centre, Beall file, 4-5.

12 Most major publications of the CFFDRS include historical synopses. Particularly useful are C.E. Van Wagner, "Development and Structure of the Canadian Forest Fire Weather Index System," Forestry Technical Report 35 (Ottawa: Ministry of Supply and Services Canada, 1987); Forestry Canada Fire Danger Group, "Development and Structure of the Canadian Forest Fire Behaviour Prediction System," Information Report ST-X-3 (Ottawa: Forestry Canada, 1992); C.E. Van Wagner, "Structure of the Canadian Forest Fire Weather Index," Publication 1333 (Ottawa: Canadian Forestry Service, 1974); and S.W. Taylor and M.E. Alexander, "Common Cause: The Canadian Experience in Forest Fire Danger Rating" (unpublished paper). On the core architecture, see S.J. Muraro, "A Modular Approach to a Revised National Fire Danger Rating System," in "Contributions on the Development of a National Fire Danger Rating System," Information Report BC-X-37 (Ottawa: Canadian Forestry Service, 1968).

On the context within the CFS's overall work, see Richard A. Rajala, "Feds, Forests, and Fire: A Century of Federal Forestry Innovation in Canada" (unpublished report, National Museum of Science and Technology, June 2000).

13 Van Wagner, "Development and Structure of the Canadian Forest Fire Weather Index System," 3.

14 Van Wagner, "Structure of the Canadian Forest Fire Weather Index," 29. The question of credit for particular contributions is a sticky one. His name graces the major technical reports, and he himself admits to doing "any background science," being "the principal system designer," devising "the core equations" of both the FWI and the FBP (Fire Behaviour Prediction), excepting Turner's work on the drought code. I find little evidence to question this assessment. C.E. Van Wagner to S.J. Pyne, 1 July 2006.

15 C.E. Van Wagner, "Canadian Forest Fire Weather Index" (Ottawa: Canadian Forest Service, 1970). On the formal explanation, see Van Wagner, "Structure of the Canadian Forest Fire Weather Index"; see 2 for a description of continuities.

16 M.E. Alexander et al., "User Guide to the Canadian Forest Fire Behaviour Prediction System: Interim Edition" (Ottawa: Canadian Forestry Service, 1984), and "Tables for the Canadian Forest Fire Weather Index System," Forestry Technical Report 25, 4th ed. (Ottawa: Canadian Forestry Service, 1984). Forestry Canada Fire Danger Group, "Development and Structure of the Canadian Forest Fire Behaviour Prediction System," Information Report ST-X-3 (Ottawa: Forestry Canada, 1992), 8. On the system's international dissemination, see Taylor and Alexander, "Common Cause," 11-12.

Two Solitudes: C.E. Van Wagner and Donald Stedman

1 C.E. Van Wagner to Stephen Pyne, October 2002, 6 (hereafter CEVW to Pyne).

2 Ibid., which contains a biographical summary.

3 Ibid., 3. Van Wagner stated the proposition many times in many venues; see, for example, C.E. Van Wagner, "Forest Fire Research in the Canadian Forestry Service," Information Report PI-X-48 (Ottawa: Canadian Forestry Service, 1984), 17.

4 C.E. Van Wagner, "Moisture Content and Inflammability in Spruce, Fir, and Scots Pine Christmas Trees," Technical Note 109 (Ottawa: Forest Research Branch, 1961); Van Wagner, "Forest Fire Research in the Canadian Forestry Service," 29.

5　C.E. Van Wagner, "Conditions for the Start and Spread of Crown Fire," *Canadian Journal of Forest Research* 7, 1 (1977): 23-24; C.E. Van Wagner, "Age-Class Distribution and the Forest Fire Cycle," *Canadian Journal of Forest Research* 8, 2 (1978): 220-27; C.E. Van Wagner, "Fuel Variation in the Natural Fire-Cycled Boreal Forest," in *Proceedings of the International Fire Management Workshop, 1978,* comp. D. Quintilio, Information Report NOR-X-215 (Ottawa: Canadian Forestry Service, 1979), 67-69; C.E. Van Wagner, "The Impact of Fire on the Nation's Timber Supply," Canadian Forestry Association, *Forestry on the Hill,* special issue 4 (1993): 26-28; and C.E. Van Wagner, "The Economic Impact of Forest Fire," paper for the Annual Meeting of Intermountain Fire Council (Banff, October 1983).

6　CEVW to Pyne, 3-4.

7　C.E. Van Wagner, "Comparison of American and Canadian Forest Fire Danger Rating Systems," Information Report PS-X-2 (Petawawa, ON: Petawawa Forest Experiment Station, 1966), 16-17.

8　C.E. Van Wagner, "Two Solitudes in Forest Fire Research," Information Report PS-X-29 (Ottawa: Canadian Forestry Service, 1971), 7.

9　Van Wagner, "Two Solitudes," 7. CEVW to Pyne, 3-4.

10　Margaret Atwood, *Survival: A Thematic Guide to Canadian Literature* (Toronto: Anansi Press, 1972), 32-33.

11　Ibid., 230. Robertson Davies, "What May Canada Expect from Her Writers?" *One Half of Robertson Davies* (Toronto: Macmillan of Canada, 1977), 140-41.

12　For biographical information, see "Donald Frank Stedman," in *The Canadian Encyclopedia* (Toronto: McClelland and Stewart, 2000); National Research Council of Canada, "Science and Tech Innovations," http://www.nrc-cnrc.gc.ca/education/sti-1930s_stedman_e.html (accessed 15 April 2005); and not least the Stedman Papers, 2 vols., LAC, RG 39, vol. 869.

13　The "loner" label is from "Donald Frank Stedman." On his correspondence with Beall, see D.F. Stedman to J.C. Macleod, 31 March 1960, LAC, RG 39 869, file 32-0-6, part 1.

14　See D.C. Rose, "Preliminary Trials on Instrumental Methods of Measuring Forestry Fire Hazard" (report, National Research Laboratories, 8 June 1936), LAC, RG 39 170, file 49357-1, "Preliminary Trials." Also, on other experiments, see, for example, H.W. Harkness, "On the Time Required for Forest Duff to Attain Hygroscopic Equilibrium," *Forestry Chronicle* 15, 3 (1939): 164-71.

15　Stedman Papers, vol. 2, file 17 for inert gases and file 20 for the speed of light.

16　D.F. Stedman to J.C. Macleod, 31 March 1960, and C.D. Niven to J.C. Macleod, 28 March 1960, LAC, RG 39 869, file 32-0-6, part 1. C.E. Van Wagner, memorandum, to D.E. Williams, 23 October 1964, LAC, RG 39 869, file 32-0-6, part 2. On the report itself (C176-64F), see progress report, 20 April 1964, MG 31, series 26, vol. 2, file 2-12.

17　J.C. Macleod to B.G. Ballard, 27 November 1964, LAC, RG 39 869, file 32-0-6, part 2; J.C. Macleod to A. Bickerstaff, 29 June 1966, LAC, RG 39 870, file 32-0-6, part 3. Forest Fire Research Institute, "Program Review 1965 and 1966" (Ottawa: Forest Fire Research Institute, 1966), 2; W.S. Peterson and T.A. Tweddle, "Forest Fire Hazard Recorder," *Forestry Chronicle* 48 (1973): 83-86.

18　Quotations are from C.E. Van Wagner, "Fire Behavior Modeling: How to Blend Art and Science," in *Eighth Conference on Fire and Forest Meteorology,* SAF Publ. 85-04 (Bethesda, MD: Society of American Foresters, 1985), 5; C.E. Van Wagner, "New Developments in Forest Fire Danger Rating," Information Report PS-X-19 (Petawawa, ON: Petawawa Forest Experiment Station, 1970), 1; and C.E. Van Wagner, "Fuel Variation in the Natural Fire-Cycled Boreal Forest," in *Proceedings of the International Fire Management Workshop, 1978,* comp. D. Quintilio, Information Report NOR-X-215 (Ottawa: Canadian Forestry

Service, 1979), 68.

19 J.C. Macleod to D.F. Stedman, 2 September 1964, LAC, RG 39 869, file 32-0-6, part 2.

20 See Taylor and Alexander, "Common Cause," 8, for a brief account of the resulting exchange.

21 Details are from CEVW to Pyne, 6.

22 Quotations are from CEVW to Pyne, 1-2. The article was C.E. Van Wagner, "Modeling Logic and the Canadian Forest Fire Behavior Prediction System," *Forestry Chronicle* 74, 1 (1998): 50-52.

Revanchism and Federalism

1 Rajala, "Feds, Forests, and Fire," 185.

2 Alexander Koroleff, "Course of Action Needed to Reduce Our Heavy Losses from Forest Fire," Woodlands Research Index 46 (F-3) (Pulp and Paper Research Institute of Canada, 1948), 1-2.

3 The exchanges are recorded in LAC, RG 39 212, file 505336-1, Sub-Committee on Forest Fire Research (August 1947 to March 1949).

4 J.R. Johnston, "The Situation with Respect to Fire Protection," *Forestry Chronicle* 30 (1954): 22-24.

5 See F.A. Harrison, "Forest Fire Research," *Timber of Canada* 19 (1958): 30-33.

6 See D.G. Fraser, "Aircraft for Forest Fire Control in Canada," paper presented at the Meeting of the Commonwealth Advisory Aeronautical Research Council in Australia, April 1962, National Research Council. For a good summary of the propagation of aircraft, see Rajala, "Feds, Forests, and Fire," 142-58. But see also D.E. Williams to Jose Isaias Gonzalez, 1 December 1965, LAC, RG 39 789, file 32-11-7 1.

7 "Workshop Meeting on Aircraft in Forest Fire Control: Summary of Discussions," Ottawa, 5 and 6 December 1963, National Research Council of Canada, ix, 1-2, 4-5, 18.

8 See S.G. Chester, "Studies of the Use of Aircraft in Forest Fire Control: Progress Report" (Richmond Hill, ON: Forest Research Branch, 1965), for presentation to the Thirteenth Annual Meeting of the Associate Committee on Forest Fire Protection. For a quick survey of developments, see D.E. Williams to J.D. MacArthur, 8 November 1965, LAC, RG 39 789, file 32-11-7 1.

9 D.G. Fraser, "Aircraft for Forest Fire Control in Canada" (manuscript, Forest Research Branch, November 1964), later revised and published as "Forest Fire Control Aircraft in Canada," *Journal of the Royal Aeronautical Society* 68 (1964): 546-52. For an overview of the program, see Ron Pickler and Larry Milberry, *Canadair: The First 50 Years* (Toronto: Canav Books, 1995), 216-17. Chapter 8 is devoted to the CL-215.

10 Pickler and Milberry, *Canadair,* 216-17.

11 For the quotations, see D.E. Williams to M.L. Prebble, 6 December 1965, and D.E. Williams to M.L. Prebble, 26 May 1967, LAC, RG 39 789, file 32-11-7 1; also informative is J.C. Macleod to Dr. H. Schwartz, 26 May 1967, same file. On the Ontario project with Trackers, see Rajala, "Feds, Forests, and Fire," 160.

12 M.L. Prebble to Jack Davis and A.W.H. Needler, 27 November 1968, including "The Use of the Airtanker in Forest Fire Suppression" (Ottawa: Forest Fire Research Institute, 1968), LAC, RG 39, Accession 94-95/770, box 1, file 1001-108/3-9. The report was later published as D.E. Williams, D.L. McLean, and B.S. Hodgson, "The Use of the Airtanker in Forest Fire Suppression," Internal Report FF-8 (Ottawa: Forest Fire Research Institute, 1968).

13 Associate Committee on Forest Fire Protection, Special Report No. 1, *National Forest Fire Seminar on Aircraft Management*, Petawawa Forest Experiment Station, 25-30 October 1970. For a summary, see Robert W. Upton, "National Forest Fire Seminar on Aircraft Management," *Pulp and Paper Magazine of Canada* 72 (1971): 3-11.

14 Task Force on Federal Government Assistance in Dealing with Forest Fire Control Emergencies, "Report of Meeting of December 16 and 17, 1970," LAC, RG 39, Accession 94-95/770, box 24/72, file 1165-36/C 7-4 3, Org. – Forestry Branch, Forest Fire Research Institute.

·15 John Gass, memo, to G.R. Maybee, 21 September 1973, historical files, Provincial Fire Centre, Shubenacadie, Nova Scotia. A good summary of the various criticisms is contained in Robert R. Ross to D.F. Merrill, 21 March 1973, CIFFC historical files, CCFFM-CIFFC, box 6, file 4.1, vol. 2.

16 Quotations are from D.H. Owen to D.F. Merrill, 30 March 1979, CIFFC historical files, CCFFM-CIFFC, box 6, file 4-1-1, vol. 2. Among major airtanker studies, see A.J. Simard and D.E. Williams, "The Airtanker Fleet Feasibility Study," Paper 19, paper prepared for the Forestry Seminar sponsored by the Canadian Council of Resource Ministers, 1970; D.G. Fraser, "Development of Aircraft Use in Forest Fire Control," paper presented at the National Seminar on Aircraft Management, 1970; A.J. Simard, "An Analysis of the Use of Aircraft for Forest Fire Suppression," paper presented at the National Seminar on Aircraft Management, 1970; A.J. Simard, "Airtankers and Wildland Fire Management: A Systems Overview," paper presented to Fall Fire Review, Bureau of Land Management, Alaska, 1974; A.J. Simard, "Airtanker Utilization and Wildland Fire Management," paper presented to the Fifth International Agriculture Aviation Congress, 1975; D.G. Fraser, "Canadian Forest Fire Aircraft: Then and Now," paper presented to the Canadian Aeronautics and Space Institute Annual Meeting, 1977; J.E. Grigel, R.G. Newstead, and R.J. Lieskovsky, "A Review of Retardant Delivery Systems Used in Fixed-Wing Airtankers," Information Report NOR-X-134 (Edmonton: Canadian Forestry Service, 1975); and A.J. Simard, "The Use of Air Tankers in Canada, 1957-1977," Information Report FF-X-71 (Ottawa: Canadian Forestry Service, 1979).

17 A useful digest of developments is available in J.W. Paisley, "The Canadian Interagency Forest Fire Centre: A Brief History" (manuscript on file at the CIFFC, 1983). See also "CIFFC Developmental Group Final Report" (27 May 1982), historical files, CIFFC. The major documents are available in LAC, RG 39, Accession 94-95/769, box 31, file 1165-36/ C8-29 1, specifically James A.C. Auld to John Roberts, 7 July 1980; John Roberts to James A.C. Auld, 13 August 1980; James A.C. Auld to John Roberts, 2 September 1980; Ontario Ministry of Natural Resources, "A Federal Presence in Forest Fire Control in Canada: A Proposal" (February 1981); CCREM, Meeting of Deputy Ministers of Forestry, 17 March 1981 (summary); CCREM Task Force on Forest Fire Control, "Forest Fire Control in Canada: A Discussion Paper for the Canadian Council of Resource and Environment Ministers" (August 1981); CCREM, Meeting of Task Force on Forest Fire Control, 3 and 4 December 1981, quotation from page 1. Note too that duplicates of all the relevant documents, and many others, are housed at CIFFC (actually in a broom closet).

18 For an earlier summary of what mutual aid meant, see S.R. Hughes, "Mutual Aid Is Important to the Control of Forest Fires in Canada," CIFFC historical files, CCFFM-CIFFC, box 6, file 4.1, vol. 2.

19 For the documents discussed, see LAC, RG 39, Accession 94-95/770, box 24/72, file 1165-36/C 704 3, Committees, Boards, Councils (Forest Fire Control).

20 For a summary of how Canadians interpreted the agreement, see D.F. Merrill, memo, to

G.A. Steneker, 11 March 1985, CIFFC historical files, CCFFM-CIFFC, box 6, file 4-1-1, vol. 3. Quotations are from Ontario Ministry of Natural Resources, "A Federal Presence," 3, and W.L. Sleeman, memo, to Mrs. Michele Fordyce, 16 December 1980, Archives of Ontario, RG-1-400, Accession 23663, box 1.

21 On competing proposals, see "Forest Fire Control in Canada: Water Bomber Aircraft and Supplemental Fire Equipment Caches," minister's briefing note, Forestry Ministers' Meeting, 1-2 September 1982, CIFFC historical files, CCFFM-CIFFC, box 6, file 4.1, vol. 3. On early developments, see CIFFC *Annual Reports* for 1983 and 1984.

22 For a good summary, see "Notes on the Development of the Canadian Interagency Forest Fire Centre, Related Agreements and Programs," LAC, RG 39, Accession 1995-96/336, box 15, file 1165-36/C276 9. For relative costs – and a spirited defence of the CL-215 – see D.F. Merrill and T. Wood, "Airtankers for Forest Fire Control in Canada," draft document for CCREM Forest Fire Task Force, CIFFC historical files, CCFFM-CIFM, box 6, file 4.1, vol. 3.

23 Cliff White, *Wildland Fires in Banff National Park 1880-1980,* Occasional Paper no. 3 (Ottawa: Ministry of Supply and Services Canada, 1985), 63, 67-69, 73. For a summary of the ASW program, see *Report of Lands, Parks, and Forests Branch for the Fiscal Year Ended March 31, 1946* (Ottawa: Edmond Cloutier, 1947), 106-7.

24 The "shortages" quotation is from *Report of the Department of Mines and Resources for the Fiscal Year Ended March 31, 1947* (Ottawa: Edmond Cloutier, 1948), 105; the other quotations are from White, *Wildland Fires,* 74-76. For developments throughout the system, see *Report of the Department of Mines and Resources Including Report of Soldier Settlement of Canada for the Fiscal Year Ended March 31, 1941* (Ottawa: Edmond Cloutier, 1941), 85-86.

25 White, *Wildland Fires,* 76-78.

26 Ibid., 78.

27 A thumbnail history is in M.J. Heathcott and S.C. Cornelsen, "Options for Fire Management in Wood Buffalo National Park," Wood Buffalo National Park files, 3. The quotation is from *Report of the Director of Forestry for the Year 1914* (Ottawa: Government Printing Bureau, 1915), 29.

28 Sidney Stephen Janzen, "The Burning North: A History of Fire and Fire Protection in the NWT" (master's thesis, University of Alberta, 1989), 79-80.

29 Ibid., 81.

30 Lumber statistics are from ibid., 102-3.

31 Harry Holman, quoted from ibid., 105.

32 J.S. Rowe, "Nature Protection: Wilderness and Natural Areas" (unpublished paper, Department of Forestry, 1962), 1.

33 "Fire Review. October 25-26, 1971. Wood Buffalo National Park" (unpublished report, Parks Canada, 1971), 2-3. The reference to the army-bulldozed line is from Mark Heathcott, comments on draft manuscript, 7 December 2005. For an overview of the thinking behind the priority ranking, see N.S. Novakowski, "Fire Priority Report: Wood Buffalo National Park" (Canadian Wildlife Service, 1970).

34 Heathcott and Cornelsen, "Options for Fire Management in Wood Buffalo National Park," 3.

35 A.D. Revill and Associates, *Ecological Effects of Fire and Its Management in Canada's National Parks,* 3 vols. (Ottawa: Parks Canada, 1978); Peter Deering, "A Direction for Fire Management in Elk Island National Park" (unpublished report, 1990), especially 15, 17; C.E. Van Wagner and I.R. Methven, "Fire Management of Canada's National Parks: Philosophy and Strategy," Occasional Papers 1 (Ottawa: Parks Canada, 1980). See, too,

Nikita Loupkhine, "Guiding Philosophy for Management of Fire and Vegetation in Canadian Parks," in *Proceedings: Symposium and Workshop on Wilderness Fire*, technical co-ordinators James E. Lotan et al., General Technical Report INT-182 (US Forest Service, 1985), 16-20.

On the role of the CFS, consider these remarks from Cliff White, comments to Stephen Pyne, 7 December 2005: "When I started working directly on fire in 1978, Dennis Dubé had recently taken over from D. Quintilio at NoFRC and, with his amazing capacity to quietly initiate and facilitate action, was stimulating fire management and research across a wide field of interests. I remember that in his office, and the adjacent one, he had over forty project files piled up, each for some individual provincial or federal initiative. About five of these were for proposed or partially finished Parks Canada fire studies and burning experiments. These project paper piles would lay dormant for some period until some young keener or bold administrator would stop in at the centre for some ideas on where to go next. Dennis would dust off the piles for the appropriate park, and, voilà, the direction for a likely course of action could be quickly discussed. After a ten-minute visit to his office, I was well connected to specialists such as Marty Alexander and Doug McCrae and on my way to doing fire history and biomass research in Banff."

36 Dave Kiil, Dennis Dubé, and Al Jeffrey, "Board of Review Report on Rolling River Fire, 1980-6, Riding Mountain National Park" (unpublished report, 31 January 1981), 2, 12-13.

37 David L. Day, Clifford A. White, and Nikita Lopoukhine, "Keeping the Flame: Fire Management in the Canadian Parks System," in *Proceedings of Interior West Fire Council 1988 Annual Meeting*, Information Report NOR-X-309 (Edmonton: Forestry Canada, 1989), 9; Kiil, Dubé, and Jeffrey, "Board of Review Report," 19.

38 I'm indebted to Cliff White for pointing out this extraordinary synergy; comments to Stephen Pyne, 7 December 2005.

39 C.A. Jeffrey, Dennis Dubé, and Dennis Quintilio, "A Review of the Wood Buffalo Fire Management Program 1981" (unpublished report to Parks Canada, 19 May 1981), 4.

40 Van Wagner and Methven, "Fire in the Management of Canada's National Parks," 10, 15.

41 J.C. Macleod, "Federal Forest Fire Research," Forest Fire Research Reports, Woodlands Section Index 2172 (F-3), *Pulp and Paper Magazine of Canada* 63 (1962): WR-414.

42 J.C. Macleod, *Research Work of the Forestry Branch*, Miscellaneous Publication 6 (Ottawa: Department of Northern Affairs and National Resources, 1956), 22. Figures and the "bleeding" quotation are from J.C. Macleod, memo, to Dr. H. Schwartz, 1 May 1968, LAC, RG 39 789, file 506-9-0 1, Environment – Fire – General.

43 See "An In-House Paper on Forest Fire Research in the Department of Forestry and Rural Development," attached to J.C. Macleod, memo, to Regional Directors, Director, Petawawa Forest Experiment Station, and Director, Forest Fire Research Institute, 25 July 1968, LAC, RG 39 789, Fire 506-9-0 1, Environment – Fire – General.

44 A.D. Kiil, memo, to R.J. Bourchier, 13 December 1977, including attachment "On the Nature, Effectiveness, and Future Direction of the CFS Fire Research Program," LAC, RG 39, Accession 1995-96/336, box 78, file 6650-1 1.

45 Subcommittee on Forest Fire Research, Canadian Committee on Forest Fire Management, "Forest Fire Research: The Need for Change: A Position Paper on Fire Research" (May 1984), LAC, RG 39, Accession 1995-96/336, box 16, file 1165-36/C276 10.

46 Ibid., 1-2; Subcommittee on Forest Fire Research, Canadian Committee on Forest Fire Management, "Forest Fire Research" (January 1986), LAC, RG 39, Accession 1995-96/336, box 16, file 1165-36/C276 10.

Fire's Outer Limits: Fire Provinces on the Fringe

1 *Annual Report of the Department of the Interior for the Year 1899* (Ottawa: S.E. Dawson, 1900), 19-20; Charles Camsell, quoted from Sidney Stephen Janzen, "The Burning North: A History of Fire and Fire Protection in the NWT" (MA thesis, University of Alberta, 1990), 44; on Elihu Stewart, see Janzen, "The Burning North," 58. As these citations suggest, my debt to Janzen's thesis is great. This chapter is enormously better for being able to build on his study.

2 Jonquil Graves, "A History of Wildlife Management in the Northwest Territories" (manuscript, Department of Renewable Resources, NWT, 1988), 27-28, 50-53.

3 Janzen, "The Burning North," 2.

4 H.A. Conroy, "Report of H.A. Conroy," in *Report of the Director of Forestry for the Year 1912* (Ottawa: Government Printing Bureau, 1912), 86; George Card, "Report, Fort Smith, N.W.T., Dec 29th, 1915," and John Conner, "Report, Fort Smith, N.W.T., Oct 3rd, 1913," LAC, RG 39 862, file 39112.

5 E.H. Finlayson, *Report of the Director of Forestry, 1913* (Ottawa: Government Printing Bureau, 1914, 20; Henry Jones, quoted from "Final Report for Season 1916, Sept 30, 1916, Fort Resolution, N.W.T.," LAC, RG 39 262, file 39112.

6 E.H. Finlayson, *Report of the Director of Forestry for the Year 1916* (Ottawa: Government Printing Bureau, 1917), 74; T.W. Harris, quoted from Janzen, "The Burning North," 52. For a good survey of early fire ranging, see Janzen, "The Burning North," 60-63.

7 E.H. Finlayson, *Report of the Director of Forestry for the Year 1917* (Ottawa: Government Printing Bureau, 1918), 63-64; *Report of the Director of Forestry for the Year 1918*, 54. For another interesting adaptation of fur trade logistics applied to fire, see H.D. Bury, "Memorandum to R.H. Campbell, November 11, 1916," LAC, RG 39 262, file 39112.

8 Details are from Janzen, "The Burning North," 76-79. Quotations are from A. Rafton-Canning, "Suggestions for Season 1921, December 31st, 1920," LAC, RG 39 112, file 40308; J.A. McDougal, quoted from Janzen, "The Burning North," 80.

9 The chronology is from Janzen, "The Burning North," 79-80.

10 Ibid., 104, 89-91.

11 E.G. Oldham, quoted from Janzen, "The Burning North," 104; *Report of the Department of Mines and Resources for the Fiscal Year Ended March 31, 1946* (Ottawa: Edmond Cloutier, 1947), 80-81.

12 *Report of the Department of Mines and Resources for the Fiscal Year Ended March 31, 1947* (Ottawa: Edmond Cloutier, 1948), 90.

13 H.L. Holman, quoted from Janzen, "The Burning North," 105.

14 Ibid., 105-6, 102-3, 109.

15 D.A. Macdonald, "Forestry Branch," *Report of the Department of Resources and Development for the Fiscal Year Ended March 31, 1950*, 95; for the 1953 fires, see *Annual Report, Department of Northern Affairs and National Resources, Fiscal Year 1953-54*, 23-24.

16 Janzen, "The Burning North," 109.

17 See, for example, "Forests and Game Section," in *Annual Report, Department of Northern Affairs and National Resources, Fiscal Year 1954-1955*, 24; on local critics, see Janzen, "The Burning North," 106-7.

18 Janzen, "The Burning North," 110.

19 For a good summary, see the Beverly and Qamanirjuaq Caribou Management Board, "A Review of Fire Management on Forested Range of the Beverly and Qamanirjuaq Herd of Caribou," Technical Report 1 (Beverly and Qamanirjuaq Caribou Management Board, 1994), 11. For the research, see G.W. Scotter, "Effects of Forest Fires on the Winter Range of

Barren-Ground Caribou in Northern Saskatchewan," *Wildlife Management Series 1, no. 18* (Canadian Wildlife Service, 1964); Scotter, "Study of the Winter Range of Barren-Ground Caribou with Special Reference to the Effects of Forest Fires," *Canadian Wildlife Service Progress Report 3* (Canadian Wildlife Service, 1965); and Scotter, "Effects of Fire on Barren-Ground Caribou and Their Forest Habitat in Northern Canada," *Transactions, North American Wildlife Conference* 32 (1971), 246-59; J.P. Kelsall, "Continued Barren-Ground Caribou Studies," *Wildlife Management Bulletin, Series 1, 12* (Canadian Wildlife Service, 1957); and J.P. Kelsall, "Cooperative Studies of Barren-Ground Caribou, 1957-58," *Canadian Wildlife Service Management Bulletin Series 1, 15* (Canadian Wildlife Service, 1960). On the Porter Lake experiment, see Caribou Management Board, "Review," 11.

20 Department of Northern Affairs and National Resources, *Annual Report: Fiscal Year 1961-1962*, 41; the quotation is from Janzen, "The Burning North," 112.

21 Janzen, "The Burning North," 112-13.

22 Ibid., 114-15. A higher statistical register comes from the official summaries because they conflate the Northwest Territories and Yukon fires; *Indian and Northern Affairs 1971/72 Annual Report*, 72.

23 Janzen, "The Burning North," 116.

24 Ibid., 117-18; *Indian and Northern Affairs 1972/1973 Annual Report*, 88. On the policies, see John McQueen, "N.W.T. Priority Zones for Forest Fire Protection," in *Fire Ecology in Resource Management: Workshop Proceedings*, ed. D.E. Dubé, Information Report NOR-X-210 (Ottawa: Canadian Forestry Service, 1978); Janzen, "The Burning North," 118; Alvin Kim Clark, "Management Implications of Integrating Values-at-Risk and Community Consultation with the Northwest Territories' Forest Fire Management Policy" (MS thesis, University of Alberta, 1993), 4-5.

25 *Indian and Northern Affairs 1973-1974 Annual Report*, 68.

26 Janzen, "The Burning North," 118-19; McQueen, "N.W.T. Priority Zones for Forest Fire Suppression," 96-102; Lorraine Allison, "The Relationship of Fire and Wildlife to Fire Management in the Northwest Territories" (unpublished report, Northwest Territories Wildlife Service, 1979).

27 Allison, "Relationship of Fire and Wildlife," 27.

28 On politics, see Kenneth Coates, *Canada's Colonies: A History of the Yukon and Northwest Territories* (Toronto: James Lorimer, 1985), 219-27.

29 Peter J. Murphy, Stanley R. Hughes, and John S. Mactavish, *Forest Fire Management in the Northwest Territories: A Review of 1979 Forest Fire Operations and Forest Fire Management Policy* (Ottawa: Minister of Supply and Services Canada, 1981). For a survey of the 1979 fire and caribou, with policy recommendations that reflect the thinking of the science-informed elite, see Robert S. Ferguson, "A Discussion Paper on the Potential Effects of Fire on the Beverly Caribou Population and Fire Management Options for Caribou Winter Range," report to the Caribou Management Board (1982), Archives of Northwest Territories, G-1994-004 [35-2].

30 On political devolution, see "Transfer of the Responsibilities of Forest Management from D.I.A.N.D. to G.N.W.T., November 12, 1981," Archives of Northwest Territories, G-1994-004 [34-1]. For useful discussions about how different sides interpreted the process, see "Fire Transfer Meeting, December 16, 1981," "Letter, to P.H. Beaubier from Herb Norwegian, July 12, 1982," and "Letter, Nellie J. Cournoyea to Honourable John Munro," 18 May 1984," Archives of Northwest Territories, G-1994-004 [34-1]; "Review of Policies and Procedures of the Forest Fire Management and Control Program in the Northwest Territories" (unpublished report presented to Northern Affairs Program, NWT Region,

Department of Indian Affairs and Northern Development, 1984, Departmental Library, Yellowknife).

31 On the agency's reaction, see "Departmental Responses to Recommendations Made by the Fire Review Panel," Archives of Northwest Territories, G-1994-004 [35-1], which lists replies, item by item; Clayton Burke, "N.W.T. Fire Management Program Committee Report. 1981," 2 November 1981, 21, Archives of Northwest Territories, G-1994-003 [2-1]; the "never accepted" quotation is from "Letter, to P.H. Beaubier from Herb Norwegian, July 12, 1982," Archives of Northwest Territories, G-1994-004 [34-1]; other quotations are from "Fire Management Committee Meeting, July 13-14, 1982," Archives of the Northwest Territories, G-1994-004 [33-1], 2. Other illuminating documents include "N.W.T. Fire Management Program Committee. Background Information. April 21, 1982," Archives of Northwest Territories, G-1994-003 [2-1], and Fort Smith Hunters and Trappers Association, "Written Submissions to Northwest Territories Forest Fire Review Panel, 1979-1980," Archives of Northwest Territories, G-1994-003 [2-1].

32 The quotation is from L. Mychasiw, "An Expression of Concepts and Principles Respecting Forest Fire Management in NWT: A Discussion Paper for Development of Fire Management Policy" (unpublished report, NWT Wildlife Service, 1982), 7.

33 For an introduction to Yukon fire geography, see S.W. Taylor et al., "Wild Fire Frequency in Yukon Ecoregions, 1946-92" (unpublished report, Canadian Forest Service, 1994).

34 Coates, *Canada's Colonies*, 87-92; the Sifton quotation is from 94.

35 The best single survey remains Harold J. Lutz, *Aboriginal Man and White Man as Historical Causes of Fires in the Boreal Forest, with Particular Reference to Alaska*, School of Forestry Bulletin 65 (New Haven: Yale University School of Forestry, 1959). References to Klondike burning are from John Parminter, "A Historical Review of Forest Fire Management in British Columbia" (MA thesis, University of British Columbia, 1978), 10.

36 John Parminter, "Largest 20 Known Fires in B.C., 1920-2001" (unpublished paper, 2002). See also developments at this time in the Northwest Territories, aptly summarized in Janzen, "The Burning North."

37 *Report of the Department of Mines and Resources for the Fiscal Year Ended March 31, 1946* (Ottawa: Edmond Cloutier, 1947), 93. The quotation on the Carmacks fire is from Al Beaver, letter to Stephen Pyne, 30 December 2005.

38 On burning for fuel wood, see Fred Fraser, memo, to C.K. LeCapelain, 24 September 1952, Yukon Archives, Gov. Ser. 1 2246, file 14; the quotation is from "Annual Summary of Forest Fire Losses. Yukon Territory. Calendar Year 1950," Yukon Archives, Gov. Ser. 1 2246, file 15, 4.

39 *Report of the Department of Resources and Development for the Fiscal Year Ended March 31, 1952*, 79; the quotation on windrows is from F.H.R. Jackson to C.K. LeCapelain, 27 August 1951, Yukon Archives, Gov. Ser. 1 2246, file 15, 1-2,; on slash and dredging, see "Memorandum, Fred Fraser to F.J.G. Cunningham, June 23, 1952," Yukon Archives, Gov. Ser. 1 2246, file 14.

40 "Memorandum, Fred Fraser to F.J.G. Cunningham, June 23, 1952," with "Memorandum for Discussion with Mr. Fred Fraser, Forest Fire Protection, Yukon Territory, Ottawa, February 12, 1952," Yukon Archives, Gov. Ser. 1 2246, file 14.

41 Department of Northern Affairs and National Resources, *Annual Report Fiscal Year 1958-1959*, 37. "Revision of Data for Minister's Reference Book: Number of Fires and Resulting Damage Occurred," Yukon Archives, Gov. Ser. 2599, file 4, 2.

42 See DIAND, Forest Resources, *The Role of Fire in the Yukon Boreal Forest: Workshop*, Whitehorse, 6 February 1996, 3; Department of Northern Affairs and National Resources,

Annual Report Fiscal Year 1965-1966, 17; quotations are from Associate Committee on Forest Fire Protection, "Yukon Territory," Annual Meeting (Ottawa: Associate Committee on Forest Fire Protection, 1969), 2-3; and E. Nyland, "Forest Fire in the Yukon," North American Forestry Commission, Fire Management Study Group, Canadian-Alaskan Seminar on Research Needs in Fire Ecology and Fire Management in the North, 7-10 October 1975, 1.

43 On the 1969 season, see DIAND, *Annual Report, 1969-1970*, 89-90; statistics are from Government of Yukon, "Wildfire Statistics from 2003 back to 1946," http://www.community. gov.yk.ca/firemanagement/sts46.html; and S.W. Taylor et al., "Wild Fire Frequency in Yukon Ecoregions," 12-13; Nyland, "Forest Fire in the Yukon," 1; on Faro, see Keith Kepke, "Yukon Fire History," in DIAND, "Developing Fire Safe Communities in the Yukon. A Summary of a Multi Government Workshop to Develop an Action Plan. January 22 and 23, 1998. Proceedings," 3. More detailed fire summaries for 1969 are available in the Yukon Archives, Gov. Ser. 1 2589, file 10. They include reports at the times of the fires.

44 Nyland, "Forest Fire in the Yukon," 2-4; for a thumbnail chronicle, see DIAND, "Fire Management in the Yukon Territory and Northwest Territories," revised April 1974, 1; quotations are from Edo Nyland and Wilf C. Taylor, "Forest Fire Control Plan," January 1972, which also lays out priorities within the protected zone.

45 DIAND, *Annual Report, 1974-1975*, 63; on aerial ignition, see E. Nyland, "Wildfire Control through Aerial Ignition in the Yukon," in North American Forestry Commission, Fire Study Group, "Canadian-Alaskan Seminar," 1-2.

46 Nyland, "Forest Fires in the Yukon," 2; G.R. Lait and W.C. Taylor, "Backfiring and Burn-out Techniques Used in the Yukon, 1972," Information Report NOR-X-43 (Northern Forest Research Centre, 1972).

47 See E. Nyland and John D. Dell, "International Teamwork Applied to Fire Protection Planning in Yukon," North American Forestry Commission, Fire Management Study Group, *Forest Fire News* (1977): 1-7.

48 "Report of the Committee on Forest Improvement and Protection. Presented to the Federal-Provincial Task Force on Forestry" (unpublished report, St. John's, 1972), 57. On fire's ecological power in Newfoundland, see also W.C. Wilton and C.H. Evans, "Newfoundland Forest Fire History 1619-1960," Information Report N-X-116 (Newfoundland Forest Research Centre, 1974), 1-2.

49 For a master chronology of Newfoundland fires, see Wilton and Evans, "Newfoundland Forest Fire History," 9, 96.

50 Ibid., 97-98, 2, 98-101. For detailed accounts of the 1892 fire, see "Fires," in *Encyclopedia of Newfoundland and Labrador*, ed. Joseph Smallwood (St. John's, NF: Newfoundland Book Publishing, 1967), 108-11; and Moses Harvey, "The Great Fire of 8 July 1892," in *By Great Waters: A Newfoundland and Labrador Anthology*, ed. Peter Neary and Patrick O'Flaherty (Toronto: University of Toronto Press, 1974), 113-18.

51 Wilton and Evans, "Newfoundland," 98-101; W.J. Carroll, *A History of the Newfoundland Forest Protection Association* (Newfoundland Forest Protection Association, 1990), 3.

52 Ibid., 3-4.

53 Ibid., 6-8.

54 Ibid., 8-9.

55 Newfoundland Forest Protection Association, *Annual Report, 1960*, Fiftieth Anniversary Issue, 6-8.

56 The Howe quotations and the scope of the 1904 fires are from Wilton and Evans, "Newfoundland," 101-7.

57 On 1925, see Carroll, *History*, 4.

58 Ibid., 9.

59 Margaret R. Conrad and James K. Hiller, *Atlantic Canada. A Region in the Making* (Don Mills, ON: Oxford University Press, 2001), 176-77.

60 *Annual Report of the Department of Natural Resources 1934-1935*, 14.

61 Carroll, *History*, 15.

62 Ibid., 15, 42-43, 17-18; on pumps, see H.V.E. Smith, *Annual Report of the Fire Patrol to the Annual Executive Meeting of the Newfoundland Forest Protection Association, November 1947*, 11. Smith cited 1935 as his reference year; L.R. Cooper to Commissioner for Natural Resources, 6 February 1936, Provincial Archives of Newfoundland and Labrador, GN 31/2, box 2, file 7/1 1.

63 Forest Officer to Secretary N.R., 10 November 1938, Provincial Archives of Newfoundland and Labrador, GN 31/2, box 2, file 7/1 2. For fire years, see Wilton and Evans, "Newfoundland," 5, 40-48.

64 Carroll, *History*, 19; on fire years, see Wilton and Evans, "Newfoundland," 3-5, 49-51.

65 Carroll, *History*, 43-44; Wilton and Evans, "Newfoundland," 110-11. Figures on sizes differ: NFPA for 1947 says 150 square miles burned in 1946 and 740 (474,000 acres) in 1947. *Annual Report, Newfoundland Forest Protection Association, November 1946*, 12-14; *Annual Report … NFPA, November 1947*, 10-13. On job-hunting fires, see "Chairman's Report," in *Annual Report … NFPA, November 1947*, 36.

66 Quotations are from Smith, *Annual Report … NFPA, November 1947*, 12-13.

67 Quoted in Carroll, *History*, 45-46; on aircraft, see Smith, *Annual Report … NFPA, November 1947*, 13.

68 Carroll, *History*, 46-48.

69 A. Martin, "Chairman's Report," in *Annual Report of the Newfoundland Forest Protection Association to the Annual Meeting, November 1949*, 3-4; detailed accounts of the fires are on 45-51.

70 Ibid., 4; *Annual Report of the Newfoundland Forest Protection Association to the Annual Meeting, November 1950*, 5, 9, 42-44.

71 *Report of the Royal Commission on Forestry* (Newfoundland: David R. Thistle, 1955), 13, 57; and within that *Report*, J.A. Brodie, "Report on Forest Protection Services, Province of Newfoundland, January 30th, 1955," 58-84; on the NFPA as a crown corporation, see 85.

72 Carroll, *History*, 48-49; "Report of the Special Committee of Nfld. Forest Protection Association on the Recommendations of the Royal Commission on Forestry with Respect to Forest Fire Protection in Newfoundland," Provincial Archives of Newfoundland and Labrador, GN 31/2, box 75, file 398/2/4 1.

73 Supervisor of Forestry Operations to A.J. Reeve, 19 June 1957, Provincial Archives of Newfoundland and Labrador, GN 31/2, box 116, file 623/19.

74 *Annual Report of the Newfoundland Forest Protection Association, 1958*, 10. See also Carroll, *History*, 48-49; for the new fire pattern, see *Annual Report of the Newfoundland Forest Protection Association, 1959*, 6.

75 Newfoundland Research Council, *Symposium on Prescribed Burning in Forestry, Agriculture, and Wildlife Management* (St. John's: Department of Mines and Resources and Memorial University of Newfoundland, 1958). A summary with official comments is available in *Annual Report of the Department of Mines and Resources for the Year Ended 31st March, 1958*, 88-89, 96; W.A. Dickson and D.E. Nickerson, "Factors Affecting Natural Regeneration on Cut-Over and Burned-Over Lands, Newfoundland" (Ottawa: Department of Northern Affairs and Natural Resources, Forestry Branch, 1958). For follow-up, see "Newfoundland

Forest Service, Forest Fire Report," in *Annual Report of the Newfoundland Forest Protection Association 1967,* 48, in which the trend toward mechanical and chemical surrogates already manifests itself.

76 For the 1959 fires, see *Annual Report of the Department of Mines and Resources for the Year Ended 31st March, 1960,* 48. For aerial tactics developed, see *Annual Report of the Department of Mines, Agriculture, and Resources for the Year Ended 31st March, 1961,* 45. See also Newfoundland Forest Protection Association, *Annual Report, 1960,* Fiftieth Anniversary Issue, 39.

77 *Annual Report of the Department of Mines, Agriculture, and Resources for the Year Ended 31st March 1962,* 48-55; on the forest's economic contribution, see I.M. Stewart, "Meteorological Conditions Associated with the Newfoundland Forest Fire Season of 1961" (unpublished report, Department of Transportation, Meteorological Branch, 1961), 1.

78 *Annual Report of the Department of Mines, Agriculture, and Resources for the Year Ended 31st March 1961-62,* 56. For an interesting critique of the season's efforts, see E.B. Ralph, "Forest Fires 1961," F.R. Hayward, "Forest Fires 1961: Problems Encountered, Lessons Learned, and Future Planning with Respect to 1961 Experience," and M.C. Vardy, "Forest Fires 1961" (unpublished papers, Department of Mines, Agriculture, and Resources Library, Corner Brook, NF); Carroll, *History,* 14, 19, 50-51; *Annual Report ... 1961-62,* 56.

79 *Annual Report of the Department of Mines, Agriculture, and Resources for the Year Ended 31st March, 1965,* 31; M.C. Vardy, "Report of the Controlling Committee," in *Annual Report ... 1967,* 6-7; Carroll, *History,* 50-53; "Report of the Committee on Forest Improvement and Protection: Presented to the Federal-Provincial Task Force on Forestry" (St. John's, NF, 1972), 72-73; and on prevention, see letter, 19 June 1957, Provincial Archives of Newfoundland and Labrador, GN 312, box 116, file 623/19.

80 *Annual Report of the Department of Mines, Agriculture, and Resources for the Year Ended 31st March 1968,* 89. For a snapshot of fire, as viewed by commercial forestry, see Atlantic Development Board, "Forestry in the Atlantic Provinces: Background Study No. 1" (Ottawa: Atlantic Development Board, 1968), 1-28 to 1-29.

81 *Report to the Government of Newfoundland and Labrador of the Royal Commission on Forestry 1970* (St. John's, NF: Royal Commission on Forestry, 1970), 26-28.

82 "Report of the Committee on Forest Improvement and Protection," 66, 76.

83 Ibid., 77-80. On the 1975 season, see "Newfoundland Forest Service: Forest Fire Report – 1975," in *Annual Report of the Newfoundland and Labrador Forest Protection Association, 1975,* 6-7, 14-15; *Annual Report of Newfoundland Forest Protection Association, 1976,* 12.

84 *Annual Report of Newfoundland Forest Protection Association, 1979,* 20; Carroll, *History,* 54; the quotation on regeneration is from C.F. Poole, *Report of the Royal Commission on Forest Protection and Management* (St. John's, NF: Royal Commission on Forest Protection and Management, 1981), Part 1: Newfoundland, 5, and Part 2: Labrador, 10-11.

Internal Combustions

1 E.P. Heaton, *Report of the Provincial Fire Marshal E.P. Heaton, Following Investigation into the Northern Ontario Conflagration of October 4th, 1922* (Toronto: Clarkson W. James, 1922), 40. On the Haileybury fire, see Archives of Ontario, MU 2207. The suite of fires from 1910 to 1922 is well documented in the provincial archives. A general survey, richly illustrated, is available in Michael Barnes, *Killer in the Bush: The Great Fires of Northeastern Ontario* (Erin, ON: Boston Mills Press, 1987); the Matheson fire also finds its way into Janet Looker, *Disaster Canada* (Toronto: Lynx Images, 2000), 116-21.

2 Heaton, *Report,* 40.

3   See *Report of the Department of Lands, Forests, and Mines of the Province of Ontario for the Year Ending 31st October 1911* (Toronto: L.K. Cameron, 1912), ix. I have relied for a general source on Barnes, *Killer in the Bush.*

4   Barnes, *Killer in the Bush,* 14-15.

5   Ibid., 17-18.

6   Ibid., 18, 22.

7   H.C. Meek to A.P. Turner, 28 October 1911, Provincial Archives of Ontario, RG 8-20, 1-1-2.

8   Ibid. A.P. Turner to Arthur F. Sladen, 10 October 1911, Provincial Archives of Ontario, RG 8-20, 1-1-2. The lieutenant governor replied that, while there was "absolutely no way of ascertaining the details of the incident," which depended solely on the survivors' testimony, the "general opinion" was that the account was true.

9   H.C. Meek to A.P. Turner, 10 October 1911; see also H.C. Meek to A.P. Turner, 29 September 1911, Provincial Archives of Ontario, RG 8-20, 1-1-2.

10   *Report ... 31st October 1911,* ix.

11   *Report of the Department of Lands, Forests, and Mines of the Province of Ontario for the Year Ending 31st October 1914* (Toronto: L.K. Cameron, 1915), x, 92.

12   *Report of the Department of Lands, Forests, and Mines of the Province of Ontario for the Year Ending 31st October 1916* (Toronto: A.T. Wilgress, 1917), xvi-xvii.

13   Ibid., xvi-xviii.

14   Ibid., xviii.

15   *Report of the Minister of Lands and Forests of the Province of Ontario for the Year Ending 31st October 1920* (Toronto: Clarkson W. James, 1921), 207. On blueberries, see Barnes, *Killer,* 68.

16   *Report of the Minister of Lands and Forests of the Province of Ontario for the Year Ending 31st October 1920* (Toronto: Clarkson W. James, 1921), 207.

17   Ibid., 207-8.

18   The description of Haileybury is from Bruce C. Dawson, "Haileybury Fire: October 4, 1922" (unpublished report, Ontario Department of Lands and Forests, Forest Protection Branch, 1967), 10; the quotations are from Heaton, *Report,* 20, 26.

19   Heaton, *Report,* 30. For additional information, see *Report of the Northern Ontario Fire Relief Committee, of Relief Extended to Sufferers in Fires in Northern Ontario, October 4, 1922,* Archives of Ontario, MU 2206.

20   *Report ... 1922,* 14.

21   My account relies on the wonderful compilation assembled by John Parminter, "Darkness at Noon: The Bloedel Fire of 1938" (manuscript, BC Forest Service, 1988).

22   Statistics are from ibid., 39-40; the quotations are from 36-37.

23   Ibid., 28, 15.

24   *Mississagi Fire: Blind River Division, Fire No. 9, 1948,* Special Notes 1948 (Ontario Department of Lands and Forests, 1964), Archives of Ontario, pamphlet 1964, box 1. A composite log of the fires was assembled later by Don Gord Campbell, "The Mississagi Fire 1948" (unpublished report, Ministry of Natural Resources, 1976), Great Lakes Forestry Centre Library, Sault Ste. Marie; it includes a map and an analysis of weather and fire behaviour. See also Q.F. Hess, "The Mississagi-Chapleau Fires in 1948 and a Quarter of a Century Later," Great Lakes Forestry Centre.

25   Campbell, "The Mississagi Fire 1948," 62; Parminter, "Darkness at Noon," 37.

26   The best summary is B.J. Stocks et al., "The 1980 Forest Fire Season in West-Central Canada: Social, Economic, and Environmental Impacts" (unpublished report, Canadian Forestry Service, 1981), Great Lakes Forestry Centre; see also James B. Harrington, "The

1980 Forest Fire Season" (unpublished report, Canadian Forestry Service, 1981), LAC, RG 39, Accession 1995-96/336, box 78, file 6650-1 2.

27 Committee on Emergency Planning, "The Evacuation of Red Lake, Cochenour, Balmertown, and Surrounding Area as a Result of Forest Fire #14, Red Lake District, 1980," submission to cabinet (Ministry of Natural Resources, 1980), Archives of Ontario, RG 1-397, Accession 21952, box 1, Evacuation of Red Lake – 1980, 1-2.

28 Ibid., 3-5.

29 For a summary review, see K. Irizawa, "Board of Review Report, Preparedness – 1980. Executive Summary" (unpublished report, 1980), and K.K. Irizawa et al., "1980 Forest Fire Preparedness" (unpublished report, 1980), Archives of Ontario, RG 1-318, box 2, file Fire Control Task Force. See also Stocks et al., "The 1980 Forest Fire Season in West-Central Canada."

30 Irizawa et al., "1980 Forest Fire Preparedness," 1, 21.

31 Ibid., 21, 23.

Continental Drift and Global Warming

1 Peter C. Newman, *The Canadian Revolution: From Deference to Defiance* (Toronto: Penguin Books, 1996), xix.

Fire Geography of Green Canada

1 A good record is available in the minutes of the annual meetings; see, in particular, the first and last, *Proceedings of the Thirty-First Meeting of the Canadian Committee on Forest Fire Control,* Thunder Bay, 25, 26, 27 January 1983, 5; and "Strategic Plan: The Canadian Committee on Forest Fire Management," in *Proceedings of the Thirty-Ninth Meeting of the Canadian Committee on Forest Fire Management,* Victoria, 22-24 January 1991, Appendix 1.

2 See *Proceedings of the Thirty-Second Meeting of the Canadian Committee on Forest Fire Control* (Saskatoon, 1984), 2. Also useful is the position paper prepared for CCREM, "Forest Fire Control in Canada," LAC, RG 39, Accession 94-95/769, box 38, file 1165-36/C276.

3 Subcommittee on Forest Fire Research, "Forest Fire Research: The Need for Change. A Position Paper on Fire Research," in *Proceedings of the Thirty-Third Meeting of the Canadian Committee on Forest Fire Management* (Whitehorse, 1985), 1, 3.

4 I.C.M. Place, *75 Years of Research in the Woods: A History of the Petawawa Forest Experiment Station and Petawawa National Forestry Institute* (Burnstown, ON: General Store Publishing House, 2002), 152-57, 187.

5 The best summary of developments and thinking at the time is Cliff White, "Keepers of the Flame: Implementing Fire Management in the Canadian Parks Service" (Natural Resources Branch, Canadian Parks Service, 1989).

6 Parks Canada, Management Directive 2.4.4, Fire Management (1986), file C 6215, 6, Parks Canada Departmental Library, Gatineau.

7 Ibid., 9.

8 R/EMS Research, "Fire Management in the Canadian Parks Service: Evaluation and Recommendations" (Canadian Parks Service, 1988); Cliff White, "Keepers of the Flame: Implementing Fire Management in the Canadian Parks Service" (Natural Resources Branch, Canadian Parks Service, 1989), vii, xi, 31.

9 White, "Keepers of the Flame," vii, xi.

10 For a description of this debate, see Stephen Woodley, "Playing with Fire: Vegetation Management in the Canadian Parks Service," in *Proceedings, Intermountain West Fire Council*

Conference, 1995 (Missoula: Intermountain Fire Council, 1996), 7. The counterarguments are summarized in Edward A. Johnson, *Fire and Vegetation Dynamics: Studies from the North American Boreal Forest* (Cambridge, UK: Cambridge University Press, 1992).

11 See Woodley, "Playing with Fire," for details of resolutions. Figures on burn targets are from an e-mail from Mike Etches, Parks Canada Senior National Fire Management Officer, 23 June 2005. For details on the evolving policy, see Parks Canada, "National Fire Management Strategy" (1 March 2005), and Parks Canada, "Unimpaired for Future Generations?" Conserving Ecological Integrity with Canada's National Parks, *Report of the Panel on the Ecological Integrity of Canada's National Parks,* vol. 2 (Ottawa: Minister of Government Works and Public Services Canada, 2000), chapter 5, "The Need for Active Management and Restoration."

12 CIFFC, Foreword, in *Annual Report, for the Year Ending March 31, 1989*; CIFFC, Foreword, in *Annual Report, for the Year Ending March 31, 1990.*

13 See annual reports. Quotations are from CIFFC, Foreword, in *Annual Report for the Year Ending March 31, 1998*; and CIFFC, Foreword, in *Annual Report for the Year Ending March 31, 1999.*

14 Albert J. Simard, co-ordinator, "National Workshop on Wildland Fire Activity in Canada: Policy Implications," Information Report ST-X-12 (Edmonton: Canadian Forest Service, 1997); CIFFC, "Strategic Plan for the Renewal of the Canadian Forest Fire Program: Five Point Plan" (CIFFC, May 2002).

15 The simplest chronicles, since 1983, are the annual reports of CIFFC. On the early Soviet trip, see R.J. Bouchier, ed., "Report of a Visit by Canadian Forest Fire Protection Specialists to the Soviet Union, August, 1968" (unpublished report, 1968). On the China project, see Richard A. White and Merrill F. Rush, "The Jiagedaqui Fire Management Project (JAIPRO): An Example of International Assistance," in *The Art and Science of Fire Management*, ed. M.E. Alexander and G.F. Bisgrove, Information Report NOR-X-309 (Edmonton: Forestry Canada, 1990), 287-96.

16 See CIFFC annual reports for 1988, 1992, 1994, and 1996. Also see CFS reports on Indonesia research. Information on New Brunswick and the Honduras project is courtesy of Keith Barr. For a good survey of Alberta's involvement, see P.J. Murphy et al., *The Alberta Forest Service, 1930-2005: Protection and Management of Alberta's Forests* (Alberta Sustainable Resource Development, 2006), 371-72.

17 See FAO NAFC final reports, by year. A good summary of the early years is "North American Forestry Commission: Recommendations, Proposals, and Follow-Up Actions, 1961-1968" (1968), LAC, RG 39 735, file 116-F12-15 6.

18 L.H. Amyhot to E.N. Doyle, 10 February 1972, LAC, RG 39 735, file 116-F12-15 6.

19 For a distilled roster of official contacts, see Dieudonne Mouafoetal, "Building Cross-Border Links: A Compendium of Canada-U.S. Government Collaboration" (Ottawa: Canada School of Public Service, 2004). See also the annual reports and proceedings of the individual compacts and councils.

20 The "wildland/urban interface" has a library of sources. For an early introduction, see Cordy Tymstra, compiler, *Fire Management in the Wildland/Urban Interface: Sharing Solutions* (Edmonton: Partners in Protection, 1995); and Canadian Wildland Fire Strategy Project Management Team, "Canadian Wildland Fire Strategy: A Vision for an Innovative and Integrated Approach to Managing the Risks," in Patricia L. Andrews and Bret W. Butler, compilers, *Fuels Management – How to Measure Success: Conference Proceedings. 28-30 March 2006*, RMRS-P-41 (Fort Collins, CO: US Forest Service, 2006), 13-15.

21 Kelvin Hirsch et al., "FireSmart Forest Management: A Pragmatic Approach to Sustainable

Forest Management in Fire-Dominated Ecosystems," *Forestry Chronicle* 77, 2 (2002): 357-63.

22 B.D. Amiro et al., "Direct Carbon Emissions from Canadian Forest Fires, 1959-1999," *Canadian Journal of Forest Research* 31 (2001): 512-25.

23 Statistics are available from many sources. See, for example, "Canada: Environmental Issues," www.eia.doe.gov/emeu/cabs/canenv.html, and Carbon Sequestration Leadership Forum, "An Energy Summary of Canada," www.cslforum.org/canada.htm; especially helpful are the many graphs and maps in the *Atlas of Canada.*

24 See Amiro et al., "Direct Carbon Emissions," for statistics and general conceptual context. Also helpful is B.D. Amiro et al., "Perspectives on Carbon Emissions from Canadian Forest Fires," *Forestry Chronicle* 78, 3 (2002): 388-90.

25 See P.J. Murphy et al., "Historical Fire Records in the North American Boreal Forest," in *Fire, Climate Change, and Carbon Cycling in the Boreal Forest,* ed. E.S. Kasichke and B.J. Stocks (New York: Springer Verlag, 2000), 274-88; and Justin Podur, David L. Martell, and Keith Knight, "Statistical Quality Control Analysis of Forest Fire Activity in Canada," *Canadian Journal of Forest Research* 32 (2002): 195-205.

26 Amiro et al., "Perspectives on Carbon Emissions," 389.

Slow Burns, Fast Flames

1 For background, see Keith Keller, *Wildfire Wars: Frontline Stories of BC's Worst Forest Fires* (Madeira Park, BC: Harbour Publishing, 2002); BC Ministry of Forests, "Garnet Fire Review" (unpublished report, 1995); Chisholm Fire Review Committee, "Final Report," submitted to Minister of Alberta Sustainable Resource Development (unpublished report, 2001); British Columbia 2003 Firestorm Provincial Review, *Report* (2004), 5; and Ross Freake and Don Plant, eds., *Firestorm: The Summer B.C. Burned* (Toronto: McClelland and Stewart, 2003).

2 British Columbia 2003 Firestorm Provincial Review, "Report" (15 February 2004), http://www.2003firestorm.gov.bc.ca, 20. See also Forest Protection Program, "Ministry of Forests Report to the 2003 Firestorm Provincial Review" (2004), http://www.2003firestorm.gov.bc.ca/firestormreport.

3 For a comprehensive summary, see *Canadian Journal of Forest Research* 34, 8, a special issue on the ICFME.

4 B.J. Stocks, M.E. Alexander, and R.A. Lanoville, "Overview of the International Crown Fire Modelling Experiment (ICFME)," in ibid., 1544.

5 Early fire statistics are from summary data in "Banff National Park Prescribed Burn Program from 1983," data on file at Banff National Park headquarters.

6 Nikita Lopoukhine, "A Canadian View of Fire Management in the Greater Yellowstone Area," in *The Greater Yellowstone Ecosystem: Redefining America's Wilderness Heritage,* ed. Robert B. Keiter and Mark S. Boyce (New Haven: Yale University Press, 1991), 157. Clifford A. White and Ian R. Pengelly, "Fire as a Natural Process and a Management Tool: The Banff National Park Experience," in *Proceedings of the Cypress Hills Forest Management Workshop,* ed. Dawn Dickinson, David A. Gautier, and Bob Mutch (Medicine Hat, AB: Society of Grasslands Naturalists, 1993), 66.

7 R.A. Redmond to J.H. Crayford, 6 August 1970, LAC, RG 39 809, file 539-1-1 1, "Prescribed Burning – Silvicultural Aspects – General"; Memorandum of Agreement between Minister of Lands and Mines and Miramichi Lumber Company, LAC, RG 39 880, file 32-11-11, part 2, "Prescribed Burns."

8 Newfoundland Research Council, "Symposium on Prescribed Burning in Forestry,

Agriculture, and Wildlife Management," Memorial University, 25 March 1958; J.H. Cayford to the Editor, *New Scientist,* 21 March 1967, LAC, RG 39 880, file 32-11-11, part 2, "Prescribed Burns."

9 C.D. Haddon, memo, to D.H. Owen, 30 November 1962, BC Archives, GR 1061, box 1, file 1, BC Forest Service, 1962 Meeting, 1. Other quotations are from J. Harry G. Smith, "A British Columbian View of the Future of Prescribed Burning in North America," *Commonwealth Forestry Review* 49 (1970): 365.

10 Perry Hagerstein, cited in James K. Agee, "A History of Fire and Slash Burning in Western Oregon and Washington," in *The Burning Decision: Regional Perspectives on Slash,* ed. Donald P. Hanley, Jerry J. Kammenga, and Chadwick D. Oliver, Institute of Forest Resources, Contribution 66 (Seattle: College of Forest Resources, 1989), 11.

11 See John Parminter, "A Review of Prescribed Burning for Wildlife Habitat Enhancement: An Examination of the Roles and Responsibilities of the Ministries of Forest and Environment, Lands, and Parks" (unpublished report, 1992); and D. Ray Halladay, "An Overview of Wildlife Prescribed Burning in British Columbia," in *Wildlife and Range Prescribed Burning Workshop, Proceedings,* Richmond, BC (Vancouver: University of British Columbia, 1987), 7-16.

12 John Parminter, "Burning Alternatives Panel: A Review of Fire Ecology, Fire History, and Prescribed Burning in Southern British Columbia," paper presented to the Sixth Annual Fire Management Symposium, Southern Interior Fire Management Committee, Kelowna, BC, 1991, 15.

Fire and Ice
1 Ian Stirling, *Polar Bears* (Toronto: Fitzhenry and Whiteside, 1998), 25-27.
2 Ian Stirling, quoted in the *Globe and Mail,* 2 November 2002, verified by e-mail correspondence with the author.

Bibliographic Essay

A comprehensive bibliography of Canadian fire is not quite as vast as the country, and a printout of index cards that contained it all would not stretch from sea to sea. But it might come close. It seems pointless to reproduce such a register, especially for a book of this length, so I have left the particulars in the notes; in cases where I did not quote directly from a source but relied on that source to decode the topic at hand, I have cited it as a supplement, again in the notes. What follows instead is a guide to the general categories and repositories of information.

Sources fall into three overall groupings. There is a published literature, generally available in at least prominent libraries. There is an unpublished grey literature of reports, studies, and reviews, usually sequestered in departmental libraries or agency back-room filing cabinets. And there are bona fide archives. Each group contributed differently.

Publications are of several types: scientific, historical, bureaucratic. The published science is instructive in understanding how and why fire exists in Canada. As always, one must handle the material gingerly because it changes so often and sometimes unexpectedly and because it is bottomless. The longer I wrote, the more colleagues would refer me to the most recent article or research note and urge me to include it. This, however, is the formula for Zeno's paradox of Achilles and the tortoise. No matter how fast I might write, I could never catch up. Rather, the value of the science lies in helping to fathom the core conditions for fire's physical presence, particularly in places (which were legion) that I was unable to inspect for myself. Additionally the history of fire science became an important motif, and for this the record of publication was a fulsome and mandatory source. Articles functioned as historical artefacts, no different from explorers' journals or reports from boards of inquiry.

Other publications of value are the usual stuff of historical scholarship – settler accounts, explorer journals, traveller observations, newspaper stories, and official statements. I mostly relied on the existing canon, scavenging through it for references to fires. More substantial were official accounts from institutions charged with fire protection. They consisted of annual reports, official inquiries, other records of public accountability, and the occasional royal commission. Since the bulk of the book relates institutional history, such sources were, by volume, the most prominent cache of evidence upon which I drew. The primary difficulty was that such agencies were continually reorganized and hence renamed and shuffled from one umbrella bureau to another. Their yearly reports were thus scattered across many shelves, and it was often tricky to track down the particular location in order to maintain a continuous chronicle. (The sleuthing involved did, however, alert me to the patrimony of institutional instability most agencies experienced.) These reports were invaluable – until the 1980s. At this point (just when exactly varied by province), they exchange narratives for box scores. They cease explaining what they are doing, thinking, planning, and instead emulate corporate stockholder reports on profits and losses. Within another decade, they cease to be "published" in the old way and dissolve into the digibits of cyberspace. They survive as data; they vanish as textual sources for narrative.

The Canadian Committee has allowed for a partial survival. Since 1953, the Associate Committee on Forest Fire Protection of the National Research Council has published its proceedings. Since 1994, the "exchange of information" that is the essence of the annual gathering has occurred under the auspices of the Canadian Interagency Forest Fire Centre, which assumed responsibility for their publication. While this entire repository consistently promises more than it delivers, it remains the solitary countrywide source of information and has been so for over fifty years. No one can ignore it. I'm grateful to Dennis Dubé for donating his complete set for my use.

Publication here edges into the grey literature. Normally such documents are among the richest veins for cultural fire history, and typically they survive in departmental filing cabinets, stacked boxes, and libraries. I found those libraries to be the most significant single depository for this project. They (usually) had a complete set of annual reports and other publications, they held what survived of the grey literature on their shelves, and they were accessible. They differed widely, however, in how much they retain and were almost all in various states of bureaucratic deconstruction. Some provinces had much, some little. Quebec saved everything, Manitoba almost nothing. In this regard, the federal agencies had more robust holdings. The Canadian Forest Service, Parks Canada, and their regional offices had working libraries that transcended the scope of the work done on site. For me, the Northern Forestry Centre in Edmonton offered a foundational introduction, to which other locales contributed those stray items that it lacked and the elusive grey literature that brings a subject to life.

Departmental librarians, however, seem to be an endangered species, and the burden has been transferred to the fire agencies, which either house old documents in someone's office or dispose of the dusty piles in the name of modernization. Each reorganization and relocation to another building contributes to the attrition. Much of Canada's institutional history of fire has gone to dumpsters. It may be that individuals have rescued records (especially if they were personally involved with a project) and that these may someday wend their way to archives. For the present, two countervailing trends are at work: one has abolished narrative reports and the preservation of grey literature, and the other has spawned a proliferating herd of consultant-generated studies over the past decade that may, to some extent, substitute; we'll see. The period from the mid-1970s to the mid-1990s, however, is bleak.

The extraordinary exception is Quebec, which through the labours of Patrick Blanchet has amassed a comprehensive collection of all relevant documents – archival, published, grey – and made it available online. The director of this singular enterprise, Julie Fortin, generously made available to me all this material during my visit to the ministry. The cache underwrote Blanchet's history of fire in Quebec, and my own sketch, and no doubt will inspire others in the future. Having such a collection at my fingertips did not make Quebec fire history easy, but it did make it possible, and richer, and more satisfying.

Overall, the archival sources are much like the grey literature except that they are both better protected and leaner. Again some provinces have preserved large swaths of their history and some almost nothing. Moreover, the archival holdings tended to skew toward those records that have some legal or fiscal significance (e.g., accidental deaths or routine fire reports) rather than those that reveal policy choices or the state of the organization at a particular time. Again the bias favours the grey literature. Most archivists were exceptionally helpful and a few ecstatic to see someone doing research other than family history. Be warned: the useful records will probably be off-site and require advance requisitioning. On-site material veers toward the genealogical.

Two other depositories, likely to be overlooked, are the Canadian Interagency Forest Fire Centre and the Northern Forestry Centre. CIFFC has a fairly complete set of records relevant to the events that led to its creation, to the US-Canada treaty, and regarding the Canadian Committee, once it transferred to CIFFC's bailiwick. Many of these documents are duplicates of those held in Library and Archives Canada but are more readily obtained. The reason is mixed. At present, they are stored in a room otherwise used for housekeeping chemicals and utensils – literally a broom closet. NoFC has many of the original reports and data sets from the early trials by Wright and Beall at Petawawa and documents that pertain to the dissemination of that program throughout the provinces.

The grand exception to this relatively bleak scene is Library and Archives Canada. The records were particularly helpful for the Canadian Forest Service, Parks Canada, the Associate Committee for Forest Fire Protection (National Research Council), and biographical material on Robert Bell and Donald Stedman. I confess that access was a problem thanks to the misnamed Freedom of Information and Privacy Protection Act, which was used to block entry to anything that might touch on First Nations concerns and other matters, the reasons for which I could never determine. Colleagues at CFS were, fortunately, able to break this logjam and get me into the grand storehouse, although I was never able to overcome blockage to many old North-West Territory records and had to rely on what I could glean from the shelves of the NWT departmental library in Yellowknife and on Stephen Janzen's densely documented master's thesis.

Finally, to a tiny degree, I generated an archive of my own through conversations with colleagues. Not being a journalist, I did not record those discussions and informed my conversants that I would not quote them unless they chose to write some statement. Rather, I took notes to help shape my understanding of the published and grey literature. There was one important anomaly: Charlie Van Wagner devoted a day for detailed conversation about his career. Most of our discussion circled around projects and publications – he was reluctant to dwell on his personal life or those of his colleagues – but he did subsequently write up an account of his official career that proved exceptionally helpful and from which I have quoted.

While I list in the notes those books on which I have relied, there are a handful that deserve highlighting now and again. Granted the need for a national narrative, I found R. Peter Gillis and Thomas R. Roach, *Lost*

Initiatives: Canada's Forest Industries, Forest Policy, and Forest Conservation (New York: Greenwood Press, 1986), repeatedly informative in keeping a thematic chronology. The equivalent for fire ecology was Ross W. Wein and David A. MacLean, eds., *The Role of Fire in Northern Circumpolar Ecosystems,* SCOPE 18 (New York: John Wiley and Sons, 1983). Two succinct topical summaries that proved useful in keeping me on a Canadian track were Ken Drushka, *Canada's Forests: A History* (Montreal and Kingston: McGill-Queen's University Press and Forest History Society, 2002), and Kenneth Johnstone, *Timber and Trauma: 75 Years with the Federal Forestry Service* (Ottawa: Forestry Canada, 1991). But what made my serial histories of the provinces possible was a suite of existing studies: Peter Murphy, *History of Forest and Prairie Fire Control Policy in Alberta,* ENR Report T/77 (Edmonton: Alberta Energy and Natural Resources, 1985); Patrick Blanchet, *Forest Fires: The Story of a War* (Montreal: Cantos International Publishing, 2003); Sidney Stephen Janzen, "The Burning North: A History of Fire and Fire Protection in the NWT" (MA thesis, University of Alberta, 1990); John Vye Parminter, "An Historical Review of Forest Fire Management in British Columbia" (MA thesis, University of British Columbia, 1978); and W.C. Wilton and C.H. Evans, "Newfoundland Forest Fire History, 1610-1960," Information Report N-X-116 (St. John's: Newfoundland Forest Research Centre, 1974). All provided handholds on a new and (for me) sometimes treacherous cliff.

Among a miscellany of productive sites having source material were Wood Buffalo National Park, the Bushplane Museum at Sault Ste. Marie, Ontario, and the backcountry of Banff National Park. The first generously opened its historical files for my inspection. The second reminded me forcibly that the stuff I wrote about, while recorded mostly in texts, was really about hard-wrought objects doing work in the world. And Banff, although viewed from a saddle on Ribbon, gave me occasion to ponder how fire truly acted in the northern landscape of rock, trees, and wind and how unbearably complex is its behaviour and how taunting to our understanding. It was a saddle-sore epiphany that stayed with me and returned with every fresh shelf of documents and carbon-copied reports retrieved from a mouldy box.

Index